PARLIAMENT OF VICTORIA
DRUGS AND CRIME PREVENTION COMMITTEE

INQUIRY INTO LOCALLY BASED APPROACHES TO COMMUNITY SAFETY AND CRIME PREVENTION

Final Report

June 2012

ORDERED TO BE PRINTED

by Authority
Government Printer for State of Victoria

No. 130 Session 2010–2012

The Report was prepared by the Drugs and Crime Prevention Committee.

Drugs and Crime Prevention Committee
Inquiry into Locally Based Approaches to Community Safety and Crime Prevention — Final Report
DCPC, Parliament of Victoria

ISBN: 978-0-9804595-8-6

Drugs and Crime Prevention Committee

Parliament House, Spring St
Melbourne Vic 3002

Phone: (03) 8682 2810
Fax   (03) 8682 2808

Email: sandy.cook@parliament.vic.gov.au
Website: http://www.parliament.vic.gov.au/dcpc

Drugs and Crime Prevention Committee — 57th Parliament

Members

Mr Simon Ramsay M.L.C. *Western Victoria* — Chair

Mr Johan Scheffer M.L.C. *Eastern Victoria* — Deputy Chair

Mr Brad Battin M.P. *Gembrook*

Mr Shaun Leane M.L.C. *Eastern Metropolitan*

Mr Tim McCurdy M.P. *Murray Valley*

Staff

Ms Sandy Cook — *Executive Officer*

Mr Peter Johnston — *Senior Legal Research Officer*

Dr Stephen Pritchard — *Research Officer (from December 2011)*

Ms Mignon Turpin — *Research Officer (September–October 2011)*

Ms Danielle Woof — *Committee Administrative Officer*

Consultants

Professor Peter Homel — *Principal Criminologist, Crime Prevention, Australian Institute of Criminology*

Ms Georgina Fuller — *Research Officer, Crime Reduction and Review Program, Australian Institute of Criminology*

Functions of the Drugs and Crime Prevention Committee

The Victorian Drugs and Crime Prevention Committee is constituted under the *Parliamentary Committees Act* 2003 (Vic) as amended.

Section 7

The functions of the Drugs and Crime Prevention Committee are, if so required or permitted under this Act, to inquire into, consider and report to the Parliament on any proposal, matter or thing concerned with:

a. the use of drugs including the manufacture, supply or distribution of drugs;

b. the level or causes of crime or violent behaviour.

Terms of Reference

Under s33 of the *Parliamentary Committees Act 2003*, the following matter be referred to the Drugs and Crime Prevention Committee — for inquiry, consideration and report on locally based approaches to community safety and crime prevention, and the Committee is asked to consider:

(a) the breadth of locally based groups and organisations addressing community safety and crime prevention issues within Victoria, particularly with regard to local government and Neighbourhood Watch;

(b) the approaches adopted by these groups to promulgating community safety and crime prevention practices, programs or initiatives;

(c) the extent to which these organisations are effective in engaging with local and state agencies in the development of policy;

(d) whether institutional or other arrangements support or impede such local groups in engaging in the development of community safety initiatives;

(e) whether there is a cost benefit to the community for current crime prevention strategies;

(f) whether alternate models for such organisations may improve outcomes; and

(g) local community safety and crime prevention arrangements in other jurisdictions, particularly within Australia, New Zealand and the United Kingdom.

Acknowledgements

The Committee wishes to acknowledge the valuable contribution of Mignon Turpin for her editing work, Matt Clare at Mono Design for the cover design, Luke Harris from Chameleon Print Design for laying out the report and Phil Balzer from Tenderprint Australia for printing it.

The Committee is most grateful to the City of Greater Dandenong for permission to reproduce the photographs for the Report cover. These photographs depict scenes that are part of a partnership agreement between the City of Dandenong, VicUrban and other public, private and community agencies to revitalise the heart of Dandenong. The City of Dandenong/VicUrbanRevitalisation Project draws from the principles of community regeneration, renewal and capacity building which underlie the approach to crime prevention and community safety discussed in this Report.

Chair's Foreword

The recent release of crime statistics in Victoria has shown that crime against the person has increased during the last year. Crime costs the community in a variety of ways. For example, the Australian Institute of Criminology found the cost of crime in Australia in 2005 to be nearly $36 billion per year. More recently a study by Professor Russell Smyth from Monash University conservatively estimated the cost of crime in Victoria 2009-2010 to be $9.8 billion.

Given these statistics it is timely that the Drugs and Crime Prevention Committee has undertaken an inquiry into community safety and crime prevention. It should be noted at the outset however that this Inquiry has not been about individual crime prevention initiatives or specific areas of crime prevention such as family violence or alcohol related crime. Rather, the focus is about the processes and models through which effective crime prevention policy and programs can be developed and implemented at local level and the partnerships that can be formed to make this happen. The recommendations arising from this Report reflect this. Having said this the Committee received considerable evidence through submissions and witness testimony in Victoria and other parts of Australia that alcohol and drug misuse is one of the key drivers contributing to crime and antisocial behaviour and that accordingly measures need to be taken to address this.

The Committee agrees that there is a definite place for criminal justice initiatives to deter and reduce offending and antisocial behaviours. However the concept of crime prevention cannot be narrowly circumscribed to traditional law and order approaches only. These approaches can be superficially attractive but they ignore the complex and multiple contributory factors that lead to criminal offending. Crime prevention strategies need to be based on social developmental, situational and environmental models approaches in addition to law enforcement measures. It is equally important to incorporate the concepts of community engagement, social capital and community capacity building into crime prevention policy and program implementation. Modern crime prevention and community engagement approaches are essentially about investing in safer, healthier and happier local communities.

A key aspect of this Inquiry was examining local approaches to crime prevention including the role and work of Neighbourhood Watch within the community. The work of local government and community agencies therefore featured strongly throughout this Report. Much crime prevention theory and research indicates that initiatives developed and implemented at a local level are some of the best ways of reducing crime and antisocial behaviour. As most crime of immediate concern to communities is local (e.g. property crime, antisocial behaviour and alcohol related crime, vandalism etc.) then the primary focus for preventive action should also be local. As such the Committee has made recommendations to the overall structure of Community Crime Prevention in this state which will allow for greater local level and community collaboration as well as more easily facilitating input from experts. These recommendations will also provide for greater coordination across government.

The Report and its recommendations address many of the complex challenges of crime prevention. The Committee is of the view that given this complexity of the task a 'one size fits all' approach is inappropriate in addressing the issues of crime and antisocial behaviour in Victoria.

The Committee's recommendations are also to be read in conjunction with a set of principles that inform and support them. These principles are based on the deliberations of the Drugs and Crime Prevention Committee and the evidence it has received during the course of this Inquiry. The recommendations are also supported by a list of best evidence indicators of 'what works' in delivering successful crime prevention and community safety interventions. A commitment to evidence based practice research, evaluation, and performance measurement supported by comprehensive data is an essential part of developing effective crime prevention programs and initiatives.

Finally, crime prevention is far less effective when agencies and departments work in 'silos' in isolation from each other. A coordinated 'all of government' approach is needed and the Committee's recommendations for an enhanced crime prevention structure and process reflect this. In short, this is a very detailed and comprehensive Report that provides significant recommendations that will help address crime and provide a mechanism for local community safety programs to be both strategic and effective.

The Committee would like to thank the many people who provided oral evidence and written submissions to this Inquiry, and to those who attended as witnesses at the public hearings in Melbourne, Frankston, Dandenong, Ballarat, Geelong, Perth and Sydney and even from the United Kingdom

The Committee would also like to express its gratitude to the staff of the Drugs and Crime Prevention Committee; Executive Officer, Sandy Cook, Senior Research Officer, Pete Johnston, Research Officers, Stephen Pritchard and Mignon Turpin and Administrative Officer, Danielle Woof for their dedicated hard work and cooperation.

The Committee also thanks Professor Peter Homel and the staff of the Australian Institute of Criminology for their excellent work in developing an online survey for distribution to all local councils and shires in Victoria, in order to gather a comprehensive picture of current crime prevention activity. The results of this important benchmarking research, which are found in Chapter 5, assisted the Committee in forming the framework for the Committee's Final Report and recommendations.

Finally, I would personally like to thank the Committee Members, Johan Scheffer, Brad Battin, Shaun Leane and Tim McCurdy for their cooperative and bipartisan approach to this Inquiry and for their efforts to table this report in Parliament on time.

Simon Ramsay M.L.C.
Chair

Executive Summary and Recommendations

Addressing crime prevention and community safety in Victoria has proven a surprisingly complex task for the Drugs and Crime Prevention Committee. In particular, some of the key challenges for this Inquiry were: establishing the extent to which local crime prevention programs and projects are being developed and implemented; what the challenges in developing these programs have been; and what evidence exists to show that such programs are (or are not) successful and being sustained. It should be noted at the outset, however, that the Inquiry is not about individual crime prevention initiatives or specific areas of crime prevention such as family violence or alcohol related crime. Rather, the focus is about the processes and models through which effective crime prevention policy and programs can be developed and implemented at local level and the partnerships that can be formed to make this happen. The recommendations listed below reflect this.

The Committee also agrees that whilst there is a definite place for criminal justice initiatives such as arrest and imprisonment to deter and reduce offending and antisocial behaviours, the concept of crime prevention cannot be narrowly circumscribed to traditional law and order approaches only. Whilst law and order approaches may be attractive in that they tackle crime at its most obvious source – the offender – they ignore the complex and multiple contributory factors that lead to criminal offending. Community safety and community engagement are therefore key aspects of any crime prevention agenda.[1]

Similarly, crime prevention should not be restricted to one particular approach. Crime prevention strategies based on social developmental, situational and environmental models and approaches are required. As discussed at length in this Report it is equally important to incorporate the concepts of community engagement, social capital and community capacity building into crime prevention policy and program implementation. A crime prevention approach that invests in social development and community capacity building is essentially about making local communities more liveable, happy and healthy places for all.

The Committee has found a wide range of crime prevention and community initiatives operating within Victoria which, whilst in many cases are inherently worthwhile, do not stem from some overarching or uniform plan or direction. Certainly the establishment of a Community Crime Prevention Unit at state government level has been a significant step forward. The Committee also acknowledges that there have been some notable achievements in developing and implementing crime prevention and community safety programs in Victoria. Many of these successful interventions have been driven by local government and community agencies. The point remains, however, that these approaches are not led by or do not emanate from a comprehensive overall crime prevention strategy at either state or municipal level. A central and integrated state Crime Prevention and Community Safety Framework that draws from and incorporates relevant aspects of the National Crime Prevention Framework is required.

At the same time the Committee believes that policy development and program implementation for crime prevention and community safety in Victoria should be structured to place more emphasis on the role of local councils and community agencies.

---

1   For a detailed discussion see Chapter 2.

Crime prevention takes place at all levels of government and society. However, much crime prevention theory and research indicates that initiatives developed and implemented at a local level are some of the best ways of reducing crime and antisocial behaviour (Homel 2009a). As such the Committee has made recommendations to the overall structure of Community Crime Prevention governance, which will allow for greater local level and community collaboration as well as more easily facilitating input from experts. It will also provide for greater coordination across government.

The Report and recommendations set out below address the myriad and complex challenges of crime prevention. The Committee is of the view that given the complexity of the task a 'one size fits all' approach is inappropriate in addressing the issues of crime and antisocial behaviour in Victoria. This is as true for local communities be they large or small, rural or urban as it is for the state as a whole.

Finally, the Committee's recommendations are to be read in conjunction with a set of principles that inform and support them. These principles are based on the deliberations of the Drugs and Crime Prevention Committee and the evidence it has received during the course of this Inquiry. The recommendations are also supported by a list of best evidence indicators of 'what works' in delivering successful crime prevention and community safety interventions.

Principles informing the recommendations

1. In addressing crime prevention and community safety, evidence based strategies are essential

   There is now general agreement in both the national and international literature as to what is the most effective range of responses available to policy-makers to address community safety and crime prevention. The indicators of best practice crime prevention interventions are listed in the 'what works' section below.

2. A 'one size fits all' approach to crime prevention does not address the specific issues, needs and requirements of individual local communities

3. Crime prevention is more effective when investing in health and education rather than just law enforcement/justice measures

   According to the International Centre for the Prevention of Crime (ICPC) all available crime statistics internationally show that a reactive and purely law enforcement/security model to address crime has not worked. 'State investment in harsher penal laws, new prison construction and the expansion of police forces have had limited impact on reducing violence and have signally failed to discourage new crimes or to improve the population's sense of security' (ICPC 2011, p.21).

4. Community capacity building and social capital are essential and integral aspects of addressing crime prevention and community safety issues in contemporary society

5. Effective crime prevention and community safety interventions require:

- A belief that crime prevention is important in and of itself

Crime prevention work needs to be valued for its own sake and not as an 'optional extra'. This is particularly true with regard to the role of police. Crime prevention should be considered an integral part of policing, and police officers who work in the area of crime prevention should be highly valued within the organisation.

- An understanding of the causes and contributory factors leading to crime and antisocial behaviour

- Clear goals and vision that are directly linked to proposed strategies

- A unified service delivery model. Crime prevention and community safety interventions are less effective when agencies and departments work in isolation from each other (silos)

- An applied commitment to evidence based practice research, evaluation, and performance measurement supported by up-to-date data

- A commitment to plan for the 'long haul'

Crime prevention strategies and programs needs to transcend the imperatives of short-term expediency, for example the electoral cycle.

- The empowerment and participation of local communities in decision making

It is important to factor in the issues that communities have already identified as important to them, rather than prescribing what issues communities have to address.

6. There is value and long-term benefit in taking a holistic community development approach to community safety and crime prevention

Such an approach includes the participation of all levels of government, non-government agencies, the private sector and local communities and their representatives.

7. Victoria Police have the primary responsibility for law enforcement in this state. They also play a key role in crime prevention

8. Effective crime prevention requires police to take a proactive community focused approach in addition to reactive policing

9. Research suggests that local government authorities are best placed to understand and reflect the particular needs and problems of their local community. A s such they are best placed to generate and deliver the most appropriate prevention interventions for their local communities

The emphasis on the role of local governments in crime prevention is strongly encouraged by international organisations such as the United Nations Office on Drugs and Crime and UN-HABITAT and the Australian Institute of Criminology (AIC). Indeed, the AIC's research has pointed to a number of reasons as to why local government is such an important player in community crime prevention. For example as Shaw has stated: 'Across Australia virtually all government crime prevention agencies include local government in the development and delivery of their respective crime prevention strategies' (2004, p.1). This is largely due to the fact that most crime of immediate concern to communities is local (e.g. property crime, antisocial behaviour, vandalism etc.) It clearly follows then that the primary focus for preventive action should also be local.

Best practice/evidence indicators of 'what works'

In developing effective crime prevention and community safety interventions the Committee recognises that there are a set of recognised and proven best evidence indicators that should be the basis for any recommendations pertaining to this Inquiry. In particular effective crime prevention requires:

1. An understanding of crime prevention theory and how it is practically applied to the development of crime prevention strategies

2. Strong and consistent leadership and supportive governance structures

3. A capacity to manage collaborative multi-agency actions

4. The engagement of key stakeholders at the local level

5. Outcome focused performance measurement systems

6. Effective communication processes designed to promote engagement and sustainability

7. The gathering and dissemination of relevant police intelligence to support evidence based strategies

8. A mixture of crime prevention approaches including situational/environmental and social crime prevention

   Crime prevention should have a broad focus and includes the prevention of antisocial and threatening behaviours which may not constitute a crime but which undermine community safety and social inclusion. Crime prevention and community safety for example can be promoted through the use of community renewal and revitalisation and capacity building projects. Crime prevention should not be restricted to a law enforcement agenda only.

   Crime Prevention through Environmental Design (CPTED) and other situational crime prevention measures such as CCTV camera systems are commonly one element of broader crime prevention strategies. The Committee believes that it is important to combine situational crime prevention measures with other longer-term community strengthening activities that empower the community to take action.

9. Strategies need to be coordinated and integrated

   It is essential that where strategies are developed and implemented to address crime prevention policy they are wherever possible part of an integrated policy framework and a 'whole of government approach'.

10. A mixture of long- and short-term initiatives

11. Consideration of the changing demographics of the local community

    Vast population growth (actual and projected) creates pressures on existing services and infrastructure. Additional to this increase in numbers, consideration needs to be given to the changing demographics of the community i.e. increase in first home buyers and increase in youth populations, increase in culturally and linguistically diverse communities and an ageing population. These changes will also mean that further consideration will need to be given to the way in which crime prevention and community safety programs are developed and implemented and targeted to these new communities.

12. A problem solving approach drawn from systematic research, analysis and review as to what the actual problems are in any given community

13. Effective partnerships and good governance models

    Successful partnerships are extremely important in developing best practice crime prevention models. The elements that need to be present in successful partnerships include:

    1. *commitment*

    2. *equity*

    3. *trust*

    4. *mutual goals/objectives*

    5. *collaboration over implementation*

    6. *continuous evaluation*

    7. *timely communication and responsiveness.*

14. Community engagement and input

15. Monitoring and evaluation

16. Only strategies and programs that have been demonstrated to be effective should be continued.

Recommendations

The Committee acknowledges the work that the Victorian government has done in the formation of a specialised Community Crime Prevention Unit, Regional Reference Groups, the establishment of specialist community crime prevention grants programs and the appointment of the first Minister for Crime Prevention in Victoria.

On the basis of the evidence, however, the Committee believes that while it may be useful to have some aspects of coordination and service delivery organised at a regional level, further emphasis and attention should be paid to the important role of local government in developing and implementing crime prevention and community safety services.

As has been discussed throughout the report local government authorities are best placed to implement crime prevention policy at the local level. Local government has the infrastructure and consultative mechanisms in place along with relationships with community partners to implement such initiatives. The Committee has found that local government authorities in Victoria are already involved in a range of community crime prevention initiatives and are willing to take on this work as long as they receive the appropriate support and resources.

The Committee has therefore made recommendations to the overall structure of Community Crime Prevention governance that will allow for greater local level and community collaboration as well as more easily facilitating input from experts. It will also provide for greater coordination across government. The proposed new developments are set out in the diagram below. The diagram shows the greater emphasis given to the role of local communities and the local tier of government in crime prevention and community safety in comparison to the current model. The existing structures are indicated in blue and the additional structures are in orange.

Recommended Structure for Crime Prevention

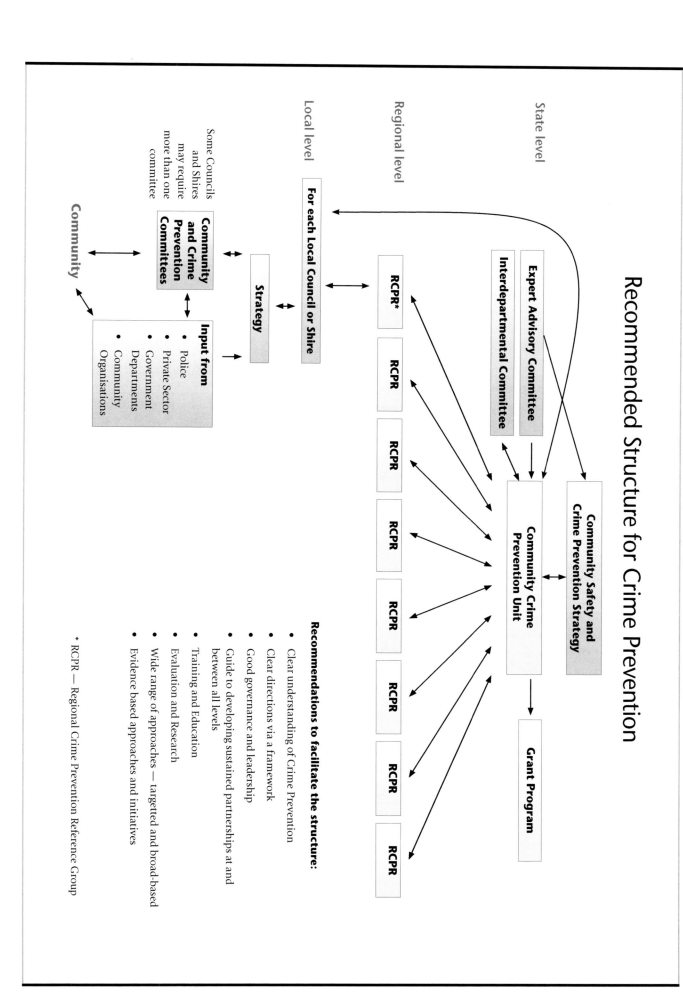

State level

Regional level

Local level

Expert Advisory Committee

Interdepartmental Committee

Community Safety and Crime Prevention Strategy

Community Crime Prevention Unit

Grant Program

RCPR*

RCPR

RCPR

RCPR

RCPR

RCPR

RCPR

RCPR

For each Local Council or Shire

Strategy

Community and Crime Prevention Committees

Some Councils and Shires may require more than one committee

Community

Input from
- Police
- Private Sector
- Government Departments
- Community Organisations

Recommendations to facilitate the structure:

- Clear understanding of Crime Prevention
- Clear directions via a framework
- Good governance and leadership
- Guide to developing sustained partnerships at and between all levels
- Training and Education
- Evaluation and Research
- Wide range of approaches — targetted and broad-based
- Evidence based approaches and initiatives

* RCPR — Regional Crime Prevention Reference Group

For the management and delivery of crime prevention to be effective at all levels, (local regional and state), the Committee has made a range of recommendations for what is required to support the enhanced structure and facilitate crime prevention in this state, particularly in local government areas. Specifically, to make this model work effectively recommendations have been made with regard to:

- Good governance and leadership
- Understanding the concept, theory and various approaches pertaining to crime prevention
- The implementation of evidence based approaches and initiatives
- Entering into sustainable partnerships
- Education, communication and training needs
- Evaluation and research
- Funding
- Communication

Each of these recommendations and the context from which they emanate has been discussed thoroughly in relevant chapters throughout this Report. Many of the Committee's recommendations including most notably a detailed explanation of the enhanced community crime prevention structure proposed for Victoria are discussed in detail in Chapter 12 which concludes this Report.

The recommendations also draw from the large body of academic literature on crime prevention and community safety and the written submissions and oral evidence received by the Committee from experts in the field and representatives from government, non-government and community organisations during the course of this Inquiry.

A Victorian Crime Prevention and Community Safety Framework

1. **The Committee recommends** that the Community Crime Prevention Unit should develop a Crime Prevention and Community Safety Framework as the means for coordinating Government action in the area. In developing the framework, the Government should ensure it consults with relevant partners in community crime prevention such as local government, police and representatives of non-government organisations.

Strategy Frameworks and associated Partnership Agreements in crime prevention, as with other areas of social and economic policy, are instruments of good governance. In turn, good governance is more than just 'government' or public administration, it is also about finding 'effective ways of continuously engaging with various sectors of society, it is therefore closely aligned with democracy and the central role that citizens play in any effective governance system' (Institute on Governance 2003, p.1).

Throughout this Report the need for a coordinated response to crime prevention has been identified as one important measure of good governance.

A coordinated response is only possible if clear directions and parameters are set for community safety and crime prevention policy. This is best achieved through the establishment of a Victorian Crime Prevention and Community Safety Framework that sets out the goals, aims and objectives of crime prevention in this state and the optimal ways to achieve them. Where applicable the Victorian Crime Prevention and Community Safety Framework should also draw from the relevant features of the National Crime Prevention Framework.

(Chapters 4 and 12)

2. **The Committee recommends** that the Crime Prevention and Community Safety Framework include clear definitions as to what is meant by crime prevention and community safety.

Defining 'Crime Prevention' and/or 'Community Safety' has been a great concern for local government in developing, implementing and responding to crime and community safety concerns. For example, according to Professor Peter Homel the concept of crime prevention is poorly or narrowly defined and understood even by those ostensibly working to achieve crime prevention goals (Homel 2005, 2009a, 2009b).

Each municipal area has its own unique demographics and profile and consequently it will also have different priorities and issues of concern in the area of 'community safety'. What is of pressing importance in one local government area, for example bushfire arson, may be largely irrelevant in another. Thus whilst clearly some flexibility in what counts for 'crime prevention and community safety' is essential, it is also imperative that in developing, implementing and funding crime prevention programs in Victoria a clear yet flexible definition of the terms 'crime prevention' and 'community safety' is understood.[2]

(Chapters 2 and 12)

3. **The Committee recommends** that the best way of implementing the Crime Prevention and Community Safety Framework and indeed crime prevention strategies generally is through the Community Crime Prevention Unit.

Effective crime prevention requires a high degree of leadership, coordination and efficiency with regard to the delivery of crime prevention and community safety initiatives in Victoria. The Committee considers the recent introduction of the Community Crime Prevention Unit to be an important first step in this direction. As such the Unit should have the lead role in coordinating and implementing statewide crime prevention and community strategy policy and programs throughout Victoria.

(Chapters 4 and 12)

Role of the Community Crime Prevention Unit

The Community Crime Prevention Unit should be responsible for a wide range of tasks and duties that are indicated in the recommendations set out below.

4. **The Committee recommends** that the role of the Community Crime Prevention Unit should include but not be restricted to:

- the development and publication of the Crime Prevention and Community Safety Framework including a community engagement strategy to indicate how the public, community organisations and the private sector can have ongoing input into crime prevention policy;

- liaising with federal and state agencies, professionals in the field, community agencies and media;

- disseminating information with regard to crime prevention and community safety;

- implementing a mapping exercise and audit to establish the current levels of services available;

- developing and coordinating training programs on crime prevention and community safety;

- developing and coordinating a research agenda and the commissioning of crime prevention research;

- assessing and providing funding for programs, research and evaluation relating to crime prevention and community safety;

- ongoing responsibility for evaluating programs that are funded;

---

2   For a detailed account of the issues pertaining to the definition of terms such as 'crime prevention' and 'community safety' see discussion in Chapter 1 of this Report.

- developing a protocol in liaison with media representatives on the reporting of community safety and crime prevention issues;

- liaising with and supporting local government and community agencies to develop Local Community Crime Prevention Strategies;

- identifying available resources and gaps in service delivery in order to plan a response to community safety and crime prevention at both state and local levels;

- identifying key personnel and agencies in the community who have expertise in dealing with community safety and crime prevention in order to establish a comprehensive referral and resource network; and

- identifying best practice initiatives and assessing their applicability to local communities.

(Chapters 6 and 12)

5. **The Committee recommends** that the Community Crime Prevention Unit provides technical support and assistance to enhance the capacity and effectiveness of local crime prevention action.

In addition to the roles outlined in Recommendation 4 the Committee believes it is essential that the Community Crime Prevention Unit plays an important role as a specialist resource to provide technical support, training and assistance to enhance the capacity and effectiveness of local crime prevention action. The objective would be to improve and enhance the capacity and effectiveness of those involved in the design, delivery and assessment of critical crime reduction and prevention initiatives that impact directly (or indirectly) on the safety and wellbeing of the community. This can be achieved by synthesising and disseminating best practice approaches to crime prevention and crime reduction, and through developing and providing training in effective methods for evaluating programs and/or measuring program outcomes. The Community Crime Prevention Unit would direct this assistance to three particular groups:

- *those responsible for the direct implementation and delivery of crime reduction and prevention activities, including law enforcement agencies, the broader criminal justice sector, state and local government agencies, and the business, non-government and community sectors;*

- *those responsible for the development, design and management of crime reduction and prevention strategies, policies and programs at the level above direct delivery. These groups include policy-makers and senior managers in law enforcement and the wider criminal justice sector, as well human services; and*

- *government and non-government agencies and professionals from other sectors whose work has a significant impact on reducing the risk of crime, or the precursors of criminal behaviour (education, human services, health, early childhood sector).*

(Chapters 6 and 12)

Community Crime Prevention Advisory Group

6. **The Committee recommends** that the Community Crime Prevention Unit should establish and support a Crime Prevention and Community Safety Advisory Group to provide ongoing formal advice to the Community Crime Prevention Unit from experts in the field.

It is the Committee's view based on the evidence that it has received and the current research available that expert input into the development of crime prevention policy in Victoria is essential. The Committee recommends, therefore, that a Crime Prevention Advisory Group should be established and supported by the Community Crime Prevention Unit. Such a Committee should comprise of government and non-government organisation representatives with specialist expertise in the area of crime prevention. Without restricting the membership of such a group, it is advisable that representatives be drawn from research institutes, police and key community agencies, private sector organisations, state government and local government peak bodies.

The Crime Prevention Advisory Group would provide ongoing advice to the Crime Prevention Unit and would have input into developing the Victorian Crime Prevention and Community Safety Framework.

(Chapters 6 and 12)

The Regional Reference Group

The Committee acknowledges the work of the Community Crime Prevention Unit in establishing regional reference groups in Victoria. Clearly these groups could have a significant role to play in supporting the work of the Unit and in particular facilitating access to necessary data and other information for crime prevention planning, implementation and review.

However, the Committee is cognisant of the experience of the United Kingdom and other places where regions have taken a lead role in developing and implementing crime prevention policy to the exclusion of local communities who have not been included in the management process. This has occurred particularly where:

> ...regional systems have been artificially overlaid on localities that have no organic or historical connection; the efficiency advantages that may flow from a more natural structure can be lost as the primary regional management task becomes the management of what is often historically derived competition or rivalry between groups and localities (Homel 2005, p.2).

This is one of the main reasons the Committee has recommended an enhanced structure of management and delivery of crime prevention and community safety to take into greater account the role of local government and local communities and their relationship to a strong central unit.

(Chapters 6 and 12)

Interdepartmental Crime Prevention Working Group

7. **The Committee recommends** that the Victorian Government establish an Interdepartmental Crime Prevention Working Party to coordinate crime prevention and community safety programs and interventions across state government departments.

Since the causes of crime are diverse and broad, crime prevention initiatives have been expanded across a wide range of government departments to include measures aimed at addressing both the social and economic determinants of crime. Whilst the Committee has not been able to ascertain the full extent of crime prevention and community safety initiatives operated by Victorian government departments, suffice to say a wide range of programs do exist that directly and indirectly address crime prevention.

Clearly there is a need for an all-of-government approach to crime prevention. However, without adequate coordination and organisation such an approach can be fragmented, inefficient and counter-productive, rather than one which strengthens the overall crime prevention capacity of government.

The establishment of an interdepartmental working party for crime prevention would help address these issues and work against a silos approach to crime prevention. Moreover, given that crime prevention policy is located in a department in which criminal justice enforcement and management is also a responsibility, the influence of an interdepartmental working party would also prevent crime prevention from becoming dominated solely by a law enforcement agenda (Solomon 2009).

(Chapters 6 and 12)

Local government

Strategies should be tailored to local conditions and needs

The Committee believes that based on the extensive evidence outlined in this Report, wherever possible the local community should be a major focus for developing initiatives to address community safety and crime prevention. In this regard the input of local government authorities is crucial. As Loxley et al state:

> The emphasis on the local community flows from the requirement to tailor prevention strategies to varying local conditions, the emerging success of community approaches and the attraction of enhancing community in order to address growing social disconnection' (2004, p.239).

8. **The Committee recommends** that the Victorian Government Framework on crime prevention and community safety provide local government with clear direction on its crime prevention responsibilities.

There is often a misunderstanding of the role of local government in crime prevention and community safety matters. Much work is required at local government and state level to clearly define the role of local government in this area.

(Chapters 7 and 12)

9. **The Committee recommends** that the Community Crime Prevention Unit work with local government authorities to develop and implement a Crime Prevention and Community Safety Plan where one does not currently exist or where it does not conform to the principles and guidelines of the new Crime Prevention and Community Safety Framework. Such a Plan should draw from the new Crime Prevention and Community Safety Framework and be based on/ informed by best practice evidence.

The Committee believes it is essential that each local council where they have not done so develop a Local Crime Prevention and Community Safety Strategy. One way in which the Community Crime Prevention Unit could assist local councils to meet this requirement is to develop and provide a Crime Prevention and Community Safety Strategy Plan Template that could serve as a base model for local councils to modify or alter according to their individual local circumstances. The New South Wales Crime Prevention Strategy Template may serve as a useful guide in the development of a similar model in the Victorian context.[3]

(Chapters 7 and 12)

10. **The Committee recommends** that local governments in developing their crime prevention and community safety strategy plans seek the views of members of the local community through a properly constituted consultation process.

(Chapters 4 and 12)

11. **The Committee recommends** that each council and shire conduct a crime prevention audit and/or needs analysis of community safety requirements in their municipality.

Such an audit and needs analysis would provide useful data and information for local government areas to develop their crime prevention and community safety strategy plan.

(Chapters 7 and 12)

12. **The Committee recommends** that each local government authority should ensure that its crime prevention and community safety strategy plan be based on evidence of current crime prevention and community safety issues and problems facing the local community.

Clearly, a comprehensive and effective Crime Prevention and Community Safety Strategy Plan must be based on evidence as to what are the most pressing crime and community safety issues facing the local community. One way in which this might be done is through the community safety audit and needs analysis referred to in Recommendation 11. In developing this Plan consideration should be given to a mix of long- and short-term goals and a mix of social, situational and environmental crime prevention responses and approaches.

(Chapters 7 and 12)

---

3   See Appendix 10 for a copy of this template.

13. **The Committee recommends** that the Community Crime Prevention Unit should undertake a Review of the feasibility and likely effects of requiring local councils to develop crime prevention and community safety strategy plans as part of a legislative mandate.

Whilst many local councils have developed community safety or crime prevention plans for their areas, many have not done so. Requiring councils to develop these important policy documents through legislation may be one way of ensuring all communities in Victoria have a systematic plan to address crime in their areas. A review as to whether mandatory requirements are desirable would need to consider the following issues:

- *Should the provision for local council Crime Prevention and Community Safety Strategy Plans be embedded in legislation? If so why? If not why not?*

- *If legislation is recommended should it be part of a new Act dedicated to crime prevention in local government?*

- *Alternatively, would it be sufficient to amend another Act that already addresses local government issues to include the relevant requirement? For example, the Public Health and Wellbeing Act 2008?*

- *Is there a danger in that amending a pre-existing Act, the issue could be 'hidden', 'lost' or minimised as a matter of importance for local government?*

Any proposed Review could also include discussion as to whether a grant of funding for crime prevention purposes should be contingent upon a local council having a Crime Prevention and Community Safety Strategy Plan in place.

(Chapters 6 and 12)

14. **The Committee recommends** that the Community Crime Prevention Unit commission research to compare the crime prevention outcomes of those local government areas that currently have crime prevention and community safety strategy plans or their equivalents with those that do not.

The Committee notes that the survey conducted by the AIC (reported on in Chapter 5) found a correlation between local councils having a formal crime prevention strategy in place and a more informed and tailored approach to crime prevention. A positive correlation was also found between the type of approaches employed, the extent and level of community and stakeholder engagement and data collection and research. However, the Committee is not aware of any local or international research that has been undertaken to establish the benefit or otherwise of local councils developing local crime prevention and community safety strategy plans. This is a significant gap in crime prevention research that should be addressed. In particular, the findings of such research could benefit the Community Crime Prevention Unit in undertaking the review recommended in Recommendation 13. Without such research there is no evidence base to establish whether mandating crime prevention plans for local councils in legislation is a feasible option.

The Australian Institute of Criminology may be a useful research body to undertake such research.

(Chapters 11 and 12)

15. **The Committee recommends** that those councils and shires that do not presently have a community safety and crime prevention committee should establish one.

Each local council in Victoria should form at least one community crime prevention committee that would draw upon local community input and expertise to address issues and problems and discuss solutions pertinent to local communities in the area of crime prevention and community safety. Membership on the committee could include representatives from Victoria Police and relevant government and non-government agencies. Whilst the membership of such committees should be flexible, the Committee believes that in large and/or diverse local government areas there may need to be more than one committee. This would particularly be the case in municipalities that cover large areas or where there are rural and urban areas within the municipal boundary that may give rise to a variety of different crime prevention and community safety issues.

(Chapters 7 and 12)

Developing partnerships at all levels

The evidence before the Committee has been overwhelming that crime prevention needs to be a shared responsibility between governments and civil society. The recently developed National Crime Prevention Framework states in this regard:

> In Australia, contemporary crime prevention has generally embraced the value of partnerships, collaborative policy development and program delivery, in recognition that the causes of crime are wide ranging, complex and frequently require a coordinated response.[4]

A report by the Institute on Governance in 2006 noted the importance of partnerships between government and 'civil society',[5] in a range of subject areas including community safety. Such partnerships, however, need to be based on principles of accountability, responsibility and leadership.

16. **The Committee recommends** that in developing partnerships with community groups, councils and shires incorporate the guidelines from the Institute on Governance's *Good Governance Principles for Partnerships* as outlined in Recommendation 17.

(Chapters 3 and 12)

17. **The Committee recommends** that any partnerships entered into between government agencies such as the Community Crime Prevention Unit, local government and non-government agencies and the private sector incorporate the Institute on Governance *Good Governance Principles for Partnerships* discussed later in this Report.[6]

The Institute on Governance believes that any partnerships formed between government, 'civil society' (such as non-government organisations) and the private sector need to be based on sound principles of governance. These principles include:

- *Legitimacy and Voice*

- *Direction and Strategic Vision*

- *Performance*

- *Accountability*

- *Fairness.*

In doing so, government and civil society can use the relative strengths of each partner in order to achieve policies and programs that address current issues in crime prevention and community safety.[7]

These partnership arrangements need to flow both horizontally (i.e. across agencies) and vertically (i.e. from the centre to the local and regional level) if they are to be effective at promoting 'joined-up' practice.

(Chapters 3 and 12)

---

4   http://www.aic.gov.au/crime_community/crimeprevention/ncpf.aspx. See also the discussion in Chapter 3.

5   Also known as non-governmental or voluntary sector organisations (see Edgar, Marshall and Bassett 2006, p.1).

6   See Chapter 4 of this Report.

7   For a discussion of good governance principles for partnerships, see Chapter 3 of this Report.

Involvement of the private sector in crime prevention partnerships

18. **The Committee recommends** that the Victorian government undertake a review of the involvement of small business and corporate enterprises in crime prevention partnership initiatives. Such a review could include but not be restricted to:

- an audit of the current involvement of small business and the corporate sector in crime prevention and community safety initiatives in Victoria

- the role of corporate social responsibility in the area of crime prevention and community safety

- how the United Nations Guidelines on the use of corporate crime prevention partnerships can be incorporated into the proposed Crime Prevention and Community Safety Framework

- the effectiveness and positive outcomes of current public/private sector projects in the areas of crime prevention and community safety

- the use of private sector volunteers to work on projects associated with crime prevention and community safety

- the barriers faced by the corporate and small business sector in becoming involved in crime prevention and community safety initiatives

- incentives that the Victorian and/or Commonwealth governments may be able to provide to the private sector to invest in crime prevention and community safety projects

- ways of promoting to the private sector the positive aspects of becoming involved with crime prevention and community safety initiatives

- ways of providing practical advice to the private sector on entering crime prevention partnerships, particularly through implementing the guidelines outlined in the *ICPC Public-Private Partnerships and Community Safety: A Guide to Action* (2011).

The Committee recognises that in Victoria small business and corporate enterprises can and have played a role in supporting crime prevention and community safety programs and initiatives. Research has also shown that the private sector is in a unique position to contribute to the safety and welfare of communities, at local, state or national level.[8]

The United Nations has also outlined several useful ways in which the private sector can make a substantial contribution to enhancing community safety and reducing crime. These include:

- *Contributing to social programs that address the causes of violence and crime*

- *Helping to reduce the opportunities and incentives to commit crime by making situational and contextual changes (situational and crime prevention through environmental design measures)*

- *Contributing to the restoration and better use of public and semi-public spaces*

- *Participating in urban renewal projects*

- *Helping to prevent crime and recidivism by developing learning programs and providing job training and employment opportunities for ex-offenders.*[9]

Whilst the involvement of the private sector in addressing crime prevention and community safety has generally been welcomed, relatively little research has been conducted in Victoria to understand the challenges in developing these partnerships or to measure the outcomes, benefit or influence of initiatives between governments and the private sector in terms of their capacity to reduce crime or have a positive impact on community safety.

(Chapters 3 and 12)

---

8   See discussion in Chapter 3.

9   For a discussion of this type of corporate social responsibility in the crime prevention context, see the Drugs and Crime Prevention Committee, *Inquiry into Youth Offending, Final Report*, particularly in the context of the Bridge Program and its work to find employment for young ex-offenders with private sector companies.

Research and evaluation

19. The Committee acknowledges on the basis of the available evidence that crime prevention and community safety initiatives are rarely subject to rigorous evaluation. **The Committee therefore recommends** that there is a need for the Community Crime Prevention Unit to ensure state-wide evidence based research, access to evaluation of programs and best practice modelling is provided or made available to councils in order to deliver effective crime prevention and community safety programs.

The importance of evaluation, monitoring and performance measurement as key features of effective crime prevention has been stressed in the recently developed National Crime Prevention Framework. However, too often evaluation is viewed as an expensive diversion from the 'main game' of delivering crime prevention services. This may be particularly the case for under-funded community and local government agencies.

Moreover, while evaluation is important, it can also require significant resources. For this reason, the Committee proposes different forms of evaluation for different types of activities: performance measurement and outcomes reporting for projects funded by small grants; external evaluation of 'clusters' of projects identified as particularly important; and more substantial evaluation of innovative or unique projects.

(Chapters 11 and 12)

20. The Committee recommends that the Victorian Government should establish a set of evaluation priority areas in consultation with key crime prevention stakeholders such as government agencies, academia, local government and community agencies.

A possible forum for the development of such an agenda could be the proposed Crime Prevention Expert Advisory Group. This group could identify key crime prevention initiatives that should be evaluated as a priority. Some examples could be projects targeting family violence or antisocial behaviours by young people.

(Chapters 11 and 12)

21. The Committee recommends that the Community Crime Prevention Unit requires recipients of small grants such as Community Safety Fund Grants to report to the Unit on performance measurements and outcomes against the initial aims of the program.

The Committee acknowledges that it can be onerous and expensive for some local government authorities and associated agencies to undertake formal evaluations of their programs. This is particularly the case for smaller agencies with limited budgets. It is still important for smaller agencies to provide evaluative data to the Community Crime Prevention Unit on the outcomes of their programs. In such cases, however, it should be done in a manner that is relatively quick, concise and 'user friendly'. Completing evaluation or performance measurement documents should not be so time-consuming as to detract from time spent on actual program delivery. One way of enabling local councils to evaluate their crime prevention programs could be for the Community Crime Prevention Unit to develop a template to facilitate these types of evaluation.

(Chapters 11 and 12)

22. The Committee recommends that the Community Crime Prevention Unit reserve specific funding within their total crime prevention program to fund external evaluation of 'clusters' of projects that are identified as being of particular importance.

(Chapters 11 and 12)

23. The Committee recommends that the Community Crime Prevention Unit select for evaluation individual projects or initiatives that appear innovative but for which there is no evidence base currently to support their worth. Such an evaluation would assess their effectiveness in achieving desired outcomes and identify the practical challenges and lessons for implementing similar projects.

Evaluation funding needs to be carefully targeted given the expense involved. In many individual cases, due to the type of intervention being implemented and the budget available for the project, a formal or high level evaluation may not be warranted. This may particularly be so in cases where the recipient agency has not received a separate or dedicated budgetary allocation for evaluation. Rather, it may be more effective to conduct sophisticated evaluation of classes or clusters of programs (for example, youth justice or domestic violence programs); or projects for which there is no evidence base. The findings, including 'lessons learned' or 'what works', could then be analysed and made available for crime prevention officers, policy-makers and project managers. The clustering method of evaluation should also be applicable to the evaluation of small grant programs.

(Chapters 11 and 12)

24. **The Committee recommends** that the Victorian Government establish an independent crime research, statistics and data collection/analysis agency to assist local government, police and community agencies with the provision of data and evidence to inform the development and implementation of crime prevention programs and initiatives. The Bureau of Crime Statistics and Research (BOCSAR) in New South Wales may serve as a useful example.

Evidence has been given to the Committee that local government access to data has often been through networking with key agencies i.e. Victoria Police and others represented on crime prevention partnerships. A large percentage of crime prevention projects have arisen out of a spontaneous recognition that there is a crime problem, where potentially more methodical problem identification might reveal a different picture of the 'real crime problem' in an area. As a result, crime and fear of crime reduction measures can often be chosen on insufficient analysis of the problem and subsequently their success can be impacted.

An independent crime research and statistics agency would lead to the development and application of an evidence base for effective crime prevention including the measurement and reporting on effective (and ineffective) crime prevention interventions throughout Victoria.

(Chapters 11 and 12)

Funding

Sufficient funding is an important aspect of developing and implementing crime prevention and community safety programs in Victoria. In particular local councils will need to be supported to undertake any expanded crime prevention and community safety roles. As such the Committee makes the following recommendations.

25. The limitations on Council activity in the community safety area can often be attributed to the lack of adequate and specifically tailored/dedicated funding. **The Committee therefore recommends** that appropriate funding opportunities be offered to local government to drive more targeted, evidence-based community safety activity.

Local level approaches to community crime prevention are extremely important.

Much of the detailed work addressing local crime prevention and community safety issues is increasingly been undertaken by local government, particularly through the use of local community safety plans. Local government municipalities and shires and their agencies are increasingly becoming significant players and stakeholders in the development of crime prevention policy and the implementation and delivery of crime prevention programs and initiatives. Whilst some councils have accepted and even embraced these challenges, others find the responsibility onerous, particularly without increased funding to compensate the extra workload. This may be particularly true of smaller rural shires.

Indeed, many local government authorities that have given evidence to this Inquiry are concerned that although they are increasingly expected to deliver policies and programs addressing crime prevention and community safety they are not provided with the resources to meet these expectations effectively.

(Chapters 4, 8 and 12)

26. **The Committee recommends** that the Victorian Government provide further and ongoing grants for community crime prevention and safety initiatives, particularly those involving partnerships. These grants should be awarded to initiatives that fulfil the objectives of the Crime Prevention and Community Safety Framework.

The Committee acknowledges the recent provision of a series of grant schemes by the Community Crime Prevention Unit for various crime prevention initiatives that local communities can apply for. It believes, however, that an additional grants scheme needs to be implemented, drawing from funding guidelines in the new Crime Prevention and Community Safety Framework.

(Chapter 12)

27. **The Committee recommends** that as a requirement of receiving Victorian Government funding for crime prevention, local governments either by themselves or in conjunction with other local councils in their regions are required to establish local safety committees that foster crime prevention and community safety partnerships.

The Committee believes it essential that all local government authorities establish crime prevention and community safety committees or equivalent to address crime prevention issues in their municipalities and shires. It acknowledges, however, that for some smaller councils particularly in rural areas of Victoria the resources and commitment required to set up such a Committee may prove onerous and/or expensive. It may therefore be feasible for two or more local councils to join together to form a district level Committee, thereby sharing the financial and resource burden involved in its establishment and ongoing operation.

(Chapter 12)

28. **The Committee recommends** that as a requirement for obtaining a crime prevention grant, councils, shires and local community organisations be required to demonstrate to the Community Crime Prevention Unit that the initiative for which they are seeking funding addresses an identified problem in the community and falls within a priority of the local crime prevention and community safety strategy. Such evidence could be provided through the local crime prevention audit/needs analysis and/or by accessing police statistics, research and other intelligence data.

The NSW Bureau of Crime Statistics and Research provides an extremely useful model as to how councils and shires can be assisted in gaining the appropriate evidence (see Recommendation 24).

(Chapters 11 and 12)

Education and Training

29. **The Committee recommends** that the Community Crime Prevention Unit should develop a series of training packages on crime prevention and community safety. These modules should support the attainment of skills and knowledge required for job roles that involve the identification, planning, development or delivery of crime prevention strategies or activities. Course content could include the following:

- Understanding crime prevention theory and practice

- The various approaches to crime prevention including social-developmental approaches and crime prevention through environmental design

- Understanding, developing and maintaining good partnerships

- What works in crime prevention

- Evaluation theory and techniques

- How to apply for grants and funding

The Committee acknowledges the need for ongoing and initial professional development and training for local crime prevention and community safety officers, members of crime prevention and community safety committees and police. The Committee also acknowledges the expense for councils, shires and local community organisations across the state developing their own training packages and believes therefore that the responsibility for funding such training be primarily with the Community Crime Prevention Unit.

These crime prevention and community safety training packages could be delivered by a variety of groups including the Community Crime Prevention Unit, by regional reference groups or by the Local Government Professionals Community Safety Special Interest Group.

(Chapters 8 and 12)

30. The Committee recommends that comprehensive units on crime prevention and community safety should be incorporated into Victoria Police probationary training as soon as possible.

Victoria Police has acknowledged that crime prevention is an important aspect of police work in Victoria. In a submission to the Committee, Victoria Police explained that whilst there are plans in the future to incorporate crime prevention in recruit training it does not provide this training at present. Training is however made available to sworn officers at detective training school and for every Senior Sergeant Qualification and Inspector Qualification Program. Whilst such training is important it is equally crucial that instruction on crime prevention and community safety be offered earlier in a police recruit's probationary training.

(Chapters 8 and 12)

31. The Committee recommends that relevant TAFE Colleges develop crime prevention modules as part of community development courses so that those responsible for developing or implementing crime prevention initiatives can receive appropriate accreditation and acknowledgement for their professional development.

Professional development is clearly an important factor to be taken into consideration in the work of crime prevention officers. This is particularly the case as this area of expertise becomes increasingly specialised. Crime prevention officers and others working in that or related fields should be encouraged to undertake tertiary studies in this area. Consideration should be given to accrediting specialist crime prevention officers who have successfully completed diplomas or degrees in crime prevention, community safety or related areas.

Educational providers RMIT, Chisholm Institute of TAFE, Holmesglen Institute of TAFE, Kangan Institute and Northern Melbourne Institute of TAFE currently offer stand-alone crime prevention units with no prerequisite. They have all also indicated that they can deliver on-campus or online units specially tailored to local government staff.

(Chapters 8 and 12)

Communication

32. The Committee recommends that Victoria Police should provide a clear statement of what the public should do when it observes any suspected criminal activity.

Whilst crime prevention may be 'everybody's business', the Committee has found during the deliberations of this Inquiry that there is some uncertainty as to what members of the general public should do in cases where they observe criminal or antisocial conduct occurring or suspect it may have occurred. This confusion is partly due to a range of agencies being associated with the reporting of such activity; for example Neighbourhood Watch, Crime Stoppers and Victoria Police itself.

Members of the general public therefore need to receive unambiguous messages as to what they should do in cases where they have observed or been aware of criminal or antisocial activity. For example, in cases of police emergencies, that they should call 000 (zero, zero, zero) or in less serious cases contact 'Crime Stoppers'.

(Chapters 7 and 12)

33. The Committee recommends that the Community Crime Prevention Unit investigate the promotion of Facebook and other forms of social media in developing and implementing crime prevention initiatives.

The Committee acknowledges that social media and the use of new technologies is an excellent way of communicating with various sectors/groups of the community.

(Chapter 12)

Crime prevention approaches

34. The Committee recommends that the Community Crime Prevention Unit liaise with, encourage and assist university architecture and planning faculties to offer or expand courses on Crime Prevention through Environmental Design.

(Chapters 2 and 12)

35. The Committee recommends the Victorian Government consider establishing a Designing Out Crime Research Centre in Victoria similar to that operating at the University of Technology, Sydney NSW.

The Designing Out Crime Research Centre in Sydney, New South Wales[10] has clearly been effective in using crime prevention through environmental design principles to combat situational and opportunistic crime in that state. It is feasible that the establishment of a similar centre in Victoria would also produce beneficial outcomes. A possible model is the formation of a private-public partnership between the Community Crime Prevention Unit and one of Victoria's architecture and/or urban planning/design schools.

(Chapters 3 and 12)

Recommendation for Neighbourhood Watch

36. The Committee recommends that Neighbourhood Watch as part of its current funding requirements be reviewed by the Victorian Government in 2013. The Review would assess the effectiveness of Neighbourhood Watch as a government funded crime prevention initiative. It should also indicate on the evidence received whether on balance further government funding should be allocated to support Neighbourhood Watch beyond 2014.

The Committee acknowledges that Neighbourhood Watch Victoria has had a long history and particularly in its early years achieved much in promoting safer communities in Victoria. In particular the work of its many committed volunteers is to be commended. Nonetheless, for reasons outlined at length in this Report[11] it is appropriate for this Committee to question the relevance and viability of the organisation in the 21st century. It may be that the proposed appointment of a Chief Executive Officer to head the organisation, a restructure of the Board, the implementation of their new strategy and a reassessment at the organisation's aims, objectives and priorities will result in positive changes. Nonetheless, the Committee believes it is imperative that the Victorian government conduct a Review of Neighbourhood Watch in 2013 to determine whether it has a viable and continuing existence. In particular, the onus should fall on Neighbourhood Watch to demonstrate to the Victorian government that it merits ongoing funding. Any Review should also include canvassing transitional and future alternative crime prevention options should it be decided that Neighbourhood Watch not receive ongoing Victorian Government assistance.

(Chapters 10 and 12)

---

10   Discussed in Chapter 3.
11   See discussion in Chapter 10.

Contents

List of Tables and Figures

Tables

Figures

List of Abbreviations

AIC	Australian Institute of Criminology
ANZCPSOG	Australia and New Zealand Crime Prevention Senior Officers' Group
AYOS	Assertive Youth Outreach Service
BOCSAR	Bureau of Crime Statistics and Research
CACP	Canadian Association of Chiefs of Police
CALD	Culturally and Linguistically Diverse
CCPP	Community Crime Prevention Plan
CCPU	Community Crime Prevention Unit
CCTV	closed-circuit television
CED	Community Engagement Division
CGD	City of Greater Dandenong
COSI	Community Safety Initiative
CPDO	Crime Prevention Diversity Officer
CPP	Crime Prevention Partnerships
CPSD	Crime Prevention through Social Development
CPTED	Crime Prevention through Environmental Design
CPV	Crime Prevention Victoria
CRP	Crime Reduction Program (UK)
CRTPD	Crime Reduction through Product Design
CSCP	Community Safety and Crime Prevention
CSMT	Community Safety Management Team
CSP	Community Safety Partnership
CSR	Corporate Social Responsibility
CST	Community Safety Team
CTC	Communities that care
DACCWA	Devon and Cornwall Community Watch Association
DHS	Department of Human Services
DOC	Designing Out Crime
EBPP	evidence based policy program
EOTS	Eyes on the Street program
GGSC	Greater Geelong Safety Committee
ICCWA	Injury Control Council of Western Australia
ICPC	International Centre for the Prevention of Crime
ITT	Interdisciplinary Triage Teams
JNW	Junior Neighbourhood Watch
LAC	Local Area Command
LGA	Local Government Authority
LGPro	Local Government Professionals
LNWA	Leicestershire Neighbourhood Watch Association
MRA	Market Reduction Approach
NARTT	Northern Assessment and Referral Treatment Team
NCCPP	National Community Crime Prevention Programme
NCPS	National Crime Prevention Strategy
NESB	non-English speaking background

NHWN	Neighbourhood & Home Watch Network (UK)
NJC	Neighbourhood Justice Centre
NNWN	National Neighbourhood Watch Network
NPT	Neighbourhood Policing Team (UK)
NSGWI	National Strategy Group on Watch Issues (UK)
NW/HW	Neighbourhood Watch and Home Watch (UK)
NW	Neighbourhood Watch
OCP	Office of Crime Prevention
ON	Operation Newstart
OSTT	Operational Safety Tactics and Training
OWL	Online Watch Link
PCC	Perth City Council
PCC	Police and Crime Commissioner (UK)
PCSG	Police and Community Support Group (UK)
PCSO	Police Community Support Officer (UK)
PSA	Police Service area
RIGS	Rural Intelligence Gathering System
SCP	Situational Crime Prevention
SCPD	Strategic Crime Prevention Division
SMT	Senior Management Team
SYLDP	The Sudanese Youth Leadership Development Program
SYNWA	South Yorkshire Neighbourhood Watch Association
UN	United Nations
UNODC	United Nations Office on Drugs and Crime
UTS	University of Technology Sydney
VLGA	Victorian Local Governance Association
YSAS	Youth Substance Abuse Services
VVNWA	Valleys and Vale Neighbourhood Watch Association
WHO	World Health Organization

Section A — Contextualising Crime Prevention and Community Safety

1. Introduction

Background to prevention approaches

In the late 19th century, Sir Arthur Conan Doyle, crime novelist and creator of fictional detective Sherlock Holmes, stated 'To avenge crime is important but to prevent it is more so'.[1]

Crime costs the community in a variety of ways including the loss of productivity, policing, criminal justice administration and court costs. The Australian Institute of Criminology approximated the cost of crime in Australia in 2005 to be nearly $36 billion per year (Rollings 2008). More recently a study by Professor Russell Smyth from Monash University conservatively estimated that the cost of crime in Victoria 2009-2010 was $9.8 billion.[2] 'This is equivalent to $1678 per person or 3.4% of Gross State Product in Victoria 2009-2010' (2011, p.20).

Acknowledging these costs, western countries over the past few decades have gone beyond an 'avenging' or law enforcement model to address crime and antisocial behaviour. It has been recognised that preventing crime through the promotion of social development, social inclusion and participation and community capacity building models[3] not only can 'work' but more importantly, for governments in particular, be far more cost-effective than criminal justice responses such as incarceration (Sutton, Cherney & White 2008).[4] Whilst law and order approaches may be attractive in that they tackle crime at its most obvious source — the offender — they ignore the complex and multiple contributory factors that lead to criminal offending. As criminologists point out, one of the chief advantages of prevention policy 'is that it moves beyond a fixation with deviance and deviants and begins to address *all* the contributing factors' (Sutton, Cherney & White 2008, p.5, Committee's emphasis). Most importantly, a crime prevention approach that invests in social development and community capacity building is essentially about making local communities more liveable, happy and healthy places for all.

Reframing crime prevention

However, despite this increasing recognition that crime prevention is important of itself, crime prevention approaches in Australia over the past 40 years have been essentially cyclical and fragmented, often relying on top-down models that were mandated from centralised state government departments. A variety of different approaches, frameworks, 'grand plans' and models have been tried in an effort to implement crime prevention programs in Victoria and across Australia, with varying degrees of success. This suggests that to a certain extent the idea of prevention per se remains an adjunct to the 'main game' of law enforcement. However, more than

---

1   Quoted in McKendry 2003, p.14.
2   These figures should not be regarded as definitive.
3   See below and discussion in Chapter 2 for examination of these concepts in the crime prevention context.
4   See below and the discussion in Chapter 11 for a discussion of cost-effectiveness and community crime prevention approaches.

100 years after Conan Doyle stated the words above, criminologists and policy-makers are still generally of the view that to reduce victimisation and deter crime, governments, in partnership with the community and private sectors, need to go beyond simple law enforcement and criminal justice measures to tackle the risk factors that contribute to criminal and antisocial behaviour.

This paradigm shift in the way crime prevention was being conceptualised was evident by the 1980s and 1990s in Victoria, Australia and overseas. Traditional law and order approaches, if not replaced, were being accompanied by other ways of addressing, reducing and preventing crime; methods that looked at the causes and contributory factors that might explain why antisocial behaviour occurs in the first place.[5]

Moreover, there has been a worldwide trend for local communities to increasingly 'own' the problems of crime in those communities and proactively work towards preventing or at least reducing such crime and antisocial behaviour (Hicks 1993).

Local is global

Increasingly crime prevention of all types is being influenced by international developments. Government policy-makers, local urban and social planners, police and community agencies across the world are examining crime prevention models to incorporate the best of 'what works' and learn lessons from what hasn't. Drawing from international practice still means, and in fact reinforces, that localised approaches tailored to individual communities remain important. What is right for a municipality in Los Angeles will not necessarily be appropriate for the suburbs of Melbourne. Yet it is largely true to say that from the 1990s onwards crime prevention policy and practice has been to a significant degree internationalised, and part of these global approaches is the move towards the importance of local communities 'owning' crime prevention initiatives.

Localised crime prevention

Crime prevention takes place at all levels of government and society. However, much crime prevention theory and research indicates that initiatives developed and implemented at a local level are some of the best ways of reducing crime and antisocial behaviour (Homel 2009a). Yet in practice, implementing a community based crime prevention strategy can be problematic. What have been the mistakes made in implementing community crime prevention models and what needs to be done to bolster local level crime prevention approaches are issues that need to be examined and these are discussed extensively in Chapter 3 and 4. This is not, however, an Inquiry into what *specific* crime prevention initiatives work or are suitable for local communities. Whether a local community employs an environmental crime prevention strategy such as better street lighting, a social prevention strategy such as parenting classes for young mums and dads or a mixture of both is less important than the models employed and the approaches taken to develop and successfully implement these initiatives.[6]

A history of crime prevention in Victoria

The history of crime prevention in Victoria mirrors generally the history of crime prevention initiatives in other western nations. The attempts of Australian state and federal governments to implement coordinated crime prevention strategies in the late 1980s and 1990s were largely drawn from the experience of the United Kingdom, France and the United States in

---

5   Most notably, social and situational or environmental crime prevention approaches. See further discussion later in this chapter and in Chapter 2.

6   For a detailed discussion of environmental, social and other crime prevention strategies, see the discussion in Chapter 2 of this Report.

the 1970s and 1980s (Sutton, Cherney & White 2008).[7] This history reflects the essentially cyclical nature of crime prevention efforts over the last 30 years or more. Or as Cherney and Sutton state: 'Cycles of instability and renewal that have simply helped further undermine relationships between central and local partners' (2007, p.66).[8] On occasion, crime prevention programs have emphasised the social aims of increasing the life chances of socio-economically disadvantaged communities via better health, education and employment opportunities. At other times a law and order approach has been paramount in which the aim has centred more on targeting and punishing the offender than addressing more widely the needs of local communities. At times crime prevention strategies have been based on a broad (and somewhat confused) mixture of both approaches. The United Kingdom's crime prevention strategy of the late 1990s encapsulated in the catchphrase of the day — 'Tough on Crime, Tough on the Causes of Crime' — was arguably an example of this muddled approach.[9]

Early approaches to crime prevention in Victoria

Despite the above criticisms of the fragmented response to crime prevention and community safety, Victoria has been seen as 'somewhat of a pathfinder for crime prevention in Australia' (Hill & Sutton 1996, p.56). From the late 1970s a number of programs were established that sought community input into preventing and reducing crime in local neighbourhoods. For example, in 1979 the Safety House Network was established to provide registered safety house 'refuges' for vulnerable children and senior Victorians to turn to when they feel unsafe or in need of urgent assistance.[10] In Victoria one of the first crime prevention strategies rolled out at state level under police auspices has been the Neighbourhood Watch program. This program, established in 1983, is one of the aspects of the Terms of Reference that will be examined in greater detail in Chapter 10. It was followed in 1987 by the establishment of the Crime Stoppers partnership between Victoria Police, the media and the general public.[11]

Early attempts at coordinating crime prevention — the 1990s

By the 1990s most state and territory governments had established specific crime prevention units, most often located in justice, courts or police portfolios (Clancey 2011). Central coordinating agencies to develop crime prevention projects became established in Victoria from the 1990s onwards. These included agencies such as the original Crime Prevention Division of the Department of Police and Emergency Services in the early 1990s and VicSafe. These agencies developed partnership strategies that sought to centralise control

---

7   Crime prevention policy and program development is largely the province of state and increasingly local governments due to the division of powers and responsibilities under the Australian Constitution. Whilst the Federal Government established a National Community Crime Prevention Program in 2004, its role has largely been confined to the distribution of funds for crime prevention programs through a national grants program, with applications largely coming from local community groups. It is essentially project rather than plan based, focusing on funding for street lighting and CCTV installations 'rather than providing an overarching crime prevention policy framework' (Clancey 2011, p.3; See also Sutton, Cherney & White 2008, pp.105–106). To a certain extent however this situation has changed with the formation of a National Crime Prevention Framework. See discussion in Chapter 3.

8   Several criminologists and policy-makers have been critical of this 'boom and bust' cycle of crime prevention policies, strategies and governance arrangements, not only in Victoria but across Australia generally. Cherney and Sutton have stated an 'absence of vision' has been responsible for the repeated failure of crime prevention policy in Australia (2007, p.68). McMillan has stated that the adoption of crime prevention strategies and policies can often be susceptible to 'fashion trends' (1992, p.75). Homel, even more critically, has argued that ineffective leadership, inflexible top-down program design, a lack of commitment to 'scientific' crime prevention and poor communication between central and local stakeholders has undermined crime prevention efforts and led to strategy fragmentation (2005).

9   See the discussion in Chapter 3 of this Report.

10   For further information on the Safety House scheme, see www.safetyhousevic.org.au

11   Crime Stoppers Victoria is a 'community based initiative which encourages members of the public to provide information on unsolved crimes, wanted people and people they know are involved in criminal activity.'
      The core activity for Crime Stoppers Victoria is to receive confidential telephone calls and online reports from the public about possible criminal activity, and ensure that the resulting information reaches those whose responsibility it is to investigate such matters.

      Crime Stoppers Victoria also develops and manages programs and initiatives which inform and educate the community about crime prevention and safety. For further information on Crime Stoppers, see http://www.vic.crimestoppers.com.au/

in a state coordinated body whilst incorporating input and participation from local bodies (both local government and community agencies). Such programs and projects included the Good Neighbourhood program (1988) loosely based on the French Bonnemaison approach (see Dussuyer 1991; McMillan 1992)[12] and the Safer Cities and Shires program (1997–2000). The Safer Cities strategy was a multi-agency approach to preventing crime and violence in the state, which encouraged local governments to become 'lead agencies' in crime prevention and community safety through the formation of Senior Management Teams (SMTs). Each SMT was to initiate an analysis of local problems and develop a community safety plan based on the assessment.[13] VicSafe also saw the first network of locally based police community consultative committees established in July 1990.[14] Other organisations established in this early period included the Victorian Community Council against Violence and the Ministerial Community Safety and Crime Prevention Council.[15]

Crime Prevention Victoria 2000–2007

From 2000 most crime prevention programs were centrally administered by Crime Prevention Victoria (CPV). CPV was for many years a division within the Department of Justice based in Melbourne and was tasked with leading a multi-agency approach in reducing crime and violence in the State of Victoria.

At that time CPV worked closely with local organisations and local communities to develop effective local responses. CPV's work program included providing support and advice, encouraging the development of innovative and cost-effective programs, and conducting strategic data analysis, research and evaluation to inform good practice in the state. In 2002, CPV launched the Victorian Government strategy 'Safer Streets and Homes: A Crime and Violence Prevention Strategy for Victoria'. Central to the implementation of the strategy was a six million dollar portfolio of locally based projects aimed at testing out what works best in crime prevention, and providing a basis for informing future work.

The project sponsored initiatives that covered three priority themes:

◆ improving safety in streets and neighbourhoods

◆ preventing family violence

◆ reducing offending and violence by young people.

CPV was downgraded from a Division within Justice to a business unit in 2007 and was subsequently abolished altogether from the Department of Justice.

The current position

When the new Liberal Coalition Government was formed in November 2010, a Ministry of Crime Prevention was established with a commitment to strengthening and supporting crime prevention and community safety initiatives. Since the Terms of Reference were given for this Inquiry, a number of new initiatives and programs have been announced by the state government pertaining to crime prevention and community safety. New directions for community safety announced this year have included:

---

12 For an extended discussion of the Bonnemaison program and other international approaches to crime prevention, see Chapter 3.

13 For a critical analysis of the Safer Cities and Shires program, see Cherney 2004.

14 For a comprehensive account of crime prevention policies, programs and strategies that were developed in Victoria in the 1980s and early 1990s, see McMillan 1992.

15 The Ministerial Community Safety and Crime Prevention Council was established to bring about a 'whole of government' approach to crime prevention and community safety. It was constituted by the Secretaries of government departments (Premier and Cabinet, Justice, Community Services) local government mayors and community representatives. For further information on this and other Victorian crime prevention agencies during this period, see the Submission from Bill Horman to the Drugs and Crime Prevention Committee, Inquiry into Locally Based Approaches to Community Safety and Crime Prevention, May 2011.

- the establishment of the Community Crime Prevention Unit within the Department of Justice to work 'in partnership with government and non-government agencies, local business and service providers to lead the development of evidence-based policies and crime prevention programmes' ('Department of Justice 2011, p.9)

- a new Grants Program for local governments and community groups to develop and implement community safety initiatives

- increased funding and support for the Neighbourhood Watch program.

These and other initiatives will be discussed at length in Chapters 6 and 10.

The role of Victoria Police

Victoria Police have the primary responsibility for law enforcement in this state. They also play a key role in crime prevention. Effective crime prevention requires police to take a proactive community focused approach in addition to reactive policing. As such, Victoria Police recognise that crime prevention is an important part of police work and that effective crime prevention engages and develops partnerships with the local community, schools, ethnic communities, local business and other groups. Accordingly, each Police Service Area (PSA) has a Crime Prevention Officer (CPO) who acts as a liaison officer to individuals and community groups and provides advice in relation to local community safety problems. The CPO is responsible for developing and implementing programs in partnership with local communities to reduce crime and the fear of crime within his or her area.

Victoria Police also has involvement with crime prevention initiatives including Neighbourhood Watch and Crime Stoppers. In relation to Neighbourhood Watch (NW) Victoria Police currently funds 26 full-time positions in the role of NW Divisional Police Coordinator. These members are responsible for direct liaison and partnership with volunteers and provide them with direction and support in relation to the conduct of the program and the development of crime prevention strategies to support a reduction of crime and enhanced community safety.[16]

The need for an Inquiry

As indicated above, crime prevention in Victoria has been arguably characterised by inconsistent approaches and a variety of models. It is certainly true that the importance of localised community approaches has been recognised and to a certain extent put in place by different local authorities. There has also been a move beyond reliance on traditional law and order approaches *only* to the development and implementation of crime prevention policies and programs that address the *causes* and preconditions of offending.

Nonetheless, it is also arguable that there is no uniformity of approach to crime prevention in Victoria. What are the best forms of governance for overseeing crime prevention policy and the optimal models for developing and implementing crime prevention programs are important questions. It is also important to find the best ways to develop effective crime prevention programs and partnerships for local communities and local circumstances. Therefore an Inquiry that considers how crime prevention should best address the needs of local communities is timely.

Terms of Reference

To the **Drugs and Crime Prevention Committee** — for inquiry, consideration and report on locally based approaches to community safety and crime prevention, and the Committee is asked to consider:

---

16   For further discussion of the role of Victoria Police with regard to crime prevention and community safety, see Chapter 6 of this Report.

(a) the breadth of locally based groups and organisations addressing community safety and crime prevention issues within Victoria, particularly with regard to local government and Neighbourhood Watch;

(b) the approaches adopted by these groups to promulgating community safety and crime prevention practices, programs or initiatives;

(c) the extent to which these organisations are effective in engaging with local and state agencies in the development of policy;

(d) whether institutional or other arrangements support or impede such local groups in engaging in the development of community safety initiatives;

(e) whether there is a cost benefit to the community for current crime prevention strategies;

(f) whether alternate models for such organisations may improve outcomes; and

(g) local community safety and crime prevention arrangements in other jurisdictions, particularly within Australia, New Zealand and the United Kingdom.

The Terms of Reference concentrate on *locally* based approaches to community safety and crime prevention. There is much good work being done at the community level to address local problems and minimise the effects of crime in the community. One of the challenges for delineating the scope of this Inquiry is establishing the extent to which such local crime prevention programs and projects are being developed and implemented, what the challenges in developing these programs have been and what evidence exists to show that such programs are (or are not) successful and being sustained. It should be noted at the outset, however that the Inquiry and this associated Report is not about individual crime prevention initiatives or specific areas of crime prevention. It is not concerned, for example, about recommending initiatives to prevent family violence or alcohol related antisocial behaviour per se, important as these issues are. Rather, as discussed below, the focus is about the processes and models through which effective crime prevention policy and programs can be developed and implemented at local level and the partnerships that can be formed to make this happen.

A key question raised by one of the Inquiry's Terms of Reference is whether the locally based approach to crime prevention is not only arguably more cost-effective but also can lead to greater social benefits than the standard ways of responding to crime (Waller 2006). Questions as to where the balance needs to be struck between traditional law enforcement and more creative crime prevention and community safety approaches, particularly at local or community level, are crucial.

Scope of the Inquiry

Crime prevention at first glance looks to be a relatively simple concept, yet in fact it is an extremely complex issue that requires serious consideration. A number of challenges confronted the Committee when it was determining the nature and scope of the Inquiry. This was particularly the case because the Terms of Reference for the inquiry are extremely broad and far-reaching. Strict parameters needed to be drawn otherwise there was a risk that the Inquiry would lose focus and direction. These challenges included:

◆ Clarifying concepts such as crime prevention and community safety.[17]

◆ Deciding whether specific crimes should be the focus of any crime prevention/safety initiatives. For example, should the Committee be considering crimes as diverse as youth offending, family violence, burglary, fraud, and/or environmental crime? Ultimately it was decided that specific types of crime need only be discussed when

---

17   Defining crime prevention is discussed later in this chapter.

illustrating a particular point pertaining to crime prevention models or approaches. It is how crime prevention strategies are facilitated in local communities that is important not the focus on particular crimes.

♦ Giving consideration to which groups of people or communities should be the focus of local crime prevention initiatives. For example, should there be a focus on rural communities, Indigenous communities, young people or seniors, or should crime prevention be universal in its application? The Committee decided that for the purposes of this Inquiry it was more important to discuss the processes by which such programs can be developed, implemented and delivered rather than focus on specific groups for whom crime prevention programs are targeted.

♦ Determining whether state and national initiatives should be examined. The Terms of Reference directed the Committee to examine local government, community and Neighbourhood Watch initiatives, not state or national level initiatives. However, the issue of whether or not it is possible to investigate local crime prevention strategies without understanding the state and national context within which they operate needed to be addressed. Similarly it needed to be questioned whether the federal system of government in Australia makes truly comprehensive crime prevention and community safety policy workable. As Sutton, Cherney and White argue, the constitutional division of powers in this country may mean various stakeholders have differing and sometimes conflicting lines of political and bureaucratic accountability (2008).[18] Again, whilst the focus of the Inquiry is on localised approaches to crime prevention, jurisdictional issues including the role and responsibilities of state and federal governments will be discussed in as much as they impact upon successfully delivering crime prevention at that level. In this regard, consideration needs to be given to the recently developed National Crime Prevention Framework.

♦ Ascertaining the nature and extent or number of crime prevention programs in Victoria, particularly at the local level. How could this best be done and how is the effectiveness of crime prevention programs measured? The Committee sought the assistance of the Australian Institute of Criminology (AIC) to explore some of these questions. It was not possible to conduct a complete audit of crime prevention activity by local government authorities (LGAs), however the survey conducted by the AIC on behalf of the Drugs and Crime Prevention Committee, together with evidence received by the Committee, provided some useful information on these issues.[19]

♦ Deliberating on whether short-term/reactive versus long-term/proactive or developmental strategies are better suited to local crime prevention in the 21st century. Should it be even put as an either/or proposition? In other words, is a mix of both types of interventions best suited to developing and implementing crime prevention policy and programs? What approaches to crime prevention work better for local communities? Are some more suited than others to local focused activity?

♦ Ascertaining whether any lessons could be learnt from the past crime prevention strategies and initiatives in Victoria and other Australian jurisdictions, and from overseas experiences of crime prevention and community safety. As indicated previously, a localised approach to crime prevention is not one that necessarily excludes international trends, models or influences. As Chapters 3 & 4 discusses,

---

18   On this issue the authors state:

      'Persuading national, regional and local governments to endorse general statements about the need for a 'whole of government approach' has been relatively straightforward. The real challenge has been finding ways to translate such 'in principle' agreement into strategies and programmes that transcend political and administrative rivalries and engender genuine cooperation at the grass roots' (Sutton, Cherney & White 2008, p.94).

19   For example through the use of written submissions and evidence obtained in public hearings.

there is much that Victorian crime prevention planners can learn from overseas models — not only 'what works' but also the pitfalls to avoid.

The Report addresses these myriad challenges. Certainly the Committee is of the view that given the complexity of the task a 'one size fits all' approach is inappropriate in addressing the issues of crime and antisocial behaviour in Victoria. This is as true for local communities as it is for the state as a whole.

Considerations for the Inquiry

The Committee received correspondence from Professor Darren Palmer of Deakin University which stated that in addressing any issues pertaining to local crime prevention three basic questions need to be asked: What is the problem, where is the problem in terms of localities and the features of those localities and what is capable of being done in terms of engaging local communities and enhancing their capacity to do something about the problems they see?[20] To such an Inquiry one needs to add the following questions: What are the underlying causes of offending and which of these causes are the most relevant to the crime or crimes being addressed? (Sutton, Cherney & White 2008). Crime prevention is essentially underpinned by understandings or assumptions of why crimes occur: 'Crime prevention always is and should be linked to broader discourses about the nature of society and preferred approaches to social control' (Sutton, Cherney & White 2008, p.13).

All of these questions are examined in greater detail throughout the Report. At first instance, however, it is necessary to look at how crime prevention and related issues have been defined; how crime prevention policy has been developed in Victoria and elsewhere in past years; and finally to briefly discuss what are some of the current initiatives in crime prevention policy development and program delivery.

Definitions and concepts

Crime prevention

Professor Peter Homel has described the concept of crime prevention as poorly or narrowly defined and understood even by those ostensibly working to achieve crime prevention goals (Anderson & Homel 2006 in Homel 2009a). Similarly, Elizabeth McMillan (1992) has called crime prevention a 'rubbery concept' with elastic boundaries; multi-faceted and multi-form policies, programs, models and objectives.[21] However, the following definition of crime prevention by criminologists Van Dijk and De Waard has generally been accepted. The authors view crime prevention as:

> The total of all private initiatives and state policies other than the enforcement of criminal law, aimed at the reduction of damage caused by acts defined as criminal by the state (Van Dijk & De Waard 1991, p.483).

A limitation of Van Dijk and De Waard's definition however is that it tends to exclude the traditional law and order approaches to crime control (for example, arrest, imprisonment, punishment and other criminal justice initiatives that are sometimes viewed as 'tertiary' crime initiatives).

---

20   Correspondence from Associate Professor Darren Palmer, Convenor, Criminology Program, Deakin University, Drugs and Crime Prevention Committee, Inquiry into Locally Based Approaches to Community Safety and Crime Prevention, Melbourne, 9 September 2011.

21   See Elizabeth McMillan 1992, *An Overview of Crime Prevention in Victoria*, at http://www.aic.gov.au/publications/ previous%20series/proceedings/1-27/~/media/publications/proceedings/15/mcmillan.ashx

More recently, in 2011 the National Crime Prevention Framework was released. The document, which was developed by the AIC on behalf of the Australian and New Zealand Crime Prevention Senior Officers' Group, explained that:

> crime prevention includes 'strategies and measures that seek to reduce the risk of crimes occurring, and their potential harmful effects on individuals and society, including fear of crime, by intervening to influence their multiple causes'.[22] These measures can be implemented by individuals, communities, businesses, non-government organisations and all levels of government, to target the various individual, social and environmental factors that increase the risk of crime, disorder and victimisation. Strategies include those that modify the physical environment to reduce the opportunities for crime to occur (environmental approaches), and those that address the underlying social and economic causes of crime and limit the supply of motivated offenders (social and structural approaches) (National Crime Prevention Framework 2011, p.4).

Crime prevention strategies can be further divided into three categories — primary, secondary and tertiary. The Committee generally takes these concepts to mean the following:

◆ Primary (or universal) strategies are those which address the general population, for example universal literacy or health programs.

◆ Secondary (or selected) strategies are those which target a sub-group such as parents or students in a school community.

◆ Tertiary (or targeted) strategies address a specific group which has demonstrated the need for support in a particular area. For example, tertiary prevention can target people who are already known offenders or environments already affected by crime. In the context of juvenile crime for example, it may include employment skills programs for young men released on parole (see Brantingham & Faust 1976; Injury Control Council of Western Australia (ICCWA) 2011).[23]

Some theorists, policy-makers and practitioners believe these types of tertiary crime prevention strategies need to be looked at as part of a comprehensive approach to effective crime reduction and prevention strategies.[24]

However, in recent years there has been a move away from the use of the term 'crime prevention' because of the stigma that program practitioners believe is at times associated with the term. [25]

Community safety

Other theorists and practitioners have a preference for the term 'community safety' in place of or in addition to crime prevention. They argue that a preoccupation with crime can result in interventions that are too narrowly focused and perceived as the sole province of the police (Morgan 1991). For example, Homel has stated: 'For too long, crime prevention has been approached as an activity that is an adjunct to the "main game" of investigating, prosecuting and punishing crime' (2009a, p.2). Moreover, attempts to distinguish anti-crime initiatives from strategies to address other harms (such as substance dependence or child abuse) means dealing separately with issues that according to Sutton, Cherney and White cannot and should not be addressed in isolation: 'A more comprehensive term such as "community safety" seems to avoid this dilemma' (2008, p.25).

---

22 United Nations Economic and Social Council (UN ECOSOC) 2002. *Guidelines for the prevention of crime*, 11th Commission on the prevention of crime and criminal justice. Resolution 2002/13, Annex. UN ECOSOC, New York.

23 Primary, secondary and tertiary crime prevention strategies are discussed further in Chapter 2.

24 Cherney and Sutton view crime prevention however as a distinct *alternative* to law and order policies. A 'tough on crime' rhetoric in Cherney and Sutton's view is incompatible with many aspects of crime prevention 'best practice' (2007, p.71).

25 Sutton, Cherney and White 2008.

The Committee agrees that whilst there is a definite place for criminal justice initiatives such as arrest and imprisonment to deter and reduce offending, the concept of crime prevention cannot be narrowly circumscribed to traditional law and order approaches only. Community safety and community engagement are key aspects of any crime prevention agenda.[26]

Community safety programs also have the potential to embrace a wider range of issues, including those pertaining to health, education and employment. Community safety, it is argued, is: 'an aspect of the *quality* of people's lives in which the risk from a range of social harms such as crime, be it real or *perceived*,[27] is minimised. It also refers to an increase in people's capacity to cope should they experience these harms' (Ekblom & Wyvekens in Morgan & Homel 2011, p.25 (Committee's emphasis)). In effect, community safety reflects a broad approach that in addition to reducing criminal activity covers other activities that impact upon community wellbeing and quality of life, such as health, road safety, injury prevention, fire and emergency situations (Armstrong & Francis 2003). It is an essentially 'positive' process.[28]

It should be stated from the outset, however, that as important as the accident and emergency aspects of community safety are, the Committee's focus as directed by the Terms of Reference is confined to an examination of protecting the community from criminal activity, disorder and antisocial behaviour.

Community development, social capital and community capacity building

The need for local community responses and local preventative strategies to address the problems of crime and antisocial behaviours is being viewed as increasingly important by international public health and social wellbeing agencies. A key focus of this approach is to incorporate the concepts of community development, social capital and community capacity building into crime prevention policy and program implementation.

Community development and community engagement

Whilst much of the community development literature concerning crime concentrates on drug and alcohol-related crime and youth offending, the principles of community development[29] — that the factors that contribute to crime are complex and multifaceted; that there is no single cause and no single solution; and that communities themselves have to address the broader societal and cultural issues that may contribute to crime — are relevant to all forms of crime and crime prevention.

The mobilisation of community action to address issues of concern to local communities is not new of course, but what possibly *has* changed is the recognition that individual based law enforcement approaches, whilst sometimes necessary, are not going to change criminal

---

26   For a detailed discussion see Chapters 2 and 3.

27   For a discussion of the perception of crime and its relationship to the reality of criminal activity, see Chapter 8.

28   The extended understanding of crime prevention as embracing community engagement was endorsed by a number of witnesses and submissions to this Inquiry, particularly those working at local government or community level. See, for example, correspondence from Mr Rob Spence, Municipal Association of Victoria (MAV) 21 May 2012; Mr Bill Horman, Neighbourhood Watch, 27 June 2011 and Mr Phillip Schier, Local Government Association of Victoria (LGAV), 27 June 2011. Representatives from all these groups told the Committee that they thought the term 'crime prevention' of itself had negative connotations that 'community safety' did not. For example, according to Mr Spence local governments would much rather stress the 'positive development exercise' of community engagement than the 'negative purely crime prevention exercises'. For Mr Horman of Neighbourhood Watch, crime prevention is essentially about 'community wellbeing, community consultation, community building and community engagement' — inclusivity rather than the exclusivity of crime prevention as it has traditionally been conceptualised.

    The concept of community development as it relates to crime prevention is discussed extensively in Chapter 2 of this Report. It has been defined in this context as a process that:

    'Stresses a collective approach to problem solving and decision making about needs, goals, priorities and programmes. In particular, it seeks to enable marginal groups to migrate into 'the acting community' of decisions and decision makers.' (Henderson, Jones & Thomas in Lane & Henry 2004, p.202).

29   For detailed discussion of the principles of community development and their relationship to public health, crime and antisocial behaviour see World Health Organization 1992; Homel 1997.

behaviour at a *population* level. From this perspective community based development strategies are about more than punishing criminal individuals, they are concerned with systemic and structural change so that the whole of the community is utilised to support crime prevention (Midford 2004).[30]

One of the key ways in which this community action model is realised is through the creation of local community safety groups and partnerships and the development of community safety plans usually in local government areas. Whilst these types of intervention are discussed at length in later chapters,[31] it is timely to state here that the idea of such groups is to bring together a broad range of community stakeholders including local residents, police, local government officials, police and representatives of various local interest groups.

A related concept is that of community engagement whereby an agency, most often a local council but sometimes the police or a private sector organisation, may provide a range of programs to engage the community and particularly people who may be at risk of criminal activity or offending.

Community engagement programs aim to provide a sense of connectedness or inclusivity within a community. Often people with few social networks or resources are at increased risk of offending, therefore creating connections is particularly important (Williams et al 2009). On a broader level, community engagement programs and community events can have an important educative effect. Family days, festivals, crime prevention weeks and sporting events may cater for members of the general public or discrete groups within it such as multicultural groups or young people.[32]

The benefits of community based approaches to crime prevention are clear. They allow opportunities for local people to have their opinions heard, their ideas taken into consideration and in many cases participate in generating solutions for their local community. This, according to Chikritzhs et al (2007), empowers people and enables them to contribute to their local community. Moreover, where a crime prevention or community safety program is developed and implemented by local community members, even where they are assisted by local council representatives or other officials, the community response is arguably more positive than when it has been externally developed or 'imposed' (Graham & Homel 2008).

Social capital and community capacity building

Although 'social or cultural capital' and 'community capacity building' are different concepts to that of 'community development', the approaches are clearly related.

---

30 An excellent example of such a community development project to address crime and antisocial behaviour is the North Metropolitan Community Violence Prevention Project in Perth, Western Australia.

This program is auspiced by the Injury Control Council of Western Australia (ICCWA). This project is primarily aimed at reducing the levels of violence in the local communities of northern metropolitan Perth. It is very much based, however, in a community development model that seeks to produce positive health and other outcomes for all members of the local community whether they are 'at risk' of committing criminal or antisocial behaviours or not. The Committee met with representatives of ICCWA in Perth in June 2011. These witnesses stressed to the Committee that holistic evidence based health promotion and community development programs that concentrate on resilience and community capacity building are an essential aspect of any intervention to reduce crime in local communities.

See for example evidence of Ms Deborah Costello, Chief Executive Officer, Injury Prevention Council of Western Australia, Evidence given to the Drugs and Crime Prevention Committee, Inquiry into Locally Based Approaches to Community Safety and Crime Prevention, Meeting, Perth, 21 June 2011. See also the strategy document — Community Violence Prevention Strategy in the North Metropolitan Area (Injury Control Council WA and North Metropolitan Area Health Service May 2011).

31 See Chapters 6 and 7.

32 Community engagement programs are especially relevant in the context of youth offending. For a detailed discussion of this issue see the Drugs and Crime Prevention, *Inquiry into Strategies to Prevent High Volume Offending by Young People, Final Report* (2009).

Social capital is based on the idea that societies need to invest in the developmental health of human populations and communities at each level (national, state and local). Social capital theory argues that any social policy addressing human needs (including by definition those pertaining to issues such as criminal or antisocial behaviour) must take into account the developmental needs of children. In other words, to address simply the symptom of the problem (for example youth crime, domestic violence) is closing the stable door after the horse has bolted. Healthy communities are assisted to support their citizens from an early age by building their capacities to develop alternatives to crime and disorder.[33] Keating, one of the key theorists of this theory, argues that:

- The key necessities for supporting healthy child development are income, nutrition, childcare, stimulation, love/support, advocacy and safety.

- Our societies have under-invested in development in the early years (0–5 years), compared to the school-age years, despite research that identifies that these early years are most important.

- To improve the quality of human development, attention needs to be paid to all levels of social aggregation: family, neighbourhood, school and the national socioeconomic environment (Keating cited in Australian National Council on Drugs (ANCD) 2001, p.22).

Keating examined the costs of failing to provide supportive contexts for developmental health, in terms of reduced school performance, increased antisocial behaviour, and reduced work participation (Keating cited in ANCD 2001).[34] Whilst Keating's analysis is still relevant, the supporting evidence is clearly out-dated. However, more recent research by the Washington State Institute for Public Policy has made comparable claims. A study by Aos et al (2011) for example found there was a significant return on investment for evidence based social and community development approaches to reduce crime compared to purely law enforcement measures.[35] The authors, however, did make the salient point that whilst in theory 'blue chip'[36] crime prevention approaches can certainly 'give taxpayers a good return on their dollar', many funded prevention programs in the United States and elsewhere have not been rigorously evaluated. Thus for some crime prevention programs there is insufficient evidence to determine whether benefits exceed costs (Aos et al 2011, p.1). Similar observations have been made in the Australian context.[37]

Community capacity building as with community engagement and development projects is essentially about providing connectedness between human beings — developing self-esteem and an ability to form positive relationships with others thus obviating the need for criminal or antisocial behaviour.[38]

There are of course other causal factors that impact upon criminal offending — structural factors such as unemployment or poverty are clearly significant. Social connectedness and community development programs are not of themselves sufficient to prevent or

---

33 For example, the *Health Development and Social Capital Project* conducted in a low socioeconomic area of Adelaide, South Australia found that 'involvement in social and community life improved health and acted as a buffer to declining socioeconomic status' (Australian National Council on Drugs (ANCD) 2001, p.8).

34 For further discussion of these concepts particularly in the context of youth offending, substance misuse and alcohol related crime, see the *Final Report* of the Drugs and Crime Prevention Committee's:
- Inquiry into Strategies to Prevent High Volume Offending and Recidivism by Young People
- Inquiry into Strategies to Reduce Assaults in Public Places in Victoria
- Inquiry into the Inhalation of Volatile Substances. And the extensive literature cited and discussed therein.

35 An earlier report by the Institute in the specific context of early intervention programs for youth to reduce juvenile crime produced similar findings. See Aos et al 2004. A more detailed discussion of cost-benefit analysis in crime prevention is given in Chapter 11 of this Report.

36 That is, programs that have been rigorously evaluated according to stringent evidence based principles and found to produce positive returns for taxpayers.

37 See for example, Morgan and Homel 2011.

38 Community capacity building is particularly noticeable in the context of youth offending where approaches such as mentoring are crucially important. For a discussion of mentoring and other examples of community programs to reduce youth offending see the *Final Report* of the Drugs and Crime Prevention, *Inquiry into Strategies to Prevent High Volume Offending by Young People* (2009).

reduce serious crime. Nonetheless, the Committee believes that the concepts discussed in this section are not naively optimistic but important aspects of an overall approach to addressing crime prevention particularly at local community level which need to be encouraged and supported.

Crime prevention classifications and typologies

Criminologists have also devised a number of ways of classifying what activities and programs come under the heading of 'crime prevention', for example typologies such as 'situational crime prevention', 'developmental' or 'social crime prevention' and so on. An extended account of these classifications, concepts and definitions is found in Chapter 2.

The Inquiry process

The previous discussion has indicated that the area of crime prevention and community safety is complex, challenging and requires measured consideration rather than 'knee-jerk' responses. The Committee has therefore embarked upon an extensive research process in order to canvass the issues and receive input and information from as many individuals, agencies and organisations as possible that have an interest in the issues raised in the Terms of Reference.

In conducting the Inquiry the Committee employed a variety of processes and methodologies to gain a comprehensive understanding of the nature, breadth, institutional support and impediments, costs and effectiveness of locally based approaches to community safety and crime prevention in Victoria.

Literature review and background briefings

The Committee commenced the Inquiry by receiving background briefings from the Department of Justice, Victoria Police, the Municipal Association of Victoria and expert criminologists specialising in the field.[39] A comprehensive review of the literature was undertaken on the theory, policy and practice of crime prevention and community safety in Victoria, other Australian jurisdictions and overseas. This review was constantly updated throughout the Inquiry.

Written submissions

Calls for written submissions were published on Saturday 30 April 2011 in the *Herald Sun* and *The Age*. Letters inviting submissions to the Inquiry were sent to key government and non-government agencies in Victoria. The Committee received 24 written submissions, which came from a range of individuals and organisations.[40]

Public hearings and teleconferences in Melbourne

Public hearings were held in Melbourne on 27 June 2011, 9, 10 and 15 August 2011, 10 October 2011, 27 February 2012 and 16 April 2012. The Committee also conducted telephone conferences with expert witnesses from interstate. In total, oral evidence was received from 133 witnesses.[41]

Regional visits and public hearings

Through its research the Committee identified that the Cities of Dandenong, Frankston and Ballarat have been developing a range of crime prevention and community safety

---

39   For a list of those who gave briefings to the Committee see Appendix 1.
40   For a list of the submissions received by the Committee see Appendix 2.
41   For a list of witnesses appearing at Public Hearings, and spoken to via teleconference see Appendix 3.

initiatives to address local community concerns regarding rising crime rates, particularly rises in the numbers of assaults in public places. The Committee decided to travel to these cities to conduct a series of forums and public hearings with local councils and their crime prevention and community safety partners to gain an understanding of the work of local communities and the issues they face in developing policy and program responses. The Committee also held meetings and a forum in the City of Geelong. Geelong was selected because it had implemented a range of successful initiatives to reduce problems of alcohol-fuelled violence in that region, which were worthy of consideration for other locations.[42]

At all regional locations, public forums were conducted to provide an opportunity for Neighbourhood Watch and community representatives to have input into the Inquiry.

Interstate visits

The Terms of Reference required the Committee to investigate whether there are alternate models for the delivery of better crime prevention and community safety outcomes within Australia. Crime prevention has had a chequered history in most of the Australian states and territories. At one stage, particularly in the 1990s, most of the states had a crime prevention unit of some type established, often liaising either formally or informally with local government. Some of these have since been disbanded (South Australia and Victoria for example). However, interesting crime prevention work is being currently undertaken in Western Australia and New South Wales and it was considered that the Committee could gain valuable insights by visiting these states.[43]

In Perth the Committee undertook a night-time tour of the CBD with representatives from Perth City Council to see first-hand the incorporation of Crime Prevention through Environmental Design (CPTED) principles as a key aspect of promoting community safety and the impact that building and environmental changes had made on the city.

Independent research

The first Term of Reference required the Committee to investigate the breadth of locally based groups and organisations addressing community safety and crime prevention issues within Victoria, particularly with regard to local government and Neighbourhood Watch. At the outset of the Inquiry the Committee established that there was no systematically compiled catalogue of groups and organisations addressing these issues in existence in Victoria.

The Committee therefore decided to commission Professor Peter Homel and staff at the Australian Institute of Criminology to assist it in developing and distributing an online survey to all local councils and shires in Victoria, in order to gather a comprehensive picture of current crime prevention activity. The survey asked councils and shires to identify local crime prevention initiatives in their area and answer specific questions in relation to their operation and effectiveness. The results of this important benchmarking research assisted the Committee in forming the framework for the Committee's Final Report and recommendations.

The Committee also designed a series of questions to seek the views of each Neighbourhood Watch chapter regarding the current work of Neighborhood Watch and the challenges confronting the organisation in providing meaningful crime prevention programs. These questions were circulated to the various chapters by the President of Neighborhood Watch Inc and the responses were forwarded to the Committee and analysed.[44]

---

42 For a list of Regional visits, Forums and Public Hearings conducted in Dandenong, Frankston, Ballarat and Geelong see Appendix 4.

43 For a list of people the committee met with in Perth and gained evidence from in Sydney see Appendix 5. It should be noted however, that NSW is currently in the process of reviewing its crime prevention model and processes, subsequent to the change of government in 2011.

44 For an analysis of the responses collected see Chapter 10. For a list of questions circulated to Neighbourhood Watch chapters see Appendix 6, and for a list of those chapters that answered see Appendix 7.

In order to gain an understanding of the nature and breadth of crime prevention policies and initiatives operating across government the Committee also sought information from various Victorian government departments. The Minister for Community Crime Prevention, Hon Andrew McIntosh, subsequently informed the Public Accounts and Estimates Committee at a public hearing on 17 May 2012 that:

> Importantly we have initiated a whole-of-government stocktake of programs contributing to crime prevention objectives to help inform this work. What this means is that every government agency, every government department, will have to do a stocktake in relation to those projects they have got in relation to crime prevention.[45]

At the time of writing the Report the findings of this review are not available. The Committee is therefore not able to comment in any depth on the range of policies and initiatives operated by government departments across Victoria. The Committee believes strongly, however, that comprehensive information about the extent and nature of such policies is crucial for ongoing decision making and policy development.

The Chair also attended a seminar of the community safety special interest group of Local Government Professionals (LGPro). LGPro is a peak body for those working in local government in Victoria. The Committee's research staff also attended a conference and seminar relating directly to the Inquiry's terms of reference.[46]

Community input into the Inquiry

In carrying out this Inquiry, the Committee has drawn upon the views and expertise of a broad range of people. The submissions, public hearings and interstate meetings have provided valuable insights into the excellent work of various community and government organisations and provided significant knowledge into what has turned out to be an extremely complex and challenging issue. The Committee is most appreciative of the time, effort and valuable contribution that all the individuals and organisations made during the progress of this Inquiry.

---

45   Minister McIntosh, Evidence given to the Public Accounts and Estimates Committee, Inquiry into budget estimates 2011–2012, Melbourne 2011.

46   For a list of the conference and seminars attended by the Committee and staff see Appendix 8.

2. Theoretical Approaches to Crime Prevention

Introduction

There are a number of ways of classifying what activities and programs come under the umbrella of 'crime prevention'. These frameworks differ according to the types of crime under consideration. Whatever approach is taken, however, it is important not to force all prevention approaches into a single unproblematic classification scheme (Hughes 1998).[47]

This chapter commences with a general overview of the ways in which crime prevention has been understood. In particular it examines the four main approaches to crime prevention: criminal justice, social, environmental and community conceptualisations. The chapter then looks at other ways in which crime prevention can be classified, such as how crime prevention projects may differ according to the object of the crime prevention strategy or the stage at which the crime prevention strategy is targeted (primary, secondary or tertiary prevention). Finally, the discussion concludes that a *mix* of crime prevention approaches is crucial.

Approaches to crime prevention

There are four basic approaches to crime prevention which can be summarised as follows:

Criminal justice approach:

Whereby the police and justice authorities enforce the law and the courts and corrections systems hold offenders accountable for their actions.

Social or developmental approach:

Whereby risk and protective factors relating particularly to young people's offending are addressed and early intervention and developmental strategies are implemented to address the underlying social and economic causes of such crime. Social approaches may also include programs to improve educational, employment, health and housing standards.

Situational or environmental approach:

Whereby strategies are developed to reduce the opportunities for crime and increase the risks associated with committing offences. This may be through the implementation of better urban design and public planning, strengthening or increasing surveillance in public places, or improving security measures in homes and businesses.

---

47 Such a conceptualisation however does not always find favour with the 'critical school' of criminologists who argue against taking a 'global' concept of crime for granted. In other words, dominant discourses of crime prevention, whether stemming from a law and order, social or environmental paradigm, are essentially about technologies of social control and regulation:

'Far from seeking to develop a coherent and critical understanding of the way crime problems occur [conventional accounts of crime] take such matters for granted. Crime thus becomes a reified behavioural outcome that needs to be prevented, contained or managed through the implementation of a range of local and national measures…Strategies for prevention thus tend to be discussed in terms of what is officially recorded and understood as 'crime'. This tactic raises a problem in that no attention is given to processes by which such knowledge is constructed. For example, it ignores the fact that some populations [such as young people or Indigenous people] are more heavily policed and therefore more likely to be criminalised than others' (Hil 1996, pp.61; see also, Watts, Bessant & Hil 2008).

In short, advocates of critical criminology argue that situational approaches that focus on the problem (for example a burgled shop) or social approaches that focus on families or children 'are not en*ough for effective long term prevention' if they pay no attention to the broader political, economic* and cultural factors that nurture crime (Lane & Henry 2004, p.204).

Community based approach:

Similar to social approaches, the community is engaged to develop interventions which seek to change the social conditions that influence offending. Community development and community capacity building approaches are often employed to achieve these ends (New South Wales Government 2008; Morgan & Homel 2011). Community or locally based approaches are a major focus of this Inquiry.

These classifications reflect *both* instrumental and expressive or symbolic functions. For example, in developing urban design policies to reduce crime in a public housing estate, the provision of better street lighting is the instrumental outcome of implementing situational crime prevention. But as well as signifying *practical* ways of reducing or preventing crime, a choice between developmental, situational or law and order crime prevention policies may signal a government's preferred approach or vision for social order (Sutton, Cherney & White 2008).

These approaches also differ according to their focus of intervention. However, often the approaches can and do co-exist, as will be discussed later in this chapter.

Criminal justice approaches

Traditional criminal justice approaches to crime prevention centre on zero tolerance policing, arrest, court hearings, imprisonment and other forms of punishment that aim to have deterrent effects.[48] The underlying principle of zero tolerance policing is that 'a strong law enforcement approach to minor crime (in particular public order offences) will prevent more serious crime from occurring and will ultimately lead to falling crime rates' (Cunneen 2004, p.151).[49] This draws from the famous analogy Wilson and Kelling drew regarding 'broken windows'. If one broken window is not repaired in a building, others may be broken in the building and then vandalism and crime may escalate in the street or neighbourhood (1982). From another perspective it may indicate that according to Felson's typology of crime,[50] potential offenders may interpret the broken windows as indicators of a lack of 'guardianship' 'and conclude that the location offers ample opportunities for crime' (Sutton, Cherney & White 2008, p.48):

> An unrepaired window is a sign that no one cares and therefore more damage will occur. Similarly if disorderly behaviour is not dealt with in a particular area then more serious crime will be the result. Small 'incivilities' such as public drunkenness, vandalism and begging create an atmosphere where more serious crime can flourish (Cunneen 2004, p.151).

---

48   This includes both general deterrence — the effect on the general population — and specific deterrence, the effect on the specific offender, potential offender or group of offenders. For a comprehensive discussion of the theory of deterrence and its relationship to the threat of imprisonment, see *Does Imprisonment Deter? A Review of the Evidence*, Sentencing Advisory Council of Victoria (2011b). In short, this research paper concluded that:

   'The research shows that imprisonment has, at best, no effect on the rate of re-offending and is often criminogenic, resulting in a greater rate of recidivism by imprisoned offenders compared with offenders who received a different sentencing outcome. Possible explanations for this include: prison is a learning environment for crime, prison reinforces criminal identity and may diminish or sever social ties that encourage lawful behaviour and prison imprisonment is not an appropriate response to the needs of many offenders who require treatment for the underlying causes of their criminality such as drug, alcohol and mental health issues' (Sentencing Advisory Council of Victoria 2011b, p.23).

49   For a critical account of zero tolerance policing, see *The Political Resonance of Crime Control Strategies: Zero Tolerance Policing* (Cunneen 2004). Cunneen's chief criticism is that in the most 'crude' form of zero tolerance policing (for example arrest for 'minor' infringements) the concept of partnership policing is forgotten (2004, p.152). For an account of crime prevention partnerships and partnership policing, see Chapters 3 and 6.

50   According to the criminologist Felson's formulation, crime is the product of three basic ingredients that coalesce at a particular time and place:
   • a motivated offender
   • a suitable target, and
   • the absence of a capable guardian.

   Therefore, drawing upon Felson's theories of crime prevention, policy development should have as its aim three main objectives:
   • To reduce the supply of motivated offenders
   • To make crime more difficult, and
   • To create structures that increase the supervision of possible offenders (Felson 1995).

Law and order initiatives are popular with the media, politicians (of all persuasions) and seemingly the public. For example, zero tolerance strategies, such as arrest for 'minor' infringements are '[g]eared quintessentially to the type of performance indicators that are immediately measurable and perfectly understandable to government: zero tolerance is about arresting people for targeted offences' (Cunneen 2004, p.154). This restricted focus on crime statistics may exclude other less easily measured indicators of effectiveness, such as those used to evaluate other approaches to crime prevention, particularly social prevention.[51] Moreover, law and order policing, for example through the use of 'crackdowns' or well publicised operations, is also more conducive to governments and media that 'demand results that can easily be represented in the public sphere'(Cunneen 2004, p.154).

However, recent surveys and research conducted by the Sentencing Advisory Council of Victoria suggesting that 'community views are not necessarily as punitive as typically portrayed… and are more complex and nuanced than is often characterised' have countered this view. The Advisory Council's research has consistently indicated that '[w]hen provided with viable alternatives to imprisonment, people are more likely to prefer alternatives to building more prisons' (Sentencing Advisory Council of Victoria 2011a, p.4 and the references listed therein).[52]

Law and order approaches are essentially tertiary interventions; that is, those which are applied after an offence has occurred (Sutton, Cherney & White 2008, p.24).

> While more police and tougher penalties may not be the most cost-effective responses, they do bear a direct and obvious relationship to crime. At the symbolic level, they help governments articulate a simple and unequivocal political message: that they will act decisively to protect the public from offenders and other 'disruptive elements' (Sutton, Cherney & White 2008, p. 94).

Another class of initiatives that could conceivably count as tertiary crime prevention are those that are aimed at either diverting offenders from the prison system once sentenced through community based measures or rehabilitating offenders such as when a person is on parole or released from prison.[53]

The above discussion should not be taken as excluding the need for 'law and order' approaches to crime prevention and community safety. Clearly in some circumstances, particularly with regard to the most serious and violent crimes, interventions such as arrest and imprisonment may be necessary evils. But as Hil argues, in most jurisdictions even those with a 'tough on crime' approach, 'punitive' justice approaches can be counterbalanced or co-exist with more liberal measures, such as group conferencing and other community based crime prevention initiatives discussed later in this chapter (1996, p.60).

Social or developmental crime prevention

> It is thought that each evil should be cured at the spot where it breaks out, and no thought is taken for the place where it actually originates and whence it spreads its influence (Goethe).[54]

Social crime prevention attempts to reduce the likelihood of individuals and/or groups coming into contact with the criminal justice system by addressing and strengthening both the formal (school, work etc.) and informal (friends, families, peer groups, community)

---

51   See discussion in Chapter 11 of this Report.

52   See *Alternatives to Imprisonment: Community views in Victoria* (Sentencing Advisory Council of Victoria 2011a, pp.1, 2; see also Gelb 2006, 2008). For a discussion of the arguments for and against law and order approaches used in the survey see Sentencing Advisory Council of Victoria 2011a, p.7.
     For a discussion of the intrinsic merits of community crime prevention versus tertiary measures such as imprisonment from a cost-benefit perspective, see the discussion in Chapter 11 of this Report.

53   A correctional policy with a rehabilitative focus may also serve to prevent or at least reduce the amount of recidivism in a community. See Spindler 1994; O'Toole 2002. For a comprehensive discussion of tertiary crime prevention initiatives to counter recidivism in the context of youth offending, see Drugs and Crime Prevention Committee, *Inquiry into Strategies to Prevent High Volume Offending by Young People, Final Report* (2009).

54   Eighteenth century German philosopher, poet and writer, translated by Hollingdale, see Goethe 1971, p.67.

networks of those individuals and groups. It commonly encompasses community development and early intervention programs, and seeks to influence the underlying social and economic causes of crime, including offender motivation.

Whilst theoretically social prevention programs can be implemented at all stages of the life cycle, in practice social prevention often focuses on the early or formative stages of life (Sutton, Cherney & White 2008). Thus interventions such as pre-natal classes, visiting infant nurses, quality preschool programs, parenting skills training, and educational, leisure and vocational programs for children and teenagers in later years are common examples of social programs that *may* have crime prevention as a major or subsidiary goal but are important nonetheless for the social benefits that accrue for their own sake (Brantingham, Brantingham & Taylor 2005).

Addressing the causes of crime

Unlike environmental or situational crime prevention strategies, social prevention seeks to address the entrenched or long-term causes of crime.[55] 'It moves beyond a fixation with deviants and deviance and begins to address all contributing elements [of crime]' (Sutton, Cherney & White 2008, p.5). Associate Professor Darren Palmer from Deakin University, whilst not discounting the effectiveness of some situational crime prevention measures, has emphasised that a broader more encompassing and long-term approach that includes social prevention measures is necessary:

> [i]f you actually want to do something far more significant, long term and lasting and sustainable and the like, you have to go into a much broader approach to crime prevention — that is, trying to look at the larger drivers of crime around those kinds of political, cultural, economic, social and educational factors and the like. Where it is not so attractive is that a lot of those things are actually long term. You do not see the benefits for some time, but in terms of their longevity they are the kinds of things that ultimately will not only be better for crime prevention but better for producing a better society.[56]

Similarly, Assistant Commissioner Wayne Gregson, a senior police officer in Western Australia, has endorsed the social and developmental approach to crime prevention over traditional law and order approaches. In evidence to the Committee in Perth he stated:

> If you ask me, you get a much better return on investment [with social prevention strategies]. If I had a choice to invest in education or policing, you get a four to one return on every dollar you spend on education. You get a much better return than what you spend on law enforcement. Law enforcement is too late down the continuum of individuals. I think early childhood education is an absolutely key pillar of prevention for later years. You cannot underestimate the return on investment for early intervention and education and I think that you see the evidence of that in a whole range of programs: the more you spend at the front end, the less you will spend later on down the judicial continuum.

---

55 What 'causes' offending however is highly contentious, controversial and arguably unanswerable. Certainly an understanding of criminal activity requires an analysis of some of the major causal or contributory factors that can be attributed to such offending, including some of the theoretical explanations taken from various streams of criminology. Often such theories form the basis of policy and program development. Yet it is also important to avoid explanations of crime that attribute offending to single causes. Why some people engage in criminal activity and others do not is a very complex issue.

Causal theories of crime have often been uni-linear; that is, they attribute a direct and often single cause to the crime. To use an overly simplistic example, 'bad' parenting can lead to juvenile alienation and ultimately to 'delinquency'. However, as Buckland and Wincup (2004) state, it is highly questionable and indeed dangerous to translate statistical association into causality or overestimate the explanatory power of one factor in isolation.

For an excellent critique of the concept of causality in criminology, see Watts, Bessant and Hil 2008. For a more general discussion of causal links to criminal and antisocial behaviour, see Drugs and Crime Prevention Committee, *Inquiry into Strategies to Prevent High Volume Offending amongst Young People, Final Report* (2009).

56 Associate Professor Darren Palmer, Convenor, Criminology Program, Deakin University, Geelong, correspondence to the Drugs and Crime Prevention Committee, Inquiry into Locally Based Approaches to Community Safety and Crime Prevention, Melbourne, 9 September 2011.

But of course governments have different priorities and it is expensive and you cannot, unfortunately, stop doing policing while you are trying to tip a bucket of resources into front-end education. Oftentimes, a cynic might say that governments of all persuasions are not likely to see a return on investment during a term of government. I might suggest that sometimes policies are aligned slightly towards cycles and political realities — big P political realities.[57]

Developmental approaches: Risk and protective factors

Developmental approaches are a key aspect of social crime prevention particularly as they apply to children in the early stages of life. They take their theoretical basis from studies of human development and social psychology. Developmental prevention strategies are frequently targeted at formative or early stages of life, for example through early childhood support schemes:

> Through educational and social development strategies, particularly in families and schools, interventions seek to reduce and prevent anti-social behaviour and promote the integration of offenders into mainstream social life (Lane & Henry 2004, p.203).

A further feature of developmental theory is the idea that processes of development, whether physical, cognitive, psychological, or social, can be hindered or damaged by adverse or disruptive events that extend beyond the normal stresses that most (children) experience at some time. Some children face additional (sometimes stressful) transitions as they move geographically (moving house, school, community and even country) or when the composition of their family changes through the death of a parent or sibling, or through divorce, separation or re-partnering of parents. Illness or trauma in childhood can also impact development, as can an environment that is physically, psychologically or socially impoverished. Economic disadvantage, parents who lack parenting or general life skills and, in extreme cases, child abuse and neglect, can all disrupt healthy development and create future problems including antisocial behaviour. The developmental pathways approach therefore draws attention to a range of risk factors that can increase the likelihood of offending behaviour.

---

57 Assistant Commissioner Wayne Gregson, Judicial Services, Western Australia Police, Evidence given to the Drugs and Crime Prevention Committee, Inquiry into Locally Based Approaches to Community Safety and Crime Prevention, Meeting, Perth, 21 June 2011.

In Canada, Crime Prevention through Social Development (CPSD) is arguably far more accepted and used by Canadian federal and provincial police forces than their equivalents in other western countries, including Australia. The use of CPSD by Canadian police in partnerships with other government and community agencies is discussed extensively in the *National Police Leadership Survey on Crime Prevention through Social Development* (Macrae et al 2005). The background to a greater reliance on CPSD is summarised by the authors as follows:

'Negligible changes in crime rates encouraged a greater interest in addressing the social and economic origins of crime, and by the mid-1980's Canada shifted resources into developing a balanced approach to crime prevention, one that incorporated both conventional crime control methods and an understanding of the social precursors to crime and victimization (Stroick, 2002).

The 1990s witnessed the formation of a National Strategy on Community Safety and Crime Prevention, whose agenda was to look beyond traditional crime control methods to address the underlying causes of crime. Using a social development approach, the National Crime Prevention Centre (NCPC) developed a federal government plan to support community safety and crime prevention. The plan encouraged the involvement of all Canadians, from various levels of government, to police agencies, to individual communities (National Crime Prevention Strategy (NCPS), 2002). Since 1998, this National Strategy has supported the development of thousands of pilot projects, inspired by the concept of Crime Prevention though Social Development (CPSD): "a long-term, proactive approach of addressing the personal, social and economic factors that lead some individuals to engage in criminal acts or to become victims of crime" (Stroick, 2002:1).

In 2003, the Canadian Association of Chiefs of Police (CACP) Crime Prevention / Community Policing Committee adopted a resolution on community safety, health and well-being, endorsing Crime Prevention through Social Development. The resolution promoted the idea that police leaders can, and should, play an essential role in supporting community safety and well-being, and the prevention of crime. To do so requires both innovative and proactive social development approaches that address root causes of crime while incorporating conventional methods of crime control. Community partnerships and collaboration are the keys to enhancing the safety and development of communities' (Macrae et al 2005, p.1).

A notable Victorian initiative brought to the attention of the Committee in the area of social and community crime prevention is the Policing and Interdisciplinary Triage Teams. See the discussion in Chapter 6 in the context of partnership policing.

The use of the concept of risk factors for youth offending was discussed and critiqued in the Drugs and Crime Prevention Committee's *Final Report, Inquiry into Strategies to Prevent High Volume Offending by Young People* (2009). Many respondents to that Inquiry acknowledged the dangers of using a developmental pathways approach in a deterministic way that sees risk factors as leading to fixed and inevitable crime pathways. However, much of the evidence received from individuals and organisations, based on their grassroots experience working with young offenders, supported the view that major risk factors could be identified and that prevention strategies to address them were warranted.

Risk and protective factors

Social prevention approaches often rely on identifying these *risk* and *protective* factors 'manifest in individual, family, peer, school, neighbourhood, community and other contexts that can affect whether people are likely to become involved in or continue offending' (Sutton, Cherney & White 2008, p.22).

Risk factors are those that may contribute to a person's likelihood of offending; for example maltreatment during childhood, being subject to Child Protection orders; economic and family disadvantage, homelessness, use of alcohol or other drugs, mixing with a criminal peer group, a history of truancy or low educational achievement. Protective factors, on the other hand, are those which may boost a person's resilience to committing criminal offences or otherwise displaying antisocial behaviours; for example strong family attachments, good educational record, and involvement in religious or other community groups or activities. One form of a social crime prevention strategy that can boost protective factors is the use of sport, outdoor and recreational programs and camps.[58] As Cameron and MacDougall state, whilst crime prevention is not the primary objective of sport and physical activity 'it might be an extremely positive by-product' (2000, p.1). Although vigorous evaluation is required, the authors' research indicates that 'Sport and physical activity programs may result in immediate crime prevention, and those that involve members of the community on a continuing basis may be sustainable' (2000, p.5). This may result from the sense of belonging and the relationships that develop through playing sport and undertaking physical activity.[59]

Social prevention in action: The *Pathways to Prevention Project*

A key example of a major social prevention project in Australia is the *Pathways to Prevention Project*, created through a partnership between Griffith University and Mission Australia and located in a lower socioeconomic area of Brisbane. The Project attempts to address causal or contributory factors leading to criminal behaviour and was based on:

> ...the assumption that mobilising social resources to support children, families and their communities before problems emerge is more effective and cheaper than intervening when problems have become entrenched (Homel et al 2006).[60]

Early childhood identification and intervention is a crucial aspect of programs such as 'Pathways'; increasing the number of child health nurses, school nurses and midwives, and providing comprehensive parent training is 'seen as the first step in identifying children at risk' (Injury Control Council of Western Australia (ICCWA) 2011, p.21). Such programs, whilst coming out of a public health model espoused by the World Health Organization (WHO), are also seen as crucial crime prevention strategies:

---

58 The use of sports programs, particularly those that are community focused could also be characterised as a form of 'community crime prevention'.

59 These programs may not be useful for young people who have no inclination or 'talent' for sporting or other physical activity (Morris, Sallybanks & Willis 2003; Morris, Sallybanks, Willis & Makkai 2003). For a discussion of some local sporting and other programs as examples of community crime prevention, see Chapter 2

60 See also Sutton, Cherney and White 2008, pp.44–45.

Evidence suggests that pre-school enrichment and social development programs, which target children early in life, can prevent aggression, improve social skills, boost educational achievement and improve job prospects. These effects are most pronounced in children from poor families and neighbourhoods. The benefits of high quality programs of this type can also be sustained into adulthood (ICCWA 2011, p.28).

Many of the strategies to prevent violence and antisocial behaviour overlap with strategies to raise healthy, well-adjusted and happy children. Preventing the maltreatment of children is a key precursor in preventing ongoing violence and crime generally (ICCWA 2011; WHO 2009a, 2009b).[61]

The key underlying concept of much social crime prevention is therefore that well designed programs aimed at *developmental* rather than *remedial* interventions 'can alter the pathways available to individuals [especially children] and their families and in doing so can reduce the likelihood of participants achieving negative outcomes' (such as being involved in criminal activity) (Manning, Homel & Smith 2006, p.201).

The strategies employed in social crime prevention, for example early childhood support or mental health initiatives, are ideally long-term (and expensive) investments. As with the Pathways Project, they also tend to be primary or universal measures rather than targeted to a specific population (for example all children rather than a subset of children 'at risk' of offending). Many social prevention measures may not even seek (at least ostensibly) to address crime and antisocial behaviour, although that may be the long-term consequence. They may be embedded in programs (and departments or ministries) whose stated aims are primarily to address education, housing or family support.[62] As such it may be difficult 'if not impossible to provide unequivocal evidence that social prevention has been effective in the short term' (Cherney & Sutton 2007, p.78).[63]

Critiques of social and developmental approaches

A growing body of research and literature across the social and natural sciences raises serious questions about the credibility of some social prevention approaches, particularly those relying upon developmental explanatory theories (see Beck 1992, 1998; Bessant, Hil & Watts 2003; Kelly, 1999, 2000; Dwyer & Wyn 2001). A particular criticism made is that some researchers have gone beyond using risk and protective factors descriptively to using them as predictive indicators of future offending (or indeed abstinence) by people. For example, Watts, Bessant and Hil (2008) argue that listing a variety of risk indicators such as single parent environments, truancy, dysfunctional families, long-term unemployment, rejection of child, or conversely protective factors such as pro-social development, family harmony, strong family norms and morality etc are:

---

61   The Community Violence Prevention Strategy of the Injury Control Council of Western Australia in partnership with the North Metropolitan Area Health Service is one such strategy.

62   Indeed some commentators have argued that the systematic delivery of services or resources to families particularly with young children may be taken for granted by many middle-class families:
'When middle class and upper class people do all they can to ensure that their offspring cope with life's major challenges and transitions, they generally do not perceive themselves as practising social [crime] prevention. They are merely doing simple things that everybody believes in, using basic services and resources that are taken for granted. Only when the discourse relates to disadvantaged populations do we begin to portray social prevention as requiring something extra whose addition to the mix requires research based guidance and monitoring' (Sutton, Cherney & White 2008, p. 43. See also Homel R 2005; Homel R et al 2006).

63   For example, many earlier social prevention programs that focus on early childhood prevention were not primarily designed to prevent crime. The *Elmira Early Infancy Project* and the *Perry Preschool Program* in the United States are good examples of these (see generally Chisholm 2000; Sutton, Cherney & White 2008, pp. 32ff for analysis of these formative programs). An increased reliance on early childhood intervention programs *specifically* as a form of crime prevention is relatively recent internationally and in Australia. Nonetheless it is still difficult to measure the cost-benefits of these programs in reducing crime per se and separating this outcome from other measurable outcomes such as child development. See Chisholm 2000; Dossetor 2011 and the discussion in Chapter 11 for an account of the cost-benefits of crime prevention.

[p]romoted as if this policy framework rests on solid empirical and scientific evidence, the use of indices of 'risk' and 'protection' points to a level of fantasy and plain silliness that is deeply worrying. Any reader can ask her or himself if [these] characteristics as indicators of antisocial behaviour are anything more than a bundle of prejudices about the world of the 'typical' young... juvenile delinquent (Watts, Bessant & Hil 2008, p.158).

One assumption inherent in the developmental pathways approach which Bessant believes warrants caution is that causal connections are identifiable and can be tracked and documented. This assumption she states is not only false but also encourages a neglect of other possible explanations for phenomena such as criminal behaviour or drug abuse. Bessant also argues that the proposition that a researcher can use aggregate data about large numbers of young people and then apply that data or any findings to a particular person and go on to argue that the individual is 'at risk' is itself flawed:

> Risk based research often involves pointing to certain average values or deviations from the norm (based on investigations of large numbers of individual cases) and then turning to an actual single individual and saying to that person 'Because you exhibit factors a, b and c you are at risk of substance abuse'. Such an assessment means moving from measures of central tendency like averages to particular cases. As the statistician Gould explains this is problematic because moving from a claim that X is true of the whole group to the claim that X is also true for each single member of the group cannot be done (Bessant 2001 in Drugs and Crime Prevention Committee 2006, p.672).

Not the least of the criticisms made of a rigid risk factors approach then is the way in which an almost actuarial table of risk factors can be used to determine various types of offending.[64]

In a more general sense, criticisms have been made of social prevention approaches that foster a viewpoint that other methods of crime prevention such as environmental approaches or even law and order measures are inherently ineffective and that 'social prevention is the only viable way to reduce crime' (Sutton, Cherney & White 2008, p. 41). Such arguments, according to Sutton, Cherney and White, ignore the fact that crime embraces a whole spectrum of activities and some, particularly those that are casual, opportunistic or 'unintentional', may be more amenable to other forms of crime prevention (2008, p.41). While social prevention measures have much to commend them, particularly those which aim to build better communities for *all* people not just those at risk of criminal activity, the task for crime prevention advocates is to achieve the appropriate balance between the various approaches at their disposal.

Environmental or situational crime prevention

Environmental crime prevention 'aims to modify the physical (and in the cyber era, virtual) contexts in which crimes can occur and potential offenders operate' (Sutton, Cherney & White 2008, p.22). Environmental crime prevention approaches are essentially pragmatic solutions

---

64 See for example Baker's analysis of the relationship between developmental and demographic factors and juvenile participation in crime (Baker 1998, pp.31ff). Whilst it may be useful to know for instance that truancy is a high predictor of involvement in malicious damage and acquisitive property crime, one needs to be careful that such models do not become used in almost self-fulfilling ways. American theorists Sampson and Laub are also critical of using developmental criminology in this predictive way:

'...we question the *prospective* or predictive power of offender groups and whether they are causally distinct with respect to later trajectories...Developmental criminology...tends to emphasise the notion that people get 'locked' into certain trajectories. One of the lessons of prospective longitudinal research is that there is considerable heterogeneity in adult outcomes that cannot be predicted in advance...we highlight a life course view that emphasises human agency and choice over the life span, underscoring how people construct their lives within the context of ongoing constraints. From this view trajectories are interpreted not from a lens of unfolding inevitability but rather continuous social reproduction'(2005, pp.13, 14). (Emphasis in original)

For a similar analysis in the Australian context, see Goodnow 2006.

which concentrate on the immediate problems confronting individuals and local communities (Lane & Henry 2004). In contrast to social crime prevention, environmental prevention measures concentrate on the *targets* of criminal behaviour. Environmental crime prevention programs and projects specifically aim to modify the physical context in which crime occurs to minimise the extent to which these environments can give opportunity to engage in criminal activities. There are two main techniques by which environmental crime prevention programs can be implemented: *broad based planning and design* and *focused situational prevention*.

Broad based planning and design

This is an approach that: '[i]s concerned with ensuring that the settings in which people, work, live and find recreation are not "built" in ways which undermine capacities for surveillance [eg. that large scale housing estates are well lit]' (Sutton, Cherney & White 2008, p.22).

This approach has grown into a specific aspect of crime prevention planning called Crime Prevention through Environmental Design (CPTED). Emerging in the 1960s and 1970s, CPTED is based on the idea that urban design, such as the design of public buildings, streets, shopping centres or parks, and the installation of measures such as improved street lighting could prevent crime by reducing opportunities to commit it.[65] Supporters of such strategies argue the cost of installation of improved street lighting for example is outweighed by the monetary benefits resulting from crime reduction (Painter & Farrington 2001).

CPTED strategies rely upon being able to influence the decisions of potential offenders to commit criminal acts. Research into criminal behaviour shows that the decision to offend or not to offend is more influenced by cues to the perceived risk of being caught than by cues to reward or ease of entry:

> Offenders often make cost-benefit assessment of potential victims and locations before committing crime. CPTED aims to create the reality (or perception) that the costs of committing crime are greater than the likely benefits. This is achieved by creating environmental and social conditions that:
>
> - Maximise risk to offenders (increasing the likelihood of detection, challenge and apprehension);
>
> - Maximise the effort required to commit crime (increasing the time, energy and resources required to commit crime);
>
> - Minimise the actual and perceived benefits of crime (removing, minimising or concealing crime attractors and rewards); and
>
> - Minimise excuse-making opportunities (removing conditions that encourage/facilitate rationalisation of inappropriate behaviour).[66]

Consistent with this research, CPTED based strategies emphasise enhancing the perceived risk of detection and apprehension and are based on the belief that the proper design and effective use of the built environment can reduce crime, reduce the fear of crime, and improve the quality of life. CPTED incorporates urban planning and architectural design theory and practice to 'influence people's perceptions of the built environment and the way public space is defined and used' (Sutton, Cherney & White 2008, p.60).

---

65   *Market Reduction Approach* (MRA) is a related crime prevention approach with regard to property crime such as theft and burglary). This approach aims to reduce property crime by focusing on '[s]hrinking the stolen goods market, by preventing supply and reducing demand for stolen goods' (Australian Institute of Criminology (AIC) 2005, p.1). Without such an active market, disposal may become risky and unrewarding for the potential offender. MRA strategies include identifying the 'hot' products most attractive to thieves, thus giving the public the opportunity to make choices about the types of product they will purchase; marking of products by owners or manufacturers; designing products with inbuilt security features; regulating second-hand goods shops that may act as deliberate or inadvertent 'handlers' of stolen goods; and launching campaigns by police and the private sector to make the public, and particularly victims, aware of their unwitting role in possibly aiding property crime (see AIC 2005).

66   See *Safer by Design,* New South Wales Police Force. Accessed 29 August 2011 at http://www.police.nsw.gov.au/community_issues/crime_prevention/safer_by_design

CPTED has been increasingly promoted by both police and local government groups to prevent crime occurring in local communities (for example, in night-time economy precincts and large housing estates). Certainly the Committee has received much evidence endorsing CPTED as a valuable tool in reducing crime in local communities For example, a submission from Mr Geoff Griffiths of Officer in Melbourne's outer south states:

> This method of crime prevention still has enormous potential for local communities, especially in the outer fringe new housing development areas like Officer. As an example, the consultants for Vic Urban working on the environmental structure plan of Officer did not know anything about CPTED. If a trained person with clout was able to review the new housing and commercial developments from a CPTED perspective the community would save millions over time. The importance of physical and environmental considerations has been lost. I had even suggested a State strategy to have University Architectural and Planning Departments have mandatory modules on CPTED.[67]

CPTED projects and audits have also increasingly become a mandatory part of the planning or developmental approval process, particularly in local government jurisdictions (see Sutton, Cherney & White 2008).[68]

In Western Australia for example, the WA Office of Crime Prevention has developed a Designing Out Crime initiative that provides funds for local governments to conduct CPTED projects.[69] CPTED and the broader situational crime prevention approaches discussed in the next section can also form part of overall city or community renewal/revitalisation programs such as a partnership currently underway between the City of Greater Dandenong (CGD) and VicUrban. Ms Lee Robson, Manager of Community Engagement at the CGD, underlined the importance of environmental approaches, and particularly CPTED, when the Committee met with officers from the CGD:

> I think there are about four points that are pretty important that we have learnt: the first one is visibility, having activity where people can see it with passive surveillance as they pass by; the second one is activating a space, making sure that there is legitimate activity, and sometimes councils need to program activities to make sure that occurs early on, right from the outset; the third one is reducing what I call territorialism, not allowing a particular group to colonise a space but by making it clear that it is available to everyone, and again that sometimes requires programming; the fourth one is all of those elements of good design — making sure an area is well lit, that there are no obstructions, that there is seating located in a place where people can

---

67 Mr Griffiths also provided the Committee with a valuable paper on CPTED written as a result of his work as the Manager for Armed Robbery Reduction in the ANZ Bank. The paper, 'Crime Prevention: A pro active response to the prevention of armed robberies. Situational Crime Prevention and Environmental Design' examines the ways in which environmental design and situational approaches can reduce the numbers of armed robberies in banks and other businesses and ensure the safety of bank staff and customers. (See submission from Mr Geoff Griffiths to the Drugs and Crime Prevention Committee, Inquiry into Locally Based Approaches to Community Safety and Crime Prevention, May 2011.)

68 Many state governments have produced CPTED design guidelines and manuals for their planning processes. In Victoria the Department of Planning and Community Development has developed *Safer Design Guidelines for Victoria.*

   See http://www.dpcd.vic.gov.au/planning/urbandesign/guidelines/safer-design-guidelines

   For an account of the various safe design guidelines in other states and territories, see Clancey 2011. Commenting on the widespread adoption of CPTED principles across the country at both state and local level, Clancey remarks:

   'The popularity of CPTED across Australia means that there is a generation of police, planners, architects and other design professionals who automatically consider crime risks in their work...While the content and style of guidelines differ across these jurisdictions, they all embed CPTED into their planning regimes and provide a policy (and in some cases statutory) recognition of CPTED' (2011, p.9).

69 Keryn Reid, Program Coordinator, Graffiti Team, Western Australia Police, spoke to the Committee about their Office of Crime Prevention's efforts to do CPTED audits in the context of graffiti prevention:

   'Our team does offer a CPTED audit. We will go out and do the Crime Prevention Through Environmental Design audits at the hot-spot locations. We do not really have the resourcing to be doing it on a daily basis, but we will do it when people come to us out of desperation and need to make some changes to the environment' (Evidence given to the Drugs and Crime Prevention Committee, Inquiry into Locally Based Approaches to Community Safety and Crime Prevention, Meeting, Perth, 20 June 2011).

   For further discussion of the Western Australian approaches to crime prevention, see Chapter 3.

legitimately sit and spend some time, that there are toilets well designed with the doors facing the streets. All of those principles about environmental design are important.[70]

This project and the concept of community renewal generally will be discussed in greater detail later in this chapter.[71]

Focused situational crime prevention

The other technique of environmental crime prevention is focused situational crime prevention (SCP) which concentrates on: 'manipulating *specific* environments or environment types [for example, banks, cars, transport interchanges] in ways that will increase the risks and efforts associated with offending and reduce associated rewards' (Sutton, Cherney & White 2008, p.22). It 'focuses on reducing crime opportunities rather than on the characteristics of criminals or potential criminals' (Australian Institute of Criminology (AIC) 2003a, p.1).

The theoretical basis for situational crime prevention is sometimes argued to be premised on 'rational choice theory', an economic based theory that portrays criminals, including young offenders, as 'rational decision makers who base their decision to commit crimes on an analysis of the risks compared to the expected profits. That is, the criminal does a rudimentary cost-benefit analysis' (Geason & Wilson 1992, p.7).

Rational choice theory assumes the following propositions:

- Offenders freely and actively choose to commit crimes.

- The decision to commit the crime is made in response to the immediate circumstances and the immediate situation in which an offence is considered.

- The motivation to offend is not constant or beyond control; that is, it is dependent on a calculation of costs and rewards rather than being the result of an inherited or acquired disposition to offend.

To put it concisely, one school of thought maintains that criminals analyse a given situation and will not proceed if the going looks tough (Geason & Wilson 1992, p.7).

Situational crime prevention endeavours to reduce the opportunities for particular categories of crime by increasing the risks and difficulties associated with committing the crime and consequently reducing the rewards (Clarke 1995; Ekblom & Tilley 2000; Painter & Farrington 2001; Smith & Cornish 2003; Sutton & White 1995; Gottfredson & Soule 2005). Thus, with regard to house burglary, systematic programs and guides for householders aimed at making breaking and entering more difficult (stronger house locks, marking of valuables with ultra violet pens, cutting down or removing shrubbery around houses that may conceal intruders etc) may be of assistance.[72] In the case of youth offending, a common preventive measure may be to keep products such as cigarettes, alcohol or aerosol paint cans in locked storage units, particularly in smaller shops.

---

70 Ms Lee Robson, Manager, Community Engagement, City of Greater Dandenong, Evidence given to the Drugs and Crime Prevention Committee, Inquiry into Locally Based Approaches to Community Safety and Crime Prevention, Public Hearing, Dandenong, 30 May 2011.

71 For an academic account of the importance of urban and social planning for crime prevention, see Whitzman 2005. In particular Whitzman concentrates on the need for *place management* as an approach to address not only crime and uncivil behaviour but also for promoting the health and wellbeing of local communities. Place management is a 'coordinated, community led process that deals with specific problems in specific places where one of the outcomes is to redress significant social and economic disadvantage and improving overall community well being' (2005, pp.32–33). Whitzman uses the example of a park in St Kilda that was used by drug dealers, itinerants and others engaging in 'antisocial' behaviour. Through the coordinated efforts of Port Phillip Council, local police, residents, landscape designers, community developer workers and sex worker representative groups, the park was renewed in such a way that security concerns were allayed and recreational opportunities enhanced without dispossessing or disenfranchising some of the more disadvantaged members of the community. See C Whitzman 2005, *Social Planning and Crime Prevention; Some lessons from innovative practices.*

72 For a comprehensive example of a policy based on situational crime prevention principles, see the Report of the ACT Burglary Victims Response Project — *Crime Victims and the Prevention of Residential Burglary* (Department of Justice & Community Safety (ACT) 2004).

Whilst it will never be possible to create systems that will deter every potential offender from committing crime or antisocial behaviour, situational prevention advocates argue nonetheless that certain preconditions may affect whether an offence occurs or is attempted:

> These [threshold conditions] relate to the number and type of opportunities offered within specific contexts. For someone who is capable of, and not adverse to, offending, the decision whether or not to commit a specific crime will be a function of both whether an opportunity presents itself and whether the likely rewards from exploiting that opportunity are sufficient to offset the perceived efforts and risks. Situational prevention revolves around identifying 'pinch points', or modifiable conditions that are susceptible to intervention, and which can reduce or pre-empt perceived opportunities for crime' (Clarke 2005 in Sutton, Cherney & White 2008, p. 51).

Two major approaches to modifying the conditions that may give rise to opportunities for crime are through *opportunity reduction* and *target hardening*.

Opportunity reduction and target hardening

The starting point for employing SCP strategies is to 'view the world from the point of view of a potential offender' (Sutton, Cherney & White 2008, p.51). SCP tries first to understand how people perceive opportunities for crime and then to remove these opportunities.

Cornish and Clarke, pioneers of modern situational crime prevention, outline five basic techniques of SCP and how they can be utilised. These are:

- *Increasing the effort*: Making it physically harder for offenders to commit the crime.
- *Increasing the risks*: Making it more dangerous for the offender to commit the crime by increasing the risks.
- *Reducing the rewards*: Making the crime less productive or rewarding for the offender.
- *Reducing the provocations*: Attending to those aspects of the potential offender's environment that may stimulate or provoke the offending behaviour.
- *Removing Excuses*: Stimulating and reinforcing the internal constraints against the offending — the moral dimension, appealing to the conscience of the potential offender and emphasising the harm [that it could] cause (Cornish & Clarke 2003 adapted in Crime Research Centre, University of Western Australia 2008, p.12).

For the potential offender, therefore, the decision whether or not to commit a specific crime 'will be a function of both whether an opportunity presents itself and whether the likely rewards from exploiting that opportunity are sufficient to offset the perceived opportunities and risks' (Tilley 2005 in Sutton, Cherney & White 2008, p.51). SCP aims to identify modifiable conditions that are susceptible to intervention such as hardening crime targets or controlling access to facilities and space. Some examples include:

- improved street lighting
- substituting glassware for plastic in hotels
- rapid removal of graffiti
- restricting aerosol paints used for 'chroming'
- tagging and barcoding merchandise
- phone entry systems
- gated estates
- Neighbourhood Watch programs
- training of staff and codes of practice to reduce potential problems in hotels and nightclubs

- crime reduction through product design (CRTPD).[73]

Not only can SCP use better design and planning techniques to reduce the opportunities to commit crimes, as CPTED does, but can also go further and include non-design interventions (for example, the training of bar staff mentioned above).

Natural surveillance

Situational crime prevention also relies upon the idea of *natural surveillance* pioneered by the American urban planners Jane Jacobs and Oscar Newman in the 1960s and 1970s (see, for example, Jacobs 1961; Newman 1972). Natural surveillance involves using planning techniques to provide opportunities for people to exert social control (increased guardianship) in the course of their routine activities to deter offenders and increase the risk of their apprehension. It is to be distinguished from technical forms of surveillance such as closed-circuit television (CCTV):[74]

The interventions proposed by Jacobs:

> [w]ere to draw people back to city centres through the establishment of mixed land uses and the provision of amenities (eg shops, pubs, restaurants, and parks) and activities that would draw people out of their homes and onto the streets both during the day and the night. Natural surveillance is all about having more 'eyes on the street' and has become a key part of the [situational crime prevention] lexicon (Sutton, Cherney & White 2008, p.61).[75]

A key aim of natural surveillance is to ensure that areas prone to criminal activity are not abandoned, that 'appropriate' activity is generated through day and night, and that any signs of crime or abandonment (graffiti and other forms of vandalism, wrecked cars, rubbish etc.) are quickly removed (see Newman 1972).

Debates over environmental/situational crime prevention approaches

Unlike social crime prevention, environmental prevention focuses more on immediate or proximate causes of crime and may use short-term and less expensive measures to combat it (for example CCTV cameras). Also unlike the universal social or developmental crime prevention programs, SCP may often be targeted to a specific target group (for example, drinkers in pubs, shoplifters etc.).

Some critics of environmental crime prevention strategies argue that these measures do not in fact address the *causes* of crime (either proximate or remote) but only the *symptoms* of crime. Moreover, such critics propose that sometimes an environmental crime prevention measure, for example the securing of a housing estate through better lighting or the use of patrols and guards, may simply *displace* crime to a neighbouring area where such initiatives are not being trialled. If situational crime prevention measures are not combined with social or community based interventions which at least attempt to address the causes of crime:

> the most likely outcome will be to displace crime rather than eliminate it all together…when individuals find specific opportunities blocked they will simply adapt by committing a new crime or selecting a different less well protected target (Sutton, Cherney & White, 2008, p.57; see also Crawford 1998).

From a broader perspective, some critics have been concerned about the perceived 'intrusiveness' of some situational measures:

---

73 Crime Reduction through Product Design (CRTPD) is clearly conceptually related to Crime Prevention through Environmental Design (CPTED). It is an approach that has 'evolved to provide security of physical objects and data against criminal activity' (Lester 2001, p.1). The use of technology to design products less susceptible to theft or vandalism (for example, anti-tampering pharmaceutical packaging, tracking systems in laptop computers, ink release mechanisms attached to retail merchandise, car immobilisers) is a key aspect of CRTPD. See Lester 2001 for a general discussion of the concept and application of CRTPD.

74 CCTV is discussed later in this chapter.

75 Indeed one of the police partnership programs in Western Australia aimed at increasing 'natural surveillance' to prevent crime and antisocial behaviour is in fact called 'Eyes on the Street'. This will be discussed in detail in Chapter 3.

> In the long term, reliance on SCP is consistent with the emergence of gated estates, the proliferation of CCTV and the advent of the fortress and surveillance society (Davis 1990 in Sutton, Cherney & White 2008, p.55).

Supporters of SCP and CPTED note that such approaches are usually within the capacity of agencies such as local government, community bodies or the private sector to implement:

> Environmental prevention — with its emphasis on opportunity reduction — can provide the basis for a program that agencies and people at local level can influence directly (Sutton, White & Cherney 2008, p.69).

Certainly from a cost-benefit perspective, despite the costs of some expensive items such as CCTV, SCP initiatives lend themselves more readily to cost-benefit analysis than other forms of crime prevention strategy:

> The reasons for this include the comparative ease by which cost estimates of the program's hardware and labour can be obtained, the crime specific target of many programs, and the reliance on a comparatively inexpensive before and after evaluation method [compared to social or developmental programs] (Chisholm 2000 p.4).

However Chisholm also sounds a warning note about the importance of recognising that if displacement factors are taken into account (for example offenders targeting areas not covered in a particular program or initiative) 'these net benefits would almost certainly be reduced' (2000, p.4).[76]

A note on CCTV

One aspect of situational crime prevention which is hotly debated is the use of CCTV and other forms of surveillance such as electronic scanning in bars and other entertainment precincts. It is not easy to accurately assess the effectiveness or value of electronic surveillance as either a deterrent crime prevention tool or a method of gaining criminal intelligence or evidence after a crime has been committed. This is largely because there have been so few rigorous evaluation studies done of CCTV installation and even fewer of the more recent forms of identity scanning technology (Parliament of Australia 2005).[77] This is quite apart from other vexing issues such as the storage of data, who has access to such data, and the civil liberties implications of this.[78]

---

76 For further discussion on cost-benefit and evaluation, see Chapter 11.

77 For a comprehensive overview of the effectiveness of CCTV surveillance and its usefulness as a deterrent against crime, see the research report produced by the Commonwealth Parliamentary Library — *An overview of the effectiveness of closed circuit television surveillance*, Parliament of Australia (2005).

78 These topics are beyond the scope of this Report. However, it is salient to point out that when the Committee received correspondence from Associate Professor Darren Palmer from Deakin University, he expressed misgivings not only about the effectiveness of surveillance technology as a crime prevention tool but, at least in the case of using identification scanners in Geelong nightclubs, the privacy implications. He pointed out that at least with CCTV there is some (minimal) regulation of data gathering and access but with scanning no such safeguards exist:

'In reality that is what they [nightclub owners] are doing as a practice, is to say, 'We meet all the privacy principles', but they are actually not strictly governed by those. They actually fall into this black hole of no regulation. It is a bit like CCTV when it first got rolled out. People started to adopt it. There were no standards, there were no restrictions over its use and so on and there were no guidelines in terms of the 28 or 30 days of keeping the records and the like. ID scanners are a bit like that. They are just slowly trying to adopt and adapt to that kind of system, but they are not required to…It is just one of those things. It is a bit like CCTV; I will use that example again. Okay, it may not deliver everything we think it will, but at least it is doing something. I think this is a bit different because you are actually creating huge databases with people's IDs and licences — name, address, photo — and, I think, limited security. In fact our observations showed that there was limited security around how the systems were operating — inappropriate access and inappropriate recording of information about people who were then being banned, because they use it to ban people. They are not meant to use it for marketing or anything like that.'

Of particular concern to Professor Palmer was the fact that there is little regulation of either CCTV or other forms of surveillance footage being accessed by media outlets. In his view there should be a legislation imposing a blanket ban on such practices (Associate Professor Darren Palmer, Convenor, Criminology Program, Deakin University, correspondence to the Drugs and Crime Prevention Committee, Inquiry into Locally Based Approaches to Community Safety and Crime Prevention, Melbourne, 9 September 2011).

Nonetheless, some local government authorities (LGAs) with whom the Committee met were enthusiastic about using CCTV in their localities, particularly in entertainment and late night precincts, although they acknowledged that CCTV was only one component in reducing or preventing crime. As Ms Lee Robson from the CGD explained:

> ...when CCTV is used as part of a suite of community safety activities it can have some positive outcomes. This council has now funded, partly, the development of CCTV around the Dandenong railway station and potentially around the Noble Park railway station. We are working very actively with Victoria Police and with other agencies, such as Metro Trains, to look at not only letting people know that it is there, that there are fresh eyes looking at what is happening in the area, but to have a suite of activities that try and promote legitimate use of any public space in that area.[79]

Her colleague, Mr Mark Doubleday, added that the use of CCTV has resulted in some significant improvements:

> Council [also] committed quite a considerable sum of money, nearly three years ago, to undertake a pilot of [the use of camera surveillance] in the Menzies Avenue Community Centre. That was done with Victoria Police and others. The results from that are indicating that there is a drop in graffiti and a perception of antisocial behaviour...Projects, such as closed-circuit TV are very expensive. They are not a silver bullet but it is one aspect where, if the ingredients in the approach are done right, if I can use that term, there are demonstrated results to be had.[80]

When the Committee met with police officers from Western Australia they placed more emphasis on the intelligence gathering and evidence collecting value of CCTV than on its deterrent effect. There is quite a significant array of CCTV cameras being used in Western Australia, particularly in the city centre. The city centre cameras are operated from a control centre located in Perth Railway Station operated jointly by the Western Australia Police and the Perth City Council. Superintendent John Leembruggen of the Western Australia Office of Crime Prevention spoke to the value of CCTV as both a crime prevention measure and evidence gathering tool:

> It is great for evidence. The guys know when they are going into those types of [entertainment] environments that it [antisocial behaviour] is getting recorded, so their behaviour obviously is always appropriate to the incident, but at the same time it is good evidence in court and things like that. And everyone knows, you go into Perth and you are going to be on camera; you go into Fremantle and you are going to be on camera. So it is quite good.
>
> And the cameras are fantastic. We have had jobs here that I have done in Perth where you can see persons of interest driving around and we have the capabilities to actually zoom in and gather information and intelligence from what was happening inside the vehicle. That is how good they are. So you can follow them everywhere and, when they hop out of the vehicle, you can follow them. Obviously there are some little areas that are black spots, but you could follow them out and as they walk around town, into shops and out of shops and things like that. It is quite amazing and great for intelligence...[81]

Senior Constable Steve Harrison in charge of CCTV surveillance for the Commonwealth Heads of Government Meeting in Perth in late 2011 also spoke to the merits *and* the shortcomings of CCTV surveillance:

79   Ms Lee Robson, Manager, Community Engagement, City of Greater Dandenong, Evidence given to the Drugs and Crime Prevention Committee, Inquiry into Locally Based Approaches to Community Safety and Crime Prevention, Public Hearing, Dandenong, 30 May 2011.

80   Mr Mark Doubleday, Director, Community Services, City of Greater Dandenong, Evidence given to the Drugs and Crime Prevention Committee, Inquiry into Locally Based Approaches to Community Safety and Crime Prevention, Public Hearing, Dandenong, 30 May 2011.

81   Superintendent John Leembruggen, Community Engagement Division, Western Australia Office of Crime Prevention, Evidence given to the Drugs and Crime Prevention Committee, Inquiry into Locally Based Approaches to Community Safety and Crime Prevention, Meeting, Perth, 20 June 2011.

For further discussion of the use of CCTV and other forms of surveillance in Western Australia in the context of the Eyes on the Street program, see Chapter 3.

Surveillance may work as a deterrent. There have been lots and lots of articles and documents written on CCTV as a tool to determine crime. The British example, which is fairly obvious, is that they put CCTV in an area and crime moves to another neighbouring area, so it does not actually change that behaviour in real terms and just sends it somewhere else. That is for overt CCTV at least anyway. With CCTV, the general thought is that people feel safer when they are in an environment where they can see big cameras and they are actually moving and they imagine they have got other people behind watching after their security and safety. Therefore, as a result of that, there is a high likelihood that there is less crime in that immediate environment.

The presence of CCTV may act as a prompt to remind people to take other security measures. So they see the camera, the camera is panning — some of those cameras will auto patrol so they will look around by themselves — once again, the inference is that someone is on the other end of it. They go, 'Right, did I lock my car? These people are looking after me, but I need to take some care for myself.'

So from a police perspective — reactive, proactive and real-time: we can use CCTV as a mechanism to draw down on the historical data forensically and we can go and find things that we think may have occurred within the view of the camera. Proactive is to use CCTV as a mechanism to, I suppose, actively police an area and then respond to something that you see there immediately.[82]

Conclusions as to the effectiveness of CCTV are summed up in the evaluation of street CCTV in Glasgow — it is not a 'universal panacea' (Ditton et al cited in New South Wales Law Reform Commission 2005). Similarly, an overview of the implementation of CCTV by the Commonwealth Parliament found that:

Available research appears to consistently indicate that CCTV surveillance works best as part of a package of crime prevention measures rather than being relied upon in isolation. As the Australian Institute of Criminology boldly notes, 'CCTV will not work by itself'. Research also suggests that CCTV may be of more value as a source of evidence than as a deterrent, and most effective against property crime. Whatever its intended use, it is clear that careful consideration needs to be given to the way in which CCTV is applied in order to maximise whatever benefits it does offer.

Although CCTV is undoubtedly a valuable tool in the prevention and investigation of crime, the inconsistent and ambiguous nature of its effectiveness would seem to suggest that the right balance of environmental factors, education, administration, resources and equipment is yet to be determined and achieved (Parliament of Australia 2005, p.3). [83]

Community based crime prevention

Community based crime prevention programs include those that operate within local community areas and involve community residents actively working with local government agencies and partnerships to address issues contributing to crime, antisocial behaviour and disorder. Community members are encouraged to play key roles in problem identification and planning solutions to problems in their communities. There is wide variation in community based crime prevention programs resulting from factors such as program focus, program rationale, community context (for example the demographics of the local community) and type of community involvement. Community based crime prevention programs are operated by neighbourhood residents, police, LGAs and community agencies. Community based crime prevention programs often rely on partnerships including community policing partnerships.[84]

Much community based crime prevention incorporates or is drawn from theories of community development and the processes of community engagement and community

---

82　Senior Constable Steve Harrison, CCTV/Blue Iris Program, Western Australia Office of Crime Prevention, Evidence given to the Drugs and Crime Prevention Committee, Inquiry into Locally Based Approaches to Community Safety and Crime Prevention, Meeting, Perth, 21 June 2011.

83　For a critical account of the 'surveillance society' in the United Kingdom, including the use of CCTV, see Chapter 9.

84　Many community crime prevention models stem from the Bonnemaison program implemented in France in the 1980s. Bonnemaison and other examples of community crime prevention models are discussed in greater detail in Chapter 3 of this Report. Community policing and other forms of community partnerships are also discussed at length in Chapters 6 and 7.

capacity building (Lane & Henry 2004; Sutton, Cherney & White 2008). Community development strategies, including those focusing on crime, are often implemented in disadvantaged communities and ideally focus on integrated multi-objective and multi-strategy responses rather than single objective programs (Lane & Henry 2004).[85] They may also be developed or implemented for particular communities with special and culturally specific needs, for example Indigenous communities.[86]

Other community based crime prevention programs are arguably more 'middle-class' in nature, aimed at first and foremost protecting individual and community property from burglary and vandalism. Neighbourhood Watch is the archetype of such a community partnership strategy.[87] The advantage of community based strategies according to some commentators is that they can incorporate the best features of both social/developmental and environmental approaches.

Renewal and regeneration

Community renewal is a community based approach that joins residents, businesses, government and local organisations together to help transform their community into a place of opportunity and activity. Increasingly it has been argued that local communities and local knowledge are at the forefront of developing and implementing many areas of social policy, including crime prevention policies. This reflects:

♦ growing recognition about the importance of investing in communities as a field of public policy

♦ evidence that community strength/cohesion buffers against impact of poverty and social isolation

♦ stronger communities produce benefits that are tangible — through community renewal and building processes.[88]

Community or Neighbourhood Renewal, as it is sometimes termed, involves residents in making choices about how best to achieve:

• ongoing community participation in decision-making

• new job and learning opportunities

• increased volunteering and support for each other

• better community facilities and more attractive open spaces

• more involvement in cultural, recreational and sporting activities

• improved feelings of safety and wellbeing.[89]

---

85 See for example the Communities that Care program discussed in Chapter 7 of this Report.

86 For a discussion of the suitability of crime prevention measures in particular communities, see Chapter 7.

87 Although arguably its role has or is changing in recent years. See discussion in Chapter 10.

88 http://www.sheltersa.asn.au/Documents/November%20Forum/Community%20Renewal.pdf

89 http://www.dpcd.vic.gov.au/communitydevelopment/community-planning/community-renewal
    The former Victorian Government's *Community Renewal Strategy* had three main stages:

    1. Local governments are funded to employ locally-based workers who bring residents, different levels of government, local businesses and other organisations together to develop an action plan for the community. Residents are given the authority to decide priorities, directions and solutions for their community.

    2. State and local government and other organisations are asked to respond to the action plan in a flexible and coordinated way, drawing funding from a number of sources together to make it work harder.

    3. Locally developed solutions are put on the ground.

       Whilst the *Community Renewal Strategy* was initiated by the former state government, the model and the principles upon which it is based are still being rolled out in many municipalities throughout Victoria. See for example, *Community Renewal Rosebud West,* a partnership between the Mornington Peninsula Shire, the Department of Planning and Community Development, local organisations, and the local community, at http://www.mornpen.vic. gov.au/; or Bayswater North Community Renewal, a similar partnership process at: http://www.maroondah.vic.gov. au/BayswaterNorthCommunityRenewal.aspx

Randolph and Judd suggest three broad renewal/regeneration strategies that can be used by urban and social planners in partnership with local governments, community agencies and local residents. These are:

Physical/spatial interventions — including housing upgrades, urban design and infrastructure improvements and de-concentration via asset sales and/or redevelopment;[90]

Social interventions — including tenant consultation/participation, community development, crime prevention initiatives, youth programs, drug and alcohol programs, employment and training, and social enterprise development;

Management interventions — including localised housing management teams, interagency and whole of government service co-ordination, place management[91] and outsourcing housing management to the community or private sectors (Randolph & Judd 2000, p.2).

Local community programs

There are numerous examples of community based renewal activities that draw from the community model of crime prevention and many of these have been presented to the Committee in submissions or through evidence to the Inquiry. For example, the CGD, as part of its community renewal program, explained how the community was very much part of its efforts to improve local areas and crime 'hot spots' through better urban design and community consultation and involvement. In addition, the employment of youth workers to engage with young people and address their needs and problems at these sites could be viewed as a form of social development that looks beyond immediate fixes to the causes or contributors of (youth) crime:

The design of public space is [very important], and we have been exploring some options through using art and engagement as a way of involving communities in planning spaces that they will ultimately use. The use of public space — or the illegitimate use of public space — is often an issue for planners. There is an area in Noble Park, for example, around the railway station which has been developed as a very small urban park — and I use the word 'park' in its broader sense — called the Noble Park Civic Space. There has been an extensive process of consultation with community groups. Over 30 different community groups were consulted extensively, often in community languages about what vision did they have for this space; how were they going to use this space. It was recorded both digitally and with drawings and we believe the space that is now being designed reflects what the community wants, and ultimately the design of that space, because it has had some buy-in, we hope, will result in a space that people can feel a sense of ownership with and, therefore, any risk of behaviour that is not particularly conducive to the community good will be lessened...We have also had youth workers working in the area with specific groups. Some of the traders have expressed concern about that, and we have been proactively engaging the traders to make sure that any issues they may have can be dealt with either by the youth workers or by the police...

These processes, of course, take time. They take resources and they take commitment.[92]

---

90 When the Committee met with the Mayor and officers of the City of Frankston they spoke of the need to 'deconcentrate' as part of making Frankston a safer place to live. In Frankston, for example, it was argued that many of the agencies or organisations that catered for disadvantaged members of the local community, for example methadone dispensers or needle exchanges, were concentrated in a particular pocket of the central activities/business district 'which means that our city is becoming quite unappealing for other members of the community'. As a consequence, the City of Frankston is examining ways it can work with the local traders, business community and community agencies to 'attract a new kind of development into the city' and revive the area around Davey Street' (in the central business and activities district). (Ms Jane Homewood, Manager, General Development, City of Frankston, Evidence given to the Drugs and Crime Prevention Committee, Inquiry into Locally Based Approaches to Community Safety and Crime Prevention, Public Hearing, Frankston, 30 May 2011).

91 For an explanation of 'place management' refer to Whitzman 2005.

92 Ms Lee Robson, Manager, Community Engagement, City of Greater Dandenong, Evidence given to the Drugs and Crime Prevention Committee, Inquiry into Locally Based Approaches to Community Safety and Crime Prevention, Public Hearing, Dandenong, 30 May 2011.

The Dandenong/VicUrban project draws from the principles of community regeneration espoused by Randolph and Judd discussed earlier in this chapter and is clearly and ideally a mix of all three approaches.[93]

Critiques of community crime prevention

For the most part the community crime prevention model has been accepted as a positive addition to the repertoire of approaches to promote safer and healthier communities, particularly at local level. This approach, however, has had its critics. For some, community crime prevention and community capacity building can be seen as a way of protecting or supporting the most stable of communities or parts thereof. Hope, for example, discusses the use of 'community safety' measures as a way of constructing a fortress mentality to keep out a growing underclass in Los Angeles (Hope 1996). Similarly, Squires cites the example of using community safety/community crime prevention rhetoric in Thatcher's England as a way of protecting the interests of the already comfortable middle class:

> Community safety strategies clearly reflect just such a rethink. They take us beyond the 'social' and 'situational' divide and comprise mechanisms for separating 'us' (the law abiding) from 'them' (those to be managed, surveilled, diverted or punished). Criminological discourse has tended to debate the contrasting merits of 'social' versus 'situational' crime prevention, although the present analysis would suggest that both are rather working to the same script...we have to see 'community safety' planning as being, in part, about the more effective insulation of 'us' and the more effective ostracism of 'them'. The argument links this aspect of crime prevention and 'community safety' strategy to the wider critique of the discourse of 'community' invoked by 'community safety' planning (Squires 1999).[94]

Mike Davis has depicted one possible culmination of these arguably socially divisive trends as the establishment of a kind of nightmarish 'urban apartheid' (1990, p.226).[95] High value 'down town' developments are:

> [c]reated where 'defensible space' strategies establish a socially cleansed exclusion zone. In nearby inner city blocks a ghetto underclass is contained by urban design and zoning policies and confronted by aggressive policing strategies more reminiscent of an occupying military power than civilian peacekeeping. In the suburbs, the gated corrals of the middle class, protected by armed private security patrols, complete the picture of social fragmentation. Yet these are still communities, albeit such seemingly beleaguered and dysfunctional ones that their enthusiasm for such notions as 'zero tolerance' (maximum licensed intolerance) only exposes the precarious nature of their confidence that official agencies can guarantee civil peace (Squires 1999). [96]

This somewhat apocalyptic vision arguably does not reflect the reality of what counts for community crime prevention at local level, at least not in Australia. Nonetheless, it does raise interesting and relevant issues as to how the 'community' in community crime

---

93   Community renewal programs are not necessarily easy to develop, implement or maintain. For a good account of the challenges, difficulties and rewards of initiating community renewal projects in Queensland, see A Stark and J McCullough 2005, 'Engaging Communities in Community Renewal: Challenges, Success Factors and Critical Questions'. Accessed 31 August 2011 at: http://www.engagingcommunities2005.org/abstracts/McCullough-Julie-Ann-final.pdf

94   Peter Squires 1999, Criminology and the 'community safety' paradigm: Safety, power and success and the limits of the local. Accessed 31 August 2011 at: http://www.britsoccrim.org/volume2/012.pdf

95   For example, Sutton, Cherney and White discuss the experience of the American 'Weed and Seed' program funded by the federal government:

'Weed and Seed involved first using criminal justice interventions (eg zero tolerance policing, arrest and imprisonment) to 'weed' neighbourhoods of individuals identified as disruptive, then 'seeding' the neighbourhood with family support, community development and other social programs. Many neighbourhoods were polarised over whether and to what extent the 'weed' component should be applied and some disadvantaged neighbourhoods successfully resisted this aspect' (Sutton, Cherney & White 2008, p. 41).

96   See Peter Squires 1999, Criminology and the 'community safety' paradigm: Safety, power and success and the limits of the local. Accessed 31 August 2011 at http://www.britsoccrim.org/volume2/012.pdf

prevention is defined.[97] Are community crime prevention/safety models inclusive of all constituents in the local area (young people, Indigenous people, migrants, the disabled etc.) or only a certain subset within them such as well-off ratepayers? Does urban/economic renewal privilege some sections of the community at the expense of others? Is the very concept of community at the heart of such strategies idealised and nostalgic? (King 1989). Is community crime prevention simply law and order in another guise?

On the basis of the evidence gathered by the Committee the answer to the above questions is probably a qualified no. Whilst there is always the chance that some aspects of community crime prevention may serve the interests of the middle class only, overall the community engagement and community safety strategies such as the Dandenong Revitalisation Project have been successful.[98]

Community engagement methods that focus on crime prevention and local examples that demonstrate or draw upon this approach are clearly the major focus of the Inquiry's Terms of Reference. As such, community programs including Neighbourhood Watch will form the basis of extensive chapters later in this Report.

Other ways of classifying crime prevention

Criminologists have developed other typologies for classifying crime prevention than those outlined previously. These include classifying crime prevention according to theoretical standpoint; the object of the crime prevention programs or policies; classifications according to temporal stage in the cycle or classifications according to the population being targeted (either as offender or 'victim').

Classifying according to theoretical standpoint

The aims, outcomes and approaches to devising a crime prevention program may vary according to the theoretical or ideological standpoint of the developer or practitioner. For example, a *technocratic* or *managerial* approach incorporates a 'what works', 'crime science' or administrative paradigm, the goal of which is to 'identify the most effective methods of crime reduction and to ensure such knowledge guides policy and practice' (Hughes 1998 in Sutton, Cherney & White 2008, p.14). A key belief of this school is rather than relying on (or at least only on) sociological based theories of crime to develop crime prevention initiatives, policy relevant criminology:

> [n]eeds to be underpinned by a scientific agenda that uses experimental methods and empirical investigation to identify 'what works'. Such a rigorous evidence based approach is seen as the best way to overcome successive government failures to implement successful programs (Sutton, Cherney & White 2008, p.14).

This school of criminology places its confidence in scientifically measurable outcomes, meta evaluations, identifiable goals, outcomes and objectives and coordination of projects across a range of stakeholders. Joined up strategies and a 'whole of government' approach are key aspects of this approach. Rationality rather than ideology is the watchword of the

---

97 Skogan in the American context, for example, describes how crime prevention funds may be utilised by different 'communities' characterised as either preservationist or insurgent. The preservationist (or exclusionary) approach to crime prevention may seek to secure safer (middle-class) neighbourhoods — for example through Neighbourhood Watch or gated communities — whereas the insurgent or inclusionary approach seeks to create better opportunities for disadvantaged neighbourhoods or communities (Skogan 1988).

98 For example, Dandenong's Metro Village 3175, part of the Dandenong Revitalisation Project, is a new master-planned community in the heart of Dandenong with architecturally designed residences financially affordable for people on lower incomes including people currently living in the Dandenong area. Metro Village 3175 is located on the site of the former Dandenong Livestock Market. In November 2005, VicUrban launched a project to develop the land into a mixed-use development consisting of 1100 residences as well as cafes and restaurants, known as Metro 3175, with 3175 signifying Dandenong's postcode. See http://www.greaterdandenong.com/documents.asp?id=3396&title=revitalising+central+dandenong

technocratic approach. Such an approach is most comprehensively exemplified by the United Kingdom's Crime Reduction Partnerships Model.[99]

An approach based in 'critical' criminology on the other hand would prefer that prevention policies and programs be located in the context of broader social, political and economic realities. Often such an approach would advocate redistributive policies to effect such change. Critical criminology advocates would usually prefer to use the language of 'community safety' rather than crime prevention (Sutton, Cherney & White 2008, Watts, Bessant & Hil 2008).

Conversely, as discussed previously, a conservative 'law and order' approach tends to address the 'offender' only; for example deterrence through threat of police detection and punishment. From such a standpoint 'zero tolerance' policing may be viewed as a major strategy to reduce and eliminate crime.

Classifying according to object of the crime prevention

The development of crime prevention programs may also vary according to the underlying object (stated or unstated) or *raison d'etre* of the approach. For example, the object may be narrowly focused: namely, reducing crime. However, a crime prevention policy may have the broader objective of a more pleasant, healthy or 'liveable' neighbourhood or community. Similarly it may take what some American criminologists have called a *preservationist* or *exclusionary* approach to crime prevention (securing safer neighbourhoods, for example through Neighbourhood Watch or gated communities) or it might promote an *insurgent* or *inclusionary* approach (creating better opportunities for disadvantaged neighbourhoods or communities).

Classifying according to stage in the cycle

Under this typology, crime prevention models or programs can be divided into three categories: primary, secondary and tertiary. They can then be further cross-divided into the categories of social and environmental programs discussed above.

Primary prevention addresses those factors or conditions relevant to crime that affects an entire population or community (Brantingham & Faust 1976). Primary social prevention programs may include early intervention programs for young children whereas a primary environmental program may be the provision of better street lighting in a particular area. In both cases a reduction in crime may be a by-product of a greater overall strategy of creating safer and happier communities rather than the primary objective of the intervention.

Secondary crime prevention, however, usually involves targeting populations deemed to be 'at risk'. An example may be a program to reduce the amount of school truancy in a particular area (truancy being one of the lead indicators of future criminal offending by juveniles).

Finally, tertiary prevention targets people who are already known offenders or environments already affected by crime:

> The objective of [tertiary prevention] is to reduce future offending and the re-victimisation of people or places already affected by crime. Examples include prison based treatment programs for convicted sex offenders and post release schemes to help offenders resettle in the community, as well as the use of situational techniques to improve guardianship of crime hot spots or premises that have recently been burgled (Sutton, Cherney & White 2008, p.23).

Examples of crime prevention programs or interventions according to the stage in the cycle can be seen in the following table.[100]

---

99   For further discussion of the UK model, see Chapter 9.

100 For a more comprehensive list and discussion of various crime prevention programs see Chapter 6 and 7 and the list in Appendix 9.

Table 2.1: Crime prevention: Typology and examples according to stage in the cycle

	Primary	Secondary	Tertiary
Social	• Programs to give all children a headstart' before they encounter formal school systems • Early school Programs to reshape concepts of masculinity • Initiatives to support parents	• Wilderness programs for 'at risk' teenagers • School truancy reduction schemes	• Tougher sentences for selected crimes • Initiative to help release prisoners secure paid jobs • Behaviour-change programs for recidivist sex offenders
Environmental	• Incorporation of prevention principles into urban planning and design of residential complexes • General prevention advice for householders, businesses	• Installation of alarms • Use of routine patrols or other special surveillance • Neighbourhood Watch	• Closure of high-risk areas • Installation of bullet-proof glass and CCTV in banks with records of repeat victimisation

Source: Sutton, Cherney & White 2008, p.24.

Classifying according to the population targeted

Crime prevention, either of the social or environmental kind, may be further classified according to the population sub-groups at which it is targeted. For example, crime prevention programs may be aimed at juveniles, women, Indigenous people or indeed specific neighbourhoods. Such groups may be either offenders or beneficiaries (victims) of the particular intervention.

Conclusion — The need for a mix of crime prevention approaches?

Crime prevention is a somewhat amorphous concept that can mean different things to different people. For some theorists and practitioners it is a distinct alternative to other criminal justice policies (Sutton, Cherney & White 2008), for others it is merely a supplement to law and order approaches.

Whatever view is taken, it is true that crime prevention consists of a diverse array of measures, projects and programs sometimes coordinated or linked into an overall framework, sometimes not. Some programs will have a clear objective with achievable aims and measurable outputs — other programs may be more ad hoc and not based on the best knowledge or evidence available.

Most commentators in the area of crime prevention today generally are of the view that a model combining the best aspects of crime prevention approaches is the most suitable, particularly as there is usually a good deal of overlap between approaches, for example situational and social approaches (Lane & Henry 2004; Sutton, Cherney & White 2008; Homel 2010b).[101] Each approach has its merits and its weaknesses. Social or developmental approaches can result in not only a reduction in crime but also 'the achievement of safe, secure, vibrant and economically vibrant communities...and enhanced social and human capital' (Homel 2010b, p.3; see also International Centre for the Prevention of Crime (ICPC) 2010). On the other hand, many developmental/social measures are expensive investments that may take a substantial period of time to achieve the intended results.

---

101 The Western Australian crime prevention model is arguably one that attempts to comprehensively combine the social and situational approaches in an overall plan. See discussion in Chapter 3.

Short-term solutions such as the installation of CCTV systems can seem politically safe and attractive to the media and a general public concerned about crime in their area. This is not, however, to discount their intrinsic worth as an adjunct to reducing crime and antisocial behaviour.

Situational or environmental measures may provide convenient 'quick fixes' and reduce crime in some locations, addressing the immediate causes of the problem and bringing about direct physical changes in the environment of a particular area. For example, research has indicated that whilst social interventions may be more effective than situational or physical interventions to reduce crime or the fear of crime on disadvantaged public housing estates, there are definitely some environmental measures that can be implemented to reduce the high level of crimes on such estates. In particular, measures such as improved lighting and more activity in areas that are otherwise unoccupied may reduce the opportunities for committing crime and as a result also decrease the fear of crime in particular locations.[102] They do not, however, serve as comprehensive solutions to address 'the structural causes associated with the more deeply entrenched social, economic and cultural dimensions [of crime]' (Homel 2009a, p.2). They also run the risk of displacing the problem from one area to another.[103]

Peter Homel has stated that whichever approach is taken or whatever mix is employed, and despite the relative merits of each experience, in Australia and overseas it has consistently been shown that the effectiveness of crime prevention initiatives is often reduced by the practical and technical problems associated with the development and implementation of crime prevention models including:

- Ineffective and inefficient processes for the transfer and uptake of available knowledge about good crime prevention practice and research, such as there is a failure to learn and apply valuable lessons;

- The absence of a skilled and professional crime prevention workforce;

- Inadequate project and program management ability; and

- Lack of knowledge and experience with performance measurement and program evaluation (Homel 2009a, p.3).[104]

Recommendations emanating from this chapter are listed on the next page.

The following chapter will examine the types of models that have been created to develop and implement crime prevention strategies and programs and approaches that have been used to avoid the problems listed above.

---

102 See Judd, Samuels and Barton, Australian Housing and Urban Research Institute at http://www.griffith.edu.au/data/assets/pdf_file/0013/81400/social-city-01-judd.pdf

103 Either geographic displacement — crime moves from one neighbourhood or area to another — or type of crime displacement — the offender changes the focus of his or her criminal activity to another target. In the latter case, Sutton, Cherney and White argue that this will not always be a negative phenomenon. They give an example of how situational crime prevention measures such as motorcar immobilisers may mean offenders may switch from car theft and joyriding to other forms of crime. Nonetheless, the use of such immobilisers has significantly reduced the dangers associated with high speed car driving, pursuits and collisions including death. 'Such displacement is still likely to be associated with net social benefits' (2008, p.42).

104 For a discussion of the need for evaluation of crime prevention programs and initiatives, see Chapter 11.

Recommendations

2. **The Committee recommends** that the Crime Prevention and Community Safety Framework include clear definitions as to what is meant by crime prevention and community safety.

34. **The Committee recommends** that the Community Crime Prevention Unit liaise with, encourage and assist university architecture and planning faculties to offer or expand courses on Crime Prevention through Environmental Design.

Section B — Policy Frameworks and Initiatives: Global and Australian approaches

3. International, National and State Policy Frameworks for Implementing Crime Prevention Initiatives

Introduction

The history of crime prevention policy development and implementation has been fraught with obstacles, false hopes and cyclical swings. This is true of crime prevention policy development in other parts of the world as well as in Australia. This chapter examines the various international and domestic models that have been used to implement crime prevention policies and programs. Some have been regarded as 'successes', others have not necessarily fulfilled the ambitions their planners had for them. The chapter commences with a brief discussion of the international influence on crime prevention through bodies such as the United Nations (UN) and World Health Organization (WHO). It then examines two notable examples of efforts to establish a comprehensive 'scientific' and collaborative approach to implementing crime prevention — the Bonnemaison Project in France and the United Kingdom's Crime Prevention Partnerships, in some respects a failed effort. Then crime prevention models across Australia, most notably Western Australia and New South Wales are examined. A discussion of the strengths and weaknesses of the approaches in these two states serves as a good lead-in to the subject of the following chapter: 'What 'works' and doesn't work in establishing good crime prevention models'.

International approaches to implementing crime prevention

Increasingly it has been recognised that the 'science' of crime prevention is an international phenomenon for which knowledge sharing knows no boundaries. A set of various crime prevention principles and frameworks for implementing crime prevention strategies has been adopted at a global level for dissemination in member states; the most important of these have been sponsored through the UN and WHO.

The United Nations, World Health Organization and crime prevention

International bodies such as the UN and WHO, on the basis of numerous commission and research reports, have agreed that governments need to go beyond law enforcement and criminal justice to tackle the risk factors that contribute towards crime and antisocial behaviour (Waller 2006). In particular, the UN established a set of principles for effective crime prevention in 2002. These are:

- *government leadership*—at all levels to create and maintain an institutional framework for effective crime prevention;

- *socio-economic development and inclusion*—integration of crime prevention into relevant social and economic policies, a focus on integration of at risk communities, children, families and youth;

- *cooperation and partnerships*—between government organisations, civil society and the business sector;

- *sustainability and accountability*—adequate funding to establish and sustain programs and evaluation, and clear accountability for funding;

- *use of a knowledge base*—using evidence of proven practices as the basis for policies and programs;

- *human rights/rule of law/culture of lawfulness*—respect for human rights and promotion of a culture of lawfulness;

- *interdependency*—take account of links between local crime problems and international organised crime; and

- *differentiation*—respecting different needs of men and women and vulnerable members of society (UN-ECOSOC 2002).[105]

Similarly, in 2003 the WHO Assembly Resolution (56-24) urged governments to implement nine crime prevention/community safety recommendations as follows:

1. Create, implement and monitor a national action plan for [local] violence prevention.

2. Enhance capacity for collecting data on violence.

3. Define priorities for, and support research on, the causes, consequences, costs and prevention of violence.

4. Promote primary prevention and local community responses.

5. Strengthen responses for victims of violence.

6. Integrate violence prevention into social and educational policies, and thereby promote gender and social equality.

7. Increase collaboration and exchange of information on violence prevention.

8. Promote and monitor adherence to international treaties, laws and other mechanisms to protect human rights.

9. Seek practical, internationally agreed responses to the global drugs and global arms trade.[106]

These recommendations form, in part, the basis of an international 'safer communities' movement.[107] In particular, the WHO established the Karolinska Institute in Sweden,[108] responsible for accrediting global cities as 'safe communities' if they met the criteria of a strict vetting process, agreed to site visits and inspections and hosting an international Safer Communities Conference.[109]

Two international responses to crime

Internationally, over the last 25 years, 'the prevailing logic for crime prevention has been that since most crime of immediate concern to communities is local (ie. property crime, antisocial behaviour, vandalism) then the primary focus for preventive action should also

---

105 For explanation of these principles in greater detail and their application to crime prevention practice, see Homel 2009a and the discussion later in this chapter.

106 See http://apps.who.int/gb/archive/pdf_files/WHA56/ea5624.pdf

107 Other important global bodies and programs connected to the international community safety movement include the UN HABITAT — Safer Cities Programme, of particular importance in the cities of the developing world; the United Nations Office on Drugs and Crime (UNODC) and the Montreal based and UN affiliated International Centre for the Prevention of Crime (ICPC). Particularly important is the ICPC's Survey Report on international crime prevention trends and effectiveness discussed later in this chapter.

108 Now based in Geneva, Switzerland.

109 The Cities of Moreland and La Trobe in Victoria became the first accredited safe cities in Australia in the mid-1990s. Melbourne held an international Safer Communities conference in 1995. The Committee has also been told that currently the City of Frankston is seeking accreditation as a WHO Safer City.

be local' (Homel 2010a, p.118). However, what counts as a local approach will often vary depending on the system of governance applicable in each country; for example unitary systems such as the United Kingdom or constitutional federations such as Canada:[110]

> In some countries such as in the United Kingdom and New Zealand, this logic has found its way into nationally mandated legislative measures to support local crime prevention action. In other countries such as the USA, Canada, Australia, parts of Europe and South America, it has simply been picked up and implemented as a strategy that best suits local circumstances. In those sorts of locations, crime prevention action as a locally organised and delivered initiative simply reflects the fact that the relevant policies and necessary services are more directly within the control of local or regional authorities rather than those at national level. In other words, how local crime prevention action is organised will be a function of the prevailing local governance arrangements (Homel 2010a, p.118).

Homel states the development of local crime prevention approaches in France is a good example of this (2010a). Partnerships to prevent or reduce crime have been an essential feature of crime prevention policy in France commencing with the Bonnemaison Project and in the United Kingdom with the UK Crime Reduction Program. These influenced the formation of many similar projects across Australia.

The Bonnemaison Project (France)

The Bonnemaison Project arose from a year-long Inquiry by the French national government's Commission on Safety and Security in the Community (1982) chaired by Gilbert Bonnemaison. It arose out of concern with the levels of rising crime and disorder in France, particularly amongst ethnic and migrant communities in Paris and the larger towns of France in 1981.[111] The Final Report of the Committee emphasised three concepts — *solidarity, integration* and *locality:*

> Working from the premise that people subject to social dislocation and exclusion from mainstream social life and opportunities were more likely to resort to crime, it argued that prevention strategies should concentrate on addressing the problems experienced by disaffected young people, immigrants, the unemployed and other 'at-risk' groups, and strive to reintegrate them into their local communities (Sutton, Cherney & White 2008, p.95).

The Committee Inquiry Report recommended a coordinated infrastructure for developing and implementing crime prevention projects. Nationally, the French government established an 80 member Crime Prevention Council chaired by the Prime Minister and including the mayors of key towns and cities of France. Regionally, Departmental Councils on Crime Prevention chaired by the Chief Administrator of the Region acted as a conduit between national and local government. The third level comprised Local Crime Prevention Committees chaired by the mayor of the relevant town and comprising representatives of national, regional and local government and community groups (Sutton, Cherney & White 2008). Local crime prevention committees were entrusted to develop and implement a coordinated crime prevention plan; 'such plans were to be based on systematic assessment not just of the town or city's crime and safety problems and their causes, but of the local resources and institutions that might help effect solutions' (Sutton, Cherney & White 2008, p.96; see also Crawford 1998, p.222). Moreover, as Homel states:

> Local crime prevention activity was organised through the development of detailed local plans that emphasised agency-based prevention involving institutions such as schools, housing authorities and employment and youth support services working together with police and other groups.

---

110 Canada has had a National Strategy on Community Safety and Crime Prevention since 1998. It divides responsibility for crime prevention between the federal government and agencies, provincial and local governments. For a detailed discussion of crime prevention models and approaches in Canada, see Peter Homel, *Lessons for Canadian Crime Prevention from International Experience* (Homel 2009b; see also Morgan & Homel 2011; www.publicsafety.gc.ca).

111 The program was named after Gilbert Bonnemaison, the Chair of the Commission of Inquiry.

Crime prevention action itself was funded through a series of contractual arrangements between the national government and the local crime prevention committees that also incorporated the need for close interagency cooperation (Homel 2010a, p.119).

Social inclusion rather than exclusion was the paramount premise for reducing offending. Moreover, health, social, youth and other welfare programs and staff that had hitherto been viewed as peripheral at best were now seen as a crucial part of the fight to prevent and reduce crime.

As Homel has remarked, Bonnemaison became a prototype, 'albeit a flexible and malleable one', for local crime prevention approaches internationally (2010a, p.119).[112] One attempt where at least some of the principles of Bonnemaison were applied with only limited success was in the United Kingdom.

The United Kingdom Crime Reduction Program

The United Kingdom Crime Reduction Program (CRP) was launched in 1999 as a result of the Home Office Crime Prevention Unit conducting a review of documented approaches to 'what works' to reduce crime. It has been referred to as 'one of the most closely studied crime prevention implementation experiences internationally' (Homel & Homel 2012). The chief aim of the program was to turn research based evidence (based on evaluations of 25 years of crime prevention research and experience) into mainstream practice — the evidence based policy program (EBPP) (see Homel 2004). Similar to the Bonnemaison Project, the aim of the project was to utilise a partnerships approach to crime prevention across every level of government in the country. Because of Britain's unitary form of government it was possible to have nationally mandated legislative measures in place to support local crime prevention plans in ways that would not be possible in Australia (Homel 2010a). In particular, the *Crime and Disorder Act* mandates that every local government authority (LGA) in Britain must develop and implement a local crime prevention partnership with police and relevant community agencies tailored to their own particular local circumstances. Coordinated nationally, the Home Office would oversee and administer these crime reduction contracts/plans entered into with local governments:

> Research and evaluation personnel were to work hand in glove with policy and resource managers to ensure that successful initiatives flourished, that necessary changes were made to those strategies that were shown to be less effective, and that resources were allocated to where they could achieve greatest impact (Homel & Homel 2012).

Local governments would be responsible for drawing up a partnership plan to reduce crime in its shire or borough often in conjunction with private sector and community groups. Indeed local governments in Britain have a *statutory duty* to work in partnerships to reduce crime through the formulation of local strategies for their areas:

> Most importantly, the CRP was designed to operate in a joined up way across government agencies at the central and regional level and in partnership with local government and community groups at the local level. In other words, it was attempting to manage the implementation of a complex innovative program with multiple interventions and outcomes simultaneously in a vertical direction (ie through a central policy level through a regional structure to local delivery) and horizontally (ie across diverse central agencies) (Homel & Homel 2012).

Unfortunately the CRP, for many reasons, was not as successful as its planners had hoped and was for the most part dismantled after its initial three-year period. A major reason was that the program was not well executed and the skills and organisational capacities

---

112 For example, the approach found in the crime prevention work of the National Crime Prevention Council and the US Conference of Mayors in the United States. (See also approaches in Holland, Germany, Ireland, Canada and Mexico discussed in Homel 2010a; and particularly in the context of Holland, see Sutton, Cherney & White 2008.)

required for such a far-reaching approach were not always in evidence (Homel & Homel 2012). Other reasons for the lack of success included:

- Poor support systems from the centre

- A lack of facilitative administrative support

- Difficulties in finding, recruiting and retraining suitably qualified and skilled staff

- Generally inadequate technical and strategic advice and guidance from the centre [ie the Home Office] and the regions; and

- Inadequate levels of project management competence and skill, particularly in financial and resource management (Homel & Homel 2012).

A full analysis of the reasons for failure is beyond the scope of this chapter although they have been well documented.[113] Suffice to quote Sutton, Cherney and White commenting on the British model:

> [p]lanning process [should] allow scope for problem-solving and flexibility. This has not always been the case. The UK *Crime and Disorder Act* includes a statutory requirement that local authorities develop crime and disorder plans. However, rather than being used as a mechanism for the centre to establish dialogue with local authorities and community groups, this statutory obligation seems to have become a target for imposing fixed targets (e.g., specified reductions in certain volume crimes). Flexibility in addressing local problems was not encouraged (2008, p.72).

The British experience, however, did have some positive aspects. One of the strengths in the British approach was the recognition that crime prevention is 'everyone's business' and that local governments and local communities must be involved in the process. As Garner Clancey of Sydney University's Institute of Criminology commented in the context of the UK model:

> Crime prevention is owned by no-one. There is no single agency that has responsibility for crime prevention. Police are obviously the prime agents, but if you look at some of the best examples, crime prevention has nothing to do with policing. It is early intervention work done by health providers, education providers. It is designing out crime that is done by architects and design professionals. As a result of that multidisciplinary approach I think we need to have a shared language. We need to build capacity within the relevant sectors to be able to talk to each other, to be able to understand the data sets that are available and to develop joint responses. ... I am not suggesting the British model has been a complete success in this regard but in terms of the nature of that legislation it is really about saying that crime prevention is an inter-agency responsibility.[114]

According to Mr Clancey the virtue of the British model whatever its weaknesses, is that it mandates the police as a lead agency to take overall direction of community crime prevention:

---

113 In particular, see the analysis in Homel, Nutley, Webb & Tilley 2004; Homel 2004; Morgan & Homel 2011, Homel & Homel 2012.

114 Mr Clancey added that one of the reasons the British model potentially works well is due to the alignment of government boundaries. They are all around local authorities:

'One of the greater frustrations I see in New South Wales is the non-alignment of agency boundaries— local police areas 81, 152 local government areas, a multitude of education districts. People are talking at different mediums at cross-purposes often because you have different players in the room just by virtue of where the geographic boundaries draw. For me that compromises the quality of the work' (Mr Garner Clancey, Adjunct Lecturer, Sydney Institute of Criminology, University of Sydney, Evidence given to the Drugs and Crime Prevention Committee, Inquiry into Locally Based Approaches to Community Safety and Crime Prevention, Public Hearing, Sydney, 19 September 2011).

Indeed when the Committee spoke to Ms Margaret Southwell, Crime Prevention Officer with the Bankstown Council in Sydney's south she stated that one of the advantages for Bankstown compared to other areas of Sydney is that their LGA boundary and the Local Area Command [Police] boundaries are identically aligned 'which makes it a bit easier to work with police' (Ms Margaret Southwell, Chair, New South Wales Local Government Community Safety and Crime Prevention Committee and Community Development Officer, Community Development, Bankstown City Council, Evidence given to the Drugs and Crime Prevention Committee, Inquiry into Locally Based Approaches to Community Safety and Crime Prevention, Public Hearing, Sydney, 19 September 2011).

> There is a great deal of clarity in that. Others are involved — corrections, health, welfare agencies… but unless there is someone at the top to drive it, to administer it, to advocate to high levels of government [it will be directionless].[115]

Overall the experience in England showed that despite the project being given significant political and financial commitment and having a well developed evidence base about 'what works' for crime prevention, 'only modest levels of innovation and system change were achieved' (Homel & Homel 2012).[116]

However The United Kingdom experience illustrated the pitfalls to be avoided for successfully implementing crime prevention policy and programs. These lessons would be particularly important for Australia.[117]

Australian approaches to implementing crime prevention strategies

It has been particularly difficult in Australia to address crime prevention in a coordinated and uniform way given the federal/state division of powers.[118] Even where there is a central authority responsible for crime prevention planning at state level, things are not always smooth sailing. For example, Cherney and Sutton state that local and regional crime prevention requires significant central state support:

> Local planning and problem solving will not occur if central governments refuse to devolve resources, authority and decision making powers to the local players who have responsibility for program delivery (Cherney & Sutton 2007, p.75).

In a federal system of government such as Australia however:

> Devolution of resources and decision making will always be difficult in Australia's multi-tiered system of government which poses significant practical obstacles to ideals of effective multi-agency partnership (Cherney & Sutton 2007, p.76).

Crime prevention at Commonwealth level

Despite the criticisms made above, the federal government does have a (minimal) role in funding and directing crime prevention policy and programs. Clearly there are issues pertaining to the prevention of federal crimes for which the Commonwealth, through the Australian Federal Police and Attorney General's Department, has direct responsibility (for example, terrorism, drug and sex trafficking and other crimes across state borders). But even in areas of state and local government responsibility the Commonwealth has a minor role to play particularly through its funding programs.

For example, there have been various embodiments of a national crime prevention strategy or initiative over the last 20 years but most, have been restricted to largely providing grants and funding for projects developed and implemented at state or local level, rather than developing policy at a national level.[119] The National Community Crime Prevention

---

115 Mr Garner Clancey, Adjunct Lecturer, Sydney Institute of Criminology, University of Sydney, Evidence given to the Drugs and Crime Prevention Committee, Inquiry into Locally Based Approaches to Community Safety and Crime Prevention, Public Hearing, Sydney, 19 September 2011.

116 Other aspects of crime prevention and policing strategies and structures operating in the United Kingdom are discussed in Chapter 9 pertaining to Neighbourhood Watch in England and Wales.

117 For a discussion of recent initiatives in crime prevention since the election of the Conservative government in 2010, see *A New Approach to Fighting Crime,* (Home Office 2011). The new forms of community safety partnerships comprised of police, local government authorities, the National Health Service, probation officers and fire and rescue services are discussed incidentally in Chapter 9 concerning Neighbourhood Watch in the United Kingdom.

118 For a comprehensive discussion of how crime prevention policy and delivery may differ depending on the tier or level of government responsible for it, see Peter Homel 2010a, *Delivering effective local crime prevention: why understanding variations in municipal governance arrangements matters.*

119 For a critique of earlier attempts at coordinating crime prevention at a national level, see Catalano 1999.

Programme (NCCPP) was established in 2004 and was administered by the Commonwealth Attorney General's Department. The NCCPP was designed to provide funding for grassroots projects designed to enhance community safety and crime prevention by preventing or reducing crime and antisocial behaviour, improving community safety and security, and reducing the fear of crime. The NCCPP Small Grants Programme, which featured a streamlined process for small crime prevention grants of up to $5000, was announced on 1 May 2007. This program has funded 417 projects.

Some commentators have been somewhat critical of this limited role in federal support for crime prevention. They have stressed the importance of establishing national frameworks for crime prevention in Australia, particularly with regard to providing technical assistance to improve performance and effectiveness of those responsible for developing and implementing diverse crime prevention and community safety projects across Australia.

For example, Ms Margaret Southwell, Chair of the New South Wales Local Government Community Safety and Crime Prevention Network, told the Committee in Sydney that:

> We do not have a national crime prevention policy. I think that is probably relevant to our Victorian counterparts, as much as it is to ourselves. There is a real lack of strong leadership at the federal level. That affects our intra-governmental efforts to coordinate what we are trying to do across the country. We would really be looking to federal government to adopt a position; some type of [approach] that I think can help us.[120]

Professor Peter Homel argues that the establishment of a national network is necessary for two main tasks in particular:

- Improving workforce skills and organisational development; and
- Strengthening and improving the effective dissemination of the crime prevention evidence base (Homel 2009a, p.5).

He claims that one way this could be done is through the establishment of a national crime prevention technical assistance fund managed through a well supported high level advisory body:

> The function of this fund would be to sponsor relevant and appropriate professional training, promote the development of events and processes, as well as guide the growth of a more effectively disseminated crime prevention evidence base.

> There would be need to create mechanisms at the national level to assist in developing and delivering these capacity-building resources in a way that enables better performance and goal achievement. Without more strategic coordination, the currently modest and largely uncoordinated levels of investment in capacity building provided through the states and territories, as well as via key national agencies, run the risk of remaining ineffective (Homel 2009, p.5).

A new crime prevention framework for Australia

Bearing the criticisms of the lack of a national framework in mind the Australian government through the Australia and New Zealand Crime Prevention Senior Officers' Group (ANZCPSOG) recently commissioned the Australian Institute of Criminology to develop a new National Crime Prevention Framework as a resource which canvasses the most effective best practice approaches to the prevention and reduction of crime. It also outlines the possible roles and functions for state/territory and national governments for the effective delivery of crime prevention throughout Australia.

---

120 Ms Margaret Southwell, Chair, New South Wales Local Government Community Safety and Crime Prevention Committee and Community Development Officer, Community Development, Bankstown City Council, Evidence given to the Drugs and Crime Prevention Committee, Inquiry into Locally Based Approaches to Community Safety and Crime Prevention, Public Hearing, Sydney, 19 September 2011.

Purpose and outcomes

The purpose of this Framework is to:

- support a coordinated approach to addressing crime and safety issues of national importance, including new and emerging crime problems;
- promote an improved level of collaboration between crime prevention agencies operating in each jurisdiction;
- improve the effectiveness of crime prevention across Australia by promoting principles of good practice and successful strategies;
- encourage increased commitment to crime prevention at all levels of government and across different sectors; and
- assist in guiding the allocation of crime prevention resources to achieve the greatest impact.[121]

This Framework does not aim 'to prescribe specific actions that must be implemented by stakeholders involved in the delivery of crime prevention. Rather, it provides guidance by way of information on best practice to assist with the development of appropriate policies, strategies and programs to address crime problems'.[122]

The Framework seeks to achieve the following outcomes:

- a reduction in crime and disorder problems that are of greatest harm and concern to the community;
- increased community safety, security and cohesion, including a reduction in the actual and perceived risk of victimisation;
- increased support for people to cope with the impact of victimisation; and
- a reduction in reoffending among those people who have already engaged in criminal or antisocial behaviour.[123]

Principles

The Framework is based on a number of underlying principles which in turn have to some degree been drawn from the *United Nations Guidelines for the Prevention of Crime*. These principles state that effective crime prevention involves:

- strong and committed leadership at all levels;
- collaboration between multiple stakeholders to address the wide-ranging causes of crime and to draw upon the skills, expertise, resources and responsibilities necessary to address those causes;
- the practical application of research and evaluation findings in the development and implementation of measures to reduce crime, targeted to areas of the greatest need and adapted to suit local conditions;
- a focus on outcomes and a commitment to demonstrating measurable results through evaluation and performance measurement, with clear lines of accountability;
- building and maintaining the capacity to implement effective crime prevention policies and interventions;
- promoting an active and engaged community, and being responsive to the diversity and changing nature of communities;
- long-term commitment to achieving sustainable reductions in crime and savings to the criminal justice system and the community; and
- coordination across sectors to embed crime prevention into relevant social and economic policies, including education, employment, health, and housing policies, particularly those directed towards at-risk communities, children, families and youth.[124]

---

121 *National Crime Prevention Framework — Overview* at http://www.aic.gov.au/crime_community/crimeprevention/ncpf.aspx
122 http://www.aic.gov.au/crime_community/crimeprevention/ncpf.aspx
123 http://www.aic.gov.au/crime_community/crimeprevention/ncpf.aspx
124 http://www.aic.gov.au/crime_community/crimeprevention/ncpf.aspx

Priority areas

Whilst the Framework recognises that across the country different states and territories will experience different types and levels of crime and community safety issues, there are a number of serious issues that affect Australians on a national level. Therefore the following areas have been identified as requiring a national and coordinated response:

- Reducing alcohol related violence
- Improving the safety of young people
- Improving the safety of Indigenous people
- Preventing child abuse and neglect
- Reducing violence against women.[125]

Implementation and review

It is envisaged that states and territories in developing and implementing new, or modifying existing, crime prevention policies and strategies will refer to the objectives, principles and priorities outlined in the National Framework:

> Responsibility for overseeing the implementation of this Framework will rest with the ANZCP SOG and its member agencies. Reporting on progress in implementing the Framework will be consistent with the current jurisdictional biannual reporting by ANZCP SOG member agencies. Reporting will focus on the delivery of crime prevention activity that is consistent with the principles and addresses the priorities highlighted in this Framework.[126]

This Framework is seen as 'a working document'. The priority areas will be subject to annual review so 'new and emerging issues can be highlighted and incorporated over time'.

Individual state and territory jurisdictions will be responsible for evaluating the effectiveness of any strategies implemented as part of the Framework. A longer-term review will be conducted to assess the effectiveness of the Framework in achieving its purpose and objects and to determine its contribution to crime prevention and reduction throughout Australia.

The use of partnerships to promote crime prevention strategies

The most popular methods for implementing crime prevention programs and policies in Victoria and Australia have been through the use of *partnership models* and *whole of government* approaches.[127] Whole of government approaches[128] are based on the assumption:

> That because we know the causes of crime are complex and multifaceted, then preventive approaches will be more effective if we combine the efforts of all the relevant government agencies, community and business groups into a single coordinated strategy (Makkai 2004).

There is much discussion of crime prevention partnerships in the international literature.[129]

A report by the Institute on Governance in 2006 noted the importance of partnerships between government and 'civil society',[130] in a range of subject areas including community safety. The authors point out that in the area of crime prevention as in other aspects of social policy it is essential that policy-makers are clear as to what they understand partnerships to mean:

---

125 For discussion of proposed approaches in each of these areas see http://www.aic.gov.au/crime_community/ crimeprevention/ncpf.aspx

126 www.aic.gov.au/crime_community/crimeprevention/ncpf.aspx

127 Crime prevention partnerships will be discussed in greater detail in Chapters 6 and 7.

128 See also the discussion later in this chapter.

129 For a discussion of the importance of good governance principles for (crime prevention) partnerships, see Chapter 4 of this Report.

130 Also known as non-governmental or voluntary sector organisations (see Edgar, Marshall & Bassett 2006, p.1).

> The word 'partnership' is [a] term that means different things to different people. Broadly speaking, a partnership may be defined simply as a collaborative venture between two or more organisations that pool resources in pursuit of common objectives. But if an NGO meets with government officials to press for change is this a 'partnership'? Is a government run consultation session a 'partnership'? In our view, these do not qualify as partnerships. Although seeking input and seeking change are both key reasons to enter into partnership. Partnership is more than a one off chance to discuss a particular policy or program. Partnerships by their very nature, represent a sustained commitment to move forward together to reach a common objective (Edgar, Marshall & Basset 2006, p.4).

It is essential in taking 'a whole of government approach' that local crime prevention governance, including the use of partnerships, is flexible and avoids a 'one size fits all' approach. Unfortunately this has not always been the case with regard to some of the crime prevention models implemented in other jurisdictions, such as in the United Kingdom (Cherney & Sutton 2007).

Crime prevention models in Australia usually involve a centralised state agency working in partnership with local government and local community agencies. Whilst there is a National Crime Prevention Initiative in place it primarily acts as the source of funds for grassroots state agencies applying by way of grant applications. However, the new *National Crime Prevention Framework* does emphasise the importance of crime prevention as a shared responsibility between governments and civil society. The Overview of the Framework states in this regard:

> In Australia, contemporary crime prevention has generally embraced the value of partnerships, collaborative policy development and program delivery, in recognition that the causes of crime are wide ranging, complex and frequently require a coordinated response.
>
> Central to good governance in successful crime prevention partnerships are the development of:
>
> - appropriate mechanisms for promoting and steering a whole of government approach to the prevention of crime, and ensuring that key stakeholders are involved in crime prevention planning at all levels;
> - forums for bringing together government, non-government, communities and businesses that promote open communication and allow all partners to contribute;
> - clearly defined roles and responsibilities for these stakeholders;
> - a shared goal and common purpose, and an understanding of how each partner contributes to this goal;
> - partnerships for the delivery of integrated solutions, comprising closely linked and coordinated interventions that can achieve shared outcomes;
> - an understanding and acceptance of the different interests, philosophies and contexts in which each partner works;
> - clear lines of accountability for the partnership, both to each other and their respective organisation;
> - a joint framework for performance measuring and reporting, with an agreed understanding of what constitutes success; and
> - clear benefits to the partnership that are evident to all those involved.[131]

Nonetheless, substantive crime prevention development and practice is essentially located at state and local government level as a result of the constitutional division of powers in Australia (crime and crime prevention being primarily state based). The central state agency may be a coordinating government department such as Justice, the Police or a combination of both. The other major partner in the enterprise is the relevant local government shire or

---

131 http://www.aic.gov.au/crime_community/crimeprevention/ncpf.aspx

council. Often local community agencies may also sit on the relevant coordinating body or at least have input into and be represented by a local government representative such as a Crime Reduction Officer or equivalent.

Whilst partnership initiatives have generally been viewed positively in Australia, they have not been without their problems. Some of the issues which have led some crime prevention partnerships and organisations to fail have included:

◆ no clear vision or agreed understanding as to what the objectives of the partnership/ strategy is

◆ no clear delineation of responsibility between state and local government representatives of the partnership

◆ a failure to realise that there are fundamental differences between the governance, powers and responsibilities of local governments in Australia compared to other local jurisdictions upon which some Australian crime prevention models are based, particularly the United Kingdom

◆ poor lines of communication between different representatives of the partnership

◆ an increase of responsibilities for local government without an appropriate or commensurate resourcing (see Morgan & Homel 2011; Sutton, Cherney & White 2008; Homel 2004, 2006).

The nature of these problems and how they can impact upon the implementation of good crime prevention practice are discussed in detail in Chapter 8 of this Report.

Private sector partnerships in crime prevention and community safety

A relatively recent development at an international level has been the proliferation of public-private partnerships (PPPs)] in the crime prevention and community safety field. At the fifth international colloquium of the International Centre for the Prevention of Crime (ICPC) in 2005 the central debate was on the use of 'strategic partnerships for effective crime prevention' (ICPC 2011, p.7). Since that date there has been an increasing number of partnership arrangements entered into between private sector companies, government agencies, 'civil society' organisations and the media worldwide, if not commonly in Australia (ICPC 2011). The reasons for the relative lack of involvement by the private sector in this country in crime prevention partnerships are unclear. Possibly one reason is that Australian business, unlike its counterparts in Europe and the USA, has not been as associated with philanthropic enterprises as these other societies. Another reason may be that the private sector as with a section of the general public may mistakenly view crime prevention as an issue that is the sole responsibility of the state's law enforcement and control apparatus:

> Disagreement exists about the role of the police and the responsibilities of the different levels of government. In this confused situation the private sector tends not to regard itself as a major player in crime and violence prevention (ICPC 2011, p.81).

The private sector may also be discouraged in participating in crime prevention projects because they may desire (expect) immediate or short-term results and crime prevention interventions to be sustainable often have to be 'long-term'. Finally, crime prevention is not necessarily a 'glamorous' area in which a company may choose to invest its corporate social responsibility (CSR) dollars. Indeed the ICPC has stated that many private sector companies are 'apt to view crime prevention as a "negative agenda" and are reluctant to be openly associated with measures to tackle it. Firms are keener to link their brands to what they regard as more positive causes' (2011, p.83).

This reluctance should not be overstated, however. While the level of private sector participation in crime prevention projects may not the same as in the USA, it is increasing and the partnerships are becoming increasingly diverse in nature. The range of stakeholders that private companies may enter into partnership with in developing crime prevention projects is indicated in Table 3.1 below.

Table 3.1: Community safety partnerships for the private sector

Public Sector	Private Sector	Civil Society	Community
Local and state government offices and structures	Industry Organisations	NGOs	Associations and Local entities
Police	Sports Associations	Academic sector	Community Leaders
Other government bodies	Chambers of Commerce	Foundations	Residents associations
	Other firms	Institutes	
		Associations	

Source: Adapted from ICPC 2011, p.43.

The private or business sector has clearly always played a role in some areas of crime prevention that are integral to its interests — for example, the protecting of private property through employing security guards, deploying private patrols or making their products or services less vulnerable to theft or fraud. But in more recent years there has been increasing support for a more altruistic approach to the private sector becoming involved in charitable, not for profit, pro bono, community or philanthropic projects reflected in the concept of CSR.[132]

The common reasons given as to why the private sector may be a welcome partner in crime prevention partnerships is usually couched in terms of their creativity, ingenuity, 'business acumen', intellectual 'know-how', access to resources (both of finance and labour), and planning and management skills (ICPC 2011, p.22). There is also a sense that:

> Private firms being to a certain extent 'new' to the area of community safety, can provide a neutral space and innovative ideas for improving coordination among the various other actors. A firm might, for example, be better placed to assemble the different stakeholders [other businesses, civil society, public and private sectors] to work together on joint crime prevention projects (ICPC 2011, p.23).

First and foremost, however, the involvement of private companies in crime prevention projects is attractive as they generally have the financial resources that other sectors lack. Private sector involvement may also contribute to more cost-effective ways of funding crime prevention initiatives (ICPC 2011).[133]

The UN and other international agencies have given the imprimatur to the involvement of the private sector in crime prevention partnerships, particularly with national and local

---

132 Community oriented PPPs are not to be confused with profit making or business PPPs entered into between the state and private consortia — for example projects to build public infrastructure.

133 Whether this is in fact the case is open to debate, for even amongst their advocates there is acknowledgement that little evaluation has been done of the effectiveness of PPPs and CSR in reducing crime or having a positive effect on community safety:

'This is a common problem, since many partnerships tend to focus more on maintaining good relations with the other parties in the arrangement, and securing quick results rather than assembling good quality data enabling them to track outcomes and impacts over time' (ICPC 2011, p.32).

See generally ICPC 2011 and in the Australian context Prenzler and Sarre (2010). For a discussion of cost-benefits, cost-effectiveness and evaluation in crime prevention, see Chapter 11.

governments. For example, the United Nations *Handbook on Crime Prevention Guidelines* (2010) outlines the ways in which the business and private sectors can make a positive contribution to community building, community engagement and community safety through:

- Contributing to social programs that address the causes of violence and the risk factors associated with it;

- Helping to reduce the opportunities and incentives to commit crime by making situational and contextual changes, including altering the design of products to prevent thefts;

- Contributing to the restoration and better use of public and semi public spaces;

- Participating in urban renewal projects;[134]

- Helping to prevent crime and recidivism by developing learning programs and providing job training and employment opportunities for ex-offenders.[135]

The emergence of PPPs is a growing trend and it will be interesting to see whether they become more popular in this country. Nonetheless, even their supporters recognise that government and the public sector will bear the main responsibility for crime prevention and community safety (ICPC 2011). This is particularly the case in the Australian states where partnerships are most often forged between a central government entity, police and local government representatives as the following examples indicate.

The experience of Western Australia — Community Safety and Crime Prevention Partnerships

Western Australia has had a long history of forging and formalising partnerships with local government and community agencies to address crime and community safety in local communities. Whilst crime prevention structures have been overhauled in the last year in Western Australia,[136] this strong partnerships model has basically remained the same.

Recent changes to crime prevention in Western Australia

Policy, planning and project delivery functions in the crime prevention area prior to July 2011 were undertaken through a separate and independent office, the Office of Crime Prevention (OCP), which was established in October 2001. As the result of a strategic review of crime prevention policy in Western Australia the functions of that office have now been dispersed amongst a number of newly created entities and as of July 2011 the agency previously known as the OCP ceased to exist other than as a unit of the Western Australia Police.[137]

Crime prevention policy in Western Australia is now coordinated by the WA Police Strategic Crime Prevention Division. The Strategic Crime Prevention Division is located within WA

---

134 A unique example of this in the Australian context is the *City of Greater Dandenong Revitalisation Plan* in Victoria.
This revitalisation/urban renewal program of a relatively disadvantaged suburb with high crime rates is delivering a diverse range of highly visible public realm improvements within the city centre including:
- The widening and improvement of Lonsdale Boulevard (the main shopping and business sector)
- The creation of an integrated new urban precinct called Metro Village 3175
- The creation of 'City Street' a green pedestrian and cycle thoroughfare connecting the city centre to the transport hub
- Improved public transport
- A new Civic Centre
- The redevelopment of the Dandenong Market sector.
Whilst the partnership consortium primarily consists of government and semi-government agencies (VicUrban; Department of Transport; City of Greater Dandenong; Metro Trains; Arts Victoria), local businesses and community organisations have also been significantly involved in the consultation and planning process.
The City of Greater Dandenong Revitalisation Plan as an example of a dynamic crime prevention and community safety approach will be discussed further in Chapter 6.

135 See the *Handbook on the Crime Prevention Guidelines: Making them Work*, United Nations Office on Drugs and Crime (UNODC) 2010, at www.unodc.org

136 See discussion below.

137 On occasion however this chapter will still refer to the Office of Crime Prevention as the unit is still in existence (albeit in a different form) and many of the structures, programs and governance models pertaining to crime prevention and community safety currently operating were in fact established under the aegis of the previous OCP.

Police Judicial Services portfolio, and is the policy and planning arm for state-wide crime prevention efforts:

> Recognising that effective crime prevention can only be achieved through joined up efforts, the Division works across government, and with all sectors of the community to plan and deliver effective crime prevention.[138]

This will also be realised through the establishment of a Crime Prevention Council chaired by the Minister for Police. The reason for this, as Assistant Commissioner Wayne Gregson told the Committee:

> [i]s that most issues cannot be addressed by one agency and, the more complex the issue, oftentimes there are many agencies involved in service delivery. So to ensure a coordinated joined-up approach...to ensure certainty of project or program delivery, we will be setting up a crime prevention council to be chaired by our minister. On that will be various CEOs of other government agencies and they will be setting the policy framework and they will be giving us some high-level strategic objectives in the whole area of crime prevention and community engagement. What we are hoping to draw from that is that each agency will then take away and, in a unified way, deliver their part of the jigsaw puzzle.[139]

Crime prevention teams have been reallocated into three Divisions along functional lines. Operational functions previously provided by the Strategic Projects team (Burglar Beware, Eyes on the Street, Neighbourhood Watch et al),[140] and all projects managed through the Graffiti Team, have been relocated to the Community Engagement Division (CED). The new Strategic Crime Prevention Division has been established to provide other functions previously conducted by OCP, including policy, planning, research and evaluation and grants administration.

Simultaneously, youth related functions (Juvenile Justice Officers) previously provided through CED have been realigned to a new Division, the Youth Policing Division. 'This change reflects the growing importance of effective youth policing to cross-Government youth crime prevention and diversion efforts'.[141]

The Judicial Services portfolio incorporates a range of other existing police crime prevention operational functions such as Indigenous and Community Diversity, youth policing, and District Crime Prevention and Diversity Officers located throughout the state.

The Strategic Crime Prevention Division:

- develops and coordinates comprehensive strategies and policies;
- supports multi-agency planning in response to priority crime issues;
- provides crime prevention advice to State and Local Government;
- provides strategic leadership in crime prevention efforts;
- undertakes and commissions research to establish best practice community safety and crime prevention strategies; and
- provides grant funding for community safety and crime prevention initiatives.[142]

---

138 http://www.crimeprevention.wa.gov.au/content

139 Assistant Commissioner Wayne Gregson, Assistant Commissioner, Judicial Services, Western Australia Police, Evidence given to the Drugs and Crime Prevention Committee, Inquiry into Locally Based Approaches to Community Safety and Crime Prevention, Meeting, Perth, 21 June 2011.

140 See discussion below.

141 The three Divisions are co-located within the Judicial Services portfolio, under Assistant Commissioner Wayne Gregson. Division leaders are:
- Assistant Director David Wray — Strategic Crime Prevention Division.
- Superintendent John Leembruggen — Community Engagement Division.
- Superintendent Peter Hatch — Youth Policing Division.

142 http://www.crimeprevention.wa.gov.au/content.

Strategic Crime Prevention in WA is supported by formal governance structures incorporating key Departments such as Child Protection, Communities, Attorney General, Corrections, Housing, Health, Drug and Alcohol, Sport and Recreation and others.

> This arrangement ensures that crime prevention policy and planning is inclusive of, but not exclusive to, WA Police. Other key sectors closely involved in delivery of WA community crime prevention include government and non-government agencies within the welfare, health, justice and education sectors.[143]

Working on the premise that 'crime is everybody's business', the new divisions have continued building safer communities through programs such as Burglar Beware, Eyes on the Street, Goodbye Graffiti, Leavers WA, Designing Out Crime, Neighbourhood Watch, Community grants and Community Safety and Crime Prevention Planning.

> These efforts seek to minimise the number of people and businesses who are victims of crime and to minimise the impact of offending on the broader community by providing leadership on crime prevention and engaging the community at all levels.[144]

A new crime prevention strategy

In addition to the restructuring of crime prevention governance in Western Australia, a new overarching crime prevention framework outlining crime prevention aims and priorities has been implemented. The Western Australia Police *Crime Prevention Strategy 2011–2014* (hereinafter the Strategy)[145] views police activity as forming but one part of a coordinated government response to preventing and reducing crime. As such, the Strategy recognises that to 'achieve maximum effect, responsibility for crime prevention needs to be shared across agencies' (Western Australia Police 2011, p.2). As discussed later in this section, the local government and agencies partnerships approach remains a key feature of the new Strategy and restructure.

Community safety and crime prevention partnerships

The current model for developing and implementing crime prevention projects in Western Australia is the Western Australian Community Safety and Crime Prevention partnerships program (CSCP). The Strategic Crime Prevention Division (SCPD) of Western Australia Police now has primary and overall responsibility for directing and coordinating the state government's approach to community safety and crime prevention. Strategic direction is provided by a state Community Crime Prevention Plan (CCPP) developed in conjunction with relevant state and local government departments and agencies.

The SCPD employs a partnership approach with state and local government agencies, non-government agencies and local organisations to develop and implement sustainable initiatives to improve community safety throughout Western Australia. One of the main ways this is realised is through the development of local CCPPs. CSCP partnerships are established with local governments in rural and metropolitan districts to establish crime prevention plans based on local needs and local priorities. Partnership agreements are signed between the OCP and either individual local governments or regional groupings. Local governments lead and coordinate their partnerships and in turn can enlist input from a range of key stakeholder groups within their local communities. A recent evaluation of the CSCP planning process states that:

> The Purpose of a CSCP Plan is to identify and prioritise concerns about community safety and crime prevention in a LGA, identify key action areas and responsibility for these actions. The Plan

---

143 http://www.crimeprevention.wa.gov.au/content.whoweare/

144 http://www.crimeprevention.wa.gov.au/content.whoweare

145 The Crime Prevention Strategy is but one of numerous strategies that form part of Western Australia's overall strategic policing plan. See generally http://www.police.wa.gov.au/Aboutus/StrategyandPlanning/PolicingStrategies/

is a tool to address local issues in a coordinated approach, improve the efficiency of services and to ensure that the most appropriate agencies are engaged to respond to the issue. CSCP Plans:

- identify and prioritise local issues of concern;
- develop practical responses to these issues; and
- evaluate and measure the effectiveness of each response.

The [former Office of Crime Prevention] has identified the aim of the CSCP Plans as being to improve community safety, improve service delivery and reduce crime within the community (Morgan & Homel 2011, p.7).

Partnerships on the ground — Intelligence and 'Third Party Policing'

The restructured crime prevention approach in Western Australia relies heavily on partnership models, particularly between lead agencies such as the police and local government and community agencies. Mr David Wray has indicated that a shift has taken place where community safety and crime prevention are not seen as second cousins to the business of (operational) policing:

Police involvement I think has been really important. In some of the local government areas there has probably been, in truth, some removal of police resourcing because, 'Local government have taken it up. We don't need to'. That does not work. Police need to be, and they are, a key partner in our new strategy framework. Our crime prevention strategy makes clear that police have a role in crime prevention and that it is going to be delivered through a partnership approach. So we will actually be measuring police on whether or not they are linking up to the local partners and looking at crime issues in the future. That is a really important step.[146]

Mr Wray believes it is imperative that police 'accept crime prevention as a mainstay part of what they do' and that this is reinforced through community partnerships. According to Mr Wray this is one of the most important policy developments in community safety in recent years:

I do want to emphasise the partnership focus — partnership has really been at the hub of every project activity that we have done. It's about good communication, active engagement, not a one-way activity for local government [or police] but...actively supporting local government in being able to do those things. It has been very successful. We have won awards — state premier's awards and national awards — around the partnership approach that we have taken. Crime prevention really is everybody's responsibility, and that includes the state government.[147]

An important partner within the Western Australia police structure in addressing crime prevention and community safety issues is the State Intelligence Division and its incorporation of 'third party policing':

Crime prevention is at the core of all WA Police activity, but we recognise that we obviously cannot do that alone and that that is a responsibility that needs to be shared across agencies and the community, with us actively coordinating that and forming one of the main coordinated responses. We have a key role, through our intelligence collection processes, in communicating crime problems to other stakeholders and the community, participating in the development of comprehensive responses and overarching crime prevention strategies.

From an intelligence perspective there are obviously a whole raft of methodologies and ways for us to do that, but our role is principally to provide our senior executive management team

---

146   Mr David Wray, Assistant Director, Western Australia Office of Crime Prevention, Evidence given to the Drugs and Crime Prevention Committee, Inquiry into Locally Based Approaches to Community Safety and Crime Prevention, Meeting, Perth, 21 June 2011.

147   Mr David Wray, Assistant Director, Western Australia Office of Crime Prevention, Evidence given to the Drugs and Crime Prevention Committee, Inquiry into Locally Based Approaches to Community Safety and Crime Prevention, Meeting, Perth, 21 June 2011.

with relevant, timely, accurate intelligence on current and future crime trends and criminal environment to assist in the process — and it is a four-step process — of identifying current, emerging or potential crime problems; planning responses to those problems and, obviously, prevention strategies; delivering those strategies as part of a broad response; and reviewing those strategies to see how effective they are and whether we need to adapt them or modify them, or scrap them and do something new, something different.[148]

Third party policing principles used by the Intelligence Division is an extension of community policing whereby third parties such as local government officers are encouraged to take on a crime prevention responsibility:

It is the responsibility of the police to build those relationships with those third parties. There can be a number of those. The list is non-exhaustive. It is anyone from parents to schoolteachers, business owners, your local car park attendants, grounds maintenance people, anybody who can give us some intelligence on what is going on in their neighbourhood... The focal point of third party policing can be people, it can be a target group such as young people, gang members, drug dealers; it can be places, for instance identified hot spots in parks, in public malls, anywhere where it is known that people hang around and engage in activities that perhaps, even if they are not unlawful, are causing disturbances and anguish for local residents; or it can be situations, some sort of criminogenic activities, bus stop placements that facilitate robberies perhaps, or late opening hours that lead to brawls within licensed premises, spray paint in hardware shops that are in high-risk areas. So third party policing involves the police using those opportunities to influence the agencies to perhaps change the location of the bus stops, or reduce the hours of the business that is causing the trouble, or the sale of spray paints to particular people, minors etcetera. So those are the sorts of things that third party policing captures.[149]

The intelligence from these third parties is fed back at a fortnightly district Tasking and Coordination Group (TCG) meeting where all sub-district officers (including crime prevention officers) discuss the prominent or pressing issues over the previous two-week period and how they can be rectified. It is a decision making group that can decide on the basis of intelligence received what strategies should be developed or resources deployed to address crime prevention and other policing matters.

Western Australia Police think highly of their community crime prevention model and partnership plans and the generally good reciprocal relationship between police and local government. Mr David Wray of the SCPD warns, however, that such relationships do not simply spring up 'overnight':

It is about knowing each other's responsibilities and where things start and stop. It is not just a matter of, 'This is your responsibility now to do it.' The local government partnerships did not happen by themselves. We have had a team actively working out there to support local governments in their planning processes, giving them the training and advice that they need along the way, and so on...Generally speaking, partnerships come down to the same sorts of things that make any relationship good.[150]

---

148 Ms Denise Lofthouse, Manager, Capability and Development, State Intelligence Division, Western Australia Police, Evidence given to the Drugs and Crime Prevention Committee, Inquiry into Locally Based Approaches to Community Safety and Crime Prevention, Meeting, Perth, 20 June 2011.

149 Ms Denise Lofthouse, Manager, Capability and Development, State Intelligence Division, Western Australia Police, Evidence given to the Drugs and Crime Prevention Committee, Inquiry into Locally Based Approaches to Community Safety and Crime Prevention, Meeting, Perth, 20 June 2011.

150 Mr David Wray, Assistant Director, Western Australia Office of Crime Prevention, Evidence given to the Drugs and Crime Prevention Committee, Inquiry into Locally Based Approaches to Community Safety and Crime Prevention, Meeting, Perth, 21 June 2011.

Partnerships with local government

Local government is equally enthusiastic about the need to work in partnership with police and other agencies in delivering crime prevention and community safety programs to their local communities. For example, Mr Michael Wood, Coordinator of the Safer Vincent Crime Prevention Partnership in the inner city council of Vincent, told the Committee how important it was to have high level partnerships with police, government and community agencies to effectively develop and implement crime prevention services in his local area:

> Essentially, that is about relationships; it is about keeping our Safer Vincent Crime Prevention Partnership on track, which is our key consultative body at the town tasked with safety and crime prevention matters; it is about leadership; it is about assisting our partnership to find solutions to antisocial and criminal behaviour issues; it is about working across all levels of department within our council and across all agencies. We have got a longstanding role, at the Town of Vincent, in safety and crime prevention. Way back in 1998 we committed to the development of our Safer Vincent Program, and this was done to meet that increasing expectation that local government would take more of a leading role in community safety and crime prevention matters. Since that time we have acknowledged that the role of community safety and crime prevention is not just the police nor council but all agencies in the community working together. We have a very mobilised crime prevention partnership, which has been honed over many years, and a fantastic working relationship with WA Police.

> This we have reflected in the signing of our partnership between the Town of Vincent and the state government Office of Crime Prevention, the development of our formal Safer Vincent Crime Prevention Partnership, which devolved from our Safer Vincent Program, and subsequent development of our safety and crime prevention plans.[151]

Community Safety Partnerships are now generally thought well of by local government officers in Western Australia. For example, Mr Wood told the Committee that whilst at first there may have been concern that local government would have new responsibilities 'foisted' on them without commensurate resourcing, overall the partnership system has been beneficial. Nonetheless:

> There is need for a constant reinvigoration of the community safety and crime prevention planning process and the partnership process…safety plans do not just exist. They need life breathed into them on a daily basis. It is important that you have all stakeholders providing input and providing that breath of life…and leadership and coordination. It is incumbent on all stakeholders to take those leadership roles.[152]

The Town of Vincent[153] as part of their partnership process has a series of unique information and intelligence sharing meetings with Western Australia Police. Vincent hosts the Central Metropolitan Police Integration Committee where a member of the police comes to Vincent to 'sit at the table' and listen to the concerns of the town and the issues of importance to the district as previously outlined to council staff in consultation meetings with the community:

> [The Committee] has evolved over time and it has been a key way of building that trust and rapport with police. Obviously police deal with some areas of confidential information that they are not always able to share with all agencies, but at these meetings we are able to talk very frankly about issues and areas of concern for the community, so we can bring community concerns to

---

151 Mr Michael Wood, Coordinator, Safer Vincent Crime Prevention Partnership, Town of Vincent, Evidence given to the Drugs and Crime Prevention Committee, Inquiry into Locally Based Approaches to Community Safety and Crime Prevention, Meeting, Perth, 21 June 2011.

152 Mr Michael Wood, Coordinator, Safer Vincent Crime Prevention Partnership, Town of Vincent, Evidence given to the Drugs and Crime Prevention Committee, Inquiry into Locally Based Approaches to Community Safety and Crime Prevention, Meeting, Perth, 21 June 2011.

153 Based in inner city Perth. Now gazetted as the City of Vincent.

that table and have the opportunity on a monthly basis to talk directly to the officer in charge and, vice versa, he can talk to us. I think more and more the recognition is that we can work hand in hand. We all have information and ways we can assist each other.[154]

The Community Safety Partnership process is also well demonstrated by the experience of the Perth City Council (PCC) in setting up their plan. PCC is in the unique situation of being both a capital city with commercial and business interests, an entertainment district based in inner city Northbridge and having residential areas of the city with concerns particular to the citizens who live there. The City's Community Safety working group meets quarterly to address these disparate issues. The Committee is comprised of membership from both local and state government agencies including the state Drug and Alcohol Office, police and resident groups. Ms Lesley Murray, the PCC's Principal Social and Community Planner explained to the Committee in detail the process through which local government enters a Community Safety Plan with the OCP:

> In 2004 we signed a partnership with the Office of Crime Prevention, where they had created model guidelines we needed to follow and how we would develop the plan. I have to say it took us two years to develop that plan. There was such a lot of consultation in it. We developed a reference group which included representatives from three community groups that existed at the time plus business groups and key agencies. They ran with the whole of the consultation process according to the planning manual which was put out by the Office of Crime Prevention.
>
> We appointed consultants, we did interviews with stakeholders, about fifty stakeholders in the City, and there was a street intercept survey.
>
> From that we developed a list of priorities which were related to thirty issues and forty-five strategies. So one of the key things about the community safety plan process is it had to consult with the local community to develop priority strategies and we worked with Murdoch University, using a risk management workshop to get those forty-five strategies and thirty issues down to four issues and four strategies. And they are the four that are listed in the first part of the current plan ... getting more activity in the city, the second was about media reporting of crime, event management and promotion and then there was one relating to anti-social behaviour and substance abuse.[155]

The PCC has stated that overall their experience of working in partnership with police and the OCP has been a positive one.

Partnerships with the media

Members of the Western Australia Police told the Committee that an essential partner in developing effective crime prevention programs is the local media, particularly in promoting accurate reporting of crime and the importance of local crime prevention strategies. In developing the Western Australian Crime Prevention Strategy, Superintendent John Leembruggen told the Committee that:

> What we did was make sure that all the local superintendents or local police — because we are really trying to localise everything — were in the paper every week. They were telling all the good news stories about what we were doing as police, and who we were working with — some of the partnerships were appearing in there — and saying that we were all working together, trying to drive out crime.[156]

---

154 Mr Michael Wood, Coordinator, Safer Vincent Crime Prevention Partnership, Town of Vincent, Evidence given to the Drugs and Crime Prevention Committee, Inquiry into Locally Based Approaches to Community Safety and Crime Prevention, Meeting, Perth, 21 June 2011.

155 Ms Lesley Murray, Principal Social and Community Planner, Sustainable Community Development, City of Perth, Evidence given to the Drugs and Crime Prevention Committee, Inquiry into Locally Based Approaches to Community Safety and Crime Prevention, Meeting, Perth, 22 June 2011.

156 Superintendent John Leembruggen, Community Engagement Division, Western Australia Office of Crime Prevention, Evidence given to the Drugs and Crime Prevention Committee, Inquiry into Locally Based Approaches to Community Safety and Crime Prevention, Meeting, Perth, 20 June 2011.

Crime prevention diversity officers

A key aspect of the partnership process in Western Australia has been the establishment of a group of 23 dedicated crime prevention diversity officers (CPDOs) in each of the regional police districts across the state. In 2009 an internal police review of the CPDO role found they were being used inconsistently — some districts placed great importance on the need for a dedicated crime prevention role, others minimised this role. The review found there was a lack of central support for CPDOs which was undermining the good work they were doing:

> One of the findings was that there was inconsistency amongst districts, and two of those do not have CPDOs at all. So far as the roles go, the crime prevention and diversity officers are pretty much at the whim of the district superintendent. If the district superintendent does not have a crime prevention emphasis within their district — and at this stage that probably has not been enforced, for want of a better word, from the top — then those crime prevention and diversity officers are able to be tasked elsewhere or they might wear the hat of a crime prevention and diversity officer but on multiple occasions they will be taken out of that role to work front-line duties when they are short on staff and that kind of thing, which then of course reflects detrimentally on the professionalism of those crime prevention and diversity officers if they have made appointments or they are attending meetings with the local council and the like. For them to have to cancel is not good for the professionalism of WA Police as a whole... From the crime prevention and diversity officers' perspective, they have felt very undervalued within their districts. Part of that is because they are taken out of their role on multiple occasions and put to do other things just to fill gaps within the district.[157]

As a result, a senior officer has recently been appointed to a new position to coordinate and oversee the placement and training of these specialist officers and implement a project to develop a crime prevention and diversity officer model, which then can be standardised across all the districts.

The Committee met with Senior Sergeant Sue Parmer, the Coordinator of this program in Perth in June 2011. She emphasised the importance of having CPDOs as an integral part of the overall Western Australian police approach to fighting crime and promoting community safety. In her view it is crucial that CPDOs in each district attend the meetings of the TCG discussed earlier:

> One of the key things which I will be working towards, and some of the districts — at least metropolitan-wise — are doing, is that they are attending their Tasking and Coordination Group [TCG] meetings, on a monthly basis. Some of them are also attending their tactical meetings, which happen on a daily basis. This is for the purpose of ensuring that crime prevention is being addressed and that crime prevention strategies are being utilised to tackle the issues happening within each district.

> What I am finding is that, where the crime prevention officers are not attending these meetings, they tend to be acting autonomously within their district and are not working towards the district outcomes. They might be contributing to the district outcomes in some way, but they are not specific to what the intelligence is saying that they should be working towards, and that is one of the key things which I am aiming to achieve in the project that I am working on. Every crime prevention officer will be part of the daily TAC meetings so that they can then go away and develop strategies and partnerships with the local councils, various other agencies, CALD groups within the community as is necessary, in order to tackle the issues they have to tackle.[158]

157 Senior Sergeant Sue Parmer, District Coordinator, Community Engagement Division, Western Australia Police, Evidence given to the Drugs and Crime Prevention Committee, Inquiry into Locally Based Approaches to Community Safety and Crime Prevention, Meeting, Perth, 21 June 2011.
158 Senior Sergeant Sue Parmer, District Coordinator, Community Engagement Division, Western Australia Police, Evidence given to the Drugs and Crime Prevention Committee, Inquiry into Locally Based Approaches to Community Safety and Crime Prevention, Meeting, Perth, 21 June 2011.

By attending the TCG meetings CPDOs would be in a position to liaise and share intelligence with Intelligence Officers in order to prioritise tasks and approaches in their local communities:

> They [CPDOs] would present [their issues] at the TCG. They would present that information, that for example, a particular location has been burgled. At a recent TCG I went to, there was a liquor store which had been targeted, I think, four times in the previous three months, so it was a priority for the CPDOs to go out there and talk to them about crime prevention...and come up with strategies to address the burglaries...

> Or if assaults, and the offenders have been identified as being African offenders, that crime prevention diversity officer will then go out and engage with the community leaders from that area and work out a strategy on what they need to do to deal with it.[159]

In addition to this 'reactive' policing, CPDOs may also organise proactive forums or community consultations with general or specific members of the public to discuss community safety issues and concerns to members of that community. Such forums may also include speakers or representatives from other government and community agencies who have knowledge or skills in a particular area.

As highlighted by the internal review of CPDOs, it is essential that these officers are well trained as specialists in the area of crime prevention including in areas such as networking, working in partnership with local government, cultural diversity and community engagement skills — areas in which crime prevention or community safety officers had not hitherto been skilled. Senior Sergeant Parmer remarked that whilst some CPDOs were naturally talented at this type of work, that did not obviate the need for specialist training in the area. Ideally this would mean that all CPDOs would eventually have undertaken the Diploma in Crime Prevention offered at the Western Australian Police Academy.

Crime prevention funds

During the period of the former OCP a number of funds and key grant programs were available to assist local government and community agencies develop and implement crime prevention and community safety programs. The three most notable of these were the Community Partnership Fund, an Indigenous Partnership Fund and a Local Government Partnership Fund. These will be rolled over in 2012 into one consolidated fund. In addition to these funds two priority grant funds, the Community Safety Grants Fund, which is for CCTV and related projects, and a Graffiti Fund which is specific to graffiti prevention projects, have been established. Mr David Wray noted the value of community crime prevention grants:

> One thing of note with crime prevention grants is certainly on a per capita basis that [Western Australia] has the greatest amount of grants available anywhere in Australia, as far as I know. The national program I think has a commitment of $50 million against it now, over four or five years. But this is a $3 million annual program and I cannot understate the importance of the grants program in bringing community members alongside your activities.[160]

These grants are particularly important in the context of local governments being able to deliver quality community safety and crime prevention programs. Local government in Mr Wray's view being the best jurisdiction to deliver on-the-ground crime prevention:

---

159   Senior Sergeant Sue Parmer, District Coordinator, Community Engagement Division, Western Australia Police, Evidence given to the Drugs and Crime Prevention Committee, Inquiry into Locally Based Approaches to Community Safety and Crime Prevention, Meeting, Perth, 21 June 2011.

160   Mr David Wray, Assistant Director, Western Australia Office of Crime Prevention, Evidence given to the Drugs and Crime Prevention Committee, Inquiry into Locally Based Approaches to Community Safety and Crime Prevention, Meeting, Perth, 21 June 2011.

The policy hub of this is the principle of subsidiarity, which is that crime prevention is best delivered by the lowest competent authority to do so — that is, you localise your responses to the crime issues that you are confronted with. That was the policy driver for the local government partnerships. What happens is local governments, when they decide to develop a crime prevention community safety plan, enter into a partnership with the state in the first instance and upon endorsement of that, both by their own councils and by the state government, they are given a $10,000 planning grant to assist them with consultation and referring to the statistics and the evidence and so on, and the development of a plan.

Once that plan has been endorsed by the state government they have been entitled to a $20,000 incentive grant as well. Basically what we're saying to them is, 'If you can assure us that you are doing appropriate planning by consulting with the community, by referring to the statistics and real crime problems, by looking at the evidence about what you're proposing to do in solution to those, then we're prepared to give you $20,000 to spend on a project or projects of your own making, of your own wish'. That has been very successful. That approach has certainly inspired the interest of local governments. Ninety-four per cent of local governments have signed partnership agreements and around 71 per cent of them have active plans in place, which is certainly the highest in Australia and quite possibly anywhere in the world.[161]

The crime prevention model in New South Wales

The New South Wales Crime Prevention Framework was established in 2008 and like Western Australia strongly promotes a partnership approach with local government and other community stakeholders. The Framework aims to ensure a coordinated approach to achieving the crime reduction goals identified in the New South Wales State Plan (2006).[162] However, it should be noted that the crime prevention policies for NSW are currently being reviewed by the Attorney General's Department and the current system may not necessarily be retained.

The State Plan set broad targets to include reductions (between 10 and 15 per cent) in the incidence of household property crime, violent crime against individuals and offender recidivism:

> The Crime Prevention Framework recognises that, to achieve its objectives, initiatives must target specific crimes using hard data to identify priority areas both at a state and local level. This ensures there is a focus on the most prevalent crime types and the communities that experience the most crime.

> The Crime Prevention Framework is designed to achieve the targets for crime reduction identified in the State Plan. Under the Framework, the broad State-wide priorities are translated into tangible extended local targets, utilising agreed crime data, and with consideration given to the current local crime environment and agencies' capacity to respond. Participating agencies focus on these prioritised crimes and locations. While each agency maintains responsibility for its core service delivery, coordination of efforts targeting agreed priority locations and crime types prevents duplication and reduces crime (NSW Government 2008, p.3).

The Crime Prevention Steering Group

The coordination of crime prevention at state level was situated within a Crime Prevention Steering Group made up of the executive officers of the three Departments central to the development and implementation of crime prevention and reduction (Police, Attorney General's Department and Department of Premier and Cabinet).

---

161 Mr David Wray, Assistant Director, Western Australia Office of Crime Prevention, Evidence given to the Drugs and Crime Prevention Committee, Inquiry into Locally Based Approaches to Community Safety and Crime Prevention, Meeting, Perth, 21 June 2011.

162 Now superseded. See discussion below.

A notable aspect of the NSW Framework is its ability to draw upon data analysis from the NSW Bureau of Crime Statistics and Research (BOCSAR). The Steering Group also coordinates all program and grant based crime prevention funding.

The Steering Group is in turn supported by the inclusion of a number of stakeholders engaged through working groups:

> Given the broad range of agencies that can contribute to the reduction of different crime types, the Steering Group engages with different stakeholders as appropriate. Stakeholders may be engaged through Working Groups whose membership is drawn from a number of key agencies (such as the Departments of Corrective Services, Juvenile Justice, Community services, Local Government, Housing, Health, and the Office of Liquor, Gaming and Racing). Working Group membership depends on the issues to be addressed (NSW Government 2008, p.4).

The Steering Group regularly consults stakeholder representative groups (such as the Victims' Advisory Board, the Local Government and Shires Associations, the Australian Hotels' Association, and Clubs NSW) and provides them with a forum in which to raise crime prevention issues, by inviting them to Steering Group meetings on a regular basis.

Local government involvement

As stated, the NSW model relies on heavy involvement from local government and their agencies. This has in part been based on the approach of the LGAs in the United Kingdom, whereby local government became very much involved in the development of specific local crime prevention plans, although unlike Britain there is little involvement or expenditure on the consequences of crime or the management of offenders.[163] The Attorney General's Department supports local councils as lead agencies for identifying and implementing local crime prevention strategies in NSW. Local governments have statutory responsibilities to produce local crime prevention plans (in some areas known as Safer Community Compacts). In particular, the Department provides councils with tools, templates and guidelines for the development and endorsement of local crime prevention strategies.[164] Such strategies are then submitted to the Department for endorsement and possible funding. The Attorney General will approve (or otherwise) these proposed plans usually on the advice or endorsement of the Minister of Police or Minister for Community Services. Copies of the approved plans or compacts are provided to the Steering Groups 'to ensure members are aware of local crime prevention and reduction activities and are able to provide their support as needed' (New South Wales Government 2008, p.6). If a compact is not achieving its goals, it might be referred to the Steering Group for consideration.

Crime prevention partnerships

A more formal approach to local government participation is the establishment of crime prevention partnerships (CPPs). Similar to the model operating in Western Australia, CPPs are implemented in 'priority crime areas' which are determined by data analysed by BOCSAR and approved by the Steering Group. They are mandated to drive crime prevention initiatives at local level to address identified priority problems (for example, consistent or serious alcohol related violence).[165]

> CPPs are a formal partnership between local council and local representatives of the NSW Police Force, relevant NSW Government agencies (which may include the Departments of Housing, Education and Training, Community Services, Health, and the Office of Liquor, Gaming and

---

163 Mr Brendan Thomas, Assistant Director-General, Crime Prevention and Community Programs, NSW Department of Attorney General and Justice, Evidence given to the Drugs and Crime Prevention Committee, Inquiry into Locally Based Approaches to Community Safety and Crime Prevention, Public Hearing, Sydney, 19 September 2011.

164 See Appendix 10.

165 The legislative basis for these plans is the *Children (Protection and Parental Responsibility) Act* 1997 which allow councils to develop crime prevention plans and have them approved by the Attorney General.

Racing), local transport companies, and other agencies as relevant and appropriate. CPP boundaries are based on NSW Police Force Local Area Command boundaries and are referred to by the name of the relevant Local Area Command.

Where established, CPPs are the operational vehicle through which coordinated crime prevention planning occurs.

CPPs meet regularly to develop local solutions to local crime problems. CPPs focus on all non-domestic violence crime-related State Plan targets (NSW Government 2008, p.6).

CPPs are chaired by the NSW Police Force Local Area Commander with a representative of the local council as Deputy Chair:

In priority areas, CPPs are tasked with developing Crime Prevention Partnership Action Plans which align their local crime prevention and reduction objectives with the extended targets set by the Steering Group. Local councils have a key role to play in the development of these Action Plans in locations where CPPs are operational.

CPP Action Plans are submitted to the Steering Group for assessment against the targets and objectives identified by the Steering Group and which are aligned with the State Plan. Once approved by the Steering Group, an Action Plan can also be submitted by the relevant local council to the Attorney General for evaluation and endorsement as a Safer Community Compact in order to access funding as regulated by the legislation (NSW Government 2008, p.6).

Whilst CPPs and Community Compacts have generally been well received in New South Wales it has been argued that some councils are in a better position to take advantage of the process and develop a compact or partnership than others. According to Ms Margaret Southwell, Chair of the Local Government Community Safety and Crime Prevention Network and a Crime Prevention Officer with Bankstown Council, this often will depend on funding:

The funding body has a great impact on councils with smaller budgets. Because we [Bankstown Council] do have a separate program budget for community safety, we do not need to rely so much on getting our plan endorsed and supported by the Department. But some smaller councils might be in a position where they need to do a lot of work to get their plan endorsed. You cannot get funding until your plan is endorsed, and we know of some councils that have been working on plans for 18 months to two years to try and get them endorsed by the department.[166]

It should be noted that with a change of government in New South Wales in 2011 the 2006 State Plan has been superseded by a new master plan — New South Wales 2021: 'A 10 year plan to rebuild the economy, return quality services, renovate infrastructure, restore accountability to government, and strengthen local environment and communities'.[167]

BOCSAR, data collection and crime prevention plans

One feature of the New South Wales model that is impressive is the use of data to inform the development of crime prevention policy and in particular the formulation of crime prevention plans by local government areas. Such plans are developed less on the basis of what the local community may *perceive* the problems to be and more on what available data there is to support it. As the Assistant Director General of Crime Prevention and Community Programs told the Committee:

---

166 Ms Margaret Southwell, Chair, New South Wales Local Government Community Safety and Crime Prevention Committee and Community Development Officer, Community Development, Bankstown City Council, Evidence given to the Drugs and Crime Prevention Committee, Inquiry into Locally Based Approaches to Community Safety and Crime Prevention, Public Hearing, Sydney, 19 September 2011.

167 http://2012.nsw.gov.au/about-nsw-2021. At the time of writing, a new crime prevention strategy has yet to be developed and published. It is thought, however, that the basic features of the 2008 strategy will remain in place including the partnership compacts between local councils and the Crime Prevention Division of the Attorney-General's Department.

One of the challenges in the locally based crime prevention plan and getting, broadly speaking, the community's views on crime problems is there is a legitimate question as to whose views you are getting. Fifty people in a room or 40 people in a room do not necessarily constitute 60,000 people, so the views you get, in my experience — and I have been involved in this process for a while — can be very seriously skewed towards people's personal interest or personal experiences. You can end up with a local crime prevention plan or a local crime prevention approach that is not really based on the crime problem at all but based on people's perceptions on what a problem might be. We had a very strong concern in terms of investing the resources and the time with the New South Wales government into going down a road where you might be funding something that is someone's perception of a problem, when the crime data tells us that the real problem is something very different.[168]

The Attorney General's Department therefore does not accept or endorse any local level crime prevention plans that have not been based on 'real recorded crime data':

There are some challenges in that. Not all crime is recorded — but it is, from our perception, the best and most reliable basis we have of evidence on what a local problem is. In terms of funding activities, in our experience a lot of the activities that people put forward to be funded were people's pet projects. We had the experience of people sort of forum shopping with projects. They have a particular view of what they want to do and they come to us. 'It's a crime prevention project, absolutely awesome'. ...[but] we really do not fund anything these days that is not directly linked to [a] definable problem.[169]

For the most part the way in which LGAs can inform their prevention plans through the use of empirical evidence is by using the resources of BOCSAR. Mr Garner Clancey of Sydney University also stressed the importance of this process when he gave evidence to the Committee:

From the outset can I say that I think one of the key challenges around this area is really around data sharing. I think localised responses to crime prevention and community safety require the exchange of data between key agencies... I also say that the best responses, in my opinion, particularly from a local crime prevention perspective are premised on a very good understanding of spatial and temporal trends in local crime...

In New South Wales we have made some great leaps forward in extracting that data from the New South Wales Bureau of Crime Statistics and Research, BOCSAR, and sharing that information with local agencies. It has helped improve local planning because people were talking about where the crime is occurring rather than this nebulous view that crime has gone up or down in the local government area. That does not tell you a great deal. Most of our local government areas are incredibly large. We do need to know where the crime is occurring and maybe some of the drivers, particularly around temporal trends.[170]

The Director of BOCSAR, Professor Don Weatherburn also testified to the importance of the Bureau in supplying LGAs with local level data and the process by which they can ascertain it:

The types of data that is typically used for the purposes of crime prevention that come from the bureau are trends in offences where the offences occur, what sorts of premises, offender

---

168 Mr Brendan Thomas, Assistant Director-General, Crime Prevention and Community Programs, NSW Department of Attorney General and Justice, Evidence given to the Drugs and Crime Prevention Committee, Inquiry into Locally Based Approaches to Community Safety and Crime Prevention, Public Hearing, Sydney, 19 September 2011.

169 Mr Brendan Thomas, Assistant Director-General, Crime Prevention and Community Programs, NSW Department of Attorney General and Justice, Evidence given to the Drugs and Crime Prevention Committee, Inquiry into Locally Based Approaches to Community Safety and Crime Prevention, Public Hearing, Sydney, 19 September 2011.

170 Mr Garner Clancey, Adjunct Lecturer, Sydney Institute of Criminology, University of Sydney, Evidence given to the Drugs and Crime Prevention Committee, Inquiry into Locally Based Approaches to Community Safety and Crime Prevention, Public Hearing, Sydney, 19 September 2011.

information, incident information, seasonal and daily patterns and spatial distribution… The way it works is that if they [local councils] express an interest, if they write back saying they are interested in this, my staff would meet with their staff to work out exactly what their concerns are, or what should be a matter of concern, and work out what maps might best suit their purposes or what sorts of reports, along those lines might best suit their purposes. We would simultaneously refer them to the Crime Prevention Division of the Department of Attorney General and Justice so if they wanted any outside assistance from that body they could obtain it — that is also free of charge — or they may wish to hire a consultant.[171]

Professor Weatherburn did acknowledge, however, that not all councils are necessarily welcoming of the process:

There is certainly a group that respond like that, that are fearful of having this information. There is another group, a growing group, who are keen to get hold of it. The initial reaction in a crime-prone local government area is to not want to deal with this and not want it publicised. But things seem to be changing quite rapidly at the moment because we recently wrote to every local government in New South Wales offering a free service, analysing their crime data for them in a bespoke manner, especially designed for them, and the take-up rate has been quite good. Marrickville Council is one I recall that was not too keen about this in the beginning but I think when they realise there are tools for addressing this crime problem, it is not all bad news, and they get enthusiastic about it.[172]

Community Safety Precincts Committees and Community 'Surgeries'

As a crime prevention measure, New South Wales Police are also actively involved in Community Safety Precinct Committees. These Committees are overseen by the Department of Premier and Cabinet and are chaired by the local area police commander. Local members of parliament, council representatives, community groups and individuals meet with police at the local police station to talk about the effectiveness of current crime prevention strategies and what could be improved. The purpose of the Committees is to:

- Ensure Local Area Commanders are communicating to their local communities;
- Encourage community partnerships to reduce crime and the fear of crime;
- Develop local solutions to local crime in partnership with local stakeholders;
- Improve public safety and reduce the fear of crime at a local level;
- Raise understanding of the relationship between policing and crime reduction; and
- Ensure Commanders take into account local community views on police visibility, police deployment and crime hotspots when deciding police tasking and deployment.[173]

The Committee sessions are held on a quarterly basis. In some precincts there may be more than one Committee, for example, the Darling River/Bourke region has at least five Committees because of the distances involved in travelling.

Superintendent Commander Heather Begg spoke to the efficacy of these Committees in September 2011:

There has been some really good work done. For example, if you have an issue with kids hanging around at night, or public transport, or about licensed premises being opened, those type of things, they can be discussed between police and community at a local level. They also work

171 Professor Don Weatherburn, Director, New South Wales Bureau of Crime Statistics and Research, Evidence given to the Drugs and Crime Prevention Committee, Inquiry into Locally Based Approaches to Community Safety and Crime Prevention, Public Hearing, Sydney, 19 September 2011.

172 Professor Don Weatherburn, Director, New South Wales Bureau of Crime Statistics and Research, Evidence given to the Drugs and Crime Prevention Committee, Inquiry into Locally Based Approaches to Community Safety and Crime Prevention, Public Hearing, Sydney, 19 September 2011.

173 http://www.police.nsw.gov.au/community_issues/cspc

closely with crime prevention partnerships. They are in 15 local area commands and they involve cross-government groups working together on crime problems within those areas. They get a lot of traction because it is a mandatory participation.[174]

A similar concept in community engagement is the adaptation or extension of the British idea of 'community surgeries' or meetings[175] between police and local people. The surgery is a less formal basis through which a citizen can talk to their local area police commander or equivalent about issues of concern to him or her:

> The idea of having a local area commander there is that they are decision-maker and that when concerns are raised at a community meeting they can make decisions about particular issues. We developed a model in New South Wales and we trialled it in the rural and metro areas. We did not want to be too prescriptive in how local area commands run their particular engagements but nonetheless we provided some examples. They might want to do a 'face the people' type session which is a typical community-type meeting. They might want to pick an area, street, a housing area etcetera where there are no problems, tell the community that they are coming by way of local media, letterbox drop, and that they would be available there to talk about whatever issues.
>
> There is a number of ways you can do it but it is about engaging the people that we do not normally talk to. It is not necessarily about a person that would continually come to a regular community safety precinct committee championing a specific issue. It is about chatting with mum and dad who get their impression from the local paper about crime, and correcting these perceptions and giving our message directly to the community.[176]

The community surgery model has been trialled in a number of areas and in a number of different ways. For example, in Moree in New South Wales, meetings were held in a Housing Commission area. These meetings were held in conjunction with the Housing Department. Representatives of the Housing Department looked at housing issues whilst the police addressed crime and crime prevention matters. In Sutherland in South Sydney police conducted 'surgeries' by visiting several local shop areas and talking informally with local shopkeepers:

> They received information about Joe Bloggs selling drugs upstairs and there was a drug bust as a result of it. It is an intel-gathering exercise as well. The feedback from the community, and also from the police, was very positive in terms of gathering information about crime, correcting misconceptions. Even at constable level — because the local command is encouraged to take a selection of their staff with them, be it a crime prevention officer or two general duties constable — it is a chance for them to interact with people and get feedback. It was a very positive thing even for our people. We developed a model and a [performance measurement process] whereby we have asked all commands to do a minimum of five per year and we have left it open in terms of how they do it.[177]

Deployment of specialist officers and the use of community leaders

The approach of the New South Wales Police with regard to using specialist personnel to address crime prevention issues for specific groups is very much based on matching need

---

174 Superintendent Commander Helen Begg, Operational Programs, Sydney, New South Wales Police Service, Evidence given to the Drugs and Crime Prevention Committee, Inquiry into Locally Based Approaches to Community Safety and Crime Prevention, Public Hearing, Sydney, 19 September 2011.

175 In England apart from the obvious medical meaning of the word, a 'surgery' is a place in which local members of the community or constituents may meet with office holders, local representatives or other officials to discuss matters affecting them in their community. Its most common usage in England refers to the consultation meetings usually held weekly between a Member of Parliament and her or his local constituents.

176 Inspector Leith Kennedy, Project Officer Customer Service and Programs, Sydney Metropolitan, New South Wales Police Service, Evidence given to the Drugs and Crime Prevention Committee, Inquiry into Locally Based Approaches to Community Safety and Crime Prevention, Public Hearing, Sydney, 19 September 2011.

177 Inspector Leith Kennedy, Project Officer Customer Service and Programs, Sydney Metropolitan, New South Wales Police Service, Evidence given to the Drugs and Crime Prevention Committee, Inquiry into Locally Based Approaches to Community Safety and Crime Prevention, Public Hearing, Sydney, 19 September 2011.

and demand rather than providing resources across the board. Therefore if an area has a particular problem associated with youth related crime it makes more sense that youth liaison officers are employed in that area in greater numbers.

Assistant Police Commissioner Carlene York explained to the Committee:

> We place our resources or the specialist resources where they can make the most difference. For example, we will have Aboriginal liaison officers. There is not a need for one of those in every command, but there might be a need for two in one command and none in neighbouring commands. They are very much focused about getting into the Aboriginal community and working with them and being our voice in that community but coming forward and saying, 'We think we might be able to do this', or, 'We think we might be able to do that'. The ethnic liaison officers — where crime is becoming a problem in some of the ethnic communities — we are looking at targeted recruitment of those officers, placing them in the communities where they can do the most, and working with us from that point of view.[178]

Another innovative strategy in the area of community engagement is the adaptation of the American concept of Citizens Academies to use community officials or leaders in an outreach program called Community Awareness Policing Program or CAPP — essentially a program about police being accessible to the community and by doing so promoting community safety. Inspector Leith Kennedy of New South Wales Police explained the rationale and the value of the program to the Committee:

> CAPP was an initiative of the Commissioner. He visited the FBI and observed the Citizens Academies whereby they rotate recognised community leaders through these academies and they have a chance to walk in the shoes of law enforcement officers. Over a number of evenings and a number of days they do structured exercises with specific learning outcomes. They leave the program generally as advocates to police or law enforcement officers and, if not, they definitely have a greater understanding of what we do, why we do things and understanding how we do things. That is the idea. The commissioner asked for that to be developed in New South Wales. We developed the CAPP program and in line with that we invite recognised community leaders to join us for a number of weeks to walk in our shoes.[179]

The Local Government Community Safety and Partnership Network

Ms Margaret Southwell, Crime Prevention Officer with Bankstown Council, acknowledges that local government must work in partnership with other agencies to be effective and that the relationship, structures and processes between local government and police are generally good. However, she also stated when she met with the Committee that one of the perceived weaknesses was a lack of connection *between* councils as to how they could foster good crime prevention and community safety approaches:

> There were not many opportunities for professional development on networking. Lots of councils were doing the same thing but there was no communication and no sharing of that knowledge …also a lot of people in the role [of crime prevention officer] are coming from a Human Services background. But there are no set qualifications. They do not have to have a criminology degree; they do not have to have experience in something particular. There is a diverse workforce who might be implementing programs in a different way.[180]

---

178 Assistant Commissioner Carlene York, Assistant Commissioner, Northern Region Commander, New South Wales Police Service, Evidence given to the Drugs and Crime Prevention Committee, Inquiry into Locally Based Approaches to Community Safety and Crime Prevention, Public Hearing, Sydney, 19 September 2011.

179 Inspector Leith Kennedy, Project Officer Customer Service and Programs, Sydney Metropolitan, New South Wales Police Service, Evidence given to the Drugs and Crime Prevention Committee, Inquiry into Locally Based Approaches to Community Safety and Crime Prevention, Public Hearing, Sydney, 19 September 2011.

180 Ms Margaret Southwell, Chair, New South Wales Local Government Community Safety and Crime Prevention Committee and Community Development Officer, Community Development, Bankstown City Council, Evidence given to the Drugs and Crime Prevention Committee, Inquiry into Locally Based Approaches to Community Safety and Crime Prevention, Public Hearing, Sydney, 19 September 2011.

For this reason the Local Government Community Safety and Partnership Network of which Ms Southwell is chair was established in 2009. Currently it has 57 members from across New South Wales, a majority being metropolitan councils although there are regional and rural councils represented as well. Ms Southwell explained the role and value of the Network as follows:

> The network was set up to be able to disseminate information and assist us in our jobs by sharing information, but also to advocate for professional development opportunities so we can get a standardised qualification or background for workers to improve professionally and assist in the day-to-day working of that role. The network also aims to facilitate improved program evaluation. We wanted to develop something to know what is best practice in the area. We wanted to be able to build something that we can use to advocate to different levels — local, state and federal government. It is quite strange that there was no consultation or communication and we wanted to set up something that we would have a better position to be able to advocate for; also recognising the strength in partnerships, creating a multidisciplinary approach and looking at how we can better, as a workforce, approach crime prevention.

> At the moment we have quarterly issues based meetings in Sydney and that might be meetings on alcohol-related crime and we would get guest speakers in to speak on those issues, to share knowledge about that. But we do have an email network that circulates information. If people have a request about a particular issue, like, 'I'm experiencing this issue, can you help me', we would send that out over the network. We have workers from Queensland and also New Zealand who participate in that email network as well.[181]

As indicated, one of the key focuses of the Network is the promotion of professional development and training for crime prevention and community safety officers. Ms Southwell also stated that some officers may only work part-time in crime prevention positions or they might be sharing that role with other responsibilities in, for example, community safety or road safety:

> People want to see professional development that will assist in their day-to-day jobs. …Basically not all councils have a community safety and crime prevention role. Most of the people are coming from a community development background, and they would have done the New South Wales Police Safer by Design course, but more and more people are coming in with a background of criminology. Further training needs have been identified in terms of CPTED and urban design, increased information on that. Also how to identify and develop evidence based approaches and how to improve evaluation techniques are needed.[182]

The Network provides a valuable forum through which such training and information sharing can be implemented

The Designing Out Crime Centre

Finally, one of the most innovative crime prevention partnerships recently established in New South Wales has been the development in 2007 of the Designing Out Crime Research Centre (DOC). The DOC was established as part of a NSW Department of Attorney General and Justice initiative in conjunction with the University of Technology Sydney (UTS) who oversee and operate the DOC.

---

181 Ms Margaret Southwell, Chair, New South Wales Local Government Community Safety and Crime Prevention Committee and Community Development Officer, Community Development, Bankstown City Council, Evidence given to the Drugs and Crime Prevention Committee, Inquiry into Locally Based Approaches to Community Safety and Crime Prevention, Public Hearing, Sydney, 19 September 2011.

182 Ms Margaret Southwell, Chair, New South Wales Local Government Community Safety and Crime Prevention Committee and Community Development Officer, Community Development, Bankstown City Council, Evidence given to the Drugs and Crime Prevention Committee, Inquiry into Locally Based Approaches to Community Safety and Crime Prevention, Public Hearing, Sydney, 19 September 2011.

The DOC was created to help reduce the levels of opportunistic crime in NSW; that is, crime that is enabled or exacerbated by particular kinds of social contexts, situations and environments, specifically:

◆ Property crime

◆ Personal crime (particularly violent crime)

◆ Alcohol-related crime

◆ Antisocial behaviour; and

◆ Perceptions of problems with public drunkenness and vandalism.

Mr Rodger Watson, Manager of the DOC explained its function and operations when the Committee met with him in Sydney:

> The Designing Out Crime Research Centre is a partnership between the New South Wales government and University of Technology of New South Wales. We operate out of the Faculty of Design Architecture and Building. That gives us a basis in urban design and the built environment. However, we do go outside that scope. We use design methodologies to explore problems and to come up with design solutions, whether they be products, systems or advice on urban environments and architecture… Our primary mode of problem exploration until recently has been utilising our design students. We engage [clients and partners] — be they state governments, the Department of Housing is one of our main clients, RailCorp, New South Wales Police, retail sectors and local government.
>
> We engage with them to explore crime problems that they may be dealing with. We go through a period of problem exploration where we gather information as we are talking to them. They come and talk to our students… Invariably these students are final year or masters design students from architecture, planning or some of the design disciplines, such as interior design or industrial design. These students form teams of up to about five or six students. They are briefed with the problem by the stakeholder…and then they go away and implement their design techniques to explore the problem and come up with solutions.
>
> We now have about 20-odd projects that we have been through that process on, ranging from public housing, transport, night-time economy, a lot of situations where drugs might be an issue. We try to take a broader crime focus, a focus that explores the situation in total and takes a socially responsive approach.[183]

Today the DOC is one of a small number of similar international research centres such as the Home Office/Design Council 'Design out Crime' project in the United Kingdom.[184]

The DOC aims to develop exemplary designs, design methodologies, tools and resources to help reduce the levels of opportunistic crime in NSW. It does this by:

• Conducting criminology-based research into the ways in which product, service or environmental design influences crime

• Developing methods for reducing the incidence and impact of crime through the redesign of products, services and/or features of the natural or built environment

• Promoting the benefits, socially and financially of crime prevention design to business, government and other tiers of the community.[185]

---

183   Mr Rodger Watson, Deputy Director, Designing Out Crime Research Centre, University of Technology, Sydney, Evidence given to the Drugs and Crime Prevention Committee, Inquiry into Locally Based Approaches to Community Safety and Crime Prevention, Public Hearing, Sydney, 19 September 2011.

184   See http://www.designcouncil.org.uk/our-work/challenges/security/design-out-crime/

185   http://www.designingoutcrime.com.au

The approach of the DOC is based on the situational crime-prevention techniques of Crime Prevention Through Environmental Design (CPTED) which inter alia focus on anti-crime measures for public spaces, including:[186]

- Territorial reinforcement
- Surveillance
- Access control
- Activity support and image management.[187]

The centre is primarily multidisciplinary and draws together the expertise from a variety of organisations, including:

- NSW Department of Attorney General and Justice
- The Faculty of Design, Architecture and Building (DAB) at UTS
- The Bureau of Crime Statistics and Research (BOCSAR)
- Faculty of Law at UTS
- Housing New South Wales
- NSW Police Force.

The Centre also develops relationships with industry and experts in other research centres to broaden its base of knowledge and expertise. Essentially the Centre uses evidence based design approaches to think 'outside the square' about crime problems to see if they can be addressed and solved in a different way.

Conclusion

Various approaches to implementing crime prevention policies and programs have been tried with different degrees of success across Australia and internationally. The experience of developing and implementing crime prevention and reduction policies and programs in jurisdictions outside Victoria has shown that there are a range of different approaches and that 'not one size fits all'. Certainly lessons can be learnt from examining the approaches of other countries and indeed the experiences of other states in this country. Many of the interventions utilised interstate and overseas have their own individual differences tailored for their own unique circumstances. Nonetheless, one common feature seems to be that each of the jurisdictions studied in this chapter have emphasised the need for crime prevention agencies to work in partnership with other relevant organisations and agencies. Some of these partnerships are 'horizontal' working across different levels of government departments and agencies; partnerships between police and local government are a prime example of this. Others are vertical with central (government) agencies working with, and drawing upon, the expertise in their local communities.

It is also essential that those agencies responsible for developing and implementing crime prevention and community programs, particularly police and local government, have access to the best possible data to inform their strategies. New South Wales is a good example of where crime prevention policy and program development is made on the basis of up-to-date and relevant information rather than supposition and guesswork. This is largely due to the close partnerships formed between community agencies, police and local government with the independent BOCSAR. The Home Office Research and Statistics Directorate performs an equally valuable role in Britain.

---

186   See discussion on CPTED in Chapter 2.
187   http://www.designingoutcrime.com/

Some of the approaches to crime prevention developed since the 1990s, particularly the United Kingdom crime prevention partnerships program, have made much of the fact that they were established according to 'scientific' principles as to 'what works'. Yet in the British case the experiment was abandoned shortly after the pilot phase had expired. So what then makes some approaches successful and others not able to achieve the initial hopes of their planners? This complex issue is the topic of the following chapter.

Recommendations

16. **The Committee recommends** that in developing partnerships with community groups, councils and shires incorporate the guidelines from the Institute on Governance's *Good Governance Principles for Partnerships* as outlined in Recommendation 18.

17. **The Committee recommends** that any partnerships entered into between government agencies such as the Community Crime Prevention Unit, local government and non-government agencies and the private sector incorporate the Institute on Governance *Good Governance Principles for Partnerships* discussed later in this Report.

18. **The Committee recommends** that the Victorian government undertake a review of the involvement of small business and corporate enterprises in crime prevention partnership initiatives. Such a review could include but not be restricted to:

    ◆ an audit of the current involvement of small business and the corporate sector in crime prevention and community safety initiatives in Victoria

    ◆ the role of corporate social responsibility in the area of crime prevention and community safety

    ◆ how the United Nations Guidelines on the use of corporate crime prevention partnerships can be incorporated into the proposed Crime Prevention and Community Safety Framework

    ◆ the effectiveness and positive outcomes of current public/private sector projects in the areas of crime prevention and community safety

    ◆ the use of private sector volunteers to work on projects associated with crime prevention and community safety

    ◆ the barriers faced by the corporate and small business sector in becoming involved in crime prevention and community safety initiatives

    ◆ incentives that the Victorian and/or Commonwealth governments may be able to provide to the private sector to invest in crime prevention and community safety projects

    ◆ ways of promoting to the private sector the positive aspects of becoming involved with crime prevention and community safety initiatives

    ◆ ways of providing practical advice to the private sector on entering crime prevention partnerships, particularly through implementing the guidelines outlined in the ICPC Public-Private Partnerships and Community Safety: A Guide to Action (2011).

35. **The Committee recommends** the Victorian Government consider establishing a Design Out Crime Centre in Victoria similar to that operating at the University of Technology, Sydney NSW.

4. What Works and What Doesn't in Developing Crime Prevention Strategies, Policies and Programs

Introduction

Crime prevention is a complex issue that is anything but straightforward to implement in practice. Although it is not possible to say a 'one size fits all' approach or template can be used to implement a successful crime prevention model, the research literature, evaluation studies, and experience of those in the field suggest there are certain approaches to 'doing' crime prevention that are more likely to be successful than others.

Crime prevention is important of itself

Research has shown that good crime prevention models and practice must stem from a philosophy that values prevention in itself and not merely as an adjunct to law and order. Sutton, Cherney and White have argued that in Australia 'prevention and community safety remain background tasks as far as the media and government crime policy are concerned' (2008, p.3). Echoing these concerns, Homel and Homel (2012) have stated that the problem in Australia is 'primarily a lack of political vision concerning science based prevention and a consequent failure to articulate and agree on goals'. As a corollary to this it is important to increase public awareness that 'doing' crime prevention is a worthwhile exercise and not a 'soft' approach:

> Crime prevention must be seen as a legitimate and effective method of addressing crime and disorder problems and bringing about sustainable reductions in those issues that impact upon people's feelings of safety within their community (Morgan & Homel 2011, p.39).

International research shows that crime prevention is most effective when it is 'embraced as an activity in its own right with its own goals and objectives' (International Centre for the Prevention of Crime (ICPC) 2010, p.9).[188] This, as Homel points out, requires high level sustained commitment and a generous level of resourcing (2009a). The following sections look at the impediments to developing and implementing good crime prevention practice and the necessary criteria that must be utilised to ensure effective crime prevention delivery.

The dos and don'ts of crime prevention implementation

Homel has argued that Australian attempts to develop and deliver coherent evidence based crime prevention policy and programs have been beset by the same problems that thwarted the UK's Crime Reduction Program (CRP). That is:

> [l]ack of effective leadership, inflexible top down program design and poor communication between local and central stakeholders (Homel in Sutton, Cherney & White 2008, p.106).[189]

---

188 In its trends survey for 2010 the ICPC has strongly exhorted governments that safety and crime prevention strategies must 'constitute public policies in and of themselves and not be annexed to other policies' (ICPC 2010, p.9).

189 It should be noted that not only is Professor Peter Homel an expert in the area of crime prevention and former Director of Crime Prevention in NSW, he was also seconded to the United Kingdom Home Office to work on a review of the Crime Reduction Program (CRP) in 2004-2005.

These and other problems have been identified in Victoria with regard to implementing crime prevention models. Some of these issues identified by Hill and Sutton have historically included:

- the low profile media coverage of crime prevention — which deprives the public of opportunities to appreciate the short and long term benefits that can accrue from properly designed and implemented programs;

- facile acceptance that addressing underlying causes is 'too hard' — there are now numerous practical illustrations that long term, properly integrated initiatives do work;

- lack of focused expertise — often responsibility for developing programs has been foisted on locally based project officers who have great enthusiasm and strong community development skills, but comparatively little expertise in the specialist field of crime prevention;

- excessive police ownership of crime prevention strategies — this can inhibit development of broad based skills and partnerships which provide the foundation for most effective programs (Hill & Sutton 1996, pp.56–57).

Whilst the above list pertains to the crime prevention strategies and programs in 1996, recent research by Peter Homel has indicated that little has changed.[190] Homel suggests that, regardless of what crime prevention approaches are employed, experience in Australia (and overseas) has shown that crime prevention effectiveness is frequently stymied by:

- ineffective and inefficient processes for the transfer and uptake of available knowledge about good crime prevention practice and research, such as that there is a failure to learn and apply valuable lessons;

- the absence of a skilled and professional crime prevention workforce;

- inadequate and inappropriate sustainable resources;

- inadequate project and program management ability; and

- lack of knowledge and experience with performance measurement and program evaluation (Homel 2009a, p.3).

What 'works'

If these are the negative aspects or how not to develop and implement crime prevention models, what are the characteristics associated with successful and sustained approaches to crime prevention and community safety? Peter Homel has presented a 'checklist' of six conditions for good crime prevention models. These are:

- A belief in the possibility of prevention

- Clear goals and vision directly linked to strategies

- A practical grasp of crime prevention theory

- Strong and consistent leadership and supportive governance structures

- A capacity to manage collaborative multi-agency action

- Outcome focused performance measurement systems

- An applied commitment to evidence based practice and research/evaluation

- Effective communication processes designed to promote engagement and sustainability (Homel 2009b, p.32).[191]

---

190   A number of reviews in Australia and overseas have testified to the 'failure' of crime prevention models in this regard. For a full account see Homel 2009a.

191   Some of these principles will be expanded in greater detail in the next sections.

A mix of centralised and localised approaches

It is generally agreed that the optimal mix for delivering effective crime prevention programs is through the collaborative efforts of representatives of central coordinating units and localised stakeholders. For example, Morgan and Homel argue in the Western Australian context that having policy and planning implementation coordinated from the Office of Crime Prevention (OCP) was important because of the support and assistance it could give local government, including through:

- Assist[ing] local government to develop [crime prevention partnership] plans

- Monitor[ing] and supporting implementation through frequent and regular contact with local government

- Continu[ing] to negotiate the involvement of key stakeholders

- Assist[ing] in the process of transferring contemporary crime prevention knowledge and examples of good practice to local government

- Disseminat[ing] detailed crime data for their local area; and

- Assist[ing] local government to access grant funding opportunities (2011, p.30).

And whilst a strong centralised coordination unit is important for local and regional crime prevention:

> Local planning and problem solving simply will not occur if central governments refuse to devolve resources, authority and decision making powers to the local players who are responsible for program delivery. The notion of 'partnership' is empty if grassroots stakeholders lack the authority to change agency policies and practices and commit resources to their part of a crime prevention and community safety plan. Rarely however have members of local or regional crime prevention committees in Australia possessed this type of authority (Cherney & Sutton 2007, p.75).

Whilst it is generally agreed that there needs to be a strong relationship between a central coordinating (government) agency and local networks, there is less agreement on which department or departments should have the ultimate responsibility for driving the process. In Australia, crime prevention units have largely been the province of Justice/Attorney-General portfolios. In Western Australia, however, overall responsibility belongs to the Police Service. Too often, according to critics such as Hill and Sutton, crime prevention can be subject to 'excessive ownership' by police authorities (1996, p.57). Such an approach has even been criticised or at least questioned by those already within coordinating justice or police portfolios. As one senior police officer with responsibility for crime prevention stated to the Committee:

> ...my personal opinion is that you would be better to have an OCP which is perhaps driven by a central government agency and not a core police agency such as the police that could also act as a coordinating body, like Premier and Cabinet or something like that or even Treasury to some extent...If it were put in education or health, there is always the risk that they get diverted off to other priorities.[192]

Some advocates believe that crime prevention policy should be driven from the 'top':

> An authoritative and well resourced crime prevention unit located within the Premier and Cabinet is the prerequisite for proper monitoring and evaluation. A whole of government commitment from the Premier down will be essential to ensure that all departments make tangible commitments to crime prevention and work in partnership with relevant agencies and community groups to achieve the common goal of making Victoria safer (Hill & Sutton 1996, p.58).

---

192 Assistant Commissioner Wayne Gregson, Judicial Services, Western Australia Police Service, Evidence given to the Drugs and Crime Prevention Committee, Inquiry into Locally Based Approaches to Community Safety and Crime Prevention, Meeting, Perth, 21 June 2011.

Western Australia has been an excellent example of a centrally located agency working in effective partnerships with local communities that are often widely geographically dispersed. As discussed in Chapter 3 the Western Australian OCP has demonstrated that: 'careful attention to effective ongoing communication with stakeholders and a commitment to the provision of strategic support can overcome many of the barriers to delivering centrally driven initiatives at a local level' (Homel 2009b, p.29).

A mix of crime prevention approaches

Cherney and Sutton (2007) argue that local based community safety responses should ideally involve a combination of shorter-term (situational) and long-term (social) measures.[193] And whilst these critics agree that implementing a crime prevention plan does require sustained long-term planning and investment this does not preclude shorter-term responses, such as temporary task forces, being assembled to address specific issues that may have arisen (2007, p.72). A good example is the problem of alcohol related violence — the optimal crime prevention approach to address this issue would rely upon multiple short-term and long-term interventions, including policing, public education and environmental/design initiatives targeted at both the general public as well as the perpetrators of such violence.[194]

The most ambitious crime preventions strategies or frameworks have used a number of multiple interventions to address linked problems, either simultaneously or contemporaneously. Sometimes this approach has been overly ambitious, fragmented or disjointed resulting in failure (the UK CRP).[195] On other occasions, such as through the Western Australian OCP, the approach has been implemented relatively successfully.

Collaborative approaches

Whether the approaches are known as 'whole of government' (Australia), 'networked government' (USA) or 'joined up government' (UK), Homel argues that there is near universal agreement today that crime prevention programs and strategies need collaborative multi-agency action:

> This is because of the near universal acceptance these days that neither the criminal justice system nor human service agencies alone are able to adequately address the complex array of the causes of crime (Homel 2009b, p.17).[196]

Collaborative structures rely on good inclusive partnerships and participation, although as Homel points out there can be a great deal of confusion as to what 'partnership' means in practice (Homel 2009b).[197] The nature of partnerships and the characteristics that make them strong will be discussed at length in Chapters 6 and 7. The following table from Homel and Homel outlines the optimal ingredients for working crime prevention partnerships:

---

193   See also discussion in Chapter 2.

194   For further discussion on alcohol related violence and interventions to address it, see Drugs and Crime Prevention Committee, *Inquiry into Strategies to Reduce Assaults in Public Places in Victoria, Final Report* 2010.

195   For the reasons why this may have been the case, see the discussion above and Homel 2009a, 2009b, 2010a; Sutton, Cherney and White 2008.

196   Lee and Woodward (2002) argue that such an approach is not unique to the field of crime prevention but is an example of a more general shift in public administration away from a 'control and command' model of governance towards governance through collaboration across different tiers and sectors of government with multiple stakeholders (Lee & Woodward in Homel 2009b, p.18).

197   As Homel points out however, some crime prevention approaches are anything but inclusionary, good examples being gated communities and the use of move-on powers in public spaces such as shopping centres (see Homel 2009b, p.30).

Table 4.1: Five principles of good governance for crime prevention partnerships

Governance principle	Conditions for success
Legitimacy and Voice Those in positions of power are perceived to have acquired their power legitimately and there is an appropriate voice accorded to those whose interests are affected by decisions	• Everyone who needs to be, is at the table • There are forums for bringing the partners together • The forums are managed so that the various voices are listened to and the dialogue is genuine and respectful • There is a consensus orientation among all those at the table
Direction/Strategic Vision The exercise of power results in a sense of overall direction that serves as a guide to action	• All parties share a joint and clearly articulated vision of their goal • Each party to the partnership sees how their organisation can contribute to the vision • Roles and responsibilities are clearly defined • The parties have adequately adjusted to any changes to the vision that have occurred over time
Performance Institutions and processes are responsive to the interests of participants, citizens or stakeholders	• There is a clear idea among participants as to what constitutes success • Performance is monitored and reported • The framework for performance measurement and reporting is developed jointly • There are sufficient resources to build and maintain the partnership • The different contexts in which the parties work are understood and accepted
Accountability There is accountability between those in positions of power and those whose interests they serve, and transparency and openness in the conduct of the work	• The accountabilities of all of the parties are clear • There are open, transparent and accountable relationship between the parties • The accountability relationships of the parties to their respective organisations is recognized and respected • The effectiveness of the partnership is reported publicly
Fairness There is conformity with the rule of law and the principle of equity	• All parties believe they receive sufficient value from the partnership • The clients of the parties, and the public, benefit from the partnership • The laws that govern each party are recognized and respected

Source: Adapted from Edgar, Marshall and Bassett (2006) in Homel and Homel (2012).

Whilst the above principles in greater or lesser degrees may be essential for good governance and the management of (crime prevention) partnerships, friction can emerge between the principles:

> For example, demands for increased accountability, and the resources required to achieve this, may work against goals for improved performance, as more time spent writing reports means less time delivering a program. This [does not mean] accountability is not important (it is!) but rather to illustrate the need to recognise the inherent conflicts within the principles and the importance of finding balance among them (Edgar, Marshall & Bassett 2006, p.3).

Evidence based policy and programs, evaluation and performance measurement

Contemporary crime prevention policy and programs rely on strong research and evidence based outcomes as to 'what works' to meet specified goals and needs. Whilst such an approach seems relatively straightforward, Nutley, Davies and Walter argue that doing 'what works' is in fact much more complex and nuanced. They believe that four key requirements need to be addressed in promoting evidence based practice:

◆ Agreement as to the nature of 'evidence';

◆ A strategic approach to the creation of evidence, together with the development of a cumulative knowledge base;

◆ Effective dissemination of knowledge, together with the development of effective means of access to knowledge; and

◆ Initiatives to increase uptake of evidence in both policy and practice (2002, p.3).

This begs the question, however, that in establishing and drawing from a knowledge base for crime prevention practice, formal research is only one source of knowledge:

> *Informal* knowledge — such as that embedded in many systems and procedures which shapes how an organisation functions, communicates and analyses situations; *tacit* knowledge — arising from the capabilities of people, particularly the skills they have developed over time and *cultural* knowledge — relating to customs, values and relationships with clients and other stakeholders, are also powerful influences on people's professional practices [and the delivery or implementation of crime prevention models]' (Homel 2009b, pp.23–24).

Equally important for implementing and sustaining good crime prevention models is the need to measure the effectiveness of crime prevention programs or procedures. The importance of evaluation, monitoring and performance measurement as key features of effective crime prevention was also stressed in the recently developed National Crime Prevention Framework. The topics of evaluation and performance measurement are the subject of Chapter 11 of this Report.

Workforce and training

Effective crime prevention models require knowledgeable planning and implementation, which is contingent upon an expert and knowledgeable workforce in the area of crime prevention. Morgan and Homel state, however, that too often in Australia and overseas crime prevention measures have been made less effective by players having:

- a poor understanding of crime prevention theory and techniques;
- the absence of a skilled and professional crime prevention workforce;
- inadequate project and program management ability; and
- the lack of knowledge and experience with performance measurement and program evaluation (Homel 2008 in Morgan & Homel 2011, p.29).[198]

Similarly, Cherney and Sutton (2007) have stated that many attempts to implement local crime prevention plans and programs have failed because of a dearth of local staff with relevant experience. In their view, Community Safety Officers[199] employed by local government or police agencies may be particularly useful in liaising between central government units and local agencies.

Planning for the 'long haul'

One problem with many crime prevention strategies, frameworks and programs is that they too often can be sustained only for particular election cycles. Good crime prevention, particularly that pertaining to social, structural or developmental measures, requires a

---

198　For the importance of evaluation in the context of crime prevention, see Chapter 11.
199　See the discussion in Chapter 7.

sustained (and expensive) [200] commitment to embedded long-term programs: 'This is because design and delivery of effective crime prevention outcomes is complex which reflects the complexity and multi-faceted nature of the underlying causes of crime' (Homel 2009a, p.2).

The STAD (Stockholm prevents Alcohol and Drug problems) program in Sweden is an excellent example of a sustained crime prevention initiative. This initiative addressed alcohol-related disorder in Stockholm by incorporating a partnership approach between police, local government agencies and bar and restaurant owners. [201] The success of the project was largely due to the 10-year period allowed for implementation from the initial development/exploration phase to adoption and 'institutionalisation':

> This realistic time frame is perhaps one of the major lessons that can be learned from STAD, since one of the major enemies of good leadership and effective governance that underpin successful crime prevention is the tendency for governments to expect results too quickly or constantly reorganise the manner in which crime prevention is delivered (Homel & Homel 2012).

The CRP in England is an example of a more complex set of initiatives that failed in part due to the shorter time frame allowed to achieve 'results'.

Funding

The funding of crime prevention initiatives is clearly very important. A recent Report by the ICPC has emphasised that regional and local agencies need *sustainable* and *institutionalised* financial resources (ICPC 2010). Homel has similarly commented that sufficient, indeed generous, funding should be allocated to not only specific short-term projects but also embedded long-term programs (2009a). Moreover, crime prevention programs should contain specific funding/budgetary measures to enable the integration of crime prevention measures:

> This includes the promotion and incorporation of measures to ensure that funds made available to deliver crime prevention activity are not misappropriated or redirected away from their intended purpose that is the prevention of crime (Homel 2009a, p.4).

In particular, this Committee supports the submissions made by a variety of local government authorities (LGAs) to this Inquiry that additional resources are needed for community safety services. With regard to LGAs and local level approaches, a common refrain heard by the Committee is that local government and their agencies are increasingly expected to provide education, social services and programs with regard to crime prevention and community safety but are not provided with appropriate infrastructure, staffing and funding levels. Moreover, long-term planning is difficult when agencies are funded for only a limited period of time with no guarantee of continued funding. Inadequate funding can particularly be a problem for smaller and rural and regional councils. Sufficient funding is crucial to ensure that agencies have appropriately trained workers to address the complex issues pertaining to crime prevention.

Homel suggests that one approach to remedy these problems is through the establishment of a crime prevention technical assistance fund, managed through a 'suitably supported, high level advisory body':

> The function of this fund would be to sponsor relevant and appropriate professional training, promote the development of events and processes, as well as guide the growth of a more effectively disseminated crime prevention evidence base (Homel 2009a, p.5).

---

200 Although much of the international literature suggests long-term investment in crime prevention programs, particularly those pertaining to social and developmental approaches, are cost-effective and result in significant returns on justice, welfare and health expenditures. See, for example, studies cited in Homel 2009a and the discussion in Chapter 2 of this Report.

201 For a full discussion of STAD, see Graham and R Homel 2008.

While the Committee realises that the costs associated with community safety programs and policy initiatives can be expensive, it believes in the long run such an approach will be cost-effective not only because such programs may reduce crime and antisocial behaviour but also because they promote positive social development and community capacity building. Homel has reviewed the research studies on the cost implications of crime prevention programs and has concluded that they *are* economically viable 'and can achieve a significant return on investment in terms of savings in justice, welfare, healthcare and the protection of social and human capital' (2009a, p.3). As such the Committee recommends that ongoing grants be provided for community crime prevention and safety initiatives, particularly those involving partnerships. These grants should in most cases, however, be awarded to initiatives that fulfil the objectives of the Community Safety and Crime Prevention Framework.

Conclusion

Research suggests that an important starting point for creating successful crime prevention models is valuing prevention in itself, not just as an adjunct to law and order policies. Notwithstanding the complexities inherent in crime prevention, policies and approaches being developed and implemented currently are better placed to succeed than many earlier attempts, as they have the benefit of seeing what policies have and haven't worked and learning from recent research literature and evaluation studies. Long-term planning, forming multi-agency partnerships to design and implement policies and measuring performance of policies are examples of factors identified by such research as being essential.

Recommendations

1. **The Committee recommends** that the Community Crime Prevention Unit should develop a Crime Prevention and Community Safety Framework as the means for coordinating Government action in the area. In developing the framework, the Government should ensure it consults with relevant partners in community crime prevention such as local government, police and representatives of non-government organisations.

3. **The Committee recommends** that the best way of implementing the Crime Prevention and Community Safety Framework and indeed crime prevention strategies generally is through the Community Crime Prevention Unit.

10. **The Committee recommends** that local governments in developing their crime prevention and community safety strategy plans seek the views of members of the local community through a properly constituted consultation process.

Section C — Locally Based Approaches to Crime Prevention and Community Safety in Victoria

5. A Survey of Local Crime Prevention and Community Safety Activity in Victoria

This chapter describes the outcomes of a quantitative survey undertaken by the Australian Institute of Criminology (AIC) on behalf of the Drugs and Crime Prevention Committee to generate a snapshot of the level of local community safety and crime prevention activity currently being undertaken in Victoria, particularly that which involves local government authorities (LGAs) and other key community groups. The chapter provides a particular focus on the practical experiences of working in crime prevention partnerships and sheds some light on many of the otherwise hidden challenges, strengths and opportunities for undertaking community safety work at a local level. It also offers some insight into options for further improving crime prevention and community safety activity at the local level across Victoria into the future.

Background

For more than a quarter of a century local community safety and crime prevention action has been based on an implicit understanding that since most crime of immediate concern to communities is local (e.g. property crime, antisocial behaviour, vandalism, etc.) then the primary focus for preventive action should also be local.

In practice this has meant that those who promote crime prevention action, both in Australia and overseas, have generally turned to local governments as a key resource for coordinating the delivery of local preventive responses. This has been based on the assumption that local LGAs are best placed to understand and reflect the particular needs and problems of their local community and are therefore also best placed to generate and/or deliver the most appropriate prevention interventions for their local communities.

This emphasis on the role of local governments in crime prevention is strongly encouraged by international organisations such as the United Nations Office on Drugs and Crime and UN-HABITAT and includes three principle characteristics:

1. The use of a comprehensive approach based on a detailed analysis of factors influencing crime and victimisation, including social, economic, environmental and institutional factors;

2. The engagement of key stakeholders at the local level; and

3. The importance of clear and consistent local leadership (International Centre for the Prevention of Crime (ICPC) 2008, p.211).

The importance and variety of partnerships in crime prevention has also been highlighted by numerous international reviews and organisation. However, there has also been a widespread recognition of significant discrepancies between the the capacity of local authorities to adequately address local concerns about crime and their lack of resources, both financial and legal (ICPC 2010b).

In Victoria there has been a significant history of LGAs working to promote local community safety and crime prevention action. However, the Victorian experience has been very similar to that in many other parts of the world in that the impact and effectiveness over time has been highly variable (Sutton et al 2008).

This experience was one of the reasons that led the Committee to commission the AIC to undertake a systematic survey of the current state of local community safety and crime prevention activity across Victoria. The Committee requested the AIC develop a survey that would assist in addressing the first four terms of reference for the Committee's Inquiry, specifically an assessment of the nature of locally based approaches to crime prevention and community safety that described:

1. The breadth of locally based groups and organisations involved, with particular regard to local government and Neighbourhood Watch (NW);

2. Approaches adopted to promulgate practices, programs or initiatives;

3. An indication of the extent to which these organisations effectively engage with local and state agencies in the development of policy; and

4. The range of barriers or facilitating factors that are contributing to the capacity of local groups to engage in the development of community safety initiatives.

Partnerships for crime prevention

One of the key tasks for this survey was to assist the Committee to examine the importance of partnerships and the role of local communities in addressing local problems. To do this it is necessary to properly understand how partnership arrangements operate in the context of local community crime prevention initiatives.

Under a typical partnership model, service provision is not viewed in terms of the core functions and responsibilities of separate agencies and interest groups who are delivering services in a particular community. Rather, it is looked at in terms of how to best organise and run services to achieve agreed community priorities and goals, regardless of where the service is sourced from or who is leading the service delivery process.

However, there is a great deal of confusion over what the term 'partnership' means in practice. The term is used widely to describe local structures, such as for planning, coordinating and delivering local crime prevention initiatives. But there is no single form that is seen as being most effective or appropriate in all circumstances.[202]

Numerous definitions exist regarding what it means to be in a 'partnership' arrangement within the public sector. For example, Bennington and Cummane (1999) list a number of elements that will be present in a successful partnership arrangement. These will include:

◆ commitment

◆ equity

◆ trust

◆ mutual goals/objectives

◆ collaboration over implementation

◆ continuous evaluation

◆ timely communication and responsiveness.

---

202   For more information see the report by Joseph Rowntree Foundation 2003.

Brinkerhoff (2002) emphasises the need for a balance between mutuality (for example, equality in decision making, joint accountability, mutual trust and respect, as well as jointly agreed purposes and values) and the specific organisational identity and features of partner agencies that both add value to the process and make each agency indispensable to others.

The bulk of attention in how to get partnership models operational has focused on the coordination and collaboration of local services within a regional and local context. As was pointed out in a review of the experience of integrated governance approaches in Australia (IPAA 2002), improved coordination is often regarded as the prime solution to government problems.

However, other research has demonstrated that without a clear and coherent plan and capacity for active technical support at the central level even the best local action is likely to fall short of the goal (Homel et al 2004). As well as this, it is clear that functional agreements between central agencies are also necessary in order to maximise local and regional collaboration. These partnership arrangements need to flow both horizontally (i.e. across agencies) and vertically (i.e. from the centre to the local and regional level) if they are to be effective at promoting joined-up action in practice.

This does not mean that the relationships within any partnership arrangements will always be equal. The nature of the power relationship between each agency involved in the partnership should be a product of what value they can add to the achievement of the joint outcomes. For example, at times it may be appropriate for a regional manager to assume leadership of an initiative, as a result of being best placed to leverage the necessary resources or most effectively to influence the policy process. In other circumstances, a local authority may be most appropriate as it has access to the most relevant resources. In other situations it may be the police, a community or voluntary organisation, a local business group, or another government agency. In fact, as explained by Edgar et al (2006) a successful partnership values and openly acknowledges the different types of power that each individual or organisation brings.

Yet, without a functioning partnership arrangement based on the principles of integrated governance, this form of flexible organisation will not be able to occur. Consequently, an examination of the nature and extent of partnership operation in the context of Victorian local community safety and crime prevention activity was central to this survey.

How the survey was undertaken

The AIC designed a formal self-completion survey that was distributed to all LGAs in Victoria. A copy of the survey is in Appendix 11 of this Report. The questionnaire itself was a modified version of an existing survey form developed for use in an international study of local government participation in community safety and crime prevention activity at the local community level.

The ICPC developed the original questionnaire on which the Victorian survey was based for an international project undertaken recently for similar purposes as the Committee's current Inquiry. However, the survey undertaken by the AIC was modified to reflect the Committee's needs and Victorian circumstances and allowed for a mixture of quantitative and qualitative items.

The survey questionnaire was divided into five sections that covered:

◆ Issues about crime and community safety in the community in which respondents live;

◆ What planning processes and associated strategies, if any, were in place to prevent crime and enhance community safety;

- What crime prevention and community safety initiatives were being pursued in each locality;

- An assessment of what changes had been observed as a result of any existing or past local crime prevention initiatives and whether there had been any formal evaluation of these initiatives; and

- A set of questions about the extent and nature of any Neighbourhood Watch activity in the area.

The questionnaire also included a number of questions which identified the LGA as being located in an urban, rural or urban fringe area. No analysis was undertaken in terms of individual LGAs.

There were also a number of questions asked about the overall focus of their community safety and crime prevention programs or strategies as well as issues to do with perceived difficulties with implementing, operating and managing crime prevention and community safety programs in general.

The final version of the questionnaire was set up to be completed electronically using the AIC's on-line survey facilities. However, an alternative version of the questionnaire was also made available to facilitate a comprehensive coverage of respondents.

The Chair of the Committee wrote to all the Chief Executives of Victorian LGAs inviting them to complete the survey and emphasising that their participation would be invaluable to assisting the Committee's work. The letter also emphasised that the survey was being undertaken by the AIC on the Committee's behalf and that all responses were to be directed to the AIC and that the AIC would undertake the analysis and ultimately provide a report for the Committee's use.

The survey was undertaken over a four-week period in September and October 2011. All but one LGA responded (78 out of 79 LGAs). While not all responses were usable in all cases, as is often the case with surveys like this, this does mean that responses were received from LGAs that covered approximately 93 per cent of the Victorian population. Of these, 32 per cent were urban LGAs; 56 per cent were rural; and 12 per cent were in areas described as being urban outer fringes. When the responses were analysed in terms of whether they were received from an LGA that was in an urban, rural or mixed locality, few if any significant differences in the responses were found. This means that there is a high level of homogeneity in the results regardless of what area the LGA was from.[203]

---

203 The primary analysis was conducted using STATA 12 statistical software. Due to the categorical nature of survey data, where applicable, a Pearson's Chi Square test with Fisher's exact test of relationship was used to test for any statistical differences in the responses. Any such differences are noted as the results are reported below.

Results of the survey

The nature of locally based approaches to crime prevention and community safety

Respondents were asked to identify the main crime and community safety issues in their LGA. The most common crime and safety issues are summarised in Figure 5.1.

Figure 5.1:   Crime and safety issues in Victoria LGAs (%)

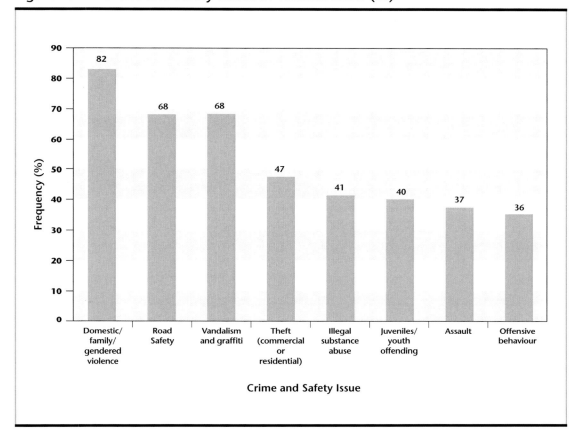

Note: Multiple responses were allowed and this summary does not include issues where the response is less than 30 per cent.

Eighty-two per cent of respondents believed that alcohol-related problems and domestic violence were key crime and safety issues in their LGA, followed by road safety (68%) and vandalism and graffiti (68%).

It is likely that the frequent mention of road safety issues by many of the respondents is the result of many local authorities having been involved with the World Health Organization's (WHO) 'Safer Communities' program. Within the WHO's Safer Communities approach, crime prevention and community safety is considered to be just one aspect to reducing and preventing a wide range of intentional and unintentional injury that can occur within a community. These forms of injury can include such things as burns, sporting or other recreational accidents as well as traffic accidents. This approach, the prevention of any forms of injury be it crime related or not, is seen as part of the task of creating a safer community.

Figure 5.2 summarises information related specifically to the focus of crime prevention and community safety programs.

Figure 5.2:   Focus of crime prevention and community safety programs (%)

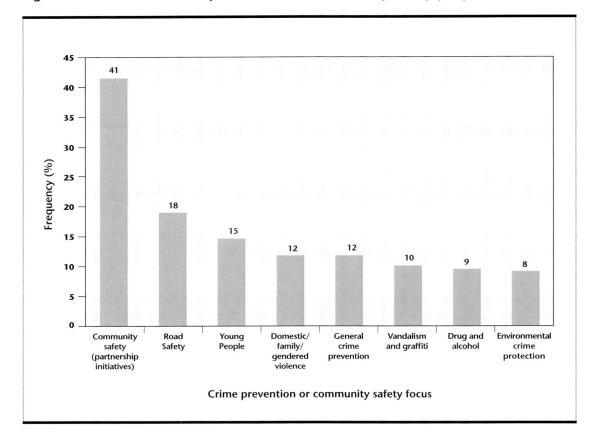

These results reflect an apparent tendency for local councils to adopt, implement or endorse programs with broad 'safety' goals. Specifically, 41 per cent of programs had community safety–partnership development as a key or secondary focus. The second most common focus was road safety. Programs with a community safety focus tended to involve significant partnerships with external stakeholders. Examples of initiatives with a community safety focus included the development of community safety committees, 'Streetwatch' teams, community safety months, lighting upgrades and information kits on topics such as how to run safer parties and car safety.

This reported emphasis on general community safety issues most probably reflects a realistic assessment of the appropriate role local government can best fulfil in contributing to the achievement of local crime prevention goals in a partnership arrangement. Research into the most effective forms of local community partnerships suggests that groups such as local authorities are generally best placed to fulfil a coordination and facilitation role:

♦ through assisting with the mobilisation of local resources;

♦ facilitating participation and access to informal networks;

♦ assisting in the establishment of flexible structures and procedures;

♦ providing a closer understanding and emotional commitment to community issues and concerns; and

♦ promoting a community-based self-help attitude (Edgar, Marshall and Bassett 2006).

While not all of these issues have been able to be directly explored using the data collected in this survey, such findings can be used to inform a better understanding of the findings throughout this chapter.

For example, when comparing the information presented in Figures 5.1 and 5.2, there is an apparent discrepancy between the focus of councils' programs and initiatives and identified crime and safety issues. Though alcohol-related problems and domestic, gendered and family violence were viewed as significant problems, only a handful of programs and initiatives were specifically directed at these issues.

However, while this may appear to be a discrepancy, it is more likely a reflection of the limitations of local councils in their ability to lead and be responsible for some specific crime prevention action. A common view is that crime prevention is primarily the responsibility of other specific agencies, in this case police and/or human services agencies. Ninety-nine per cent of respondents reported that police were responsible for crime prevention and community safety in their area, followed by community associations (62%) and schools (62%). Therefore, an alternative explanation is that local councils view their role in such issues as involving less 'frontline' prevention activity and more that of supporting the work of justice and human service agencies while enhancing the wider set of protective factors within their local community.

This idea is supported by the degree to which local councils defined their approach to crime prevention as either social or environmental. There are two broadly defined approaches to crime prevention known as social and environmental approaches (Sutton et al 2008). In practice, these two approaches are generally used in combination. However, many strategies and programs will often give an emphasis to one approach or the other.[204]

In essence, the environmental approach seeks to change the specific characteristics of the environment that contribute to criminal events occurring. Environmental measures can involve activities such as improved security through strengthening locks; improving surveillance; improving street lighting; installing closed circuit television; putting locks on windows; introducing safer money handling procedures; and limiting the amount of money held on premises. Essentially these sorts of measures seek to prevent crime by creating an environment in which the incentive to commit a crime is reduced and its commission is more difficult.

The social (or structural) approach is commonly directed at trying to influence the underlying social and economic causes of crime that can be seen to exist in a particular community and differentially affect specific members of that community. This approach may include action to improve housing, health and educational achievement as well as attempting to improve community cohesion through a variety of community development measures.

204 See discussion in Chapter 2.

Figure 5.3: **Orientation of local council approach to crime prevention and community safety (%)**

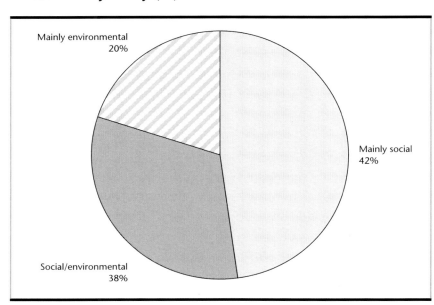

n= 76

As shown in Figure 5.3, 80 per cent of respondents indicated their approach to crime and community safety could be classified as mainly social or a combination of social and environmental crime prevention. While these categories are broad descriptions of orientations, this finding is consistent with previous research into local community crime prevention activity in Australia (Homel 2005; Cameron & Laycock 2003).

The orientation of many LGAs towards a social approach to crime prevention and community safety appears to be reflected in the sort of initiatives and programs they undertake, as illustrated in Figure 5.4.

Figure 5.4: **Types of crime prevention and community safety programs implemented by local councils (%)**

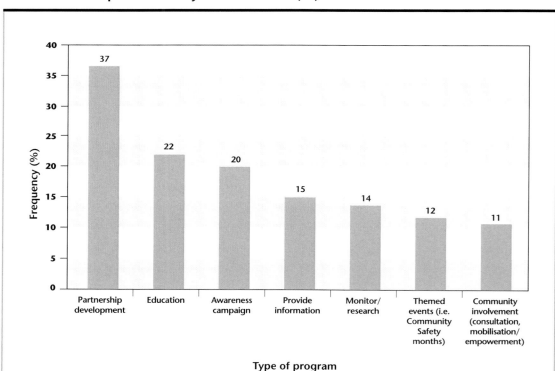

The most common type of initiatives and programs involved the development of partnerships with key stakeholders (37%).

The following are examples of the various ways in which local authorities reported that partnerships were developed in crime and community safety programs:

◆ Eastern Regional Family Violence HELP Card Project 2010-11: six eastern metropolitan region councils collaborated to put together informational cards regarding family violence. Cards were distributed across each council's local area.

◆ Local Safety Committees: the composition of the committees varied between local government areas, however common members included the council, police, emergency services, and representatives from agencies such as VicRoads and Neighbourhood Watch. The role of the committee varied as well, though common duties included implementing and guiding the council response to specific crime and safety issues in the area.

◆ Youth drug and alcohol awareness campaigns: in order to teach young people about drug and alcohol safety, many councils implemented awareness programs that partnered with local schools, community health workers, department of community services and, in some instances, local businesses.

Other programs implemented by local councils focused on education (22%), awareness campaigns (20%), information provision such as flyers or kits (15%) and monitoring and researching crime prevention and community safety issues (14%). A number of initiatives involved both education and awareness aspects, such as the domestic violence help cards. However, education programs involved some form of skill or information acquisition such as teaching newly arrived refugees to swim or strategies for bush fire safety. Altogether though, the types of programs highlighted by respondents suggest an emphasis on improving underlying social factors that can lead to victimisation or offending, such as a lack of awareness of, or education about, crime related issues.

Based on the program descriptions provided by respondents, partnerships were primarily utilised to form committees with a community safety focus. The role of these committees varied between programs, with some created to guide long-term community safety objectives, while others functioned as more transient forums for the discussion and consideration of strategies and responses to specific issues. A key aim of many of the committees was to raise awareness of safety issues, for instance organising safety audits or community safety awareness months.

In summary, the results presented in Figures 5.1–5.4 suggest that the LGAs in Victoria are pursuing a predominately social approach to crime prevention and community safety in their communities. As such, the focus and method of crime prevention and community safety are geared towards strengthening community ties and promoting community awareness, rather than undertaking more targeted crime prevention measures traditionally pursued by criminal justice agencies such as police.

The role of partnerships

Due to the importance of external involvement in an effective partnership model of crime prevention and community safety, local councils were asked a number of questions designed to assess their level of engagement in local and governmental partnerships.

As already shown in Figure 5.4, 37 per cent of crime prevention and community safety initiatives involved partnership development activity. Examples of the type of LGA activity likely to include partnership development included chairing or participating in committees or liaising between stakeholders. Local councils' engagements with specific stakeholders are presented in Table 5.1.

Table 5.1: Frequency of engagement with selected stakeholders

Stakeholder	Number	%
Police	112	52
Community/interest groups	63	29
Local businesses	38	18
Health agencies (incl. Fed/State/Local and community health agencies)	30	14
VicRoads	28	13
Schools	27	13
Government agencies nfd*	25	12
Emergency services	22	10
LGA residents	22	10

Note: Table 5.1 includes stakeholders where the proportion engaged is greater than 10%.
*nfd: not further defined

The results indicate that local councils are engaging in formal partnerships with a broad range of agencies and organisations, many of which fall outside the traditional crime prevention and community safety associations. The most common stakeholder involved in council activity is the Victorian Police (52%). Examples of how police were involved in local crime and community safety activity include:

◆ monitoring information obtained from newly installed CCTV cameras

◆ providing input on various councils and working groups

◆ direct involvement with the program such as in initiatives that target juvenile offenders.

Other partnerships existed with community and interest groups (29%) and local businesses (18%). This suggests that rather than limiting themselves to traditional partners, local councils are involved with a wide range of stakeholders.

Fourteen per cent of LGAs engaged with government and non-government health agencies and 12 per cent of respondents reported engaging with other government agencies (not further defined). Only seven per cent of respondents reported involving Department of Justice in their crime prevention or community safety projects, four per cent involved Department of Human Services, and three per cent the Department of Planning. These results suggest a lack of local engagement with government stakeholders, other than police or local health authorities, particularly with the higher levels of government. This is of particular importance when considering the important influence of higher government policy on crime and community safety activity at a local level.

Influence of government on local crime and community safety initiatives

When respondents were asked indicate the extent to which their crime prevention and community safety activity was in direct response to government policy, 73 per cent responded that local government policy was the primary influence on their activity. This compares to 34 per cent for state and 12 per cent for federal government policy. Further, 12 per cent of local councils indicated that state policy did not directly influence their activity in any way, while 27 per cent felt the same with regards to federal policy.

Figure 5.5:   The extent community safety and crime prevention initiatives are a direct response to Federal government policy (%)

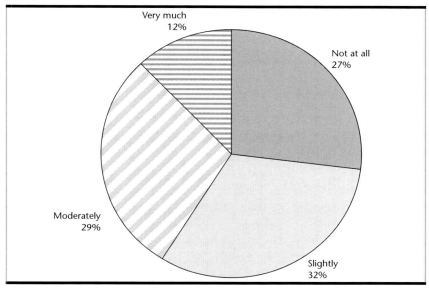

n= 41

Figure 5.6:   The extent community safety and crime prevention initiatives are a direct response to State government policy (%)

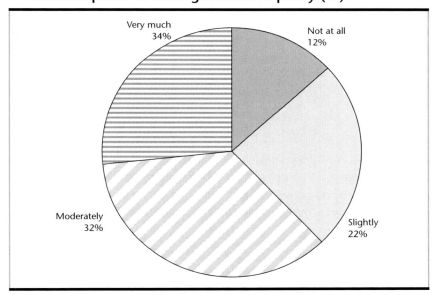

n= 41

Figure 5.7: **The extent community safety and crime prevention initiatives are a direct response to local government policy (%)**

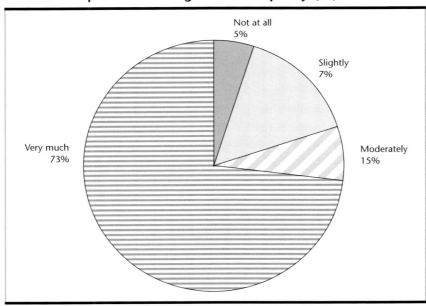

n= 41

Comments from respondents indicated that the relatively low influence that state and federal policies played in the formulation of local crime prevention programs and strategies could in part be explained by an apparent lack of guidance, communication and coordination between local councils and higher levels of government. As two respondents explained:

> 'Partnerships and collaboration with locally based groups and Victoria Police are strong but collaboration with state government including the coordination of crime prevention efforts between state (excluding police) and local government could be improved' (Respondent 7).

> 'Differing priorities, values, approaches between Council, [other] levels of Government, partners, community etc.' (Respondent 19).

Other respondents noted that while it was sometimes difficult or impractical for state government agencies to engage in multi-agency partnerships in the same way that local governments do, there was a role for the state government agencies to play as strategic partners assisting in setting program priorities and directions.

Thus, the key finding that emerges from these results is that local governments are engaging with a diverse range of stakeholders in an effort to carry out effective crime prevention and community safety strategies. However, there is also evidence that local councils do not seem to be well connected to other levels of government.

One respondent pointed to a way of improving this situation by suggesting that:

> 'There is a need for State Government to work with Local Government to clearly define roles, responsibilities and terms of reference in relation to program development and delivery in the areas of crime prevention and community safety. By taking this unified approach, policy statements, programs, activities and future directions will be closely aligned (avoiding replication or competition) and give best value outcomes to the wider communities' (Respondent 23).

It is of interest that this apparent lack of connection to state and federal strategic and policy directions does not seem to extend to the financial connection. State government is identified as a primary funding source by 82 per cent per cent of local authorities, followed by the federal government (29%). So it seems that while these two levels of government appear to be significant for funding, they are not deemed to be so from a policy and program priority perspective.

The impact of a crime prevention and community safety strategy

Respondents were asked to indicate if their council's approach to crime and safety was built upon a formal strategy. This question was used as a way of gaining some insight into the influence, if any, that the presence of a formal crime prevention strategy has on local crime prevention and community safety activity.

Figure 5.8: Crime prevention and community safety strategies in place (%)

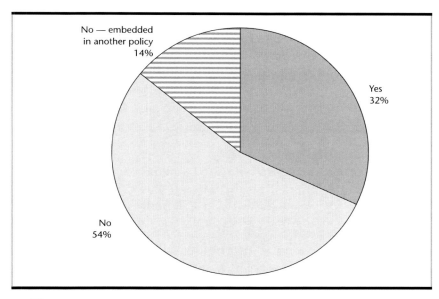

n = 76

Thirty-two per cent of respondents indicated that they had a formal crime prevention and/or community safety plan in place to guide their strategies for their communities. However, a further 14 per cent (n=11) indicated that crime prevention strategies were incorporated into a wider local government community welfare or health strategy formally operating in their council area. This is an important issue to note, as while an embedded policy still acknowledges crime and safety, current international best practice (such as the 2002 UN *Guidelines on Crime Prevention*) argue that a stand-alone policy is optimal. Regardless of this however, over half (54%, n=41) of respondents indicated their local council did not use a formal crime prevention or community safety strategy. The reasons councils gave as to why they did not have a formal strategy included a lack of resources in order to develop and implement one and the view that crime was not considered a major issue in their local area.

Figure 5.9:   Social and environmental focus, by presence of a formal strategy (%)

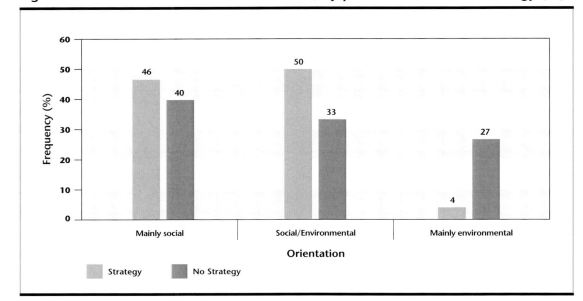

A significant association was found to exist between the presence of a formal strategy and whether or not the council pursued a mainly social or mainly environmental crime prevention agenda.[205] Based on the data presented in Figure 5.9, this association would seem to suggest that councils without a strategy more commonly reported following a mainly environmental crime prevention agenda than those with a strategy.

The available data does not allow for any causal link to be drawn between the presence of a strategy and an adherence to a particular crime prevention orientation. However, the data does show that there is no statistically significant evidence to indicate that the absence of a crime prevention or community safety strategy was a general disadvantage, when measured in terms of existing specific crime prevention activity. Further research on this possible correlation would be worthwhile.

However, it could be that the type of interventions and programs involved in the adoption of a social crime prevention orientation may well produce a need for more complex programs/interventions and partnership arrangements, something that in turn leads to the need to have some form of strategic document in place to assist in the implementation and management process.

Barriers to crime prevention

All respondents were asked to identify barriers to successful crime prevention and community safety activity action. This information is summarised in Figure 5.10.

---

205   $\chi^2(2)= 5.71, p=0.05$

Figure 5.10: Identified barriers to effective crime prevention and community safety activity (%)

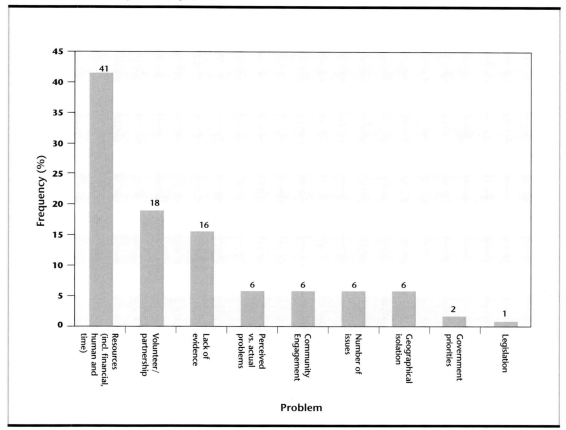

By far the most commonly cited difficultly in implementing crime prevention and community safety strategies and programs was a lack of resources, including funding, time and personnel. Eighteen per cent of respondents indicated that they had difficulties dealing with volunteers or partnerships. This included issues such as not enough partners or volunteers to adequately meet the needs of the program, lack of engagement with partners and differing priorities regarding roles and philosophy. Sixteen per cent of respondents felt that a significant barrier to crime prevention and community safety activity was the lack of evidence and data available to help inform their approach.

While the main issue regarding resources centred on funding (16%), the second most common resource problem related to a lack of skilled and qualified staff. The resulting skills shortage negatively impacts the ability of LGAs to implement strong crime prevention and community safety initiatives. Often councils relied on volunteers (whose time is limited) or on a single council staff member whose priorities were spread over a number of different areas.

Further, the issue of the absence of suitably qualified or skilled staff is compounded by its relationship with another commonly cited barrier to effective crime prevention activity: a lack of available data and evidence to inform locally based prevention initiatives (16%). This lack of evidence is directly related to a shortage of staff who possess adequate training and/or qualifications to manage crime prevention and community safety. Addressing this skill deficiency would assist in improving the quality of the initiatives implemented by LGAs in Victoria.

Figure 5.11: Evaluations conducted, by presence of formal strategy (n)

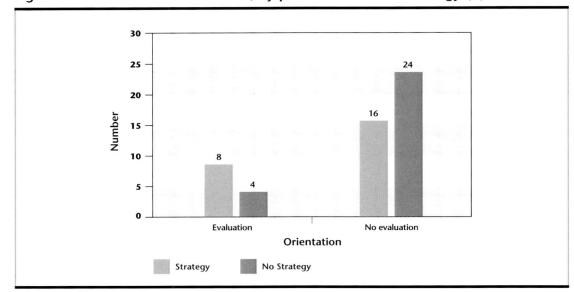

As shown in Figure 5.11, few LGAs are undertaking any form of evaluation with only 12 councils indicating they have been conducting an evaluation. Whether or not it is reasonable to expect LGAs to be undertaking formal evaluation work on their own strategies and activities, this lack of critical review and assessment activity has the potential to inhibit the growth of an already limited knowledge base about effective strategies for local community crime prevention. This in turn has a direct impact on the ability of other local councils to implement their own crime prevention strategies using the formally evaluated experience of others. Furthermore, the lack of robust strategic evaluations means it is difficult to determine the specific and general efficacy of local crime and safety programs.

How a strategy informs the approach

Though not directly assessed in the survey, a number of indicators within the results suggest having a formal strategy in place produces a more informed and tailored approach to crime prevention and community safety.

Figure 5.12: Data sources used to inform crime prevention and community safety issues, by formal strategy (%)

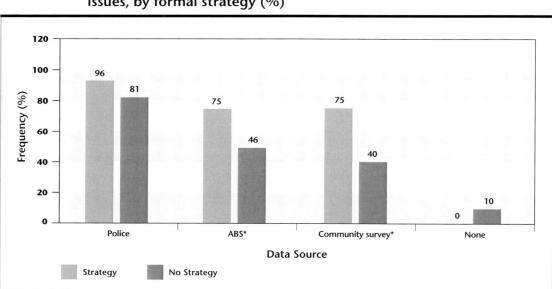

Note: * indicates a significant relationship

Analysis found that significant associations existed between whether a formal strategy was in place in a particular community and the type of information used to identify crime prevention and community safety issues and plan for responses. For example, there is a significant association between an LGA having a formal strategy and using a community survey as part of their planning process.[206] This seems to suggest that councils with a formal crime prevention strategy were more likely to directly consult the community when identifying crime and safety issues.

Similarly, during the development of the strategy, local councils reported high levels of external stakeholder input. Ninety-one per cent of respondents reported consulting with external stakeholders during the strategy formulation phase and 71 per cent engaged in joint strategy implementation, though only eight per cent received any type of funding to undertake this activity. Further, 96 per cent of respondents rated external stakeholder input at this stage as either very useful or useful.

Results also indicated that 83 per cent of local councils sought input into their strategy through consultations with the community or targeted populations. In 75 per cent of cases input was gained by conducting a community survey and in 71 per cent this input was obtained through holding public meetings.

On a more general level, it appears that around half of all councils (49%) reported difficulty in accessing useful data for the purposes of community safety planning and 78 per cent had difficulty in collecting and collating the data they did have access to. These data access difficulties were then reflected in the fact that only 40 per cent reported that they had systems in place to monitor, refresh and update this information.

Strategies tailored to specific communities

Strategies were also tailored to address crime and safety issues relevant to specific populations.

Figure 5.13: Communities identified in crime prevention and community safety strategy (%)

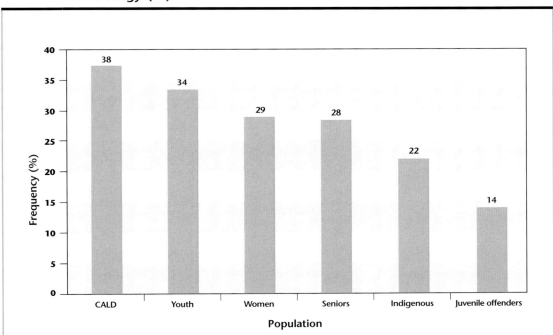

206 $\chi^2(1) = 7.88$, p<0.01

As shown in Figure 5.13, the frequency that a specific population is identified for special attention varies. This most likely reflects differing community composition and associated requirements and problems. However, taken together these results produce a picture of a more informed response to crime and safety issues within the LGA. Specifically, those councils with a formal strategy appear to draw on information from a wider range of sources and have more direct consultation with external stakeholders and the community during the initial planning stages. Further, as shown in Figure 5.13, councils are more likely to report developing and implementing programs or initiatives for specific vulnerable communities as part of their crime prevention strategies.

Partnerships with Neighbourhood Watch

Almost two-thirds of local councils (65%) reported that there was a Neighbourhood Watch (NW) chapter in their area. Twenty-two per cent indicated that they were unaware of whether there was a NW chapter in their area. There were no significant differences between urban or rural councils in terms of this issue.

Figure 5.14: **Councils reporting the presence of Neighbourhood Watch in their LGA (%)**

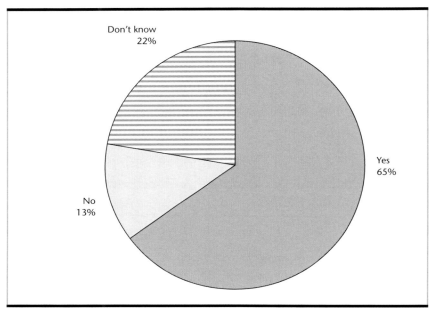

n= 76

Fifty-six per cent believed there was an ongoing role for NW in terms of their local crime prevention and community safety strategies; however 30 per cent did not express a view on this proposition.

Neighbourhood Watch was reported as being involved in local action in a number of ways. The most common activities included:

◆ advising residents on security measures (43%)

◆ disseminating information on crime prevention and community safety issues (49%)

◆ liaising between the community and police (41%).

A further third (35%) said that NW played a role in helping to identify specific community crime and safety issues, one of the original functions that the NW program was set up to fulfil.

The way in which NW chapters were involved in local community safety work varied. Some are active members of community safety committees; others worked as volunteers to help gather information on community safety and crime prevention issues in the area. Other NW chapters were more directly involved in local crime prevention programs through disseminating basic crime prevention and safety information and providing staff for stalls during community safety events.

While only a limited set of views were received from respondents, it appears that NW programs are viewed as useful resources in the crime prevention and community safety agendas of local councils. However, it is also worth noting that there was a lack of consensus regarding the overall relevance of NW.

Some respondents were positive in their evaluations stating:

> 'The group are a vital link for police and council to different sectors of the community that might not be reached otherwise' (Respondent 30).

> 'Neighbourhood watch are instrumental in Council's Community Safety month. They hold two information tables throughout the month and actively promote personal and home safety' (Respondent 16).

Others were less positive, referring to NW programs as 'out dated and irrelevant' and suggesting that they tended to focus on the problem of crime not the solution. However, 95 per cent was of the view that there was some sort of ongoing role for NW in their community's crime prevention and community safety activities. In addition, several respondents suggested that with a change or refreshing of the NW model it could again become a useful element of their community safety programs.

Conclusion

It is clear that the majority of LGAs in Victoria are committed to playing a significant role in the development, coordination and delivery of crime prevention and community safety policies and programs in their local area. While only a minority have specific crime prevention and community safety strategies to guide their activity, a number of others have embedded this strategic process into wider community welfare or health strategies, possibly as a result of being required to produce Health and Wellbeing plans.[207] A small number (around five) suggested that they are in the process of developing such strategies.

Importantly, these survey results have shown the potential value of having a crime prevention and community safety strategy in place regardless of whether it stands alone or is integrated into a wider social plan within the LGA. While not definitive, the findings suggest that local communities that have such plans may well be operating with a framework that will enable a more sustainable program of crime prevention and community safety work to be carried on within the local community. Furthermore, such a finding would be consistent with international good practice and advice for effective crime prevention action.

For some other LGAs, crime prevention and community safety remains a relatively low priority, being seen as the responsibility of other agencies such as police. This may be a quite reasonable position when viewed from the perspective of relatively low crime rates in many communities. However, when viewed through a prevention lens, it is a more problematic position, as crime prevention is essentially about being able to anticipate emerging problems and being prepared to take action to prevent those problems developing and becoming entrenched.

Too often, consideration of the need for developing and implementing a crime prevention strategy is the result of community concern about existing crime problems, problems that could potentially have been prevented from emerging had appropriate preventive action

---

207 See Chapter 7

been taken beforehand. This is another argument for LGAs taking the lead in developing a comprehensive crime prevention strategic plan for their communities as a part of their normal social planning processes. These plans should be regularly updated to reflect changes in the social, demographic, economic and crime characteristics in their communities as well as to accommodate developments in state and national crime prevention priorities.

This is consistent with the finding that the most common and probably the most significant function that LGAs fulfil in their crime prevention and community safety role is that of coordination and facilitation, although it is clear that many also have a significant role in direct service delivery. The coordination and facilitation role is a critically important one because it provides a focus for local leadership on issues of concern to the community, something that has been identified internationally as a vital function for effective and sustainable crime prevention action.

However, one of the most consistent issues identified by the LGAs was that they do not feel adequately equipped to make informed decisions regarding crime prevention and community safety. This was not so much about the lack of adequate financial resources, although this was a problem identified by many, as it was about a lack of skills and technical capacity for maximising the potential benefit to their communities when they do manage to get crime prevention and community safety programs going.

This is highlighted by two related findings. First, there is a high level of difficulty in accessing what is seen to be useful and valuable material for planning local crime prevention activity even though councils generally reported that they had attempted to access this material. Second, there is an almost complete lack of any effective evaluation and performance monitoring work for existing initiatives. As has also been highlighted internationally, the absence of good assessment work inhibits ongoing learning and program development and, ultimately, service improvement (ICPC 2010b).

The survey has also highlighted that while national and state authorities are identified as the major funding bodies for local crime prevention work, it appears that state and national crime prevention policies and priorities are not a major influence on local priorities. It could be argued that the historical tendency on the part of both national and state governments to engage in the crime prevention and community safety agenda in an inconsistent and uncoordinated way has exacerbated this situation (Homel 2006). However, this is probably also a function of the way that LGAs have employed a wide variety of different models for how to plan for and deliver crime prevention and community safety outcomes for their communities. While on the one hand it is reasonable and appropriate for local communities to organise their approach to community crime prevention in a way that best suits their circumstances and the needs of their communities, on the other hand it is also reasonable to expect that these approaches and organisational models would be based on best available evidence for effective strategies.

However, as suggested by the findings, the apparent absence of effective local mechanisms for accessing good practice advice on the most effective and useful approaches to achieving crime prevention and community safety goals inevitably means that the effectiveness and efficiency of local crime prevention action will be compromised and less than optimal. As highlighted by Edgar et al (2006), responsibility for overcoming this problem must be a shared one as different stakeholders will be able to provide access to the different parts necessary for solving the crime prevention puzzle.

The critical element then is the achievement of best value in the effective management of partnerships and collaborative working. The survey has revealed that LGAs have identified this as one of their potentially most important contributions to local crime prevention and community safety, yet it is one of the most difficult tasks to effectively deliver. Partnerships, if managed badly, can be costly and extremely ineffective (Homel 2006).

6. Implementing Crime Prevention Programs: The Victorian Government and its Agencies

Introduction

Crime prevention has had a long although not completely successful history in Victoria. There are a multitude of programs and initiatives today across Victoria that impact in some way on crime prevention or community safety. Many of these, however, do not necessarily or formally fall under the umbrella of crime prevention or community safety per se. Programs focusing on youth development, health or education, for example, are likely to have an impact on crime prevention in that they can produce beneficial outcomes that act as preventive factors or lessen the risks that a person may become involved in criminal activity.[208] Because of this vast array of specifically dedicated crime prevention programs and other initiatives that may have a positive effect on lessening crime and antisocial behaviour it is impossible to outline all programs in Victoria relevant to crime prevention. This chapter therefore focuses on programs and initiatives that are identified as being primarily and specifically about crime prevention.

This chapter begins with a brief history of crime prevention approaches in Victoria then sets out the current approaches by the state government and its agencies, most notably Victoria Police, to addressing crime prevention. The following chapter will discuss in similar terms the crime prevention and community safety initiatives undertaken by local government authorities (LGAs) and community organisations. The approach both chapters take is to discuss the general and conceptual issues applicable to crime prevention amongst different stakeholders such as the police and local government. This discussion will be illustrated by case studies highlighting innovative crime prevention and community interventions. In many cases these initiatives are based on the partnership approaches discussed in Chapter 3. As such, there may often be some overlap as to the 'ownership' of a particular program.[209] The chapter does not include discussion of programs such as Neighbourhood Watch. Whilst Neighbourhood Watch could arguably fall within the rubric of community crime prevention, given the specific remit to discuss it in this Inquiry's Terms of Reference it is separately discussed in Chapter 10 of this Report.

A brief history of crime prevention approaches in Victoria

Despite Victoria leading the way in crime prevention in Australia in a number of respects, formal programs have tended to be cyclical and have fluctuated over the last 30 years.[210] As described in Chapter 1, these cycles of change have had a destabilising and undermining effect on the relationships between central and local partners.[211]

---

208 For further discussion of crime prevention in the context of youth development and social engagement see the Drugs and Crime Prevention Committee, Inquiry into Strategies to Prevent High Volume Offending and Recidivism by Young People, *Final Report* (2009).

209 For example, a program implemented jointly by Victoria Police and a LGA could be equally discussed in the section pertaining to police initiatives as it could in the examination of local government programs.

210 See Chapter 1.

211 See Chapter 1 for a more detailed discussion of these issues.

From the late 1970s Victoria was something of a 'pathfinder for crime prevention in Australia' (Hill & Sutton 1996, p.56), having established and run innovative programs which focused on local neighbourhood crime prevention. Notably, these initiatives included Safety House, providing assistance and refuge to vulnerable children and senior Victorians and Neighbourhood Watch and Crime Stoppers, both significant nation-wide crime prevention partnerships between local residents and police.

Crime prevention was centrally coordinated through dedicated crime prevention agencies from the 1990s. These included the original Crime Prevention Division of the Department of Police and Emergency Services in the early 1990s and VicSafe. These agencies developed and implemented strategies that drew together centralised state coordinated bodies with local bodies (both local government and community agencies). This included multi-agency approaches like the Safe Cities strategy, and the development of locally based police consultative committees through VicSafe.

The lesson learned from Safer Cities and Shires, according to Cherney (2007), was that 'without commitment to the devolution of resources, authority and decision-making powers, partnerships will struggle to effectively deliver State-wide policies on crime prevention and community safety' (p.238). Homel (2009b) similarly attributes the abandonment of the Safer Cities and Shires strategy to both 'a lack of commitment by the central agencies responsible for leading the initiative to establish adequate support and collaborative program delivery mechanisms' (p.28) and a 'lack of consistent leadership and an unwillingness to devolve resources, authority and decision-making powers to local inter-agency partnerships responsible for actually implementing the local level initiatives' (p.28).

From 2000, crime prevention programs were typically centrally administered by Crime Prevention Victoria (CPV). CPV provided support and advice, assistance in the development of innovative and cost-effective programs, strategic data analysis, research and evaluation. In 2002, CPV launched the Victorian Government strategy 'Safer Streets and Homes: A Crime and Violence Prevention Strategy for Victoria.' However, in 2007 CPV was downgraded from a Division to a business unit within the Department of Justice and was later abolished altogether.

From 2007 until 2010 Victoria Police continued to have responsibility for managing or co-managing a number of crime prevention initiatives (including Neighbourhood Watch and Crime Stoppers, along with the employment of Crime Prevention Officers (CPOs) in each police division). However, during this period there was no central coordinating agency or unit to develop, fund, oversee and evaluate crime prevention and partnership programs.

Current state government approaches to crime prevention

A new beginning

Following the 2010 state election, a stand-alone crime prevention portfolio, the Community Crime Prevention Unit (CCPU), was established under the direction of Minister Andrew McIntosh. To address community safety and crime prevention in Victoria, $39 million was allocated in the 2011/2012 budget over four years to support initiatives in these areas,[212] to be administered by the CCPU which was located within the Department of Justice. Ms Julianne Brennan was appointed as its first Director.

The role of the Unit in the area of crime prevention is to:

- Use research and analysis to identify the drivers of crime, and fear of crime, and appropriate responses

- Promote co-ordination across government to embed crime prevention into relevant social and economic policies and services

- Identify and target priority crimes and behaviours in the community with specific strategies to reduce crimes against people and property

- Build and maintain engagement and capability in local communities to implement effective crime prevention responses to local issues.[213]

The Director of the CCPU spoke to the role and function of the Unit and the approach of the government to crime prevention when she gave evidence to the Committee:

> One of the most common assumptions that we face is that crime prevention is really about police and correctional and justice responses, but when you...see the interrelationship of the factors, it's quite clear that this is something that actually requires the community and government as a whole to work together to make an impact. So while the police, courts and corrections are integral to addressing crime prevention, and having a comprehensive approach to that, the kinds of drivers of crime and criminal activities, and indeed victimisation, are complex and really require a collaborative effort; it's beyond the mandate of the justice system alone. In particular, we need to rely on health, education, community development and infrastructure systems as well, which are an important part of addressing some of those underlying drivers of crime and social disorder.[214]

Some of the key ways in which the multifaceted approach to crime prevention promoted by the CCPU can be realised is through the use of partnerships and coordination, both horizontally across government departments and vertically from the centre to the newly established regional reference groups.

The operational framework for the Victorian government's crime prevention and community safety strategy is set out in Figure 6.1. It should also be noted that it is the Committee's interpretation and has not come from the Department of Justice.[215]

---

212 Ms Julianne Brennan, Community Crime Prevention Office, Department of Justice, State Government of Victoria, Evidence given to the Drugs and Crime Prevention Committee, Inquiry into Locally Based Approaches to Community Safety and Crime Prevention, Public Hearing, Melbourne, 27 February 2012.

213 Presentation to the Drugs and Crime Prevention Committee, by Ms Julianne Brennan, Director, Community Crime Prevention Office, Department of Justice Inquiry into Locally Based Approaches to Community Safety and Crime Prevention, Public Hearing, Melbourne, 27 February 2012.

214 Ms Julianne Brennan, Community Crime Prevention Office, Department of Justice, State Government of Victoria, Evidence given to the Drugs and Crime Prevention Committee, Inquiry into Locally Based Approaches to Community Safety and Crime Prevention, Public Hearing, Melbourne, 27 February 2012.

215 Whilst the structure of the CCPU is according to Ms Brennan 'evolving', the Committee nonetheless believes there are some ways in which the role and structure of the unit could be developed further, see discussion in Chapter 12.

Figure 6.1: Current crime prevention structures

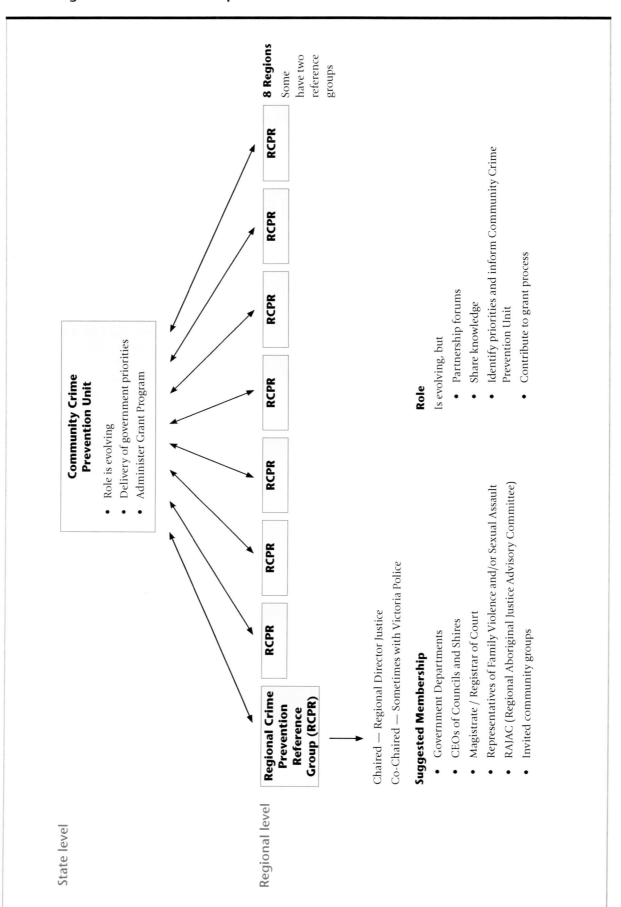

Regional reference groups

In recognition of the key role that local communities have in community crime prevention, the Department of Justice has established crime prevention reference groups corresponding to the Department of Justice administrative regions to support the work of the department and establish partnerships between government departments, local government and the local community.[216] Due to the size of some of the larger areas, some regions have more than one reference group.[217]

The reference groups are chaired by the Department of Justice Regional Directors for the corresponding region, with some also co-chaired by a representative of Victoria Police. Invitations to attend are offered to Chief Executive Officers from each of the local councils within the regions. Some groups also have representatives from key government departments, like the Department of Health, the Department of Human Services (DHS) or the Department of Education and Early Childhood Development. Other invitees can include a 'family violence or sexual assault representative, either the regional integration coordinator or the chair of local regional groups',[218] 'judicial and legal representatives' and chairs of the Regional Aboriginal Justice Advisory Committees, culturally and linguistically diverse (CALD) community representatives and community health services. On occasion the group will also include representatives of business and local associations and chairs of local community safety committees.[219] Ms Julianne Brennan explained to the Committee that the reference groups would evolve over time, but that from a 'government perspective it is seen as critical that there is representation from other key departments... such as health, education, Department of Planning and Community Development, DHS in particular sitting around the table.'[220]

The role of the reference groups, according to Ms Brennan is to act as a conduit between the work of the Justice Department and the crime prevention initiatives of local government and local communities:

> The reference groups are designed to support the work of the department but more broadly to establish partnerships across government represented in those regions with local government and with the local community. So very much about playing a vital role in developing locally based initiatives for community safety and crime prevention, with a strong recognition that one size does not fit all in this space; the challenges that are faced by communities in Mildura or Bendigo are often quite different from those that are faced by communities in East Gippsland or in the Grampians, for example. The establishment of the regional crime prevention reference groups is

---

216 The Department of Justice regions are North-Western (incorporating Banyule, Brimbank, Darebin, Hobsons Bay, Hume, Maribyrnong, Melbourne, Melton, Moonee Valley, Moreland, Nillumbik, Whittlesea, Wyndham, Yarra), Southern-Metropolitan (incorporating Bayside, Cardinia, Casey, Frankston, Glen Eira, Greater Dandenong, Kingston, Mornington, Port Phillip, Stonnington), Eastern Metropolitan (incorporating Boroondara, Knox, Manningham, Maroondah, Monash, Whitehorse, Yarra Ranges), Hume (incorporating Alpine, Benalla, Greater Shepparton, Indigo, Mansfield, Mitchell, Moira, Murrindindi, Strathbogie, Towong, Wangaratta, Wodonga), Gippsland (incorporating Bass Coast, Baw Baw, East Gippsland, Latrobe City, South Gippsland, Wellington), Grampians (incorporating Ararat, Ballarat, Golden Plains, Hepburn, Hindmarsh, Horsham, Moorabool, Northern, Grampians, Pyrenees, West Wimmera, Yarriambiack), Barwon South West (incorporating Colac Otway, Corangamite, Glenelg, Greater Geelong, Moyne, Queenscliff, Southern Grampians, Surf Coast, Warrnambool) and Loddon Mallee (incorporating Buloke, Campaspe, Central Goldfields, Gannawarra, Greater Bendigo, Loddon, Macedon Ranges, Mildura, Mount Alexander, Swan Hill).

217 Ms Julianne Brennan, Community Crime Prevention Office, Department of Justice, State Government of Victoria, Evidence given to the Drugs and Crime Prevention Committee, Inquiry into Locally Based Approaches to Community Safety and Crime Prevention, Public Hearing, Melbourne, 27 February 2012.

218 Ms Julianne Brennan, Community Crime Prevention Office, Department of Justice, State Government of Victoria, Evidence given to the Drugs and Crime Prevention Committee, Inquiry into Locally Based Approaches to Community Safety and Crime Prevention, Public Hearing, Melbourne, 27 February 2012.

219 Ms Julianne Brennan, Community Crime Prevention Office, Department of Justice, State Government of Victoria, Evidence given to the Drugs and Crime Prevention Committee, Inquiry into Locally Based Approaches to Community Safety and Crime Prevention, Public Hearing, Melbourne, 27 February 2012.

220 Ms Julianne Brennan, Community Crime Prevention Office, Department of Justice, State Government of Victoria, Evidence given to the Drugs and Crime Prevention Committee, Inquiry into Locally Based Approaches to Community Safety and Crime Prevention, Public Hearing, Melbourne, 27 February 2012.

bringing together those various parties to ensure that there is a local focus on: what are the issues that are facing our community, what are our priorities?[221]

Ms Brennan added that the reference groups will perform a key function in 'engaging the community in not only identifying the issues but identifying the appropriate local responses'.[222] The CCPU in conjunction with bodies such as the Australian Institute of Criminology (AIC) will assist the reference groups by providing and disseminating evidence based resources such as crime prevention tool kits and templates which in turn will assist communities at local level to develop crime prevention interventions.

In this sense the reference groups function as:

> [a] point of partnership collaboration between the department and broader government, so the other government departments are there and particularly the local government that represents the local community. It is a partnership forum that's designed to both move information up through community crime prevention about what are the issues in the local region, help us understand what are the different issues facing each region and use that to inform our future practice and the framework and the priorities as we move forward but also as a mechanism for us to disseminate information down and out to the community about good practice, about education and engagement in crime prevention initiatives.[223]

Key government priorities for crime prevention in Victoria

Since the election of the coalition government in 2010, a number of key priority areas have been established for crime prevention and community safety. These include strategies to address graffiti, reducing violence against women and children and a greater participation by local communities in developing crime prevention programs through the establishment of a number of grants programs. Another important priority for the government has been the need to ensure that in most cases community crime prevention programs that are funded by the government and/or administered by the CCPU are subject to evaluation and/or performance measurement. These are all key aspects of the government's Community Crime Prevention Program.

The Community Crime Prevention Program

One of the immediate priorities of the CCPU is the delivery of the government's Community Crime Prevention Program (CCPP), a major funding initiative. Ms Julianne Brennan explained to the Committee that this Program has been developed as the CCPU has 'recognised that communities are best placed to identify and prioritise the issues...and develop responses' and that the Unit's role is 'to support them to do so.'[224]

Minister Andrew McIntosh announced that $39 million had been allocated for the CCPP, which consists of:

- $19.7 million for public safety infrastructure — over four years

- $5.25 million for a community safety fund — over four years

- $13.5 million for the anti-graffiti plan — over four years

---

221 Ms Julianne Brennan, Community Crime Prevention Office, Department of Justice, State Government of Victoria, Evidence given to the Drugs and Crime Prevention Committee, Inquiry into Locally Based Approaches to Community Safety and Crime Prevention, Public Hearing, Melbourne, 27 February 2012.

222 Ms Julianne Brennan, Community Crime Prevention Office, Department of Justice, State Government of Victoria, Evidence given to the Drugs and Crime Prevention Committee, Inquiry into Locally Based Approaches to Community Safety and Crime Prevention, Public Hearing, Melbourne, 27 February 2012.

223 Ms Julianne Brennan, Community Crime Prevention Office, Department of Justice, State Government of Victoria, Evidence given to the Drugs and Crime Prevention Committee, Inquiry into Locally Based Approaches to Community Safety and Crime Prevention, Public Hearing, Melbourne, 27 February 2012.

224 Ms Julianne Brennan, Community Crime Prevention Office, Department of Justice, State Government of Victoria, Evidence given to the Drugs and Crime Prevention Committee, Inquiry into Locally Based Approaches to Community Safety and Crime Prevention, Public Hearing, Melbourne, 27 February 2012.

- $550,000 to Neighbourhood Watch — over four years.[225]

These budget initiatives are being rolled out to help build community crime prevention capacity at the local level 'by supporting the community to help identify local crime concerns and interventions and promote involvement and understanding of the way locals can personally help and also minimise their own vulnerability to crime'.[226]

The following are the key components of the government's community crime prevention program for the next four years.

The Anti-Graffiti Plan

Graffiti has been identified by the CCPU as being a significant issue for the community.[227] The Anti-Graffiti Plan includes Graffiti Prevention and Removal Grants between $5,000 and $25,000 for projects including purpose built graffiti trailers, portable removal systems, removal kits, paint vouchers, anti-graffiti coating kits and vouchers, information, education or diversionary initiatives, local based projects and design projects such as the installation of mural art. These grants are complimented by the Graffiti Removal Program, which uses offenders on community based work orders to clean up identified graffiti 'hotspots' and disseminate graffiti information resources, and the Rapid Response Program, which also uses offenders on community based work orders to provide a rapid response to graffiti reports from partner councils.[228]

The Grants Program

As part of the Victorian Government's commitment to having crime prevention programs developed by and for the local communities affected by crime in their areas, a new funding stream has been initiated via community grant programs, which are in addition to dedicated government programs such as the Anti-Graffiti Plan. These include:

- Public Safety Infrastructure Fund Grants
- Community Safety Fund Grants Program
- Reducing Violence Against Women and Children Grants.

Public Safety Infrastructure Fund Grants

This fund provides grants of up to $250,000 for councils to develop public safety infrastructure, such as alarm, lighting and CCTV systems, which will assist community safety and crime prevention in public places. This can pay for the establishment of security systems, relating to the enhancement of existing, or the installation of new, public safety or security assets, or urban design initiatives that help to increase safety, security and confidence in public places, but cannot be used to fund existing projects or ongoing or non-infrastructure costs like staffing, project management or maintenance or servicing.

Objectives of the Infrastructure Fund Grants include to '[b]uild the knowledge base about best practice public safety infrastructure solutions, and capture and share lessons

---

225 http://www.premier.vic.gov.au/media-centre/media-releases/1426-minister-launches-community-safety-grants-for-local-crime-prevention-initiatives.html

The Government's support of Neighbourhood Watch and the organisation generally is discussed in further detail in Chapter 10.

226 Ms Julianne Brennan, Community Crime Prevention Office, Department of Justice, State Government of Victoria, Evidence given to the Drugs and Crime Prevention Committee, Inquiry into Locally Based Approaches to Community Safety and Crime Prevention, Public Hearing, Melbourne, 27 February 2012.

227 Ms Julianne Brennan, Community Crime Prevention Office, Department of Justice, State Government of Victoria, Evidence given to the Drugs and Crime Prevention Committee, Inquiry into Locally Based Approaches to Community Safety and Crime Prevention, Public Hearing, Melbourne, 27 February 2012.

228 Ms Julianne Brennan, Community Crime Prevention Office, Department of Justice, State Government of Victoria, Evidence given to the Drugs and Crime Prevention Committee, Inquiry into Locally Based Approaches to Community Safety and Crime Prevention, Public Hearing, Melbourne, 27 February 2012.

learned'.[229] In addition to and in support of this grant program the CCPU has provided a guide to developing CCTV for public safety in Victoria, which outlines considerations and provides advice in relation to the use of CCTV.

Community Safety Fund Grants Program

The Community Safety Fund Grants Program will fund local crime prevention and community safety projects for community groups, sporting organisations, businesses and local government up to $10,000. Some examples of eligible projects, listed in information guides, include (but are not limited to): security alarms for community facilities; external lighting systems; security screens, fencing and locks; crime prevention information packs; and community safety awareness activities.[230]

The program will not fund projects that: normally receive funding or ongoing costs from another source; seek retrospective funding for projects that have already been started or completed; projects that require ongoing funding beyond the scope of the proposed initiative; or projects that provide ongoing services or programs of work.[231] No evaluation will be required for projects under this program due to the small allocation of funds, although the CCPU has indicated that a template for evaluation will be made available.[232]

Reducing Violence Against Women and Children Grants

Reducing Violence Against Women and Children Grants focus on preventing violence *before* it happens, through early intervention and prevention initiatives. In this sense, 'early intervention' relates to the identification and reduction of risk factors, as opposed to providing services once violence has occurred. The grants are taken to support partnerships at a regional and sub-regional level to deliver programs across a three-year period. Dedicated grant funding will also be available for programs developed by Indigenous communities.

$4.8 million of the new funding program is being made available in grants of up to $600,000 for one project in each Department of Justice region to be implemented over three years. Dedicated funding of $2.4 million is also being provided for programs developed by Koori communities. The Department's Koori Justice Unit is consulting with Regional Aboriginal Justice Advisory Committees about these grants.[233]

Applicants must be a LGA or a not-for-profit organisation that is an incorporated association, an incorporated cooperative, a company or an organisation established under Commonwealth or state/territory legislation (but not a state government department, statutory authority, school or educational institution).[234] Projects cannot be research focused, apply or operate across regions, be currently funded, support services for women and children who have experienced family violence or sexual assault or be for behaviour change services for men who have used violence against women.[235]

According to Ms Julianne Brennan, the regional reference groups will play a key role in the grant administration processes. In particular, the reference groups will identify regional

229 Public Safety Infrastructure Fund: Grant Guidelines,p.3, accessed at http://www.justice.vic.gov.au/resources/9/8/98265 00047cb6f2ca799f76acb98c873/psifgrants-guidelines-web+ready.pdf
230 http://www.justice.vic.gov.au/resources/5/c/5c600a80478e9ce5bebabf3b0ecf4c59/faqs+-+addendum+included.pdf
231 http://www.justice.vic.gov.au/home/community+crime+prevention/community+safety+fund+grants/
232 Ms Julianne Brennan, Community Crime Prevention Office, Department of Justice, State Government of Victoria, Evidence given to the Drugs and Crime Prevention Committee, Inquiry into Locally Based Approaches to Community Safety and Crime Prevention, Public Hearing, Melbourne, 27 February 2012.
233 http://www.justice.vic.gov.au/resources/0/c/0ca052804a59ab3f8eceff23d54abd95/application+guidelines+web+read y.doc
234 http://www.justice.vic.gov.au/resources/1/1/116506804a59ab3f8ed8ff23d54abd95/question+and+answers+informati on+sheet+web+ready.doc
235 http://www.justice.vic.gov.au/resources/1/1/116506804a59ab3f8ed8ff23d54abd95/question+and+answers+informati on+sheet+web+ready.doc

priorities, match expressions of interest to these and make recommendations to the CCPU in relation to the short-listing of the grants process.[236]

Project and program evaluation

The CCPU recognises that evaluation is important to ongoing effectiveness and success and so has tailored 'evaluation mechanisms depending on the type of project and the size of the project'.[237] For the smaller $10,000 local community grants, evaluation templates are provided to recipients and results will be fed into a programmatic evaluation.[238] The larger grants will have a formal evaluation requirement. In addition to this, the CCPU will do programmatic evaluations internally engaging providers 'to look at the processes that we[re] followed, what the response from the community is and whether it's hitting those targets about engaging local community into the process'.[239]

The Department of Justice has recognised that the evaluation of programs that it funds in full or part is crucial in the development and implementation of crime prevention programs.[240] Ms Julianne Brennan stressed to the Committee the need for comprehensive evaluations as part of any evidence based approach to crime prevention. In doing so, however, she stressed that it is important to acknowledge that smaller less funded local agencies may be far less able to perform sophisticated evaluations than a nationwide organisation such as Mission Australia or the Salvation Army.

The issues of evaluation, performance measurement and cost-effectiveness in the development and implementation of crime prevention and community safety programs are discussed further in Chapter 11 of this Report.

Working across departments

The State Government currently contributes to community safety and crime prevention through a broad range of initiatives, services and programs across a number of departments and agencies. In particular, work done through the Departments of Education and Health and Human Services overlaps with the programs offered by the Department of Justice and Victoria Police. For example, the DHS,[241] the Department of Health[242] and the Department of Education and Early Childhood Development[243] all run programs and initiatives focusing on the prevention of violence independently of the programs run through the Department of Justice or the CCPU.

A key objective of the CCPU is improving the coordination and effectiveness of the services that exist, as well as developing new programs to address the gaps. CCPU Director Ms Julianne Brennan described the role as:

236 Ms Julianne Brennan, Community Crime Prevention Office, Department of Justice, State Government of Victoria, Evidence given to the Drugs and Crime Prevention Committee, Inquiry into Locally Based Approaches to Community Safety and Crime Prevention, Public Hearing, Melbourne, 27 February 2012.

237 Ms Julianne Brennan, Community Crime Prevention Office, Department of Justice, State Government of Victoria, Evidence given to the Drugs and Crime Prevention Committee, Inquiry into Locally Based Approaches to Community Safety and Crime Prevention, Public Hearing, Melbourne, 27 February 2012.

238 Ms Julianne Brennan, Community Crime Prevention Office, Department of Justice, State Government of Victoria, Evidence given to the Drugs and Crime Prevention Committee, Inquiry into Locally Based Approaches to Community Safety and Crime Prevention, Public Hearing, Melbourne, 27 February 2012.

239 Ms Julianne Brennan, Community Crime Prevention Office, Department of Justice, State Government of Victoria, Evidence given to the Drugs and Crime Prevention Committee, Inquiry into Locally Based Approaches to Community Safety and Crime Prevention, Public Hearing, Melbourne, 27 February 2012.

240 For a discussion of the CCPU's evaluation requirements for grants programs see Chapter 11.

241 http://www.dhs.vic.gov.au/about-the-department/plans,-programs-and-projects/projects-and-initiatives/women/preventing-violence-against-women-initiatives

242 http://www.health.vic.gov.au/healthpromotion/downloads/violence_ph.pdf

243 http://www.education.vic.gov.au/healthwellbeing/respectfulsafe/unacceptable.htm

[p]romoting co-ordination across all levels of government to embed crime prevention into relevant policies and services; identifying and targeting priority crime behaviours and introducing specific strategies to address those; and then building and maintaining engagement and capability in local communities to implement effective crime prevention initiatives.[244]

The CCPU has indicated that in order to develop best evidence crime prevention programs it is essential to conduct an audit or review of what crime prevention programs are currently being implemented at government level. Minister McIntosh informed the Public Accounts and Estimates Committee at a public hearing in May 2011 that a whole-of-government stocktake of programs contributing to crime prevention objectives would help inform the work of the CCPU.[245]

At the time of writing the Report the findings of this audit are unfortunately not available. The Committee is therefore not able to comment in any depth on the range of policies and initiatives operated by government departments across Victoria. The Committee believes strongly, however, that comprehensive information about the extent and nature of such policies is crucial for ongoing decision making and policy development.

Department of Justice partnerships

The Department of Justice has recognised that crime prevention and community safety are not simply activities that are involved with prosecuting and punishing crime by police and law enforcement officials. As such it has forged a number of formal and informal partnership programs with a variety of stakeholder groups. These range from representation on Commonwealth Government crime prevention bodies such as the Australia and New Zealand Crime Prevention Senior Officers' Group and the Ministerial Council on Police and Emergency Management to working with business groups, welfare peak bodies, community organisations such as Youth Law and academic think-tanks such as the Crime Prevention Through Environmental Design (CPTED) course at RMIT University. This diverse group of partners is testament to the need to take an all-encompassing view of community safety and crime prevention that goes well beyond narrowly prescribed criminal justice models.[246]

Similarly, the Department of Justice auspices other crime prevention initiatives that engage a variety of partners and promote numerous approaches to addressing community safety. One such example is the Neighbourhood Justice Centre (NJC) located within the Yarra municipality of inner city Melbourne. This is a unique partnership between the Department of Justice, local government and community safety and crime prevention service providers. It is worth considering here because it offers a prime example of an independently evaluated and reviewed collaboration of multiple stakeholders at a single location. While it began by offering primarily tertiary preventive services and programs, it has more recently expanded to include primary and secondary preventive activities as well.[247]

Established by the *Court Legislation (Neighbourhood Justice Centre) Act* 2006, the NJC is a 'one-stop shop'[248] of on-site services for victims, civil litigants and community facilities. It provides a court (including a children's court), on-site treatment and support services, counselling, mediation and crime prevention programs and community meeting and networking facilities. Modelled on New York's Red Hook Community Justice Centre, it is the only centre of its kind in Australia. The Centre was evaluated in 2010 and it was

244 Ms Julianne Brennan, Community Crime Prevention Office, Department of Justice, State Government of Victoria, Evidence given to the Drugs and Crime Prevention Committee, Inquiry into Locally Based Approaches to Community Safety and Crime Prevention, Public Hearing, Melbourne, 27 February 2012.

245 Minister McIntosh, Evidence given to the Public Accounts and Estimates Committee, Inquiry into budget estimates 2011–2012, Melbourne 2011.

246 For a list of other partners and partnership projects undertaken by the Department of Justice, see Appendix 12.

247 http://www.neighbourhoodjustice.vic.gov.au/site/page.cfm

248 Rob Hulls, (then) Attorney-General, 'Attorney-General's Column', *Vic Bar News*, May 2007, p.9.

reported that recidivism rates were reduced by seven per cent, 14 per cent better than other courts.[249] Since the establishment of the NJC, the crime rate in Yarra has reduced by 12 per cent. Residential burglaries are down 26 per cent, motor vehicle theft is down 38 per cent and other (mainly commercial) burglaries are down 20 per cent.[250]

The role of Victoria Police in crime prevention and community safety

The most popular methods for implementing crime prevention programs and policies in Victoria and Australia have been through the use of partnership models whereby different stakeholders in the community develop crime prevention and community safety programs in conjunction with government or other non-government or community agencies and organisations.[251] The key players in community crime prevention operating in Victoria today are Victoria Police, local governments and their agencies and non-government and community organisations. The rest of this chapter discusses some of the 'stand-alone' and partnership programs entered into by Victoria Police in the area of crime prevention and community safety, giving examples of some innovative program case studies.[252]

Victoria Police as a Crime Prevention Stakeholder

The involvement of modern policing with crime *prevention* is drawn from the original Peelian principles of policing. Sir Robert Peel, founder of modern policing, identified the prevention of crime and disorder as primary activities for police. Peel also advocated that the effectiveness of police should not be measured by the number of arrests, but by the lack of crime.[253]

Victoria Police recognise that crime prevention is an important part of police work and that effective crime prevention engages and develops partnerships with the 'local community, schools, ethnic communities, local business and other groups'.[254] Indeed under the *Police Regulation Act* each Victorian police officer when taking the oath of office acknowledges his or her duty to prevent crime.[255]

Throughout the state Victoria Police are involved in community safety and crime prevention in various capacities. Apart from their traditional role of policing defined services areas, responding to service calls and providing targeted operations corresponding to local crime issues, police are involved in numerous collaborative crime prevention partnerships with local government and community groups across the state aimed at community capacity building and social inclusion. The wide ranging role of the police and the partners they work with in the area of crime prevention was described by Deputy Commissioner Tim Cartwright when he gave evidence to the Committee in:

> Our role in crime prevention extends from the most local — simple things like advising people on how and where to lock their bikes safely — right through to national and international complex issues around paedophilia, sexual servitude, organised crime and crime importation. They all have aspects of crime prevention, and our relationships with other agencies, with other government departments of course vary in complexity just as much. At the base the local government areas are still critical to everything we do. They share similar objectives about community safety. We

---

249 *Evaluating the Neighbourhood Justice Centre in Yarra, 2007–2009*, Victorian Government Department of Justice, February 2010.

250 http://www.neighbourhoodjustice.vic.gov.au/webdata/resources/files/NJC_evaluation_main_document.pdf

251 Crime prevention partnerships are discussed in greater detail in Chapter 3.

252 Chapter 7 will discuss how crime prevention programs are developed and implemented by local government and community organisations.

253 Submission of Victoria Police to the Drugs and Crime Prevention Committee, Inquiry into Locally Based Approaches to Community Safety and Crime Prevention, April 2012.

254 'Our Focus' from http://www.police.vic.gov.au/content.asp?Document_ID=271 accessed on 20 March 2012.

255 Submission of Victoria Police to the Drugs and Crime Prevention Committee, Inquiry into Locally Based Approaches to Community Safety and Crime Prevention, April 2012.

have our relationships of course with the areas within the Department of Justice in Victoria, the Department of Human Services, the Department of Health, and typically we will work closely with those agencies in achieving similar objectives. At the local level the service organisations like Lions and Rotary are still very important to us, and in local government, as I have said, there will be voluntary agencies. Universities increasingly give us assistance in all sorts of ranges and areas. At the state level we have those government departments, at the national level we have things like the National Motor Vehicle Theft Reduction Council, which I sit on, and Crime Stoppers Australia, and of course Neighbourhood Watch at the local level as well. They are all critical to us.[256]

Crime prevention structures in the Victorian Police

The responsibility for crime prevention in Victoria Police is located in the central, regional and local divisions. Each of the three levels involves intelligence-led crime prevention principles through 'Intelligence Assessments'. For specific crime problems 'Intelligence Practitioners' develop relevant initiatives which have a focus on crime prevention.[257]

At a central level the Crime Department's Crime Strategy Group, the State Tasking and Coordination Committee and the Safer Communities Unit identify and manage crime prevention initiatives. The Safer Communities Unit has been restructured as a result of a departmental review. It is now part of the Media and Corporate Communications Department and is managed by an Inspector and four Victoria Public Service (VPS) staff.

Regionally, the Regional Tasking and Coordination unit processes and identifies priorities and coordinates activities at regional level.

At the local level, Divisional and Police Service Areas (PSAs) are directly involved in the coordination of crime prevention activities. At this level CPOs are directly engaged. Fluctuation or spikes of crimes in certain PSAs may call for local level management.[258]

Victoria Police have stated that the restructuring of policing functions has given crime prevention a greater yet more decentralised priority in police business:

> We have regional community engagement inspectors located in each of the four regions. They are responsible for coordinating the activities of all of our proactive programs — our liaison officers, our crime prevention officers and our Neighbourhood Watch officers

> One of the shifts we have seen recently is a shift to a focus on the regions taking accountability for these sorts of activities more than the centralised model, which is what we had formerly. Now the crime prevention officers belong to the regions but they get strategic advice and training coordinated by the centre. Strategies developed by the centre will then be passed out to the regions and put in place that way.[259]

There has also been a slight move away from specialisation of roles. Deputy Commissioner Cartwright told the Committee that:

> I would say that generally we are trying to move away from the specialised roles to end up with a group of people who can support each other, so we would want to see community engagement skills in there, a mix of crime prevention skills and Neighbourhood Watch knowledge all under the

256 Deputy Commissioner Tim Cartwright, Victoria Police, Evidence given to the Drugs and Crime Prevention Committee, Inquiry into Locally Based Approaches to Community Safety and Crime Prevention, Public Hearing, Melbourne, 16 April 2012.

257 Submission of Victoria Police to the Drugs and Crime Prevention Committee, Inquiry into Locally Based Approaches to Community Safety and Crime Prevention, April 2012.

258 Submission of Victoria Police to the Drugs and Crime Prevention Committee, Inquiry into Locally Based Approaches to Community Safety and Crime Prevention, April 2012.

259 Deputy Commissioner Tim Cartwright, Victoria Police, Evidence given to the Drugs and Crime Prevention Committee, Inquiry into Locally Based Approaches to Community Safety and Crime Prevention, Public Hearing, Melbourne, 16 April 2012.

one umbrella so that whatever the problem is you can pull that group of expertise together and focus on them. At the moment we tend to have silos, [and in the past] that has been a challenge.[260]

Notwithstanding this retreat from specialist roles Victoria Police still sees a place for the position of a discrete Crime Prevention Officer to address crime and community safety at local level.

Crime Prevention Officers (CPOs)

Police engagements with local communities are shaped by both demographically and geographically specific needs and issues that relate to local crime and safety matters. Accordingly, each police PSA has a CPO who acts as a liaison officer to individuals and community groups and provides advice in relation to local community safety problems.[261] The CPO is responsible for developing and implementing programs in partnership with local communities to reduce crime and the fear of crime within his or her area.

> The CPO acts as a liaison officer to individuals, community groups, local government and corporations. They provide advice, source, develop, and implement crime prevention strategies relevant to local community safety priorities in addressing problems/issues.[262]

There are up to 43 full-time and some part-time dedicated CPOs positioned across Victoria. These members are highly skilled at developing crime prevention initiatives and have qualified in the course of CPTED. In recent years Victoria Police have moved to a Crime Desk model where specially trained staff examine crime scenes and support investigations. These 'Crime Scene Officers' also attend the CPTED course and are well positioned to offer advice to victims and other community members in relation to crime prevention. All of the above-mentioned police officers are Operational Safety Tactics and Training (OSTT)[263] qualified and can also be used on the front line depending upon operational needs.[264]

Traditional police involvement with crime prevention

Traditional policing operations are clearly the primary function of Victoria Police. These roles include responses to service calls, arrest and investigatory work, and targeted operations such as those around public order, alcohol and drugs abuse, street offending, burglaries and robberies or road safety. In a narrow sense such tasks can be viewed as crime prevention or at least crime reduction, but they are essentially *reactive* approaches. As important as such work is, the focus of this Inquiry is on the broader definitions of crime prevention and community safety and the *proactive* role of the police in addressing these issues.[265]

The proactive role of the police in crime prevention was expressed well by Inspector Charles Allen of the Greater Dandenong Police when he gave evidence to the Committee:

> Victoria Police is acutely aware that [traditional] responding is treating the symptoms of problems, and to impact on the problems we first of all need to have a full understanding of what the

---

260 Deputy Commissioner Tim Cartwright, Victoria Police, Evidence given to the Drugs and Crime Prevention Committee, Inquiry into Locally Based Approaches to Community Safety and Crime Prevention, Public Hearing, Melbourne, 16 April 2012.

261 'Crime Prevention Officers' from http://www.police.vic.gov.au/content.asp?Document_ID=292 accessed on 20 March 2012.

262 Submission of Victoria Police to the Drugs and Crime Prevention Committee, Inquiry into Locally Based Approaches to Community Safety and Crime Prevention, April 2012.

263 Operational Safety Tactics and Training includes such matters as firearms practice, defensive tactics, conducting searches of persons or premises, and vehicle intercepts.

264 The fact that CPOs can be deployed to other operational duties has, however, been criticised in some quarters. According to this view it is thought that the role of the CPO should be dedicated solely to proactive crime prevention and community safety initiatives and not relegated to an adjunct position after operational duties are finished. See Chapter 3 of this Report.

265 Whilst the work of police associated organisations such as Crime Stoppers and Neighbourhood Watch can at least in part be considered proactive programs, they are discussed separately later in this Report.

problems are. Often the problem or the solution to the problem may generally sit outside what is viewed as a traditional policing response and we may not [always] have the prime role in addressing that problem. However, we also understand our role as important social capital in working with our community partners and partner organisations dealing with social problems.[266]

Police training in crime prevention

Currently there is no specific crime prevention training offered to Victoria Police recruits or probationers. Recruit Training however is moving towards the development of a crime prevention education package as result of a sworn member from the Safer Communities Unit being assigned to Victoria Police's education and training unit.[267] The Detective Training School also incorporates two work shop sessions relating to high volume crime and disruption crime initiatives.[268] Protective Security Officer Training also incorporates one session delivered by a Crime Prevention Officer.

Crime Prevention through Environmental Design courses are also offered to all sworn staff by Victoria Police and are self funded. These courses are run bi-annually and offer a comprehensive curriculum over 2 weeks with theory and practice in reducing crime, risk shifting and target hardening of premises.[269]

A senior Victoria Police officer also offers half day community engagement presentations to every Senior Sergeant Qualification Program and Inspector Qualification Program utilising case studies from Local Area Commanders (LAC's) and divisional managers. Crime Prevention Officers, Neighbourhood Watch Liaison Officers and other dedicated liaison officers all participate in courses dedicated to their particular line of work. For example, the most recent 3 week Youth Resource Officer course finished in April 2012. Partnering with non government organisations (NGOs), Victoria Police also ran an intensive Gay and Lesbian Liaison Officer (GLLO) course last year for portfolio GLLOs from across the State, concentrating on the high levels of unreported domestic violence and physical injury that is suffered by members of these communities.[270]

Despite such welcome initiatives the Committee still believes that Victoria Police recruits are not receiving comprehensive or uniform training in crime prevention at any stage during the two year probationary training period. As such the Committee has recommended comprehensive and consistent training in crime prevention during the probationary period.

A new approach — community engagement and partnerships in crime prevention

A community partnership approach to policing has become a specific part of the state government's approach to crime prevention. Victoria Police has now an extensive range of partnerships that contribute to crime prevention at both the state and local level. In a presentation to the Committee, CPPU Director Ms Julianne Brennan indicated that:

- Whilst the Department of Justice has a key role in the lead, coordination and collaboration across government, the strength of Victoria Police activity is in the facilitation, implementation and engagement in partnerships, particularly at the local level

---

266 Inspector Charles Allen, Greater Dandenong Police Service Area, Victoria Police, Evidence given to the Drugs and Crime Prevention Committee, Inquiry into Locally Based Approaches to Community Safety and Crime Prevention, Public Hearing, Dandenong, 30 May 2011.

267 Submission of Victoria Police to the Drugs and Crime Prevention Committee, Inquiry into Locally Based Approaches to Community Safety and Crime Prevention, April 2012.

268 For example one of these sessions focuses on the Box Hill train station as a case study looking at how crime prevention relates to intelligence led responses, community and private industry involvement, and the placement of environmental design, including CCTV.

269 For a discussion of CPTED including 'target hardening', see Chapter 2.

270 Submission of Victoria Police to the Drugs and Crime Prevention Committee, Inquiry into Locally Based Approaches to Community Safety and Crime Prevention, April 2012.

- There are over 100 sworn and unsworn police employees who have various liaison roles and responsibilities for the partnership in and delivery of various crime prevention programs

- Victoria Police participates in or leads some 500 locally based crime prevention programs.[271]

Victoria Police spoke to the importance of crime prevention partnerships in a submission to the Committee:

> Victoria Police seek to develop links within the local community, schools, ethnic communities, local business and other groups to reduce the incidence and impact of crime. Victoria Police understands the importance of community and other partnerships in reducing crime and in providing a safer place to live. Partnerships are achieved through community based crime prevention programs such as Neighbourhood Watch and Crime Stoppers and a network of full time Crime Prevention Officers. Community consultation and education are key parts of this process. Current knowledge about effective crime prevention strategies comes from evaluation, research and anecdotes about successful and unsuccessful programs and strategies used in the past. Some of these strategies have very little to do with the police, while others involve the police in important ways. Crime prevention efforts involving the police represent just one stream among many types of crime prevention efforts. Police, however, cannot do this work alone and it is important that there is an integrated whole of Victoria Government approach to crime prevention. Police play a vital role, and on many occasions a leading role, but not the only one.[272]

Victoria Police also participates in the activities of local Community Safety Committees with local councils and other key stakeholders. The level of coordination is managed and progressed through Local Area Commanders and special units within Victoria Police including community focused departments. In general terms the subject matter will define the appropriate area of the force. In all cases a liaison officer will be appointed and is responsible for reporting on the initiatives' progress.[273]

On occasions Victoria Police might run campaigns alongside the Department of Justice. An example of this was the 'Assault reduction strategy' in 2009. Another example of a Victoria Police operation that included proactive crime prevention and partnership components was 'Operation Guardian' conducted in 2010.[274]

In relation to the Neighbourhood Watch Program, Victoria Police currently funds 26 full-time positions in the role of Neighbourhood Watch Divisional Police Coordinator. These members are responsible for direct liaison and partnership with volunteers and provide them with direction and support in relation to the conduct of the program and the development of crime prevention strategies to support a reduction of crime and enhanced community safety.[275]

Some of these partnership programs are profiled in the following sections.

---

271 Presentation to the Drugs and Crime Prevention Committee by Ms Julianne Brennan, Director, Community Crime Prevention Office, Department of Justice, Inquiry into Locally Based Approaches to Community Safety and Crime Prevention, Public Hearing, Melbourne, 27 February 2012.

272 Submission of Victoria Police to the Drugs and Crime Prevention Committee, Inquiry into Locally Based Approaches to Community Safety and Crime Prevention, April 2012.

273 Submission of Victoria Police to the Drugs and Crime Prevention Committee, Inquiry into Locally Based Approaches to Community Safety and Crime Prevention, April 2012.

274 'Operation Guardian' implemented crime prevention initiatives to reduce crime and assaults upon Victoria's Indian population. Between 2009/10, International students predominately from India were being assaulted and robbed in large numbers. This was a state-wide issue with ramifications and poor publicity for the Victorian Government, Victorian Tourism, tertiary education/colleges and Victoria Police. Investigation indicated that Indian students were working in industries across Victoria which exposed them to higher levels of being victims of crime. (e.g. taxi industry, 24-hour convenience stores) This was a state-wide problem managed centrally and focused on re-active patrols, risk management, crime prevention initiatives and community education. Simply because of the size and scope of the project, this warranted central management and involved many stakeholders. See Submission of Victoria Police to the Drugs and Crime Prevention Committee, Inquiry into Locally Based Approaches to Community Safety and Crime Prevention, April 2012.

275 Submission of Victoria Police to the Drugs and Crime Prevention Committee, Inquiry into Locally Based Approaches to Community Safety and Crime Prevention, April 2012.

Police partnership case studies[276]

The Assertive Youth Outreach Service and the Dandenong Police

An example of community development work undertaken by Police that extends beyond 'enforcement' and engages with specific social or ethnic groups is the Assertive Youth Outreach Service (AYOS). This program is run by Greater Dandenong Police in partnership with the Victorian Multicultural Commission, the City of Greater Dandenong, the Youth Support and Advocacy Service (YSAS) and other community agencies. AYOS is a component of the City of Greater Dandenong's 'Connections For At Risk Young People' initiative, which was piloted in 2009.

There is a specific focus on the needs of young refugees, which in practice in this municipality has meant the outreach has been primarily to members of the local Sudanese community.[277] The AYOS program provides a service to local youth to assist them develop a sense of community. A key aspect of this program is building a sense of social inclusion and community for individuals who may otherwise feel excluded or disconnected. The program also works to develop positive relationships between police and youth. AYOS offers support relating to personal safety, monitoring for intoxication and overdose, help with health, accommodation and material aid needs. It provides harm minimisation strategies, information on drug-related harms (including the Needle Syringe Program) and helps young people with mental health, social and legal problems.[278]

Crime prevention and community safety is achieved through the combination of services only possible through the collaboration of the various partners. Partnership has been critical to the success of AYOS.[279] As Inspector Allen highlighted, '[t]he strength and success of this service has been the strength of the relationships between the service providers'.[280] Mr Warren Eames, Manager of Community Programs at YSAS, also spoke to the importance of the partnership approach when he presented to the Committee:

> I would emphasise the strength of the relationship between youth services and police, both routine and formal communications but also a fantastic, more informal relationship building which I think has benefited both sectors in terms of understanding the imperatives of each service. The real key to this, apart from Assertive Outreach, the late night work that has occurred has been...engaging and integrating mainstream services for this group for a whole range of outcomes in terms of not only social but also primary health, family engagement and support around involvement with the legal system as well.[281]

The Sudanese Youth Leadership Development Program

The Sudanese Youth Leadership Development Program (SYLDP) is another capacity building program led by Victoria Police in the Greater Dandenong area in conjunction with the City of Greater Dandenong, local Sudanese community groups, the Victorian Multi-Cultural Commission, the Community Support Grants Program and Rotary. A major aim of the program is to break down the mistrust felt by younger members of the Sudanese community, particularly young men, towards the local police. The SYLDP currently runs for 10 weeks and is being offered to 24 Sudanese youths from the Greater Dandenong area.

---

276 In addition to these case studies that are examined in detail, Appendix 13 outlines a comprehensive list of crime prevention initiatives that Victoria Police are currently engaged in either as a sole organisation or in partnership with other stakeholders.

277 http://www.ag.gov.au/Crimepreventionandenforcement/Pages/NationalYouthPolicingModel.aspx

278 http://www.ysas.org.au/specialist-programs/assertive-street-outreach

279 http://www.ag.gov.au/Crimepreventionandenforcement/Pages/NationalYouthPolicingModel.aspx

280 Inspector Charles Allen, Greater Dandenong Police Service Area, Victoria Police, Evidence given to the Drugs and Crime Prevention Committee, Inquiry into Locally Based Approaches to Community Safety and Crime Prevention, Public Hearing, Dandenong, 30 May 2011.

281 Mr Warren Eames, Manager, Community Programs, Youth Support and Advocacy Service (YSAS), Evidence given to the Drugs and Crime Prevention Committee, Inquiry into Locally Based Approaches to Community Safety and Crime Prevention, Public Hearing, Dandenong, 30 May 2011.

The program consists of workshops that will cover topics including leadership styles, project management, submission writing, public speaking and employment readiness. Participants will also have the opportunity to discuss their right and responsibilities and law and order matters.

At the completion of the program, the group will be encouraged to develop a project that will benefit their community. This may include organising a sports or arts event or a program that would support community development.

Inspector Bruce Wemyss, one of the key police organisers of the program, spoke to the Committee about the benefits of the partnerships and particularly the importance of having young people from the community heavily involved in the design and development of the project:

> What we did is bring a whole lot of young people that were picked by their own community to sit down with us and design a program that would benefit them and they had some ownership. The group of boys that were chosen helped us develop the program and as a result of that we have a series of young people now within the local community that we would class as people we can go to, as young people, to give us advice and guidance on issues affecting youth, particularly in this case…Sudanese youth.

> This is an interchangeable program. It would be a matter of sitting down with any particular culture and saying, 'What are the needs? What are the things you need to learn more about as a potential leader in your community?' We would sit there and help develop that. It is not a traditional role for us as police to present this course and I was not in a position where I could present everything. I am not for example an expert on employment issues. We had people coming in to talk about those things. We had an employment readiness session where young people could come in and work with local service providers in preparing themselves for employment. We had people come in and talk about public speaking from toastmasters. We had local council representatives come in and talk about issues that related to council business — applying for grants, funding for projects.[282]

Mr Tito Agout, a young Sudanese man, is one of the original participants of the program who after working in partnership with the police and other community representatives is now seeking to become a police officer himself:

> It was really a good program for us because we do learn about leadership styles. We also learn about police roles and how we could become leaders in our communities and how we can be connecting police with our youth… Me personally, I have learned a lot in this program and I have learned about the police force, and it has given me the confidence of how to become a leader too and how I could help my community with Victoria Police and other communities.[283]

Dandenong Police Working Together with Maori and Pacific Islander Communities

In 2008 Dandenong Police began engaging with Maori and Pacific Island youth after noticing the increasing representation of this group in the crime statistics for the greater Dandenong region. Increasingly this group became more and more involved in violent offending and antisocial behaviour. Recognising this cultural group as particularly vulnerable to crime, Victoria Police began a series of community safety and crime prevention initiatives focused on 'diversionary' activities — to build youth resilience through sport, and also to build relations between youth and police. These early initiatives spanning 2008–2011

282 Inspector Bruce Wemyss, Community Engagement Inspector, Greater Dandenong Police Service Area, Victoria Police, Evidence given to the Drugs and Crime Prevention Committee, Inquiry into Locally Based Approaches to Community Safety and Crime Prevention, Public Hearing, Dandenong, 30 May 2011.

283 Mr Tito Agout, Representative from Sudanese Youth Leadership Development Program, Evidence given to the Drugs and Crime Prevention Committee, Inquiry into Locally Based Approaches to Community Safety and Crime Prevention, Public Hearing, Dandenong, 30 May 2011.

were focused mainly around backyard rugby programs, and largely driven by the CPOs of Dandenong Police.

The police have since been working in partnership on these and other projects with 'Three Seas', a community based initiative and registered non-government organisation (NGO) that gives leadership and guidance to projects involving the Maori and Pacific Islander communities in the greater Dandenong region. The work of 'Three Seas' is discussed further in Chapter 7.

Rationalising referral pathways — the police and Interdisciplinary Triage Teams

The concept of Interdisciplinary Triage Teams (ITT) provides for early intervention when people in need of assistance first come in contact with police. It rationalises referral pathways at the police/community services interface by establishing teams of community service professionals. This is a whole-of-government, cross-sectoral approach, that empowers local people to solve local problems. Mr John Thexton, one of the key initiators of this approach, spoke to the Committee about the frustrations police had with the referral system in the context of people with mental illness whom they have encountered in the course of their duties:

> Basically, the concept started around about 2000 when I had a meeting with Plenty Valley Community Health. The concern then was that people with drug and alcohol issues were continually coming to the notice of police. What we thought was that if we were able to intervene as close to the time of arrest as possible, we would be able to get them into drug and alcohol counselling and try to prevent their recidivism. Obviously a lot of the families of the various people who were involved were at their wits' end. The people who we were looking to help at that particular stage were quite often people who were addicted to heroin or other drugs, and basically they were stealing to support their habit. They were committing large numbers of burglaries, street robberies and that type of thing... But as I think everybody acknowledges, nobody has just one issue; quite often they are interrelated. Basically what we had was a small segment of the population that took up an enormous amount of police and emergency services time and resources... if this segment of the population can be engaged and can receive appropriate assistance, re-attendance by police and emergency services can be dramatically reduced. That has a number of implications for policing. One is that the police can then concentrate on other issues. As I say to my members, there are plenty of crooks out there; we do not need to be catching the same ones all the time. So it frees up police resources.[284]

Individual sectors of the health and community services have also recognised the need to take a more integrated approach. A submission to the Committee on the work of the ITTs states that:

> This approach offers the next step in going beyond integration of services within sectors and departments at a local level. It demonstrates that an integrated response across a wide range of community services can be achieved, whilst bridging the justice/health interface.[285]

People involved in the concept include operational police, experienced police family violence advisers, leaders in community services and academics. Also included are community service professionals from a number of disciplines who say that working in this team environment has not only improved their professional relationship with police but has also had a positive influence on how they work within the community service sector to achieve better outcomes for people referred by police. A submission to the Committee by people involved with the formation of the ITTs states that:

---

284 Mr John Thexton, Evidence given to the Drugs and Crime Prevention Committee, Inquiry into Locally Based Approaches to Community Safety and Crime Prevention, Public Hearing, Melbourne, 9 August 2011.

285 Submission from Mr John Thexton, Dr Rae Walker, Ms Eleni Wellings and Dr Raul Foglia to the Drugs and Crime Prevention Committee, Inquiry into Locally Based Approaches to Community Safety and Crime Prevention, May 2011.

A significant component of police work involves working with members of our community who are in crisis, who have committed offences, are at risk of doing so, or who are linked with such people as victims or family members. Many would potentially benefit from a range of health and welfare services. Effectively addressing health and welfare issues that contribute to increased risk of offending, revictimisation or harm is an important crime, violence and social disorder prevention strategy. A key issue for operational police who come into contact with people who have health and welfare needs is to develop the capacity to effectively link these people to the primary health care system and a key issue for primary health care is to develop systems that effectively deal with a population group that frequently has special needs and can be difficult to engage.[286]

The justice/health relationship according to the authors of the submission has been developed in an ad-hoc, issue by issue approach, which has 'generated a plethora of referral criteria and burgeoning referral pathways, creating gaps, confusion and frustration particularly for operational police leading to missed opportunities for enhanced social outcomes and community safety'.[287] The adoption of an ITT approach essentially rationalises the referral process for police. The ITTs of community health professionals include Alcohol and Other Drugs, Mental Health, and Family Violence and Child and Family counsellors who are established at a municipal/police service area level. These teams provide police and other emergency services a dedicated point of referral to:

♦ respond to any issue not requiring an immediate crisis response by contacting the person referred within 24 hours, taking advantage of a 'window of opportunity' to positively intervene

♦ respond to victims and offenders or any person in need of assistance who agrees to a referral.

'Interdisciplinary Triage Teams create an efficient system of work by using existing resources — i.e. the police — to link these most marginalised and hidden populations to appropriate services'.[288] Mr John Thexton told the Committee that in effect the ITT process is building on relationships and partnerships that have often been in existence but engaging them in a more systematic and rational way:

In some respects and in reality police are basically an outreach service and a way of connecting people who are, as we have already laid out, difficult to engage. In many localities there are already good relationships between police and primary health-care agencies, but what we are talking about here is enhancing that. Basically what we are talking about is taking an interdisciplinary approach, because at the moment there are a whole lot of referral pathways from police to community services — for example, you have drug and alcohol — which is a fragmented and limited way of getting people across to those services. It is perhaps most advanced in relation to family violence, where referrals are made. There is a whole range of areas that really have no formal referral pathways.

[We are] basically enabling police to make referrals to one area and then community services coming together and forming interdisciplinary teams. Some of the advantages of that are that in the past people have fallen through the cracks because they do not fit the criteria or whatever. Also the advantage of this concept is that a lot of it is really about building relationships. The program is located in the police station, so it is about building relationships with the police, it is about building relationships with the community services and it is about maintaining those relationships.

---

286 Submission from Mr John Thexton, Dr Rae Walker, Ms Eleni Wellings and Dr Raul Foglia to the Drugs and Crime Prevention Committee, Inquiry into Locally Based Approaches to Community Safety and Crime Prevention, May 2011.

287 Submission from Mr John Thexton, Dr Rae Walker, Ms Eleni Wellings and Dr Raul Foglia to the Drugs and Crime Prevention Committee, Inquiry into Locally Based Approaches to Community Safety and Crime Prevention, May 2011.

288 Submission from Mr John Thexton, Dr Rae Walker, Ms Eleni Wellings and Dr Raul Foglia to the Drugs and Crime Prevention Committee, Inquiry into Locally Based Approaches to Community Safety and Crime Prevention, May 2011.

> In country Victoria it works well. In one respect it has to work in country Victoria because you have limited resources, therefore people have to work together.[289]

Northern Assessment Referral and Treatment Team

The key model established to use an interdisciplinary triage approach is the Northern Assessment Referral and Treatment Team (NARTT).

This was established in May 2003 and initially funded as a pilot program by the then Crime Prevention Victoria. The program operates in the police service areas covering the municipalities of Darebin and Whittlesea in the northern suburbs of Melbourne. It receives referrals from three 24-hour police stations and operates from Plenty Valley Community Health. The NARTT pilot evaluation of 2004 describes this effective Interdisciplinary Triage Team approach in detail. The evaluation found:

> NARTT performs a valuable, effective and integral role in the local service sector. It is complementary to existing programs and services, adding value to the local service network; has met and exceeded funding agreement objectives; and has developed an outstanding and reliable partnership with partnership police stations, contributing to groundbreaking cultural shifts and opportunities for separate sectors to come together.[290]

Since 2003 the NARRT model and its conceptual basis of interdisciplinary triage has been replicated in other areas of Victoria and has been well received. These areas have included rural districts such as Echuca and Goulburn. The submission about NARTT includes the following quote from a Leading Senior Constable in rural Victoria:

> As operational members we attend numerous incidents where the job we have responded to is often just a person who needs some time spent with them due to them being lonely, depressed, suicidal, suffering some form of financial hardship or dealing with issues be that with a partner, sibling, child or parent. The job is often not a criminal matter. We don't have the time, resources or expertise to stay with them & hear all their troubles & issues. This is why [this] system is such a useful tool. We find if they know someone will contact them & discuss their issues at length, there is some light at the end of the tunnel and all isn't doom and gloom, which is often how it appears when we first arrive. The perception by the person concerned is also that we also care and have been of some assistance.[291]

Operation Newstart

Operation Newstart (ON) is a partnership between Victoria Police and the Department of Education and Early Childhood Development providing early intervention for young people aged 14 to 17 who are enrolled in Victorian state secondary colleges and are deemed to be at significant educational and social risk. Characteristically, participants demonstrate these risk factors:

1. Low level truancy

2. First contact with police

3. Emerging mental health issues

4. Experimentation with alcohol and other drugs

5. Family conflict

6. An unstable peer group.[292]

---

289 Mr John Thexton, Evidence given to the Drugs and Crime Prevention Committee, Inquiry into Locally Based Approaches to Community Safety and Crime Prevention, Public Hearing, Melbourne, 9 August 2011.

290 Submission from Mr John Thexton, Dr Rae Walker, Ms Eleni Wellings and Dr Raul Foglia to the Drugs and Crime Prevention Committee, Inquiry into Locally Based Approaches to Community Safety and Crime Prevention, May 2011.

291 Submission from Mr John Thexton, Dr Rae Walker, Ms Eleni Wellings and Dr Raul Foglia to the Drugs and Crime Prevention Committee, Inquiry into Locally Based Approaches to Community Safety and Crime Prevention, May 2011.

292 Submission from Mr Phil Wheatley for the Executive, Operation Newstart, to the Drugs and Crime Prevention Committee, Inquiry into Locally Based Approaches to Community Safety and Crime Prevention, May 2011.

Many of ON participants have had a previous history of involvement with the juvenile justice system including:

- 13% having contact with police officers
- 33% having been cautioned by police
- 15% having made a court appearance prior to entering the program.[293]

Intervention is facilitated by a full-time police officer and a full-time outdoor education teacher who together, and in conjunction with a number of external agencies, provide multi-layered outdoor, recreational, vocational and therapeutic experiences during a complete school term (approximately 10 weeks).

This is an intensive program for students who are at real risk of becoming totally disengaged from schooling, their families and their communities. Such young people have a heightened risk of committing crime, reckless driving, becoming victims of crime and involvement in reckless risk-taking behaviour.

ON programs are established in response not just to a community need but, significantly, also in response to an initiative taken at *local* level such as, 'The initiative of a local police officer, a student wellbeing coordinator, a teacher, parent, social worker in the local CAMHS [Child & Adolescent Mental Health Services], a youth worker employed in local government'. Once taken, the decision to form an ON program involves many other local stakeholders:[294]

> ON has always been aware of the importance of involving its facilitators in enhancing operational police members' interactions with youth. This has been most highly developed in Operation Newstart Western where every newly appointed constable (Probationary Constable Extended Training members) spends 2 weeks on the program. At the end of each program each member provides a critique and is also assessed by the facilitators on their participation and input. Operation Newstart Casey has recently been approved to implement a one day training program for a range of operational members. This is an area where ON can envisage facilitators having an expanded role, with benefits including less complaints against police, better outcomes for youth in critical incidents and as part of a strategy to reduce levels of disengagement from Victoria Police by operational police members.[295]

The results of ON have generally been very positive. Following the ON program, participants reported significant improvement in their socio-emotional wellbeing. Parents and teachers also reported improvement in several aspects of emotion and behavioural control. Data was analysed for 168 referrals accepted into the ON program, of which 132 completed the program and 36 did not. Overall, those who did not complete ON had more frequent encounters with the law including field contact, court appearances and charges. Participants who completed ON have made significantly fewer court appearances.[296] In 2010 ON was one of five projects recognised at a national level as a winner of an Australian Crime and Violence Prevention Award.[297]

Representatives from the Newstart program however told the Committee that Victoria Police has indicated its intention, for operational reasons, to reduce its commitment from

---

293 Submission from Mr Phil Wheatley for the Executive, Operation Newstart, to the Drugs and Crime Prevention Committee, Inquiry into Locally Based Approaches to Community Safety and Crime Prevention, May 2011.

294 Submission from Mr Phil Wheatley for the Executive, Operation Newstart, to the Drugs and Crime Prevention Committee, Inquiry into Locally Based Approaches to Community Safety and Crime Prevention, May 2011.

295 Submission from Mr Phil Wheatley for the Executive, Operation Newstart, to the Drugs and Crime Prevention Committee, Inquiry into Locally Based Approaches to Community Safety and Crime Prevention, May 2011.

296 Submission from Mr Phil Wheatley for the Executive, Operation Newstart, to the Drugs and Crime Prevention Committee, Inquiry into Locally Based Approaches to Community Safety and Crime Prevention, May 2011.

297 Representatives from the Newstart program however told the Committee that Victoria Police has indicated its intention, for operational reasons, to reduce its commitment from a full-time police officer for each program to a part-time position for each program. At the moment negotiations are taking place with Victoria Police to 'find the best outcome for Operation Newstart in that regard' (Mr Phil Wheatley, Executive Director, Operation Newstart Victoria, Evidence given to the Drugs and Crime Prevention Committee, Inquiry into Locally Based Approaches to Community Safety and Crime Prevention, Public Hearing, Geelong, 10 August 2011).

a full-time police officer for each program to a part-time position for each program. At the moment negotiations are taking place with Victoria Police to 'find the best outcome for Operation Newstart in that regard'.[298] The Committee questioned Deputy Police Commissioner Tim Cartwright about the future of Operation Newstart when he gave evidence to the Committee. He confirmed that to a certain extent the program was being downscaled due to budgetary considerations:

> One of the challenges we face is where we put our limited resources, so Newstart has been reviewed. We are still involved but not to the same level that we were. My understanding was that each of the Newstart had a full-time police officer involved with a full-time education officer, so we would see that officer doing nothing for the year other than the Newstart, which was terrific for those kids but a very limited application of the small resources we have had, so we made a decision, around Newstart at least, to draw back a bit around that. It is always a challenge for us, the balancing act; it is where you get best bang for your buck.[299]

The Police and Community Youth Assist Program

The Police and Community Youth Assist Program is a local program (initially piloted in the Frankston area) that identifies young people at risk of involving themselves in antisocial and criminal behaviour and aims to divert them away from crime through diversion, intervention and prevention strategies. It works as a major partnership between Victoria Police, Mission Australia, the City of Frankston and a considerable number of other community agencies.[300]

The program offers individually tailored action plans and 'sustainable pathways' based on a case management framework. It aims to enhance the health and wellbeing of young persons and to encourage sustainable education and employment.

The program relies heavily on police Youth Resource Officers to explore the use of discretion where appropriate to divert a young person from the negative outcomes of the criminal justice system.

It also aims to provide the young person where possible with access to intensive support programs including mental health services, accommodation, alternatives to school, drug and alcohol programs, family welfare and counselling services and employment services, with the ultimate aims of reducing antisocial behaviour, recidivism and of promoting social inclusion.

---

298 Mr Phil Wheatley, Executive Director, Operation Newstart Victoria, Evidence given to the Drugs and Crime Prevention Committee, Inquiry into Locally Based Approaches to Community Safety and Crime Prevention, Public Hearing, Geelong, 10 August 2011).

299 Deputy Commissioner Tim Cartwright, Victoria Police, Evidence given to the Drugs and Crime Prevention Committee, Inquiry into Locally Based Approaches to Community Safety and Crime Prevention, Public Hearing, Melbourne, 16 April 2012

300 Other community support agencies involved with the program include:
  • Anglicare
  • FIFS Frankston Integrated Family Services & Child First
  • PYFS Peninsula Youth and Family Services
  • YSAS Youth Substance Abuse Service
  • PENDAP Peninsula Drug & Alcohol Program, Peninsula Integrated Health
  • Peninsula Sexual Assault Centre
  • Frankston Integrated Health Centre
  • Peninsula Community Legal Centre
  • Frankston Ambassadors (Frankston Council, Outreach)
  • CAMHS, Child and Adolescent Mental Health Service Crisis Centre
  • Headspace Peninsula
  • Salvation Army (Emergency Accommodation)
  • Taskforce Community Agency (Employment, Education & Support Services)
  • LLEN, Local Learning Employment Network (Employment, Education and Training Co-ordinator)
  • Chisholm Institute (Educational Facility)
  • Hands On Learning (Alternate Learning Options within Secondary Colleges)
  • Department of Human Services, Adolescent Team
  • Department of Education, Southern Region.

One of the key people involved with developing the program is Leading Senior Constable Renée Bloomfield, a Youth Resource Officer with the Frankston Police. She spoke to the Committee about the benefits of working in partnership with other agencies to help prevent and reduce youth crime in the Frankston area:

> Five years ago we looked at the role of youth resource officer and said, 'What contributes to youth crime? What are the causal factors? What are the issues that impact upon youth being antisocial and contribute to community behaviour?' We looked at documents, such as the World Health Organization social determinants of health, also much of the Australian Institute of Criminology Research done by Ross Homel and his associates. We also looked then at some of the issues that pertained particularly to Frankston and we had documents that had been undertaken by the Frankston Partnership which is the executive committee of Frankston Police, Frankston Council, Department of Justice, Department of Education and Early Childhood Development, DPCD [Department of Planning and Community Development] and I think the Brotherhood of St Laurence...What we are starting to understand from a policing perspective is that youth and crime is very complex and as articulated by Ross Homel from the Australian Institute of Criminology, in order to take preventative strategy it needs to be a multifaceted partnership approach.
>
> ...It needs to be able to look at many of the risk factors...and take a collaborative community approach to address many of these complex issues. Recognising that a steering committee was established that links with over 20 community support agencies in Frankston — Frankston Council being one of them — the strategy was equipped to deal with any youth issue that came before us. In short, Victoria Police explored our traditional and contemporary measures of policing to ensure that we do provide positive outcomes for young people.[301]

Youth welfare agencies have been enthusiastic about integrated and coordinated approaches such as Youth Assist and see them as more positive responses to youth at risk than the punitive measures of increased surveillance and 'move on' laws. For example, a joint submission from Youthlaw, The Youth Affairs Council of Victoria and the Peninsula Community Legal Centre to the Frankston City Council states there is a need to:

> Enhance existing programs [such as] the Frankston Police & Community Youth Assist Program that offer holistic approaches to youth issues and adopt multi-agency involvement to address complex issues.[302]

Victoria Police officers have also been enthusiastic about the aims and efforts of the program.[303]

The Youth Assist Program has been favourably evaluated by the Youth Research Centre at the University of Melbourne.

---

301 Leading Senior Constable Reneé Bloomfield, Youth Resources Office, Frankston, Victoria Police, Evidence given to the Drugs and Crime Prevention Committee, Inquiry into Locally Based Approaches to Community Safety and Crime Prevention, Public Hearing, Frankston, 30 May 2011.

302 Submission from Peninsula Community Legal Centre, Youthlaw and the Youth Affairs Council of Victoria to Frankston City Council. Accessed at www.yacvic.org.au

303 A Victoria Police media release speaks to the benefits of the program as follows:
'Frankston Police have teamed up with Mission Australia this April to identify and assist at-risk youth who are prone to being involved in criminal behaviour.
Since its beginning in July 2007, the "Youth Assist Program" has already provided early intervention and prevention strategies to 145 youths aged up to 17 years old. Once at-risk youths have been identified, the program aims to reduce the onset of crime and prevent recidivist offending behaviour. Where possible, youths are encouraged to enter the work place or re-commence studies, and many have successfully been reunited with their families and the community.
Frankston Youth Resource Officer, Leading Senior Constable Renee Bloomfield, said the program aims to enhance the health and wellbeing of young people:
"The program allows us to tailor individual actions plans to encourage at-risk teenagers to pursue education and employment pathways," said Leading Senior Constable Bloomfield.
Each individual that comes through the program has different needs, which is why it is important for police to engage support from a wide range of community partners.
This includes community groups that specialise in drug and alcohol abuse, family violence, adolescent support and counselling, health support, legal studies, family counselling, emergency accommodation and education, employment and training' (Victoria Police Media Release — *Youth Assist Program*, 27 August 2008, Accessed on 6 May 2009 at http://www.police.vic.gov.au/content.asp?Document_ID=16901)

Conclusion

This chapter has examined new approaches to the development and implementation of crime prevention and community safety programs in Victoria. It has looked at the commitment of the state government to establish a new dedicated crime prevention unit that not only will fund a number of grants programs for community based crime prevention initiatives but will also coordinate and implement strategies across Victoria through its regional reference groups. The discussion has also centred on the crime prevention programs of one of the government's most important agencies — the Victoria Police — and its move towards a more proactive community policing partnership style.

The police, however, are only one, albeit important, organisation that has a major involvement in the implementation of crime prevention and community safety programs. LGAs and their associated agencies are equally important in this area. Community organisations, by themselves or in partnership with others, are also crucial stakeholders in modern crime prevention. These latter groups are the subject of the next chapter.

Recommendations

4. **The Committee recommends** that the role of the Community Crime Prevention Unit should include but not be restricted to:

   ◆ the development and publication of the Crime Prevention and Community Safety Framework including a community engagement strategy to indicate how the public, community organisations and the private sector can have ongoing input into crime prevention policy;

   ◆ liaising with federal and state agencies, professionals in the field, community agencies and media;

   ◆ disseminating information with regard to crime prevention and community safety;

   ◆ implementing a mapping exercise and audit to establish the current levels of services available;

   ◆ developing and coordinating training programs on crime prevention and community safety;

   ◆ developing and coordinating a research agenda and the commissioning of crime prevention research;

   ◆ assessing and providing funding for programs, research and evaluation relating to crime prevention and community safety;

   ◆ ongoing responsibility for evaluating programs that are funded;

   ◆ developing a protocol in liaison with media representatives on the reporting of community safety and crime prevention issues;

   ◆ liaising with and supporting local government and community agencies to develop Local Community Crime Prevention Strategies;

   ◆ identifying available resources and gaps in service delivery in order to plan a response to community safety and crime prevention at both state and local levels;

   ◆ identifying key personnel and agencies in the community who have expertise in dealing with community safety and crime prevention in order to establish a comprehensive referral and resource network; and

   ◆ identifying best practice initiatives and assessing their applicability to local communities.

5. **The Committee recommends** that the Community Crime Prevention Unit provides technical support and assistance to enhance the capacity and effectiveness of local crime prevention action.

6. **The Committee recommends** that the Community Crime Prevention Unit should establish and support a Crime Prevention and Community Safety Advisory Group to provide ongoing formal advice to the Community Crime Prevention Unit from experts in the field.

7. **The Committee recommends** that the Victorian Government establish an Interdepartmental Crime Prevention Working Party to coordinate crime prevention and community safety programs and interventions across state government departments.

Continued overleaf.

Recommendations (cont.)

13. **The Committee recommends** that the Community Crime Prevention Unit should undertake a Review of the feasibility and likely effects of requiring local councils to develop crime prevention and community safety strategy plans as part of a legislative mandate.

30. **The Committee recommends** that comprehensive units on crime prevention and community safety should be incorporated into Victoria Police probationary training as soon as possible.

7. Implementing Crime Prevention Programs: Local Government Authorities and Community Organisations

Introduction

The previous chapter examined in depth the role of the State Government and its new Community Crime Prevention Unit in developing, funding and implementing crime prevention and community safety programs throughout Victoria. It also discussed the important role the Victoria Police play in this regard. A key component of successful crime prevention strategies is the need for the government and the police to support and/or work in partnership with a variety of other organisations and agencies. Two of the most important of these are local government authorities (LGAs) and non-government or community organisations. The input of these separate but interrelated bodies to Victorian crime prevention is significant.

Local government – 'More than just roads, rates, and rubbish'[304]

Local government in Victoria has played a key role in crime prevention and community safety, although less so perhaps than in other states. Whilst some jurisdictions such as England and New South Wales mandate local government involvement as a condition of grant or funding assistance, Victoria has tended to take arguably a less coercive role.[305]

The role of local government in the area of crime prevention and community safety

Local government is increasingly having a role as a key player in the development and implementation of community crime prevention programs. As Shaw has stated, 'Across Australia virtually all government crime prevention agencies include local government in the development and delivery of their respective crime prevention strategies' (quoted in Australian Institute of Criminology (AIC) 2004, p.1). The AIC has given a number of reasons as to why local government is well placed to lead and deliver community crime prevention programs:

1. Research shows that a great deal of crime is very local in nature (e.g. domestic burglary, anti-social behaviour, and certain forms of violence). There is also growing evidence about the effectiveness of locally organised crime prevention action.

2. Local government is frequently well placed to coordinate and manage crime prevention responses across the community.

3. There is an increasing community expectation that local government will assume some level of responsibility for initiating or directing action for crime issues that are seen to be affecting local amenity and quality of life. In this sense, the local authority is the level of democratic process closest to, and reflective of, the needs of communities.

---

304 Quote from Councillor Joan Donovan, Council Representative, Macedon Ranges Local Safety Committee, Macedon Ranges Shire Council, Evidence given to the Drugs and Crime Prevention Committee, Inquiry into Locally Based Approaches to Community Safety and Crime Prevention, Public Hearing, Melbourne, 9 August 2011.

305 See discussion in Chapter 3.

4. Local government frequently has the most appropriate management infrastructure and skill base for delivering the multi-agency programs that are often required (AIC 2004, p.1).

Yet it is equally true, as the AIC points out, that not all all LGAs will have an equal capacity to provide a leadership and a coordination role. Nonetheless, evidence to this Inquiry has shown there is certainly a wish in local government circles to have greater involvement in the development of community safety initiatives for their local communities.

In Victoria, local government provides important input into state government programs, police operations and community organisation activities.[306] Local governments also engage in crime prevention and community safety activities directly, through council run programs and strategies, and indirectly, through the consideration of crime prevention and safety factors in education, health, community development and planning.[307]

The role of local government and its crime prevention or community safety officers has been described well by Mr John Maynard a senior officer at the City of Sydney. Whilst his comments refer to his experience of crime prevention in New South Wales, for the most part they are arguably also applicable to Victoria:

> I think there is recognition that local government does have a role to play in crime prevention. It is the level of government closest to the people. Of course we have always played an indirect role in crime prevention through the provision of street lighting and infrastructure and so forth, and even clean streets can affect people's perceptions of crime. We also have a long history in our community services in local government working with Aboriginal communities, people with disabilities and so forth, those broader capacity building initiatives which in and of themselves can be useful in reducing and preventing crime.
>
> *Obviously the key to what we are trying to do is to work in partnership.* There is no 'one size fits all', no silver bullet, no magic formula with what we are trying to do. Essentially we rely on partnerships which we are able to establish which have trust, transparency, commitment to quality, accountabilities and clear definitions of roles and responsibilities. If we can get all of those things right we are well on the way to getting somewhere in terms of working in genuine partnership with all of our stakeholders.[308] (Committee's emphasis)

The role of the crime prevention officer or equivalent at council level is equally important. Although, as the AIC survey in Chapter 5 indicates, many LGAs may not have a staff member solely dedicated to crime prevention per se, usually there will be someone in a position that encompasses a broader community safety role. Again an example of this type of role from the City of Sydney is applicable:

> We can split the function of the local government officer into three: firstly, it is around education and information. We work with the police around reinforcing those community safety messages, such as, take your valuables with you when you park your car; report crime; get to know your neighbours, look out for your neighbours; crime prevention, like charity, begins at home, and other key messages around protecting yourself in public places and protecting your personal property as well. We do that through community events, community consultation and we work with our identified communities.

306 Ms Maree McPherson, Chief Executive Officer, Victorian Local Governance Association, Evidence given to the Drugs and Crime Prevention Committee, Inquiry into Locally Based Approaches to Community Safety and Crime Prevention, Public Hearing, Melbourne, 27 June 2011.

307 See for example, Mr Philip Schier, Senior Policy Officer, Victorian Local Governance Association, Evidence given to the Drugs and Crime Prevention Committee, Inquiry into Locally Based Approaches to Community Safety and Crime Prevention, Public Hearing, Melbourne, 27 June 2011.

308 Mr John Maynard, Senior Project Coordinator, Safe City, City of Sydney, Evidence given to the Drugs and Crime Prevention Committee, Inquiry into Locally Based Approaches to Community Safety and Crime Prevention, Public Hearing, Sydney, 19 September 2011.

Secondly, we work on situational prevention. That is all that public domain stuff which you may have heard about.... We look at things like what type of social fabric developers are trying to create, how a communal space is used.

Thirdly, we do social crime prevention. We will look at specific target groups within our local government area and work on targeted issues. For example, we have a lot of international students in our City of Sydney local government area. They come into the country often with language issues, very unfamiliar with the environment they come to reside in. They will walk around with their iPods on, texting on their mobile phones, and they might have had a few drinks. They are susceptible and they are targeted. We make sure we are getting to colleges and student institutions. We have translated information where possible to assist the police in again promoting the community safety message.[309]

The Australian Institute of Criminology survey

One of the findings of the AIC survey, discussed in Chapter 5, was that the majority of LGAs in Victoria are committed to playing a significant role in the development, coordination and delivery of crime prevention and community safety policies and programs in their local area.[310] While it is notable that only a minority of councils have formulated *specific* crime prevention and community safety strategies, many others have either embedded this strategic process in wider community welfare or health strategies or reported that they are in the process of developing such strategies.

The AIC survey also concluded that whilst the most common function that LGAs fulfil in their crime prevention and community safety role is that of coordination and facilitation, it is clear that many also have a significant role in direct service delivery. Another key finding of the survey was that where community safety and/or crime prevention activities were undertaken by LGAs many of them were done in formal partnerships with police or community agencies. Both these findings (that is direct service delivery and entering into formal partnerships) are certainly true of the councils that gave evidence to the Committee and are profiled in this chapter.

Community safety committees and community safety plans

As indicated above, the AIC survey found that many local government authorities in Victoria have a version of a community safety committee and/or a community safety plan or strategy document that guides the local government response to crime, antisocial behaviour and community safety issues in the local community. Relatively few of these however are specifically titled 'Crime Prevention Strategies'. In addition, many councils may also have specific strategies on particular crime prevention subject areas such as a drug and alcohol action plan or an anti-graffiti strategy.

Local based community safety and crime prevention strategies typically reflect the needs of the areas to which they apply in either specific or general terms. Accordingly, approaches, strategies and plans respond to and address local community safety and crime issues, some of which will be relevant to all municipalities and some of which will be more specific to particular places. For example, the City of Greater Geelong engages in programs that address location-specific problems, for example, developing strategies relating to beach parties.[311]

---

309 Mr John Maynard, Senior Project Coordinator, Safe City, City of Sydney, Evidence given to the Drugs and Crime Prevention Committee, Inquiry into Locally Based Approaches to Community Safety and Crime Prevention, Public Hearing, Sydney, 19 September 2011.

310 See Chapter 5.

311 Cr Jan Farrell, Community Safety Portfolio, City of Greater Geelong, Evidence given to the Drugs and Crime Prevention Committee, Inquiry into Locally Based Approaches to Community Safety and Crime Prevention, Public Hearing, Geelong, 8 August 2011.

Community safety strategies and committees for selected individual local government authorities are discussed later in this chapter.

A survey by the Victorian Local Government Association

A survey conducted by the Victorian Local Governance Association (VLGA) of local government approaches to community safety and crime prevention found 'considerable variability in the degree to which councils are directly involved in community safety and crime prevention activity'.[312] There tended to be a greater diversity of activities in metropolitan councils, where there are a greater range of social and environmental factors in play and a greater diversity of stakeholders. Consequently, council plans and strategies in metropolitan areas tended to reflect this diversity and complexity. As Mr Schier, a senior policy officer of the VLGA observed, 'the larger metropolitan councils tend to have a greater involvement and a more diverse range of activities',[313] resulting in a greater commitment of resources.

In the inner suburbs, councils are more likely to employ a dedicated community safety or crime prevention officer, whereas in the outer metropolitan areas the emphasis is more broadly on cultural safety and in smaller rural councils the role is even smaller.[314] As Mr Schier pointed out, unlike inner metropolitan councils which are often actively engaged in specific crime prevention activities, smaller rural councils are more likely to be 'supporting police and working through a community safety committee where police and community agencies were represented rather than seeing it as a direct role for council'.[315] Overall, representatives from local government peak bodies thought that councils generally preferred to engage their communities under the positive banner of 'community safety' than the perceived negative label of 'crime prevention'. This is supported by the survey results of the Drugs and Crime Prevention Committee's study reported in Chapter 5, which also suggested a tendency for councils to implement or endorse broad safety goals.

While for many councils crime prevention approach is under the larger category of 'community safety', many also approach safety as a subset of health and wellbeing.[316] Approached in this way, council's plans and strategies generally do not address crime prevention in any detailed or focused way and do not clearly define council responsibilities in the area or in developing policy. This tendency may be further reinforced by the view, articulated by Mr Schier of the VLGA, that crime prevention is '[e]ssentially...seen as core police business which council can support rather than core council business.'[317] Understood

---

312   Mr Philip Schier, Senior Policy Officer, Victorian Local Governance Association, Evidence given to the Drugs and Crime Prevention Committee, Inquiry into Locally Based Approaches to Community Safety and Crime Prevention, Public Hearing, Melbourne, 27 June 2011.
       It should be noted however that the response to the survey was somewhat limited. Only 11 of the 79 Victorian Local Government Areas made formal responses to the survey. See submission from Mr Philip Schier, Senior Policy Officer, Victorian Local Governance Association to the Drugs and Crime Prevention Committee, Inquiry into Locally Based Approaches to Community Safety and Crime Prevention, June 2011. The survey results and commentary form part of this submission.

313   Mr Philip Schier, Senior Policy Officer, Victorian Local Governance Association, Evidence given to the Drugs and Crime Prevention Committee, Inquiry into Locally Based Approaches to Community Safety and Crime Prevention, Public Hearing, Melbourne, 27 June 2011.

314   Mr Philip Schier, Senior Policy Officer, Victorian Local Governance Association, Evidence given to the Drugs and Crime Prevention Committee, Inquiry into Locally Based Approaches to Community Safety and Crime Prevention, Public Hearing, Melbourne, 27 June 2011.

315   Mr Philip Schier, Senior Policy Officer, Victorian Local Governance Association, Evidence given to the Drugs and Crime Prevention Committee, Inquiry into Locally Based Approaches to Community Safety and Crime Prevention, Public Hearing, Melbourne, 27 June 2011.

316   For example, Banyule City Council, Bass Coast City Council, Bayside City Council, Brimbank City Council, Casey City Council, Glenelg Shire Council, Hume City Council, Indigo Shire Council, Manningham City Council, Maribyrnong City Council, Maroondah City Council, City of Port Phillip, Stonnington City Council and the City of Whitehorse.

317   Mr Philip Schier, Senior Policy Officer, Victorian Local Governance Association, Evidence given to the Drugs and Crime Prevention Committee, Inquiry into Locally Based Approaches to Community Safety and Crime Prevention, Public Hearing, Melbourne, 27 June 2011.

in this way, LGAs only have responsibility for crime prevention where it overlaps with areas of clear council responsibility, as Mr Schier explained:

> where it fits clearly at the community level – that is, the level at which local government connects with local communities...if it can be shown to have a clear link to areas where councils have responsibilities, such as public spaces. Those things include street-level violence when an issue in a pub spills out onto the street or where you have a concentration of nightclubs and so on in a particular area... [Also] where it is a broader community education role, such as youth programs on road safety or drug and alcohol education. It may then be a primary care partnership with local government, schools and the police all working together on something like that.[318]

The incorporation of safety and crime prevention under the umbrella of health and wellbeing may also partly derive from reporting requirements set out in the *Public Health and Wellbeing Act* (Vic) 2008. The Act requires all local councils to 'prepare a municipal public health and wellbeing plan within a period of 12 months after each general election', reporting and addressing data about health status and health determinants, identifying goals and strategies based on available evidence, providing for community involvement and detailing partnership with government departments and agencies.[319]

Understandably, an approach to community and safety in terms of health and wellbeing is likely to focus on limiting the impact of crime or safety matters on individuals, within the scope of council activities or responsibilities. Rather than addressing the underlying causes of crime, for example, the likely focus would be on minimising or reducing its impact in terms of the health and wellbeing of community members.

It is unclear whether this broad approach is a result of the economic or budgetary limitations, a lack of clearly defined responsibilities[320] or whether a more general approach is a reflection of local priorities or issues. Councils have limited resources to address a diverse range of matters. This will occasionally mean that certain areas of council responsibility will be prioritised at the expense of others. In such cases, particularly with smaller outer metropolitan or rural councils, a general approach may support the view that crime prevention is best left to Victoria Police.[321] This is supported by the analysis of the survey data on local government approaches undertaken by the AIC for the Committee (see Chapter 5). As noted in the survey findings, 99 per cent of local government respondents reported that police, rather than local councils, were primarily responsible for crime prevention and community safety in their area.

In order to understand the various approaches taken by local government to crime prevention, it is useful to examine in depth how various municipalities across Victoria that gave evidence to the Inquiry approach community safety.

---

318 Mr Philip Schier, Senior Policy Officer, Victorian Local Governance Association, Evidence given to the Drugs and Crime Prevention Committee, Inquiry into Locally Based Approaches to Community Safety and Crime Prevention, Public Hearing, Melbourne, 27 June 2011.

319 Section 26 (1) *Public Health and Wellbeing Act 2008* (Vic)

320 This will be addressed in the following chapter.

321 Submission from Mr Philip Schier, Senior Policy Officer, Victorian Local Governance Association to the Drugs and Crime Prevention Committee, Inquiry into Locally Based Approaches to Community Safety and Crime Prevention, June 2011.

The City of Greater Dandenong: A case study in diverse approaches to crime prevention and community safety

The City of Greater Dandenong (CGD) is a local government area in Victoria, located in the southeastern suburbs of Melbourne. It has an area of 130 square kilometres and has an estimated population of 137,600 people.

The CGD is a community of complex and various characteristics, including a rising and ageing population, culturally diverse residents and a high level of migrant settlement. A notable feature of Greater Dandenong is the diversity of countries of origin and spoken languages of residents. CGD is the most culturally diverse locality in Victoria with more than half of its population born overseas.

The CGD is also a relatively disadvantaged community with the lowest incomes in Melbourne, poor educational outcomes among young people, high rates of unemployment and the second highest level of youth disengagement in Melbourne.[322]

Quite apart from these demographic features the Committee decided to use the CGD to illustrate how one LGA can incorporate a number of different crime prevention streams into its overall approach for addressing local community safety issues. These include social developmental approaches, situational and environmental crime prevention and community renewal/revitalisation and capacity building.[323]

Mr Mark Doubleday, Director of Community Services for the CGD, spoke to the multifaceted aspects of crime prevention and community safety in the CGD in evidence to the Committee:

> Local government and this council is particularly unique with some of its focus. It has a spread of service areas, such as youth services, family support services – we are one of the few councils that has a family welfare service – an extensive community development unit, a focus on community events, as well as other areas, such as urban design. In the social sphere we have quite a commitment of resources that the intention is they are intervention and prevention orientated, developmental, and seeking to engage with local community with particular demographics in a way that addresses particularly the perception through the various areas that they look at.[324]

Crime and the City of Greater Dandenong

While the level of crime in CGD has remained stable in recent years, the rate of *violent* offences has risen substantially over the past five years and is now 70 per cent higher than the average in metropolitan Melbourne.[325] Moreover *public perception* of personal safety remains the lowest in Victoria 'with safety in streets and public places frequently raised during the community consultation process'.[326] Rates of family violence and child abuse are also high in CGD with police attendance at family violence incidents being the second highest in Melbourne and the rate of child abuse substantiations the highest in the southern region of the Department of Human Services (DHS).[327]

To in part address these negative indicia, the CGD has developed a number of action plans and strategies. These are profiled in the next sections.

---

322 See *City of Dandenong Community Well-being plan 2010-2013*. For example, at the time of the last census, one in seven of 20-24 year olds in the CGD were not in paid employment or education.

323 Some aspects of CGD programs and approaches have been discussed in other chapters of this Report. In particular, see Chapter 2.

324 Mr Mark Doubleday, Director, Community Services, City of Greater Dandenong, Evidence given to the Drugs and Crime Prevention Committee, Inquiry into Locally Based Approaches to Community Safety and Crime Prevention, Public Hearing, Dandenong, 30 May 2011.

325 *A Profile of Health and Well-being in Greater Dandenong 2010*. See www.greaterdandenong.com

326 See City of Dandenong Community Well-being plan 2010–2013.

327 See City of Dandenong Community Well-being plan 2010–2013.

Community Wellbeing Plan 2010–2013

In Dandenong, the 'Community Wellbeing Plan 2010–2013' shows how Council promotes health and wellbeing for all its residents. It identifies key priorities and strategies that respond to the changing health needs of Greater Dandenong residents. The Plan is the result of extensive consultation with residents, service agencies, organisations and council staff. The Council has worked in partnership with these stakeholders to develop and implement the Plan.

The Plan provides information on the broad range of council activities that impact upon health and wellbeing. In particular it outlines a number of aims, goals, programs and projects on health and mental health, drug and alcohol use, child development, employment, housing, refugee and migrant assistance, travel and transport, environmental initiatives, sustainable communities, participation in education, equity and social inclusion.[328] In short, the Plan promotes a Social Model of Health[329] that takes a holistic approach to quality of life issues including community safety. The Plan encompasses community development, community capacity building and early intervention programs that indirectly seek to influence the underlying social and economic causes of crime, antisocial behaviour and community dysfunction.

In addition, the CGD has developed a separate strategy document that *specifically* addresses issues of crime and community safety within the municipality, while sharing the same community capacity building goals that the Community Wellbeing Plan promotes.

Community Safety Plan 2011–2014

The introduction to the Community Safety Plan 2011–2014 states that:

> A safe community is where people want to live, work and interact with one another. It is where homes, workplaces, public transport, community spaces and neighbourhoods are welcoming and people trust one another, feel safe and are free from harm. *Community safety is therefore more than policing and crime.* It has a connection with many aspects of community life and wellbeing.[330] (Author's emphasis)

The purpose of this plan is:

- To clearly outline the role of the City of Greater Dandenong in relation to community safety
- To ensure a consistent *whole-of-organisation* approach to community safety
- To identify the priority areas and key strategies in community safety for the City of Greater Dandenong
- To provide a strategic context for the Community Safety Advisory Committee.[331]

The CGD describes its role in crime prevention and community safety as one based on partnerships, collaboration and advocacy endorsing many of the conceptual approaches to crime prevention discussed throughout this Report. In particular it states:

---

328 See also the associated document *A Profile of Health and Wellbeing in Dandenong* for an overview of social and health indicators for the municipality. Accessed at http://www.greaterdandenong.com/Resources/SiteDocuments/sid1_Health%20Profile%20Final%202010.pdf

329 A social model of health views the wellbeing of any community as being influenced by complex social, economic and physical environments which are interrelated:
'The City of Greater Dandenong, like any municipal body, works across a range of areas to deliver facilities and services to its residents. There is a need therefore for a 'social' view of health to be taken into consideration when designing a wellbeing plan. An integrated approach on a broad scale has been demonstrated to be most effective in addressing health and wellbeing issues, rather than only focusing on reacting to illnesses or a resulting lack of wellbeing' (City of Greater Dandenong Health and Well-being Plan 2010–2013. Accessed at http://www.greaterdandenong.com/Resources/SiteDocuments/doc8798.pdf

330 City of Greater Dandenong Community Safety Plan 2010–2014. Accessed at http://www.greaterdandenong.com/Resources/SiteDocuments/sid1_Community%20Safety%20Plan.pdf

331 City of Greater Dandenong Community Safety Plan 2010–2014. Accessed at http://www.greaterdandenong.com/Resources/SiteDocuments/sid1_Community%20Safety%20Plan.pdf

Council exercises a regulatory role in enforcing a number of State regulations as well as local laws where community safety is a key issue: amenity management, fire prevention, animal control, parking control and school crossing supervision. In addition, Council influences actual and perceived levels of safety through agency partnerships, advocacy, quality infrastructure and design, community education, sustained funding for targeted programs and the shared use of data, knowledge and information as common elements for success.

Agency partnerships are viewed by Council as particularly important. Council recognises that partnership based strategies are the key to expanding crime prevention from the domain of the police to the responsibility of the entire community. This approach to crime prevention is likely to have greater success than single agencies working alone. Isolated projects are often unable to deal effectively with the variety of factors that influence community safety, therefore local government action requires support from a range of stakeholders including other levels of government, local agencies and members of the community.[332]

In conjunction with the Community Wellbeing Plan, the Safety Plan covers a wide range of both social developmental and environmental crime prevention approaches including:

- Safer public places
- Urban Design and Social Inclusion
- Hotspots in Greater Dandenong
- Alcohol and Other Drugs
- Preventing family violence
- Elder abuse
- Safety in the home
- Families and Young Children
- Road safety and
- Public Transport.[333]

Community Safety Advisory Committee

The CGD has established a Community Safety Advisory Committee to guide Council's thinking regarding key aspects of safety across the municipality. This strategic group includes senior members of Victoria Police, State Government, community agencies, transport providers, Neighbourhood Watch, Council's Media and Communications Department and Council's Youth Services.

The purpose of the Community Safety Advisory Committee is to:

- Create a safer Greater Dandenong (perception and reality);
- Provide leadership in the area of community safety;
- Positively reinforce the safety message;
- Provide high-quality and informed advice to Council to assist in planning for safer communities;
- Initiate and/or drive programs for community engagement; and
- Bring community leaders together to focus on integrated outcomes.[334]

---

332 City of Greater Dandenong Community Safety Plan 2010–2014. Accessed at http://www.greaterdandenong.com/ Resources/SiteDocuments/sid1_Community%20Safety%20Plan.pdf

333 City of Greater Dandenong Community Safety Plan 2010–2014. Accessed at http://www.greaterdandenong.com/ Resources/SiteDocuments/sid1_Community%20Safety%20Plan.pdf

334 http://www.greaterdandenong.com/Resources/SiteDocuments/sid1_Community%20Safety%20Plan.pdf

The Advisory Committee meets bi-monthly and oversees the development and progress of the Community Safety Plan. It will also report to Council annually on progress made, and on emerging issues and trends regarding community safety.

Representatives of local Neighbourhood Watch branches are included on the Advisory Committee in recognition of 'the role that Neighbourhood Watch plays in promoting greater community awareness of safety issues'.[335]

Community Support Grants

The CGD's Community Support Grants Program provides financial support of up to $20,000 to community groups and organisations to carry out programs, projects, and activities that will benefit local residents and promote community capacity building.[336] The Grants Program aims:

- To build the capacity and confidence of the community to meet its own needs;
- To help people to overcome social or economic disadvantages;
- To foster social inclusion by encouraging participation in community activities;
- To improve access and inclusion for all residents;
- To improve community safety and perceptions of community safety;
- To encourage a sense of community and local identity; and
- To promote harmony among people of diverse backgrounds.[337]

Situational and environmental approaches

Environmental crime prevention programs and projects specifically aim to modify the physical context in which crime occurs to reduce the number of places where criminal activities can occur.[338] Situational prevention approaches focus on reducing crime opportunities rather than on the characteristics of criminals or potential criminals. Programs utilising situational methods manipulate *specific* environments or environment types (for example, shopping malls) in ways that will increase the risks and efforts associated with offending and reduce the associated rewards.

Another specific aspect of environmental crime prevention is the concept of Crime Prevention through Environmental Design (CPTED) – the idea that urban design, such as the design of public buildings, streets, shopping centres or parks and measures such as improved street lighting can prevent crime by reducing opportunities.

The City of Dandenong has applied both situational and CPTED measures in promoting community safety throughout the municipality. As an example of the former it has invested heavily in the placement of CCTV cameras and technology in the commercial and entertainment precincts of Dandenong.[339] It has also specifically mandated the use of CPTED as a key approach to reduce crime and antisocial behaviour in its Community Safety Plan.

> Appropriate planning and design of urban environments can improve feelings of safety and community participation. Council seeks to create safer communities through the use of safer design principles such as the multi-disciplinary approach known as Crime Prevention Through

---

335 For a discussion of Neighbourhood Watch, see Chapter 10. Members of the Dandenong Neighbourhood Watch group gave evidence to the Committee at a Public Hearing in Dandenong, 30 May 2011.

336 For a discussion of the concept of community capacity building, see Chapter 1.

337 City of Greater Dandenong Community Support Grants Program Guidelines and Information Booklet http://www.greaterdandenong.com/Resources/SiteDocuments/doc22547.pdf

338 For a detailed discussion of environmental crime prevention, see Chapter 2.

339 A detailed discussion of the City of Greater Dandenong's use of CCTV is found in Chapter 2 of this Report.

Environmental Design (CPTED). This seeks to increase community use of public spaces, reduce opportunities for crime and anti-social behaviour and create liveable communities.[340]

The use of CPTED is particularly noticeable in the CGD's grand plan for renewing the heart of the municipality – the City of Greater Dandenong Revitalisation Plan.

City of Greater Dandenong Revitalisation Plan – An exercise in community renewal

The State Government's $290 million funded Revitalising Central Dandenong initiative was developed with the aim of rejuvenating the city centre and making it a safe place to live, work and visit.

The Revitalising Central Dandenong initiative is being delivered by the Victorian Government, through VicUrban, in partnership with the CGD[341] and is an excellent example of employing the principles of partnership planning, as Chapter 3 of this Report discussed, including the use of the private sector to develop community development initiatives.

In November 2007 the then Premier of Victoria John Brumby MP and the Mayor of the CGD launched the Revitalising Central Dandenong Urban Master Plan. The plan detailed a 15–20 year vision for the largest urban renewal project in Victoria since the Melbourne Docklands. The plan maps a dynamic future for central Dandenong as it seeks to attract more people, jobs and businesses to the city centre.

The revitalisation program is delivering a diverse range of highly visible public realm improvements within the city centre including:

◆ The widening and improvement of Lonsdale Boulevard

◆ The creation of an integrated new urban precinct called Metro Village 3175

◆ The creation of 'City Street' a green pedestrian and cycle thoroughfare connecting the city centre to the transport hub

◆ Improved public transport

◆ A new Civic Centre

◆ The redevelopment of Dandenong Market

◆ A 'Cultural Precinct' with restaurants, shops and entertainment from a variety of ethnic groups.

Mr Kevin Van Boxtel, Manager of the Revitalising Dandenong Project, spoke to the Committee about the objectives of the Project in making Dandenong a safer, more pleasant and productive environment than has been the case:

> The project itself is really about re-establishing central Dandenong as the capital of the south-east...there are three key objectives. The first one is to attract private sector investment as a flow-on effect of government investment, $1 billion over that 20-year period; the second is to strengthen our base in terms of economic and social sustainability in the longer term – and third to improve the overall amenity, safety and urban environment of the city centre itself.[342]

---

340 City of Greater Dandenong Community Safety Plan 2010–2014. Accessed at http://www.greaterdandenong.com/Resources/SiteDocuments/sid1_Community%20Safety%20Plan.pdf

341 Other partners include the Dandenong Development Board, Vic Urban, Department of Transport, Metro Trains, Arts Victoria and private sector corporations and businesses.

342 Mr Kevin Van Boxtel, Manager, Revitalising Central Dandenong, City of Greater Dandenong, Evidence given to the Drugs and Crime Prevention Committee, Inquiry into Locally Based Approaches to Community Safety and Crime Prevention, Public Hearing, Dandenong, 30 May 2011.

Many of the projects involve bringing vibrancy and vitality to the central city. The program is primarily focused at pedestrians in streets and the 'reclaiming' of public spaces that are encountered between the station and the market, areas which have traditionally been feared as crime 'hot spots':[343]

> Through this whole process of the city changing through infrastructure works and through new investment in private land, council has continued to run, over the last three to four years, a very strong program that is geared around our community. Some of the [projects] like the Little India cultural precinct, the Afghan Bazaar cultural precinct, run food tours, and hold floral displays. At the moment we are just about to hold our nocturnal night walk which is an activity we hold once a year where we get people coming into the city centre at night and walking through that environment. Some people have not necessarily experienced that previously and it is about getting people comfortable with that space at a different time to when they would normally enter of their own accord. [In short] there is a lot of work that happens through both council and VicUrban that is geared towards activation and use of our public realm and public streets.[344]

Ms Lee Robson, the CGD's Manager of Community Engagement, told the Committee that by starting afresh the CGD has been in a unique position to use some of the best principles of CPTED and situational crime prevention to create some cutting edge design features:

> The design of public space is all important and we have been exploring some options through using art and engagement as a way of involving communities in planning spaces that they will ultimately use. The use of public space – or the illegitimate use of public space – is often an issue for planners...The design end is all important because about 80 per cent of the heavy lifting has to be done at the design stage. It is very hard to retrofit something afterwards. What we have seen in central Dandenong is a wonderful opportunity to reinvent some public spaces.[345]

Ms Robson also said that some valuable lessons had been learnt by the Council during the revitalisation project:[346]

> I think there are about four points that are pretty important that we have learnt: the first one is visibility, having activity where people can see it with passive surveillance as they pass by; the second one is activating a space, making sure that there is legitimate activity, and sometimes councils need to program activities to make sure that occurs early on, right from the outset; the third one is reducing what I call territorialism, not allowing a particular group to colonise a space but by making it clear that it is available to everyone, and again that sometimes requires programming; the fourth one is all of those elements of good design – making sure an area is well lit, that there are no obstructions, that there is seating located in a place where people can legitimately sit and spend some time, that there are toilets well designed with the doors facing the streets. All of those principles about environmental design are important.[347]

Some of the specific projects developed to enhance community wellbeing and safety are listed below.

---

343 A hot spot is 'an area where a complex or ongoing mix of antisocial behaviour occurs that contributes to low levels of perceived or actual safety'. In Dandenong hot spot areas have traditionally been associated around Dandenong Railway Station and its immediate precinct (Ms Lee Robson, Manager, Community Engagement, City of Greater Dandenong, Evidence given to the Drugs and Crime Prevention Committee, Inquiry into Locally Based Approaches to Community Safety and Crime Prevention, Public Hearing, Dandenong, 30 May 2011).

344 Mr Kevin Van Boxtel, Manager, Revitalising Central Dandenong, City of Greater Dandenong, Evidence given to the Drugs and Crime Prevention Committee, Inquiry into Locally Based Approaches to Community Safety and Crime Prevention, Public Hearing, Dandenong, 30 May 2011.

345 Ms Lee Robson, Manager, Community Engagement, City of Greater Dandenong, Evidence given to the Drugs and Crime Prevention Committee, Inquiry into Locally Based Approaches to Community Safety and Crime Prevention, Public Hearing, Dandenong, 30 May 2011.

346 Further discussion on the Revitalising Dandenong project is found in Chapter 2 of this Report.

347 Ms Lee Robson, Manager, Community Engagement, City of Greater Dandenong, Evidence given to the Drugs and Crime Prevention Committee, Inquiry into Locally Based Approaches to Community Safety and Crime Prevention, Public Hearing, Dandenong, 30 May 2011.

Projects

Cultural precinct initiatives

- Cultural precinct branding – Little India
- Cultural precinct branding – Afghan Bazaar
- Little India cultural tours
- `Afghan Bazaar cultural tours

Public realm improvements

- Living colour floral displays
- Alfresco dining
- Flag poles
- Palm Plaza seating project
- Way finding signs
- Grass Cubes Palm Plaza

Public art

- Transformed – Temporary Public Art Program
- Winter art projection
- 'Vessels of Light' public art project
- Viachroma
- Depot
- The Offering
- The Dandenong Book of Prayer
- Nocturnal walk

Lighting Projects

- Gateway lighting treatment
- The Colour of Night
- Palm Plaza lighting upgrade.

The CGD has over the past 10 years used a variety of social developmental, environmental and community capacity building approaches to reduce crime, enhance community safety and promote community health and wellbeing in what is still one of Melbourne's most disadvantaged local government areas. The Committee will follow with interest the efforts of the municipality in addressing many of the myriad problems that face not only Dandenong but similar communities across the greater city of Melbourne and beyond.

Regional crime prevention – the City of Geelong

Having examined a case study of how crime prevention and community safety issues are addressed in an outer suburban area of Melbourne, it is useful to look at how similar concerns are dealt with in a regional area such as Geelong.

The Council approach to community safety is articulated through the Geelong Community Safety Strategy 2010–2013 (Safety Plan). The Safety Plan operates under the key objectives of:

◆ working together

◆ safety in our community

◆ safety in the home

◆ safety on our roads.

The plan is reviewed every three years and is kept relevant by a reporting mechanism that sees each of the four objectives reported on three times per year.[348]

The terms 'crime prevention' and 'community safety' have not been defined by the strategy. 'However, it is implicit in their use that the former relates to activities, design and behavior that can prevent crime from taking place, while the latter refers to a wider range of strategies that enhance people's sense of feeling safe in a place, their connection to their environment and engagement with the people in that space'.[349]

The City of Greater Geelong provides a good example of a local government that engages in a broad range of activities and programs that draw together numerous stakeholders.[350] The council works in collaboration with Victoria Police and the community in a range of initiatives that cover a diverse and broad municipality. Since 2009 the council has had a community safety portfolio, which responds to general community safety, crime prevention, drug and alcohol planning, in conjunction with a variety of multi-partner groups including the Geelong Local Safety Committee, a Drugs Action Plan Committee, Gambling Advisory Committee, a Graffiti Reference Group, Barwon Action Drug Committee, the Prevention of Violence Against Women working group and Road Safe Barwon.[351] The council auspices the Family Violence Program, the Liquor Accord, the Safe City Cameras and Nightlife Radios Program, the Safe City Taxi Rank, Central Geelong NightBus, Hoon Hotline and the Graffiti program.[352]

The council has also engaged in research in partnership with Deakin University focusing on a range of community safety and crime prevention issues, including the evaluation of programs and studies on Drug and Alcohol in the Night-Time Economy, community perceptions of drug and alcohol treatment programs and prevention initiatives, and a review of private security.[353]

---

348 Submission from Mr Paul Jamieson, Community Development Manager, City of Greater Geelong to the Drugs and Crime Prevention Committee, Inquiry into Locally Based Approaches to Community Safety and Crime Prevention, May 2011.

349 Submission from Mr Paul Jamieson, Community Development Manager, City of Greater Geelong to the Drugs and Crime Prevention Committee, Inquiry into Locally Based Approaches to Community Safety and Crime Prevention, May 2011.

350 Submission from Mr Paul Jamieson, Community Development Manager, City of Greater Geelong to the Drugs and Crime Prevention Committee, Inquiry into Locally Based Approaches to Community Safety and Crime Prevention, May 2011.

351 Cr Jan Farrell, Community Safety Portfolio, City of Greater Geelong, Evidence given to the Drugs and Crime Prevention Committee, Inquiry into Locally Based Approaches to Community Safety and Crime Prevention, Public Hearing, Geelong, 8 August 2011.

352 http://www.geelongaustralia.com.au/community/safety/ accessed on 21 March 2012.

353 Assoc. Prof. Darren Palmer, Convenor, Criminology Program, Deakin University, Evidence given to the Drugs and Crime Prevention Committee, Inquiry into Locally Based Approaches to Community Safety and Crime Prevention, Public Hearing, Geelong, 8 August 2011.

Greater Geelong Safety Committee

The City of Greater Geelong like many other local government authorities has established a committee for involving local community agencies in developing interventions for promoting community safety. The Greater Geelong Safety Committee (GGSC) is an alliance between the City of Greater Geelong, Victoria Police, State Government Departments and community representatives.

The GGSC believes 'that through a holistic partnership approach we can make Geelong an even safer place to live, work and play'.[354] The GGSC's key priority is to create an integrated approach to community safety.

The GGSC has around 20 regular members at a monthly meeting and often brings in other people to address specific issues such as road safety or the prevention of violence against women. The GGSC also has a Neighbourhood Watch representative at most meetings with strong collaboration between the Council and Neighbourhood Watch. The local Neighbourhood Watch President has taken a strong interest in the partnership model and is committed to developing new approaches to community safety.[355]

Localised issues and localised responses

In addition to the overarching GGSC, the City of Greater Geelong has a number of supporting committees that operate in conjunction with the GGSC and are linked into the Safety Plan. These include the Barwon Drug Action Plan Committee, the Prevention of Violence Against Women working group, Road Safe Barwon and the Graffiti Reference Committee. One example of how partnership work and networking through local committees can help solve problems at a very local level was given to the Committee by Councillor Jan Farrell in the context of alcohol-related violence on the Ocean Grove foreshore:

> Ocean Grove is a small town with a population of about 11,000 people. It has always been a rite of passage for young people to enjoy New Year's Eve on the beach. On New Year's Eve 2005 there were major issues around alcohol and violence to the point where a large group of young people went into the local caravan park [and exhibited antisocial behaviours]. There were not a lot of police in the area on the night and we had not had this kind of problem before and there was a lot of distress caused in that community on that New Year's Eve. At 9 o'clock the next morning my phone rang and it was the local caravan park operator who was ringing to say, 'What are we going to do about it? Your council, your problem, you fix it'. At 5 o'clock that afternoon we were in a meeting with that venue operator and the officer in charge of Bellarine Police Station and we started a process about how we were going to very clearly support our young people to continue to have that right to be on the beach on New Year's Eve, but also how to minimise the risk of harm to both themselves and to local residents.

> Since that time a local committee has been convened and supported, by the local [police] sergeant. It now includes a wide range of groups – the CFA; the local coast manager; Barwon Coast Council; St John Ambulance; the traders, the owners of the caravan park. Those meetings are convened on an as needs basis. They ramp up coming through October, November, December, and there is always an evaluation process at the end of that. Some of the initiatives that have been put in place, Barwon Coast as the land manager has put in a lot of money around lighting. One of the obvious initiatives was to light the place. They have also developed fireworks on New Year's Eve which has brought lots more families into the area. Instead of it being a young people only event, lots more families are coming to it.

354 Submission from Mr Paul Jamieson, Community Development Manager, City of Greater Geelong to the Drugs and Crime Prevention Committee, Inquiry into Locally Based Approaches to Community Safety and Crime Prevention, May 2011.
355 For a discussion of Neighbourhood Watch, see Chapter 10 of this Report.

Council has assisted with by-laws around alcohol. No open alcohol containers in the area. Also we provide road management. One of the issues was some of the young people using their cars as a portable esky. They would have access backwards and forwards to their cars during the afternoon and evening and that is no longer an option. One of the other things that has been incredibly important has been the support of Victoria Police, often riding with our by-laws people from about 3 o'clock in the afternoon. Leading up to New Year's Eve there are visits to the local packaged liquor about supporting the initiatives of not selling alcohol in glass containers on New Year's Eve. There are also a lot of patrols during the afternoon so we can identify where things happen.

One of the important parts of this is that it has been *a local issue and it has been a local response*, lots of partners around the table. I am not saying that we will not, one year, have the same issues again, but we have minimised the risk of those issues happening at a local level. We have also reclaimed the space for families in Barwon Heads and Ocean Grove who are quite comfortable coming into that space now. Most importantly, we have allowed the young people in that area to not be excluded from that space. One of the issues that we see time and time again is around a response to young people and the way they behave in excluding them from spaces. What we should be doing is bringing more people into those spaces and making those spaces more comfortable for young people to be in.[356]

The City of Geelong considers that the response taken in Geelong to issues of community safety and crime prevention including issues such as violence in the coastal holiday areas can be categorised into the three broad themes. Before adopting an approach to any issue it believes the following questions need to be addressed:

- *Planning* – Does an issue/intervention fit into existing plans? Can this be linked to existing plans or strategies?

- *Partnerships* – What partnerships exist to support an intervention? Do new partnerships need to be developed? Who are the key partners?

- *Evidence base* – Is there an existing evidence base for the work? Can this contribute to the data in some way? Does the existing evidence support a particular approach?[357]

Other local government initiatives

The Committee has taken evidence from representatives of a number of local government areas across Victoria during the course of this Inquiry. Some of these are inner city or suburban Melbourne areas (City of Yarra, City of Dandenong, City of Frankston, City of Casey). Others concern rural and regional Victoria (City of Geelong, City of Ballarat). Evidence has been given from a semi-rural or 'peri-urban' council (Shire of Macedon Ranges) and the central city of Melbourne has also been represented (City of Melbourne).

What all these municipal bodies have in common is that to greater or lesser extents they rely on entering partnerships with other stakeholders to develop and implement local crime prevention and community safety projects and programs. These programs are far too numerous to detail individually in a Report of this type. The following section therefore gives only a basic account of some of the most salient features of a few selected councils.

---

356   Cr Jan Farrell, Community Safety Portfolio, City of Greater Geelong, Evidence given to the Drugs and Crime Prevention Committee, Inquiry into Locally Based Approaches to Community Safety and Crime Prevention, Public Hearing, Geelong, 8 August 2011.

357   Submission from Mr Paul Jamieson, Community Development Manager, City of Greater Geelong to the Drugs and Crime Prevention Committee, Inquiry into Locally Based Approaches to Community Safety and Crime Prevention, May 2011.

The City of Yarra

The City of Yarra is based in inner city Melbourne taking in the suburbs of Richmond, Collingwood, Fitzroy and Abbotsford. Like other inner city councils it faces the unique issues attributable to having both a significant population of disadvantaged residents as well as a notable group of affluent people in the more gentrified areas of the municipality. As Mayor of Yarra, Ms Alison Clarke told the Committee: 'Trying to get those two groups – the advantaged and disadvantaged – to get together [to address the problems] is a tricky one'.[358]

As such, the City of Yarra faces particular localised crime and safety issues. Some of these are related to its proximity to the central business district, a large public housing population (about 10 per cent of the total municipal population) and busy entertainment precincts.[359]

Other key safety issues in the City of Yarra include the negative impacts of alcohol and illicit drug consumption on the community. The entertainment precincts of Swan Street in Richmond, Brunswick and Smith Streets in Fitzroy and Collingwood are often associated with amenity impacts for the community, public drunkenness, and occasionally antisocial behaviour. Victoria Street in North Richmond and Abbotsford currently has the highest volume of heroin dealing in Victoria which brings with it crime, amenity and safety impacts for the community. Further, the City of Yarra has a visible Aboriginal community of which some members have long-term problematic use of alcohol.[360] Mayor Allison Clarke told the Committee that in addressing these problems the Council had moved away from *solely* a traditional law and order response, for example the enforcement of local laws against drinking in public, to one that took more of a social development approach:

> There has been an expectation that the law will somehow fix them [drug, alcohol and antisocial behavioural problems], but I think people are starting to be a little more realistic about that now. I had a meeting with the Smith Street traders a couple of weeks ago. They had a particular issue because there was a group of Aboriginal people who were drinking in the street and sometimes hassling people and so forth. They were keen that this local law would stop them from doing that. It did for a little while, and now they are coming back. The issue is one of addressing a group who have got multiple disadvantages. We have been trying to get them engaged in other programs rather than the [punitive] deterrent effect… We have been trying to address it in a more strength-based community development way rather than a law-and-order way, given their backgrounds. The police sometimes ask them to pour their drinks out and move on, but they cannot be there all the time. As soon as they go away the problem comes back. The traders are coming to an understanding that you cannot just have a law and suddenly it is fixed. We are still going to have to do the strength-based community development stuff with these people, and it will be a long project. There is nothing simple in local government. We have got our heads around that pretty well by now.[361]

The Yarra City Local Safety Committee

To address some of these problems since 2004, Yarra City Council in conjunction with Yarra Police Services Area convened a Local Safety Committee (the Committee) to bring together diverse agencies to identify and respond to local safety issues. Members of the Committee include Victoria Police, Yarra City Council, Department of Health, Office of Housing, the

358 Cr Alison Clarke, Mayor, City of Yarra, Evidence given to the Drugs and Crime Prevention Committee, Inquiry into Locally Based Approaches to Community Safety and Crime Prevention, Public Hearing, Geelong, 10 August 2011.

359 Submission from Mr Craig Kenny, Director, Community Programs, Local Safety Committee, City of Yarra to the Drugs and Crime Prevention Committee, Inquiry into Locally Based Approaches to Community Safety and Crime Prevention, May 2011

360 Submission from Mr Craig Kenny, Director, Community Programs, Local Safety Committee, City of Yarra to the Drugs and Crime Prevention Committee, Inquiry into Locally Based Approaches to Community Safety and Crime Prevention, May 2011

361 Cr Alison Clarke, Mayor, City of Yarra, Evidence given to the Drugs and Crime Prevention Committee, Inquiry into Locally Based Approaches to Community Safety and Crime Prevention, Public Hearing, Geelong, 10 August 2011.

Neighbourhood Justice Centre, Yarra Drug and Health Forum, Youth Support and Advocacy Services, North Yarra Community Health and North Richmond Community Health.

The Committee provides a forum to share information among members which enables diverse agencies to understand one another and form synergies which in turn facilitates a more coordinated and collaborative approach to responding to the community. 'The Forum is a great example of how the community can be engaged at the local level, thereby providing a conduit to government and other agencies in terms of policy development'.[362] Mr Ross Goeman, Acting Manager of Community Planning and Advocacy for the City of Yarra spoke to the benefits of the Committee and the partnerships that have flowed from it when he gave evidence to the Drugs and Crime Prevention Committee:

> There has been some *really good* work between Victoria Police and particularly the community health centres, particularly around a lot of those high-profile police operations. For a couple of those they had coordinated drug and alcohol workers at the Richmond police station during the operation to provide direct face-to-face referral services, which were apparently very successful. It certainly facilitated very good relationships. A year or a year and a half ago, perhaps two years ago, some work was done around the high-rise estates. There was the perception that young people were problematic or there was problematic behaviour in the estates. The local safety committee coordinated some researchers to go out and look at that, and they found that largely it was not an issue.[363] (Speaker's emphasis)

'Taking Action Together'

An initiative called 'Taking Action Together' facilitated through the Local Safety Committee in 2010 is another example of a locally based partnership approach to alleviate the impacts of illicit drugs in the City of Yarra, in particular around Victoria Street in North Richmond and Abbotsford. In developing practical solutions, 70 representatives of a range of agencies including State Government; Department of Health and VicHealth, came together to share and identify potential solutions. Thirty-four actions were agreed to.

Many of the solutions are based on principles of a cross-sector approach and close engagement with the community impacted by illicit drugs including injecting drug users. For example a very successful action out of Taking Action Together was the development of a street art mural in a laneway. The laneway is commonly used for injecting drugs, which created amenity and safety concerns for the community. Though a simple action, it was successful on many levels in that it:

◆ engaged illegal graffiti artists to develop productive, commissioned activity;

◆ created an open space and thoroughfare for visitors, traders and residents of and around Victoria Street;

◆ formed positive, constructive partnerships between Victoria Street traders and Yarra City Council in seeking traders' support for the mural; and

◆ achieved outcomes of improved amenity and safety in that particular area through the minimisation of discarded syringes and incidences of public injecting.

As the Yarra City submission to this Inquiry stated:

---

362 Submission from Mr Craig Kenny, Director, Community Programs, Local Safety Committee, City of Yarra to the Drugs and Crime Prevention Committee, Inquiry into Locally Based Approaches to Community Safety and Crime Prevention, May 2011.

363 Mr Ross Goeman, Acting Manager, Community Planning and Advocacy, City of Yarra, Evidence given to the Drugs and Crime Prevention Committee, Inquiry into Locally Based Approaches to Community Safety and Crime Prevention, Public Hearing, Geelong, 10 August 2011.

The experiences from this locally based approach demonstrate that collaboration among local agencies including Police and Council, community members and State Government is necessary to facilitate improvements in community safety.[364]

In short, the submission argues that the initiatives of Yarra City Council in conjunction with its associated agencies are excellent examples of a partnership approach to crime prevention and community safety.

The City of Frankston

Frankston City Council provides an example of a local government that engages in a broad range of crime prevention and community safety activities. This includes targeted activities, focusing on specific crime or safety issues, as well as the 'implementation of broader approaches such as exploring creative opportunities for young people or building capacity within communities that will make them more welcoming and inclusive'.[365]

The council has a Community Safety Management Team (CSMT) that receives reports on all crime prevention and community safety programs, engages with stakeholders and develops strategies to address emerging issues. The CSMT includes representation from police, health services, education, youth services and other community representatives. The council has also developed a comprehensive draft strategy in consultation with community organisations, Victoria Police, the Department of Planning and Community Development and the Department of Justice.[366] The CSMT also includes a Community Safety Coordinator, Graffiti Management Coordinator, Fire Prevention Officer, Community Safety Officer, Community Safety Officer/Investigation/Mobile Cameras, Ambassador Program Coordinator, Ambassador Program Officers and an Administration Officer.

Programs and achievements of the Community Safety Committee include:

- The Frankston City Ambassador Program, launched in December 2006. A program coordinator and program officer deter antisocial behaviour and improve perceptions of safety in the Central Activities District and Frankston foreshore areas with their presence and relationship with the community. The officers work with local traders, services, community members and police.

- The Frankston Drink Safe Project commenced in 2005 with funding from the National Community Crime Prevention Program.

- The Safer City Centre based in Young Street, opposite Frankston railway station, provides police and Council services with a 'one stop shop'. This concept is a first for Australia, and was recognised with the 2003 Gold Award for Excellence in Local Government in Crime and Violence Prevention and the 2004 LGPro (Local Government Professionals) award for excellence.

- Installation of CCTV cameras throughout Young Street and at the Frankston Safe Taxi Rank. These cameras will be continuously monitored at Frankston Police Station.

- A safety audit was carried out by volunteers around the Frankston railway station and transit interchange. As a result, lighting was improved, and changes were made to the layout of the public toilets.

---

364 Submission from Mr Craig Kenny, Director, Community Programs, Local Safety Committee, City of Yarra to the Drugs and Crime Prevention Committee, Inquiry into Locally Based Approaches to Community Safety and Crime Prevention, May 2011.

365 Submission from Mr Steven Dickson, Compliance and Safety Manager, Frankston City Council to the Drugs and Crime Prevention Committee, Inquiry into Locally Based Approaches to Community Safety and Crime Prevention, May 2011.

366 See http://www.frankston.vic.gov.au/Local_Laws_and_Safety/index.aspx accessed on 21 March 2012.

◆ Problems with young people gathering in reserves at night and causing disturbances to neighbours have been dealt with through the use of security guards at selected reserves on Friday and Saturday nights. Some reserves have been deemed 'no entry' areas at night to further reduce the problem.

◆ Development of a drug and alcohol action plan.

◆ The Safe Taxi Rank, a combined project of various local licensed premises, Frankston Taxis and Council, operates to provide safe late night transport.

◆ A Liquor Accord operates to promote the responsible service of alcohol and reduce the incidence of alcohol-related harms.

Police initiatives and partnerships in crime prevention in the City of Frankston have been discussed in Chapter 6.

City of Casey

The City of Casey is located in the outer south-eastern suburbs of Melbourne. Casey is Victoria's most populous municipality, with a 2006 census population of 214,960 residents. The municipality's population growth rate during both 1996–2001 and 2001–2006 was higher, in absolute terms, than other rapidly growing outer Melbourne municipalities.

While the City of Casey does not having a crime prevention strategy per se, it is committed to 'community safety' through the development of a Community Safety Department and Team and evidenced in Council strategies and plans such as the Municipal Health and Wellbeing Plan and the Community Safety Strategy.[367]

City of Casey Municipal Health and Wellbeing Plan

The Casey Council's vision for community safety, including reducing crime and antisocial behaviour is articulated through its Municipal Health and Wellbeing Plan 2009–2013 mandated under the *Public Health and Wellbeing Act* 2008:

> Through community consultation this plan clearly articulates 'community safety' as one of seven key priorities. Casey's concept of community safety is defined as a community in which 'all residents and visitors can work, live and play in a safe and secure environment, free of risk to health and wellbeing'. Community safety relates to both the perception of risks to wellbeing, as well as the actual incidence of crime and injury in the public sphere and in the home. Council's current priorities to enhance community safety are:
>
> • Family violence prevention;
>
> • Road trauma reduction;
>
> • Fire/emergency management;
>
> • Intentional (crime) & unintentional (accident) injury prevention;
>
> • Disease prevention including immunisation and food safety; and
>
> • Alcohol harm minimisation.[368]

Community Safety Team

The Community Safety Team (CST) is engaged in a number of community safety, road safety and school crossing activities including CPTED assessments; addressing resident

---

367   Submission from Mr Richard Maugueret, Acting Manager, Community Safety, City of Casey to the Drugs and Crime Prevention Committee, Inquiry into Locally Based Approaches to Community Safety and Crime Prevention, October 2011.

368   Submission from Mr Richard Maugueret, Acting Manager, Community Safety, City of Casey to the Drugs and Crime Prevention Committee, Inquiry into Locally Based Approaches to Community Safety and Crime Prevention, October 2011.

and business trader safety concerns relating to antisocial behaviour; Neighbourhood Watch; and the operation of the Graffiti Management program (Education, Eradication and Enforcement). It also addresses residents' road safety concerns and delivers Road Safety Awareness programs, including the management and operation of the Casey Safety Village and the City of Casey Hoon Hotline. The CST works closely with the Council's Health Promotion teams in promoting community safety messages, for example through alcohol and drug minimisation and family violence prevention programs. It similarly liaises with Council's Fire Prevention team to address issues pertaining to fire safety and awareness.

Community Safety Partnerships

Casey Council has entered a number of partnerships with government and non-government agencies in order to deliver its community safety programs. This is formally done with state government agencies through the Safer Casey Partnership. This is:

> A local, strategic 'whole of Government' approach to facilitating interagency targeted community safety actions and fostering exchange of critical information. Agencies involved include City of Casey, Victoria Police (Police Service Area Inspector is a Co-Chair of the committee), Country Fire Authority (CFA), Southern Health (represented by Cardinia-Casey Community Health Service), VicRoads, Department of Education & Early Childhood Development (DEECD), Department of Human Services (DHS), Department of Justice (DOJ), South Eastern Region Migrant Resource Centre (SERMRC) and other community representatives as required. The individual agencies that are members of Safer Casey Partnership are working to improve the wellbeing of all people in Casey by reducing the impact of intentional and unintentional injury and harm on individuals, families, schools, workplaces, business and communities.[369]

The Safer Casey Partnership is the key strategic committee where community safety and crime prevention matters are considered. A submission from the Council to this Inquiry states that this committee effectively brings together all key agencies across the municipality to address crime and community safety issues, although problems have been encountered with staff changes across the different organisations and varying representation at meetings.[370]

> The success of the network has not necessarily been in the area of project delivery or outcome focus, but rather on the concept of partnership. It provides opportunities for the various organisations to consider joint programs and service delivery. This can be evidenced in the positive working relationship developed through the Casey Safety Village. This unique Safety Village concept showcases the Casey Road Safety Education Centre (CRSEC) and Country Fire Authority Learning Centre. It delivers road and fire safety educational programs to kindergarten and primary school children. This collaborative effort between the two organisations is evidence to the success of the Safer Casey Partnership.[371]

The CST and other council officers also sit on a Council and Police Liaison Committee with members of the Community Engagement Team from the Casey Police Service Area. The Committee meets on a quarterly basis to identify emerging crime issues and associated crime prevention strategies; identify partnership projects to positively impact perceptions of safety; and general information exchange (criminal damage, graffiti and other forms of antisocial behaviour). Where appropriate, the Committee also helps to inform the Safer Casey Partnership and other local council committees and police operations.

---

369 Submission from Mr Richard Maugueret, Acting Manager, Community Safety, City of Casey to the Drugs and Crime Prevention Committee, Inquiry into Locally Based Approaches to Community Safety and Crime Prevention, October 2011.

370 One of the common challenges faced by local councils in developing local partnerships, see Chapter 8.

371 Submission from Mr Richard Maugueret, Acting Manager, Community Safety, City of Casey to the Drugs and Crime Prevention Committee, Inquiry into Locally Based Approaches to Community Safety and Crime Prevention, October 2011.

Casey Council Community Safety Programs

The City of Casey's submission to this Inquiry outlined many examples of programs and projects that could loosely be included under the rubric of crime prevention and community safety.[372]

Macedon Ranges Shire

Rural or semi-rural councils like Macedon Ranges Shire Council, where crime is not as concentrated or prominent and consequently priorities may differ, face different challenges to their city and suburban counterparts. In the Macedon Ranges Shire Council the perception is that much of the crime comes in from neighbouring areas.[373] Crime prevention and safety is therefore approached across nine townships as Councils see one of their roles as trying 'to maintain young people within those townships and encourage them to have a sense of connection and therefore a sense of belonging and respect for their local towns'.[374] Other priorities include road safety and mental health.[375]

A key body for addressing crime prevention and community safety in the shire is the Macedon Ranges Local Safety Committee. This organisaton uses a cross-sector, multi-agency approach to identify and influence key current and emerging safety and crime prevention issues. Members comprise representatives from the community, police, council, education, health and welfare sectors.

> The Safety Committee fosters strategic alliances and builds ongoing and effective networks, partnerships and collaborations with individuals and groups in the local community, police and council as well as the education, health and welfare sectors.

> The Safety Committee has a particular focus on prevention, which requires it to keep abreast of existing and emerging health, safety, crime and wellbeing issues. Having members from diverse sectors with broad networks helps the Safety Committee achieve this.[376]

Local police representatives who are on the Safety Committee spoke to the benefits of this approach when they gave evidence to the Committee. For example Detective Sergeant Shane Brundell said:

> [e]veryone [on the Committee] is from different areas, but they are at such a level in their own little agencies that they have clout, and so when we sit together as a safety committee there is no barrier to the discussions. Everything is effectively on the table, because the greater picture is that we all want the same goal at the end of the day. We discuss everything, and no-one says 'No'. Everyone is prepared to give it a go, and we try. So we are prepared to put our hand up at the end of the day for the benefit and safety of the community, and it is really good to see and it is really good to be part of that team.[377]

---

372 Submission from Mr Richard Maugueret, Acting Manager, Community Safety, City of Casey to the Drugs and Crime Prevention Committee, Inquiry into Locally Based Approaches to Community Safety and Crime Prevention, October 2011.

373 Sergeant Geoff Neil, Officer-in-Charge, Macedon Ranges Traffic Management Unit, Gisborne, Victoria Police, Macedon Ranges Local Safety Committee, Evidence given to the Drugs and Crime Prevention Committee, Inquiry into Locally Based Approaches to Community Safety and Crime Prevention, Public Hearing, Melbourne, 9 August 2011.

374 Ms Pauline Neil, Coordinator, Youth Development Unit, Macedon Ranges Shire Council, Evidence given to the Drugs and Crime Prevention Committee, Inquiry into Locally Based Approaches to Community Safety and Crime Prevention, Public Hearing, Melbourne, 9 August 2011.

375 Detective Sergeant Shane Brundell, Macedon Ranges Crime Investigation Unit Representative, Gisborne, Victoria Police, Macedon Ranges Local Safety Committee, Evidence given to the Drugs and Crime Prevention Committee, Inquiry into Locally Based Approaches to Community Safety and Crime Prevention, Public Hearing, Melbourne, 9 August 2011.

376 Submission from Dr Lorraine Beyer, Sustainable Communities Planner, Macedon Ranges Local Safety Committee, to the Drugs and Crime Prevention Committee, Inquiry into Locally Based Approaches to Community Safety and Crime Prevention, June 2011.

377 Detective Sergeant Shane Brundell, Macedon Ranges Crime Investigation Unit Representative, Gisborne, Victoria Police, Evidence given to the Drugs and Crime Prevention Committee, Inquiry into Locally Based Approaches to Community Safety and Crime Prevention, Public Hearing, Melbourne, 9 August 2011.

His colleague Sergeant Geoff Neil agreed stating:

> As a local safety committee we are virtually made up of our local health services, education, business, community, local government and police. We are not a high-level committee but I think we are good at what we do because we are the ones who are working on the ground and putting it on the ground. We get guidance, of course, from further up the food chain, but our commitment to achieving the common good is fantastic. We are all committed to the committee and making it work. We trust each other implicitly. We have respect for each other. It is a very open committee, and there is a free flow of information… we resolve the issues; we pick them up early.[378]

The Shire has also produced a Community Safety and Crime Prevention Plan developed with key stakeholders and with wide community consultation:

> [The Plan] is designed to be a unifying document which will help the community as well as key local and state agencies, sectors and groups to cultivate a coordinated and systematic approach to safety and crime prevention in the Macedon Ranges. The Local Safety Committee approached the Macedon Ranges Shire Council to support its development and it was subsequently launched in May 2011 and distributed throughout the Shire. The six Priority Areas highlighted in the Plan are:
>
> 1. Safe Places & Spaces
>
> 2. Friendly & Connected Neighbourhoods
>
> 3. Safe & Secure Women
>
> 4. Mental & Physical Wellbeing
>
> 5. Safety & Wellbeing
>
> 6. Alcohol & Licensing.[379]

In addition to its collaborative cross-sector approach on many current and emerging safety and crime prevention issues, the Macedon Ranges Local Safety Committee supports a number of larger programs addressing specific areas of concern with regard to crime, antisocial behaviour and community safety. Many of these are based in preventing young people in the shire from becoming involved in criminal or antisocial activity.[380]

Community organisations and crime prevention

Much community based crime prevention incorporates or is drawn from theories of community development and the processes of community engagement and community capacity building (Lane & Henry 2004; Sutton, Cherney & White 2008). As was discussed in Chapter 2, community development strategies, including those focusing on crime, are often implemented in disadvantaged communities and ideally focus on integrated multi-objective and multi-strategy partnerships rather than single objective programs (Lane & Henry 2004).[381] They may also be developed or implemented for particular communities with special and culturally specific needs, for example Indigenous communities.[382]

---

378 Sergeant Geoff Neil, Officer-in-Charge, Macedon Ranges Traffic Management Unit, Gisborne, Victoria Police, Evidence given to the Drugs and Crime Prevention Committee, Inquiry into Locally Based Approaches to Community Safety and Crime Prevention, Public Hearing, Melbourne, 9 August 2011.

379 Submission from Dr Lorraine Beyer, Sustainable Communities Planner, Macedon Ranges Local Safety Committee, to the Drugs and Crime Prevention Committee, Inquiry into Locally Based Approaches to Community Safety and Crime Prevention, June 2011.

380 These programs include 'Live 4 Life', 'Pole Position', 'Learner Driver Mentor Program' and Youth Camps. For details, see Submission from Dr Lorraine Beyer, Sustainable Communities Planner, Macedon Ranges Local Safety Committee, to the Drugs and Crime Prevention Committee, Inquiry into Locally Based Approaches to Community Safety and Crime Prevention, June 2011. See also Council safety and crime prevention plan, accessed at http://www.mrsc.vic.gov.au/Files/SafetyPlanMRSC0311.pdf

381 See for example the 'Pathways to Prevention' program discussed in Chapter 2 of this Report.

382 For a discussion of the suitability of crime prevention measures in particular communities, see Chapter 2.

At the non-government organisation level, crime prevention and community safety is addressed by many charitable groups and organisations, community volunteers, professional service providers, community programs and initiatives. Groups like Anglicare, Jesuit Social Services, Berry Street and the Salvation Army, for example, deliver a range of services across Victoria that engage with crime prevention and community safety issues generally, like residential services and homelessness, drug and alcohol services and violence prevention.[383] The following programs are drawn from evidence given to the Committee by way of written submission or at Public Hearings.[384] The common theme of the following programs is that they rely on working in partnership with a variety of agencies and organisations to achieve their goals.

Salvation Army programs – Street Teams and the 'AXA 614 Youth Bus'

The Salvation Army has long been associated with addressing the needs of the disadvantaged. Whilst many of their programs are directly or indirectly involved with community safety and community engagement, this section concentrates on innovative programs the Committee received evidence about.

Street Teams

As part of its community engagement activities the Salvation Army runs a weekend Youth Street Teams program in conjunction with the City of Melbourne, Victoria Police and other youth and welfare agencies. Its aim is to combat binge drinking and other forms of antisocial behaviour in the Melbourne CBD whilst assisting young people who may be at risk. Major Brendan Nottle of the Salvation Army spoke to the Street Teams program when he gave evidence to the Committee:

> With street teams, the idea came out of two things. We had been working with the police and the City of Melbourne on a number of pilot programs around trying to work with young people who are getting really drunk on Friday and Saturday nights and getting caught up in or actually perpetrating violence that is fuelled by alcohol. At the same time the City of Melbourne ran a website called 'Your city: your space', and they encouraged young people to contribute ideas to that website about how they thought things could happen to change the outcomes of alcohol-fuelled violence in the city. One of the ideas that some young people came up with was to actually have young people on the streets on Friday and Saturday nights who would act as positive role models. We have taken that idea and really developed it in close conjunction with the City of Melbourne.

> What we do, and we have been doing this since the beginning of December last year, is every Friday and Saturday night have 20 young people get together at about 10.30 at night at the Salvation Army building at Bourke Street. They are coordinated by experienced and qualified youth workers, and then there is an overall coordinator for the night. Before the night starts, on both Friday and Saturday nights, the overall coordinator has to report to Melbourne East police station and Melbourne West police station. We are involved in briefing the police about our presence on the streets that night, how we can be contacted and what we are available to do. We also go to Crown Casino now and brief the security teams at Crown Casino.[385]

The 'Salvos' work in close cooperation with Victoria Police to address potential violent or antisocial behaviour before it spirals out of control. Through the proactive efforts of the youth coordinators and volunteers potential problems are 'nipped in the bud':

---

383 See http://www.anglicarevic.org.au/ and http://www.salvationarmy.org.au/victoria

384 Some community crime prevention programs that are in part led by community organisations have already been discussed in the sections on local government or police where these other organisations may be a lead partner. Mission Australia's involvement in the Youth Assist Program in Frankston is a prime example of this.

385 Major Brendan Nottle, Commanding Officer, Salvation Army, Evidence given to the Drugs and Crime Prevention Committee, Inquiry into Locally Based Approaches to Community Safety and Crime Prevention, Public Hearing, Melbourne, 9 August 2011.

It has turned out to be a really effective program because there are two things that develop as the night goes on. One is that we have the coordinator in a van, which is well marked with Salvation Army shields, and they have another person with them. They respond to telephone calls from the police and security at Crown Casino, rather than the police having their resources tied up with young people who are drunk and perhaps unconscious sometimes. There are often young girls who will go into nightclubs down on King Street. They will go outside on their own for a smoke or some fresh air, and then they cannot get back in. They leave their handbag inside, so they become very vulnerable very quickly. The police will call us to those situations, and we will take responsibility for that particular young person. That could mean taking them back to the Salvation Army, helping them sober up, trying to make contact with their friends so that they can reconnect with their friends or actually getting them in the van, taking them home and just getting them out of the city.[386]

An added bonus is that there are fewer demands upon police resources at what is normally a time of peak police activity:

That concept has developed further to the point now where, when police charge a young person for being drunk and disorderly and they are locked up for 4 hours – sometimes when a person is released perhaps they will get into strife and get locked up again, and in the state of mind they are in sometimes the on-the-spot fine, the penalty notice or the banning from the city do not have any impact on them – the police will call us and we will take that young person out of the city. We will deal with any young person as long as they are not violent, because then that is putting our teams at risk. It has become a program that I think is really valued by the police because it actually takes pressure off them and frees them up to go back to their core business, which is law and order. It is doing a similar thing with security at Crown as well.[387]

The AXA 414 Youth Bus

An associated aspect of the Streets Program is the Salvation Army's 'AXA 414 Youth Bus'. The bus is a coach that has been fully refurbished into a mobile 'youth centre on wheels'. It is equipped with wireless internet connected PCs, Xboxes, a plasma TV, three surround sound systems, hang out couches, chess tables, a mini kitchen and a private counselling room.

The AXA614 Youth Bus is designed to be a safe place off the streets for Melbourne's homeless and marginalised youth. It is a tool for the Street Teams to interact and engage with vulnerable and isolated young people 'with the intention of building relationships and seeing their lives transformed'.[388] Major Nottle sees it as an essential complement to the work of the Street Teams:

The bus is out from 6.30 p.m. to about 10.00 or 10.30 at night Monday to Thursday. We park it down outside St Paul's Cathedral on Flinders Street. Some nights it goes down to the Alexandra Gardens skate park and also down on Flinders Street at the end of Flinders Street station near Queen Street. We work with 70 to 100 under 25s a night at the bus. They are all in significant need. In terms of a lot of the young people we see, on average 30 to 40 of those young people, are from residential care units. They are in the care of the state.

They often gravitate into the city because they get bored at home. In some cases there have been people aged as young as 13 who are living in a house on their own, meaning with no other young person, with four youth workers. Young people just get bored out of their brain and gravitate to the city. They often meet up with other young people. They often get caught up in really negative

---

386 Major Brendan Nottle, Commanding Officer, Salvation Army, Evidence given to the Drugs and Crime Prevention Committee, Inquiry into Locally Based Approaches to Community Safety and Crime Prevention, Public Hearing, Melbourne, 9 August 2011.

387 Major Brendan Nottle, Commanding Officer, Salvation Army, Evidence given to the Drugs and Crime Prevention Committee, Inquiry into Locally Based Approaches to Community Safety and Crime Prevention, Public Hearing, Melbourne, 9 August 2011.

388 http://www.salvationarmy.org.au/axa-614-bus.html

behaviour around the city. Often that is where they get involved in talk like, 'There is the bus. That is the barbecue on the side'. [389]

Again as with the Street Teams an essential part of the Youth Bus project is the partnerships with which the Salvation Army has entered into to 'make it work':

> I should also say that the [Melbourne City] council has been really excellent in the way they have worked with us. Our sense is that the council is very keen to see a lot of the issues around alcohol-based violence addressed, and they are really prepared to back anything that they think is going to work. It is not just in terms of money; it is a very active involvement and participation by council. They sit down with us regularly, see how things are going and contribute ideas. They are a really good sounding board. I think those sorts of commitments from council have been really helpful as well.

> We work really closely with the police around this particular project as well. The police will come to us and say they have seen young people or a particular young person who is causing some trouble around the city. We will really cooperate with police around helping them sort those issues out with the young people.

> The other interesting issue around this is that not only do we have our youth workers, we also have qualified youth workers, a drug and alcohol worker and a lawyer from Youthlaw who comes out on the bus. They are working really closely with the Department of Human Services and the police in trying to get young people home. They also work really closely around trying to accommodate homeless young people who appear at the bus. [390]

Mr Dean Griggs, Manager of Community Safety and Wellbeing at the City of Melbourne states that one of the benefits of the Street Teams and AXA Bus project is that they are conceivably transferable to other areas of community safety interventions:

> I think the simplicity of the street teams is that they are very applicable to other areas. You may not run them for the same number of hours…You would need to tailor it to a particular area, but I think as a model it is a ripper, and it does have that applicability. … I think there is potential for it at events, if there are concerts or even on New Year's Eve, or using it earlier on in the evening. At the moment it is very much 11.00 p.m. to 5.00 a.m. on Friday and Saturday nights. But as a model I think it is very transferable. We would be happy to talk to other councils about how we put it together. [391]

In light of the favourable reception to the project, the Salvation Army is in the process of discussing with Metro Trains and the transit police about rolling the teams out on the rail network, potentially complementing the work of the new Protective Service Officers 'in a really positive way':

> They do the law and order work, and [our] guys are available to do the softer work that needs to happen around connecting with homeless people, people who are alcohol affected, people suffering from mental health issues and people who are homeless. These teams are there to work and perhaps extricate those people from those situations, so it helps to develop that perception of safety on the rail network as well. [392]

---

389 Major Brendan Nottle, Commanding Officer, Salvation Army, Evidence given to the Drugs and Crime Prevention Committee, Inquiry into Locally Based Approaches to Community Safety and Crime Prevention, Public Hearing, Melbourne, 9 August 2011.

390 Major Brendan Nottle, Commanding Officer, Salvation Army, Evidence given to the Drugs and Crime Prevention Committee, Inquiry into Locally Based Approaches to Community Safety and Crime Prevention, Public Hearing, Melbourne, 9 August 2011.

391 Mr Dean Griggs, Manager, Community Safety and Wellbeing, City of Melbourne, Evidence given to the Drugs and Crime Prevention Committee, Inquiry into Locally Based Approaches to Community Safety and Crime Prevention, Public Hearing, Melbourne, 9 August 2011.

392 Major Brendan Nottle, Commanding Officer, Salvation Army, Evidence given to the Drugs and Crime Prevention Committee, Inquiry into Locally Based Approaches to Community Safety and Crime Prevention, Public Hearing, Melbourne, 9 August 2011.

The Dock

Initiatives like The Dock provide an example of a community program that engages with issues relevant to a specific group or area. The Dock is a not-for-profit centre established by Police and the Three Seas organisation for Polynesian youth living in the Greater Dandenong, Casey, Frankston and Monash local government areas.[393] The primary objective of Three Seas is to enhance community ownership of initiatives, to pool resources, skills, and programs through partnering and networking with other agencies and organisations, and to generate youth focused support projects.[394]

The Dock itself is a building in Stud Road Dandenong. It was offered rent free to base youth programs for primarily local Maori and Pacific Islander youth. Called 'The Dock' because it represents both a safe port where ships harbour, and a 'place, all too familiar to Maori and Pacific Island youth, in a Court of Law'[395] – The Dock was created as a place from which projects directed at Maori and Pacific Islander youth could be launched, as well as a place for the community to gather. The centre provides a range of community development, mentoring and capacity building activities. The services directly respond to the social and economic conditions that contribute to the over-representation of Maori and Pacific Islander youth in detention, particularly in Dandenong.[396]

Three Seas, in association with its partners that include the police and the Education Department, plans to run a range of community led projects both at and outside The Dock including:

- A Youth Drop in centre providing access to 'down time' activities and services in a safe and supervised environment. The drop in centre will be the bait in which to attract at risk youth into the centre where services and projects are accessible to them.[397]

- A School Support Project. Linking in with other local community based organisations it will develop a 'Before School Breakfast Project'; A 'Lunch Box Project'; and an 'After school homework support Project'.

- In association with Victoria Police and other local community groups – a Back Yard Rugby Project; Carpark Basketball; Netball; Weight training and 'Fitness for fatties'.[398]

Berry Street – Safe and Caring Community Project

Berry Street is an independent Community Service Organisation and Australian charity. Established in 1877, protecting and caring for children has been its primary goal. Berry Street's vision is that 'all children have a good childhood, growing up feeling safe, nurtured and with hope for the future'.[399] Berry Street provides a diverse range of services across metropolitan, regional and rural Victoria, Australia. Among these are community

---

393 Ms Isabel Calvert, Secretary, Three Seas Steering Committee / The Dock, Evidence given to the Drugs and Crime Prevention Committee, Inquiry into Locally Based Approaches to Community Safety and Crime Prevention, Public Hearing, Dandenong, 30 May 2011.

394 Submission from Ms Isabel Calvert, Secretary, Three Seas Steering Committee, to the Drugs and Crime Prevention Committee, Inquiry into Locally Based Approaches to Community Safety and Crime Prevention, May 2011.

395 See submission from Ms Isabel Calvert, Secretary, Three Seas Steering Committee, to the Drugs and Crime Prevention Committee, Inquiry into Locally Based Approaches to Community Safety and Crime Prevention, May 2011.

396 See discussion earlier in this chapter. The Dock however is facing challenges in being able to sustain its programs. These will be discussed in Chapter 8 in the context of challenges in providing community safety programs.

397 See submission from Ms Isabel Calvert, Secretary, Three Seas Steering Committee, to the Drugs and Crime Prevention Committee, Inquiry into Locally Based Approaches to Community Safety and Crime Prevention, May 2011.

398 Three Seas has many other community/youth development and crime prevention projects planned for 'The Dock' which are too numerous to be listed here. For further detail see the submission from Ms Isabel Calvert, Secretary, Three Seas Steering Committee, to the Drugs and Crime Prevention Committee, Inquiry into Locally Based Approaches to Community Safety and Crime Prevention, May 2011.

399 See http://www.berrystreet.org.au/

strengthening programs that are aimed at social inclusion, the reduction of antisocial conduct and community capacity building, particularly in rural communities.[400]

One of its key initiatives in this area is the Safe and Caring Community Project, a program Berry Street auspices in conjunction with the rural Murrundindi Shire and local police. This program addresses bullying and violent behaviour among school youth in the local catchments.

The community development approach at the core of the Safe and Caring Community Project is characterised by:

- Locally identified and agreed issues
- 'Whole of Community' philosophy
- Multiple, coordinated responses
- Meaningful partnerships with local government, schools, police and government and community agencies
- Sharing of key community values
- Medium to long term 'process' (rather than a short-term 'fix').[401]

Mr David Hall, Senior Manager of Safe and Caring Communities, explained the project to the Committee when he gave evidence in August 2011:

> The Safe and Caring Communities project came about because we identified that there was a high level of antisocial behaviour [in Alexandra and district]. The level of respect and responsibility was not what we would have felt was appropriate. This project came about following a visit to me by the local school principal, who said that he had been approached by the local shire council. There had been a complaint about bullying at the secondary college, and his attitude at that time was, 'Why are they sticking their nose in my business? The school is school business'. I said to him, 'Since when has bullying been the province of schools? Isn't it something that belongs to the whole of the community?'. I think the light bulb went on. We subsequently met with the mayor and one of the shire councillors and the opportunity I saw was that we had the taking up of a particular issue by our local shire council and our secondary college.

> The concept was then taken to the police and community consultative committee. This concept was put to them. We said, 'Here is an opportunity to really expand what that committee is about. It is an opportunity to take on a new role. We do not have to form a new committee; there is already something happening'. That immediately gave us the input of the local police, all the other schools and a range of other partners.[402]

Subsequently the formation of Safe and Caring Communities became a forum in which a number of government and community stakeholders (police, schools, sports clubs, service organisations) could work together to address not only bullying in schools but a whole range of antisocial behaviours that could eventually lead to criminal conduct. It was essential according to the founders of the program that the issue of bullying and antisocial behaviour more generally was not seen as something restricted to the school environment. Rather, it should be viewed as a form of behaviour that was being expressed in all parts of the community, particularly as many of the young people involved, as both protagonists and victims, were not necessarily attending school. As such it needed to be addressed in all parts of community life. As Mr Julian Pocock from Berry Street told the Committee:

---

400 Berry Street also offers comprehensive programs and assistance in the areas of Disability Services; Education; Family Services; Home Based and Residential Care; Therapeutic Services and Counselling; and Youth Services. For further information see http://www.berrystreet.org.au/

401 Submission from Mr Julian Pocock, Director, Public Policy and Practice Development, Berry Street to the Drugs and Crime Prevention Committee, Inquiry into Locally Based Approaches to Community Safety and Crime Prevention, May 2011.

402 Mr David Hall, Senior Manager, Safe and Caring Communities, Berry Street, Evidence given to the Drugs and Crime Prevention Committee, Inquiry into Locally Based Approaches to Community Safety and Crime Prevention, Public Hearing, Geelong, 10 August 2011.

We need[ed] to make sure that in our approach to community-based crime prevention we have a broader platform of intervention than the school system, because the reality is that still a very significant proportion of young people do not complete year 12, are not at school in those later years and are often disengaged along the way. We need our messages to be in the other places where those young people are, and often that is not at school. That is why this particular project has taken the view that an issue like bullying [or other forms of antisocial behaviour] cannot be seen as just belonging to or being resolvable within a school context. It is important that children and young people in that community get a consistency of message in the home and in all the contexts in which they are operating.[403]

Indeed, in some respects bullying was merely one aspect of a program that is essentially about community capacity building in a rural area that was hit badly by the 2009 bushfires. As Mr Hall told the Committee:

In terms of community development you need an opportunity for something to come up. I had identified that there was a need for something. Under-age drinking was a possibility, but it had not stood out.

Graffiti was not a problem in the community. But when the bullying came up, that was one thing that everyone could identify with as a starting point. We have since moved: we now have an under-age drinking subcommittee. All areas of community safety now fit under the umbrella. In terms of mobilising the community, it was about getting an issue, and it was whatever. If there had been a car accident and some young people had been killed, we would have started with that. It is really about seeing what is going to mobilise a community at that particular time and working out how to use that opportunity to then expand and further develop it. It is really about seeing what is going to mobilise a community....[404]

Important outcomes from the project include:

- the value and long term benefit of taking a holistic community development approach to community safety and crime prevention

- the importance of starting with the issues that communities have already identified as important to them, rather than prescribing what issues communities have to address – in the case of the *Safe and Caring Community Project* the issue that the community wanted to address was bullying

- ensuring that crime prevention has a broad focus and includes the prevention of anti-social and threatening behaviours which may not constitute a crime but which undermine community safety and social inclusion

- promoting a consistent set of values that permeate through local schools and the local community such as tolerance, understanding and respectfully resolving conflict

- understanding that patterns of behaviour, good and bad, are established early in life and are modelled in the important institutions, groups, social settings and clubs that children and young people participate in – modelling respectful relationships in all these places for children and young people is central to community safety and crime prevention.[405]

Another positive role of the project has been the greater networking between police and community agencies to proactively address antisocial behaviour in the Shire:

---

403 Mr Julian Pocock, Director, Public Policy and Practice Development, Berry Street, Evidence given to the Drugs and Crime Prevention Committee, Inquiry into Locally Based Approaches to Community Safety and Crime Prevention, Public Hearing, Geelong, 10 August 2011.

404 David Hall, Senior Manager, Safe and Caring Communities, Berry Street, Evidence given to the Drugs and Crime Prevention Committee, Inquiry into Locally Based Approaches to Community Safety and Crime Prevention, Public Hearing, Geelong, 10 August 2011.

405 Submission from Mr Julian Pocock, Director, Public Policy and Practice Development, Berry Street to the Drugs and Crime Prevention Committee, Inquiry into Locally Based Approaches to Community Safety and Crime Prevention, May 2011.

[Police] have started to see the benefit. It has made their job easier. Part of the program was breaking down the barriers between the police and the rest of the community. That has been extremely effective. The involvement of the police in the schools for instance has increased significantly in a very positive manner.[406]

Berry Street argues that the community development approach to community safety and crime prevention, as demonstrated through the Safe and Caring Communities Project, is transferable and can enhance community safety and crime prevention at the local community level. As Mr David Hall told the Committee:

We have tried to take that whole umbrella and say, 'If we're really to have a community that we want to live in and raise our children in, then we've got to be able to impact on every part of that community in order to make that community a safer and stronger community'.[407]

Communities that Care

Communities that Care (CTC) is a not-for-profit training and consulting company formed through a collaboration between the Royal Children's Hospital and the Rotary Club of Melbourne with the objective of 'implementing, evaluating and disseminating strategies that can increase the delivery of effective prevention services in Australian communities'.[408] The CTC vision is to promote the healthy development of children and young people through long-term community planning to prevent health and social problems including becoming involved in crime and antisocial behaviours.

CTC is primarily a community mobilisation and community engagement model rather than a traditional approach to crime prevention and community safety.[409] It operates as a training and technical assistance resource that has been designed to enhance the healthy development of children and young people. It also aims to promote the community's capacity to plan and deliver effective developmental prevention services. The CTC approach includes undertaking a survey across the state to gauge the risk and protective factors that make young people vulnerable to (or resilient against) antisocial and harmful behaviour. Professor John Toumbourou the Chief Executive Officer of CTC spoke to this approach when he gave evidence to the Committee:

The survey is designed to measure what we describe as risk and protective factors... The idea is that there are some things we can measure [such as] family conflict, or bullying, ...they are risk factors that will affect the healthy development of children and increase the likelihood that those children are going to end up with problems. They can be problems that might involve them in violence, or they might be involved in hazardous alcohol use. All these things put children at risk of injury, and we know that these things are sort of a cluster of things that we want to reduce.

Communities that Care is working in a similar way to [the] safer communities programs. In fact we have a very close partnership [with them]. What we do is offer a framework by which this type of work can happen. We have the child and youth survey, which is an important instrument, but we also do training work for coalitions in the community by which we try to encourage different areas within the community, with local governments being major partners that we work with. We

406 Mr David Hall, Senior Manager, Safe and Caring Communities, Berry Street, Evidence given to the Drugs and Crime Prevention Committee, Inquiry into Locally Based Approaches to Community Safety and Crime Prevention, Public Hearing, Geelong, 10 August 2011.

407 Mr David Hall, Senior Manager, Safe and Caring Communities, Berry Street, Evidence given to the Drugs and Crime Prevention Committee, Inquiry into Locally Based Approaches to Community Safety and Crime Prevention, Public Hearing, Geelong, 10 August 2011.

408 http://www.rch.org.au/ctc/

409 See Chapter 1 for a discussion of community engagement, community mobilisation and community capacity building.

work with child and youth professionals, we work with the health sector and we often work with police as well on our Communities that Care local community committees.[410]

The CTC process was designed in the USA and initiated in Australia as a long-term community planning process aimed at preventing a range of health and social problems including alcohol and drug abuse, violence and crime, school failure and community disengagement. The School of Psychology at Deakin University and the Centre for Adolescent Health located at Melbourne's Royal Children's Hospital have been collaborating to provide research and technical support for this best-practice initiative, while significant fund raising and administrative support has been provided through the Rotary Club of Melbourne.[411]

Four registered CTC coalitions currently operate in Australia.

These are:

◆ Communities that Care – Mornington Peninsula

◆ Strengthening Generations – Ballarat

◆ Communities that Care – Myrtleford

◆ Investing in our Youth – Bunbury, Western Australia.

Initial activities focus on community involvement by mobilising the support of key leaders and setting up a relevant prevention organisation or committee. Once communities achieve basic organisational 'readiness', the next phase seeks to identify the major risk and especially protective factors that are influencing local child and adolescent adjustment outcomes within the family, school, community, peers and at the individual level:

> The reason we measure protective factors is that we are trying to encourage these community coalitions to develop healthy environments, not just in the family but also at school and in the broader community. The program brings together coalitions that can use that data and then train them to do the next phase, which is the development of the prevention strategies plan. Communities that Care encourages a greater investment in evidence-based prevention at a local level, and this is the sort of work that has been going on quite well at Mornington Peninsula.[412]

Community profile information is systematically developed from youth surveys and other sources and used to establish local prevention and intervention priorities and health promotion targets. A plan is then established to select and implement evidence-based prevention programs that have been designed to address the selected priorities and targets. Prevention is seen as crucial in addressing potential problems before they become worse, for example identifying a problem with school truancy and putting in place programs to address it may result in fewer young people committing criminal acts later in life:

> Prevention is key. One of the dilemmas I think we have all got, is that often what we have to do when we are in governance roles is respond to those issues that are the order of the day. For example, often the order of the day can be that where there has been a crime or you have somebody who is running amok because of a mental illness, you cannot afford to not do anything about it; you have to respond. Often the responses at that crisis end are very expensive, with very little likelihood that you will be able to solve the root of the problem, whereas the preventive

410 Professor John Toumbourou, Chief Executive Officer, Communities that Care Ltd, Evidence given to the Drugs and Crime Prevention Committee, Inquiry into Locally Based Approaches to Community Safety and Crime Prevention, Public Hearing, Geelong, 10 August 2011.

411 Submission from Professor John Toumbourou, Chief Executive Officer, Communities that Care Limited to the Drugs and Crime Prevention Committee, Inquiry into Locally Based Approaches to Community Safety and Crime Prevention, May 2011.

412 Professor John Toumbourou, Chief Executive Officer, Communities that Care Ltd, Evidence given to the Drugs and Crime Prevention Committee, Inquiry into Locally Based Approaches to Community Safety and Crime Prevention, Public Hearing, Geelong, 10 August 2011.

approach tries to turn the lens on things that might not seem a problem for governance. For example, it is not really a problem for us sitting in this room that there is a child who is exposed to high family conflict, but actually what we do know is that if we leave that situation and we do not have a response to it, then the likelihood is that that child might become in the future a mental health client. So trying to reduce these pathways to problems makes sense, because the investment can be shown through economic return studies to be three, four, fivefold in terms of overall savings.[413]

Finally, monitoring and evaluation are implemented to assess the effectiveness of the local community plan. A series of training programs, assessment resources and consultations are provided to support communities. Through these steps the CTC process assists communities to build local capacity to address the root-causes of child and adolescent problems.[414]

Other examples of programs tailored to local needs can be found in relation to specific environmental issues, such as beach parties or night-time transportation,[415] hooning and drug use.[416] In many cases community organisations and groups deliver these programs or initiatives in partnership with local and state government or Victoria Police.

Community groups and organisations are perfectly positioned to effectively respond to local crime prevention and safety issues.[417] However, they frequently lack the resources to fully realise their goals.[418] While in many cases programs run by state or local government or community groups involve partnerships between the local community, government departments and agencies, police and services providers, support is varied across the state. Nevertheless, there are many good examples of programs built on well-developed partnerships.[419]

Conclusion

This chapter and Chapter 6 have examined current crime prevention and community safety programs in Victoria. Some of these programs have been traditionally focused. Others are concerned more broadly with community engagement and community capacity building, in other words a reduction in crime is an indirect, albeit desired, result of the overall aims and objectives. Even programs that are not ostensibly about crime prevention or community safety per se may nonetheless have significant impacts upon crime and antisocial behaviour. This is particularly the case in the context of social policy initiatives in the area of health, education or youth welfare (Homel et al 2004).

Nearly all the programs discussed, however, have relied on either government or non-government agencies working in collaborative partnerships with other local stakeholders. Most of these partnerships have been flexible and innovative, avoiding a 'one size fits all' approach.

---

413 Professor John Toumbourou, Chief Executive Officer, Communities that Care Ltd, Evidence given to the Drugs and Crime Prevention Committee, Inquiry into Locally Based Approaches to Community Safety and Crime Prevention, Public Hearing, Geelong, 10 August 2011.

414 Submission from Professor John Toumbourou, Chief Executive Officer, Communities that Care Limited to the Drugs and Crime Prevention Committee, Inquiry into Locally Based Approaches to Community Safety and Crime Prevention, May 2011.

415 Mr Darren Holroyd, President, Geelong Nightlife Association, Evidence given to the Drugs and Crime Prevention Committee, Inquiry into Locally Based Approaches to Community Safety and Crime Prevention, Public Hearing, Geelong, 8 August 2011.

416 Mr Steven Dickson, Manager, Compliance and Safety, City of Frankston, Evidence given to the Drugs and Crime Prevention Committee, Inquiry into Locally Based Approaches to Community Safety and Crime Prevention, Public Hearing, Frankston, 30 May 2011.

417 Peter Homel 2005, *Regional organisation for crime prevention delivery*, Australian Institute of Criminology, Canberra.

418 Challenges are addressed in the next chapter. For examples of the challenges relating to a lack of resources see Ms Isabel Calvert, Secretary, Three Seas Steering Committee / The Dock, Evidence given to the Drugs and Crime Prevention Committee, Inquiry into Locally Based Approaches to Community Safety and Crime Prevention, Public Hearing, Dandenong, 30 May 2011.

419 See also Chapter 10 on Neighbourhood Watch.

Nonetheless, developing and implementing these interventions has not been without challenges and problems. There are numerous barriers that can stand in the way of successfully 'doing' crime prevention. The reasons that some programs or approaches may thrive and others don't get off the ground or don't continue are the subject of discussion in Chapter 8.

Recommendations

8. **The Committee recommends** that the Victorian Government Framework on crime prevention and community safety provide local government with clear direction on its crime prevention responsibilities.

9. **The Committee recommends** that the Community Crime Prevention Unit work with local government authorities to develop and implement a Crime Prevention and Community Safety Plan where one does not currently exist or where it does not conform to the principles and guidelines of the new Crime Prevention and Community Safety Framework. Such a Plan should draw from the new Crime Prevention and Community Safety Framework and be based on/informed by best practice evidence.

11. **The Committee recommends** that each council and shire conduct a crime prevention audit and/or needs analysis of community safety requirements in their municipality.

12. **The Committee recommends** that each local government authority should ensure that its crime prevention and community safety strategy plan be based on evidence of current crime prevention and community safety issues and problems facing the local community.

15. **The Committee recommends** that those councils and shires that do not presently have a community safety and crime prevention committee should establish one.

32. **The Committee recommends** that Victoria Police should provide a clear statement of what the public should do when it observes any suspected criminal activity.

8. Challenges for Policy-makers and Local Groups in Developing Locally Based Crime Prevention Initiatives

In Victoria, community organisations, police and the various levels of government contribute to community safety and crime prevention in different, but frequently interrelated, ways. Their perspectives on issues will differ due to the nature of their relationships to local communities (Homel cited in Cherney & Sutton 2007). Although their responsibilities overlap, as discussed in the last two chapters, each plays a distinct role in addressing crime prevention and community safety at a local level.[420]

Whilst there are many examples of police, government and local communities working together effectively on a range of community safety and crime prevention strategies and initiatives,[421] the Committee heard evidence that a range of challenges exists that limit or impede the implementation of successful crime prevention and community safety initiatives and programs. In particular, issues were raised concerning the lack of a state-wide framework, strategy or policy; inconsistent definitions of crime prevention and community safety; and uncertainty about who is responsible for what. Evidence was also heard suggesting that a lack of funding and resources, along with a lack of research data and information on best practice, has created difficulties, particularly for community organisations and local government.

This chapter will outline the various challenges that policy-makers and local groups have experienced in developing locally based crime prevention initiatives, with particular emphasis on issues relating to governance, frameworks, definitions of community safety and crime prevention, resources, research and evaluation. The challenges experienced by Neighbourhood Watch representatives in delivering their initiatives are discussed in Chapter 10.

Governance and policy frameworks

Governance

As has been discussed previously, local government is arguably best placed to bring together the various partners and stakeholders involved in community safety and crime prevention at the local level because of their unique relationship with police, community organisations and the local community.[422] As Cherney and Sutton (2007) have observed, harnessing local expertise is critical to effective crime prevention and local government brings to community safety and crime prevention partnerships the '[c]apacity to mesh local and expert knowledge [which is] also central to promoting innovation'. (p.69) Similarly, Homel (2005) has argued that past problems in crime prevention in Victoria have resulted from a tendency to impose programs from the federal or state level, without sufficient

---

420 See the discussion of this in Chapters 6 and 7.

421 As described in Chapter 6. For specific examples see Mr Steven Dickson, Manager, Compliance and Safety, City of Frankston, Evidence given to the Drugs and Crime Prevention Committee, Inquiry into Locally Based Approaches to Community Safety and Crime Prevention, Public Hearing, Frankston, 30 May 2011.

422 Mr Steven Dickson, Manager, Compliance and Safety, City of Frankston, Evidence given to the Drugs and Crime Prevention Committee, Inquiry into Locally Based Approaches to Community Safety and Crime Prevention, Public Hearing, Frankston, 30 May 2011.

local input. Homel argues that previously a 'lack of effective leadership, inflexible top-down program design and poor communication between stakeholders has undermined Australian crime prevention and been a major cause of strategy fragmentation' (Homel 2005 cited in Cherney & Sutton 2007, p.69).

The Committee heard evidence suggesting that these issues may still exist in terms of the interface between state level activities and local needs. Mr Craig Kenny of the City of Yarra, for example, observed that the existing state level crime protection structures were not optimal for delivering crime prevention and community safety outcomes at a local level. This is particularly an issue given the role the state has in funding local activities. As Mr Kenny explained:

> [t]he current State Government legislation and policy governing community safety does not facilitate responses to community safety which address the core of the problem. Further, while local government, Police and agencies are expected to respond to health, safety and amenity issues of the community, these agencies are not empowered to manage resources to adequately respond to the needs of the community.[423]

In his submission to the Committee Mr Kenny recommended: 'recognition from the State Government that a bottom-up approach facilitates a more holistic and effective response which will enable more sustainable solutions to community safety'.[424]

A policy framework

The Committee heard evidence that the lack of a clearly defined framework for community safety and crime prevention in the state also poses a significant challenge to local government and community organisations.[425] The survey reported on in Chapter 5 also found that local government authorities (LGAs) believed there was a lack of support, assistance and local engagement by state government despite it having considerable influence over local crime prevention policy and being a major source of funding for crime prevention programs.

The *Frankston City Council Community Safety Strategy 2012–2016* also points to the lack of guidance from the state level: '[t]here is no overarching federal or state policy to respond to crime and community safety concerns'.[426] However, the Strategy notes there are welcome indications that the State Government will provide a clear policy framework in the near future as it has recently established the new Community Crime Prevention Division in the Department of Justice.[427]

Inconsistent approaches

Variations in how crime prevention is viewed

There is no consistent or standard approach to how crime prevention and community safety is viewed and therefore approached by local governments across the state. As discussed in the previous chapter, many local councils approach crime prevention as a subset of community safety, which is in turn addressed under the umbrella of health and wellbeing. While some have highly specialised crime prevention programs, others are limited by being confined within these parameters.

---

423 Submission from Mr Craig Kenny, Director, Community Programs, Local Safety Committee, City of Yarra to the Drugs and Crime Prevention Committee, Inquiry into Locally Based Approaches to Community Safety and Crime Prevention, May 2011.

424 Submission from Mr Craig Kenny, Director, Community Programs, Local Safety Committee, City of Yarra to the Drugs and Crime Prevention Committee, Inquiry into Locally Based Approaches to Community Safety and Crime Prevention, May 2011.

425 In particular, see submissions from the VGLA, Frankston City Council, City of Greater Geelong and City of Yarra.

426 Frankston City Council Community Safety Strategy 2012-2016, Frankston City Council, p.8.

427 Frankston City Council Community Safety Strategy 2012-2016, Frankston City Council, p.8.

It has been argued that considering crime prevention as a subset of community safety, health and wellbeing is appropriate for a general or broad local government approach,[428] however categorising crime prevention this way may also reflect a lack of engagement with specific crime prevention issues.[429]

Dr Carolyn Whitzman and Rui Zhang (2006) found in their review of community safety indicators in Victoria, a common definition of community safety encapsulates:

> freedom from crime and violence as well as the fear of crime and violence. Other definitions include safety from accidents (unintentional injury). Both understandings of community safety see it as a subset of 'health and wellbeing' issues integral to a liveable community, and connected to broader social, environmental and economic sustainability (p.3).

This emphasis on health and wellbeing may reinforce the delineation some councils make between council responsibilities for civic and community welfare or wellbeing and police responsibility for law enforcement and crime prevention. This 'division' of responsibilities is evident in the findings of the survey discussed in Chapter 5, where the lack of local government programs addressing issues such as alcohol-related problems and domestic, gendered and family violence is linked to local governments' tendency to see their role as supporting the work of welfare and justice agencies rather than taking a leading role.

Taking such an approach may well result in councils providing general information on safety issues, responding to community concerns and addressing hazards to safety that fall clearly under council responsibility while leaving primary responsibility for crime reduction, prevention and enforcement measures to the police.[430] As Mr Schier from the Victorian Local Governance Association (VLGA) notes with reference to the VLGA survey findings, while many councils saw crime prevention (in its traditional sense) as a key responsibility, for others it was not seen as core business:

> It is true that across the board most councils mentioned that they felt that their role was supporting Victoria Police in police work and crime prevention rather than being a prime responsibility of local government... They say, 'Where does this fit with council?' It is within that broader community wellbeing area... To a large degree it was not seen as core business. Essentially it is seen as core police business which council can support. They said, 'We have not got a lot of resources in this area'. There seemed to be a little bit of frustration coming through from a couple of the responses saying, 'We have limited resources and we are having to act more on perceptions than perhaps on realities'.[431]

Misunderstanding of the role of local government

Variations in understandings are not confined to local governments' approaches to crime prevention and community safety, but are also evident in community views about the role of local government as Mr Richard Maugueret, City of Casey explains:

> There is often a misunderstanding by the community of the role of local government in community safety matters. As a result, community expectations are sometimes not aligned with Council operations. Much work is required at local government and state level, to clearly define the role of local government in crime prevention and community safety matters'.[432]

---

428 Submission from Mr Philip Schier, Senior Policy Officer, Victorian Local Governance Association to the Drugs and Crime Prevention Committee, Inquiry into Locally Based Approaches to Community Safety and Crime Prevention, June 2011.

429 See Chapter 7 for further discussion.

430 See Chapter 7.

431 Mr Philip Schier, Senior Policy Officer, Victorian Local Governance Association, Evidence given to the Drugs and Crime Prevention Committee, Inquiry into Locally Based Approaches to Community Safety and Crime Prevention, Public Hearing, Melbourne, 27 June 2011.

432 Submission from Mr Richard Maugueret, Acting Manager, Community Safety, City of Casey to the Drugs and Crime Prevention Committee, Inquiry into Locally Based Approaches to Community Safety and Crime Prevention, October 2011.

Mr Maugueret stated further that:

> ...there is a need for State Government to work with Local Government to clearly define roles, responsibilities and terms of reference in relation to program development and delivery in the areas of crime prevention and community safety. By taking this unified approach, policy statements, programs, activities and future directions will be closely aligned (avoiding replication or competition) and give best value outcomes to the wider community. Ultimately, this will ensure that constituents across the State have a clearer understanding of what is 'community safety/crime prevention' and what it means to them. There is a real need in the industry to raise the profile of community safety both at a local government level but more importantly across the State.[433]

Variations in definitions of community safety and crime prevention

Evidence to the Committee also showed there to be considerable variation in definitions of 'crime prevention' and 'community safety' by local governments across the state, as well as in approaches to implementing such programs.[434] This may be partly due to different local issues influencing or shaping local perceptions and approaches, however at least in some cases this appears to be due to a lack of clear and consistent definitions of these terms and uncertain understanding about how these concepts fit into council responsibilities. Whitzman and Zhang's review (2006) found within the broad definition of community safety 'more uncertainty than answers' (p.13). Community safety plans demonstrated significant differences in approach and priorities:

> The review of community safety plans found there is no consensus across metropolitan Melbourne regarding how to define community safety. There was a lack of consistency when it came to defining, addressing, reporting and measuring community safety. Local responses to community safety were largely disconnected from senior governmental responses. Furthermore, programs and initiatives were poorly evaluated (if they were evaluated at all), with no clear targets or ways to measure progress (p.13).

Mr Maugueret also expressed concerns relating to the definition of community safety and crime prevention:

> Defining 'Community Safety' has been a great concern for Council staff developing, implementing and responding to crime and community safety concerns. It is appreciated that each municipal area has its own unique demographics and environments, however, there is no clear definition of the term 'community safety' in Victoria. Is the term 'Crime Prevention' deemed the same as 'Community Safety'? As a result, there is a need for State Government to work with Local Government to clearly define roles, responsibilities and terms of reference in relation to program development and delivery in the areas of crime prevention and community safety.[435]

Working in silos

Since the causes of crime are diverse and broad, crime prevention has been expanded beyond deterrence, detection and incapacitation to include measures aimed at addressing the social and economic determinants of crime. These measures address the 'social and structural factors such as access to and achievement of health, education, employment and

---

433 Submission from Mr Richard Maugueret, Acting Manager, Community Safety, City of Casey to the Drugs and Crime Prevention Committee, Inquiry into Locally Based Approaches to Community Safety and Crime Prevention, October 2011.

434 Submission from Mr Philip Schier, Senior Policy Officer, Victorian Local Governance Association to the Drugs and Crime Prevention Committee, Inquiry into Locally Based Approaches to Community Safety and Crime Prevention, June 2011.

435 Submission from Mr Richard Maugueret, Acting Manager, Community Safety, City of Casey to the Drugs and Crime Prevention Committee, Inquiry into Locally Based Approaches to Community Safety and Crime Prevention, October 2011.

housing opportunities' (Homel 2004, p.1). For this reason aspects of crime prevention have been incorporated into activities across a range of government departments and agencies.

However, without adequate coordination and organisation a multi-agency approach can be fragmented, inefficient and counter-productive, rather than one which strengthens the overall crime prevention capacity of government. Even where agencies are not working directly on crime prevention, their activities may result in a negative impact on crime prevention. Changes to areas like transport, environment and education, for example, are likely to have an impact on crime. As Professor Peter Homel explained by reference to a Western Australian review of government crime prevention initiatives:[436]

> government agencies work in a disconnected insular way, which means that some of the measures that they implement may be crime promoting rather than preventing when seen from the perspectives of other agencies.

The Committee heard evidence from Deputy Commissioner Tim Cartwright and Inspector Tony Langdon of Victoria Police[437] that a silo mentality still remained a challenge in Victoria. As Deputy Commissioner Cartwright stated, 'I see that one of the greatest impediments is working in 'silos' and not taking advantage of the enormous range of support we have in the community'.[438] Other witnesses who spoke at Public Hearings shared this view, reporting that working this way could lead to fragmentation or isolation of programs, agencies or departments.[439]

In order for crime prevention agencies to work effectively together it may be necessary to:

> reform the ways in which central and local agencies work to achieve identified goals, by ensuring that they break out of their narrow operational 'silos' and cooperate in new partnership arrangements and policy structures (Sutton, Cherney & White 2008, p.15).

Lack of resources

Limited funding

The Committee received considerable evidence that local councils are increasingly expected to be responsible for the development, implementation and management of a broader range of crime prevention and community safety programs and initiatives than previously. Whilst some councils have accepted and even embraced these challenges, others find the responsibility onerous, particularly without increased funding to compensate for the extra workload. This may be particularly true of the smaller rural shires.[440]

The tendency to take a broad or general approach to community safety may also be a result of funding restrictions. Councils and community organisations have limited resources to

436 See, for example, Anderson and Tresidder 2008, *A review of the Western Australian Community Safety and Crime Prevention Partnership Planning process: Final report*, AIC, Canberra.

437 Deputy Commissioner Tim Cartwright, Victoria Police; Inspector Tony Langdon, Safer Communities Unit, Community Engagement Division, Victoria Police, Evidence given to the Drugs and Crime Prevention Committee, Inquiry into Locally Based Approaches to Community Safety and Crime Prevention, Public Hearing, Melbourne, 16 April 2012.

438 Deputy Commissioner Tim Cartwright, Victoria Police, Evidence given to the Drugs and Crime Prevention Committee, Inquiry into Locally Based Approaches to Community Safety and Crime Prevention, Public Hearing, Melbourne, 16 April 2012.

439 For example, Assistant Commissioner Wayne Gregson, Judicial Services, Western Australia Police; Mr Frank Covill, Member, Geelong Local Safety Committee; Associate Professor Rae Walker, Health Promotion Coordinator, La Trobe University; Ms Julie Edwards, Chief Executive Officer, Jesuit Social Services; and Mr David Hall, Senior Manager, Safe and Caring Communities, Berry Street. Evidence given to the Drugs and Crime Prevention Committee, Inquiry into Locally Based Approaches to Community Safety and Crime Prevention.

440 For examples see the comments of Mr Steven Dickson, Manager, Compliance and Safety, City of Frankston, Evidence given to the Drugs and Crime Prevention Committee, Inquiry into Locally Based Approaches to Community Safety and Crime Prevention, Public Hearing, Frankston, 30 May 2011; Cr Jan Farrell, Community Safety Portfolio, City of Greater Geelong and Ms Lisa Armstrong-Rowe, Community Development Officer, City of Greater Geelong, Evidence given to the Drugs and Crime Prevention Committee, Inquiry into Locally Based Approaches to Community Safety and Crime Prevention, Public Hearing, Geelong, 8 August 2011.

address a diverse range of matters. This will occasionally mean that certain areas of crime prevention or community safety will be prioritised at the expense of others. In such cases, particularly with smaller outer metropolitan or rural councils,[441] a general approach may increase the likelihood that crime prevention is left to Victoria Police or that it is not seen as a council responsibility.[442]

The Committee heard evidence that some councils believe they are taking on more than they can manage in terms of resources available to them. Mr Jamieson, from the City of Greater Geelong, explains: 'Council has demonstrated approaches and strategies responding to the community's safety concerns. However, Council can struggle to find the capacity amidst the growing demand for services.'[443]

Mr Steven Dickson from the Frankston City Council expressed a similar view: 'It is considered that local government in responding to community demand is assuming higher levels of activity in areas which would traditionally be the responsibility of Police…On a practical level, challenges in developing and delivering community safety and crime prevention programs relate to the availability of staff and financial resources.'[444]

Dr Lorraine Beyer of the Macedon Ranges Local Safety Committee stated that their committee is 'impeded in its work by a lack of financial resources,' and that the Safety Committee has no funding or capacity to apply for funding.[445] Significantly, Dr Beyer notes that the few funding opportunities that do arise do not suit the flexible and changing needs of the Local Safety Committee's work 'as they don't enable flexibility to address local issues in a more immediate way'.[446] Rather than tailor the work of the Local Safety Committee to the funding opportunities, she believes:

> [t]he Local Safety Committee could achieve much more through expanding programs that work locally, and supporting other agencies when an issue arises that needs immediate and flexible response.[447]

Similarly, Mr Craig Kenny from the City of Yarra listed the issues that limited their 'Taking Action Together' initiative[448] which sought to alleviate the impacts of illicit drugs in the municipality:

> Limited capacity — most organisations are already fully committed and it is difficult to prioritise new and additional work despite the intention to do so…[and] [l]imited coordination and support — there are limited additional resources available for project management.[449]

---

441 Submission from Mr Philip Schier, Senior Policy Officer, Victorian Local Governance Association to the Drugs and Crime Prevention Committee, Inquiry into Locally Based Approaches to Community Safety and Crime Prevention, June 2011.

442 Also see Chapter 5.

443 Submission from Mr Paul Jamieson, Community Development Manager, City of Greater Geelong to the Drugs and Crime Prevention Committee, Inquiry into Locally Based Approaches to Community Safety and Crime Prevention, May 2011.

444 Submission from Mr Steven Dickson, Compliance and Safety Manager, Frankston City Council to the Drugs and Crime Prevention Committee, Inquiry into Locally Based Approaches to Community Safety and Crime Prevention, May 2011.

445 Submission from Dr Lorraine Beyer, Sustainable Communities Planner, Macedon Ranges Local Safety Committee, to the Drugs and Crime Prevention Committee, Inquiry into Locally Based Approaches to Community Safety and Crime Prevention, June 2011.

446 Submission from Dr Lorraine Beyer, Sustainable Communities Planner, Macedon Ranges Local Safety Committee, to the Drugs and Crime Prevention Committee, Inquiry into Locally Based Approaches to Community Safety and Crime Prevention, June 2011.

447 Submission from Dr Lorraine Beyer, Sustainable Communities Planner, Macedon Ranges Local Safety Committee, to the Drugs and Crime Prevention Committee, Inquiry into Locally Based Approaches to Community Safety and Crime Prevention, June 2011.

448 The 'Taking Action Together' initiative (as discussed in Chapter 7) is a locally based approach to alleviating the impacts of illicit drugs in the City of Yarra, developed by 70 representatives of a range of agencies. Submission from Mr Craig Kenny, Director, Community Programs, Local Safety Committee, City of Yarra to the Drugs and Crime Prevention Committee, Inquiry into Locally Based Approaches to Community Safety and Crime Prevention, May 2011.

449 Submission from Mr Craig Kenny, Director, Community Programs, Local Safety Committee, City of Yarra to the Drugs and Crime Prevention Committee, Inquiry into Locally Based Approaches to Community Safety and Crime Prevention, May 2011.

Mr Kenny added that one year after 'Taking Action Together' began, 'of the 34 actions agreed to, six have been completed, eight are underway, nine may still be completed and 11 had no action'.[450]

Mr Maugueret from the City of Casey also described a range of issues relating to a lack of resources and external funding. He explained that the challenge was not just obtaining external funding for community safety and crime prevention programs, but also ensuring that externally funded programs continue after the funding period:

> Consideration...[needs to be] given by the funder to the 'exit strategy' or sustainability of programs that were previously externally funded. This adds a strain to Council operations and limits the potential to look at being dynamic and innovative with community safety planning and program delivery.[451]

Funding and budget constraints were also seen by Victoria Police as an impediment to developing comprehensive and successful crime prevention policies and programs.[452]

The Committee notes that the Victorian Government has recently announced a range of funding initiatives.[453]

The lack of funding for existing initiatives

The Committee was told that the major challenge facing many highly effective crime prevention programs currently in place is a lack of resources. In Greater Dandenong, for example, it was reported that there is a direct link between a specific set of issues that place Maori and Pacific Islanders in a position of significant disadvantage and their high levels of over-representation in detention.[454] In evidence to the Committee, Ms Isabel Calvert of Three Seas said: 'There is something going wrong that is causing juveniles of the Maori and Pacific Island population to end up in detention.'[455] She stated further that unfortunately this group is often not identified as a priority for funding because they fall under the category of 'New Zealander':

> The disadvantaged Maori and Pacific Island population are not identified because they come into the country under a New Zealand passport. As a result of that, disadvantaged Maori and Pacific Islanders are not seen as priority groups for funding purposes, for grants or for agency priorities and strategies...we as a community cannot access a whole range of funding opportunities... The result of these challenges is that we are getting many more juveniles in our detention system than should be there.[456]

The Three Seas organisation, discussed in the previous chapter, provides community development and capacity building focused on Maori and Pacific Islanders. The programs run through Three Seas were initiated by Victoria Police in partnership with the community,

450 Submission from Mr Craig Kenny, Director, Community Programs, Local Safety Committee, City of Yarra to the Drugs and Crime Prevention Committee, Inquiry into Locally Based Approaches to Community Safety and Crime Prevention, May 2011.

451 Submission from Mr Richard Maugueret, Acting Manager, Community Safety, City of Casey to the Drugs and Crime Prevention Committee, Inquiry into Locally Based Approaches to Community Safety and Crime Prevention, October 2011.

452 Submission from Victoria Police to the Drugs and Crime Prevention Committee, Inquiry into Locally Based Approaches to Community Safety and Crime Prevention, April 2012.

453 See Chapter 6 for a description of the grants.

454 Ms Isabel Calvert, Secretary, Three Seas Steering Committee / The Dock, Evidence given to the Drugs and Crime Prevention Committee, Inquiry into Locally Based Approaches to Community Safety and Crime Prevention, Public Hearing, Dandenong, 30 May 2011.

455 Ms Isabel Calvert, Secretary, Three Seas Steering Committee / The Dock, Evidence given to the Drugs and Crime Prevention Committee, Inquiry into Locally Based Approaches to Community Safety and Crime Prevention, Public Hearing, Dandenong, 30 May 2011.

456 Ms Isabel Calvert, Secretary, Three Seas Steering Committee / The Dock, Evidence given to the Drugs and Crime Prevention Committee, Inquiry into Locally Based Approaches to Community Safety and Crime Prevention, Public Hearing, Dandenong, 30 May 2011.

but have faced considerable difficulty obtaining funding.[457] 'The Dock', an initiative of Three Seas, is a venue based in Stud Road, Dandenong, which was to be 'where the 14 countries of the Pacific Island community and New Zealand can come together and collectively pool their resources — community and human resources — to address youth issues in the region'.[458]

For local police this represented the next logical step in community development. As Inspector Charles Allen noted, the development of 'The Dock' highlights:

> ...the key issues that community is building capacity so the community can take ownership, creating structures that are sustainable to continue that. It is consistent with what we are saying and certainly across agencies we identified intractable issues within the South Pacific Islander community... The whole feeling behind The Dock is being able to capacity build so the community can take responsibility sustainably for community issues.[459]

Unfortunately, due to a lack of resources, Ms Calvert told the Committee:

> [w]e cannot afford to use ... [the Dock] and we cannot afford to have projects run out of it because we cannot open the doors because of the costs involved in running that place. This is a place that is critically needed for the Pacific Island community.[460]

Ms Calvert stated that the challenges will be overwhelming unless a range of tactical and strategic things happened and outlined the funding areas necessary for The Dock and other Three Seas programs to operate:

1. We need the same access to funding and support as other disadvantaged groups — without discrimination based on nationality.

2. In the immediate term, we need financial assistance to ensure compliance with relevant legal requirements to operate out of the premises; and

3. We need paid, full time staff to supervise projects and activities.

4. In the medium term, we need practical engagement with service providers, and Victorian agencies.

5. We need the Victorian Government to rethink its application of support to 'priority' communities to allow for this clearly disadvantaged group to access funding opportunities — at an equal level to other disadvantaged groups.

6. We need Victoria Government agencies to recognise the needs of Maori and Pacific Islander migrants and apply human resources and intellectual resources to addressing these issues.

7. We need to see the issues facing Maori and PI residents in Australia, on the policy agenda, at State, Federal and bilateral (ANZ) levels.[461]

Ms Calvert also emphasised the need for a whole of government approach:

457 Ms Isabel Calvert, Secretary, Three Seas Steering Committee / The Dock, Evidence given to the Drugs and Crime Prevention Committee, Inquiry into Locally Based Approaches to Community Safety and Crime Prevention, Public Hearing, Dandenong, 30 May 2011.

458 Ms Isabel Calvert, Secretary, Three Seas Steering Committee / The Dock, Evidence given to the Drugs and Crime Prevention Committee, Inquiry into Locally Based Approaches to Community Safety and Crime Prevention, Public Hearing, Dandenong, 30 May 2011.

459 Inspector Charles Allen, Greater Dandenong Police Service Area, Victoria Police, Evidence given to the Drugs and Crime Prevention Committee, Inquiry into Locally Based Approaches to Community Safety and Crime Prevention, Public Hearing, Dandenong, 30 May 2011.

460 Ms Isabel Calvert, Secretary, Three Seas Steering Committee / The Dock, Evidence given to the Drugs and Crime Prevention Committee, Inquiry into Locally Based Approaches to Community Safety and Crime Prevention, Public Hearing, Dandenong, 30 May 2011.

461 Ms Isabel Calvert, Secretary, Three Seas Steering Committee / The Dock, Evidence given to the Drugs and Crime Prevention Committee, Inquiry into Locally Based Approaches to Community Safety and Crime Prevention, Public Hearing, Dandenong, 30 May 2011.

...across both State and Federal agencies, and with the Govt of NZ, to address these issues. As a high priority, we need the Australian Government to research and understand the impact of a poorly thought-out policy on NZ migration and welfare support, and to address the significant negative impacts of that policy.

Without addressing the policy issues around these problems, locally based initiatives will struggle to bring about long term change. We acknowledge the need for Maori and PI communities ourselves to act collectively to bring about change. Sustainable change rests with the community, but it's almost impossible to succeed against the backdrop of discriminatory policies.

If we can get the Dock operating – it will be one step in the right direction. But we need help to get even this far.[462]

Clearly there are programs like the Dock being run in the community that address the needs of high risk groups. Often such programs involve productive partnerships between community groups and police and have the potential to deliver significant and sustainable results. However, it is not unusual for such community programs to be in desperate need of resources. Where these programs do not fit within the parameters of the Community Crime Prevention Grant Program,[463] it may mean resources are not allocated in the most cost-effective or productive manner.[464]

The need for sustainable crime prevention research initiatives was raised by Associate Professor Darren Palmer of Deakin University. As Mr Palmer explained:

In the Geelong region, we — myself, particularly with my colleague Peter Miller — have been able to attract a considerable amount of external funding, as well as funding from the local area. This is really important because you can develop your research, develop your baseline knowledge around the programs, the impact that they are having, but you have to have ongoing sustainability to that research in terms of funding, in terms of people and the like. What we have seen in the past in Victoria, and again elsewhere — it is not only about Victoria — is there might be this kind of brief period of excitement where funding is provided for various things but then it dries up and you lose your capacity to keep on monitoring what is going on.[465]

Lack of skilled personnel — Inadequate training

The Committee's survey of local government reported on in Chapter 5 found that one of the most consistent concerns identified by LGAs was that they do not feel adequately equipped to make informed decisions regarding crime prevention and community safety. Other witnesses before the Committee voiced similar concerns. The resources lacking in these situations are specific knowledge and expertise, which may also be related to financial resources — training may offer a way of developing existing resources in a cost-effective way.[466] Evidence presented to the Committee at interstate hearings also highlighted the value of training to enhance and increase local crime prevention and community safety

---

462 Ms Isabel Calvert, Secretary, Three Seas Steering Committee / The Dock, Evidence given to the Drugs and Crime Prevention Committee, Inquiry into Locally Based Approaches to Community Safety and Crime Prevention, Public Hearing, Dandenong, 30 May 2011.

463 For a discussion of the grant program, see Chapter 6.

464 In order to determine the best delivery of programs, in terms of cost-benefit or reduction of crime and promotion of community safety, an assessment of current and proposed approaches may be necessary. Cost-benefit analysis will be discussed in Chapter 11.

465 Assoc. Prof. Darren Palmer, Convenor, Criminology Program, Deakin University, Evidence given to the Drugs and Crime Prevention Committee, Inquiry into Locally Based Approaches to Community Safety and Crime Prevention, Public Hearing, Geelong, 8 August 2011.

466 Inspector Charles Allen, Greater Dandenong Police Service Area, Victoria Police, Evidence given to the Drugs and Crime Prevention Committee, Inquiry into Locally Based Approaches to Community Safety and Crime Prevention, Public Hearing, Dandenong, 30 May 2011.

capacity and effectiveness.[467] Lack of training has meant that staff responsible for activities in the area of community safety and crime prevention may be unable to adequately respond to existing and emerging needs.[468]

Mr Eames from the Youth Support and Advocacy Service informed the Committee that recruiting staff had been difficult: 'I think one of the greatest challenges has been the recruitment of staff that have a broad range of skills which means skills in community development, skills in case management, who also have the capacity and the preparedness to be pounding the pavement at midnight in some scary places...[469]

Mr Garner Clancey has argued that this lack of training is not a new problem confronting crime prevention in this country:

> ... a study in the late 1990s revealed that approximately 80% of crime prevention officers from around Australia who completed a training needs assessment stated that they had received no more than six days training in crime prevention (Wyatt et al, 1999). It could be argued that there have only been limited improvements since this time (Homel 2009) (Clancey 2011, p.15).

Similarly Professor Peter Homel has warned:

> Skill deficits within the crime prevention workforce are the major contributor to current difficulties in the capacity to deliver effective crime prevention programs. This is, in turn, a major hindrance to achieving the long-term sustainable prevention of crime (Homel 2009a, p.5).

Clearly there is a need to ensure that staff receive appropriate and sufficient training to ensure they have the skills and understanding to enable them to work effectively in the field of crime prevention and community safety. Workforce and organisational development along with the active dissemination of good practice is urgently required.

Time needed for benefits to be apparent

One of the challenges in undertaking crime prevention programs, particularly those with a community development focus, is the time it takes to see any positive outcomes. As Mr Julian Pocock from Berry Street pointed out to the Committee, 'These types of projects can take around ten years or more to see the full benefit'.[470] However there is often an expectation by government agencies and members of the community that programs should produce an immediate or short-term response and when they don't the program is seen to be unsuccessful/or wanting. In addition, funding is often only available for short-term community projects and local government organisations tend to encourage projects that have short-term outcomes (see Chapter 5). This means that longer-term projects that do have the capacity to change people's attitudes and behaviour and can improve the liveability of the community are overlooked for short-term fixes. One of the key findings from Berry Street's 'Safe and Caring Community Project' was the value and long-term benefit of taking a holistic community development approach to community safety and crime prevention. According to Peter Homel a key requirement of effective crime prevention programs is that they have a commitment to producing long-term outcomes. As he explained:

---

467 Senior Sergeant Sue Parmer, District Coordinator, Community Engagement Division, Western Australia Police, Evidence given to the Drugs and Crime Prevention Committee, Inquiry into Locally Based Approaches to Community Safety and Crime Prevention, Meeting, Perth, 21 June 2011.

468 See, for example, the discussion of resources and expertise in Chapter 5.

469 Mr Warren Eames, Manager, Community Programs, Youth Support and Advocacy Service, Evidence given to the Drugs and Crime Prevention Committee, Inquiry into Locally Based Approaches to Community Safety and Crime Prevention, Public Hearing, Dandenong, 30 May 2011.

470 Submission from Mr Julian Pocock, Director, Public Policy and Practice Development, Berry Street to the Drugs and Crime Prevention Committee, Inquiry into Locally Based Approaches to Community Safety and Crime Prevention, May 2011.

...thinking about crime prevention must move beyond specific short-term projects to embedded, long-term programs. This is because design and delivery of effective crime prevention outcomes is complex (Homel 2009) which reflects the complexity and multifaceted nature of the underlying causes of crime (Hope 1995; Sutton Cherney & White 2008: Weatherburn 2004) (Homel 2009a, p.2).

Municipal growth

High growth rates in some local government areas are presenting particular challenges to councils. These include putting pressure on existing services and a need to 'frequently update strategies to respond to emerging issues'.[471] A prime example of this is the City of Casey:

> The City of Casey is located in Melbourne's south-eastern suburbs...and is Victoria's largest and one of the fastest growing municipalities. It is a rapidly developing residential area, with large areas of land still allocated for urban development and surrounding rural areas.... [It] encompasses a total land area of about 400 square kilometres...[Its] population stands at over 260,000 residents with approximately 124 new people moving into the area each week. The population is expected to reach approximately 370,000 within the next two decades... [T]his vast growth creates pressures on existing services and infrastructure. The immediate need to accommodate for this growth needs to be done within restricted budgets. Additional to this increase in numbers, consideration needs to be given to the changing demographics of the community i.e. increase in first home buyers and increase in youth populations, increase in CALD communities and an ageing population. These changes will also mean that further consideration will need to be given to the way in which we tailor, plan and implement community safety programs to these new communities.[472]

Problems relating to perceptions of crime

Council strategies are shaped by a number of factors, including public perceptions of safety and crime, and police statistics.[473] Typically councils will respond to the issues that appear to be the most pressing and significant in their area, sometimes without the assistance of reliable or accurate evidence. As Mr Jamieson from the City of Greater Geelong explained, 'The challenge of perception and reality regarding crime and community safety is an ongoing issue for Council and all with an interest in this area'.[474]

This issue is twofold: first, without adequate data local government may not be able to gain a clear understanding of the problems within their municipality; and second, councils must also respond to community concerns. Consequently, local government may invest in measures that demonstrate a commitment to issues while not necessarily addressing them effectively or in the most cost-effective manner. This may lead to further problems. As Mr Schier from the VLGA observed, 'Diverting considerable resources...responding to the perception [of crime] may reduce the resources you have to work on things that might actually match the data'.[475]

---

471 Submission from Mr Richard Maugueret, Acting Manager, Community Safety, City of Casey to the Drugs and Crime Prevention Committee, Inquiry into Locally Based Approaches to Community Safety and Crime Prevention, October 2011.

472 Submission from Mr Richard Maugueret, Acting Manager, Community Safety, City of Casey to the Drugs and Crime Prevention Committee, Inquiry into Locally Based Approaches to Community Safety and Crime Prevention, October 2011.

473 The challenges associated with setting and identifying priorities will also be discussed in Chapter 11.

474 Submission from Mr Paul Jamieson, Community Development Manager, City of Greater Geelong to the Drugs and Crime Prevention Committee, Inquiry into Locally Based Approaches to Community Safety and Crime Prevention, May 2011.

475 Mr Philip Schier, Senior Policy Officer, Victorian Local Governance Association, Evidence given to the Drugs and Crime Prevention Committee, Inquiry into Locally Based Approaches to Community Safety and Crime Prevention, Public Hearing, Melbourne, 27 June 2011.

Mr Richard Maugueret, City of Casey, also emphasised the need for analysis of a suspected problem in developing crime prevention programs rather than acting on perceptions:

> A large percentage of crime prevention projects have arisen out of a spontaneous recognition that there is a crime problem, where potentially more methodical problem identification might reveal a different picture of the 'real crime problem' in an area. As a result, crime and fear of crime reduction measures can often be chosen on insufficient analysis of the problem and subsequently their success can be impacted. In this regard there is a real need for state-wide evidence based research, access to evaluation of programs and best practice modelling to support Councils in delivering community safety programs.[476]

A particular challenge in this area is the influence of the media with regard to crime and safety issues. In Mr Schier's view, media 'focus on particular incidents can magnify the sense and perceptions in the community about levels of risks and safety'.[477] This may create false or distorted perceptions of problems.

Similarly, Councillor Des Hudson from the Ballarat City Council reported distortions created by media reporting on crime in his municipality. As Cr Hudson observed, 'media attention that is placed on young people often will have sectors of the community thinking that all young people are out of control or likely to be antisocial. We know that is not the case'.[478] For the Ballarat Council, therefore, the challenge is responding to false perceptions created or cultivated by media reporting.

In an attempt to counter the effects of negative media the City of Greater Geelong has put into place proactive measures. As Paul Jamieson explains: 'There are a number of strategies in place attempting to balance this, such as celebrating positive community events and working with the media to look beyond the headlines'.[479] Further, the council has developed a detailed media strategy which 'provides a platform to ensure media reporting focuses on the topic rather than sensational headlines'.[480]

Frankston City Council Community Safety Strategy 2012–2016 reported facing similar challenges, noting that:

> Despite crime rates decreasing, Council's perceptions of safety survey (2010) showed that:
>
> 26% of respondents felt that crime had increased in the past year;
>
> 40% believed that the level of crime had stayed the same; and only
>
> 15% reported a perceived reduction in the level of crime.[481]

In response, Frankston City Council has, amongst other things, proposed to:

> [p]rovide training to local community organisations on effectively getting positive news stories about Frankston published by media;

---

476 Submission from Mr Richard Maugueret, Acting Manager, Community Safety, City of Casey to the Drugs and Crime Prevention Committee, Inquiry into Locally Based Approaches to Community Safety and Crime Prevention, October 2011.

477 Mr Philip Schier, Senior Policy Officer, Victorian Local Governance Association, Evidence given to the Drugs and Crime Prevention Committee, Inquiry into Locally Based Approaches to Community Safety and Crime Prevention, Public Hearing, Melbourne, 27 June 2011.

478 Cr Des Hudson, People and Communities Portfolio, City of Ballarat, Evidence given to the Drugs and Crime Prevention Committee, Inquiry into Locally Based Approaches to Community Safety and Crime Prevention, Public Hearing, Ballarat, 18 October 2011.

479 Submission from Mr Paul Jamieson, Community Development Manager, City of Greater Geelong to the Drugs and Crime Prevention Committee, Inquiry into Locally Based Approaches to Community Safety and Crime Prevention, May 2011.

480 Submission from Mr Paul Jamieson, Community Development Manager, City of Greater Geelong to the Drugs and Crime Prevention Committee, Inquiry into Locally Based Approaches to Community Safety and Crime Prevention, May 2011.

481 Frankston City Council Community Safety Strategy 2012–2016, Frankston City Council.

[e]stablish a program of positive news releases creating an improved perception of community safety in Frankston;

[w]ork with local communities through the local area planning process to adopt a "place identity" that encourages ownership of the local area and promotes the area positively;

[c]ontinue to promote Frankston's attributes such as the foreshore with a view to creating jobs and developing the economy;

[c]ampaign for residents to talk up Frankston by building on the Frankston TV initiative; and

[p]ro-actively identify and respond to derelict and unsightly properties, which create negative perceptions of safety and tend to attract graffiti, litter, vandalism and present a fire risk.[482]

Lack of evaluation and research

Local government or community based organisations may have an excellent understanding of community dynamics, specific issues and problems, but they may not always respond productively to those problems. This may in part be due to discrepancies between perceptions of crime or safety, lack of funding or lack of expertise, as discussed above. It may also relate to a lack of reliable and useful information about the issues that exist or the best solutions to those problems.[483]

In 2004, Professor Don Weatherburn of the New South Wales Bureau of Crime Statistics and Research suggested that 'in many respects...crime prevention has, in effect, been "flying blind"', due to a lack of detailed information about crime (2004, p.162). It seems the situation has changed little since that time as Professor Ross Homel (2011) also told the Committee:

> If I have to highlight one enormous weakness in Australia, at the moment, in this area of community-based work and human services generally, it is the lack of attention to systematic data collection and quality improvement — improving the practice in organisations by actually knowing who they are seeing, for how long, in what kind of programs, and what impact those contacts are having. It goes without saying that if you don't have that kind of information, you are really flying blind.[484]

It is clearly very difficult to develop a specific strategy if there is little or no data available about the particular area of crime prevention and community safety for which the strategy is being developed. Domestic and family violence is one area of crime that is particularly difficult to measure based on available crime figures. Problems with data and research are compounded by the fact that domestic and family violence related crimes are known to be under-reported. As Professor Weatherburn observes in relation to the task of assessing the rate of domestic assault:

> I do not think the figures on domestic assault would be too much use...in judging whether the risk of domestic assaults are going up, for the simple reason that, frankly, no-one knows whether this is a change in the willingness of local residents to report it.[485]

482 Frankston City Council Community Safety Strategy 2012-2016, Frankston City Council, p.16.

483 The importance of evaluation and research will be discussed in greater detail in Chapter 11. It should be pointed out however that LGAs in some states are in a better position than others to rely on good research and data to develop crime prevention programs. This is particularly true of NSW where local governments can draw upon the resources and expertise of BOCSAR. See Chapter 3.

484 Professor Ross Homel, Foundation Professor, Criminology and Criminal Justice, Griffith University, Evidence given to the Drugs and Crime Prevention Committee, Inquiry into Locally Based Approaches to Community Safety and Crime Prevention, Public Hearing, Melbourne, 9 August 2011 (via a phone hook-up).

485 Professor Don Weatherburn, Director, New South Wales Bureau of Crime Statistics and Research, Evidence given to the Drugs and Crime Prevention Committee, Inquiry into Locally Based Approaches to Community Safety and Crime Prevention, Public Hearing, Sydney, 19 September 2011.

Similarly, Mr Cairns of the City of Greater Dandenong characterised family violence as 'a hidden issue',[486] while Dr Beyer, Ms York and Ms Southwell all reported to the Committee that family and domestic violence is known to be 'under-reported'.[487] Under-reporting may be even more prevalent amongst non-English speaking or immigrant populations, where cultural factors, for example, create further challenges.[488] This is also likely to be a significant problem for rural communities since, as Carrington and Scott (2008) have observed, the 'higher frequency of physical and sexual abuse [in rural areas is] compounded by significantly less social support and limited access to services' (p.645).

Whilst LGAs and community organisations appreciate the importance of undertaking evaluation they are presented with a range of challenges/hurdles in doing so.

Mr Paul Jamieson from the City of Greater Geelong observed that one of the challenges his municipality faces is 'the need to ensure rigorous evaluation for projects in order to then have an evidence base for further work. Clearly Council needs to collect data about what interventions have an impact so resources can be better targeted'.[489] However, even when LGAs and community groups acknowledge the importance of evaluation and research they may not have the time, resources or expertise to do so. Dr Beyer of the Macedon Ranges Local Safety Committee noted that '[t]he value and cost benefits of the crime prevention and safety initiatives in the Macedon Ranges Shire have not been calculated, largely because there are no resources to do so'.[490]

That evaluation of council crime prevention programs are the exception rather than the rule was made apparent in the survey undertaken by the AIC for the Committee, discussed in Chapter 5, which found that few LGAs are undertaking any form of evaluation. Of the 78 LGAs that responded to the survey only 12 councils indicated they had been undertaking evaluation.

This situation is not confined to Victoria. Mr Garner Clancey has argued that across Australia there has been:

> …limited investment in evaluation — English et al (2002: 121) found that that '…fewer than 10% of 170 state and territory crime prevention programs and projects identified had been evaluated'. It could be argued that similar problems remain, some nine years after this article was written (Clancey 2011, p.15).

Armstrong and Francis (2003) made a similar point when Jefferies, Payne and Smith (2002) from the Australian Institute of Criminology (AIC) compiled a Register of 110 Crime Prevention Projects that have been reported and published in Australia from 1990–2002. They reported that systematic evaluations were undertaken in 33% of the cases, informal or anecdotal in 12% and no attempt at evaluation in 12%. In 48% it was not known if

---

486 Mr Brendan Carins, Acting Coordinator, Community Development, City of Greater Dandenong, Evidence given to the Drugs and Crime Prevention Committee, Inquiry into Locally Based Approaches to Community Safety and Crime Prevention, Public Hearing, Dandenong, 30 May 2011.

487 Dr Lorraine Beyer, Planner, Sustainable Communities, Macedon Ranges Shire Council, Evidence given to the Drugs and Crime Prevention Committee, Inquiry into Locally Based Approaches to Community Safety and Crime Prevention, Public Hearing, Melbourne, 9 August 2011; Assistant Commissioner Carlene York, Assistant Commissioner, Northern Region Commander, New South Wales Police Service; Ms Margaret Southwell, Chair, New South Wales Local Government Community Safety and Crime Prevention Committee and Community Development Officer, Community Development, Bankstown City Council, Evidence given to the Drugs and Crime Prevention Committee, Inquiry into Locally Based Approaches to Community Safety and Crime Prevention, Public Hearing, Sydney, 19 September 2011.

488 Inspector Bruce Wemyss, Community Engagement Inspector, Greater Dandenong Police Service Area, Victoria Police, Evidence given to the Drugs and Crime Prevention Committee, Inquiry into Locally Based Approaches to Community Safety and Crime Prevention, Public Hearing, Dandenong, 30 May 2011.

489 Submission from Mr Paul Jamieson, Community Development Manager, City of Greater Geelong to the Drugs and Crime Prevention Committee, Inquiry into Locally Based Approaches to Community Safety and Crime Prevention, May 2011.

490 Submission from Dr Lorraine Beyer, Sustainable Communities Planner, Macedon Ranges Local Safety Committee, to the Drugs and Crime Prevention Committee, Inquiry into Locally Based Approaches to Community Safety and Crime Prevention, June 2011.

evaluations had taken place. There was not sufficient information in the report to comment on the quality of the evaluations (Armstrong & Francis 2003).

Another aspect of LGAs' evaluations revealed through a review by the Drugs and Crime Prevention Committee of LGA community safety plans and crime prevention strategies was that there was very little information contained in the documents indicating what was being evaluated and for what purpose.[491]

Evaluation and research issues will be discussed further in Chapter 11.

Challenges relating to understanding and working with 'the community'

Some municipalities in metropolitan Melbourne are highly diverse, both culturally and linguistically. For example, the City of Greater Dandenong, a large municipality, has residents from 151 different nations, more than half of whom were born overseas.[492] The council area also has considerable variation in terms of economic, educational and health indicators.[493] In such cases, the community priorities and needs may differ significantly within the municipality. This can pose difficulties for local government. Mr Eames from Youth Support and Advocacy Service told the Committee, 'one of the greatest challenges has been finding a way to address need in a broad range of areas with a diversity of cultural groups'.[494]

In some areas, certain sections of the community may have competing or conflicting interests and needs. The City of Yarra, for example, indicated significant variation in terms of social and economic indicators across their municipality, which may result in a community that is heterogeneous and complex, rather than homogenous and unified. Since social and economic disadvantage have well-established links to crime rates,[495] community development and capacity building can be an effective crime prevention strategy.[496]

Challenges relating to partnerships

The Committee heard evidence outlining many instances of effective and productive partnerships.[497] Nevertheless, the establishment and maintenance of community safety and crime prevention partnerships poses a range of challenges to local government and community organisations. The key challenges relate to a lack of coordination between partners and resources required for developing and maintaining partnerships.[498] These challenges are not new. Adrian Cherney's 2004 review of the Victorian program 'Safer Cities and Shires' highlighted the 'problems that can arise when participating agencies are unclear about their respective roles and responsibilities within partnership forums' (p.242).

---

491 A survey of local government community safety and crime prevention strategies, plans and policies found that 39 made no reference to crime prevention or community safety and 17 only did so as a sub-category of health and wellbeing. No reference was made to an evaluation of programs, strategies or policies.

492 http://www.communityindicators.net.au/wellbeing_reports/greater_dandenong

493 http://www.communityindicators.net.au/wellbeing_reports/greater_dandenong

494 Mr Warren Eames, Manager, Community Programs, Youth Support and Advocacy Service, Evidence given to the Drugs and Crime Prevention Committee, Inquiry into Locally Based Approaches to Community Safety and Crime Prevention, Public Hearing, Dandenong, 30 May 2011.

495 http://www.communityindicators.net.au/metadata_items/crime

496 See Chapters 1 and 7.

497 For example, Inspector Charles Allen, Greater Dandenong Police Service Area, Victoria Police; Mr Warren Eames, Manager, Community Programs, Youth Support and Advocacy Service; and Mr Tito Agout, Representative from Sudanese Youth Leadership Development Program, Evidence given to the Drugs and Crime Prevention Committee, Inquiry into Locally Based Approaches to Community Safety and Crime Prevention, Public Hearing, Dandenong, 30 May 2011.

498 As reported above and in Chapter 7. See also evidence of Mr John Thexton, given to the Drugs and Crime Prevention Committee, Inquiry into Locally Based Approaches to Community Safety and Crime Prevention, Public Hearing, Melbourne, 9 August 2011.

Partnerships between local government and state or federal governments or between community organisations and state or federal governments have often been reported to be unsatisfactory or difficult to establish and maintain.[499] This is particularly significant given the role state and federal governments have in relation to the funding and coordination of community safety and crime prevention.[500]

As Homel explained, the imbalance in power relationships can impede effective partnerships:

> For example, there can be different reasons for participating in partnerships, with accompanying differences in resources and access to information. In a true partnership, information needs to be shared and used to enable all agencies to work together to develop crime prevention strategies relevant for a local community. This power differential between agencies on the ground can be counter-productive and lead to partnership in name only — rather than a useful and creative approach to crime prevention on a local level amongst equal partners (Homel 2009b, p.30).

Challenges confronting rural communities

During the Inquiry the committee received evidence that various aspects of life in rural and regional towns and cities facilitated the development of partnerships and the development of community crime prevention and community safety initiatives. Many of the towns already have a real sense of community belonging and have well established networks of people in place from which to develop partnerships. Police are also often seen to be a part of the community.[501] However, rural communities also experience a variety of challenges in implementing crime prevention initiatives. Obviously the distance from neighbouring towns and cities can create specific problems. As Mr Hall from Berry Street explained to the Committee:

> One of the unfortunate things about a rural community is that the access to funded services is very limited. Our family violence worker for that area comes across from Broadford, so you are looking at nearly an hour and a half travel to get a worker into the area.[502]

Limited research and services around areas such as domestic and family violence present serious challenges as this crime may occur at a higher rate in rural and regional communities than in major cities. The Australian Government Attorney-General's Department of Crime Prevention has noted in this regard:

> Women in rural and remote communities can experience higher rates of domestic violence... Rates of family violence and violence against women are disproportionately high within regional, rural and remote Indigenous communities ...[however]... the rate at which crimes are reported to police is lower outside major cities, particularly in communities where there are more informal social controls (2011, p.3).

In relation to sexual and domestic violence, Leivore (2003) has observed 'a complex interplay of personal circumstances, social values, attitudes and geography may simultaneously increase rural women's vulnerability to sexual violence and pressure them into silence about abusive situations' (p.79), whilst Jobes et al (2004) found also that 'rural officers... used some discretion in their enforcement of the law' (p.117).

---

499 See Chapters 3 and 6.

500 Submission from Mr Paul Jamieson, Community Development Manager, City of Greater Geelong to the Drugs and Crime Prevention Committee, Inquiry into Locally Based Approaches to Community Safety and Crime Prevention, May 2011.

501 Detective Sergeant Shane Brundell, Macedon Ranges Crime Investigation Unit Representative, Gisborne, Victoria Police, Macedon Ranges Local Safety Committee, Evidence given to the Drugs and Crime Prevention Committee, Inquiry into Locally Based Approaches to Community Safety and Crime Prevention, Public Hearing, Melbourne, 9 August 2011.

502 Mr David Hall, Senior Manager, Safe and Caring Communities, Berry Street, Evidence given to the Drugs and Crime Prevention Committee, Inquiry into Locally Based Approaches to Community Safety and Crime Prevention, Public Hearing, Geelong, 10 August.

These factors may contribute to an under-reporting of crime, particularly in small 'close-knit' communities. Speaking on this issue more generally, Chief Inspector Maxwell told the Committee that 'we know that rural crime is dramatically under-reported across New South Wales and I would suggest across Australia from communications we have seen thus far'.[503] The prevalence of under-reporting would suggest that crime in rural communities, in comparison to urban areas, may be significantly higher than is often assumed (Leivore 2003). Similarly, detailed analysis of crime statistics in New South Wales by Jobes et al (2004) 'dispels the notion that all small communities have less crime than larger urban centres' (p.134).

Under-reporting and consequently lack of data on offences such as sexual, domestic and family violence presents one of many challenges for rural communities in developing programs to prevent and reduce these crimes. Other challenges are outlined in the following list prepared by the AIC, reflecting the concerns expressed in public hearings. The challenges include:

Limited access to services

- Limited availability of services and high staff turnover can make it difficult for many people in regional areas to access important services.

Increased cost of service provision

- Travelling to provide outreach services incurs significant costs in staff time and practical costs associated with transport (Bull 2007a).

Lack of specialist services

- Some workers, such as family and domestic violence support workers, may have a general focus that requires the ability to deal with a number of community issues, performing multiple tasks and responding to competing agendas (Bull 2007a).

Limited local expertise

- Difficulties associated with attracting skilled professional staff to regional areas have been well documented.

- Training and professional development for local staff can be difficult, with additional costs incurred if travel to regional or city locations is required (ANCD 2002; Bull 2007a).

Local politics

- There is evidence of higher levels of social and political conservatism in some rural communities. This can translate into resistance or opposition to crime prevention initiatives that are perceived as soft options.

- There may be significant social divisions within the community and suspicion of outsiders.

Issues relating to confidentiality

- In small communities there is a risk that people will not disclose that they have a problem because of the risk of being identified within the community.

Lack of culturally appropriate services

- There are growing numbers of people from culturally and linguistically diverse backgrounds residing in regional areas of Australia, and high proportions of Indigenous people.

- Some communities may lack culturally relevant or appropriate services.[504]

---

503 Chief Inspector Joshua Maxwell, Human Resources, South West Sydney, New South Wales Police Service, Evidence given to the Drugs and Crime Prevention Committee, Inquiry into Locally Based Approaches to Community Safety and Crime Prevention, Public Hearing, Sydney, 19 September 2011.

504 http://www.crimeprevention.gov.au/NationalCommunityCrimePreventionProgramme/Documents/Tip_Sheet_11.pdf

Conclusion

Despite much praiseworthy and valuable work done in the community safety and crime prevention area, community organisations, police, state and local governments interact and collaborate in vastly different ways across Victoria. While this may be partly the result of variations in issues across different localities, the lack of a state-wide framework or strategy, uncertainty about the definitions of crime prevention and community safety and the corresponding responsibilities of local and state governments may also contribute to the inconsistency in approaches. Other limiting factors, particularly for local government and community organisations, are a lack of resources including skilled and qualified staff, and access to crime prevention and safety data and research.

Recommendations

25. The limitations on Council activity in the community safety area can often be attributed to the lack of adequate and specifically tailored/dedicated funding. **The Committee therefore recommends** that appropriate funding opportunities be offered to local government to drive more targeted, evidence-based community safety activity.

29. **The Committee recommends** that the Community Crime Prevention Unit should develop a series of training packages on crime prevention and community safety. These modules should support the attainment of skills and knowledge required for job roles that involve the identification, planning, development or delivery of crime prevention strategies or activities. Course content could include the following:

    ◆ Understanding crime prevention theory and practice

    ◆ The various approaches to crime prevention including social-developmental approaches and crime prevention through environmental design

    ◆ Understanding, developing and maintaining good partnerships

    ◆ What works in crime prevention

    ◆ Evaluation theory and techniques

    ◆ How to apply for grants and funding

31. **The Committee recommends** that relevant TAFE Colleges develop crime prevention modules as part of community development courses so that those responsible for developing or implementing crime prevention initiatives can receive appropriate accreditation and acknowledgement for their professional development.

Section D — Neighbourhood Watch and its Role in Contemporary Crime Prevention

9. Neighbourhood Watch and Home Watch — The United Kingdom Experience

Introduction

Neighbourhood Watch is one of the most well known of the community crime prevention programs that has proliferated since the 1960s. The program began as a police-driven crime prevention program based on the community and the police working together to make neighbourhoods safer. Generally the objectives of Neighbourhood Watch are comparable worldwide. Those pertaining to the organisation in the United Kingdom (UK) are reflective of the aims and goals of this crime prevention initiative:

- To prevent crime by improving security, increasing vigilance, creating and maintaining a caring community and reducing opportunities for crime by increasing crime prevention awareness.

- To assist the police in detecting crime by promoting effective communication and the prompt reporting of suspicious and criminal activity.

- To reduce undue fear of crime by providing accurate information about risks and by promoting a sense of security and community spirit, particularly amongst the more vulnerable members of the community.

- To improve police/community liaison by providing effective communications through Neighbourhood Watch messaging systems which warn Co-ordinators of local crime trends which they can disseminate to their scheme members, and by members informing the police of incidents when they occur.[505]

Neighbourhood Watch or equivalent systems can be found in many countries throughout the world (Huck & Kosfeld 2007). This chapter, however, examines the experience of Neighbourhood Watch and Home Watch in the UK (hereafter written as NW/HW) as it has one of the most comprehensive and diverse networks of Neighbourhood Watch groups and associated community crime prevention organisations (ERS Research and Consultancy 2010a, 2010b).

It is important to note, however, that the experience of NW/HW in the UK cannot be directly extrapolated to Australia. The genesis and history of the movement, although having some similarities, are in many respects also different enough to make direct comparisons of limited value. The different policing systems and local government structures in the United Kingdom and Australia also have different implications for how Neighbourhood Watch functions in these two countries.

Whilst there may be many positives associated with the operation of NW/HW in the UK, critics have argued its operations cannot be divorced from an increasing culture of intrusiveness into the lives of its citizens; one whereby privacy and confidentiality have arguably been compromised to an extent not apparent in Australia. These criticisms made of NW/HW in the

---

505 http://www.ourwatch.org.uk.

context of what has been termed by some as the 'surveillance society' are a key aspect of this chapter. What for example have been some of the criticisms made of NW/HW particularly in its role as 'the eyes and ears of the police'? Has it for instance been co-opted as an agent of the 'surveillance society'? Similarly the chapter examines some of the barriers that prevent more people from being involved in its activities, particularly young people and the many people from Britain's ethnic or non-English-speaking backgrounds (NESBs). Some of these will be similar to barriers operating in Australia, others may be different.

Despite these criticisms and notwithstanding any differences between Australia and the UK, lessons can still be learnt from the British experience as to how an arguably moribund, even irrelevant, organisation can rejuvenate itself to become a modern and dynamic community organisation addressing community safety and crime prevention across a country as diverse as the UK. Whilst the British model undoubtedly still has weaknesses and faces challenges, not the least of which is making itself attractive outside white middle-class England, there are lessons to be learned as to how NW/HW in the UK has modelled itself for the 21ˢᵗ century.

Background

The UK's first Neighbourhood Watch was set up in Mollington in Cheshire in 1982 following the success of a similar scheme in Chicago in the United States.[506] Since coming to the UK in the early 1980s, Neighbourhood Watch has evolved into wider regional associations and, finally, a coordinated national network. Whilst the organisation has always been popular, for a time during the 1990s and early 2000s it ran the risk of appearing complacent and moribund (Laycock & Tilley 1995; Davies & Jenkins 2010).

Neighbourhood Watch – The early and middle years

A review of NW/HW in 1995 found that the organisation had changed significantly from its inception in 1982 as 'the eyes and ears of the police' to a more community based organisation supported by the police (Laycock & Tilley 1995, p.v). In its original form it was primarily viewed in restricted terms – as a surveillance mechanism reporting suspicious activity to the police (Husain 1988; Bennet 1990). By 1988 the emphasis had shifted to include community activities beyond surveillance, 'a whole package of activity ranging from on the one hand crime-related issues such as property marking and security surveys to, on the other, coffee mornings and street cleaning activities' (Laycock & Tilley 1995, p.3).

By the late 1980s NW/HW was also being scrutinised more critically as a community safety initiative.

Criticisms of Neighbourhood Watch and Home Watch

There were a variety of criticisms made of Neighbourhood Watch in England and Wales in the 1980s and 1990s.

Lack of clear direction

Whilst NW/HW was never anything less than popular according to many surveys (British Crime Survey 1992; Laycock & Tilley 1995),[507] its rather nebulous and wide-ranging agenda meant that the organisation as a whole was shapeless and lacked direction:

---

506 For the background as to how and why Mollington became the 'home' of Britain's first Neighbourhood Watch group, see *The Good Neighbours who Fought Back,* Simon Edge, *The Daily Mail,* February 24, 2007, p.43.

507 The British Crime Survey (BCS) of 1992 for example indicated that 20 per cent of households were members and of those who were not 71 per cent would be willing to join (Dowds & Mayhew 1994). Despite some less than active involvement in the movement it was also thought that any move to disband Neighbourhood Watch would meet with a chorus of disapproval if not dismay by many in the community:

'It would symbolise police indifference to public support. It would thus damage police-public relationships [and policing by consent]. It would certainly fly in the face of police efforts to reinforce partnership with the public. It would risk turning some members of the public away from working with the police towards their own version of community policing – vigilantism – the danger of which has generally been avoided within Neighbourhood Watch' (Laycock & Tilley 1995, p.12).

In many respects, Neighbourhood Watch has become an empty vessel into which differing practice contents can be poured, albeit for the excellent reason of maintaining the local focus and community control. This has, however, left it as an initiative almost impossible to evaluate in any sensible way, particularly since it has been implemented or in some cases partially implemented in widely varying types of community where any possible effect on crime and crime rates will necessarily be variable. Nor has it been abundantly clear in the definitions of Neighbourhood Watch which particular offence it is supposed to affect. The obvious starting point in this respect was domestic burglary, but a number of studies have spilled over into evaluating the effect on theft of and from motor vehicles, vandalism and criminal damage, and indeed street crime more generally. Furthermore, in many local authority estates, for example, it is not always the most serious crimes such as burglary which cause difficulties for the majority of residents. Rather it is the overall quality of life, packs of dogs, litter, graffiti, troublesome neighbours – a dripping tap 365 days of the year that wears people down. And it is tackling these issues which command community support (Laycock & Tilley 1995, p.3).

Limited areas of appeal and application

One of the criticisms of NW/HW at this time was that it was at its most popular in areas which had relatively low crime rates and were reasonably affluent (Husain 1999; Bennet 1990; Laycock & Tilley 1995). 'Most schemes were in low-risk areas and relatively few in the high risk areas covering the poorest council estates, multi-racial areas and high status non-family areas which are often located in inner city regeneration pockets' (Laycock & Tilley 1995, p.4).[508]

The association of NW/HW with the property-owning classes was acknowledged by the police to be a drawback at an early stage:

> 'The middle-class image', said Superintendent Turner, 'is a problem...' This led to the belief of 'many officers' that NW will be much more difficult to set up in the areas where they are most needed such as the vast down-at-heel council estates (McConville & Shepherd 1992, p.7).

McConville and Shepherd also argued that whilst NW/HW may be popular that popularity is largely confined to white middle-class areas; for many people surveyed by the authors 'NW was seen as socially divisive, orientated around property and essentially a middle class project' (1992, p.84):

> The official statistics needs also to be treated with caution because they imply that NW has a universal appeal and that its spread across the country is unrelated to socio-economic and socio-political factors. The emphasis upon home security and property ownership would suggest, however, that NW would be more likely to take hold in some areas (such as home-owning, economically advantaged and stable communities) and less likely to succeed in others (characterized, for example, by rented accommodation, economically disadvantaged individuals and shifting populations). Moreover, insofar as NW has been initiated and promoted by the police, it cannot be taken for granted that the police would make equivalent (or greater) efforts to establish NW in areas (such as some traditional working-class communities) where their own legitimacy is contested and where their presence is accepted only reluctantly (1992, p.9).

The 1995 review of NW/HW by Laycock and Tilley, whilst for the most part positively disposed towards the organisation, recognised the concerns of those who believed NW/HW had the potential to be overly intrusive (and discriminatory), stating that:

> [i]n the very high crime areas (which are rare), Neighbourhood Watch is a particularly difficult concept to introduce; to some sub-groups of the community it is unwelcome and to others it is potentially threatening in its overt involvement of the police with the danger of intimidation which it introduces. In these contexts, some sensitivity is required if crime-related schemes are to be introduced (Laycock & Tilley 1995, p.12).[509]

---

508 The same results were found in the BCS of those years; see for example the BCS 1992.

509 See also the discussion on barriers to becoming involved in NW/HW activities later in this chapter.

Variable level of support

There was evidence that whilst NW/HW was attracting widespread general support, the level of that support was variable. In other words, with the exception of NW/HW coordinators, 'support' as in approval did not necessarily translate into 'commitment' or involvement from members:

> In practice, Neighbourhood Watch members may be required to do no more than put a label in their window declaring their membership. Many fail to attend meetings, do not mark their property and do not have security surveys. This possibility of what might be called token membership of Neighbourhood Watch schemes contributes to their apparent popularity. The more that is required by way of commitment from the general public, the less popular will be any initiative.

> The Neighbourhood Watch movement, in making relatively few demands on its membership, is particularly attractive to those members of the community who would like to be seen to contribute, but to do so on their own terms. Relatively little is demanded of members and the extent to which demands are made on Neighbourhood Watch coordinators will vary with the scheme and its area, but in any case, the coordinators themselves will generally have a considerable amount of control over the effort they expend in relation to their own scheme (Laycock& Tilley 1995, p.9).

Concerns expressed by police

Finally police also had their own misgivings about how NW/HW was developing in the 1980s and 1990s. Whilst generally supportive, they were concerned that it was not necessarily a cost-effective use of their resources, particularly if they were responsible for establishing and maintaining the schemes; it could also result in the 'residualisation of policing' (Crawford 2006, p.112).[510]

> The perspective from the police service is somewhat different and it is certainly possible to question whether Neighbourhood Watch is popular in certain sections of the police force. Some police officers are of course, very supportive of the concept. They see it as an opportunity to encourage and cultivate a partnership with the community and to work together. And indeed Neighbourhood Watch is a very positive movement and has a great deal to offer, but the down side is that it demands police resources on a scale which some police officers find difficult to justify. The popularity of Neighbourhood Watch in police forces is, therefore, qualified, and needs to be more carefully thought through in achieving a balance between meeting community needs or demands and police resource allocation. In particular, attention needs to be paid to the demands of reactive policing, which although understandable, are not obviously supportive of the longer-term commitment required of community policing, including Neighbourhood Watch (Laycock & Tilley 1995, p.10).

The other related concern of the police was the one discussed previously, that because NW/HW activity occurred primarily in low crime areas an allocation of funds and resourcing to support requests of NW/HW groups and members in low crime areas meant police 'have consequently fewer resources available for the more proactive and demanding work in high crime areas' (Laycock & Tilley 1995, p.11).

These concerns of police were summarised in the 1995 Review when it was stated that:

> There is a real danger that without change more and more police will come to perceive Neighbourhood Watch as a millstone, requiring signs of support merely to keep a smallish but articulate sub-section of the population happy (Laycock & Tilley 1995, p.13).

Moving forward

A variety of concerns about the direction NW/HW was heading in – the role of the police; how it would be funded and how effective it was as a crime prevention organisation – led to a

---

510   This is certainly arguable with other forms of citizen initiatives either volunteer based or commercial such as private police patrols, private security guards etc.

major rethinking in the early 2000s as to how an alternative vision of the organisation 'which remains true to the spirit of the movement' could be articulated (Davies & Jenkins 2010).

In 2004, with Home Office support, a National Strategy Group on Watch Issues (NSGWI) was formed to look strategically at how NW/HW could work in partnership with other agencies to address crime prevention and community safety issues:

> The NSGWI supported the movement through difficult times. But, because its membership included representatives ranging from the police and fire services to local government, business, housing and tenants organisations, the group could see how – with the right national structure in place – the movement could do much more (Davies & Jenkins 2010, p.2).

As a result of the experience of NSGWI members in working with other community groups, the Home Office funded a series of three symposia around the country which led to a major restructuring in the operations of NW/HW and the formation of an overarching national network.

The 2007 restructure

By 2007 the previous national body had folded and many members felt the need for a new organisation to share best practice, foster peer learning and provide a voice for the movement at a national level. At the symposia held on the direction of NW/HW it was agreed that a new way of organising the movement was necessary: 'They didn't want an expensive top-heavy system, but they did want a national representative structure for the movement to enable members to consult and to pass information and highlight issues that could then be dealt with at the right level' (Davies & Jenkins 2010, p.2).

A series of exploratory meetings and events were held in each region of England and Wales, involving representatives of NW/HW at both local and regional levels. Delegates were invited to discuss and vote on their preferred way of achieving a new form of representation at the national level in England and Wales.

Members representing all of the 10 regions agreed overwhelmingly that:

(a) They wanted to see a regional and national structure.

(b) They wanted a [police] force area Neighbourhood Watch/Home Watch representative to go to regional meetings.

(c) They wanted a regional Neighbourhood Watch/Home Watch representative and a deputy to go to national meetings (Davies & Jenkins 2010).

After the proposal was accepted by the NSGWI in April 2007, the new Neighbourhood and Home Watch Network was formed (NHWN).

Building capacity

In 2009 NW/HW began to organise in England and Wales on a semi-professional basis. It had established a constitution through its Network Board, engaged paid staff and set up national office facilities. It was also receiving regular funding through the Home Office.

The official national website forum was also launched at this time.[511] The site includes news, resources and contact information for the NHWN and for regional NW/HW representatives. This period of activity also coincided with radical changes to the structure and approach of policing in Britain, most particularly the formation of Neighbourhood Policing Teams (NPTs) which aimed to create stronger bonds between local citizens and area police.[512]

---

511   http://www.ourwatch.org.uk
512   See discussion later in this chapter.

The ultimate aim of this phase of change was 'to communicate with, grow and extend the diversity of the 173,000 local schemes and to establish a clear brand'[513] (Davies & Jenkins 2010, p.2). There was also a heightened emphasis on the need for the 'new look' NW/HW to collaborate with organisations and agencies outside the movement, including police, local government agencies and especially voluntary and community sector organisations (VCS).[514] Commentators were also generally positive about the direction in which NW/HW was heading and particularly having a new national 'flagship':

> The appearance of a national organisation focused on representing and equipping local residents is a significant step in the movement's history... At a national level policy makers and decision makers are eager to engage with the movement and seek its views and opinions on how local residents can be empowered more effectively to bring crime down. The new regional structure, in place since 2007, already allows more effective partnership working with the police and other strategic partners. The new organisation, with its potential to speak about what works at a local level, can bring even more weight to those discussions (Jenkins & Davies 2010, p.5)

At the launch of a new NW/HW training package, the Minister for Crime Prevention and Antisocial Behaviour Reduction, Baroness Browning said:

> Neighbourhood Watch is a great example of how communities can come together to help reduce crime and antisocial behaviour and make our streets safer. But it's important we keep this movement alive by encouraging new and more diverse membership, as well as embracing new and different ways of communicating.[515]

The rest of this chapter examines how NW/HW in the UK attempts to do this.

Current organisation and structure

Today NW/HW is the largest grassroots voluntary organisation in the UK. A variety of schemes have subsequently been established, and 10 million people are now claimed to be members with 173,000 local conveners.[516]

The day-to-day organisation of NW/HW schemes in the UK is devolved to regional and sometimes town groupings. Outside of the NHWN Board there is no uniform national structure as such, so the format, role and administration of Neighbourhood Watch are very localised.

The NHWN (England & Wales) is a registered charity and a Limited Company run by a Board of Directors. The Board liaises with an Advisory Group made up of one volunteer

---

513 For example, through using the Design Council of Britain to design a new logo, image and a new website.

514 See discussion later in this chapter for more detail on partnership formation.

515 *Our Vision for Safe and Active Communities*. A Report by Baroness Newlove, Champion for Active and Safer Communities, March 2011. Accessed at http://www.ourwatch.org.uk/resource_centre/document_library/our_vision_for_safe_active_communities

516 http://www.ourwatch.org.uk

Some critics however have been and are still critical of such claims as to its popularity. For example, as early as 1992 McConville and Shepherd argued that it is unclear as to how accurate the claims made for NWHW by its advocates are. Whilst it is some time after these comments were made the questions the authors raised may still be pertinent:

'... it is unclear for example what is meant when it is claimed that over three and a half million households are covered by NW (*Guardian*, 10 August 1989). And what does a person have to do in order to qualify as a member: Attend an inaugural meeting? Attend meetings regularly? Be on a co-ordinator's membership list? Place stickers in a window? Undertake surveillance activity? Live in a road where there is a scheme?

Answers to these kinds of questions are important in thinking about NW. There is, for example, little purpose in collecting official figures on the number of schemes if there is no agreement about or understanding of what exactly is being counted (cf Husain and Bright, 1990). Moreover, any analysis which seeks to measure the crime prevention impact of NW must be flawed if it does not take into account the differences between schemes. And any measurement of crime prevention must tease out what, if anything, acts as a deterrent to would-be criminals – stickers, signs, surveillance activity of residents, patrolling, increased security systems. On issues of this sort, official accounts of NW are unhelpful' (McConville & Shepherd 1992, pp.5–6).

For further critiques as to the 'popularity' of Neighbourhood Watch see discussion later in this chapter.

representative from each of the nine English regions plus Wales (making 10 members of the Advisory Group in total).[517] Each regional representative is chosen by NW/HW in the region itself by whatever method suits them. The only condition is that they must be a member of NW/HW and they must not be a paid member of police staff:

> The role of the Advisory Group is to liaise between grassroots Neighbourhood and Home Watch groups and members in their regions and the NHWN Board of Directors. This involves, among other things, feeding back 'news and views' from the regions to NHWN and keeping members in the region informed of developments at a national level.[518]

Within each region there are a number of police force areas – 43 in total across England and Wales. Each force area has a volunteer Neighbourhood or Home Watch representative who assists the regional representative in linking with individual Watch groups.

As previously explained, at a regional level there is no uniform system of organisation. However, taking the East Midlands region as typical, a regional model may include an umbrella organisation such as the Leicestershire Neighbourhood Watch Association (LNWA). The LNWA for example is comprised of a number of local Neighbourhood Watch bodies within the county, each with its own coordinator. These local associations need to be registered with the Leicestershire Constabulary in order to be members of and supported/ represented by the LNWA. The LNWA in turn, as with many county Neighbourhood Watch organisations, has a service agreement with the Leicestershire Constabulary. Across the county there may also be Area Support Teams where local coordinators can 'attend their meetings and seek advice, share successful tactics, or meet other coordinators'.[519] This model is quite different for example from a city such as London where the London Neighbourhood Watch Association represents Neighbourhood Watch groups in each of the 32 London Boroughs. The Borough groups are linked to Neighbourhood Policing Teams (NPTs) of the City of London Police and the Metropolitan Police.[520]

Funding sources also vary across the board. Whilst a certain amount of state funding may be available from the Home Office or local government authorities (LGAs), according to Mr Jim Maddan, Chair of the NHWN, England and Wales, this is never enough. Indeed, Mr Maddan told the Drugs and Crime Prevention Committee that whilst the Home Office has indicated their support and respect for NW/HW and the work it does, ironically this has resulted in the government requesting the organisation to take on extra tasks and roles without a commensurate increase in funding. For example, NW/HW is now in charge of coordinating and administering public liability insurance for volunteer and community groups. It also must be responsible for the costs of all the branding and licensing of NW/HW products including the public signage pertaining to NW/HW in local streets and areas.[521]

As a result, many individual NW/HW groups also work hard to raise their own funds. Some have been involved in obtaining licences to run lotteries or running bingo games, supermarket stalls, raffle drives and the engaging of assistance from local businesses (ERS Research and Consultancy 2010a, p.119). Many NW/HW groups also charge annual subscription levies of their members (ERS Research and Consultancy 2010a).[522]

---

517 The regions are East Midlands; East of England; London; North East; North West; South East; South West; Wales; West Midlands; and Yorkshire and Humberside.
Note that Scotland and Northern Ireland do not form part of the National UK Network. For details on the separate Neighbourhood Watch in Scotland, see http://www.aosnw.co.uk/
For Neighbourhood Watch in Northern Ireland, see http://www.psni.police.uk/index/support/support_neighbourhood_watch.htm

518 http://www.ourwatch.org.uk/our_work/our_board/

519 http://www.ourwatch.org.uk/our_work/in_the_regions/east_midlands/regional_links_em/

520 http://www.ourwatch.org.uk/our_work/in_the_regions/london/

521 Comments of Mr Jim Maddan, Chair, Neighbourhood and Home Watch Network, England and Wales to the Drugs and Crime Prevention. Teleconference, 16 April 2012.

522 For example a Neighbourhood Watch group in Cricklewood, London charges a five pound annual subscription levy for members which is reduced to two pounds for pensioners and the unwaged (ERS Research and Consultancy 2010a).

A note on UK policing and its relationship to NW/HW

NW/HW groups, whatever their constitution or make-up, have strong relations with local policing units. This is arguably more the case than their equivalents in Australia, at least in the current iteration of Neighbourhood Watch in this country.[523] A brief account of the structure of policing in England and Wales and its relationship to NW/HW is therefore warranted in order to understand the context and development of Neighbourhood Watch in England and its relationship to policing in that country.

Policing in England and Wales as it relates to community safety, crime prevention and NW/HW is centred on partnership models with local government and community groups. The most important bodies in this regard are the Community Safety Partnerships (CSPs), NPTs and Police Community Support Officers (PCSO). The role of the newly established Police Commissioner will also have an impact on the work of NW/HW.

Community safety partnerships (CSPs)

CSPs are made up of representatives from the police and police authority, the local council, and the fire, health and probation services (the 'responsible authorities'). CSPs, formerly known as Crime and Disorder Reduction Partnerships, were set up as statutory bodies under Sections 5–7 of the *Crime and Disorder Act* 1998.[524]

The responsible authorities work together 'to develop and implement strategies to protect their local communities from crime and to help people feel safe. They work out local approaches to deal with issues including antisocial behaviour, drug or alcohol misuse and re-offending'.[525]

CSPs also work with, and rely upon, community groups such as NW/HW and their representatives and registered local landlords. There are currently 310 CSPs in England, and 22 in Wales:

> Each responsible authority contributes their own particular local knowledge, professional expertise and resources to ensure that the issues of most concern to local people are prioritised and addressed.[526]

Neighbourhood policing teams (NPTs)

NPTs consist of small teams of police officers (usually 10–15) who are dedicated to policing a certain community or area. These officers are not deployed to duties elsewhere unless in extraordinary circumstances.

They are familiar and accessible to their local community, helping to identify local priorities and working with residents and partner organisations such as the local authority to find solutions to local crime and disorder problems.[527]

There are 3600 NPTs throughout the UK. This type of policing is designed to 'make the police more visible, reduce fear and aid interaction between the public and the police, and it aids in local knowledge, gaining intelligence and tip-offs from the public'.[528]

---

523 This is not to state that Neighbourhood Watch has not had strong relationships with police in Victoria. Indeed, Neighbourhood Watch in its early years was very much tied to strong police involvement (see Davids 1995 and the discussion in Chapter 10). The strength or closeness of the relationship will also vary from district to district and area to area so that even today there may be some Neighbourhood Watch groups that have strong police/citizen relationships. It is fair to say however that the present *structure* of (community) policing in the UK, for example the presence of Neighbourhood Policing Units, lends itself more to a strong Neighbourhood Watch model.

524 It was thought the new name indicated a more positive, inclusive approach, that is, community safety, whilst obviously including the reduction or prevention of crime as a broader concept that would also take into account community capacity building and community engagement. See Buckley 2010 and the discussion later in this chapter.

525 http://www.homeoffice.gov.uk/crime/partnerships/

526 http://www.homeoffice.gov.uk/crime/partnerships/

527 http://cfnp.npia.police.uk/neighbourhoodpoliceofficers.aspx

528 http://cfnp.npia.police.uk/neighbourhood_policing.aspx

NPTs are led by a police officer, usually of Sergeant/Inspector rank, and may include PCSOs, special constables, local council staff and members of voluntary organisations, including NW/HW.

Usually NPTs are responsible for patrolling an area of around four square miles (10 km²) of urban area or around 10 square miles (26 km²) of rural area. The Criminal Justice and Local Policing Unit of the Home Office has explained the role and rationale of NPTs as follows:

> Local Policing aims to provide people who live or work in a neighbourhood with:
>
> - Access – to local policing services through a named point of contact
>
> - Influence – over policing priorities in their neighbourhood
>
> - Interventions – joint action with partners & the public
>
> - Answers – sustainable solutions & feedback on what is being done.
>
> This means that neighbourhood teams:
>
> - publicise how to get in touch with them
>
> - find out what the local issues are that make people feel unsafe in their neighbourhood and ask them to put them in order of priority
>
> - decide with partners and local people what should be done to deal with those priorities and work with them to deliver the solutions
>
> - let people know what is being done and find out if they are satisfied with the results.[529]

Police community support officers (PCSOs)

PCSOs are unsworn officers who 'provide a visible presence in the community, helping the police to tackle antisocial behaviour and offering reassurance to the public'.[530] PCSOs help reduce crime and antisocial behaviour by dealing with minor offences and supporting front-line policing.

> PCSOs patrol in uniform and can:
>
> - Work with the public to identify and address their concerns
>
> - Contribute to the management of local neighbourhoods
>
> - Help to support people who are affected by crime and disorder.
>
> Depending on their role, PCSOs may also be given powers, including:
>
> - The power to detain someone pending the arrival of a constable
>
> - The power to direct traffic and remove vehicles
>
> - The power to issue fixed penalty notices in relation to a range of anti-social behaviour.[531]

PCSOs work closely in association with NW/HW groups and local police units.[532] For example, a case study on the operation of the Woldingham Neighbourhood Watch, based in an affluent village in Surrey stated:

> There is a close and mutually advantageous relationship between the NW Coordinator and the local PCSO, with each supporting the work of the other and benefiting accordingly...for the past

---

529   http://cfnp.npia.police.uk/neighbourhood_policing.aspx

530   http://cfnp.npia.police.uk/pcso.aspx

531   http://cfnp.npia.police.uk/pcso.aspx

532   See for example the work of the Police and Community Support Group in Leicester. This Neighbourhood Watch adjunct group works closely with police in specific crime prevention activities. For example, this group regularly hosts fundraising efforts for their local PCSOs, including for the purchase of two bikes. Another Neighbourhood Watch group *The Beeches, Neighbourhood Watch Uppingham* has even purchased a community defibrillator for use amongst residents of the estate in which the Neighbourhood Watch group is operating and have trained 15 residents on how to use it (see ERS Research and Consultancy 2010a, pp.25, 30).

4½ years the village has had a dedicated PCSO who knows the area and its residents and provides a visible deterrent (ERS Research and Consultancy 2010a, p.78).

Similarly, the Sovereign Park Neighbourhood Watch, based in a new housing estate in the northern city of York, has commented:

> Get to know your PCSO and involve them in everything you do. They can offer direct practical help but also provide access to other support and information and their endorsement lends credibility to communications with official bodies not least the Police and Council (ERS Research and Consultancy 2010a, p.115).

Police and crime commissioners (PCCs)

From November 2012, for the first time ever, the public in England and Wales will elect a civilian Police and Crime Commissioner who will be accountable for how crime is tackled in their police force areas.[533] The role of Police and Crime Commissioners is to reduce crime and deliver an effective and efficient police service within their force area. By being directly elected by the people, the British government believes the senior echelons of the police force will be more answerable to the communities they serve in ways that appointed officials cannot.

Specifically, PCCs will be able to set the priorities for the police force within their force area, respond to the needs and demands of their communities more effectively, ensure that local and national priorities are suitably funded by setting a budget and hold to account the local Chief Constable for the delivery and performance of the force. In particular, PCCs will appoint (and will be able to dismiss) Chief Constables, although the Chief Constable will appoint all other officers within the force.[534]

There is also a commitment under the new system to give the public access to key crime and policing information and a minimum platform of street level data through their neighbourhood policing team and groups such as NW/HW (Home Office 2010, p.16).

PCCs will also be responsible for developing a 'five year police and crime plan' setting priorities for policing and crime prevention for their local districts. In doing so they must take into account the views of community stakeholders such as local councils, volunteers and groups such as NW/HW. It is also expected that PCCs will work closely with members of CSPs, NPTs and community agencies such as NW/HW in addressing community safety and crime prevention priorities at local level.[535]

The new police structure and organisation, particularly the emphasis on local community policing as represented in NPTs, has led to stronger partnerships emerging between police and local chapters of NW/HW according to Mr Jim Maddan, the Chair of the national NHWN. A unique feature of the relationship between police and NW/HW is that Coordinators of NW/HW have the opportunity to meet with members of the local policing teams approximately every six weeks and discuss priorities and strategies for the local area for the ensuing three months. Conversely, local community police officers regularly attend meetings of NW/HW chapters on their 'beat' to discuss matters of local importance. Finally, NW/HW members,

---

533 Whilst civilian members of the public can stand for election as a PCC they will not be eligible to stand if they are a serving; civil servant, judge, police officer, member of the regular armed forces, employee of a council within the force area, employee of a police related agency, employee of another government agency, politically restricted post-holder, member of police staff (including PCSOs) or member of a police authority (see http://www.homeoffice.gov.uk/police/police-crime-commissioners/questions/elections/

534 The idea of PCCs has been promoted as empowering the public to have a direct say in how policing is conducted in their local areas through the direct election of the PCC. However, concerns have been expressed that the new system may lead to the 'politicisation' of policing in the UK, particularly as candidates supported by the political parties may seek election. The Home Office has responded to this criticism by stating that whilst PCCs may appoint or remove Chief Constables all operational decisions of the Chief Constable will remain at the discretion of the police alone. See *Policing in the 21st Century: Reconnecting police and the people.* Home Office, London, 2010, p.9.

535 In the consultation document leading up to the establishment of the PCC scheme, strong support was indicated for the retention and promotion of both PCSOs and NW/HW (Home Office 2010, p.32).

especially coordinators will have the opportunity to meet with their elected PCCs to air any concerns pertaining to crime or antisocial behaviour in their local chapter. This close 'two-way' level of communication between police and NW/HW is arguably one of the reasons the organisation is flourishing in relative terms in England and Wales.[536]

Neighbourhood Watch/Home Watch: Its strengths and positive impacts

The following section examines the strengths and positive outcomes of NW/HW in contemporary Britain.

Strengths

Diversity of programs

One of the unique aspects of the NW/HW movement in the UK is the sheer breadth of the type of watch groups in existence. Seemingly every aspect of life is covered by some type of community activity that combines intelligence gathering, surveillance and social activities. The diversity of these activities is too great to detail in the context of this chapter, however Appendix 14 of this Report gives a selection of activities as varied as 'Boat Watch' and 'School Watch' and everything in between. These include numerous 'Rural Watches', NW/HW groups located in churches, universities and on canals and those that aim to cater for children. In many ways these programs are indicative of the community or social development approach evident in numerous NW/HW chapters throughout the UK.

Encouraging volunteerism

The recent Home Office Report *Policing in the twenty-first century: Reconnecting police and people* indicated strong support for NW/HW in England and Wales and the concept of volunteerism in crime prevention generally. Respondents to a Home Office survey of NW/HW participants also were largely supportive of NW/HW stating that in addition to a reduction in crime and some material benefits such as cheaper insurance premiums, discounts from local businesses or volunteer awards/recognition,[537] membership had some less tangible benefits.[538] These, as will be discussed later, included having influence and input into local policy-making, particularly with local councils, and a greater sense of community wellbeing and 'belonging' within their local communities (ERS Research and Consultancy 2010a).

Establishing meaningful partnerships

As in Australia, Neighbourhood Watch in the United Kingdom clearly relies on forging good partnerships to assist in its crime prevention activities. These vary from very formal service level agreements with local area or neighbourhood policing units,[539] local government

---

536   Comments of Mr Jim Maddan, Chair, Neighbourhood and Home Watch Network, England and Wales to the Drugs and Crime Prevention Teleconference, 16 April 2012.

537   In terms of material benefit it has been suggested in the UK that monetary benefits such as local government tax breaks should be considered in order to encourage volunteerism in groups such as Neighbourhood Watch (see Home Office 2010, p.33).

538   The Report's authors chose 63 case studies of NW/HW groups across the nine regions of England and one of Wales. The final list of case study groups came from the nominations of Neighbourhood Watch regional directors submitted to the authors. Once the case studies were chosen fieldwork for the Report comprised of:
   • 'Face to face interviews with senior group members
   • Focus groups with group members
   • Wider resident consultations
   • Partner/stakeholder consultations
   • Member surveys; and
   • Observation through attendance at local group meetings' (ERS Research and Consultancy 2010a, p.6).

539   See for example 'the *Leicestershire Constabulary and the Leicestershire & Rutland County Neighbourhood and Home Watch Service Agreement*. Accessed at http://www.ourwatch.org.uk/uploads/pub_res/SLA_Leicestershire.pdf

and other agencies to more casual arrangements.[540] Commentators have observed that as with other forms of community crime prevention initiatives collaborative arrangements of both a formalised and casual nature are extremely important in developing and sustaining support for local initiatives (Davies & Jenkins 2010).[541]

Formal mechanisms

NW/HW at national, county and local level depends on good partnership structures. As an example of formal arrangements, the Devon and Cornwall Community Watch Association (DACCWA) believes setting up a formal service level agreement with the Police 'allow[s] the group to undertake more focussed activity with the Police' (ERS Research and Consultancy 2010a, p.84). Moreover the DACCWA also has signed an 'information protocol':

> Signing an information protocol with the Police has greatly increased the scale of information volunteers have access to. Subject to completing data protection training, this facilitates more efficient distribution of information to scheme members, reducing the burden on Police staff to first remove sensitive information (i.e. a burglary victim's address) as this is done by the volunteer. This is only possible since DACCWA is a registered organisation and therefore able to sign a protocol. It also reflects the professional approach taken to recruiting, training and managing volunteers (ERS Research and Consultancy 2010a, p.86).

Sometimes individual NW/HW groups may join across a particular area as one group to work in partnership with local police command and local government. Using greater economies of scale, more crime prevention and community safety interventions can thus be delivered across a wider area. For example, Leicester's Police and Community Support Group, comprised of a number of local Neighbourhood Watch chapters, works together with local police, schools, residents' associations, universities and churches to address a range of issues of importance to their local communities (ERS Research and Consultancy 2010a, pp.29ff.).

Indeed many NW/HW groups have stated the absolute importance of 'umbrella groups' to enable individual chapters or their coordinators to make contact with each other, meet, share information or even just socialise – regular contact being 'the key to sustaining interest in Neighbourhood Watch' (ERS Research and Consultancy 2010a, p.52). Umbrella groups may be particularly important in providing advice and support to embryonic NW/HW groups 'to get them off the ground' (ERS Research and Consultancy 2010a, p.99). As a spokesperson for the Chippenham and Rural Villages Neighbourhood Watch umbrella group in Wiltshire stated:

> Regular communication with NW coordinators from the umbrella group will ensure they feel included and supported, even if it's only via email. Providing an initial welcome pack helps to make coordinators feel 'part of something' (ERS Research and Consultancy 2010a, p.82).

Informal arrangements

A key partnership feature of many NW/HW groups is the informal liaison between the NW/HW chapter and the local PCSO. For example PCSOs usually know well, and have closer relationships with, NW/HW group members, particularly convenors. They attend chapter and district meetings and are generally more involved with local community activities than sworn officers whose priorities might lie elsewhere (ERS Research and Consultancy 2010a).

---

540 Some examples of organisations other than police, police support or local government that NW/HW groups across England and Wales may work in partnership with include: Schools; Youth workers and Youth Offending Teams; Probation officers; Landlords/Tenant groups; Universities; Churches and places of worship; Ethnic community groups; Residents associations; MPs; Government Departments (particularly health, transport, social services); Aged associations; Business and service groups and Environmental groups.

541 See also discussion in Chapter 3.

Other NW/HW groups, particularly those that try and 'engage' more young people into their activities, may have links with local council or community youth workers and indeed council workers and youth advocates may serve on local chapter boards.[542]

Whilst there is no one uniform partnership approach between NW/HW and other agencies in England and Wales it is generally agreed that partnerships, however formal or informal, work well between NW/HW groups, police and other agencies (ERS Research and Consultancy 2010a). Ultimately the perceived benefits of the partnership approach in the UK are due to their reciprocal nature:

> In most cases partnership working with the police has been crucial. It has given residents access to information, advice, guidance and support and resources, and it has given the Police [and other agencies] a means of engaging with communities (ERS Research and Consultancy 2010a, p.2).[543]

Other partnerships

The other strong partnership links that are evident in the UK are those between the NW/HW group and local businesses and professional groups. For example, the Eaglesfield Park Neighbourhood Watch group in London secures financial and other resources from multiple local businesses in the area. The tennis club sponsors its newsletter in return for advertising space, the local shops donate prizes for community events such as fetes and open days and the bowling club provides the group with a meeting space 'which is seen as lending more formality and credibility than having meetings in houses' (ERS Research and Consultancy 2010a, p.46). Similar arrangements with private enterprise occur across the country and with various types of NW/HW groups, both general and specialist.

Positive impacts

The Research survey *Showcasing Neighbourhood Watch Achievements* conducted in 2010 found that for the most part NW/HW groups across England and Wales in all their various guises were having a positive impact in reducing crime and antisocial behaviour, promoting community cohesion and enhancing social capital. As the introduction of the Final Report stated:

> Residents report becoming much more aware of the need to secure their homes and other property, and of becoming much more vigilant. It is also apparent that residents are more confident about reporting suspicious activity and, where they have witnessed crimes taking place, presenting evidence in prosecution. As a result a number of police forces were able to confirm that crime had reduced in Neighbourhood Watch areas and correspondingly, residents were able to report reductions in the fear of crime. It is clear that in many parts of the country Neighbourhood Watch has played a *significant role in improving people's quality of life* and in fostering community spirit (ERS Research and Consultancy 2010a, p.3). (Committee's emphasis)

Not only do residents across the country believe they have a better awareness of crime prevention issues and are more willing to liaise with police officers and PCSOs, but also police have reported that one impact of NW/HW groups is that it has helped them to 're-engage with the public'. This:

---

542 For example, a partnership between The Groves Neighbourhood Watch in Hull and local council youth workers has been particularly successful in breaking down barriers between younger and older residents in the neighbourhood 'even to the extent of speaking to each other in the street. This might appear relatively insignificant but has actually reassured some older people that young people should not necessarily be feared' (ERS Research and Consultancy 2010a, p.120).

543 Indeed some NW/HW groups have even established offices or 'drop in centres' within the local or area police station. See for example, the Sherwood and Mapperly Park Neighbourhood Watch, Nottingham (ERS Research and Consultancy 2010a, p.34). Another NW/HW umbrella group (South Tyneside Association of Neighbourhood Watches) has even been assisted by the local police legal team in setting up NW/HW chapters and the development of their constitutions. 'This allowed the police to be involved at the start and in doing so their involvement served to 'rubber stamp' the Association's purpose and appeal to local Neighbourhood Watch groups' (ERS Research and Consultancy 2010a, p.62).

[d]irectly supports the Government's priority of policing by consent and encouraging a more client driven Police service. Regular communication with Neighbourhood Watch helps the Police access local intelligence which they would otherwise struggle to obtain. This in turn has enabled the Police to deliver targeted interventions, helping to reduce crime in the area (ERS Research and Consultancy 2010a, p.34).

The Report suggests that this reciprocal benefit/impact is best illustrated from the responses of the rural 'Borderwatch' in Richmondshire:

From the perspective of the Police/Community Safety Partnership, the Neighbourhood Watch scheme has achieved a level of community engagement far in excess of that which existed previously, in terms of both numbers engaged and the quality of the engagement, as evidenced by the scale and nature of volunteering, attendance at police events and in feedback of those involved. Local people also believe that they now get a better service from the Police and, consequently their appreciation of the Police has grown (ERS Research and Consultancy 2010a, p.109).

Another major impact has been the endeavours of some NW/HW groups to engage in new ways with members of the community that hitherto had not been associated with or interested in the movement – notably young people and people from ethnic minority backgrounds. Increasingly some NW/HW groups are delivering projects, either alone or in partnership, which seek to give these people a 'voice'.[544]

Finally, part of the perceived benefit in belonging to NW/HW groups in Britain and associated partnerships is the ability for local groups to influence local government and particularly improve the delivery of public services in their area 'including seeking a greater police presence/more patrols and improvements to street cleaning, street lighting and leisure provision for children and young people (ERS Research and Consultancy 2010a, p.3).

Technology and training

Technology

It would seem that the UK NW/HW groups are more advanced than their Australian equivalents with regard to using technology to get 'the message across'. Many NW/HW groups use electronic forms of communication such as emails, alerts, and websites to involve their members (and others) in their activities. Facebook and other forms of social media are also employed.[545] The National Neighbourhood Watch Network (NNWN) also has a sophisticated website which contains inter alia links for news and events, a research and resource centre and perhaps most impressively a system for local community information by which the user puts in his or her postcode into the field and comprehensive information including maps are provided within a one to 10 mile radius.[546] In addition to this national network, many individual associations have developed their own computer based alert, information and messaging systems. For example in Nottingham:

One of the Sherwood and Mapperly Park Neighbourhood Watch [SAMPNW] members, who is also the owner of a local ICT business, identified the potential to improve its efficiency by updating its ICT systems and developing a website (www.sampnw.co.uk) as well as engage

---

544   See for example the experience of the Streetly Community Neighbourhood Watch which established the offshoot Streetly 'Youth 4em' which is a community based network of young people who collaborate with the senior members of NW/HW to address crime and antisocial behaviour in the local district. The Neighbourhood Watch/Forum groups hold regular joint barbeques giving young people a unique opportunity to interact with local residents, police, NHS and youth services representatives "thereby breaking down the barriers between young people and local agencies and demonstrating the breadth of issues that Neighbourhood Watch can address' (ERS Research and Consultancy 2010a, p.102).

545   As discussed below some critics do not approve of the use of Facebook and other forms of social media by NW/HW and other community groups.

546   See http://www.ourwatch.org.uk/your_local_area

non-traditional NW members, particularly young people, by developing online technology for receiving and reporting crime information. Through the Neighbourhood Alert facility local residents can receive crime reports, alerts by text, voice or email and can report incidents and problems in their streets on the system. A mapping facility within the alert system also shows the scale and distribution of membership, which is a powerful visual tool to demonstrate to partners the significance and coverage of NW (ERS Research and Consultancy 2010a, p.33).

Another example, from a rural community, is the East Hertfordshire Rural Intelligence Gathering System (RIGS). RIGS provides an on-the-spot solution to communicating reports of suspicious behaviour to other members of the community and the police by sending messages via a pager. Pagers were preferred options because of poor mobile phone signals in some of the county's rural areas and because 'it is a lot more cost effective and easy to send a message out to one common number as opposed to 260 different mobile phone numbers' (ERS Research and Consultancy 2010a, p.36).

The OWL (Online Watch Link) is another innovative communications scheme that was developed by the East Herts Constabulary and is gradually being taken up across the country:

> This is an online information exchange system that facilitates communication and exchange of crime reports and prevention information between the Police and NW Co-ordinators and members, which is managed by NW Liaison officers. Of the 841 NW Co-ordinators in Dacorum, 630 receive OWL messages via e-mail and the remainder by phone through the OWL system. In recognition of the contribution that the OWL system makes in delivering better public services, Herts Constabulary received a national e-government award for best e-Government and technology driven services. The system has since been bought by other police authorities and Herts Constabulary continues to promote the system through delivering presentations to police authorities around the country (ERS Research and Consultancy, 2010a, p.43).[547]

The Eaglesfield Neighbourhood Watch scheme in London is also enthusiastic about the use of local websites for alerting people quickly to incidents of crime and antisocial behaviour stating: 'A website is a low cost initiative once set up and enables crime messages to be shared quickly via e-alerts. It can also open up communications with neighbouring groups and enable everyone to observe trends beyond Neighbourhood Watch group boundaries' (ERS Research and Consultancy 2010a, p.46). However they also sound a cautionary note that it is still important to retain 'old fashioned' methods such as monthly or quarterly newsletters, community noticeboards on the estate, and door knocks and face-to-face communication 'in order to maintain contact with those without computers and retain a '"personal feel"' (ERS Research and Consultancy 2010a, p.46). Eaglesfield residents also maintain 'old fashioned' incident logs whereby members of the Neighbourhood Watch group record their observations of crime and antisocial behaviour and report them to the police and local council.

This point is well taken. A variety of groups surveyed stressed the need to use a variety of methods to engage residents to NW/HW 'from knocking on people's doors and running a stall at a local fair to using the OWL system and Facebook, as this supports wider engagement'.[548]

Whilst the use of technology and social media to promote NW/HW activities is generally viewed as a positive advance in keeping the organisation 'relevant' in the 21st century, the use of these forms of communication by members to investigate and report on 'suspicious'

---

547   Using sophisticated new technologies is also one of the strengths of the South Yorkshire Neighbourhood Watch Association (SYNWA). In autumn 2009 it launched the SYNWA website at that time believed to be the first of its kind in the UK.

548   Representative from Neighbourhood Watch, Tring, Hertfordshire quoted in ERS Research and Consultancy 2010a, p.42.

activity is regarded as less benign by some critics. These issues are discussed later in this chapter in the section pertaining to criticisms of NW/HW.

Provision of training

It is one thing to have these technological innovations in place but it is another to know how to use them. Training, particularly for NW/HW coordinators, on technological and other issues is a key aspect of the organisation's approach in the UK. Coordinators in particular do training courses across a range of topics particularly associated with the criminal justice system, including field trips to local courts and presentations given by judges, drug officers, probation officers and others. 'Coordinators are [then] able to pass on this knowledge to their members, helping them to support the Police effectively and better understand their role within the criminal justice system' (ERS Research and Consultancy 2010a, p.67).

In addition, the National NHWN offers a wide variety of training courses for police, NW/HW members and other interested parties on many aspects of crime prevention, community safety and community development.[549] As part of its training curriculum NHWN has also developed Britain's first recognised training qualification for community advocates (Advanced Award for Community Advocates):

> The qualification which was developed in partnership between the Safety Net Associates Group and the Neighbourhood and Home Watch Network is designed to address the skills needs of volunteers within community organisations, such as Neighbourhood Watch and Home Watch, staff from public bodies who support them and any other charity or organisation that has to be an advocate. Across three areas learners will develop the knowledge and skills required to act as advocates for community organisations.[550]

The National NHWN has recently obtained Home Office bursaries to fully fund 20 volunteers to study the Advanced Award for Community Advocates. The bursaries will cover the full cost of the qualification and are available for NHWN members. It is envisaged the qualification will enable candidates to:

- Describe the structure of their own Community Partnership and the extent to which their organisation holds influence within it

- To explain what communication techniques are effective in promoting effective partnership work

- To be able to describe how their Community Partnership's concerns and priorities are developed and promoted

- To describe how to influence decisions made by Community Partnerships, other public bodies and voluntary organisations

- To explain the legislation and policies which allow and require community organisers to be involved in decision-making processes by Community Partnerships and public bodies

- To describe how to formulate priorities from community concerns

- To describe how they, as community advocates, can be involved and lead on projects designed to tackle local priorities

- To develop effective partnerships with public bodies and voluntary organisations

- To identify concerns and priorities within their communities

- Develop strategies and methods to tackle the identified concerns and priorities

---

549 These include courses such as:
  - A Guide for Police Community Support Officers on Neighbourhood Watch
  - Neighbourhood Watch Liaison Officers Skills Scan and Personal Development Plan
  - Supporting Older Neighbours
  - Registering and Mapping a Neighbourhood Watch Scheme.
550 See http://www.ourwatch.org.uk/resource_centre/training/advanced_award_for_community_organisers/

Upon completion of the qualification candidates will be able to:

- Understand and demonstrate how Community Partnerships are structured, their role within them, how to influence how concerns and priorities are developed and promoted

- Understand the principles of community cohesion, what is required for communities to become more cohesive and how this benefits communities

- Understand how public and voluntary organisations are required to work together to develop concerns into priorities and how these priorities can be tackled through effective partnership working

- Demonstrate how as community advocates you go beyond influencing into doing by taking positive social action.[551]

Notwithstanding this impressive training curriculum, as discussed later in this Report some critics have argued there are significant gaps in the content of training made available to NW/HW coordinators and members particularly in areas such as ethics, privacy and confidentiality.

Leadership and communication

NW/HW groups in the UK stress the importance of strong leadership and regular communication to sustain interests in local groups. As the Review of Neighbourhood Watch groups in England in 2010 stated:

> The quality and commitment of Neighbourhood Watch Coordinators is absolutely crucial to a scheme's success. It is their efforts that give it local credibility with residents, the police and other agencies and their efforts which have gone a long way to securing its achievements (ERS Research and Consultancy 2010a, p.2).

In particular, enthusiastic and committed coordinators and the use of the umbrella groups discussed earlier can ensure 'grassroots' members that they feel included and supported:

> The coordinator is regarded as vital to the scheme's success, providing the commitment, drive and skills required to galvanise support amongst residents and represent their views to the relevant authorities. Other members provide support and attend meetings but all agree that having a strong leader is invaluable (ERS Research and Consultancy 2010a, p.111).

Being a good coordinator is a real skill according to representatives from a Neighbourhood Watch group in York. To sustain enthusiasm and relevance amongst local groups a coordinator must be able to:

> [i]dentify people willing and able to take on relevant responsibilities, but make sure that new people are always welcome, thus avoid becoming a clique. [They need to] identify what skills are available among members of the community and make best use of them. Similarly [they need] to harness the enthusiasm of members – it can become infectious! (ERS Research and Consultancy 2010a, p.115).

Innovative technological communication methods and even the use of something as basic as an initial 'welcome pack' are also important tools in keeping interest in Neighbourhood Watch high (ERS Research and Consultancy 2010a, p.82).

Broadening its remit – Social capital, community bonding and the reduction of isolation

Social cohesion

In Britain there has been a marked shift from NW/HW being solely a crime prevention organisation to one that is engaged in developing community spirit or social capital. Addressing this development in a review of NW/HW activities in 2010 the authors of *Showcasing Neighbourhood Watch Achievements* stated:

---

551   See http://www.cspacademy.ac.uk/CommunityAdvocatesBursaries.htm

> Some [Neighbourhood Watch] groups operate more like community development projects, addressing issues of social inclusion and community cohesion; seeking to deal with the causes of local problems not just the effects. Indeed Neighbourhood Watch is, to a large extent, about community spirit and neighbourliness. People want to feel part of a community and in many cases Neighbourhood Watch schemes have provided the mechanism through which this has been made possible (ERS Research and Consultancy 2010a, p.3).

As residents from Peel Estate Neighbourhood Watch in Wythenshawe, near Manchester, told the researchers of the 2010 Review such activities reassure residents that they 'are not on their own' and that NW/HW makes residents 'actively involved in looking out for each other'. Moreover, this group (and many others) 'provide[d] the opportunity to bring together local residents who would otherwise not have had the opportunity to get to know each other, addressing issues of isolation and making the area more resilient to criminal threats' (ERS Research and Consultancy 2010a, p.72). This was particularly important for the elderly, specifically targeted by the NNWN as it 'Recognise[s] the potential of Neighbourhood Watch to look out for vulnerable elderly people and help them improve the safety of their homes' (Davies & Jenkins 2010a, pp.3–4). This emphasis on the needs of, and concern for, the elderly is demonstrated in other ways in various NW/HW chapters. For example, Mr James Maddan told the Drugs and Crime Prevention Committee that some NW/HW groups were using volunteers with mobile phones and other communication networks to locate people suffering from Alzheimer's disease who had wandered from their homes or otherwise gone missing. Mr Maddan added that such interventions also saved local police time and money by obviating the need for them to be involved in such searches unless absolutely necessary.[552]

A variety of responses from other groups across the country also testified to the Review consultants how NW/HW not only reduced their fear of crime but also promoted social and community cohesion:

> Involvement in Neighbourhood Watch has helped create a stronger sense of community and neighbours who previously did not speak to each other are in more regular communication and look out for each other. In this way the scheme has had significant impacts on community cohesion in the area. Residents feel that improvement in the scheme has improved their awareness about crime prevention and they believe there is improved police presence, reduced crime levels and fear of crime (ERS Research and Consultancy 2010a, p.34).

In particular, some members believe that NW/HW groups have also helped to act as a bridge between 'old' and 'new' members of the community (ERS Research and Consultancy 2010a, p.96).

Social activities

This sense of neighbourliness has extended to NW/HW in part being a forum for social interaction and social events and activities. One Coordinator in London (Wandsworth) claims that social events are the 'key' to a successful NW/HW group (ERS Research and Consultancy 2010a, p.52). This is particularly the case when taking a holistic approach to NW/HW to maintain interest. It is equally important to ensure that NW/HW '[i]s not too negative or solely focused on crime as this can promote fear amongst the vulnerable' (ERS Research and Consultancy 2010a, p.52).

There are numerous examples of such social occasions among NW/HW groups in England. For example, 'Rural Watch' in Hertfordshire brings people living and working in rural communities together through 'barn meetings' where people have the chance to meet and interact face-to-face including on a social level (ERS Research and Consultancy 2010a, p.38). In the Berryfields Estate NW/HW in Cornwall community spirit is fostered through youth boxing projects

---

552 Comments of Mr Jim Maddan, Chair, Neighbourhood and Home Watch Network, England and Wales to the Drugs and Crime Prevention, Teleconference, 16 April 2012.

organised in association with the local police and even carol singing at Christmas (ERS Research and Consultancy 2010a, p.81). In Stevenage, 'Dog Watch' is a program targeted at dog walkers whereby each month 'a group of people walk their dogs together and keep a watch on the area. The walks are also a good way of meeting new people and socialising. The walks are organised and attended by a Dog Watch Coordinator, together with one of the group's dog mascots'[553] (ERS Research and Consultancy 2010a, p.40). A member of the NPTs also attends these walks as they are a way for police to meet the public on an informal basis.

Another social activity in which NW/HW volunteers (and others) may become involved is the holding of street parties, particularly at times of national or local celebration. For example, NW/HW chapters across the country will be organising street parties and long lunches to celebrate Her Majesty Queen Elizabeth's 60th Jubilee Year throughout 2012. Mr Jim Maddan told the Committee that not only were such functions an occasion for social fun and pleasure, they also served the useful purpose of acting as a recruitment drive for future members and volunteers for NW/HW.[554]

Environmental activities

Group activities also may involve a mix of practical and social aims. Environmental improvement projects such as tree or bulb planting, rubbish clearance or grass cutting of common parkland areas are examples of these.[555] Such activities can occur in urban and rural areas. For example, the Harling Court Neighbourhood Watch, based in a housing block estate in Wandsworth in London, involves residents in improving the block aesthetically and negotiating with the local council on issues pertaining to cleanliness and basic services. Another London based Residents Association/Neighbourhood Watch group states that:

> Aesthetic improvements such as hanging baskets get residents communicating with each other as they create a starting point for informal conversations in the street. Where improvements are installed a small plaque enables residents to see [what has been] achieved (ERS Research and Consultancy 2010a, p.50).

In Wythenshawe, experience of heavy snowfalls has motivated the local Neighbourhood Watch to establish a system for the storage and application of salt on footpaths. Other groups have established community gardens 'to further instil a sense of community pride.' For example, the Hunters Gate Neighbourhood Watch in Durham has leased land from the village church to create garden allotments. 'The concept is that the spaces can be created and maintained by villagers for the benefit of the village, with the flowers and vegetables from the allotments distributed within the community to those in need' (ERS Research and Consultancy 2010a, p.56). The Groves Neighbourhood Watch in Hull has put pressure on the local authority to establish an enhanced street cleaning service, cutting back of trees and bushes, improved street lighting and the installation of alley gates.

It has been argued that these 'quick win' projects 'can help build momentum and enthusiasm, getting people actively involved and encouraging them to believe in the Group, themselves and their communities. They also offer a practical context to engage partners, creating a sense of shared achievement that benefits relationships' (ERS Research and Consultancy 2010a, p.70).

Diversification of role

Many NW/HW groups in Britain are extending their role from crime prevention per se to a broader remit to include 'community safety'. This is particularly the case in the area

---

553 Clearly the Dog Watch also has a primary 'functional' purpose of reporting and observation. People are encouraged to be observant whilst walking their dogs and pass on information about crime or suspicious behaviour observed to police and/or local councils. The rationale is that 'Dog walkers especially are out walking at all times of day and often in areas that are not so well used by other residents' (ERS Research and Consultancy, 2010a, p.40).

554 Comments of Jim Maddan, Chair, Neighbourhood and Home Watch Network, England and Wales to the Drugs and Crime Prevention, Teleconference, 16 April 2012.

555 See for example the environmental improvement schemes of the Wythenshawe Neighbourhood Watch in Manchester (ERS Research and Consultancy 2010a, p.71).

of natural disasters and other emergencies. For example, in London over 100 NW/HW coordinators have been designated 'Emergency Volunteers'. They have:

> [p]articipated in training sessions and presentations from organisations including the Counter Terrorist Branch, the London Fire Brigade on fire safety and domestic flooding and the National Health Service on dealing with flu pandemics. This approach is about building capacity within the community and producing a pool of people who could help out in the event of emergency. It is also seen in the context of making NW more holistic and not solely focused on crime, which is perceived as a good way of sustaining interest (e.g. when crime levels are low) particularly where residents may be hesitant to join a group which is solely focused on combating crime because of fear of reprisals (ERS Research and Consultancy, 2010a, p.53).

Criticisms of Neighbourhood Watch and Home Watch

Whilst NW/HW has certainly had its advocates and supporters, it has also been the subject of criticism and concern, particularly with regard to its place and role in what some consider to be Britain's 'surveillance society'. According to conventional wisdom, Neighbourhood Watch has been viewed at best as a valuable community resource, at worst as a group of interfering but harmless meddlers. Some critics, however, at least in England, view NW/HW as far less benign. Much of this criticism is centred on the place of Neighbourhood Watch in the wider 'surveillance society' that has been apparent in Britain since the 1990s. The next section looks at these developments in order to contextualise later criticisms of NW/HW.

Context of the criticism – Britain as the 'surveillance society'

While NW/HW in the UK has broadened its role from being largely a surveillance mechanism in the 1980s–1990s to encompass community safety and social activities, the use of surveillance instruments in the societies in which it operates have increased substantially, as this 2006 study highlights:

> We live in a surveillance society. It is pointless to talk about surveillance society in the future tense. In all the rich countries of the world everyday life is suffused with surveillance encounters, not merely from dawn to dusk but 24/7. Some encounters obtrude into the routine, like when we get a ticket for running a red light when no one was around but the camera. But the majority are now just part of the fabric of daily life. Unremarkable.
>
> It is not just that CCTV may capture our image several hundred times a day, that check-out clerks want to see our loyalty cards in the supermarket or that we need a coded access card to get into the office in the morning. It is that these systems represent a basic, complex infrastructure which assumes that gathering and processing personal data is vital to contemporary living (Surveillance Studies Network 2006, p.1).

In 2006 a comprehensive report by the Surveillance Studies Network (hereinafter the Surveillance Report) on behalf of the United Kingdom Information Commissioner described the UK as being the 'most surveilled country' among the industrialised western states (Surveillance Studies Network 2006, p.1).[556]

Similarly, in February 2009 a report by the House of Lords Constitution Committee, *Surveillance: Citizens and the State*,[557] warned that the increasing use of surveillance by the government and private companies is a serious threat to freedoms and constitutional rights, stating that:

---

556 Note that the 2006 Report was updated in 2010. The update repeated many of the claims and findings of the 2006 Report adding that the moves towards a surveillance society were if anything expanding and intensifying with CCTV systems becoming even more widespread and in fact routine in most urban public spaces. See Allan Travis 2010, 'Surveillance society soon a reality, report suggests,' *The Guardian*, 11 November. Accessed at www.guardian.co.uk/2010/nov/11/surveillance-society-soon-reality

557 See http://www.publications.parliament.uk/pa/ld200809/ldselect/ldconst/18/1802.htm

The expansion in the use of surveillance represents one of the most significant changes in the life of the nation since the end of the Second World War. Mass surveillance has the potential to erode privacy. As privacy is an essential pre-requisite to the exercise of individual freedom, its erosion weakens the constitutional foundations on which democracy and good governance have traditionally been based in this country.[558]

The rise of CCTV as a surveillance tool

According to these reports the most worrying features of the 'surveillance society', at least according to civil liberties groups and some members of the general public, was the burgeoning use of closed circuit television (CCTV) systems.[559] In the Surveillance Report it was stated that in the 1990s in particular 78 per cent of the Home Office crime prevention budget was spent on the installation of CCTV infrastructure:[560] 'There may be now as many as 4.2 million CCTV cameras in Britain: one for every 14 people, and a person can be captured on over 300 cameras each day' (Surveillance Studies Network 2006, p.19). This is notwithstanding that repeated studies and evaluations including those conducted by the Home Office have indicated that CCTV has little overall effect on crime levels (2006, p.19).[561] For example, an evaluative review by Welsh and Farrington in 2006 discussed in Sutton, Cherney and White (2007) found that of the many hundreds of open-street CCTV systems put in place in the UK and the US since the early 1990s:

> [j]ust 19 had been the subject of rigorous evaluation. While these studies found an average 8 per cent decrease in crime in areas which had installed CCTV compared with a 9 per cent increase in control areas, not all interventions had been equally successful. CCTV worked better to reduce offending in car parks and other closed or semi-closed environments than in more open settings such as city centres and housing estates. There is little evidence that CCTV deters violent crime or offending that is alcohol-related. [However]…Open-street CCTV is popular with police because it can help them rationalise their use of resources. Rather than allocating large numbers of officers to routine street patrols, appropriately trained local government personnel can use the cameras to surveille relevant areas, and help direct police attention to places where trouble seems to be brewing. Camera footage can also provide evidence of, and can be used in investigating, offences after they have occurred (Sutton, Cherney & White 2007, p.56).

Equally concerning to some critics is that increasingly there are blurred boundaries between state and private sector interests when they are both involved in information gathering, privacy and surveillance.[562] The Surveillance Studies Network notes for example that:

> …more and more tasks of government are carried out through a sometimes complex combination of public, private, voluntary-sector and market mechanisms, and sometimes by only one of these types. Increasingly, a variety of local partnership arrangements bring together a variety

---

558 http://www.publications.parliament.uk/pa/ld200809/ldselect/ldconst/18/1802.htm

559 For a discussion of CCTV in the context of crime prevention generally and in Australia see Chapters 2 and 6 of this Report.

560 Indeed in the City of Westminster, in central London, microphones are being fitted next to CCTV cameras. Westminster council claims that they are simply part of an initiative against urban noise, and will not 'be used to snoop', but comments from a council spokesman appear to imply that they have been deliberately designed to capture an audio stream alongside the video stream, rather than simply reporting noise levels. (See 'Council plans to listen in on street life', *The Telegraph*, 4 May 2005. Accessed at http://www.telegraph.co.uk/news/?xml=/news/2005/05/04/nmic04.xml&sSheet=/news/2005/05/04/ixhome.html

561 See also Norris, C & Armstrong G (1999), *The maximum surveillance society: The rise of closed circuit television*, Perpetuity Press, Oxford.
     Many witnesses to this Inquiry including serving police officers were also doubtful of the capacity of CCTV to stop or prevent crime, that is, its ability to act as a deterrent. They did, however, in many cases view it as a useful investigatory tool or way of gathering evidence for use in criminal proceedings. See discussion in Chapter 2 of this report.

562 Indeed as the Surveillance Report points out, surveillance is not only conducted by governments and private organisations it is also increasingly carried out by 'ordinary people' on social network sites and through popular culture in television programs such as Big Brother:
     'After the bombings in London in 2005, both television companies and police were encouraging people to use their mobile phone cameras to take pictures of suspicious characters. Growing numbers of people, particularly children and young people, are also putting their lives up for display, and in turn watching others' lives, though online webcams and social networking sites like My Space' (Surveillance Studies Network 2006, p. 15).

of agencies and professions so that their skills can be better focused on providing services to individuals in a more integrated way (Surveillance Studies Network 2006, p. 36).[563]

This is exemplified by the fact that the vast majority of CCTV cameras in situ in Britain are not operated by the UK Government but by private companies, especially to monitor the interiors of shops and businesses.[564] [565]

Other manifestations of surveillance

Other aspects of the surveillance society that have given rise to concern have been the proliferation of databases containing personal identifying information operated by both government departments and private organisations, the use of mobile phone and vehicle tracking, and other tracking systems that can identify and plot human movement.[566] Even more worrying, according to some commentators, is that surveillance, tracking systems or identity checks may vary in intensity both geographically and in relation to social class, ethnicity and gender.[567] 'Surveillance, privacy-invasion and privacy-protection differentiate between groups, advantaging some and, by the same token, disadvantaging others' (Surveillance Studies Network 2006, p.6).

Perhaps, however, the greatest levels of disquiet have been raised with regard to the interception of the citizenry's private communications. In 2002 the British Government announced plans to extend the *Regulation of Investigatory Powers Act* (RIPA), so that at least 28 government departments would be given powers to browse citizens' web, email, telephone and fax records, without a warrant and without a subject's knowledge.[568] Public and security authorities made a total of 440,000 requests to monitor people's phone and internet use in 2005-2006. In the period 11 April to 31 December 2006 the UK government issued 253,557 requests for communication data, which as defined by the RIPA includes who you phoned, when they phoned you, how long they phoned you for, subscriber information and associated addresses.[569]

Many of the features of this Labour Government scheme were scrapped in 2009 after heavy criticisms of the civil liberties and privacy implications of the legislation. The Home Office has confirmed, however, that new laws allowing police and security services to extend the

---

563 Welsh and Farrington state that the Home Office's claim that the UK Crime Prevention program was one of the most 'evidenced –based' ever developed was belied by the huge proportion of money used from its budget towards CCTV: '[there] was a tension between the program's stated philosophy, of being 'evidence-based' and only proceeding to large-scale implementation after an approach had been piloted and demonstrated to be cost-effective, and the political need for prevention to be high-profile and perceived by the public as providing an umbrella of safety and security.
The first and most obvious symptom of this tension was the government's decision to set aside an additional £150 million for the installation of town-centre CCTV systems. This commitment was made in the absence of research evidence that closed-circuit television always constituted the most cost-effective response to the problems confronting town centres' (Welsh & Farrington 2002 in Sutton, Cherney & White 2007, p.103). For further discussion of problems associated with the UK Crime Prevention Program, see Chapter 3.

564 For example, according to 2009 Freedom of Information Act requests, the total number of local authority operated CCTV cameras was around 60,000 over the entirety of the UK. See http://www.bigbrotherwatch.org.uk/home/2012/02/price-privacy-councils-spend-521m.html

565 For a discussion of the use of CCTV in Australia see Chapter 2.

566 For example, in London, the 'Oyster' card payment system can track the movement of individual people through the public transport system, although an anonymous option is available, while the London congestion charge card uses computer imaging to track car number plates.

567 For example in the United States and the United Kingdom more attention may be paid at border control to people with Arab sounding names or of middle eastern appearance particularly since September 2011 (Surveillance Studies Network 2006).

568 '"Massive abuse" of privacy feared', *BBC News Online*, 6 November 2002. Accessed at http://news.bbc.co.uk/1/hi/sci/tech/2038036.stm

569 'Interception figures could mask monitoring of millions'. Out-law on line. Accessed at http://www.out-law.com/page 77–88

monitoring of the public's email and social media communications[570] will be introduced by the Cameron Government and detailed in the Queen's opening of Parliament in May 2012. It is envisaged the new scheme will require internet service providers to gather the information and allow access to government intelligence operatives and other agencies.[571]

It is in the context of these types of changes that concerns have been raised about the less benign aspects of NW/HW and its role as one part of the surveillance society.[572]

NW/HW as a form of social control

Echoing the more general critiques of the surveillance society there have been criticisms from the left that NW/HW is primarily an exercise in social control – part of a concerning trend of governments requiring individuals to 'take more responsibility for their own and society's security' (Ayling 2007, p.74) – what Carr was later to call the 'new parochialism' (Carr 2005). Neighbourhood Watch has often been called the 'eyes and ears' of the police and according to some commentators a key apparatus of the surveillance society:

> NW is perhaps best known for the encouragement it gives to residents to engage in surveillance activity. People are urged to be the 'eyes and ears of the police', to look out for any suspicious activity and to contact the police in case of doubt. This conception of NW sets out to appeal to people's self-interest as well as to encourage a sense of partnership with the police in the fight against crime. Residents are encouraged to recognise the fact that the police cannot be everywhere at the same time (McConville & Shepherd 1992, p.90).

Neighbourhood Watch doing the work of the State

Critics on the left and indeed on the libertarian right, have characterised citizens' groups such as NW/HW as part of a shift from 'state-centric' government oversight (the police, army etc) to what French theorist Michel Foucault would call 'governance' by a wide variety of agencies including 'self policing' (Foucault 1979; Rhodes 1997). 'Citizens are then only one "node" of many in networks of policing governance' (Ayling 2007, p.74).[573] Crime prevention is constituted as the normal responsibility of active and responsible citizens:

> A common-sense approach would suggest that, however it is defined or intended, crime prevention extends throughout all of the formal and informal networks of the criminal justice system. The contemporary emphasis on crime prevention points also to an increasingly intricate relationship between the criminal justice system, elements of corporate finance, like the insurance industry, as

---

570 For an account of how social media plays a role in not only responding to but *shaping* public policy including criminal justice policy see Matthew R. Auer, *The Policy Sciences of Social Media* (2011). Referring to Facebook, Auer usefully quotes the public policy theorist Harold Lasswell in his premonitory anticipation of privacy concerns in the Information Age: 'Although the issues are not in principle new, a data rich world can have individual records of unheard of detail promptly available....It is conceivable that human beings will undergo general revulsion against the invasions of privacy that become more common as man's auxiliary brains are put to more and more detailed use' (Lasswell 1965 in Auer 2011, p.731). Ironically Mr Lasswell made these comments in 1965.

571 Booth, Robert 2012, 'Government plans increased email and social network surveillance', *The Guardian*, 1 April. Accessed at www.guardian.co.uk/world/2012/apr/01/government-email-social-network-surveillance

572 One of the key issues that has concerned lawmakers and civil libertarians alike has been how the proliferation of surveillance, information gathering and identity checking mechanisms and other invasions of privacy can best be regulated. This is a subject which is beyond the scope of this Report. However, for a detailed account of what legislative and regulatory provisions and safeguards have been put in place in Britain see Surveillance Studies Network 2006, Part D. pp.76–90.

573 Indeed Watts, Bessant and Hil argue that in its *extreme* form this type of communitarian paradigm was reflected in the tactics of totalitarian regimes of both the extreme right (The Gestapo) and the left (the Stasi):

'The German Gestapo created neighbourhood networks of informants to make up for the numerical deficiencies of Gestapo agents, a system that the secret police or Stasi of the communist regime in Eastern Germany took over holus-bolus after 1945. The sinister overtones of that exercise has, if anything been heightened since the terrorist attacks in New York on 11 September and the Underground bomb attacks in London in 2005 by...governments mobilising support for citizens to inform authorities about 'suspicious persons' (2008, pp.157–158).

Such a critique of course is by no means equating English members of NW/HW with Nazi supporters. It merely purports to point out that some forms of 'communitarianism' has not and does not always have the benign face that organisations such as NW/HW present (See also Gellately 2002).

well as the security industries, and citizens mobilized into projects like The Neighbourhood Watch. It certainly also includes community safety programmes and a wide array of 'risk management' policies. Crime prevention is now being constituted as a normal responsibility, not solely of governments, but of all *active and responsible* citizens. This has been accentuated since the 11 September 2001 attacks in the USA when, as part of the so-called ' war on terror', governments in the UK, the USA and Australia have called on their citizens to be alert and report 'suspicious people' to the authorities (Watts, Bessant & Hil 2008, p.151. (Authors' emphasis)

In the context of the surveillance society NW/HW could be viewed as a 'hybrid' between rationalist Weberian[574] or bureaucratic methods of control and the forms of informal social networks or social ties that had been traditionally used as a form of social control. Now that there has been a 'conscious attempt to delegate responsibility for crime' to all responsible citizens:

> [N]eighbourhood Watch is put forward as one of the central vehicles through which collective community action may be co-ordinated and expressed by 'active' citizens... to make dealing with crime a civic duty rather than simply a matter that can be laid at the door of the police. Sentiments of these kinds were sometimes linked to the view that the fight against crime imposed a civic responsibility upon everybody and that it was unreasonable to expect the police to deal with the problem on their own. In a few cases, however, residents [have] expressed misgivings about what they saw as the transfer of responsibilities from the police to the public (McConville & Shepherd 1992, pp.78, 80).

Technology, media and training as instruments of social control?

Misgivings have also been expressed about the use to which technology and media have been put by the Neighbourhood Watch Network overall and individual chapters of the organisation across Britain. The examples discussed earlier in the context of technology and training such as the RIGS and the OWL are of concern to some commentators. These critics view using technology or social media to communicate reports of suspicious behaviour to other members of the community and the police as a form of surveillance bordering on vigilantism.

It is also of concern that little training would appear to have been given to NW/HW on their role and the use of technology and media. This raises a number of questions for this Committee including:

◆ Should the training of NW/HW members have a greater focus on ethics, law, privacy, confidentiality and citizenship?

◆ How are citizens involved in NW/HW equipped to constructively assess the appropriateness and standards of police conduct in the community? What are the protocols for NW/HW members who see police behaving inappropriately towards young people or members of 'minority ethnic' communities?

◆ To what extent do the NW/HW structures and processes assist the media to run stories that over-dramatise crime and generate community insecurity? Do the media have greater access to stories through NW/HW? Can NW/HW really influence the media to report in the public interest rather than commercial interest?

◆ Can an appropriate balance be struck between the use of social media to promote the activities of NW/HW and its use as an investigatory/reporting tool that may arguably compromise the privacy and confidentiality of people suspected of 'suspicious' or antisocial activities?

---

574 As an extension of the sociologist Max Weber's account of bureaucratic and administrative organisation in modern life, the surveillance society can be viewed more as the outcome of modern organisational practices, businesses, government and the military than as a covert conspiracy. According to such a view 'surveillance may be viewed as progress towards efficient administration, a benefit for the development of Western capitalism and the modern nation-state' (Surveillance Studies Network 2001, p.1).

Does Neighbourhood Watch really reduce the fear of crime or is it an exercise in 'false consciousness'?

Another criticism from the left is one based on the sociologist Emile Durkheim's view of crime as an essentially integrative function leading to a false consciousness on the part of the citizenry. According to this point of view whether NW/HW reduces crime or not it will act at a catalyst in bringing people together and re-creating a lost sense of community (Du Bow & Emmons 1981):

> By shocking the sentiments of ordinary people crime stimulates them to act individually and collectively: Community solidarity and morale are thereby increased, and informal social control exercised by the collectivity is strengthened. In the United States of America, this kind of thinking has been taken up by advocates of the 'social control' model, who see crime and fear of crime as indicators of the erosion of informal social control processes that are believed to establish and maintain order in society (Wilson, 1975; Wilson and Kelling, 1982; Kelling, 1986). The central argument is that 'collective neighbourhood efforts can influence crime and fear of crime... community crime control works' (Kelling 1986, p.91).

> This social control model has been highly influential on official thinking about crime issues and is central to official conceptions of NW/HW. Even if NW/HW does not have a marked influence upon rates of crime or if its effects are hard to measure, the expectation is that it will help deal with the problem of fear of crime: 'Implicit in NW is that fear of crime will be alleviated as residents come to have more of a sense of control over crime, both through their own efforts and those made on their behalf by neighbours' (Mayhew et al 1989 in McConville & Shepherd 1992, pp.78–79).

Research by McConville and Shepherd, however, showed that on the contrary NW/HW's strategy of seeking to exploit fear of crime runs the risk of increasing fear of crime; 'An increase in the fear of crime can lead to a further fracturing of social relations, thus weakening, not strengthening, community spirit and informal social control over crime and incivilities' (1992 p.102). According to such critics consideration should be given to the distinction between community building activities that enhance community cohesion and neighbourliness and activity that co-opts citizens into the 'surveillance society'.

Other criticisms of NW/HW in the UK

Confidentiality and security concerns

Concerns were also expressed that the deployment of NW/HW members or other volunteers working with police could result in misuse of confidential police information:

> The kinds of controls that police organisations have over their employees...often may not be applicable to volunteers. And even if they are, there may be understandable questions over the degree of allegiance volunteers feel to an organisation that does not pay them...and sometimes undervalues their contribution. The risk is real that the privacy of other citizens and also of the police themselves could be compromised by misuse by volunteers of confidential information to which they have access in that capacity (Ayling 2007, p.86).[575]

Limited ability to create community capital and social cohesion

Critics of NW/HW have also expressed cynicism about the extent to which the organisation creates community capital or social cohesion, one of the vaunted justifications for its existence. Although not specifically concerning NW/HW members, Leach argues that community crime prevention volunteers such as 'citizen patrols':

---

575 Ayling was discussing confidentiality issues in the context of all volunteers who work with police, not specifically NW/HW members. It is arguable that NW/HW volunteers may not have great access to police documents in the course of their activities to the same degree as other types of volunteer such as citizen patrols etc, although in theory the concerns are arguably still valid.

Effectively redefine the community they purport to represent to exclude certain groups that are undesirable in the opinion of [patrol] participants. [Initiatives] of this nature may erode rather than strengthen security by deepening mistrust and inequalities in the community,[and] engender conflict as a result (Leach 2006, p.7).

Similarly, Crawford argues that the types of social capital that citizens such as NW/HW members build 'when they band together to ensure their own security' is exclusive rather than inclusive (2006, p.137). The most extreme end of these types of intervention may see community participation and 'neighbourliness' deteriorate into ugly vigilantism (Davids 1995; Ayling 2007).

Vigilantism

Putative vigilantism can be seen in a number of British NW/HW chapters that have organised nightly patrols of their citizens to apprehend or at least report on apparent wrongdoers. For example, the Borderwatch group in Richmondshire involves about 50 volunteers spread across four 'beat areas' to help combat rural crime. Each area has its own watch coordinator and an attached police officer to work in support. 'Volunteers offer detailed local knowledge, being aware of people and vehicles from outside the area and knowing on which land people are allowed to be and which they are not allowed to be' (ERS Research and Consultancy 2010a, p.108).

The volunteer groups mount late night and early morning patrols to surveil local areas:

> Each patrol involves a minimum of two people, though they can involve 3 or 4 people on occasion. They work to a rota established by the designated police officer, to ensure that responsibilities are shared and that good coverage can be maintained such that patrols can be mounted every night. The officer also participates in some patrols.

> Those involved are required to observe, note and report, but not try to apprehend or confront anyone acting suspiciously. Clear guidance notes are provided, setting out a list of dos and don'ts and all volunteers are given a full briefing by the lead Police Officer. Patrols support any suspicious activity to the police, mainly using radios that link them directly to a control room at Richmond. Some groups have been provided with night sights and there is an ambition to purchase more of these... Group activities and associated intelligence gathering/witness evidence have resulted in arrests and convictions at court for crime and wildlife incidents such as poaching. In the three weeks after the scheme was launched the police reported that burglaries from farms, garages and sheds fell 9% compared with the same period a year earlier (ERS Research and Consultancy 2010a, p.109).

There is also an apparent move to incorporate citizen groups and watch groups into border surveillance practices. 'This is in its most advanced form in the USA, where programmes such as Highway Watch, Citizen corps, Coast Watch and River Watch train citizens to "look out for unusual activities"' (Surveillance Studies Network 2006, p.37).

Barriers to greater participation in NW/HW activities

The barriers to the successful and relevant operation of NW/HW groups in the UK are similar to those in other jurisdictions including Australia. Primarily they concern the image of Neighbourhood Watch as being a 'pastime' for a predominantly white middle-class and largely elderly demographic or, as a respondent to a Review of Neighbourhood Watch in England stated 'older retired white "curtain twitchers" with too much time on their hands' (ERS Research and Consultancy 2010b, p.14).

This section examines some of the structural and other barriers that make certain members of society, particularly young people and people from NESBs, reluctant to become involved in NW/HW activities.

The need for diversity of membership

As in Australia, criticisms have been made of the relatively mono-cultural membership of NW/HW groups throughout the UK. A survey of NW/HW membership in England and Wales indicated that whilst there was a stated priority for many groups to diversify their membership 'this aspiration appears to have met with limited success' (ERS Research and Consultancy 2010a, p.24). The demographic of Neighbourhood Watch groups remains primarily white, older and middle-class, although of course this will vary to greater or lesser extents depending on the geographic area of the country. Rural and affluent urban areas for example have a higher percentage of white middle-class members than inner urban areas of the big cities such as London, Birmingham Manchester or Liverpool. This is particularly the case where there are concentrations of public housing estates. Conversely, in the middle-class areas many NW/HE groups are part of or closely associated with resident association/neighbourhood improvement groups. This is particularly the case in those relatively affluent areas that do not experience a high level of crime (ERS Research and Consultancy 2010a, p.24). Moreover in such areas, particularly in rural localities, membership may often be restricted to a small core of enthusiasts who are already heavily active in all parts of village community life (ERS Research and Consultancy 2010a, p.76).[576]

People from ethnic minority backgrounds

The Review, *Exploring Barriers to Participation in Neighbourhood and Home Watch Schemes*, was commissioned by the NNWN in 2010. Its aim was to explore why people from ethnic minority backgrounds were not participating in NW/HW schemes and how these barriers could be overcome. The two most common reasons explaining this lack of participation were broadly a lack of awareness of NW/HW and/or negative perceptions of the scheme, particularly a feeling that it is of limited or no relevance to their culture or lives. In particular the self-sufficiency of some ethnic groups within segregated communities meant they saw little point in engaging with 'outsider' groups:

> They do not generally participate in Neighbourhood Watch and in many cases have developed their own communication systems through which to identify, highlight and address community safety issues. As such, [minority ethnic] groups have not sought to engage with existing Neighbourhood Watch schemes which in the main have not actively attempted to recruit them to become part of the Neighbourhood Watch movement (ERS Research and Consultancy 2010b, p.7).

Other reasons were related to an inability to speak English and a lack of education, particularly amongst elderly residents:

> There is also a general lack of interest and a lack of understanding of what Neighbourhood Watch is about. The lack of knowledge amongst the elderly is also linked to the cultural differences between how communities operate in the UK and [India] (ERS Research and Consultancy 2010b, p.9).[577]

Other reasons for a reluctance to participate in NW/HW included:

- Lack of time/other commitments.

- Lack of relevance to those living in areas of low/falling levels of crime.

- Fear of reprisals, which seem especially acute amongst minority communities.

- Some behaviours being determined by more traditional views in respect of the role of women and which raise additional challenges in respect of gender issues.

---

576 Interestingly in one close-knit affluent village – Woldingham, Surrey – coordinators have been recruited for *each* road in the village or 40 volunteers covering an average of 20 houses each. When a new resident 'joins' the village the area coordinator approaches the resident to join Neighbourhood Watch after the road coordinator becomes aware of their arrival (ERS Research and Consultancy 2010a, p.77).

577 Something as basic as funding for translation services might be of assistance in attracting people from NESBs to become, if not members, at least aware of NW/HW. For example, the SouthYorkshire Neighbourhood Watch Association engages local Polish communities in Doncaster through running a pilot translation scheme and interpretation hotline with regard to Neighbourhood Watch's activities in the area (ERS Research and Consultancy 2010a, p.113).

- Lack of role models – the 'Catch 22' of a lack of new minority volunteers due to a lack of existing minority volunteers

- Stereotypical perceptions of Neighbourhood Watch groups, as comprising white, elderly, middle class, 'curtain twitchers' (ERS Research and Consultancy 2010b, p.2).

The Report concluded that despite these barriers it was important to recognise that minority ethnic communities are by no means homogenous and that the barriers mentioned above may be less in evidence in some sections of the community, particularly educated middle-class sections of the population. Indeed this may reflect a more general barrier to participation in NW/HW schemes that is equally applicable to mainstream communities, that is, in communities characterised by high levels of deprivation there may be a belief that if 'society generally appears not to care too much about them, why should they subscribe to its institutions?' (ERS Research and Consultancy 2010b, p.19).

On the other hand, where there has been success in establishing and sustaining NW/HW groups it has been based largely on the same principles that apply to NW/HW organisations in 'mainstream' areas, namely: 'putting in effort to recruit volunteers and the use of powers of persuasion to demonstrate the relevance/usefulness of Neighbourhood Watch' (ERS Research and Consultancy 2010b, p.19).

The Report also found that if people from NESB populations were already working in positions of authority or influence, particularly as police officers or police community support officers, this could be central to the establishment and success of NH/HW groups in areas with high concentration of minority populations. For example, one PCSO from a Pakistani background worked tirelessly to support a local NW/HW group in a neighbourhood with a high proportion of Pakistani residents:

> He is able to devote significant time and effort to the process of engaging [minority ethnic] groups, using personal contacts, community networks, local mosques and community centres to identify and engage appropriate black and minority ethnic representatives and importantly support their active participation (ERS Research and Consultancy 2010b, p.6).

As such the Report recommended encouraging the deployment of specific police officers and PCSOs, particularly from minority backgrounds, to recruit volunteers from ethnic communities and support the establishment of new Neighbourhood Watch groups in areas where they reside (ERS Research and Consultancy 2010b, p.21). Certainly the use of partnerships is a key aspect of successful recruiting of minority populations to Neighbourhood Watch (ERS Research and Consultancy 2010a, p.73).

Young people

With regard to the recruitment of young people to NW/HW schemes, a separate research report commissioned for NW/HW and funded by the British Home Office similarly noted a range of barriers to participation.[578] The Report[579] found that for many young people the organisation was of limited relevance. For example, young people were more likely to view NW/HW as an organisation solely for elderly or middle-aged people. The Report found nonetheless that NW/HW as an organisation could serve a useful role in engaging young people in worthwhile community activities that would act as a deterrent in becoming involved in crime. It was noted as important, however, that such activities, be they of a sporting, leisure, artistic or outdoor nature, involve the whole community of young people

---

578 That the importance of NW/HW in the UK is not undervalued can be gauged from the relatively generous amount of funding the Home Office allocates to research on matters affecting the organisation. In 2010 alone four major research reports were produced by universities or private research consultancies

579 *An evaluation undertaken by Crime and Disorder Reduction Partnerships in the North West which aimed to engage young people in crime prevention and reduction initiatives.* Undertaken on behalf of Neighbourhood and Home Watch North West by Laura Buckley, University of Central Lancashire. May 2010.

and not just those deemed to be 'at risk'. To do otherwise runs the risk of further isolation and stigmatisation (Buckley 2010, p.9). It was found that some NW/HW groups in Britain had successfully involved young people in a range of diversionary, engagement and proactive projects in areas as diverse as fire safety projects, self-defence classes and life skills training.

Conclusion

Neighbourhood Watch as a community based crime prevention and community safety initiative clearly has many similarities and commonalities in its various iterations across the world. Nonetheless in England and Wales there are also notable differences in the way in which Neighbourhood Watch, Home Watch or their subsidiary and associated groups operate.

It has generally been acknowledged that throughout England and Wales, NW/HW groups operate more akin to community development projects than traditional crime prevention or law and order outfits. As the Review of Neighbourhood Watch in England in 2010, *Showcasing Neighbourhood and Home Watch Achievements*, noted there has been a move in England for local groups to 'address[ing] issues of social inclusion and community cohesion; seeking to deal with the causes of local problems not just the effects' (ERS Research and Consultancy 2010a, p.2). Indeed as the Report concluded, NW/HW is to a large extent more about community spirit and neighbourliness than about crime fighting; 'People want to feel part of a community and in many cases Neighbourhood Watch schemes have provided the mechanism through which this has been made possible' (ERS Research and Consultancy 2010a, p.2).[580] In short, the experience of NW/HW in England and Wales, especially since the reforms introduced in 2007, show how a well funded community organisation with strong structures and enthusiastic partnership involvement, particularly from local government, can mobilise community support to address local concerns including but by no means restricted to crime and community safety.

Despite the positives of NW/HW in the UK there are, as this chapter has examined, some challenges for the organisation. Not everyone in Britain is convinced of its relevancy or effectiveness; it has proven difficult to extend membership outside of a relatively confined white, middle-class membership. Young people and people from ethnic minority backgrounds have been particularly resistant to joining NW/HW or indeed any other mainstream community safety initiatives. Of some concern is the fact that NW/HW in some respects has become part of the web of surveillance and information gathering that to a certain extent characterises modern Britain, with all the risks inherent in that. This is by no means a reason to disband NW/HW in England and Wales. Even its most strident critics have not suggested that. Nonetheless whilst lauding its successes it is equally important that those involved with the organisation in England and Wales bring attention to the problems and challenges facing NW/HW and ways in which to address them.

These challenges are not unique to NW/HW in the UK. Neighbourhood Watch in Australia has and is also addressing a raft of issues pertaining to structure, function, funding and indeed even its very relevance as a community crime prevention organisation. The situation of the Neighbourhood Watch model in Victoria, Australia is considered in the next chapter.

---

580 That this rosy if not 'cosy' and benign view of NW/HW is not subscribed to by all commentators is apparent in the critique of Ayling. Her view is that the organisation can act as a somewhat disturbing extension of private policing. See discussion earlier in this chapter.

10. Neighbourhood Watch in Victoria: A Case for Renewal?

Background — the early years

Neighbourhood Watch was first established in Victoria in Frankston in 1983 as part of a police pilot program to reduce crime in the area, particularly residential burglaries and property theft. Victoria Police then adopted the program for state-wide implementation and this was followed by other states and territories introducing similar community based crime prevention programs. Schemes in which communities actively participated in crime prevention were already operating overseas, for example in the United States and as the previous chapter has discussed in the United Kingdom (Holloway, Bennett & Farrington 2008).[581]

Initial aims and objectives

The broad objective of the Neighbourhood Watch program was to increase community involvement in crime prevention, thus reducing neighbourhood crime and improving safety for residents. To achieve this, Neighbourhood Watch areas were established, with distinctive signage, and a partnership formed with a local police coordinator.

The program operated on the premise that, within a declared Neighbourhood Watch area:

> ...citizens support each other in crime prevention by reporting suspicious behaviour, people and vehicles, looking out for their neighbours' properties and being active in seeking to prevent crimes from occurring (de Ridder & Johns 2007, p.3).

The underlying assumption was that the increased likelihood of being seen and being apprehended would deter someone from committing a crime (de Ridder & Johns 2008). If theft did occur, strategies such as property marking would improve the chances of detecting the perpetrators and retrieving stolen property. Programs to instruct those residents forming a Neighbourhood Watch area in crime prevention strategies were instigated by their local police liaison officer (PLO).

The major focus of Neighbourhood Watch was to reduce opportunity for crime — situational crime prevention[582] — rather than investigate and deal with the social causes of crime. Crime prevention programs therefore concentrated on improving residents' awareness about public safety and attitude to reporting crime, for example through a regular newsletter about crime in the area, and on reducing their vulnerability to crime using property marking methods, such as engraving on electrical products, and effective security devices (Mukherjee & Wilson 1987).

A police management objective in establishing Neighbourhood Watch, separate to community protection objectives, has also been suggested:

> At management level, the pressure was on police managers to achieve improvement in crime reduction without financial increases and hence growth of police numbers. Hence, a number of separable but consonant discourses for the establishment of Neighbourhood Watch seem in evidence (Davids 1995, p.71).

---

581 See also discussion in Chapter 9.
582 For further discussion see Chapter 2.

There was, however, a shared expectation by both residents involved and Victoria Police that the Neighbourhood Watch program would be beneficial.

Merits of the program

In the first years after its state-wide launch in 1984, Neighbourhood Watch was considered to be beneficial in reducing the number of burglaries in Victoria and nationally. In 1987, Mukherjee and Wilson stated that in Victoria 'the police report that by May 1985 residential burglaries were 16.04 per cent lower than the first five months of 1984' (1987, p.2). One year earlier, an appraisal of community policing by Bayley for the National Police Research Unit had claimed that, 'wherever Neighbourhood Watch has been tried in Australia it has achieved its stated goal of lowering the incidence of burglaries' (Bayley 1986, p.8).

Other benefits believed to flow from Neighbourhood Watch for those involved included: reducing fear of crime; increasing social cohesion by bringing people from disparate groups together; combating 'feelings of isolation and helplessness by introducing an element of control and participation into people's lives' (Beyer in Davids 1995, p.60) and creating a more positive relationship between citizens and police.

After the first decade, however, the growth of Neighbourhood Watch slowed and its performance and relevance began to be questioned.

Reasons for the decline of Neighbourhood Watch

A range of factors have contributed to the decline in support for and relevance of the Neighbourhood Watch program which, for most areas, is now between 26 and 28 years old. These relate to the changing nature of high-level crime and society. Although some factors may be relatively recent it would seem from evidence received by the Committee that many have been issues of concern for a long time and continue to be so. These concerns are discussed later in this chapter.

Neighbourhood Watch members, social researchers and the general public consider the factors discussed below to be the major reasons for the organisation's current decline in support and relevance.

Reduction in burglary — As de Ridder and Johns point out in their *Review of Neighbourhood Watch*:

> It is noteworthy that at the time NWH was introduced there was a significantly different crime profile in Victoria. Burglary was a statistically much more prevalent offence than it is currently and many members of the community were motivated to support police in seeking to prevent burglary and theft in their local areas (2007, p.6).

According to a 2009 Neighbourhood Watch discussion paper, burglary is way down the list of things that most concern members of the community, 'and communities now fear things like hoon driving, violence or becoming a victim of fraud'.[583] As Deputy Commissioner Tony Cartwright, Victoria Police stated:

> Neighbourhood Watch does not produce what we formerly saw it produce. In my view it was formed around a particular problem, which was household burglaries. As I said, we have reduced that problem significantly.[584]

---

583 Neighbourhood Watch Victoria Board of Management 2009 discussion paper, 'Re-alignment of Police Regional Boundaries', included in the submission from Neighbourhood Watch Board of Management to the Drugs and Crime Prevention Committee, Inquiry into Locally Based Approaches to Community Safety and Crime Prevention, May 2011.

584 Deputy Commissioner Tim Cartwright, Victoria Police, Evidence given to the Drugs and Crime Prevention Committee, Inquiry into Locally Based Approaches to Community Safety and Crime Prevention, Public Hearing, Melbourne 16 April 2012.

Aging of volunteers involved and lack of younger members — According to the Neighbourhood Watch Board of Management, the program has not been able to attract new and younger members, with the current age range of most members being 70–80 years.[585] As a result, it has become difficult to find people willing to take on committee roles and give fresh leadership to Neighbourhood Watch areas.

Out-dated program and technological advances — The Neighbourhood Watch model has not kept step with changing times and has been considered irrelevant by many for some time. As Mr Andrew Brideson, Victorian State President of Neighbourhood Watch, told a Public Hearing:

> Neighbourhood Watch is virtually dead in the City of Stonnington, yet when you drive around, every lamppost on every corner has a Neighbourhood Watch sticker that says, 'You live in a Neighbourhood Watch area'. That is from the past; it is not what currently exists…Who is watching?[586]

In many areas, printed newsletters convey old information and crime statistics that are often two months out-of-date by the time they come from police and are disseminated.[587] This lack of modern technology in imparting up-to-date information was remarked on to the Committee in submissions and public hearings.

> A key issue here is the complete absence of information technology in most areas. Some areas have a token approach to the internet and so on, but there has been very little demonstrated commitment to become part of NHW on line.[588]

> One of the big driving forces of Neighbourhood Watch has been producing a [printed] newsletter…That has been the flagship of Neighbourhood Watch, but those days are gone…We have got computers, so send people emails.[589]

As well, over the 26 or so years since Neighbourhood Watch began, there has been increasing use of CCTV to monitor environments, and mobile phones equipped with cameras, emails and internet real-time information have become readily available. Indeed the use of this technology and the associated popularity of *Crimestoppers* could be suggested as key reasons as to why there has been decreasing levels of involvement in Neighbourhood Watch programs.

Competition from other groups and retaining volunteers — More recently formed community safety response groups that are more functional and are able to target specific areas of safety may have replaced the local street-level surveillance approach of Neighbourhood Watch.[590]

Retaining volunteers is a problem encountered by many organisations, for example Meals on Wheels and Animal Shelters. One reason for this may be, as a Victoria Police submission suggests, is that volunteers 'tend to remain with emergency response type volunteer services as

---

585 Submission from Mr Andrew Brideson, President, Board of Management, Neighbourhood Watch Victoria Inc., to the Drugs and Crime Prevention Committee, Inquiry into Locally Based Approaches to Community Safety and Crime Prevention, May 2011.

586 Mr Andrew Brideson, President, Board of Management, Neighbourhood Watch Victoria Inc., Evidence given to the Drugs and Crime Prevention Committee, Inquiry into Locally Based Approaches to Community Safety and Crime Prevention, Public Hearing, Melbourne, 27 June 2011.

587 Mr Bernie Durkin, Executive Manager, Strategic Projects, Western Australia Office of Crime Prevention, Evidence given to the Drugs and Crime Prevention Committee, Inquiry into Locally Based Approaches to Community Safety and Crime Prevention, Meeting, Perth, 21 June 2011.

588 Submission from Mr Andrew Brideson, President, Board of Management, Neighbourhood Watch Victoria Inc., to the Drugs and Crime Prevention Committee, Inquiry into Locally Based Approaches to Community Safety and Crime Prevention, May 2011.

589 Mr Bernie Durkin, Executive Manager, Strategic Projects, Western Australia Office of Crime Prevention, Evidence given to the Drugs and Crime Prevention Committee, Inquiry into Locally Based Approaches to Community Safety and Crime Prevention, Meeting, Perth, 21 June 2011.

590 Mr Philip Schier, Senior Policy Officer, Victorian Local Governance Association, Evidence given to the Drugs and Crime Prevention Committee, Inquiry into Locally Based Approaches to Community Safety and Crime Prevention Committee, Public Hearing, Melbourne, 27 June 2011.

they feel empowered when assisting people, are regularly trained and see results of their hard work'.[591] The submission adds that this 'is not always the case with Neighbourhood Watch'.[592]

Restructuring of police operations and change in relationship — Significant restructuring of policing operations have occurred since Neighbourhood Watch began, such as the implementation of police service areas (PSAs). One consequence has been reduced localised interactions, for example a lack of police attendance at Neighbourhood Watch meetings. Changes to policing have also resulted in specific police squads being formed to proactively police specific organised crime, for example Organised Crime Theme Desks (de Ridder & Johns 2007, p.6), which may have reduced police need for involvement in the Neighbourhood Watch program. This differs greatly from the Neighbourhood Policies Model in England discussed in Chapter 9.

Negative responses to Neighbourhood Watch — Some people who have emigrated from countries characterised by more repressive regimes have reacted negatively to members of this program, in all likelihood due to bad experiences with police in these countries. Mr Bruce James, Dandenong Neighbourhood Watch President, related his experience of this response:

> There were areas where you had — how can I put it — people that come from different countries where they did not like the police in any shape or form. When we went around knocking on the doors and they said 'Neighbourhood Watch, associated with the police', boom. That was the reaction that you received.[593]

Respect for Neighbourhood Watch within local communities has also waned, as a submission to the Inquiry illustrates:

> There seems to be a lack of respect for NHW and its role in the community by local government and other agencies. It seems that NHW is viewed as a group of old age volunteers who are intent on 'spying' on their neighbours.[594]

Displacement of crime and privacy issues – There have also been negative responses in studies of the effectiveness of the scheme. For example, a 2005 Australian study found significant evidence that Neighbourhood Watch was ineffective at preventing crime and created a displacement of crime to other neighbourhoods (Fleming 2005). It has also been suggested that the activities of Neighbourhood Watch themselves could lead to an increased fear of crime at a local level (Crawford 1998 cited in Sutton, Cherney & White 2008).

Further, a 2006 study identified the risk of Neighbourhood Watch volunteers compromising the privacy of citizens and also of police through misuse of confidential information, which had the potential to compromise investigations or even endanger lives (Davids 2006 cited in Ayling 2007).

Interstate and overseas Neighbourhood Watch situation

The problems listed above that have contributed to the decline in effectiveness of and support for the Neighbourhood Watch program have also been experienced by Neighbourhood Watch and its equivalents in other states and overseas.[595]

---

591 Submission from Victoria Police to the Drugs and Crime Prevention Committee, Inquiry into Locally Based Approaches to Community Safety and Crime Prevention, April 2012.

592 Submission from Victoria Police to the Drugs and Crime Prevention Committee, Inquiry into Locally Based Approaches to Community Safety and Crime Prevention, April 2012.

593 Mr Bruce James, President, Dandenong Neighbourhood Watch, Evidence given to the Drugs and Crime Prevention Committee, Inquiry into Locally Based Approaches to Community Safety and Crime Prevention, Public Hearing, Dandenong, 30 May 2011.

594 Submission from Rhonda Rotherham, Division Coordinator, Neighbourhood Watch Greater Geelong, and Surf Coast Committee to the Drugs and Crime Prevention Committee, Inquiry into Locally Based Approaches to Community Safety and Crime Prevention, May 2011.

595 In addition to the material discussed in Chapter 9 on the situation of Neighbourhood Watch in the United Kingdom, see Cahalen 2010; Dempsey and Forst 2010; Rosenbaum 1988 for a discussion of the issues and challenges facing Neighbourhood Watch in the USA. See also in that context the website of Neighbourhood Watch in America, http://www.usaonwatch.org/about/history.

The recent history of Neighbourhood Watch in Victoria

Neighbourhood Watch, at state and local levels, has experienced changes in structures, relationships with police and the amount of support it receives from the community and business. And at the time of writing this Report a new Strategic Plan for Neighbourhood Watch is being developed. Details of this Plan, however, are yet to be finalised. This section therefore outlines the state level's existing structure, objectives, responsibilities and engagement with local level Neighbourhood areas. Proposed aims, directions and initiatives of the forthcoming Strategic Plan will be summarised in the final section of this chapter.[596]

State level organisation — structure, roles and responsibilities

Neighbourhood Watch Victoria is an incorporated association, overseen by a Board of Management elected annually. The current Board consists of a:

◆ President

◆ Vice President

◆ Secretary

◆ Treasurer

◆ Program representative

◆ Chief Commissioners Representatives (2)

◆ Immediate Past State President.

The role of the Board is to control and manage the business affairs of the Association. In fulfilling its responsibilities the Board must have regard to the Statement of Purposes which requires it:

1. To foster and enhance the partnership between police and the community and thereby improve the safety, security and the quality of life for all Victorians.

2. To manage and provide strategic leadership for the Victorian Neighbourhood Watch Program.

3. To formulate strategies and policies in order to achieve the following objectives:

   (a) to minimise the incidence of preventable crime.

   (b) to deter criminal activity by increasing the probability of apprehension.

   (c) to reduce the fear of crime.

   (d) to increase the reporting of crime and suspicious activity.

   (e) to improve the degree of personal and household security through education programs.

   (f) to expand the program's involvement in wider community safety and crime-prevention initiatives.

4. To serve as an information exchange and the primary conduit between the various Neighbourhood Watch Divisions, thus facilitating the formulation and implementation of strategies and policies.[597]

This Statement encapsulates Neighbourhood Watch's concept of crime prevention.

There is also a State Forum consisting of elected members of the Association, which assists the Board with its deliberations. The Forum is comprised of the:

---

596 See the section 'A new strategy — 2011 onwards'. Note also that the new strategy proposes a change in defining Neighbourhood Watch areas — from police service area (PSA) or local area command (LAC) to local government area.

597 Neighbourhood Watch Victoria Inc. Constitution, included in the submission from Mr Andrew Brideson, President, Board of Management, Neighbourhood Watch Victoria Inc., to the Drugs and Crime Prevention Committee, Inquiry into Locally Based Approaches to Community Safety and Crime Prevention, May 2011.

◆ Divisional Delegates

◆ Divisional Police Coordinators

◆ Executive Director

◆ Program Representative

◆ Treasurer

◆ Secretary.

The Forum is the primary communication avenue between the Divisions and the Board, and so acts as an information exchange. It advises the Board on the status of the program within the Divisions and the efficacy or otherwise of program initiatives and strategies.[598]

The current structure of Neighbourhood Watch Regions and Divisions in Victoria, which is similar to that of Victoria Police, is comprised of four regions:

◆ Eastern — six Divisions and 17 PSAs

◆ North West Metropolitan — five Divisions and 14 PSAs

◆ Southern Metropolitan — four Divisions and 11 PSAs

◆ Western — six Divisions and 13 PSAs.

The boundaries of PSAs are the same as those of local government areas. Previous to 2010 there were five regions but this was changed by the Board of Management in consultation with Victoria Police following the latter's change to four regions.

Victoria Police participation

The Safer Communities Unit, based at the Flinders Street Police Complex, has been 'the engine room'[599] for Neighbourhood Watch, providing management at the state-wide level and producing the quarterly magazine *Sentinel*. The Unit consisted of a state manager, an executive director and at least six other officers who managed Neighbourhood Watch. Due to an internal restructure, however, the Unit is in the process of being handed over to the Media and Corporate Communications Department of Victoria Police. The Committee understands that apart from the Inspector in charge there will be no sworn police officers employed in the new structure as at the end of June 2012.[600]

At the time of writing this report, 25 Neighbourhood Watch Police Coordinators are employed to work with PSAs, some on a part-time basis and four who share their time as Crime Prevention Officers. There are also 38 Crime Prevention Officer positions including three Transit Officers. However, the positions and roles of Police Coordinators and Crime Prevention Officers are now subject to review.

Current policies

Helping to build safe and secure communities continues to be the broad policy for Neighbourhood Watch. The following strategic goals for achieving this are listed in its Strategic Plan 2008–2013:

---

598 Neighbourhood Watch Victoria Inc., 'Notes to the Accounts', included in the submission from Mr Andrew Brideson, President, Board of Management, Neighbourhood Watch Victoria Inc., to the Drugs and Crime Prevention Committee, Inquiry into Locally Based Approaches to Community Safety and Crime Prevention, May 2011.

599 Submission from the Mr Andrew Brideson, President, Board of Management, Neighbourhood Watch Victoria Inc., to the Drugs and Crime Prevention Committee, Inquiry into Locally Based Approaches to Community Safety and Crime Prevention, May 2011.

600 Mr Andrew Brideson, President, Neighbourhood Watch Victoria Inc., in correspondence to the Drugs and Crime Prevention Committee, 7 April 2012.

- improve the image and reputation of NHW more broadly in the community

- develop and deliver Community safety education programs

- increase participation in NHW across Victoria

- engage with young people to become involved with the program

- engage and enthuse our membership with targeted development program

- complement, partner and support other organisations with similar mandates

- engage and improve crime prevention and community safety initiatives.[601]

Neighbourhood Watch also aims to improve information communication to increase productivity and effectiveness; adopt a community benefit approach in all projects; increase inclusiveness in the community; rejuvenate communication strategies; review and reduce costs where possible and maximise returns on investments; broaden the skills of volunteers and become a centre of excellence in areas of crime prevention and community safety.[602]

Currently, however, policies and projects are to a large extent 'in a state of limbo', as there is an expectation that a State Manager will be appointed. A new strategic plan has also been formulated and should be enacted later in the year.

State-wide projects — funding and prioritising

Neighbourhood Watch does not run state-wide projects; rather, projects are run by each local area. However, the general focus and priority for state-level Neighbourhood Watch is the BE SAFE program, which consists of:

Bridging Gaps — expanding the volunteer base to include a broader cultural and age demographic and establish a greater skills base and exchange of ideas.

Educating — developing programs to assist leaders and managers and raise professionalism and confidence within the program framework.

Supporting — adding to the existing promotional materials such as monthly bulletins and *Sentinel* magazine by developing themed resources addressing local crime and safety issues and expanding the website to include resource acquisition capability online.

Awareness — promoting Neighbourhood Watch through further publications, revising methods of information distribution and raising awareness and use of the website.

Fostering Partnerships — in order to provide funding for projects and program initiatives and deliver these to the Victorian community.

Empowering Communities — enabling communities through education and engagement to influence strategies that create safer environments.[603] How many projects can be run and for how long, however, is largely dependent on the availability of funding and the extent of cooperation from other agencies.

---

601 Neighbourhood Watch Victoria Inc. Strategic Plan 2008–2013, included in the submission from Mr Andrew Brideson, President, Board of Management, Neighbourhood Watch Victoria Inc., to the Drugs and Crime Prevention Committee, Inquiry into Locally Based Approaches to Community Safety and Crime Prevention, May 2011.

602 Neighbourhood Watch Victoria Inc. Strategic Plan 2008–2013, included in the submission from Mr Andrew Brideson, President, Board of Management, Neighbourhood Watch Victoria Inc., to the Drugs and Crime Prevention Committee, Inquiry into Locally Based Approaches to Community Safety and Crime Prevention, May 2011.

603 Summary of the 'Be Safe' program discussed in detail in Neighbourhood Watch Victoria Inc. Strategic Plan 2008–2013, included in the submission from Mr Andrew Brideson, President, Board of Management, Neighbourhood Watch Victoria Inc., to the Drugs and Crime Prevention Committee, Inquiry into Locally Based Approaches to Community Safety and Crime Prevention, May 2011.

Sources of funding

In the past there have been various funding sponsorships and 'in kind' arrangements for advertising and training, however recently these have been cancelled or have been one-off payments rather than ongoing funding.

The Board's only current ongoing source of funding is from advertising placed in *Sentinel*. A recent sponsorship deal for a $10,000 one-off donation and commission on each security system sold has recently been made with the iPATROL company.[604] Other funding sources have been public donations and a $60,000 'lifeline grant' from the previous Victorian Labor government in 2010 to pay for public liability insurance, conference costs and redevelopment of the website.[605]

In the 2011–12 state budget, however, the Victorian government has allocated $550,000 over four years to revitalise the organisation with a funded office and state manager and also provided $25,000 for development of a new Neighbourhood Watch strategic plan.[606]

Involvement with wider community and private sector in planning and delivering crime prevention programs

Due to a lack of resources at its disposal the Neighbourhood Watch Board is not currently able to plan or deliver any programs with the wider community. As a result of the changes to the Safety Communities Unit, Victoria Police can no longer be relied upon for resourcing community programs.[607]

Relationship with local levels

Many of the reasons for the decline of Neighbourhood Watch are still being dealt with and this situation appears to be straining relations between some sections of the Neighbourhood Watch Board, Neighbourhood Watch areas and Victoria Police.

Although PSA committees have direct access to the Board and are encouraged to place issues on the agenda, it appears they generally perceive the Board to be a 'toothless tiger' that does not make decisions, or if it does such decisions can be disregarded.[608]

The general lack of efficient working relationships is evident in the Board of Management's comments on the failure of many Neighbourhood Watch areas to supply data about their membership and activities:

> Many areas have failed to supply data and it could be assumed that these areas have ceased to exist but with the lack of confidence in the data provided it is only an assumption.

> It has been extremely difficult to collect the data due to either Police Coordinators or volunteer office bearers withholding this information. It is hard to understand reasons for this despite repeated requests since February 2011.

---

604 Mr Andrew Brideson, President, Neighbourhood Watch Victoria Inc., in correspondence to the Drugs and Crime Prevention Committee, 20 October 2011.

605 Neighbourhood Watch President's 2010/11 Annual Report, included in the Submission from Mr Andrew Brideson, President, Board of Management, Neighbourhood Watch Victoria, Inc., to the Drugs and Crime Prevention Committee, Inquiry into Locally Based Approaches to Community Safety and Crime Prevention, May 2011.

606 Mr Andrew Brideson, President, Board of Management, Neighbourhood Watch Victoria Inc., Evidence given to the Drugs and Crime Prevention Committee, Inquiry into Locally Based Approaches to Community Safety and Crime Prevention, Public Hearing, Melbourne, 24 October 2011.

607 Mr Andrew Brideson, President, Neighbourhood Watch Victoria Inc., in correspondence to the Drugs and Crime Prevention Committee, 20 October 2011.

608 Mr Andrew Brideson, President, Neighbourhood Watch Victoria Inc., in correspondence to the Drugs and Crime Prevention Committee, 20 October 2011.

This situation highlights a problem in trust and communication between all levels of the organisation particularly brought about by the feeling of uncertainty and insecurity as to the future.[609]

The Neighbourhood Watch President's 2010/11 Annual Report points to specific ramifications of this breakdown in the relationship between the PSAs and the Board:

> After twelve months at the helm I still do not know the true size of the organization, the precise structure of the organization or the state of the finances in many areas. Such basic information, I consider, is essential to the efficient management of an organization and is proving to be an obstacle in obtaining sponsorship.
>
> My lack of such basic statistics also makes it extremely difficult for strategic planning.[610]

A detailed discussion of how local level Neighbourhood Watch groups operate is given below.

Formal evaluations of programs — how is success measured

There has been little academic research into the success or otherwise of Neighbourhood Watch programs. In a 2004 meta-analysis of Neighbourhood Watch, Bennett, Holloway and Farrington found mixed results from studies into its effectiveness, with half the studies finding a benefit and half finding no benefit. This study also found that a significant amount of the research conducted up to the mid 1990s was methodologically flawed (Bennett, Holloway & Farrington 2004 cited in de Ridder & Johns 2007) which brought into question the validity of the findings. Indeed according to Laycock and Tilley's review of Neighbourhood Watch programs in England, most if not all attempts to evaluate Neighbourhood Watch have been unsatisfactory with each of them having serious methodological flaws (1995).

Fleming, in a later review of the evaluation literature of Neighbourhood Watch both in Australia and overseas, found the results of Neighbourhood Watch's effectiveness suggest that it is at best equivocal:

> Despite widespread enthusiasm and support for Neighbourhood Watch by large numbers of people in Australia and overseas, there is significant evidence suggesting that it is ineffective at preventing crime (Sherman and Eck, 2002), has a displacement effect (Barr and Pease 1990, Mukherjee and Wilson 1987) and is only marginally successful in white middle class areas where crime rates are already low (Bright 1991). Nor are the assumed subsidiary benefits such as reduced fear of crime and the increased flow of information between police and community, substantiated by available evidence (Fleming 2005, p.1).

A recent study by Kang (2011) that also reviewed the effectiveness of Neighbourhood Watch as a crime reduction mechanism found the results 'uncertain', although the author did acknowledge the function of Neighbourhood Watch as a mechanism to promote community cohesion, social interaction and friendship networks should not be minimised (Kang 2011, p.4; see also Dalgleish & Myhill 2004; Huck & Kosfeld 2007).

Professor Darren Palmer a criminologist based at Deakin University, Victoria, summed up the standing of Neighbourhood Watch in the academic community in correspondence to the Committee:

---

609 Submission from Mr Andrew Brideson, President, Board of Management, Neighbourhood Watch Victoria Inc., to the Drugs and Crime Prevention Committee, Inquiry into Locally Based Approaches to Community Safety and Crime Prevention, May 2011.

610 Neighbourhood Watch President's 2010/11 Annual Report, included in the Submission from Mr Andrew Brideson, President, Board of Management, Neighbourhood Watch Victoria Inc., to the Drugs and Crime Prevention Committee, Inquiry into Locally Based Approaches to Community Safety and Crime Prevention, May 2011.

The international research evidence is very clear in terms of its limited effectiveness. A lot of resources, a lot of opportunity costs around those resources go into Neighbourhood Watch but the benefits that come out of that effort are very limited.[611]

In correspondence to the Committee the Neighbourhood Watch President confirmed that no formal evaluation of Neighbourhood Watch programs has been undertaken.[612] Consequently, measuring success accurately is not possible. In his 2010/11 Annual Report, however, the President pointed out that the past year had seen a net loss of volunteers, the closure or amalgamation of many Neighbourhood Watch areas and in many cases less interaction between local police and Neighbourhood Watch leading to a disconnect[613] — this suggests a less than rosy picture for operations overall. Perhaps given this rather negative, or at least ambivalent appraisal, the questions that should be asked then are those posed by Laycock and Tilley in their review of Neighbourhood Watch in England:

> Instead of enquiring 'Does it work?' it makes more sense to ask, 'How and under what conditions can Neighbourhood Watch maximise intended and positive outcomes and minimise negative ones? This both reflects the diversity of practice and condition and also helps focus discussion of policy implications, since in addition to informing arguments about whether or not support for the movement is worthwhile, it also invites consideration of how and where potential benefits can most effectively and economically be gained (1995, p.21).

Neighbourhood Watch at the local level

Neighbourhood Watch at the local level in Victoria relies on volunteers to work towards improving community safety and undertaking crime prevention programs in their local area, working closely with police. The following section gives an overview of how they operate and the activities they undertake.

Structure

Neighbourhood Watch areas are formed at the request of communities if they meet certain criteria based on the size and population of the area, the crime rate and the amount of community interest. Positions within a Neighbourhood Watch group are voluntary and include Zone leaders, an Area Coordinator, Publicity Officer/Newsletter Editor, Secretary and Treasurer.

While most areas are organised along the PSA model, there are some that are not. For example, Bendigo uses a Divisional structure and many country areas have a 'town based' model. Large distances between towns, cost of fuel and the aging membership base do not fit well with a single PSA Committee.

Local level views and understandings — responses to the Committee's survey

In order to gain an understanding of the situation for Neighbourhood Watch local areas, the Committee designed a series of questions which the President of Neighbourhood Watch Inc. Victoria sent out to all local groups.[614] Thirteen areas responded to the survey and three others responded to the Inquiry's Terms of Reference. All the responses were forwarded to the Committee and analysed. This section comprises a summary of the responses to each question.[615]

---

611 Associate Professor Darren Palmer, Convenor, Criminology Program, Deakin University, Deakin University, correspondence to the Drugs and Crime Prevention Committee, Inquiry into Locally Based Approaches to Community Safety and Crime Prevention, Briefing, Melbourne, 9 September 2011.

612 Mr Andrew Brideson, President, Neighbourhood Watch Victoria Inc., in correspondence to the Drugs and Crime Prevention Committee, 20 October 2011.

613 Neighbourhood Watch President's 2010/11 Annual Report, included in the Submission from Mr Andrew Brideson, Board of Management, Neighbourhood Watch Victoria Inc., to the Drugs and Crime Prevention Committee, Inquiry into Locally Based Approaches to Community Safety and Crime Prevention, 9 September 2011.

614 The list of questions is reproduced in Appendix 6.

615 For a list of Neighbourhood Watch chapters that responded to the list of questions see Appendix 7.

PSAs understanding of the concept of crime prevention

The majority of Neighbourhood Watch areas saw crime prevention as being reducing preventable crime and providing residents with a sense of safety and security. Preventable crime encompassed burglary, theft from and of vehicles, criminal damage such as graffiti, other theft such as handbag theft, and deceptions and scams.

In regard to methods of prevention, the emphasis of most committees was on educating residents in ways of improving personal and household security by properly securing their own property and valuables. Other responses included assisting police in preventing crimes through reactive responses such as reporting to police situations that may indicate a crime is being or about to be committed. One committee's understanding of crime prevention was 'that each resident…look out for his/her neighbour i.e. Community Policing'.[616]

Areas of each PSA

This question was intended to ascertain the geographical extent of the Neighbourhood Watch groups but was interpreted differently by most of the responding committees. Nevertheless, it is clear that some PSAs in country areas are spread over very large distances; some PSAs encompass disparate areas of outer metropolitan suburbs, new housing estates, rural townships and semi-rural areas, while others are entirely made up of a number of densely populated metropolitan suburbs.

PSAs role in crime prevention for their local districts

This question elicited a variety of responses in several categories, including the following:

Supporting police and authorities

◆ provide a conduit for police and other government authorities to disseminate crime prevention information and initiatives to the general public

◆ alert responsible authorities to criminal or antisocial issues raised by members of the public

◆ encourage residents to keep a lookout in their immediate area and report suspicious activity that may indicate criminal action or intent

◆ work together in conjunction with police, council and other community groups and organisations in the local residential and business sectors

◆ liaise with local police to enable the group to keep abreast of local safety and security issues

◆ report incidences of graffiti to the Council.

Involving and communicating with the community

◆ provide a forum for local interest groups and communities to raise issues of concern that affect safety and relate to crime in their areas and to provide support and assistance to them to address these issues

◆ welcome and encourage the participation of all residents of, and visitors to, our community

◆ encourage the community to be aware and involved in Neighbourhood Watch

◆ support regular communication to residents and businesses, for example through the production and distribution of Neighbourhood Watch newsletters

◆ distribute brochures via stalls at public events, shopping centres, railway stations etc

---

616 Greater Dandenong Neighbourhood Watch, response to the Drugs and Crime Prevention Committee, Inquiry into Locally Based Approaches to Community Safety and Crime Prevention, May 2011.

- carry out special letterbox drops if requested by relevant Police Unit for offences committed within their shire or local area

- provide information about crime and crime prevention via community radio, the local press, websites and emails.

- manage projects that educate and motivate members of the community to take action to prevent crime and encourage them to have a positive attitude towards the police.

Deterring criminal activity

- reduce criminals' desire to commit a crime by removing tools they need to do so, such as knives, weapons and potential weapons around the house

- provide residents with ways to prevent crime and feel safe in their homes, including safety tips and techniques

- improve safety and security within homes and the community.

Developing and implementing safety programs

- develop and implement broader community safety projects and initiatives

- promote and maintain a safe and strong connected community

- support the development of community registers to assist the elderly and vulnerable people in our community

- carry out a range of community safety programs including 'Safe Plate' days, 'Fifty in My Street' campaigns[617]

- conduct programs that implement preventative or deterrent measures to people who may commit a crime, including working bees to clean off graffiti, pick up litter and affix one-way screw to vehicle number plates, engrave bikes with licence numbers and engrave electrical goods with identification.

Sources for determining the needs and priorities with regard to crime prevention

A recurring theme in answers to this question was that up-to-date crime statistics are no longer supplied by Police,[618] or available elsewhere, resulting in a major drawback for providing current information about local crime and related issues to members and the general public, as these responses point out:

> This task was previously assisted with provision of crime statistics by the Police Victoria but the last 12–18 months has seen this information source severely eroded. Other sources such as My Place which also should contain this type of detail are badly out of date with data only available quarterly, and then usually a further month for the data to be compiled (therefore 4–7 months out of date).[619]

> ...Previously when street by street crime statistics were supplied by the police, individual NHW areas tailored their crime prevention messages in their newsletters to try to address incidents occurring in their immediate area.[620]

Without current police statistics, most groups appear to rely on feedback from members of the public, input from the Neighbourhood Watch Coordinator, local newspaper reports, public forums and individual members' observations. One group reported that crime trend

---

617 See discussion below for discussion of 'safe plate' days.

618 From 2009 Victoria Police only provided statistics at a local government area level.

619 Banyule (and Nillumbik) Neighbourhood Watch, response to the Drugs and Crime Prevention Committee's list of questions, Inquiry into Locally Based Approaches to Community Safety and Crime Prevention, May 2011.

620 Manningham Neighbourhood Watch, response to the Drugs and Crime Prevention Committee's list of questions, Inquiry into Locally Based Approaches to Community Safety and Crime Prevention, May 2011.

information about the nature and location of current issues is forwarded to them direct from the Police Tasking and Coordination meeting held fortnightly.[621]

The nature of locally initiated and conducted projects

While most of the projects have as their focus preventing theft and burglary, there was wide variation in the number of projects PSAs conduct. The membership size, age demographic of members, the group's relationship with local police, councils, schools, businesses and the community generally, how recently the PSA has been established, as well as the availability of funding, no doubt all play a large part in the productivity of each group. As one response stated:

> It should be noted at this point that there is only a handful of NHW volunteers who undertake any crime prevention activities. They are also generally 70 years plus in age and are obviously limited in the scope and time that they are able to devote to any projects.[622]

There was, however, only one Neighbourhood Watch group that said they had no projects currently being conducted.

Projects listed by many PSAs that responded are outlined below.

Safe-Plate days — which is done in association with Victoria Police, involves affixing one-way screws to vehicle number plates to reduce the likelihood of plates being stolen and possibly used on other vehicles to carry out criminal activities. Groups reported funding and/or hands-on support for this event have come from Victoria Police, local hardware stores, car dealers, the Lions Club, Mens' Shed volunteers, gold coin donations from recipients of this project, the RACV, local councils and Neighbourhood Watch members. One group stated that at each 'Safe Plate' day they 'usually fit 300 plus vehicles and give out 400 plus pamphlets',[623] while another group said it has two full-day 'Safe Plate' events planned for later this year.[624]

Bike marking — this consists of identification markings being engraved on bikes and scooters. Some groups do this in association with local police and Mildura Neighbourhood Watch reported that this event is run at local schools in partnership with the Mildura Rural City Council and Sunraysia Community Health and incorporates a bike safety presentation to students.[625]

Car Park Audits, Operation COSI, Look, Lock, Leave — these are three similar projects involving Victoria Police and Neighbourhood Watch members checking parked cars to make sure they are locked and no valuables are left in them. Car Park Audits and Look, Lock, Leave target specific car park and street locations that have been identified by police as being hot spots for theft from and of vehicles and check no valuables are on display. Neighbourhood Watch volunteers work under the guidance of Victoria Police, usually the crime prevention officer who checks registration details of 'offending' vehicles and forwards letters and security information to the owners. Operation COSI (community safety initiative), held at railway stations and selected shopping centres, involves handing out police-supplied pamphlets to train and car park users at peak periods and checking each car for visible

621   Greater Geelong and Surf Coast Neighbourhood Watch, response to the Drugs and Crime Prevention Committee's list of questions, Inquiry into Locally Based Approaches to Community Safety and Crime Prevention, May 2011.

622   Western Division 2 Neighbourhood Watch, response to the Drugs and Crime Prevention Committee's list of questions, Inquiry into Locally Based Approaches to Community Safety and Crime Prevention, May 2011.

623   Monash Neighbourhood Watch, response to the Drugs and Crime Prevention Committee's list of questions, Inquiry into Locally Based Approaches to Community Safety and Crime Prevention, May 2011.

624   Whitehorse Neighbourhood Watch, response to the Drugs and Crime Prevention Committee's list of questions, Inquiry into Locally Based Approaches to Community Safety and Crime Prevention, May 2011.

625   Mildura Neighbourhood Watch, response to the Drugs and Crime Prevention Committee's list of questions, Inquiry into Locally Based Approaches to Community Safety and Crime Prevention, May 2011.

valuables, unlocked doors and keys left in the ignition. A police letter is sent to owners of any vehicles considered at risk.

Graffiti clean-up, Litter collection — these involve Neighbourhood Watch working bees. Methods include painting over fences and walls that have graffiti on them, in some cases using paint supplied by local councils or removing paint with chemicals. In one Neighbourhood Watch area the city council supplies the chemicals for the graffiti removal project and provides training for members in their use. Glen Eira Neighbourhood Watch addressed this is by having relevant murals painted on large blank walls, such as the painting of Pharlap on a wall near the Caulfield racecourse.[626] Other methods included holding information sessions for residents to increase their awareness of such activities in their neighbourhood, working with younger people to encourage a positive attitude towards communal property, assisting police by reporting instances and removing graffiti by painting over it or removing it with chemicals.

Newsletter, brochure and flyer production and distribution, public meetings and letter drops are undertaken by most Neighbourhood Watch groups. Local carnivals, festivals and family days also provide opportunities for many PSA members to set up stalls to distribute leaflets and talk with the general public about their various crime prevention programs, give advice and recruit new members.

Other projects that PSAs reported conducting included:

Bin Sticker projects — 'Park Safe' bin stickers, in part funded by local council are applied to household waste bins in residential areas where there is a high rate of theft from motor vehicles. In Torquay, stickers with the Neighbourhood Watch logo and 'Report all crimes and suspicious activity — Call 000' are applied to household bins. The local Lions Club contributes to the cost of this project.[627]

So You Know posters — these posters inform people of the penalties for antisocial behaviour. They are produced by Geelong police, funded by the City of Greater Geelong and distributed by Neighbourhood Watch volunteers.[628]

Personal Safety and Awareness presentations — these are conducted by Neighbourhood Watch at local schools on demand and at local clubs and women's groups.

Community Safety Audit — volunteers walk through streets wearing Neighbourhood Watch identification and carrying mobile phones, cameras and clipboards with audit sheets to identify community safety issues, and possible crime trends. Police are advised of any rising trends and volunteers have contact with other stakeholders such as the council, EPA Victoria, real estate property managers, Vic Roads and local business owners.[629]

Generally funding and other forms of local support for projects comes from shire councils, Victoria Police, advertisers in Neighbourhood Watch newsletters, local businesses, service clubs, sports clubs, donations from the public and members' fund-raising activities such as sausage sizzles.

Priorities for projects may sometimes be decided on the basis of police information, sometimes by events in the local area and often by the resources available. As one respondent put it:

---

626 Glen Eira Neighbourhood Watch, response to the Drugs and Crime Prevention Committee's list of questions, Inquiry into Locally Based Approaches to Community Safety and Crime Prevention, May 2011.

627 Greater Geelong and Surf Coast Neighbourhood Watch, response to the Drugs and Crime Prevention Committee's list of questions, Inquiry into Locally Based Approaches to Community Safety and Crime Prevention, May 2011.

628 Greater Geelong and Surf Coast Neighbourhood Watch, response to the Drugs and Crime Prevention Committee's list of questions, Inquiry into Locally Based Approaches to Community Safety and Crime Prevention, May 2011.

629 Submission from Mr Gerard Traynor, Volunteer, Morwell Neighbourhood Watch / Safer Communities Group to the Drugs and Crime Prevention Committee, Inquiry into Locally Based Approaches to Community Safety and Crime Prevention, May 2011.

Projects are prioritised on the basis of the greatest expected benefit for the community relative to the volunteer and financial resources involved.[630]

It is interesting to note that when Neighbourhood Watch groups were asked whether there was a diversity of needs across the division the majority of PSAs regarded their community safety needs to be consistent across the division, although Monash Neighbourhood Watch pointed to the need to publish pamphlets in a range of languages.[631]

Ways of involving local community and private sector organisations in planning and delivering crime prevention programs

Respondents listed many of the projects above, such as 'Safe Plate' day, 'Bicycle marking' and regular Neighbourhood Watch newsletters, as also being ways of reaching out to or involving local community in delivery of crime prevention programs.

Other methods included extending invitations to representatives of various organisations to give presentations at Neighbourhood Watch sector and PSA meetings, inviting guest speakers to public information meetings on safety and security issues, consulting with businesses in relation to anti-theft programs, using Facebook for communicating information and ideas, visits to local schools, consulting with councils about community action and writing to or telephoning local businesses and organisations asking for their involvement.

One PSA group in an area that encompasses city and rural environments liaises with the local Country Fire Authority (CFA) about fire prevention strategies[632] and disseminates CFA information in its Neighbourhood Watch newsletters.[633]

The wide variation apparent in responses to the previous question is also evident in responses to this one, with some areas successfully engaging with a variety of sectors of the community, while planning and delivery of programs in other Neighbourhood Watch groups is almost entirely conducted by their volunteers and relevant Police members.

Measuring the success of projects

Formal evaluations

All the Neighbourhood Watch groups that responded to the Committee's list of questions stated that no formal evaluation of their programs had been undertaken.

The only references to formal performance measurement of any kind were to a state-level Neighbourhood Watch financed study by Caulfield Institute students some years ago; Victoria Police reviews of the value of the Neighbourhood Watch model; and a form local police had on which to tick a box if the police matter under consideration had been instigated by a Neighbourhood Watch source. This was found to be 'unsuccessful'.[634]

One respondent replied:

> No. As we do not have the manpower to do such an evaluation due to the changes from small groups to a PSA. We have lost all our volunteer base of people that did the delivery of newsletters etc.[635]

---

630 Manningham Neighbourhood Watch, response to the Drugs and Crime Prevention Committee's list of questions, Inquiry into Locally Based Approaches to Community Safety and Crime Prevention, May 2011.

631 Monash Neighbourhood Watch, response to the Drugs and Crime Prevention Committee's list of questions, Inquiry into Locally Based Approaches to Community Safety and Crime Prevention, May 2011

632 Such an approach is not uncommon in the United Kingdom and United States where Neighbourhood Watch is increasingly becoming involved (on a small scale) in areas such as emergency management, homeland security, disaster relief and pandemic management. See Chapter 9.

633 Greater Geelong and Surf Coast Neighbourhood Watch, response to the Drugs and Crime Prevention Committee's list of questions, Inquiry into Locally Based Approaches to Community Safety and Crime Prevention, May 2011.

634 Monash Neighbourhood Watch, response to the Drugs and Crime Prevention Committee's list of questions, Inquiry into Locally Based Approaches to Community Safety and Crime Prevention, May 2011.

635 Greater Frankston Neighbourhood Watch, response to the Drugs and Crime Prevention Committee's list of questions, Inquiry into Locally Based Approaches to Community Safety and Crime Prevention, May 2011.

There was also general agreement in responses to this topic that little formal statistical measurement of projects is available at the local area level. The lack of detailed street by street crime statistics that once were available has made measuring current offence rates in local areas difficult, if not impossible.[636]

However, police statistics for an entire shire or city council area on a specific crime can be matched with Neighbourhood Watch projects that have targeted that particular crime to get an overall picture of whether or not incidences of that crime have decreased. For example, one group stated that 'following a series of Look, Lock, Leave exercises over several months', crime trend reports on theft showed a significant decrease.[637]

Difficulties in measuring success statistically in local areas are explained by Manningham Neighbourhood Watch:

> Comparisons of statistics can now only be made at the municipal level which tends to hide the results of any specific action taken at the very local level. A further difficulty in making these comparisons is determining not only the respective influence of NHW and the police, but also the effects of changes to legislation that may have occurred during the period when the project was implemented.[638]

Informal evaluation

Other less formal ways of evaluation and measurement have been used, including:

- noticing changed behaviour patterns, such as less graffiti and litter and fewer hoons' vehicles

- by the public interest shown through the number of people attending public meetings (an attendance of 50–60 people is considered a success by one Neighbourhood Watch group)[639] or helping with a project

- in the case of 'Safe 'Plate' projects, by the number of vehicles serviced, which it is hoped correlates with a reduction in number plate thefts and 'drive-offs' from fuel outlets

- feedback to members from residents, businesses and partnership agencies

- comments from the general public expressed at public events

- reporting various illegal activities to police that has assisted in reducing hoon driving, graffiti and riding of unregistered motorbikes.[640]

One Neighbourhood Watch area measured the success of its graffiti removal/recording project by the consequences that followed:

> Latrobe City thinks so highly of the program that it invited the Volunteer Coordinator to present at an annual Community Safety Forum on the project. This project has also led to Victoria Police members becoming aware of the resource and using it recently to gather information which led to a youth being charged with over sixty offences of criminal damage.[641]

In general, however, Neighbourhood Watch groups were somewhat ambivalent about how successful their programs have been. The following comments indicate this:

---

636 From 2009 Victoria Police only provided statistics at a local government area.

637 Whitehorse Neighbourhood Watch, response to the Drugs and Crime Prevention Committee's list of questions, Inquiry into Locally Based Approaches to Community Safety and Crime Prevention, May 2011.

638 Manningham Neighbourhood Watch, response to the Drugs and Crime Prevention Committee's list of questions, Inquiry into Locally Based Approaches to Community Safety and Crime Prevention, May 2011.

639 Whitehorse Neighbourhood Watch, response to the Drugs and Crime Prevention Committee's list of questions, Inquiry into Locally Based Approaches to Community Safety and Crime Prevention, May 2011.

640 Submission from Mr Gerard Traynor, Volunteer, Morwell Neighbourhood Watch / Safer Communities Group to the Drugs and Crime Prevention Committee, Inquiry into Locally Based Approaches to Community Safety and Crime Prevention, May 2011.

641 Morwell Neighbourhood Watch, response to the Drugs and Crime Prevention Committee's list of questions, Inquiry into Locally Based Approaches to Community Safety and Crime Prevention, May 2011.

'Success usually follows all our projects'.[642]

'...volunteers are confident that their efforts do make a difference — but it is difficult to assess this against any benchmark standard'.[643]

'It is very hard to have a successful event without the support of the community. Just now that is the biggest worry facing all NHW groups, the lost interest in NHW'.[644]

Recent concerns, challenges and impediments

State level

Weaknesses and impediments

Respondents to the 2007 Review of Neighbourhood Watch (de Ridder & Johns) listed the following as weaknesses in or impediments to Neighbourhood Watch that were contributing to the movement becoming less relevant:

- a lack of accountability at all levels within Neighbourhood Watch

- Victoria Police moving away from its commitment to Neighbourhood Watch

- being only about older members of the community, many of whom are resistant to change

- police coordinators being stuck in the past, lacking in fresh ideas and not connected to mainstream policing

- a lack of commitment, coordination and consistent policy direction from Victoria Police and the Neighbourhood Watch Board in relation to Neighbourhood Watch.

Despite the 2007 Review making many recommendations for renewal, it would appear that few if any have been implemented and little has changed with regard to these issues, leading to the relevance of Neighbourhood Watch increasingly being questioned.

In its submission to the current Inquiry, the Neighbourhood Watch Board stated:

> The structure of NHW and many of the people involved in NHW have been holding back the movement. There are many well-meaning but very set in their ways people involved in NHW who are a disincentive to newcomers...

> Each area and division has clung on to the structure of the movement based on the early 1980s model. This has been negative and makes the movement seem out of touch and of limited value.

> The structure of NHW internally has also been problematic. The NHW Board of Management (BOM) operates in isolation and without any real capacity to influence what occurs at ground level. Some local areas are openly defiant of attempts to direct or influence.[645]

More recently (July 2011), funding has been made available by the Victorian state government for Neighbourhood Watch Victoria Board of Management to employ a state manager for four years to oversee the volunteer side of the program. The state manager will be responsible for building and maintaining partnerships with state and local government, and this appointment is being described as a first step in strengthening the Neighbourhood Watch program.[646]

---

642 Glen Eira Neighbourhood Watch, response to the Drugs and Crime Prevention Committee's list of questions, Inquiry into Locally Based Approaches to Community Safety and Crime Prevention, May 2011.

643 Maroondah Neighbourhood Watch, response to the Drugs and Crime Prevention Committee's list of questions, Inquiry into Locally Based Approaches to Community Safety and Crime Prevention, May 2011.

644 Greater Frankston Neighbourhood Watch, response to the Drugs and Crime Prevention Committee's list of questions, Inquiry into Locally Based Approaches to Community Safety and Crime Prevention, May 2011.

645 Submission from Mr Andrew Brideson, President, Board of Management, Neighbourhood Watch Victoria Inc., to the Drugs and Crime Prevention Committee, Inquiry into Locally Based Approaches to Community Safety and Crime Prevention, May 2011.

646 Mr Andrew McIntosh, Minister for Crime Prevention, Media Release, 8 July 2011, State Government of Victoria.

Challenges

The reduction in active Neighbourhood Watch areas in Victoria in recent years has been significant — from approximately 1300 areas in the past to approximately 300 currently.[647]

In his 2010/11 Annual Report, the President of Neighbourhood Watch Victoria described Neighbourhood Watch as 'being at the crossroads'.[648] For it to survive into the next decade he suggested that meeting the following requirements was essential:

◆ securing ongoing sponsorship and funding — if ongoing private sector sponsorship cannot be secured, funds for staff and marketing campaigns need to come from government

◆ adopting the latest technology to improve the speed and scope of communication — all communications between volunteers, Victoria Police and the community need to be via the internet or i-phones within the next couple of years, and the Neighbourhood Watch website must be redeveloped

◆ Victoria Police reconnecting with the community by employing at least one community police officer for each local government area. Victoria Police began Neighbourhood Watch to get support in dealing with crime in the community, and is regarded as the key agency. However, the balance has changed and instead of Neighbourhood Watch being the support for police, it has come to be supported by the police

◆ members being prepared to think about contributing to community safety rather than just safety in their backyards — this to be done through wider community engagement, building a sense of community

◆ forming local government community safety committees with Neighbourhood Watch taking the lead role — building on the strengths of local government and using it as a vehicle to keep the crime prevention program alive.[649]

The submission from the Neighbourhood Watch Board emphasised the need for engagement with local and state agencies. It considered that:

> NHW is totally ineffective in engaging with local and state agencies, other than the police, at local levels. NHW stands alone. Limited support is given by a few Members of Parliament and local government offices who photocopy local newsletters. With regard to policy discussion and development, nothing occurs.[650]

As a 2009 Neighbourhood Watch discussion paper stated after changes to Victoria Police divisional and regional boundaries and the subsequent need for changes to Neighbourhood Watch areas and police involvement, 'The challenge is to achieve change in a movement that has changed little in 25 years'.[651]

The need for change was echoed by most witnesses at the Inquiry's public hearings and in submissions to the Committee. For example, the Secretary of the Neighbourhood Watch Victoria Board, in regard to modernising methods of communication and conveying

---

647 Neighbourhood Watch Strategic Plan 2011–2016, p.5.

648 Neighbourhood Watch President's 2010/11 Annual Report, included in the Submission from Mr Andrew Brideson, President, Board of Management, Neighbourhood Watch Victoria Inc., to the Drugs and Crime Prevention Committee, Inquiry into Locally Based Approaches to Community Safety and Crime Prevention, May 2011.

649 Neighbourhood Watch President's 2010/11 Annual Report and the Submission from Mr Andrew Brideson, President, Board of Management, Neighbourhood Watch Victoria Inc., to the Drugs and Crime Prevention Committee, Inquiry into Locally Based Approaches to Community Safety and Crime Prevention, May 2011.

650 Submission from Mr Andrew Brideson, President, Board of Management, Neighbourhood Watch Victoria Inc., to the Drugs and Crime Prevention Committee, Inquiry into Locally Based Approaches to Community Safety and Crime Prevention, May 2011.

651 Neighbourhood Watch Victoria Board of Management 2009, 'Re-alignment of police regional boundaries: Opportunities and challenges for a new PSA-based model of Neighbourhood Watch', Discussion paper, included in the submission from Mr Andrew Brideson, President, Board of Management, Neighbourhood Watch Victoria Inc., to the Drugs and Crime Prevention Committee, Inquiry into Locally Based Approaches to Community Safety and Crime Prevention, May 2011.

information, told the Inquiry: 'We need to change the whole modus operandi to 21st century communications. That is what we are looking for in terms of development of the organisation'.[652] According to Deputy Commissioner Tony Cartwright, Victoria Police, efforts to develop the organisation have not however resulted in the changes needed:

> It is no secret that we have worked with Neighbourhood Warch in recent years to try many different avenues to reinvigorate it, and I would be prepared to say that they have not been largely successful.[653]

Local level

Almost all submissions, responses to the Committee's survey and witnesses at the Inquiry's public hearings expressed concern about the ability of Neighbourhood Watch areas to operate effectively, or at all, in the long term if significant change was not implemented.[654] One submission gave the example of 39 Neighbourhood Watch areas in the division five years ago now being reduced to 18,[655] while another stated that of the 35 areas that existed previously only 11 are currently active.[656] Similarly, many of the 2010 Annual Reports from PSAs showed considerably more members leaving groups than the number of new members being recruited.[657]

Specific concerns expressed included: a dwindling number of volunteers to carry out programs, little general public interest, a lack of funding for modern technology, a lack of leadership within Neighbourhood Watch and confusion about the relationship between the organisation and Victoria Police. As one respondent noted with regard to this relationship:

> Who is the leader?

> If you ask some Victoria Police members they say it is the community's program and therefore they must lead it. If you ask the volunteers they say it is the police that lead it. And herein lays the problem. Each partner is saying it is the other's program.[658]

Challenges faced in operating Neighbourhood Watch programs in the local area

The factors listed as challenges to operating programs were consistent across most of the responses this issue elicited. They included the following.

Maintaining volunteer levels and attracting people prepared to take leadership/office bearer roles — Volunteer numbers are declining due to old age, relocation, feeling disenfranchised

652 Mr Brian Samuel, Secretary, Board of Management, Neighbourhood Watch Victoria Inc., Evidence given to the Drugs and Crime Prevention Committee, Inquiry into Locally Based Approaches to Community Safety and Crime Prevention, Public Hearing, Melbourne, 27 June 2011.

653 Deputy Commissioner Tim Cartwright, Victoria Police, Evidence given to the Drugs and Crime Prevention Committee, Inquiry into Locally Based Approaches to Community Safety and Crime Prevention, Public Hearing, Melbourne 16 April 2012.

654 As Bernie Durkin of the Western Australian Office of Crime Prevention stated in the Western Australian context: 'The Neighbourhood Watch *model* is outdated but not the *concept* of Neighbourhood Watch' (Mr Bernie Durkin, Executive Manager, Strategic Projects, Western Australia Office of Crime Prevention, Evidence given to the Drugs and Crime Prevention Committee, Inquiry into Locally Based Approaches to Community Safety and Crime Prevention, Meeting, Perth, 21 June 2011).

655 Submission from Ms Rhonda Rotherham, Division Coordinator, Neighbourhood Watch Greater Geelong and Surf Coast Committee to the Drugs and Crime Prevention Committee, Inquiry into Locally Based Approaches to Community Safety and Crime Prevention, May 2011.

656 City of Bayside Neighbourhood Watch Annual Report 2010/11, included in the submission from the Mr Andrew Brideson, President, Board of Management, Neighbourhood Watch Victoria Inc., to the Drugs and Crime Prevention Committee, Inquiry into Locally Based Approaches to Community Safety and Crime Prevention, May 2011.

657 For example, in 2010 Mildura PSA gained 7 new members and lost 30; the City of Kingston in 2010 did not gain any new members but lost 160; Swan Hill PSA in 2010 gained 6 new members and lost 30; and in 2010 Manningham gained 41 and lost 101 members. However, there was at least one PSA that reversed this trend — Benalla PSA gained 29 members in 2010 and lost 14.

658 Morwell Neighbourhood Watch, response to the Drugs and Crime Prevention Committe's list of questions, Inquiry into Locally Based Approaches to Community Safety and Crime Prevention, May 2011.

by the withdrawal of crime statistics and police attendance at meetings[659] or, according to one respondent, 'general frustration with the lack of government support, particularly over the past 2 years'.[660] In addition, it is increasingly difficult to recruit new members, particularly younger people, people from a culturally diverse background and those willing to take office bearer positions. This difficulty is attributed to a lack of public interest in Neighbourhood Watch, a perception that Neighbourhood Watch groups consist of 'older residents who only hold boring meetings'[661] and society becoming 'time poor'.[662] It has also been suggested that the 'antiquated methods of typing or writing out newsletters, meeting notes and election results which are then delivered by hand is seen as time consuming by young people'.[663]

Conversely, however, some people with whom the Committee met have concerns that if Neighbourhood Watch disbanded or changed to a more technological based operation there would be negative repercussions for the many volunteers who are currently involved in its activities. For example, Ms Lisa Armstrong-Rowe, Community Development Officer with the City of Geelong stated that whilst putting Neighbourhood Watch 'on the net' is a 'fantastic opportunity':

> One of the concerns we have had in the past is if Neighbourhood Watch does not continue there is a lot of volunteer hours gone from the community. We recently had Neighbourhood Watch here distributing the 50 in 'My Street' bin stickers, a great job for Neighbourhood Watch to go and do on rubbish night, on Thursday night, go out and put a sticker on every bin in 20 or 30 streets.

> The same with the 'Remove It, Lock it, or Lose It' stickers, encouraging people not to leave valuables. Police have a high number of thefts from motor cars, so getting stickers on rubbish bins out in the streets saying, 'Keep your valuables out of your car'. That is really good stuff that Neighbourhood Watch can do but how does the model look going forward if [it is not volunteer based].[664]

Obtaining continuing police support — There is uncertainty surrounding the police coordinator role; when there is no sworn police coordinator, either through leave, or vacant positions, the programs can lack the professional support, assistance and knowledge necessary for local groups to be effective.[665] Police commitment to Neighbourhood Watch generally is also often questioned — one annual report highlighted the difficulty members have retaining confidence in their PSA's future when police attendance at and frequency of meetings has gone from 25 meetings a month with police attending each one, to six larger meetings a month and no regular police attendance.[666] The lack of local street-by-street crime statistics which had been supplied by police, and the need to have these reinstated in order to plan relevant programs of crime prevention, has been raised by many respondents.[667]

---

659 Whitehorse Neighbourhood Watch Annual Report 2010/2011, , included in the submission from Mr Andrew Brideson, President, Board of Management, Neighbourhood Watch Victoria Inc., to the Drugs and Crime Prevention Committee, Inquiry into Locally Based Approaches to Community Safety and Crime Prevention, May 2011.

660 Banyule (and Nillumbik) Neighbourhood Watch, response to the Drugs and Crime Prevention Committee's list of questions, Inquiry into Locally Based Approaches to Community Safety and Crime Prevention, May 2011.

661 Safer Communities Group — Cardinia Shire, response to the Drugs and Crime Prevention Committee's list of questions, Inquiry into Locally Based Approaches to Community Safety and Crime Prevention, May 2011.

662 Whitehorse Neighbourhood Watch, response to the Drugs and Crime Prevention Committee's list of questions, Inquiry into Locally Based Approaches to Community Safety and Crime Prevention, May 2011.

663 Submission from Victoria Police to the Drugs and Crime Prevention Committee, Inquiry into Locally Based Approaches to Community Safety and Crime Prevention, April 2012.

664 Ms Lisa Armstrong-Rowe, Community Development Officer, City of Greater Geelong, Evidence given to the Drugs and Crime Prevention Committee, Inquiry into Locally Based Approaches to Community Safety and Crime Prevention, Public Hearing, Geelong, 8 August 2011.

665 Safer Communities Group — Cardinia Shire, response to the Drugs and Crime Prevention Committee's list of questions, Inquiry into Locally Based Approaches to Community Safety and Crime Prevention, May 2011.

666 Manningham Neighbourhood Watch Annual Report, 2010/2011, included in the submission from Mr Andrew Brideson, President, Board of Management, Neighbourhood Watch Victoria Inc., to the Drugs and Crime Prevention Committee, Inquiry into Locally Based Approaches to Community Safety and Crime Prevention, May 2011.

667 For example, Greater Geelong and Surf Coast Neighbourhood Watch and Monash Neighbourhood Watch, in their response to the Drugs and Crime Prevention Committee's list of questions, Inquiry into Locally Based Approaches to Community Safety and Crime Prevention, May 2011, and Western Region Division 5 in its 2010 Annual Report.

In their submission Victoria Police informed the Committee that:

> A review has been undertaken in some areas. It has been decided that in some areas, the role of Neighbourhood Police Coordinator could be shared with other tasks or functions. The Police coordinator for example might also take on the role of Crime Prevention. In some areas, these members have changed their title to 'Community Engagement' Officers rather than specific roles. This has been well received by members of the public and they are very supportive of these new roles. These officers will still perform the role of Neighbourhood Watch coordinator and crime prevention functions with a significant focus on engaging the community.[668]

Obtaining sufficient funding, sponsorship, resources — many respondents listed a lack of appropriate resources to receive and communicate current information and run programs as a challenge to address, with some specifying the need for a current or major sponsor as a key issue needing to be resolved.[669]

Despite having the means to address the problems of hoon drivers and graffiti, to some extent at least, one PSA expressed concern about the time taken for the equipment to be operative.

> Priority for the last two years has been to access a mobile camera to assist in identification of perpetrators of graffiti and hoon drivers. Cameras are now available but the setting up of their use is incredibly slow. There is little value in setting up graffiti databases without proof regarding the person who created the material. Similarly hoons are best identified by pictorial evidence rather than unsupported recording of licence plate number.[670]

Getting the involvement and support of local councils — while having a supportive local council is regarded as greatly improving the effectiveness of and resources for community safety and crime prevention activities, in some Neighbourhood Watch areas forging relationships with council has proved difficult. One submission to the Committee stated that a Neighbourhood Watch offer to the council to operate in an area where residents were concerned about burglaries and antisocial behaviour elicited no response from the council.[671] Mr Rob Spence, the Chief Executive Officer of the Municipal Association of Victoria, acknowledged that the relationship between Neighbourhood Watch and local councils had deteriorated significantly in the past 15 years:

> We are headed up two different paths [when it comes to crime prevention]. The councils have got a community development mindset and the Neighbourhood Watch is very much about crime statistics and protecting yourself. One side is an optimistic view and the other is a bit of a pessimistic view about the way forward.

> This separation has occurred over time. If we check around the councils, they will have relationships with Neighbourhood Watch but they will not be strong...Our discussions with Neighbourhood Watch have indicated that [while] there has been an effort to try and re-establish relationships with councils it is a question of attitude. As I said one is optimistic and the other is a bit pessimistic and getting into a common alignment of what we want to achieve would be a good thing.[672]

668 Submission from Victoria Police to the Drugs and Crime Prevention Committee, Inquiry into Locally Based Approaches to Community Safety and Crime Prevention, April 2012.

669 For example, Maroondah Neighbourhood Watch, response to the Drugs and Crime Prevention Committee's list of questions, Inquiry into Locally Based Approaches to Community Safety and Crime Prevention, May 2011; Neighbourhood Watch Western Region Division 5 Annual Report 2010/11, included in the submission from Mr Andrew Brideson, President, Board of Management, Neighbourhood Watch Victoria Inc., to the Drugs and Crime Prevention Committee, Inquiry into Locally Based Approaches to Community Safety and Crime Prevention, May 2011.

670 Banyule (and Nillumbik) Neighbourhood Watch, response to the Drugs and Crime Prevention Committee's list of questions, Inquiry into Locally Based Approaches to Community Safety and Crime Prevention, May 2011.

671 Submission from Ms Rhonda Rotherham, Division Coordinator, Neighbourhood Watch Greater Geelong and Surf Coast Committee to the Drugs and Crime Prevention Committee, Inquiry into Locally Based Approaches to Community Safety and Crime Prevention, May 2011.

672 Mr Rob Spence, Chief Executive Officer, Municipal Association of Victoria, correspondence to the Drugs and Crime Prevention Committee, Inquiry into Locally Based Approaches to Community Safety and Crime Prevention, Public Hearing, Melbourne, 21 May 2012.

A challenge faced by some rural Neighbourhood Watch areas is the greater travel distances required as a result of the recent PSA changes that were described by one group as very 'citycentric'.[673] This has a negative effect on volunteer numbers as well as resources.

In response to the Committee's survey question about challenges faced in operating programs, only one Neighbourhood Watch area listed 'the rising crime rate' as an issue.[674]

A further issue that has been raised in the research literature on community crime prevention, and which would appear to be a substantial challenge for Neighbourhood Watch at a state and a local level, is how to generate community responses to crime in areas where there is most need:

> …community responses to crime are easiest to generate in exactly those areas where they are least needed, and they are hardest to establish where the need is greatest. The poor and the rich are socially divided by 'security differentials' that increasingly become significant characteristics of wealth, power and status. Community safety activity is easier to sustain in homogeneous, middle-class suburbs than heterogeneous, working-class neighbourhoods (Sutton, Cherney & White 2008, p.117).

Similarly, another researcher found that 'the areas with highest crime rates are the most reluctant to organize' (Hope 1995, cited in Sherman 1997, ch.8).[675]

Challenges faced in operating state-wide projects

Most Neighbourhood Watch areas reported that many of the challenges for operating state-wide projects were the same as those faced in running local programs, particularly the challenges presented by low numbers of volunteers and a lack of resources. Another factor given was the lack of effective coordination of programs. It was suggested that this was due in part to inadequate communications systems, such as an unsatisfactory Neighbourhood Watch website[676], and to significant variations in the level of coverage across the state and in PSA areas.[677]

Degree of support provided by local and state authorities

There was a very mixed response to the question of how much support local and state authorities gave Neighbourhood Watch groups. While the majority of groups who addressed this issue reported getting good support from local council, there did not appear to be much support from state government. Some areas reported good assistance from police but not from council, while others reported more support from local council than from state agencies.

Comments ranged from: 'Local authorities (council, police) are 100% behind Neighbourhood Watch'[678] and 'Good support from the City of Monash'[679] to 'Contact maintained with Neighbourhood Watch coordinator for our area…[n]o other contact

673 Mitchell/Strathbogie Neighbourhood Watch Annual Report 2010/11, included in the submission from Mr Andrew Brideson, President, Board of Management, Neighbourhood Watch Victoria Inc., to the Drugs and Crime Prevention Committee, Inquiry into Locally Based Approaches to Community Safety and Crime Prevention, May 2011.

674 Mildura Neighbourhood Watch, response to the Drugs and Crime Prevention Committee's list of questions, Inquiry into Locally Based Approaches to Community Safety and Crime Prevention, May 2011.

675 This is certainly true of the United Kingdom model. Neighbourhood Watch conversely seems to be most popular and has higher membership in areas with the lowest crime rates. See discussion in Chapter 9.

676 The committee notes that this website has recently been redeveloped.

677 Banyule (and Nillumbik) Neighbourhood Watch, response to the Drugs and Crime Prevention Committee's list of questions, Inquiry into Locally Based Approaches to Community Safety and Crime Prevention, May 2011.

678 Greater Dandenong Neighbourhood Watch, response to the Drugs and Crime Prevention Committee's list of questions, Inquiry into Locally Based Approaches to Community Safety and Crime Prevention, May 2011.

679 Monash Neighbourhood Watch, response to the Drugs and Crime Prevention Committee's list of questions, Inquiry into Locally Based Approaches to Community Safety and Crime Prevention, May 2011.

or support provided by local or state authorities'[680] and 'Nothing specific however local councils are supportive when events are held'.[681]

Weaknesses in the current Neighbourhood Watch model

Two areas were most frequently cited by respondents as being weaknesses in the current Neighbourhood Watch model. The first was a lack of direction from the Board of Management, which was described by one group as giving no support to local PSAs,[682] and more specifically as showing:

> … an almost complete lack of guidance or direction on how the newly created Neighbourhood Watch PSA Committee and the Neighbourhood Watch Area Committees are to operate, what are their respective responsibilities, and how they relate to each other…[683]

Insufficient input from police and uncertainty about continued commitment from police to Neighbourhood Watch programs was the second weakness cited. Such commitment was seen by all as essential: 'The need for close liaison and support from the police means that NHW stands or falls on the attitude of the police'.[684] While a few areas reported receiving strong support from police,[685] others expressed feelings that police did not value their contributions[686] and attributed the existence of 'instability issues' to the uncertainty about the commitment of Victoria Police.[687]

These areas of weakness were also identified as such in the 2007 Review of Neighbourhood Watch final report (de Ridder & Johns).

The organisation's lack of self-promotion and reduced public profile was also considered a weakness in the current model. One respondent stated that:

> Until NHW is advertised nationally on major television, radio and newspaper mediums it will continue to decline through the lack of recognition from the general public. NHW needs to be in the public eye as often and as widespread as Crimestoppers now is.[688]

Improvements, reforms and alternative models

State level suggestions for reforms and improvements

The submission from the Neighbourhood Watch Board of Management suggested that a whole-of-government approach to community safety, implementing local government safety committees and continuing to develop and renew the PSA and town based Neighbourhood Watch models would ensure improvement in delivery of community safety programs.[689]

680   Whittlesea Neighbourhood Watch, response to the Drugs and Crime Prevention Committee's list of questions, Inquiry into Locally Based Approaches to Community Safety and Crime Prevention, May 2011.

681   Western Division 2 Neighbourhood Watch, response to the Drugs and Crime Prevention Committee's list of questions, Inquiry into Locally Based Approaches to Community Safety and Crime Prevention, May 2011.

682   Greater Frankston Neighbourhood Watch, response to the Drugs and Crime Prevention Committee's list of questions, Inquiry into Locally Based Approaches to Community Safety and Crime Prevention, May 2011.

683   Maroondah Neighbourhood Watch, response to the Drugs and Crime Prevention Committee's list of questions, Inquiry into Locally Based Approaches to Community Safety and Crime Prevention, May 2011.

684   Manningham Neighbourhood Watch, response to the Drugs and Crime Prevention Committee's list of questions, Inquiry into Locally Based Approaches to Community Safety and Crime Prevention, May 2011.

685   For example, Manningham Neighbourhood Watch, response to the Drugs and Crime Prevention Committee's list of questions, Inquiry into Locally Based Approaches to Community Safety and Crime Prevention, May 2011.

686   Greater Geelong and Surf Coast Neighbourhood Watch, response to the Drugs and Crime Prevention Committee's list of questions, Inquiry into Locally Based Approaches to Community Safety and Crime Prevention, May 2011.

687   Mildura Neighbourhood Watch, response to the Drugs and Crime Prevention Committee's list of questions, Inquiry into Locally Based Approaches to Community Safety and Crime Prevention, May 2011.

688   Western Division 2 Neighbourhood Watch, response to the Drugs and Crime Prevention list of questions, Inquiry into Locally Based Approaches to Community Safety and Crime Prevention, May 2011.

689   Submission from Mr Andrew Brideson, President, Board of Management, Neighbourhood Watch Victoria Inc., to the Drugs and Crime Prevention Committee, Inquiry into Locally Based Approaches to Community Safety and Crime Prevention, May 2011.

The submission listed the following as necessary for renewal:

◆ appointment of full-time staff

◆ appointment of an editor for *Sentinel*, newsletters, promotional materials and media releases

◆ a redeveloped website and appointment of an information technology employee to improve communications

◆ funds for staff and for marketing campaigns.[690]

At a public hearing the Neighbourhood Watch President spoke further on community safety crime prevention committees built on the Western Australian model:

> Simply you have a community safety crime prevention committee with a local government representative. You have a police representative, who presumably would be the alter ego of the Neighbourhood Watch coordinator. You have school groups, aged groups, ethnic groups and you have any other community groups involved in that crime prevention community safety committee. They can then go away and do all the research and set up a program of how we can improve safety in the community. It just does not have to be about crimes... *It is really community safety in the broadest possible terms.*[691]

These comments relate to the experience of Western Australia which has recognised the 'hard reality' that if Neighbourhood Watch does not change it will 'not go beyond two years the way it is going'. As such the Western Australian division of the organisation has developed a new strategic plan with greater emphasis on the use of partnerships with other community and government organisations, including at a time of changing demography in the west more outreach to multicultural communities. It has also acknowledged the need to embrace modern technology and place greater emphasis on addressing antisocial behaviour rather than restricting its remit to the burglaries that it was originally established to report on.

Local level suggestions for reforms and improvements

Neighbourhood Watch groups responded to the question about ways of improving outcomes with a wide range of suggestions. These included:

◆ establish closer ties with other areas of community policing

◆ develop programs with relevant state and local government authorities

◆ run advertising campaigns on buses, trams and at railway stations

◆ run education programs in schools

◆ obtain TV sponsorship, for example a regular spot on a daily program

◆ Police Minister and all parliamentarians to wear Neighbourhood Watch badges in public

◆ attract substantial funding to purchase better resources and run better programs

◆ get government interpreting assistance to produce pamphlets in languages other than English

---

690 Submission from Mr Andrew Brideson, President, Board of Management, Neighbourhood Watch Victoria Inc., to the Drugs and Crime Prevention Committee, Inquiry into Locally Based Approaches to Community Safety and Crime Prevention, May 2011.

691 Mr Andrew Brideson, President, Board of Management, Neighbourhood Watch Victoria Inc., Evidence given to the Drugs and Crime Prevention Committee, Inquiry into Locally Based Approaches to Community Safety and Crime Prevention, Public Hearing, Melbourne, 27 June 2011. Committee emphasis.

- ◆ develop electronic communication to communicate with residents and distribute newsletters

- ◆ become involved with other projects that support local communities such as the Red Cross[692]

- ◆ expand the interaction from local streets to whole of town, as well as to nearby towns to prevent moving law enforcement issues from one town to the next.[693]

Research suggestions for reforms

Studies and research into the existing Neighbourhood Watch Victoria model, though few in number, suggest that most assessments have found its objectives still reflect the dynamics of policing and community involvement in crime prevention that were evident when the scheme was introduced in the early 1980s (see for example de Ridder & Johns 2007). This is quite different from the experience of the United Kingdom and to a lesser extent the United States. In both jurisdictions the movement seems to have 'moved on'.[694]

Reassurance policing

A shift advocated by some researchers is to move the emphasis away from statistical situational crime prevention and onto 'community reassurance' through promoting neighbourliness and social cohesion and enhancing partnerships between police, other agencies and the community (Fleming 2005).

> …research suggests that significant progress can be made in reducing crime while reassuring the public, building community capacity, improving the quantity and quality of police-citizen contact and enhancing police legitimacy. As a secondary consideration the project may even minimise the incidence of preventable crime (Fleming 2005, p.5).

This change in focus is evident in the United Kingdom's recent police force reforms. The *Police Reform Act 2002* (UK) incorporates the idea that communities need reassurance from the police. 'Reassurance' includes raising confidence in and satisfaction with the police and increasing feelings of safety in the community, including reducing the fear of crime (Fleming 2005).[695]

Alternative initiatives

Eyes on the Street program — Western Australia

The Eyes on the Street (EOTS) program is a crime prevention initiative of the Office of Crime Prevention in Western Australia. Originally part of the Burglar Beware program, it is now a crime prevention program in its own right aimed at increasing intelligence gathering from a range of public workers. The EOTS objectives are to:

- Establish partnerships between state and local government, businesses and WA Police to reduce crime and criminal activity;

- Provide local workers with an opportunity to participate in intelligence gathering and reporting to assist police;

- Increase police intelligence;

---

692 Responses from seven Neighbourhood Watch PSAs to the Drugs and Crime Prevention list of questions, Inquiry into Locally Based Approaches to Community Safety and Crime Prevention, May 2011.

693 Submission from Mr Gerard Traynor, Volunteer, Morwell Neighbourhood Watch / Safer Communities Group to the Drugs and Crime Prevention Committee, Inquiry into Locally Based Approaches to Community Safety and Crime Prevention, May 2011.

694 See discussion in Chapter 9.

695 A discussion of community policing models in the United Kingdom in addition to an examination of that country's experience of Neighbourhood Watch is given in Chapter 9 of this Report.

- Deter crime and criminal activity;
- Increase public confidence through high visibility campaigning (Crime Research Centre 2008, p.7).

To achieve its objectives EOTS employs three main strategies:

- Training targeted community employees in the recording and reporting of intelligence;
- Increasing criminals perception of being seen; and
- A marketing and advertising campaign to raise community awareness of the initiative and increase perceptions of safety (Crime Research Centre 2008, p.7).

While EOTS and Neighbourhood Watch both focus on expanding surveillance as a means of crime prevention, an evaluation of EOTS suggested the following reason why that program is likely to be more successful than Neighbourhood Watch:

> ...By attempting to mobilise existing natural surveillance the NW approach failed to appreciate that those motivated to get involved were most likely to already be in low crime neighbourhoods. Where the substantial burglary problem exists is in poorer areas where community integration is less and where burglary is but one indicator of community distress... EOTS potentially may be useful where NW failed as it depends less on residential involvement and more on the involvement of paid government workers (Crime Research Centre 2008, p.16).

The majority of findings from the Crime Research Centre's evaluation of EOTS were promising, with all stakeholder groups responding positively and widespread approval of the program being expanded state-wide. Limitations of current police information technology systems for tracking and providing data, insufficient information on reports submitted and the high amount of contact with partner organisations required to generate significant volume of reporting were areas that were less positive.

Eyewatch — New South Wales

In New South Wales, Neighbourhood Watch until relatively recently has followed a similar trajectory to the organisation in Victoria. It has had its times of great popularity and other times where it has appeared less relevant. The value of traditional or more conventional forms of Neighbourhood Watch, according to Mr Brendan Thomas of the NSW Department of Justice is that they can act as a useful conduit for information relay:

> I think Neighbourhood Watch, community people actively involved in crime prevention, can be a good conduit for us to get the proper information to them about what the crime rates are and what the risks are in your local area.[696]

However, Professor Don Weatherburn of the Bureau of Crime Statistics and Research (BOCSAR) believes that Neighbourhood Watch, at least with regard to its role in disseminating crime data and information, is if not redundant at least less valuable than it might once have been. This is particularly the case in a state like New South Wales which has a sophisticated agency to distribute up-to-date crime statistics and data to whomever requests them:

> When Neighbourhood Watch started many citizens were probably drawn to it because they did, for the first time, get direct information about crime in their neighbourhood and that was extremely interesting. These days — certainly in New South Wales — that would be passé. Anybody can have that information. You can see it on the web. The effectiveness of Neighbourhood Watch does depend a bit on the demography and lifestyle of the residents. [For example]...in western Sydney, most neighbourhoods are pretty much empty during the day which is when the burglars strike. There is no-one to watch. It is not as if you have retired people there who can keep a

---

696 Mr Brendan Thomas, Assistant Director-General, Crime Prevention and Community Programs, NSW Department of Attorney General and Justice, Evidence given to the Drugs and Crime Prevention Committee, Inquiry into Locally Based Approaches to Community Safety and Crime Prevention, Public Hearing, Sydney, 19 September 2011.

lookout for your property. In a street like mine, say, in the eastern suburbs, you have four retired people in one street and it might be more effective in that context. My instinct would be to treat Neighbourhood Watch as a possible option and apply it where it seems sensible to do so, rather than a one size fits all approach to crime prevention.[697]

Superintendent Begg believes the overall success of Neighbourhood Watch in New South Wales has been variable:

Neighbourhood Watch has been around a long time and we have tried to revitalise that, not always with success, but it does work in some areas. It has got to the stage where, yes, it is not a strategy that will be successful in maybe my local area commands but it is a strategy that is successful in some of them. Where it is successful, where there are communities that want that, put out a lot of newsletters, police go to those Neighbourhood Watch meetings and interact with the community, we get information, there is a good relationship there and we will continue on with it. It has gone past the stage where we say everybody has to have one.[698]

However, in addition to traditional forms of Neighbourhood Watch an innovative program called Project Eyewatch has been established. Project Eyewatch, described as '21st century Neighbourhood Watch',[699] was developed in 2010 to encourage the younger generation to participate in Neighbourhood Watch and make contact with the police. Following research by a small operations group, Facebook was used to trial a pilot site in a closed group environment and then a pilot project was rolled out.

Currently 35 command teams have been through the training process that melds the police and civilians together, teaches how the Facebook system works and how it will be used, not only to send out information but also to 'build community using a social network environment in closed groups which will afford those communities significant protection'.[700] A police layer of security is used as well to stop undesirable people coming into those groups. The project will also look at how to engage people in the mobile framework through the use of iPads and smart phones. Using current technologies people will not be restricted to coming to meetings but can be involved in facilitative forums in the community.[701]

Whilst undoubtedly such technological innovations, as in the United Kingdom, may in the long run contribute to the survival of a remodelled Neighbourhood Watch, not all commentators have viewed the trend towards Facebook and other forms of social/ technological media as uniformly beneficial. For example, Ms Margaret Southwell, Chair of the New South Wales Local Government Community Safety and Crime Prevention Network, told the Committee:

One of the concerns that has been raised by Neighbourhood Watch members, they are all seniors, is about Facebook and having access to that. A lot of them do not use the internet. That is a real concern for them. The other thing is that the Neighbourhood Watch meeting is a chance

---

697 Professor Don Weatherburn, Director, New South Wales Bureau of Crime Statistics and Research, Evidence given to the Drugs and Crime Prevention Committee, Inquiry into Locally Based Approaches to Community Safety and Crime Prevention, Public Hearing, Sydney, 19 September 2011.

698 Superintendent Commander Helen Begg, Operational Programs, Sydney, New South Wales Police Service, Evidence given to the Drugs and Crime Prevention Committee, Inquiry into Locally Based Approaches to Community Safety and Crime Prevention, Public Hearing, Sydney, 19 September 2011.

699 Superintendent Commander Helen Begg, Operations Programs, Sydney, New South Wales Police Service, Evidence given to the Drugs and Crime Prevention Committee, Inquiry into Locally Based Approaches to Community Safety and Crime Prevention, Public Hearing, Sydney, 19 September 2011.

700 Chief Inspector Joshua Maxwell, Human Resources, South West Sydney, New South Wales Police Service, Evidence given to the Drugs and Crime Prevention Committee, Inquiry into Locally Based Approaches to Community Safety and Crime Prevention, Public Hearing, Sydney, 19 September 2011.

701 Chief Inspector Joshua Maxwell, Human Resources, South West Sydney,, New South Wales Police Service, Evidence given to the Drugs and Crime Prevention Committee, Inquiry into Locally Based Approaches to Community Safety and Crime Prevention, Public Hearing, Sydney, 19 September 2011.

for them to come out and meet and talk with people. In turns of reducing social isolation for the senior community, it is good for them to get out and meet those people.[702]

Nonetheless, 25 Neighbourhood Watch groups have begun changing over to this online process, with the biggest group consisting of 450 members who share information about what is going on in their community.[703] Chief Inspector Maxwell, New South Wales Police Service, cited that group as an example of what they are aiming to achieve — a high value community network where 'community are police; police are community' and social networking capabilities are engaged '24/7'.[704] Precinct members apply to be part of a particular precinct group and undergo police checks to ensure they are not part of a criminal element. Precincts can be geographical, issue motivated or based on ethnic origin.

Information is fed to police through the local area command (LAC) page, then back to groups and the general community. Issues discussed to date include alcohol-related crime, youth crime, graffiti and traffic issues.[705]

The sponsor for Eyewatch is the NSW Police and Emergency Services Minister who expressed his expectations for the project on a video put on YouTube, which was shown to the Committee at the public hearing.

A new strategy — 2011 onwards

During the period of this Inquiry, a new Neighbourhood Watch Strategic Plan 2011–16 was developed at the behest of the Victorian Minister for Crime Prevention and the Department of Justice.[706] This followed the Neighbourhood Watch Board of Management identifying an urgent need for a review of the existing strategy. To assist with this revitalisation of Neighbourhood Watch the Victorian government allocated funding for Neighbourhood Watch in its 2011–12 state budget, committing $550,000 over four years to set up an office with a state manager.[707] The Victorian government also provided $25,000 for a consultancy to assist in developing the strategic plan for the next five years.[708]

Although some details of the new Plan are still to be finalised, the following is a summary of the stated aims and direction of the 2011–2016 Strategic Plan and of the new initiatives being developed.

702 Ms Margaret Southwell, Chair, New South Wales Local Government Community Safety and Crime Prevention Committee and Community Development Officer, Community Development, Bankstown City Council, Evidence given to the Drugs and Crime Prevention Committee, Inquiry into Locally Based Approaches to Community Safety and Crime Prevention, Public Hearing, Sydney, 19 September 2011.
This is not necessarily the experience of the Neighbourhood Watch State Office, Western Australia. A representative told the Committee that in that state the number of people logging on to Neighbourhood Watch websites and electronic newsletters had grown phenomenally: 'People are saying to us, "Happy to have the information, but don't necessarily want to go to the meetings and be part of that structure". So that is where the technology comes in'.

703 Chief Inspector Joshua Maxwell, Human Resources, South West Sydney, New South Wales Police Service, Evidence given to the Drugs and Crime Prevention Committee, Inquiry into Locally Based Approaches to Community Safety and Crime Prevention, Public Hearing, Sydney, 19 September 2011.

704 Chief Inspector Joshua Maxwell, Human Resources, South West Sydney, New South Wales Police Service, Evidence given to the Drugs and Crime Prevention Committee, Inquiry into Locally Based Approaches to Community Safety and Crime Prevention, Public Hearing, Sydney, 19 September 2011.

705 Chief Inspector Joshua Maxwell, Human Resources, South West Sydney, New South Wales Police Service, Evidence given to the Drugs and Crime Prevention Committee, Inquiry into Locally Based Approaches to Community Safety and Crime Prevention, Public Hearing, Sydney, 19 September 2011.

706 Mr Andrew Brideson, President, Neighbourhood Watch Victoria Inc., in correspondence to the Drugs and Crime Prevention Committee, 20 October 2011.

707 Mr Andrew Brideson, President, Board of Management, Neighbourhood Watch Victoria Inc., Evidence given to the Drugs and Crime Prevention Committee, Inquiry into Locally Based Approaches to Community Safety and Crime Prevention, Public Hearing, Melbourne, 24 October 2011.

708 Ms Julianne Brennan, Director, Community Crime Prevention, Department of Justice, Evidence given to the Drugs and Crime Prevention Committee, Inquiry into Locally Based Approaches to Community Safety and Crime Prevention, Public Hearing, Melbourne, 27 February 2012.

Aims and direction

The overarching aim of Neighbourhood Watch remains the same: to assist in creating informed and empowered communities in which people feel safe and secure.[709] However, there is now an understanding that the community no longer needs Neighbourhood Watch to be organised solely to prevent property crime and that it could be more relevant if it develops initiatives to build 'whole of community' resilience as is clearly evident in the United Kingdom.[710]

The strategic direction proposed in the new Plan to achieve this is to:

1. build partnerships between Neighbourhood Watch and private and public sector organisations

2. develop a community place-based safety model

3. re-educate individuals 'as to what "we" can do as a community to feel safe and secure'.[711]

These aim to address 'a perceived reluctance by the community to take responsibility for its safety and security' and 'a lack of "family" belonging that is alienating youth and ethnic groups, further driving community disconnect'.[712] A summary of initiatives for achieving the desired direction follows.

1. Partnerships and alliances

Partnerships

Neighbourhood Watch sees partnerships with the following groups continuing or being developed:

◆ emergency services (Police, Ambulance, Fire)

◆ local government

◆ the community (including local businesses)

◆ volunteers

◆ Safety House — a not-for-profit organisation that promotes safety for Victorians, especially the young and the elderly, through a network of 'safe houses'

◆ other community based crime prevention programs (eg. Crime Stoppers)

◆ funders and sponsors

◆ Neighbourhood Watch Australasia.[713]

With regard to the proposed partnership with Safety House, the Neighbourhood Watch Strategic Plan 2011–16 states that:

> Whilst the merger with Safety House will go some way to invigorating the membership base of NHW this alone in the NHW Board's opinion will not ensure the survival of NHW. The NHW Board ultimately considers that further mergers will be necessary given the number of competing community-based organisations.[714]

Alliances

Recently an alliance was formed between Neighbourhood Watch and a contracting company in which the contractors, who have all undergone police checks, will all automatically become

709 Neighbourhood Watch Strategic Plan 2011–2016, p.4.
710 Neighbourhood Watch Strategic Plan 2011–2016, p.6.
711 Neighbourhood Watch Strategic Plan 2011–2016, p.4.
712 Neighbourhood Watch Strategic Plan 2011–2016, p.11.
713 Neighbourhood Watch Strategic Plan 2011–2016, p.7.
714 Neighbourhood Watch Strategic Plan 2011–2016, p.6.

members of Neighbourhood Watch and be the 'eyes and ears' of both Neighbourhood Watch and Crime Stoppers. Initially this will be a trial program conducted in two areas, in which crime statistics and reports will be monitored and analysed.[715] A review of the trial program is to take place in April 2012 with a report to the Board of Management due in May 2012. There may be an expansion of the program if the results of the trial are positive.[716]

Other initiatives to build partnerships

These include developing a:

◆ marketing strategy

◆ community engagement plan

◆ funding plan

◆ business plan.[717]

2. Community place-based safety model

The following initiatives are proposed for developing a community place-based safety model:

◆ reconfirm the governance structure and restructuring where required

◆ update policy manual if revised framework is required

◆ provide a support pack for ongoing and new committees

◆ develop an internal communication plan

◆ develop a community engagement plan.[718]

3. Re-educate individuals 'as to what "we" can do as a community to feel safe and secure'

In order to inform community members and increase the membership of Neighbourhood Watch the following actions are to be undertaken:

◆ develop ideas for increasing community participation

◆ develop an inclusivity strategy that focuses on broadening the cultural and age demographic, skills and experiences of Neighbourhood Watch volunteers and members

◆ offer professional development training

◆ define volunteer roles where appropriate for specialist skills

◆ develop a community education plan.[719]

---

715   Mr Andrew Brideson, President, Board of Management, Neighbourhood Watch Victoria Inc., Evidence given to the Drugs and Crime Prevention Committee, Inquiry into Locally Based Approaches to Community Safety and Crime Prevention, Public Hearing, Melbourne, 24 October 2011.

716   Mr Andrew Brideson, President, Neighbourhood Watch Victoria Inc., in correspondence to the Drugs and Crime Prevention Committee, 7 April 2012.

717   Neighbourhood Watch Strategic Plan 2011–2016, p.12.

718   Neighbourhood Watch Strategic Plan 2011–2016, p.13.

719   Neighbourhood Watch Strategic Plan 2011–2016, p.14.

Changes proposed by Victoria Police

Recently the Committee has been told that Victoria Police is developing a program similar to the NSW Project Eyewatch model, in which the social network site Facebook is used to send out information and build community groups that aim to afford those communities protection. A submission from Victoria Police stated that the EyeWatch project would be 'implemented in conjunction with Neighbourhood Watch to bring Neighbourhood Watch into the 21st century'.[720] The submission also listed Geelong, Brimbank, Darebin, Yarra Ranges and Hobsons Bay as being the five PSAs in which EyeWatch is currently being trialled. It is proposed that if the trial is successful the program may be rolled out across 54 PSAs.[721]

Victoria Police believes the likely benefits of this new system will include:

◆ more active engagement by the community about local issues and their solution resulting from an easy, free and accessible 24/7 available platform for the community to actively engage with police

◆ increased engagement by the younger generation due to a more attractive system

◆ more accurate and timely feedback provided to members of the public. [722]

While the intention is to encourage younger generations to engage with the police, it would seem inappropriate for the majority of current Neighbourhood Watch members who are of an age demographic that does not always have the level of computer literacy or the technology resources required to participate in such a system. Similarly, Deputy Commissioner Tony Cartwright stated that one of the challenges for Neighbourhood Watch is 'that it is now a largely older demographic and it is probably not comfortable with some of the modern technologies that we have the opportunity to use like Eyewatch'.[723]

Conclusion

Neighbourhood Watch Victoria was established 28 years ago by Victoria Police to involve local communities in actively reducing crime, particularly burglaries and property crime. In its early years in particular it was widely recognised as an organisation strongly promoting and working towards achieving safer communities. The Committee acknowledges and commends the work of its committed volunteers, many of whom have been involved in Neighbourhood Watch for long periods.

However, it is apparent to the Committee that the practices and priorities of Neighbourhood Watch have remained largely unchanged since its inception, leading to a dramatic decline in membership and widespread discontent within the organisation. At the same time, rapid changes have occurred in the demographics and activities of our society and in technology, particularly communication methods and crime detection devices. In addition, police structures and methods, have led to questions being asked in many quarters about the relevance and future of Neighbourhood Watch in the 21st century. Such questioning was common to the evidence the Committee received during this Inquiry.

---

720 Submission from Victoria Police to the Drugs and Crime Prevention Committee, Inquiry into Locally Based Approaches to Community Safety and Crime Prevention, April 2012.

721 Submission from Victoria Police to the Drugs and Crime Prevention Committee, Inquiry into Locally Based Approaches to Community Safety and Crime Prevention, April 2012.

722 Submission from Victoria Police to the Drugs and Crime Prevention Committee, Inquiry into Locally Based Approaches to Community Safety and Crime Prevention, April 2012.

723 Deputy Commissioner Tim Cartwright, Victoria Police, Evidence given to the Drugs and Crime Prevention Committee, Inquiry into Locally Based Approaches to Community Safety and Crime Prevention, Public Hearing, Melbourne 16 April 2012.

In an attempt to revitalise Neighbourhood Watch the Victorian Government's 2011–12 budget allocated funding over four years for the appointment of a Chief Executive Officer to head Neighbourhood Watch, a restructure of the Board and development of a new strategy. While this may lead to a rejuvenated and productive organisation, the Committee believes it is imperative that Neighbourhood Watch as part of its current funding requirements be reviewed by the Victorian Government in 2013. The Review would assess the effectiveness of Neighbourhood Watch as a government funded crime prevention initiative. It should also indicate on the evidence received whether on balance further government funding should be allocated to support Neighbourhood Watch beyond 2014. In particular, the onus should fall on Neighbourhood Watch to demonstrate to the Victorian government that they merit ongoing funding. Any Review should also include canvassing transitional and future alternative crime prevention options should it be decided that Neighbourhood Watch not receives ongoing Victorian Government assistance.

Recommendation

36. **The Committee recommends** that Neighbourhood Watch as part of its current funding requirements be reviewed by the Victorian Government in 2013. The Review would assess the effectiveness of Neighbourhood Watch as a government funded crime prevention initiative. It should also indicate on the evidence received whether on balance further government funding should be allocated to support Neighbourhood Watch beyond 2014.

Section E — The Way Forward

11. Crime Prevention Initiatives: The Need for Further Research and Evaluation

Introduction

Research plays a crucial and central role in shaping the direction of social and justice policy, programs and initiatives in Australia and internationally. The need for evidence based interventions has been widely recognised and accepted by all stakeholders in the area of crime prevention and community safety, not the least of which are the agencies, organisations and individuals that gave evidence to this Inquiry. In particular, one of the constant themes to come out of this Inquiry has been the need for more comprehensive data with regard to both the level of crime and the nature of crime prevention initiatives in local communities. There has also been a constant concern in evidence given to the Inquiry that whilst there have been some significant and sophisticated evaluations undertaken of crime prevention programs in Victoria,[724] they are not conducted as frequently or comprehensively as should be the case.

This chapter will address some of these concerns. It examines the need for better research and data provision in order to systematically develop and implement best practice crime prevention programs. It then looks at how seldom crime prevention programs are evaluated and what the reasons for this may be. In doing so an examination as to whether cost-benefit analysis can be useful in the development of crime prevention programs is given. Finally, the chapter discusses some of the ways in which evidence based best practice including the conduct of comprehensive program evaluation can be facilitated. These include the assistance of central crime prevention agencies and specialist research bodies.

The limitations of current crime prevention programs

Outlining a connection between the weaknesses of Australian crime prevention programs and the lack of research, Professor Peter Homel has argued that without sufficient research Australian crime prevention has been:

> [p]lagued by a lack of clear and coherent leadership (at both national and state/territory levels), an emphasis on short-term goals and outcomes, regularly shifting but low levels of funding, and repeated radical changes in direction (2005, p.365).

As Homel explains, a key reason for these shortcomings has been the 'absence of commitment to a research and evaluation process designed to build up an evidence base for determining policy and program priorities' (2005, p.365). He concludes that, without an evidence base, '[o]ne of the greatest problems has been the continuing commitment to community-based crime prevention strategies with loosely defined goals and objectives in the absence of real evidence and cost effectiveness' (2005, p.365). It follows, therefore,

---

724   The evaluation of Operation Newstart is a good case in point. See discussion later in this chapter.

that without research and evaluation it is difficult, if not impossible, to determine whether strategies are actually effective.

Based on the work of the Committee and the evidence of numerous stakeholders, the Committee believes that any strategies, programs and interventions developed and implemented to prevent or reduce crime and antisocial behaviour must be evidence based or grounded in evidence based research. It is not always clear, however, what is meant by the term 'evidence based',[725] nor whether disparate stakeholders in the area of crime prevention are necessarily of a like mind when it comes to determining what counts as evidence based research. Some policies and programs that are popular with sections of the media and public may have no demonstrable effectiveness when measured according to the rigorous requirements of a scientific or academic evaluation. The traditional law enforcement interventions discussed in Chapter 2, whilst sometimes appearing to be necessary, may for example not be supported by evidence. Conversely, options that have shown merit in reducing crime and promoting social cohesion or community capacity building, such as social developmental programs like the Pathways Project,[726] may be viewed as 'soft options' by some people and rejected and not prioritised.

Therefore, despite its rational appeal, the issue of 'evidence based' approaches in addressing crime is by no means as straightforward as it may appear on the surface (in Stephenson, Giller & Brown 2007).

The relationship of research to crime prevention

There are a variety of factors which need to be considered when developing and implementing effective crime prevention policy and programs. Some of these are as follows.

Research is important at all stages of the project cycle

The research process is crucial at *all* stages of the crime prevention 'project' — from initial inception and planning to the evaluation of programs. Once the issues are properly identified, research will also offer guidance in terms of the best ways to address these issues. In order to determine if programs are effective and to develop and build an evidence base, the programs must be properly evaluated. Research, therefore, is important from the design stage of crime prevention strategies and programs, through to implementation and evaluation stages.

Research needs to be locally based

Obviously, to be able to adequately address community safety and crime issues in a particular area it is necessary to understand what the issues are at *local level* (Homel 2009b). A good understanding of local issues requires access to reliable crime data, associated social and community indicators of wellbeing and relevant research. As Homel has advised:

> [p]rojects and programs on crime prevention should be designed based on the results of participatory diagnosis or participatory local safety audits, be grounded in sound theoretical methods and be monitored and evaluated systematically (2009a, p.4).

Associate Professor Darren Palmer of Deakin University made a similar point to the Committee in the context of the regional City of Geelong:

> We need to ensure that we do focused research on particular regions, localities and the like. We have been very fortunate in Geelong. There is a group of us as researchers who have been quite successful

---

725　Social programs that are evidence based draw from robust research and sound, usually empirical, data. Moreover, evidence of suitability and sustainability of crime prevention programs should also be taken from an accumulation of comprehensive evaluations (mega analyses) of like programs (Saltz 2005). Using an evidence-based approach to social policy has the potential to decrease the tendency to run programs which are socially acceptable (e.g. drug education in schools, youth 'boot camps') but which often prove to be ineffective when evaluated. See also discussion below.

726　See discussion in Chapter 2.

in going for grants and getting the money to actually do the research. That is not necessarily true of most other regional and rural locations in Victoria. I think that is a real gap, because [other areas of Victoria] are actually different places, politically, culturally, economically, socially. You do need to really fully understand what is going on in a particular locality to make sense of what you need to do. We can abstract it and say, 'Drugs and alcohol are a problem'. Yes, I can accept that, but they work their ways through different localities differently and we need to understand that more.[727]

The need for an evidence base

Welsh and Farrington, two of the leading pioneers in crime prevention research, have stressed the absolutely crucial need to situate crime prevention on a rigorous evidence base. They point out that '[c]rime prevention should be rational and should be based on the best possible evidence' (2005, p.338). The basic principles of evidence based practice are that all practical decisions made should be based on research studies and that these research studies are selected and interpreted according to some specific norms characteristic for evidence based practice (Aos 2010). Research not only provides the basis for a later evaluation[728] of what practices or activities have proven to be effective, but also how local considerations may impact on achieving crime prevention objectives. This highlights the need for data collection and ongoing research in developing and maintaining effective community safety and crime prevention strategies or programs.

At the program or strategy development phase, Professor Steve Aos[729] (2010) recommends the collection of data on every relevant crime prevention program where a control is present and the collation of the data to allow for an estimation of the rate of success or effectiveness, the risk of failure, the cost and cost savings and the possible effect on areas like education, health, housing, employment, since there are likely to be flow-on benefits. According to Aos (2010), the greater the amount of data, the more authoritative and certain the estimation of the effectiveness, cost, benefit and risk will be. An 'ideal' model for the use of research based evidence in crime prevention policy development is schematically outlined in Figure 11.1.

Figure 11.1: An ideal model for utilising research in crime prevention

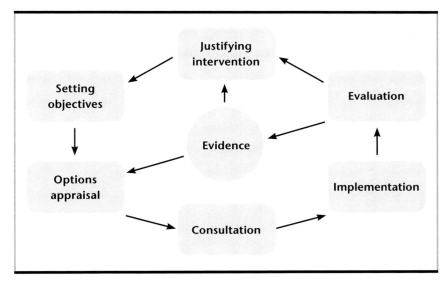

Source: Homel, P (2011).

---

727 Associate Professor Darren Palmer, Convenor, Criminology Program, Deakin University, Deakin University, correspondence to the Drugs and Crime Prevention Committee, Inquiry into Locally Based Approaches to Community Safety and Crime Prevention, Briefing, Melbourne, 9 September 2011.

728 The issue of evaluation of crime prevention programs is discussed separately later in this chapter.

729 Professor Steve Aos currently lectures at the Washington State Institute for Public Policy, an Institute in Washington State in the United States which advises the State Legislature on crime prevention.

A call for data

One of the key components of a good evidence base for crime prevention is access to sufficient and reliable (local) data. Measuring the effects of crime prevention programs can pose significant challenges to researchers — not the least of which is the availability of appropriate data and information systems to facilitate evaluation (Morgan & Homel 2011).

During this Inquiry there was a general consensus on the urgent need for better, more rigorous and comprehensive data collation and dissemination in the area of crime prevention. One reason for this expressed by many witnesses to the Inquiry, particularly those from local government backgrounds, was that too often people had a skewed idea as to the levels and nature of crime in their communities. In other words, the perceptions of crime occurring were not necessarily commensurate with the reality. For example, Councillor Jan Farrell, Chair of the City of Geelong's Community Safety Committee told the Inquiry:

> Public perception [of levels of crime] is pretty important because quite often what appears on the front page of the local newspapers can become the driving force of our responses and we have to be careful that we make sure that any responses that do come are properly based, properly founded and have some evidence base to them.[730]

The importance of research for local community safety and crime prevention programs is also acknowledged by community organisations and service providers. This is particularly true where initiatives are applied in innovative ways or to particular areas or groups. As Mr Steve Bentley of the City of Greater Geelong explained:

> I do believe that a commitment to...data collection is essential. As you go down the path and you trial different things and you want to know what works and what does not, to measure and do that over a long period of time so you can narrow down what does work, and setting up networks where people can get together and share their information, share their learning. But they will still have to take that and then apply it to their local area. That is important. Allocating long-term resources to measuring what difference you make is important.[731]

Associate Professor Darren Palmer, who has been involved in a number of crime prevention projects in the Geelong area, noted that the lack of detail in the data, particularly with regard to Victoria Police, can impede the ability of researchers and practitioners to develop, implement or evaluate effective crime prevention programs:

> We have had very significant problems in terms of police-based data...where the main problem occurs is, firstly, the time it actually takes to get access to the police data is incredible and, secondly, the police data they give you is post-code based data for privacy reasons. With postcode data you cannot get down to the street level to find out what is going on. To give you an example, in Geelong the postcode 3220 covers several suburbs well outside the city centre, so they get the data on assaults in 3220 [but] we do not know whether it is city centre based or not. So it makes it very difficult to interpret what you are actually seeing.[732]

Whilst statistical data is important, equally relevant is qualitative data, particularly drawn from the experiences of offenders themselves. Professor Palmer also argued that there needs

---

730 Cr Jan Farrell, Community Safety Portfolio, City of Greater Geelong, Evidence given to the Drugs and Crime Prevention Committee, Inquiry into Locally Based Approaches to Community Safety and Crime Prevention, Public Hearing, Geelong, 8 August 2011.

731 Mr Steve Bentley, Place Manager, City of Greater Geelong, Evidence given to the Drugs and Crime Prevention Committee, Inquiry into Locally Based Approaches to Community Safety and Crime Prevention, Public Hearing, Geelong, 8 August 2011.

732 Associate Professor Darren Palmer, Convenor, Criminology Program, Deakin University, Evidence given to the Drugs and Crime Prevention Committee, Inquiry into Locally Based Approaches to Community Safety and Crime Prevention, Meeting, Geelong, 8 August 2011.

to be a much greater capacity to do ethnographic research in crime prevention, particularly around policing practices, because the police are key drivers of crime prevention activity:

> But the capacity to do this kind of ethnographic research is quite limited. There is not a tradition of doing it in Australia, and certainly not in Victoria, and in other places in Australia where it has been done it tends to go through various kinds of other bodies.[733]

Unfortunately such research tends to be expensive and time consuming. Nonetheless, as with any area of social policy it is essential that *all* forms of research relevant to the area of investigation is undertaken. It is clear that quantitative data is needed to address crime prevention and community safety. But such data needs to be complemented by qualitative techniques including studies in ethnography and social research.

Research assistance — An expert body?

One feature of the New South Wales crime prevention model that could be replicated in this state is the use of an independent crime statistics and research body to inform the development of crime prevention policy and in particular the formulation of crime prevention plans by local government areas.

For the most part the way in which local government authorities can inform their prevention plans through the use of empirical evidence is by using the resources of the New South Wales Bureau of Crime Statistics and Research (BOCSAR). The functions and role of BOCSAR have already been discussed at length.[734] In short, however, this crime research, statistics and data analysis agency assists local government, police and community agencies with the provision of data and evidence to inform the development and implementation of crime prevention programs and initiatives. This Committee believes the establishment of a centre in Victoria similar to that of BOCSAR in New South Wales is warranted. Such a centre would lead to the development and application of an evidence base for effective crime prevention including the measurement and reporting on effective (and ineffective) crime prevention interventions throughout Victoria.[735]

'Expert' knowledge is important but not the only source of information

Clearly academic research bodies such as BOCSAR are important. However another important consideration to take into account in developing successful crime prevention programs is to 'avoid the assumption that expert knowledge invariably is superior to lay assessments…for example, expert risk assessment that ignores local knowledge about specific variations can fail dismally' (Cherney 2007, p.69).

Similarly, Nutley and Davis argue that findings from research or *formal knowledge* are just one source of knowledge about good practice:

> *Informal knowledge* (such as that embedded in many systems and procedures, which shapes how an organisation functions communicates and analyses situations), *tacit knowledge* (arising from the capabilities of people, particularly the skills they have developed over time) and *cultural knowledge* (relating to customs, values and relationships with clients and other stakeholders) are also powerful influences on people's professional practices (Nutley & Davies 2001 in Homel 2009b, pp.23–24).

---

733 Associate Professor Darren Palmer, Convenor, Criminology Program, Deakin University, Deakin University, correspondence to the Drugs and Crime Prevention Committee, Inquiry into Locally Based Approaches to Community Safety and Crime Prevention, Melbourne, 9 September 2011.

734 See Chapter 3.

735 This is not the first call for such an independent crime statistics and research body. Indeed the Drugs and Crime Prevention Committee in its *Inquiry into Crime Trends — Fifth Report* (2002) made such a recommendation. It was also a key recommendation of the Victorian Ombudsman in his *Investigation into an allegation about Victoria Police Crime Statistics* Report in June 2011.

The need for evaluation

One question that is often asked is whether 'crime prevention' is effective? Very little comprehensive research has been done to satisfactorily address this issue although it is understandable that such concerns are at the forefront of those responsible for resource allocation and budget priorities. It is a constant lament of researchers, policy-makers and practitioners that in crime prevention very little formal evaluation has been undertaken of either broad strategy types (for example, diversionary measures) or specific programs (Australian Institute of Criminology (AIC) 2002; Homel 2004, 2006, 2009a; Homel et al 2004; Morgan & Homel 2011; Sutton, Cherney & White 2008).[736]

> Rarely is evaluation a systematic part of project planning, which has key implications for lesson learning. Often the pressure on practitioners and policymakers is to get 'quick wins'; that is to get projects up and running, which leads to evaluation being an afterthought, left until a project has run its course. However an important best practice principle of program evaluation is for it to be ongoing and part of the early design of a crime prevention strategy (Sutton, Cherney & White 2008, p.71.).

Mr Garner Clancey of Sydney University's Institute of Criminology made similar comments when he met with the Committee:

> We have to start, firstly, at capturing the evidence better. I am sure everyone has said this to you. We do not do evaluation particularly well in this country, would be my argument. We often fund the programs and then do not allocate the funding at the outset to the longitudinal piece of research. This work has to be evaluated longitudinally. It is really about improving our data capture and evaluation measures before you can then start sharing the good stories.[737]

The importance of evaluation in crime prevention

Evaluation of the results of crime prevention programs has become increasingly important for a number of reasons including:

- because of the growing costs of crime;
- to ensure that the investment of government resources is directed to programs that can achieve the desired outcomes;
- to provide evidence of the results being achieved; and
- to meet the funding requirements for accountability (Armstrong & Francis 2003, p.2).

Sutton, Cherney and White also believe the concept of accountability is especially important in order for governments to win support for a shift away from 'law and order' and to support local initiatives that do so: 'it is essential that strategies and programs are able to demonstrate that their "alternative" crime prevention investments are "producing results"' (2008, p.70).

It is therefore crucial that most programs or interventions with regard to crime prevention, particularly the larger and more expensive ones, are thoroughly evaluated:

> Evaluation research is necessary in order to measure whether the policy has any impact, and to provide a 'reality-check' to high expectations often attached to promising new initiatives in this area. Evaluation also needs to be ongoing. Evidence from one time period may not necessarily

---

736 The following witnesses gave evidence to the Committee indicating how little effective evaluation of crime prevention programs was undertaken in Australia and how essential this was: Associate Professor Peter Homel, Associate Professor Darren Palmer, Mr Steven Dickson, Mr Michael Wood, Professor Ross Homel, Ms Jan Shield, Mr Brendan Thomas, Superintendent Commander Helen Begg, Professor Don Weatherburn and Mr Garner Clancey. Details on when these witnesses appeared before the Committee can be seen in Appendices 3, 4 or 5.

737 Mr Garner Clancey, Adjunct Lecturer, Sydney Institute of Criminology, University of Sydney, Evidence given to the Drugs and Crime Prevention Committee, Inquiry into Locally Based Approaches to Community Safety and Crime Prevention, Public Hearing, Sydney, 19 September 2011.

be applicable to situations emerging in another era. And evidence from developed countries may not always be applicable to developing countries. Furthermore, communities often want locally based evidence, or at least evidence that is close to home to justify their interventions rather than rely on dated findings from far afield. While there may be general agreement about the [academic] support for a specific strategy, there may be doubt among policy-makers that these findings will apply to their jurisdiction.

Evaluation research provides a useful but often under-utilised resource to decision-makers. Should resources be devoted to those policies that have at best a modest effect, or should they be directed to policies that have a chance for a broader and more substantial impact? Decisions about which strategies to implement, phase out, or modify should be informed by findings from systematic evaluation (Babor et al 2004, p.98).

But how is evaluation best undertaken in the context of crime prevention and community safety?

The process of evaluating crime prevention interventions

Effective crime prevention involves ongoing monitoring and evaluation of strategies and programs, and the dissemination of findings to the broader sector. There are two basic approaches for measuring the effectiveness of crime prevention programs. These are:

performance measurement, which involves the development of systems to regularly monitor performance information, review program performance and to inform decisions as to how to improve the operation and effectiveness of a strategy[738]; and

evaluation, which helps to determine how well a program has been implemented or whether a chosen strategy has achieved its stated objectives in order to build an understanding of what works in crime prevention, identify good practice, and determine what can be done, and in what circumstances, to prevent crime.[739]

In turn, evaluative strategies and methods can be characterised by *'outcome evaluation'* — in its most basic sense examining the impact of the intervention or 'Did the program work? The other main method is 'process evaluation' which is concerned with examining the implementation of the intervention or program — Did the 'underlying mechanisms that drove the implementation of [a] strategy...hinder or facilitate its delivery? (Sutton, Cherney & White 2008, p.80).[740]

Cameron and McDougall also believe that any process of evaluation for crime prevention programs should include *cost-benefit analysis* at the time of planning the intervention in order to ensure the most 'productive use of funding in the future' (2000, p.6). Cost-benefit analysis and cost-effectiveness are discussed separately later in this chapter.

The recently developed National Crime Prevention Framework[741] states that all these approaches (outcome and process evaluations and cost-benefit analyses) need to be considered during the initial planning and development stages of a project:

---

738 For a comprehensive and technical account of performance measurement models for crime prevention programs, see Morgan and Homel 2011.

739 *National Crime Prevention Framework*, Australian Institute of Criminology 2011 at http://www.aic.gov.au/en/crime_community/crimeprevention/ncpf/ncpf-overview.aspx

740 For a detailed technical account of the different methods and forms of crime prevention evaluation, including outcome, process, experimental methods and systematic reviews, see Chapter 5 of Sutton Cherney and White 2008.
      The authors make the point that in terms of evaluating any program or intervention, be that in the realm of the natural or social sciences, the 'gold standard' is the randomised controlled experiment, however '[w]ithin the crime prevention field there can be few opportunities to conduct randomised control experiments' (Sutton, Cherney & White 2008, p.82). But as Aos (2010) has noted, it is possible to use existing research studies that are sufficiently similar and rely on mega studies of already evaluated programs. Sutton, Cherney and White (2008) acknowledge the value of 'replicating' studies or experiments conducted in similar contexts, as '[r]eplication helps to build the validity of results' (2008, p.83).

741 See discussion in Chapter 3.

Measuring and improving the effectiveness of crime prevention involves a combination of performance measurement and evaluation. Selecting an appropriate evaluation model involves a consideration of the characteristics of a program, the purpose of the evaluation, the available options, and determining methods to gather the views of key stakeholders. Evaluation can be directed towards:

- the program as a whole, which will include the assessment of the overall impact of the program (i.e. the aggregate impact of the various initiatives delivered as part of the program) and the appropriateness, efficacy and efficiency of mechanisms used to support the delivery of crime prevention;

- individual projects or initiatives, providing evidence as to their effectiveness in achieving desired outcomes, including explanations as to the reasons for the observed effect, as well as identifying practical challenges and lessons for implementing similar projects; or

- clustered groups of projects (classified according to location, intervention type, target groups etc.) to draw conclusions regarding the effectiveness of specific interventions, and the relative contribution of certain contexts and project characteristics.[742]

Decisions regarding which interventions should be subjected to more rigorous evaluation can be based on an assessment of the potential practical and policy significance of the findings, and of the ability of the intervention to be effectively evaluated:

By focusing evaluation on clusters of projects that are identified as being important and/or of interest, individual projects can be freed to focus on performance managing their work and the knowledge base on effective crime prevention practice can be developed in a strategic and systematic way.

Determining the most effective approach to supporting evaluation work will be based on an assessment of the existing capacity and potential needs of those likely to be entrusted with the responsibility for evaluation. Experience has shown that the actual work of evaluation needs to be supported by appropriate mechanisms to ensure that regular and timely feedback on findings from evaluations can be passed back to program managers to support continued program improvement. Similarly, research and evaluation findings need to be disseminated in a format that is accessible to policy makers and to non-experts working in the sector.[743]

Considerations to be taken into account in evaluating crime prevention programs

There are a number of important considerations in designing and conducting an evaluation study, particularly in the area of crime prevention. The Commonwealth Attorney-General's Department has set out a number of principles for evaluating community crime prevention programs which state the following should be factored into any planned evaluation:

- its [the program's] purpose, focus and timing, as these relate to the use of the evaluation information for making judgments and decisions

- the practicalities associated with collecting relevant evaluation data (i.e. its feasibility)

- the technical adequacy of the evaluation data

- the nature of the strategies put in place to safeguard the rights of key stakeholders in the evaluation process (i.e. probity).[744]

Another important consideration in designing and conducting an evaluation study is the rationale which underlies the program:

742 National Crime Prevention Framework, Australian Institute of Criminology 2011 at http://www.aic.gov.au/en/crime_community/crimeprevention/ncpf/ncpf-overview.aspx

743 National Crime Prevention Framework, Australian Institute of Criminology 2011 at http://www.aic.gov.au/en/crime_community/crimeprevention/ncpf/ncpf-overview.aspx

744 *Principles for Evaluating Community Crime Prevention Projects*, Crime Prevention Division, Attorney General's Department, Commonwealth of Australia.http://www.crimeprevention.gov.au/Publications/PublicSafety/PECCPP/Pages/default.aspx

Ekblom and Pease (1995) point out that 'distinct evaluative requirements attach to different types of prevention' (1995: 585); while Pawson and Tilley (1994) note that evaluations need to take into account the mechanisms through which effects are assumed to be determined.

In most cases, a different evaluation strategy would be appropriate for a programme based on an opportunity reduction approach (for example 'lock it or lose it' campaigns) than for an offender-oriented crime prevention programme (for example providing youth at risk of offending with employment-related skills). In the former case, a model involving impact evaluation using a goal-based approach and quasi-experimental methods are more likely to be appropriate than in the latter case where process evaluation, an illuminative/responsive approach and naturalistic methods might yield more useful information, at least for a new program.[745]

Different evaluative methods may also be required for programs which seek to influence behaviour (for example truancy or behaviour modification programs), compared to programs that provide products or services (such as security services).

The challenges and problems of crime prevention research and evaluation

There are clearly great challenges in researching the 'effectiveness' of crime prevention, not least of which is measuring what counts for 'success' in any given program. For example, whilst a program such as Neighbourhood Watch may be effective in reducing the level of crime recorded in a particular local neighbourhood, it is also possible that crime levels may rise in a neighbouring district that does not have the program — the effect criminologists call *displacement*. Similarly, a program developed to provide young people with meaningful employment or leisure opportunities may result in no or minimal drop in juvenile crime rates, however it may contribute significantly to the overall health or wellbeing of the young people subject to the intervention. Can such a program be therefore counted as a success? As Sutton, Cherney and White state in this regard:

> Some forms of crime prevention (particularly social) work best when embedded in other programs (eg education, family support, employment creation) whose ostensible purpose is not preventing crime. This can make evaluation difficult because the demonstration of clear results may be evident in other ways (eg reduced truancy rates, less family breakdown and stressful family environments, improved feelings of community connectedness, reversal of educational deficits) rather than via immediate reductions in crime (2008, pp.70–71). (See also Macrae et al 2005; Lane & Henry 2003.)

Some of the most common problems associated with the evaluation of crime prevention programs were outlined by criminologist Professor Peter Homel at an AIC presentation in November 2011. These include:

- A lack of knowledge, experience and expertise among those for managing and conducting evaluations
- Problems with access to and analysis of data
- Failure to commit adequate funding and technical resources
- Use of narrow models for evaluation (e.g. focus on outcomes at the expense of process, and vice versa)
- Absence of a committed or systematic method for applying findings to policy and programs (Homel 2011).

In addition, some other common problems and challenges associated with crime prevention evaluation are detailed in the following sections.

---

745 *Principles for Evaluating Community Crime Prevention Projects*, Crime Prevention Division, Attorney General's Department, Commonwealth of Australia. http://www.crimeprevention.gov.au/Publications/PublicSafety/PECCPP/Pages/default. aspx

Unforeseen consequences

Sometimes without proper evaluations of programs, there may be unforeseen and possibly harmful consequences. In youth offending and youth justice crime prevention programs for example, one particular research question that an appropriately controlled evaluative study could answer is the extent to which certain strategies, particularly diversionary strategies, may contribute to *net-widening*:

> As contentious as such questions can be, it would seem axiomatic that public policy makers would want to know the degree to which their efforts to divert young people from the juvenile justice system are achieving that effect, rather than creating the more common result of increasing the total volume of young people brought under the control of the juvenile justice system (Commonwealth of Australia 2003, p.91).

A related issue particularly in the context of youth offending programs is the extent to which programs are servicing those with the highest levels of need and the greatest risk of offending or re-offending. Scarce resources can then be used to allocate the most intensive programs to those for whom they are best suited through 'differentiated case management' (Day, Howells & Rickwood 2003; 2004).[746]

Evaluating community development programs

One of the challenges for evaluators is to develop evaluation mechanisms for community development programs in particular. Such mechanisms need to be able:

> to engage with the dynamic, diverse and complex programs delivered in different contexts, by a multitude of actors operating within a diverse range of relationships and to produce the reliable evidence required for valid assessments of a program's performance (Armstrong & Francis 2003, p.4).

In the community crime prevention area this includes evaluators having to address the 'messy contexts' of community based programs and their multiple goals:

> The focus of community development is broad rather than discrete. It is a means for engaging, at one and the same time, with diverse groups of people, on a variety of issues. This strength presents problems when trying to measure impacts. Cause and effect are not easily identified when there are multiple strategies occurring simultaneously, and multiple perceptions of priorities and outcomes. The long-term nature of many community development approaches also makes the measuring of outcomes difficult, as does paucity of funding for long term evaluation.

> [Good] evaluations, such as the *Pathways to Prevention*[747] project emphasise the importance of linking outcomes with the process goals of community development... Concern is not only with what happened as the result of an intervention but with understanding why and how it happened, in order to ensure the transferability of experience and the sustainability of change (Lane & Henry 2003, p.208).

Cultural and social context

Program evaluation also needs to be considered in the context of its cultural context and take into account the social and cultural values and assumptions of groups with an interest in the program. For example, a number of practical issues pertaining to evaluation, which are particularly problematic in relation to Indigenous crime prevention initiatives, have been identified:

> They include the ephemeral life-time of many projects; insecure and short-term funding, given the need for the development and implantation of long-term changes; the lack of project documentation;

---

746 For further discussion of the difficulties associated with evaluating youth offending programs in particular, see Drugs and Crime Prevention Committee 2009, *Inquiry into Strategies to Prevent High Volume Offending by Young People, Final Report,* Parliament of Victoria, Melbourne.
747 Discussed in Chapter 2.

poor evaluation; the imposition of inappropriate evaluation measures or unrealistic expectations and outcome measures. It is also evident that it is easier to evaluate clearly defined and discrete projects, such as specific training or drug and alcohol treatment programmes, than the results of multiple interventions, such as community interventions, which involve a complex range of partners, services and action (International Centre for the Prevention of Crime (ICPC) 2003, p.10).

The ICPC report (2003), citing Cunneen, argues that while it may be desirable to be able to demonstrate the impact and effectiveness of projects in Indigenous communities, evaluation of the *process* may be more important:

The effects of developing crime prevention strategies in terms of developing capacity, self-confidence and an ability to deal with such major social issues may be more important. Cunneen highlights three important requirements for evaluation:

- the importance of ownership of the evaluation by the community

- the collection of data which is compatible with Indigenous experience

- the purpose of the evaluation should be to assist communities to work towards positive change (ICPC 2003, p.10).

It should not therefore be assumed that a template of crime prevention evaluation processes can apply equally to disparate communities across or even within the same locality.

Constraints on community agencies

Unfortunately few comprehensive evaluative studies such as the evaluation of Pathways to Prevention, discussed previously, have been undertaken.[748] One of the reasons for this may be that for smaller agencies in particular, running crime prevention programs can be expensive. The cost of evaluations, particularly long-term outcome evaluations, may be too expensive for many agencies to commission. Whilst independent evaluation may be the best practice, because many of the agencies are community organisations their capacity to fund a university to do an evaluation is quite limited. Moreover,[749] it is not only the issue as to whether evaluations are in fact being conducted that needs to be considered but also whether community agencies which deliver crime prevention programs are actually in a position to evaluate their programs and service delivery even if they wish to do so. As Mr Michael Wood from the Town of Vincent in Perth told the Committee, even in those cases where your gut instinct indicates you have developed a successful local crime prevention program 'you rarely actually spend the time to really qualify and measure [our] successes'.[750] This is not just a question of financial resources. It also needs investment in time and a certain amount of

---

748 One of the more successful and comprehensive evaluations in Victoria has been of Operation Newstart discussed in Chapter 6. The evaluation of this program showed the program was highly beneficial.

In a submission to this Inquiry it was stated that Operation Newstart:

- gained the support of Save the Children Australia to provide $30,000 towards an independent evaluation of Shepparton Newstart by the Nous Group (August 2010) http://www.nousgroup.com.au/database/news/1290750780document_stc_-_operation_newstart_evaluation.pdf

- Implemented an internationally recognized evaluation tool in each program, the Strengths & Difficulties Questionnaire (SDQ) http://www.sdqinfo.org an analysis of which was completed by the Royal Children's Hospital Integrated Mental Health Service, (August 2010)

- is a partner in a longitudinal study, conducted by Melbourne University, the Centre for Adolescent Health and the Murdoch Children's Research Institute, (Outdoor Youth Programs Research Partnership) Ref: http://outdoorcouncil.asn.au/doc/OYP_Research_Partnership_Prospectus.pdf. See submission from Mr Phil Wheatley for the Executive, Operation Newstart, to the Drugs and Crime Prevention Committee, Inquiry into Locally Based Approaches to Community Safety and Crime Prevention, May 2011.

749 Superintendent Commander Helen Begg, Operational Programs, Sydney, New South Wales Police Service, Evidence given to the Drugs and Crime Prevention Committee, Inquiry into Locally Based Approaches to Community Safety and Crime Prevention, Public Hearing, Sydney, 19 September 2011.

750 Mr Michael Wood, Coordinator, Safer Vincent Crime Prevention Partnership, Town of Vincent, Evidence given to the Drugs and Crime Prevention Committee, Inquiry into Locally Based Approaches to Community Safety and Crime Prevention, Meeting, Perth, 21 June 2011.

expertise by staff in evaluative processes, particularly if the only option for the agency is to do an 'in-house' study.[751]

As Sutton, Cherney and White state, evaluation can be time consuming and distracting from the 'main game' of actually implementing a program or strategy. There are many reasons why practitioners may not wholeheartedly embrace the challenge of having their programs evaluated:

> [e]valuation can only add to the cost of designing and implementing a crime prevention strategy: money that at times may be seen as better spent on intervention itself. Evaluation can also require skills and knowledge that practitioners may lack and require procedures and processes…that may seem daunting to the non-technically trained. Finally, practitioners and policymakers can regard evaluation as threatening particularly if they have invested large amounts of time and resources (or banked their reputations on) a program. It can indicate that a scheme has been a failure and a waste of resources (2008, p.72).

These concerns were also expressed by other staff in local government and community organisations. At a seminar in November 2011 of Victorian 'Local Government Professionals (LGPro) — Special Interest Group for Community Safety', members stated that whilst they appreciated the need for rigorous evaluations of their programs it was simply not feasible given that they had neither the time nor the funds to undertake them. Similar comments were expressed by those officers who responded to the Committee's survey of local government authorities (LGAs) in Chapter 5 of this Report.

Ongoing funding and sustainability

In its response to a survey of crime prevention activity of LGAs undertaken by the Victorian Local Governance Association (VLGA),[752] Frankston City Council noted that '[e]valuations are conducted for programs that receive funding (as is usually a requirement of the funding) or when required for Councillor interest/further funding applications/ Award applications'.[753] This raises an issue relating to the sustainability of programs that do not receive funding for evaluation. If research and evaluations are only able to be conducted where there is external funding of a specific project or program, data is unlikely to be complete and comprehensive, typically only covering the life-span of the associated program or project. As Associate Professor Darren Palmer noted in relation to a similar problem in Geelong:

> you have to have ongoing sustainability to that research in terms of funding…What we have seen in the past in Victoria, and again elsewhere — it is not only about Victoria — is there might be this kind of brief period of excitement where funding is provided for various things but then it dries up and you lose your capacity to keep monitoring what is going on.[754]

It may also be the case that such evaluations are limited in their scope, focusing only on whether the program or project delivered its objectives. Full evaluation should extend beyond the objectives to investigate what is achieved, how it was achieved and how this impacted on crime and safety more broadly. As Mr Richard Maugueret of the City of Casey notes, beyond the evaluation of objectives the evaluation of projects is also needed to establish the full impact they have had on crime and community safety. This not only

---

751 The need for crime prevention or community safety officers or indeed anyone responsible for developing and implementing crime prevention programs to be sufficiently trained in crime prevention, development, implementation and evaluation has been discussed in Chapter 8.

752 See discussion in Chapter 6.

753 Submission from Mr Philip Schier, Senior Policy Officer, Victorian Local Governance Association to the Drugs and Crime Prevention Committee, Inquiry into Locally Based Approaches to Community Safety and Crime Prevention, June 2011.

754 Associate Professor. Darren Palmer, Convenor, Criminology Program, Deakin University, Evidence given to the Drugs and Crime Prevention Committee, Inquiry into Locally Based Approaches to Community Safety and Crime Prevention, Public Hearing, Geelong, 8 August 2011.

involves noting changes in crime rates, but also an estimation of the effectiveness of the programs in terms of what they have prevented:

> One of the challenges is the need to ensure rigorous evaluation for projects in order to then have an evidence base for further work. Clearly Council needs to collect data about what interventions have an impact so resources can be better targeted. In crime prevention it is difficult to measure the crimes that 'never happened' as a result of good prevention.[755]

However, these more comprehensive and sophisticated evaluation studies are expensive and usually beyond the scope of smaller community agencies. It is the Committee's belief that greater assistance from the Community Crime Prevention Unit (CCPU) is required to fund community crime prevention programs either individually or in clusters of like projects and has made a series of recommendations to this effect.[756] In many individual cases, due to the type of intervention being implemented and the budget available for the project, a formal or high level evaluation may not be warranted. This may particularly be so in cases where the recipient agency has not received a separate or dedicated budgetary allocation for evaluation. Rather, it may be more effective to conduct sophisticated evaluation of classes or clusters of programs or projects (for example, youth justice or domestic violence programs). The findings, including 'lessons learned' or 'what works', could then be analysed and made available for crime prevention officers, policy-makers and project managers.

Localising crime prevention evaluation

Earlier in this chapter it was stated that research in crime prevention needed to have a strong local area component. This is also generally true of the evaluation aspect of crime prevention research. This chapter has stressed that crime prevention and community safety programs should be based on local needs and take into account local participation. Ultimately, many criminologists view successful crime prevention as being centred in building positive community relationships guided by comprehensive planning, inclusive coordination and most of all strategic vision. For example, Homel states that one of the key factors essential to successful implementation of crime prevention programs *and* their evaluation is local participation, particularly by those involved in the planning and design of the programs:

> Projects and programs on crime prevention should be designed based on the results of participatory diagnosis or participatory local safety audits, be grounded in sound theoretical methods and be monitored and evaluated systematically. A process of open exchange of relevant ideas and experience between all participants in the planning, delivery and review process should be encouraged. Good practices should be identified and widely promoted through research projects, interdisciplinary workshops and conferences, and other methods such as awards (Homel 2009a, p.4).

The role of the central authority

This emphasis on local based involvement does not necessarily exclude the involvement of a central or state coordinating mechanism or crime prevention unit. They can indeed play an important role in the promotion of research, evidence based project development and evaluation:

> Building capacity around evaluation is perhaps one of the most important roles that central agencies can play. This is particularly crucial if central policy units want to increase the success rate of their crime prevention strategies, because evaluation ensures that key lessons can be identified and problems avoided in future programs. Skill development around evaluation can help local practitioners as well as the development of 'tool kits' that assist in problem diagnosis. One of

---

755 Submission from Mr Richard Maugueret, Acting Manager, Community Safety, City of Casey to the Drugs and Crime Prevention Committee, Inquiry into Locally Based Approaches to Community Safety and Crime Prevention, October 2011.

756 See Chapter 1.

the most helpful capacity building functions that central policy unit experts can undertake is to connect local and regional project teams who may be tackling similar crime problems and who can share experience and pool knowledge. Such knowledge can encompass not only specific crime reduction techniques but also the best ways to go about developing and implementing a crime prevention plan (Sutton, Cherney & White 2008, p.88).

The Committee agrees with such an analysis and is encouraged that the State Government's CCPU has in fact set the promotion of evaluation and assisting through the provision of the types of toolkits mentioned above as one of its objects. The CCPUs regional reference groups could also operate in similar ways to that envisaged by Sutton, Cherney and White.

The Committee was encouraged by the remarks of Ms Julianne Brennan, Director of the Victorian CCPU, that evaluation generally and the funding of evaluation for community crime prevention programs was a priority for government:

> Evaluation is critical and I think it's really important to understand sometimes the difficulty in evaluating crime prevention programs. Quite often, because of the nature of the work and what you're trying to do, it can be very difficult in the short term, and particularly smaller projects, to show a clear evaluation of how much crime did you prevent in that initiative and quite often it's about the engagement and the process. What we're doing is tailoring the evaluation mechanisms depending on the type of project and the size of project. So for $10,000 local community grants, for example, it would be unreasonable to expect local community groups to put a significant amount of that money aside for an evaluation. But what we have done is worked with the AIC and our interstate colleagues and developed a very simple template that will help us get at least some idea of if these are the things that you said you wanted to achieve with this project, did you achieve them? Then we will do a programmatic evaluation on top of that.

> In relation to the bigger grant funds where we've got, for example, the public safety infrastructure funds of $250,000, it is actually a requirement that before funding is given to a local government they must submit an evaluation plan, particularly if it relates to CCTV, and that they have in place processes upfront to ensure they're capturing the information to measure whether they said what they were hoping to achieve with that was in fact achieved. For those programs there are more significant funding amounts so we will have a formal evaluation requirement in them.[757]

Networking best practice

One of the issues that arose in the course of this Inquiry was that for many stakeholders in the crime prevention sector, particular smaller community agencies, there are few opportunities to share information on best practice initiatives in crime prevention and community safety — to determine what has worked and what hasn't in the community sector. As Superintendent Helen Begg told the Committee:

> One thing that I do not think we are as good as we could be is about sharing best practice. If somebody has done something really good here, how are we letting people know. That is a real opportunity in terms of crime prevention. It does not mean to say that every program is going to work in every community, but it saves people reinventing the wheel.[758]

One model that has been reasonably successful in disseminating best practice initiatives at least at local government level has been through the Local Government Community Safety and Partnership Network in New South Wales.[759]

---

757 Ms Julianne Brennan, Director, Community Crime Prevention, Department of Justice, Evidence given to the Drugs and Crime Prevention Committee, Inquiry into Locally Based Approaches to Community Safety and Crime Prevention, Public Hearing, Melbourne, 27 February 2012.

758 Superintendent Commander Helen Begg, Operational Programs, Sydney, New South Wales Police Service, Evidence given to the Drugs and Crime Prevention Committee, Inquiry into Locally Based Approaches to Community Safety and Crime Prevention, Public Hearing, Sydney, 19 September 2011.

759 The Network is discussed in Chapter 3 of this Report.

The network was set up to be able to disseminate information and assist us in our jobs by sharing information, and also to advocate for professional development opportunities so we can get a standardised qualification or background for workers to improve professionally and assist in the day-to-day working of that role. The network also aims to facilitate improved program evaluation. Some of the things I highlighted with these projects is the difficulty to evaluate. We wanted to develop something to know what is best practice in the area. We wanted to be able to build something that we can use to advocate to different levels — local, state and federal government.[760]

A similar network exists in Victoria — the 'Local Government Professionals (LGPro)' — is a new special interest group for Community Safety or Crime Prevention officers or managers within local government, or people who may have community safety activities included in their position description such as crime and/or injury prevention, road safety, emergency management, graffiti management. The objective of the group is to share ideas, policies and processes, discuss priorities, increase knowledge, network and establish professional development activities.[761]

The economic benefits of crime prevention

Rationale

Crime costs the community in a variety of ways including the loss of property, loss of earnings or productivity, policing, criminal justice administration and courts costs (Homel 2009a). The AIC approximated the cost of crime in 2005 to be nearly $36 billion per year (Rollings 2008). More recently a study by Professor Russell Smyth from Monash University conservatively estimated that the cost of crime in Victoria in 2009-2010 was $9.8 billion.[762] 'This is equivalent to $1678 per person or 3.4% of Gross State Product in Victoria 2009-2010' (2011, p.1). It is widely recognised that crime prevention initiatives substantially reduce crime and in doing so deliver a significant cost saving to the community. This emphasises the economic aspects of crime prevention. As Chisholm (2000) has observed:

> The bottom line is the crime and the methods used to prevent it are costly. What is important for society as a whole, and policy makers in particular, is to ensure that scarce tax dollars, that could be used for a host of competing alternatives, are efficiently allocated to effective programs or policies. This does not necessarily mean that resources should be allocated to those crime prevention initiatives that are most effective in reducing crime, but that additional tax dollars be allocated in a way to maximise the return (lower crime) per dollar spent (p.1).

In order to ensure that crime prevention programs and strategies are delivering the best value for money, economic analysis and evaluation is necessary.

Measuring the cost of crime prevention[763]

There are many ways of measuring the cost and benefit of crime prevention and community safety programs and strategies (Sutton, Cherney & White 2008; Welsh & Farrington 2005). According to Dossetor (2011), the three most common approaches that are employed to analyse the economic dimension of crime prevention are cost savings, cost-effectiveness and cost-benefit analysis. Sometimes the terms 'cost savings', 'cost-effectiveness' and 'cost-benefit'

---

760 Ms Margaret Southwell, Chair, New South Wales Local Government Community Safety and Crime Prevention Committee and Community Development Officer, Community Development, Bankstown City Council, Evidence given to the Drugs and Crime Prevention Committee, Inquiry into Locally Based Approaches to Community Safety and Crime Prevention, Public Hearing, Sydney, 19 September 2011.

761 See http://www.lgpro.com/forum/

762 These figures should not be regarded as definitive.

763 For further discussion of the definitions, strengths and weaknesses of cost-savings, cost-effectiveness and cost-benefit analysis see Chisholm 2000 and Dossetor 2011.

are used interchangeably. However, whilst they provide a similar economic approach, they measure different things and provide different information. Furthermore, while cost-benefit analysis sounds relatively straightforward, it is far more complicated than comparing the benefits to the costs of a program (Sutton, Cherney & White 2008). The following definitions summarise cost-benefit analysis, cost-savings analysis and cost-effectiveness analysis:

1. Cost-benefit analysis compares a program's benefits to a stakeholder with the costs to that stakeholder. This approach places benefits and costs in comparable terms, usually dollars. Benefits that cannot be expressed in dollar terms cannot be compared and are included only for discussion. Cost-benefit analysis helps to determine a program's value to the stakeholder. Analysis is often undertaken from the perspective of the broader community.

2. Cost-savings analysis is restricted to the costs and benefits realised by a program's funding body (frequently a government agency). Only the costs to the funding body are taken into account, and the benefits are expressed as dollars. This kind of analysis is used to determine whether a publicly funded program 'pays for itself' — enabling a program to be justified not only on the basis of services provided, but also in financial terms as well.

3. Cost-effectiveness analysis determines how much is spent on a program to produce a particular outcome (or how much of a particular benefit will result from a given expenditure). While this can be done for multiple benefits, each benefit is analysed individually. No attempt is made to present the benefits as a single aggregate measure (AIC 2003b, p.1).

The advantage cost-benefit analysis has over cost-savings or cost-effectiveness analysis is that it is able to include a broad range of social and non-economic factors to measure the economic benefit of a program or strategy. As Aos et al (2001) observe, cost-benefit analysis can:

assist decision-makers in allocating scarce public resources among competing demands... These estimates can be helpful in directing public resources toward the economically successful programs and away from the unsuccessful programs, thereby producing a net overall gain...even in the absence of new funding sources (p.1).

How a cost-benefit analysis is conducted

According to Chisholm (2000), the standard procedure for conducting a cost-benefit analysis starts with the definition of the scope of the analysis, by establishing the range of benefits and identifying the parameters of comparison. For example, with an anti-graffiti education program, the first step would be determining what factors the evaluation will consider as benefits and costs. This might include a reduction in property damage, increased sense of safety or even a flow-on effect to other crime matters. Once the scope has been defined, it is important to know that the apparent benefits are a result of a program and not some other factor. To be able to demonstrate this, comparison with other areas that have not been involved in the program would be necessary to provide a basis for the identification of the actual benefits attributable to the program, as opposed to those attributable to other factors or influences.

The next step is the estimation of the program's effects and the translation of these effects into monetary value. This involves determining, in dollars, how much the program saved and how much it cost. This is one of the most challenging aspects of cost-benefit analysis since it requires calculating the benefit of intangible and non-economic factors in monetary terms. Professor Aos (2010) states that at the Washington State Institute for Public Policy they estimate the costs and benefits of matters like psychological or emotional costs. They are based on Court rulings setting out payments or penalties relating to compensation and damages, such as damages for psychological or emotional suffering. The damages for emotional suffering, for example, give a monetary value as a cost to society or victim and, on the basis of this, the prevention of suffering can be taken to be a saving or benefit with the same monetary figure represented as a positive value.

Another related approach to determine the value of certain intangible items is 'willingness to pay' (Aos 2010). This also accords with the approach recommended by Mr Brendan Thomas of the NSW Department of Attorney General and Justice who explained that this methodology 'tries to put a value on a particular problem by how much an individual is willing to pay to avoid it'.[764]

Once the program effects have been given value, the changes in cost and benefit over time are calculated and the reliability of these estimates is assessed. This stage involves considering changes to cost and benefit over a period of time. These changes might include an accrual of savings or costs, changing overheads, changing social or demographic variables or an estimation of the reliability or 'risk factor' of cost benefit modelling (Aos 2010). The following figure illustrates the steps involved in cost-benefit analysis.

Figure 11.2: Standard procedure for cost-benefit analysis

Define the scope of the analysis.

Establish the range of benefits to compare and identify the limits of the comparison.

Obtain estimates of program effects (comparing control and treatment groups before and after).

The benefits of a program are obtained from the effectiveness of the program.

Estimate the monetary value of all costs and benefits.

The central tenet of any cost/benefit analysis is the estimation of the monetary value of program effects.

Calculate the present value and assess profitability.

Account for inflation and the time value of money by discounting the stream of all costs and benefits over time using the social discount rate.

Describe and incorporate the distribution of costs and benefits.

Although a positive net present value tells us that the program was profitable for society as a whole, it reveals nothing about who actually gains and loses.

Conduct sensitivity analysis.

Estimating the costs and benefits of a crime prevention program relies upon certain assumptions, for example the effectiveness of the program and the cost of crime. Sensitivity analysis alters these assumptions and tests whether or not the program is still cost-beneficial.

Source: Barnett 1993 cited in Chisholm 2000, p.2.

---

764 Mr Brendan Thomas, Assistant Director-General, Crime Prevention and Community Programs, NSW Department of Attorney General and Justice, Evidence given to the Drugs and Crime Prevention Committee, Inquiry into Locally Based Approaches to Community Safety and Crime Prevention, Public Hearing, Sydney, 19 September 2011.

The strengths of cost-benefit analysis

Since it is widely acknowledged that the benefits of some crime prevention programs extend beyond the immediate area of crime deterrence and law enforcement (Sutton, Cherney & White 2008), cost-benefit analysis may be useful in capturing and valuing these programs' wider impact or effect. This is particularly relevant to developmental and community capacity building crime prevention projects that may have wide-reaching social benefits extending beyond crime prevention. Investment in educational crime prevention programs, for example, may deliver a reduction in crime, but also, indirectly, improvements in education, employment and health (Aos 2010). As Chisholm (2000) observes:

> by definition, a social benefit-cost analysis should consider all the social costs and benefits of a proposed program. Subsequently, if an early childhood program produces ancillary benefits beyond a reduction in criminal involvement, then these should be incorporated into the analysis (p.3).

The translation of all factors to monetary terms may also provide the basis for a comparative estimate of returns for different programs, activities or initiatives (Aos et al 2001). According to Aos et al, '[t]his allows direct "apples-to-apples" comparisons of the economics of different types of programs designed for widely varying age groups [or purposes]' (2001, p.1). By converting all factors to comparable terms, vastly different approaches can be compared. As Henry Ergas (2009) has argued, '[a]n advantage of the systematic use of CBA [cost-benefit analysis] is that it allows consistent values to be used *across* projects for assessing particular project inputs or outcomes' (p.33).

The benefits of this form of analysis can also be accumulative. As an evidence base grows this would assist the design and development of subsequent programs. As Chisholm (2000) notes:

> If the results from a benefit-cost analysis are fully transparent, future researchers will be able to recalculate the original results and be able to estimate benefit-cost ratios for specific benefits (p.3).

Cost-benefit analysis is also an attractive approach for ensuring that investment in crime prevention produces a healthy 'return'. As Chisholm (2000) points out, 'benefit-cost analysis can be used to determine which programs give the "biggest bang for the buck"' (p.5). Similarly, Drake et al (2009) observe that 'public policy makers need to be smart investors: some programs work, some programs do not, and careful analysis is needed to inform policy decisions' (p.183).

The challenges and limitations of cost-benefit analysis

The lack of research

Despite the strong arguments for economic analysis of crime prevention programs, very few cost-benefit or cost-effectiveness analyses have been undertaken in the criminal justice or crime prevention fields in Australia (Dossetor 2011). Whilst the Committee received considerable evidence showing that stakeholders generally agreed there was a need for economic analysis to be undertaken,[765] it did not receive examples of current crime prevention initiatives that were in the process of undertaking cost-benefit analysis. In order to properly conduct cost-benefit analysis, a range of data is required allowing comparison and accurate costing. This includes information on the measurable outcomes of a program, crime statistics and all relevant social and economic indicators, as well as comparative data on suitably similar areas. As Brendan Thomas of the NSW Department of Attorney General and Justice has pointed out, '[o]ne of the challenges we had in the whole cost-benefit area

---

765 For example, Mr Philip Schier, Senior Policy Officer, Victorian Local Governance Association, Evidence given to the Drugs and Crime Prevention Committee, Inquiry into Locally Based Approaches to Community Safety and Crime Prevention, Public Hearing, Melbourne, 27 June 2011; Assoc. Prof. Darren Palmer, Convenor, Criminology Program, Deakin University, Evidence given to the Drugs and Crime Prevention Committee, Inquiry into Locally Based Approaches to Community Safety and Crime Prevention, Public Hearing, Geelong, 8 August 2011.

in Australia is a dearth of costing information'.[766] The lack of research and evaluation is a major obstacle for cost-benefit analysis in Victoria. While the lack of research, evaluation and data collection necessary for cost-benefit analysis may offer some explanation for the low number of analyses undertaken in Australia, the complexity may also be a key factor.

Complexity

As Chisholm (2000) notes, while the idea of cost-benefit may seem simple for those not fully aware of what it involves, cost-benefit analysis is actually deceptively complex:

> Issues such as what the appropriate value of the social discount rate should be (for instance, what the cumulative discounted savings and costs over time should be), how to quantify the values of life and limb, and what benefits to include, all combine to make the actual task of evaluating a crime prevention program using benefit-cost analysis extremely difficult (p.2).

These complexities led to the estimation of costs and benefits of social factors being characterised as 'a certain analytical migraine' (DiIulio & Piehl 1995 quoted in Chisholm 2000, p.2). This may offer some explanation for why, in addition to the issues relating to the lack of research, evaluation and data collection, cost-benefit analysis is rarely conducted. It would also suggest that cost-benefit analysis is likely to require resources beyond the means of small organisations or local councils.[767]

Translation into monetary terms

A further difficulty relating to the translation of various factors into monetary terms concerns the lack of an objective basis for the valuation of non-economic items. Thus, while cost-benefit analysis is often taken to be a relatively objective method of analysis, being predominately quantitative rather than qualitative, the estimation of cost will often be a subjective exercise. As Sutton, Cherney and White point out, since 'assigning monetary value to costs and benefits can be an inherently subjective undertaking' (2008, p.79), the attribution of value to non-economic items may ultimately undermine claims to objectivity.

The subjective dimension of the estimation of costs and benefits of items may therefore open the analysis to the possibility of manipulation and distortion. For this reason, full transparency would be necessary to demonstrate that estimations were not manipulated to produce a particular cost-benefit. As Chisholm (2000) notes:

> Whilst reliable benefit-cost analysis can be used to determine which programs give the "biggest bang for the buck", it is just as important to be aware of the many hidden dangers that accompany bottom line benefit-cost ratios. To ensure accountability on behalf of those program practitioners who use benefit-cost analysis, it is imperative that the results from any benefit-cost analysis be fully transparent (p.5).

In response to this difficulty, Dossetor has suggested that, in order for cost-benefit analysis to provide a reliable method of assessing and comparing crime prevention programs, items would need to be standardised. As Dossetor explains:

> Moving forward, a need exists for standardising measurement and valuation of benefits to enable comparison of cost-benefit ratios between programs. A standard list of core program benefits (criminal justice costs resulting from recidivism, avoided victimisation costs etc) for certain types of intervention would resolve many of the variations in what is included and excluded for each analysis. Itemising all individual benefits and the dollar value attributed to each benefit, and

---

766 Mr Brendan Thomas, Assistant Director-General, Crime Prevention and Community Programs, NSW Department of Attorney General and Justice, Evidence given to the Drugs and Crime Prevention Committee, Inquiry into Locally Based Approaches to Community Safety and Crime Prevention, Public Hearing, Sydney, 19 September 2011.

767 Submission from Mr Philip Schier, Senior Policy Officer, Victorian Local Governance Association to the Drugs and Crime Prevention Committee, Inquiry into Locally Based Approaches to Community Safety and Crime Prevention, June 2011.

rationale behind these calculations, would allow greater comparison between programs and remove the issue of unsubstantiated final figures (2011, p.42).

A further challenge is that often the benefits of crime prevention programs will not be measurable in the short term. As Chisholm has observed, 'governments and policy makers need to be aware [that]…for certain types of programs, the benefits may be realised beyond their term of office' (2000, p.6). For this reason the cost-benefit of certain programs, particularly those that are developmental and educational, are likely to be vastly different at different stages or times.

An economic 'bottom-line'?

It is important to note that while cost-benefit analysis is useful for measuring crime prevention programs in economic terms, not all benefits or priorities will be amenable to translation into monetary terms. This form of analysis may lend itself to the prioritisation of economic benefit over social or community benefit or social justice. As Aos (2011) has explained, '[b]enefit-cost analyses can help you study policy options for the crime reduction goal, but it is pretty much silent on the justice goal'.

Examples of cost-benefit analysis

Whilst there have been very few crime prevention programs that have undertaken cost-benefit analysis in Australia, there have been some excellent economic evaluations of international programs. For example, describing the economic benefits of crime prevention programs targeting juveniles in the United States, Dossetor (2011) reports considerable economic returns on an intervention project at the Mendota Juvenile Treatment Center (MJTC) in Wisconsin USA and another community-based treatment program in Mississippi. As Dossetor notes, with the juvenile treatment centre in Wisconsin 'for each $1 that was invested in this program, taxpayers received $7.18 in benefits from reduced recidivism' (Dossetor 2011, p.19), while for community based treatment for juveniles in Mississippi '[f]or each $1 that was invested in this program, taxpayers received nearly $2 in short-term benefits from reduced justice system expenditure' (Dossetor 2011, p.21).[768]

The Washington State Institute for Public Policy has also evaluated the costs and benefits of certain juvenile and adult criminal justice policies and violence prevention programs for the Washington State legislature by reviewing over 400 research studies conducted in the United States and Canada (Aos et al 2001). The evaluation found that substantial financial benefit could be made from a number of crime prevention programs, particularly those directed at juveniles and high risk offenders or potential offenders. Aos et al reported that several of these 'high return' programs produced:

> benefit-to-cost ratios that exceed twenty dollars of benefits for each dollar of taxpayer cost. That is, a dollar spent on these programs today can be expected to return to taxpayers and crime victims twenty or more dollars in the years ahead (2001, p.5).

The Committee notes that an example of one of the few cost-benefit analyses that was conducted in Victoria is the 2007–2009 evaluation of the Neighbourhood Justice Centre in the City of Yarra.[769] The Department of Justice 2010 report on the evaluation calculated the 'achieved value for money', by comparing cost and benefit.[770] The report noted that 'there were certainly limitations to the benefit-cost analysis, due mainly to the unavailability of appropriate data' (p.24), highlighting that the lack of research limited the scope of the economic evaluation. The main measures of cost-effectiveness that the evaluators examined were:

768 For discussion of the cost benefit analysis of these programs see Dossetor 2011.
769 http://www.neighbourhoodjustice.vic.gov.au/webdata/resources/files/NJC_evaluation_main_document.pdf   accessed 18 April 2012.
770 The economic evaluation of the Neighbourhood Justice Centre was conducted by Price Waterhouse Coopers, but is reported on by the Department of Justice.

- Changes in re-offending

- Changes in the number of offences and severity of re-offending

- Community Correctional Order completion

- Breaches of intervention orders

- Differences in sentencing outcomes

- Increases in guilty pleas at the first hearing

- Increased community-work hours completed (2010 p.24).

The report states that 'Benefit-cost modelling showed that for every $1 invested in the Neighbourhood Justice Centre (NJC), the expected return would range between $1.09 and $2.23' (p.i).

The need for economic analysis in the future

Despite the difficulty in undertaking cost-benefit analysis, the Australian and New Zealand Crime Prevention Senior Officers' Group 'National Crime Prevention Framework' (2012) points out that '[c]rime prevention can reduce long term costs associated with the criminal justice system and the costs of crime' (p.3). Some programs will obviously deliver greater economic benefits than others. To be able to determine which programs deliver the greatest reduction in costs it is necessary to undertake some form of economic evaluation. Consequently, the *National Crime Prevention Framework* states 'there is...the need to undertake cost benefit analyses as part of evaluations of program outcomes in order to determine the cost effectiveness of crime prevention policies, programs and projects' (2012, p.17). Cost-benefit analysis is a particularly useful form of assessing crime prevention programs, as Dossetor observes, because it 'can assist evaluators in estimating direct and indirect costs, as well as the tangible and intangible costs and benefits of crime prevention programs' (2011, p.43).

However, while cost-benefit analysis may provide useful information on the effectiveness of programs in economic terms, it is premised on the availability of extensive data and, as Sutton, Cherney and White observe, 'requires a high level of technical competency' (2008, p.80) to undertake. For these reasons, the Committee suggests that the CCPU should investigate the most appropriate way to conduct cost-benefit analyses on its major funding initiatives.

Conclusion

The need for evidence based interventions has been widely recognised and accepted by those working in the crime prevention and community safety sectors. It is important that the results of evaluations can be utilised to improve programs and strategies to address crime and community safety. The strategies discussed in this Report and the recommendations made by the Committee are evidence based, grounded in 'joined up thinking' and research and avoid siloed approaches to the issues at hand.

Despite the difficulties in developing and evaluating crime prevention programs outlined in this chapter, a recent evaluation research report on the framework for community based local crime prevention in Western Australia (Morgan & Homel 2011) gives some hope that a model can be devised which helps identify problems that reduce the effectiveness of crime prevention programs. This would then enable strategies to be developed to deliver desired outcomes. The report identifies that evaluating crime prevention initiatives is no easy task and one that is tempting to put in the 'too hard basket' for many smaller and under-funded community agencies. Nonetheless, evaluating programs, establishing an evidence base of 'what works' and jettisoning those programs that make little if no difference to preventing or reducing crime is an essential element of modern and sustainable crime prevention implementation.

Whilst the need for evidenced strategies is clearly important, it may be that on occasion the evidence for promising initiatives is not always strong, at least at the outset. Sometimes it may be important to go with 'promising' approaches and then later evaluate. In other words, sometimes it may be appropriate to 'risk' the implementation of a new strategy even if the evidence for its 'success' is not conclusive prior to such implementation. A certain amount of 'trial and error' may be acceptable in some circumstances. As Cherney states, 'because of its [crime prevention's] very nature it always be difficult if not impossible to provide unequivocal evidence that social prevention [in particular] has been effective in the short term. Crime prevention policies which equate "what works" with being capable of producing unequivocal evidence of short term reductions in crime will often be unable to support [social] prevention' (2007, p.78).

Recommendations

14. **The Committee recommends** that the Community Crime Prevention Unit commission research to compare the crime prevention outcomes of those local government areas that currently have crime prevention and community safety strategy plans or their equivalents with those that do not.

19. **The Committee recommends** that the Victorian Government should establish a set of evaluation priority areas in consultation with key crime prevention stakeholders such as government agencies, academia, local government and community agencies.

20. The Committee acknowledges on the basis of the available evidence that crime prevention and community safety initiatives are rarely subject to rigorous evaluation. **The Committee therefore recommends** that there is a need for the Community Crime Prevention Unit to ensure state-wide evidence based research, access to evaluation of programs and best practice modelling is provided or made available to councils in order to deliver effective crime prevention and community safety programs.

21. **The Committee recommends** that the Community Crime Prevention Unit requires recipients of small grants such as Community Safety Fund Grants to report to the Unit on performance measurements and outcomes against the initial aims of the program.

22. **The Committee recommends** that the Community Crime Prevention Unit reserve specific funding within their total crime prevention program to fund external evaluation of 'clusters' of projects that are identified as being of particular importance.

23. **The Committee recommends** that the Community Crime Prevention Unit select for evaluation individual projects or initiatives that appear innovative but for which there is no evidence base currently to support their worth. Such an evaluation would assess their effectiveness in achieving desired outcomes and identify the practical challenges and lessons for implementing similar projects.

Recommendations

24. **The Committee recommends** that the Victorian Government establish an independent crime research, statistics and data collection/analysis agency to assist local government, police and community agencies with the provision of data and evidence to inform the development and implementation of crime prevention programs and initiatives. The Bureau of Crime Statistics and Research in New South Wales may serve as a useful example.

28. **The Committee recommends** that as a requirement for obtaining a crime prevention grant, councils, shires and local community organisations be required to demonstrate to the Community Crime Prevention Unit that the initiative for which they are seeking funding addresses an identified problem in the community and falls within a priority of the local crime prevention and community safety strategy. Such evidence could be provided through the local crime prevention audit/needs analysis and/or by accessing police statistics, research and other intelligence data.

12. Future Directions for Crime Prevention in Victoria

Introduction

As the influential criminologist Stanley Cohen has noted, the history of crime prevention is 'replete with good intentions gone wrong and of hope turned to despair' (1996, p.10). Certainly many crime prevention models and programs have started off promisingly only to collapse under the weight of their own expectations. The Crime Prevention Partnerships model in the United Kingdom (UK) is one such example. And whilst there have been successes such as the partnerships approach developed in Western Australia, it is not too far from the truth to state that 'Crime prevention initiatives come and go, as do the ideas and philosophies that inform them' (Watts, Bessant & Hil 2008, p.166). Such at least has been the up and down experience of crime prevention in Victoria.

Notwithstanding the arguably erratic nature of crime prevention policy and initiatives the Committee does acknowledge that there have been some notable achievements in developing and implementing crime prevention and community safety programs in Victoria. Many of these successful interventions have been driven at least in part by local government and community agencies. It is a credit to these organisations that they have been successful even where their local programs are underfunded and understaffed. The point remains however that these approaches are often piecemeal and uncoordinated not led by or emanating from a comprehensive overall crime prevention and community safety strategy at either state or municipal level. A central and integrated state crime prevention and community safety strategy is therefore required.

The Committee hopes that the findings of this Inquiry and the recommendations for enhancing the current crime prevention model will help to forge a sustainable approach to community safety that breaks this cyclical process. This concluding chapter sums up the key findings of the Committee based on academic research and the evidence from experts, representatives of government and non-government organisations and members of the community. In particular, it looks at 'what works' in delivering effective crime prevention and community safety for local communities. First, however, in order to put these findings in perspective it is necessary to reiterate the principles and evidence indicators that have informed the Committee's recommendations for this Inquiry.

Principles and evidence informing the recommendations

The following principles based on the evidence received underlie and support the Committee's recommendations which are detailed in the Executive Summary and discussed throughout this Report.

Principles informing the recommendations

1. In addressing crime prevention and community safety evidence based strategies are essential

   There is now general agreement in both the national and international literature as to what is the most effective range of responses available to policy-makers to address crime prevention and community safety. The indicators of best practice crime prevention interventions are listed in the 'what works' section below.

2. A 'one size fits all' approach to crime prevention and community safety does not address the specific issues, needs and requirements of individual local communities

3. Crime prevention is more effective when investing in health and education rather than just law enforcement/justice measures

   According to the ICPC all available crime statistics internationally show that a reactive and purely law enforcement/security model to address crime has not worked. 'State investment in harsher penal laws, new prison construction and the expansion of police forces have had limited impact on reducing violence and have signally failed to discourage new crimes or to improve the population's sense of security' (ICPC 2011, p.21).

4. Community capacity building and social capital as outlined in this Report are essential and integral aspects of addressing crime prevention and community safety issues in contemporary society

5. Effective crime prevention and community safety interventions require:

   ◆ A belief that crime prevention is important in and of itself

   Crime prevention work needs to be valued for its own sake and not as an 'optional extra'. This is particularly true with regard to the role of police. Crime prevention should be considered an integral part of policing and police officers who work in the area of crime prevention should be highly valued within the organisation.

   ◆ An understanding of the causes and contributory factors leading to crime and antisocial behaviour

   ◆ Clear goals and vision that are directly linked to proposed strategies

   ◆ A unified service delivery model. Crime prevention and community safety interventions are less effective when agencies and departments work in isolation from each other (silos)

   ◆ An applied commitment to evidence based practice research, evaluation, and performance measurement supported by up-to-date data

   ◆ A commitment to plan for the 'long haul'

   Crime prevention and community safety strategies and programs need to transcend the imperatives of short-term expediency, for example the electoral cycle.

   ◆ The empowerment and participation of local communities in decision making

   It is important to factor in the issues that communities have already identified as important to them, rather than prescribing what issues communities have to address.

6. There is value and long-term benefit in taking a holistic community development approach to crime prevention and community safety

   Such an approach includes the participation of all levels of government, non-government agencies, the private sector and local communities and their representatives.

7. Victoria Police have the primary responsibility for law enforcement in this state. They also play a key role in crime prevention.

8. Effective crime prevention requires police to take a proactive community focused approach in addition to reactive policing

9. Research suggests that local government authorities (LGAs) are best placed to understand and reflect the particular needs and problems of their local community. As such they are best placed to generate and deliver the most appropriate prevention interventions for their local communities

   The emphasis on the role of local governments in crime prevention is strongly encouraged by international and national organisations such as the United Nations Office on Drugs and Crime and UN-HABITAT and the Australian Institute of Criminology (AIC). Indeed, the AIC's research has pointed to a number of reasons as to why local government is such an important player in community crime prevention.[771] For example, as Shaw has stated: 'Across Australia virtually all government crime prevention agencies include local government in the development and delivery of their respective crime prevention strategies' (AIC 2004, p.1). This is largely due to the fact that most crime of immediate concern to communities is local (e.g. property crime, antisocial behaviour, vandalism etc.). It clearly follows then that the primary focus for preventive action should also be local.

The recommendations are also supported by a list of best evidence indicators of 'what works' in delivering successful crime prevention and community safety interventions.

Best practice/evidence indicators of 'what works'

In developing effective crime prevention and community safety interventions the Committee recognises that there are a set of recognised and proven best evidence indicators that should be the basis for any recommendations pertaining to this Inquiry. In particular, effective crime prevention and community safety requires:

1. A practical grasp of crime prevention theory

2. Strong and consistent leadership and supportive governance structures

3. A capacity to manage collaborative multi-agency actions

4. The engagement of key stakeholders at the local level

5. Outcome focused performance measurement systems

6. Effective communication processes designed to promote engagement and sustainability

7. The gathering and dissemination of police intelligence

8. A mixture of crime prevention approaches including situational/environmental and social crime prevention

   Crime prevention should have a broad focus and includes the prevention of antisocial and threatening behaviours which may not constitute a crime but which undermine community safety and social inclusion. Crime prevention and community safety for example can be promoted

---

771 See discussion in Chapters 3 and 7

through the use of community renewal and revitalisation and capacity building projects. Crime prevention should not be restricted to a law enforcement agenda only.

Crime Prevention Through Environmental Design (CPTED) and other situational crime prevention measures such as CCTV camera systems are commonly one element of broader crime prevention strategies. The Committee recommends that it is important to combine situational crime prevention measures with other longer-term community strengthening activities that empower the community to take action.

9. Strategies need to be coordinated and integrated

It is essential that where strategies are developed and implemented to address crime prevention policy they are wherever possible part of an integrated policy framework and a 'whole of government approach'.

10. A mixture of long- and short-term initiatives

11. Consideration of the changing demographics of the local community

Vast population growth (actual and projected) creates pressures on existing services and infrastructure. Additional to this increase in numbers, consideration needs to be given to the changing demographics of the community i.e. increase in first home buyers and increase in youth populations, increase in CALD communities and an ageing population. These changes will also mean that further consideration will need to be given to the way in which crime prevention and community safety programs are developed and implemented and targeted to these new communities.

12. A problem solving approach drawn from systematic research, analysis and review as to what the actual problems are in any given community

13. Effective partnerships and good governance models

Successful partnerships are extremely important in developing best practice crime prevention models. The elements that need to be present in successful partnerships include:

1. commitment

2. equity

3. trust

4. mutual goals/objectives

5. collaboration over implementation

6. continuous evaluation

7. timely communication and responsiveness.

14. Community engagement and input

15. Monitoring and evaluation

16. Only strategies and programs that have been demonstrated to be effective should be continued.

Key positions of the Drugs and Crime Prevention Committee on crime prevention and community safety

The following discussion draws on some of the key principles and evidence indicators outlined above and expands the discussion as to why they are such important aspects of an overall approach to good crime prevention and community safety models.

Being clear about definitions and concepts

The Committee throughout this Report has found it is essential to use an all-embracing and inclusive definition of what is meant by 'crime prevention'.

The Committee agrees that whilst there is a definite place for criminal justice initiatives such as arrest and imprisonment to deter and reduce offending, the concept of crime prevention cannot be narrowly circumscribed to traditional law and order approaches only. Community safety and community engagement are key aspects of any crime prevention agenda.[772]

Similarly, crime prevention should not be restricted to one particular approach. Crime prevention strategies based on social developmental, situational and environmental models and approaches are required. As discussed at length in this Report it is equally important to incorporate the concepts of community engagement, social capital and community capacity building into crime prevention policy and program implementation.[773]

The importance of local government

Local government is increasingly having a role as a key player in the development and implementation of community crime prevention programs, as has been discussed throughout this Report. As Shaw has stated: 'Across Australia virtually all government crime prevention agencies include local government in the development and delivery of their respective crime prevention strategies' (2004, p.1). This may be through a legislative mandate as in New South Wales or through comprehensive partnership agreements as in Western Australia.

Local government, however, is very well placed to lead and deliver community crime prevention programs. The AIC has given a number of reasons as to why this is the case:

- Research shows that a great deal of crime is very local in nature (e.g. domestic burglary, anti-social behaviour, and certain forms of violence). There is also growing evidence about the effectiveness of locally organised crime prevention action (e.g. burglary reduction programs in the UK, responses to disorder at major events in different parts of Australia, and local gun control initiatives in the USA).

- Local government is frequently well placed to coordinate and manage crime prevention responses across the community. For example, local government often has existing community consultative mechanisms that can easily be utilised in the problem solving process, which is so important for effective crime prevention action.

- There is an increasing community expectation that local government will assume some level of responsibility for initiating or directing action for crime issues that are seen to be affecting local amenity and quality of life. In this sense, the local authority is the level of democratic process closest to, and reflective of, the needs of communities.

- Local government frequently has the most appropriate management infrastructure and skill base for delivering the multi-agency programs that are often required. Typical services provided by local government that may be relevant to the crime prevention process include: environmental design; land use and zoning (including the establishment of alcohol free zones); waste management; provision of street lighting; public events management; local human services; and community recreational services (AIC 2004, p.1).

---

772 For a detailed discussion see Chapter 2
773 See discussion in Chapter 3.

Yet it is equally true as the AIC points out that not all all LGAs will have an equal capacity to provide a leadership and a coordination role. Nonetheless, the evidence to this Inquiry has shown that there is certainly a wish in local government circles to have greater involvement in the development of community safety initiatives for their local communities. Certainly, as most crime of immediate concern to communities is local (e.g. property crime, antisocial behaviour, vandalism etc.) then the primary focus for preventive action should also be local.

These considerations highlight the need for a central government coordinating unit as recommended by this Committee to complement the role of local government in the crime prevention partnership 'by assisting and supporting local government through the provision of appropriate and adequate technical support and other resources such as funding, skills development, access to necessary research and data, and policy guidance' (AIC 2004, p.1).

Victoria Police and crime prevention

Another important stakeholder in the field of crime prevention and community safety is of course the Victoria Police. Indeed as acknowledged in this Report, Victoria Police have the primary responsibility for law enforcement in this state. As such they play a key role in crime prevention. This role however has extended well beyond traditional approaches to law enforcement and criminal justice. Effective crime prevention requires police to take a proactive community focused approach in addition to reactive policing.

Increasingly therefore the police are expected to be involved in approaches to crime prevention that are based in a community safety and community capacity building role. In many cases this will be in partnership with local government and other community agencies. Given the importance of the police role with regard to crime prevention the Committee has made a recommendation to ensure that training can equip the police to perform these important functions.

The need for good governance and partnerships

The Committee has found the need for crime prevention to be a shared responsibility between governments and civil society. The new National Crime Prevention Framework states in this regard:

> In Australia, contemporary crime prevention has generally embraced the value of partnerships, collaborative policy development and program delivery, in recognition that the causes of crime are wide ranging, complex and frequently require a coordinated response.[774]

Central to good governance in successful crime prevention partnerships is the development of:

- appropriate mechanisms for promoting and steering a whole of government approach to the prevention of crime, and ensuring that key stakeholders are involved in crime prevention planning at all levels;
- forums for bringing together government, non-government, communities and businesses that promote open communication and allow all partners to contribute;
- clearly defined roles and responsibilities for these stakeholders;
- a shared goal and common purpose, and an understanding of how each partner contributes to this goal;
- partnerships for the delivery of integrated solutions, comprising closely linked and coordinated interventions that can achieve shared outcomes;
- an understanding and acceptance of the different interests, philosophies and contexts in which each partner works;

---

774 http://www.aic.gov.au/crime_community/crimeprevention/ncpf.aspx. See also the discussion in Chapter 3.

- clear lines of accountability for the partnership, both to each other and their respective organisation;

- a joint framework for performance measuring and reporting, with an agreed understanding of what constitutes success; and

- clear benefits to the partnership that are evident to all those involved.[775]

However, as discussed in the context of the UK experience, these elements of a good working partnership can sometimes be more aspirational than real. It is essential in taking a 'whole of government approach' that local crime prevention governance, including the use of partnerships, is flexible and avoids a 'one size fits all' approach. Unfortunately this has not always been the case with regard to some of the crime prevention models implemented in other jurisdictions, such as in the UK.[776]

One aspect of crime prevention partnerships that has been to some extent overlooked in Australia are collaborations between the private and government sectors in developing and implementing crime prevention and community safety initiatives. Whilst this Report has not to any great extent examined crime prevention partnerships involving the private sector, with both small business and larger corporations, the emergence of these partnerships appear to be a growing trend. The Committee believes on this basis it is important that the government review private partnerships as one aspect of addressing crime prevention in this state, bearing in mind of course that the public sector will bear the main responsibility for crime prevention and community safety.

The importance of strong leadership

An essential aspect in the development and implementation of good crime prevention policy and program delivery is strong and consistent leadership. This is particularly true in systems which have central and/or regional structures guiding local service delivery. One of the key principles of good governance developed by the United Nations has been the need for strategic vision by leaders entrusted with the responsibility of developing and implementing crime prevention policy:

> Leaders [should]...have a broad and long term perspective on good governance and human development along with a sense of what is needed for such development. [Leaders should also] have an understanding of the historical, cultural and social complexities in which that perspective is grounded (United Nations Development Program in Edgar, Marshall & Bassett 2006, p.2).

Leadership and the promotion of this 'vision' should result in all partners in the crime prevention 'enterprise' having a clear and well defined understanding of the purpose and goals of the partnership with each participant being aware of the ways in which they can best contribute and be accountable (Edgar, Marshall & Bassett 2006, p.10). This is particularly important in cases where ultimate direction or leadership may emanate from a central authority.

In such cases a somewhat contradictory or at least multifaceted approach is needed.

First, central management needs to be well resourced and equipped to give positive direction to the regions and local organisations:

> This means the centre itself must be appropriately staffed and adequately resourced if it is to contribute positively to the delivery process...In particular the centre [and the regions] need to be capable of providing well supported strategic guidance and technical assistance to local services that are both flexible and responsive to local needs and capable of learning from successful innovations (Homel et al 2004, pp 5,6).

A Home Office review of British crime prevention partnerships in 2011 found that effective leadership for making crime prevention partnerships work required:

---

775   http://www.aic.gov.au/crime_community/crimeprevention/ncpf.aspx. See also the discussion in Chapter 3.
776   See discussion in Chapter 3.

- Shared vision, values and norms of partners involved to establish a collaborative advantage
- Full integration of project aims into partner organisation aims
- Clear project brief, roles and responsibilities
- Core groups to oversee a problem solving approach; and
- Strong leadership and strategic direction (focused on providing a central coordination effort, getting buy in from partners and managing the project (Berry et al 2011, piii).

This strong central direction is particularly important in those cases where local government authorities may not have an equal capacity to provide a leadership and coordination role, for example in smaller or more remote rural and regional areas (AIC 2004, p.1).

The second and arguably contradictory aspect of good leadership is that local governments (and community organisations) be not unnecessarily fettered in their management of local crime prevention policy and program implementation. As was stated in the context of the United Kingdom Crime Partnerships model:

> Successful delivery of the Government's vision cannot be imposed simply through top-down performance management and the strategy is therefore to develop a criminal justice operating framework that provides local services with greater flexibility to determine how this vision is to be delivered effectively and efficiently (HM Treasury 2007 in Solomon 2009, p.59).

Such an approach reflects the principle of subsidiarity underlying the management of good crime prevention policy. That is, whilst crime prevention activity may take place at many levels (international, national, state, regional and local):

> [t]he division of tasks and structures [should be] structured in accordance with the subsidiarity principle, meaning that the investment of authority with ensuing resources and responsibilities is at the local (municipal or town) level (Homel 2009b, p.26).

Certainly, one of the key problems identified in the failure of Victoria's 'Safer Cities and Shires' program during the late 1990s was the lack of consistent leadership and:

> An unwillingness to devolve resources, authority and decision making powers to the local inter agency partnerships responsible for actually implementing the local level initiatives (Homel 2009b, p.28).[777]

Conversely, as discussed in Chapter 3, the crime prevention partnerships program developed by the Western Australian Office of Crime Prevention in conjunction with the AIC shows that:

> [w]hile problems are very likely to recur when a centrally driven initiative seeks to promote local delivery, a process of continuous engagement and effective two way communication can overcome the worst of these difficulties (Anderson & Tressider 2008 in Homel 2009b, p.29).

Strong leadership in crime prevention therefore requires both consistent and robust direction from the centre that guides, assists and supports local organisations yet at the same time does not unduly restrict their ability to manage or lead at a local level.

Finally, a hallmark of good leadership according to Homel is consistency, that is those responsible for developing and/or implementing crime prevention policy, particularly those in positions of central authority, do not continually 'chop and change' crime prevention direction due to political or other imperatives not based on a good evidence base:

> The enemy of good leadership and good governance structures is a tendency for governments to continually reorganise the manner in which crime prevention work is delivered. While it is important to review and refresh crime prevention practice in order to ensure that it is based on

---

777   For a critical discussion of the *Safer Cities and Shires* program and the problems associated with its delivery see Cherney 2004.

the best available evidence and is as effective and efficient as possible, change also requires time to achieve its maximum impact (Homel 2009b, p.33).

Research and evaluation

One question that is often asked is whether 'crime prevention' is effective. Very little comprehensive research has been done to satisfactorily address this issue although it is understandable that such concerns are at the forefront of those responsible for resource allocation and budget priorities. There are clearly great challenges in researching the 'effectiveness' of crime prevention, not least of which is measuring what counts for 'success' in any given program. For example, whilst a program such as Neighbourhood Watch may be effective in reducing the level of crime recorded in a particular local neighbourhood, it is also possible that crime levels may rise in a neighbouring district that does not have the program – the effect criminologists call 'displacement of crime'. Similarly, a program developed to provide young people with meaningful employment or leisure opportunities may result in no or minimal drop in juvenile crime rates, however it may contribute significantly to the overall health or wellbeing of the young people subject to the intervention. Can such a program be therefore counted as a success?

Despite these and other difficulties in quantifying what counts as a successful outcome, a recent evaluation research report on the framework for community based local crime prevention in Western Australia (Morgan & Homel 2011) gives some hope that a model can be devised which helps identify problems that may impact on the effectiveness of crime prevention programs and subsequently enable strategies to be developed to deliver desired outcomes.

Crime prevention programs, it is generally agreed, should be subject to rigorous evaluation. The importance of evaluation, monitoring and performance measurement as key features of effective crime prevention has been stressed in the recently developed National Crime Prevention Framework. However, too often evaluation is viewed as an expensive diversion from the 'main game' of delivering crime prevention services. This may be particularly the case for under-funded community and local government agencies.

For example, evidence has been given to the Committee that local government access to data has often been through networking with key agencies such as Victoria Police and others represented on crime prevention partnerships. A large percentage of crime prevention projects have arisen out of a spontaneous recognition that there is a crime problem, where potentially more methodical problem identification might reveal a different picture of the 'real crime problem' in an area. As a result, measures to reduce crime and fear of crime can often be chosen on insufficient analysis of the problem, which can affect their level of success.

This Report has discussed that evaluation funding needs to be carefully targeted given the expense involved. In many individual cases, due to the type of intervention being implemented and the budget available for the project, a formal or high level evaluation may not be warranted. This may particularly be so in cases where the recipient agency has not received a separate or dedicated budgetary allocation for evaluation. Rather, it may be more effective to conduct sophisticated evaluation of classes or clusters of programs or projects (for example, youth justice or domestic violence programs). The findings, including 'lessons learned' or 'what works', could then be analysed and made available for crime prevention officers, policy-makers and project managers.

Evaluation and measurement should wherever possible also be based on local analysis, local needs and local participation. This does not necessarily exclude the establishment of a central or state coordinating mechanism, such agencies and units have been utilised in past years and indeed this Committee has recommended the establishment of a centre in Victoria similar to that of the Bureau of Crime Statistics and Research (BOCSAR) in New South Wales. But ultimately many criminologists and policy-makers view the basis of successful crime prevention as being building positive community relationships guided by comprehensive planning, inclusive coordination and most of all strategic vision. Whether current crime prevention approaches and initiatives meet these aims is open to question.

Training, education and communication

Effective crime prevention models require knowledgeable planning and implementation, which in turn is contingent upon an expert and knowledgeable workforce in the area of crime prevention. As Morgan and Homel state, however, too often in Australia and overseas crime prevention measures have been made less effective by players having:

- a poor understanding of crime prevention theory and techniques;

- the absence of a skilled and professional crime prevention workforce;

- inadequate project and program management ability; and

- the lack of knowledge and experience with performance measurement and program evaluation (Homel 2008 in Morgan & Homel 2011, p.29).[778]

Similarly, Cherney and Sutton (2007) have stated that many attempts to implement local crime prevention plans and programs have failed because of a dearth of local staff with relevant experience.[779]

The Committee acknowledges the need for initial and ongoing professional development and training for local crime prevention and community safety officers, members of community safety and crime prevention committees and police. The Committee also acknowledges the financial cost involved for councils, shires and local community organisations across the state in developing their own training packages. It believes therefore that the responsibility for funding such training be primarily with the Community Crime Prevention Unit (CCPU).

Good crime prevention and community safety interventions require clear and unambiguous communication of their aims, content and goals. However given the wide range of government and community agencies involved in developing and implementing crime prevention programs there is always the risk that uncertainty can arise as to who may be responsible for any given area or program. For example, it has come to the attention of the Committee that some members of the public may be confused as to what they should do in cases where they observe criminal or anti social conduct occurring or suspect it may have occurred. This confusion is partly due to a range of agencies being associated with the reporting of such activity; for example Neighbourhood Watch, Crime Stoppers and Victoria Police itself. Therefore members of the general public need to receive unambiguous messages as to what they should do in cases where they have observed or been aware of criminal or antisocial activity.

Moreover, increasingly new technologies and social media are being used to communicate information about government and non government programs in the field of social policy and community engagement. This is a resource that could readily be utilised in the promotion of crime prevention and community safety. As discussed in Chapter 9 social media such as Facebook has already been used quite extensively by Neighbourhood Watch in England and is starting to be incorporated into the activities of Neighbourhood Watch in this country. The Committee acknowledges the benefit of using these new technologies as one means of communicating crime prevention messages to the community. Accordingly it recommended that the Community Crime Prevention Unit investigate the use of social media in communicating and promoting its activities to various sectors of the community.

---

778 For the importance of evaluation in the context of crime prevention, see Chapter 11.
779 See discussion in Chapter 8.

Funding

While local initiatives addressing crime prevention and community safety are extremely important, the state and even the Commonwealth government do have an important coordinating and funding role in service delivery, depending on their particular areas of policy responsibility. In particular, the Committee supports submissions made by a variety of LGAs to this Inquiry that additional resources are needed for community safety services. With regard to LGAs and local level approaches, a common refrain heard by the Committee is that local government and their agencies are increasingly expected to provide education, social services and programs with regard to crime prevention and community safety but are not provided with appropriate infrastructure, staffing and funding levels. Moreover, long-term planning is difficult when agencies are funded for a limited period of time with no guarantee of continued funding.[780]

Inadequate funding can be particularly a problem for smaller and rural and regional councils. Sufficient funding is crucial to ensure that agencies have appropriately trained workers to address the complex issues pertaining to crime prevention and community safety.

While the Committee realises that the costs associated with community safety programs and policy initiatives can be expensive, it believes in the long run such an approach will be cost-effective not only because it may reduce crime and antisocial behaviour but also because it promotes positive social development and community capacity building. As such the Committee recommends that ongoing grants be provided for community crime prevention and safety initiatives, particularly those involving partnerships. These grants should be awarded to initiatives that fulfil the objectives of the Victorian Crime Prevention and Community Safety Framework.

The way forward – Getting the structure right

The Committee acknowledges that the Victorian government has done much in the last year to put crime prevention 'on the map'. Not the least of which has been the formation of a specialised CCPU, Regional Reference Groups, and the establishment of specialist community crime prevention grants programs.

The Committee on the basis of the evidence, however, believes that while it may be useful to have some aspects of service delivery organised at a regional level, further emphasis and attention should be paid to the important role of local government in developing and implementing crime prevention and community safety services.

As such the Committee recommends that the structure for policy development and program implementation should be one that places more emphasis on the role of local councils and community agencies and the utilisation of good governance principles.

An enhanced model

Effective crime prevention requires a high degree of coordination and efficiency with regard to the delivery of crime prevention and community safety initiatives in Victoria. The Committee has made recommendations to the overall structure of Community Crime Prevention governance which will allow for greater local level and community collaboration as well as more easily facilitating input from experts. It will also provide for greater coordination across government. The proposed new developments are set out in diagrammatic form as Figure 12.1: The existing structures are indicated in blue and the additional structures are in orange.

---

780 See discussion in Chapter 8.

Figure 12.1: Suggested crime prevention structures

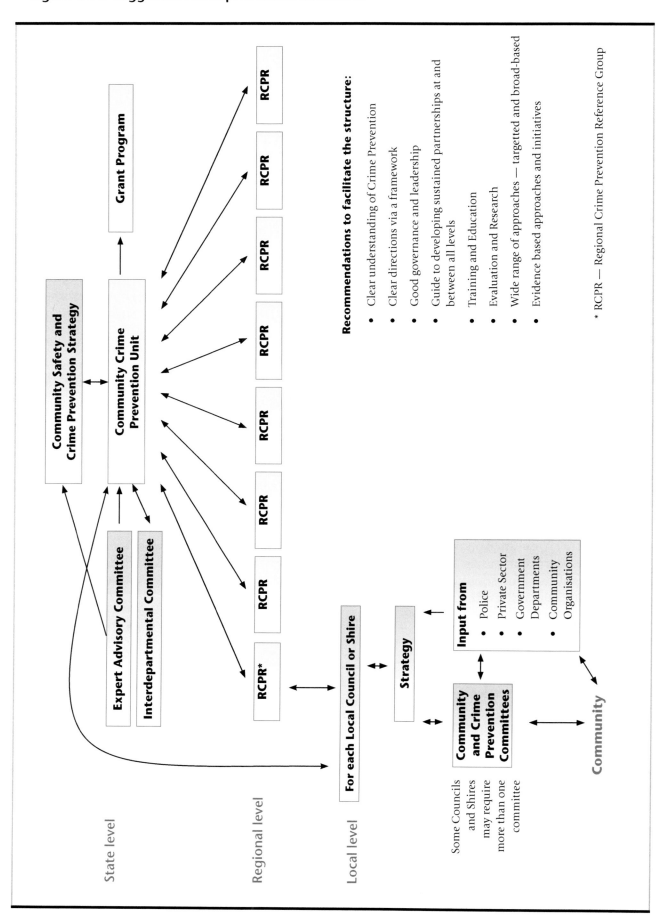

The Community Crime Prevention Unit (CCPU)

Effective crime prevention requires a high degree of coordination and efficiency with regard to the delivery of community safety and crime prevention initiatives in Victoria. The Committee considers the recent introduction of the CCPU to be an important first step in this direction.

The CCPU should be responsible for a wide range of tasks and duties that are indicated in the recommendations set out in the Executive Summary and are repeated below. These are:

- the development and publication of a Victorian crime prevention and community safety framework including a community engagement strategy to indicate how the public, community organisations and the private sector can have ongoing input into crime prevention and community safety policy;

- liaising with federal and state agencies, professionals in the field, community agencies and media;

- disseminating information with regard to crime prevention and community safety;

- developing and coordinating training programs on crime prevention and community safety;

- developing and coordinating a research agenda and the commissioning of crime prevention research;

- assessing and providing funding for programs, research and evaluation relating to crime prevention and community safety;

- ongoing responsibility for evaluating programs that are funded;

- developing a protocol in liaison with media representatives on the reporting of crime prevention and community safety issues;

- liaising with and supporting local government and community agencies to develop Local Community Crime Prevention Strategies;

- identifying available resources and gaps in service delivery in order to plan a response to crime prevention and community safety at both state and local levels;

- identifying key personnel and agencies in the community who have expertise in dealing with crime prevention and community safety in order to establish a comprehensive referral and resource network;

- implementing a mapping exercise and audit to establish the current levels of services available; and

- identifying best practice initiatives and assessing their applicability to local communities.

In addition to the roles detailed above the Committee believes it is essential that the CCPU plays an important role as a specialist resource to provide technical support, training and assistance to enhance the capacity and effectiveness of local crime prevention action. The objective would be to improve and enhance the capacity and effectiveness of those involved in the design, delivery and assessment of critical crime reduction and prevention initiatives that impact directly (or indirectly) on the safety and wellbeing of the community. This can be achieved by synthesising and disseminating best practice approaches to crime prevention and crime reduction, and through developing and providing training in effective methods for evaluating programs and/or measuring program outcomes. The CCPU would direct this assistance to three particular groups:

◆ those responsible for the direct implementation and delivery of crime reduction and prevention activities, including law enforcement agencies, the broader criminal justice sector, state and local government agencies, and the business, non-government and community sectors;

◆ those responsible for the development, design and management of crime reduction and prevention strategies, policies and programs at the level above direct delivery. These groups include policy-makers and senior managers in law enforcement and the wider criminal justice sector, as well human services; and

◆ government and non-government agencies and professionals from other sectors whose work has a significant impact on reducing the risk of crime, or the precursors of criminal behaviour (education, human services, health, early childhood sector).

One of the most important of these tasks is the development and implementation of a Crime Prevention and Community Safety Framework as it sets the direction for crime prevention in Victoria.

A Victorian Crime Prevention and Community Safety Framework

The CCPU should, as a priority, formally develop a new Crime Prevention and Community Safety Framework for Victoria as the means for coordinating Government action in the area. Throughout this Report the need for a coordinated response to crime prevention has been identified as one important measure of good governance.

A comprehensive crime prevention strategy for Victoria clearly needs to be one that is suitable for and addresses local needs and issues in this state. Notwithstanding this, state approaches to crime prevention can and are influenced by developments at the federal level. A key initiative in the last year has been a greater role for the Commonwealth in crime prevention and community safety. In particular, the Australian government through the Australia and New Zealand Crime Prevention Senior Officers' Group (ANZCPSOG) recently commissioned the Australian Institute of Criminology to develop a new National Crime Prevention Framework as a resource which canvasses the most effective best practice approaches to the prevention and reduction of crime. It also outlines the possible roles and functions for state/territory and governments for the effective delivery of crime prevention throughout Australia.

The Committee believes that in developing a Crime Prevention and Community Safety Framework for Victoria the CCPU should where applicable draw from its federal counterpart. In particular it should pay close attention to the best practice guidelines the Commonwealth has provided to assist with the development of appropriate policies, strategies and programs to address crime problems. Bearing in mind of course that at all times any such policies or programs must be applicable to Victorian circumstances and in the best interest of all Victorians.

In developing the Framework appropriate for Victoria the Government should ensure it consults with relevant partners in community crime prevention such as local government, police and non-government organisation representatives. The Framework should set out clear goals, aims and objectives of and directions for crime prevention in this state and the optimal ways to achieve them.

Any proposed framework to address crime prevention also needs to incorporate the principles of 'good governance' discussed earlier in this chapter. Good governance is more than just 'government' or public administration, it is also about finding 'effective ways of continuously engaging various sectors of society. Governance is therefore closely aligned with democracy and the central role that citizens must play in any effective governance system' (Edgar, Marshall & Bassett 2006, p.1).[781]

---

781   See also discussion in Chapter 3.

While clearly 'macro' policies that operate at a national or state level are extremely important, it is often at the micro or community level that the most effective crime prevention occurs. It is therefore essential to provide a framework that operates at many levels: the local and the global, the targeted and the general.

The establishment of a Crime Prevention and Community Safety Advisory Group

It is the Committee's view based on the evidence that it has received and the current research available that community input into the development of crime prevention policy in Victoria is essential. The Committee recommends, therefore, that a Crime Prevention and Community Safety Advisory Group should be established and supported by the CCPU. Such a Committee should comprise of experts in the field and government and non-government representatives with relevant expertise in the area of crime prevention. Without restricting the membership of such a group, it is advisable that representatives be drawn from research institutes and key community agencies, private sector organisations and local government peak bodies. In addition, representatives from state and local government departments and agencies such as Victoria Police should also be included.

Interdepartmental Crime Prevention Working Group

Since the causes of crime are diverse and broad, crime prevention initiatives have been expanded across a wide range of government departments to include measures aimed at addressing both the social and economic determinants of crime. Whilst the Committee has not been able to ascertain the full extent of crime prevention and community safety initiatives operated by Victorian government departments, suffice to say a wide range of programs do exist that directly address crime prevention. In addition, there are many initiatives that often are developed which have impacts on community safety and crime prevention but are not necessarily conceptualised as such. Youth engagement or child welfare programs located in Health or Education Departments are key examples.

Clearly there is a need for an all-of-government approach to crime prevention. However, without adequate coordination and organisation such an approach can be fragmented, inefficient and counter-productive, rather than one which strengthens the overall crime prevention capacity of government. Even where departments are not working directly on crime prevention, their activities may result in a negative impact on crime prevention. Changes to areas like transport, environment and education, for example, are likely to have an impact on crime. As Professor Peter Homel discussed in the context of the Western Australian review of government crime prevention initiatives:[782]

> Government agencies work in a disconnected insular way, which means that some of the measures that they implement may be crime promoting rather than preventing when seen from the perspectives of other agencies.[783]

The establishment of an interdepartmental working party for crime prevention would help address these issues and work against a siloed approach to crime prevention. Moreover, given that crime prevention policy is located in a department in which criminal justice enforcement and management is also a responsibility, the influence of an interdepartmental working party would also prevent crime prevention from becoming dominated by an enforcement agenda (Solomon 2009, p.57).

---

782 See, for example, Anderson and Tresidder 2008, *A review of the Western Australian Community Safety and Crime Prevention Partnership Planning process: Final report*, AIC, Canberra.

783 Correspondence from Professor Peter Homel, Australian Institute of Criminology to the Drugs and Crime Prevention Committee, 28 May 2012.

The role of the Regional Reference Groups

The Committee acknowledges the work of the CCPU in establishing regional reference groups in Victoria. Clearly these groups could have a significant role to play in supporting the work of the CCPU and in particular facilitating access to necessary data and other information for crime prevention planning, implementation and review.

However, the Committee is cognisant of the experience of the UK and other places where regions have taken a lead role in developing and implementing crime prevention policy to the exclusion of local communities who have not been included in the management process. This has occurred particularly where:

> ...regional systems have been artificially overlaid on localities that have no organic or historical connection; the efficiency advantages that may flow from a more natural structure can be lost as the primary regional management task becomes the management of what is often historically derived competition or rivalry between groups and localities (2005, p.2).

As Homel has explained, 'joining up the efforts of central agencies and local authorities and communities is also extremely important if the benefits of crime reduction and prevention efforts are to be maximised (2005, p.1).

Making it work at the local level

As has been discussed throughout the report local government authorities are best placed to implement crime prevention policy at the local level. Local government has the potential infrastructure and consultative mechanisms in place along with relationships with community partners to implement such initiatives. The Committee has also found that where local government authorities in Victoria are already involved in a range of community crime prevention initiatives and are willing to take on this work, they are concerned about the additional work load created without commensurate funding.

The Committee therefore believes that if crime prevention is to be bolstered at the local level more need to be done to formalise the structure of governance and the support given to LGAs and local communities.

At the local level the Committee recommends that each council or shire should develop a Crime Prevention and Community Safety Strategy. This strategy would be based on the Victorian Government Strategy and definitions of crime prevention and community safety that are contained therein. However this local strategy would be tailored to meet the needs of the local community. In making this recommendation the Committee acknowledges that there are some councils that already have a crime prevention strategy in place.

Each LGA should also form at least one community crime prevention committee that would draw upon local community input and expertise via membership on the committee of representatives from Victoria Police and relevant government and non-government agencies. The Committee acknowledges that within many local government areas there are various demographic areas with particular concerns which might necessitate additional crime prevention.

As constantly advocated throughout this report the Committee believes that a partnership approach be developed between central, regional and local policy-makers and practitioners.

Supporting the structure

For the management and delivery of crime prevention to be effective at all levels, local regional and central, the Committee has made a range of recommendations for what is required to support the enhanced structure detailed above. In particular to make this model work effectively recommendations have been made with regard to:

+ Understanding the concept, theory and various approaches pertaining to crime prevention

+ The importance of evidence based approaches and initiatives

+ Good governance and leadership

+ The need for entering into sustainable partnerships

+ Education, communication and training needs

+ Evaluation and research.

Each of these recommendations and the context from which they emanate has been thoroughly discussed in the Executive Summary and in relevant chapters throughout this Report.

Lessons from the British experience

In developing crime prevention policy in Victoria, lessons can be learned from other jurisdictions. For example, crime prevention delivery in the UK has been primarily organised at local level through Crime and Disorder Reduction Partnerships,[784] which place an obligation on local councils and police in partnership with health and other agencies to develop and implement strategies for tackling crime in their local communities. Local authorities were to be supported in developing these partnerships by policy-makers at both regional and central levels of government.

Although there were many problems associated with the UK model, as discussed in Chapter 9, the basic concept is still viewed as being sound.[785] The lesson to come out of the UK, however, was that while the local authority/partnership was the most important level of administration in terms of program delivery, the central agency still needs to be 'an active part of the delivery process' (Homel et al 2004, p.5). Indeed a criticism of the earlier stages of the crime prevention model in the UK was that the central government agency was too removed from the operations of local partnerships, restricting itself to developing the formulating policy and strategic frameworks, organising financial support and a monitoring and reviewing role. According to one highly experienced person working closely with local communities at the time, 'it neglected the fact that local communities need to be assisted to make informed local decisions' (Homel et al 2004, p.13). Moreover, Homel et al note that the review of the Crime Reduction Partnerships demonstrated that:

> [w]ithout a clear and coherent plan and capacity for active technical support at the central level even the best local action is likely to fall short of the goal. As well as this it is clear that functional inter-agency agreements between central agencies are also necessary in order to maximise local and regional collaboration. These partnerships need to flow horizontally (ie across agencies) and vertically (ie from the centre to the local and regional level) if they are to be effective in practice at promoting joined up action…Without a functioning partnership agreement based on the principles of integrated governance this form of flexible organisation will not be able to occur (Homel et al 2004, p.20).

Victoria is not the UK and the organisational scheme for crime prevention organisation proposed by the Committee differs in some respects from the British Crime Prevention Partnership model. For example the systems of local government in the two jurisdictions are in many respects different. Nonetheless, as was noted in Chapter 3 there is much that can be learnt from both the successes and failures of the experience in the UK. Not the least

---

784 See Chapter 9.

785 In particular, criticism was made that there was inadequate guidance and advice to local authorities from the central and regional levels of management on a range of strategic and tactical issues such as recruitment problems and project slippage. In addition there were inadequate levels of project management competency among those responsible for project implementation at all levels (local, regional, central) (Homel et al 2004, p.13).

of which is the need for very clearly delineated areas of responsibility and lines of authority and accountability to be understood from the start. Also it is essential, as the experience in the UK showed, that effective crime prevention partnerships can only be developed and 'nurtured' if 'appropriate investment in adequate resources and staff competencies at every level of the delivery chain' is guaranteed' (Homel et al 2004, p.22).

Ultimately it was found in the UK that for effective crime prevention and crime reduction to be a reality 'Programme delivery at all levels of the delivery stream [local, central and if relevant regional] need to be treated as a single integrated system' (Homel et al 2004, p.5). The Western Australian experience of crime prevention discussed in Chapter 3 is a good case study of how a centrally driven integrated system that seeks to promote local delivery can work[786] (Anderson & Tressider 2008):

> Even when confronted with vast distances and a dispersed population, often in isolated communities, the Western Australian Office of Crime Prevention demonstrate[ed] that careful attention to effective ongoing communication with stakeholders and a commitment to the provision of strategic support can overcome many of the barriers to delivering centrally driven initiatives at local level (Homel 2009b, p.29).

Pre-conditions for good crime prevention outcomes

In addition to getting the structure right there are a number of conditions which need to be put in place if crime prevention frameworks and initiatives such as the model this Committee is recommending are to have a chance of sustained success. According to Homel (2009b) these are:

- A practical grasp of crime prevention theory
- Strong and consistent leadership and supportive governance structures [as discussed above]
- A capacity to manage collaborative multi-agency action
- Outcome focused performance measurement systems
- An applied commitment to evidence based practice and research/evaluation [as discussed above]
- Effective communication processes designed to promote engagement and sustainability
- Long term adequate resourcing informed by good data about problems and strategically appropriate responses (Homel 2009b, pp.32, 34).

The last point is particularly important. As indicated above, sufficient funding not only of individual crime prevention programs but also of the governance structures used to implement them is essential. Central and/or regional management must be staffed with 'technically competent and policy literate' staff capable of providing direct and meaningful support and guidance to and analysis of individual projects at local level (Homel 2009b, p.27). If regional bodies are in place they must be capable of interacting and informing both central management and local stakeholders.

The future of Neighbourhood Watch

The Committee acknowledges that Neighbourhood Watch Victoria has had a long history and particularly in its early years achieved much in promoting safer communities in Victoria. In particular the work of its many committed volunteers is to be commended. Nonetheless, for reasons outlined at length in this Report[787] it is appropriate for this Committee to question the relevance and viability of the organisation in the 21st century.

---

786 Despite recent changes to the structure of the Office of Crime Prevention, the rudiments of the governance aspects, including the communication networks, remain the same.

787 See discussion in Chapter 10.

It may be, however, that the proposed appointment of a Chief Executive Officer to head the organisation, a restructure of the Board, the implementation of the new strategy and a fresh look at the organisation's aims, objectives and priorities will result in positive changes. Nonetheless, the Committee believes it is imperative that Neighbourhood Watch as part of its current funding requirements be reviewed by the Victorian Government in 2013. The Review would assess the effectiveness of Neighbourhood Watch as a government funded crime prevention initiative. It should also indicate on the evidence received whether on balance further government funding should be allocated to support Neighbourhood Watch beyond 2014. In particular, the onus should fall on Neighbourhood Watch to demonstrate to the Victorian government that they merit ongoing funding. Any Review should also include canvassing transitional and future alternative crime prevention options should it be decided that Neighbourhood Watch not receives ongoing Victorian Government assistance.

Concluding remarks

This Report has constantly stated that while state governments can make valuable contributions to crime prevention and community safety, most obviously through the coordinating and funding role of a central crime prevention unit, it is ultimately local communities through and with their local government representatives who are most involved with and concerned about making their communities safe. Crime prevention and community safety therefore must be based on local collaborations and local input and at the same time draw on general theories and principles of crime prevention and case studies of 'what works' across Australia and overseas.

Crime prevention initiatives must also be subject to rigorous review and evaluation, particularly when in receipt of government funding. Yet as suggested in the recommendations, this does not mean that every program in every community agency must spend great amounts of time and money in conducting technical reviews. There are ways, as this Report has made clear, of undertaking program evaluation that may be less onerous for those practicing at the 'coal face' than otherwise would be case. In addition as Sutton, Cherney and White state:

> Such evaluation does not mean that crime prevention is a matter for experts only. Crime prevention is and ought to be seen not only as an everyday activity but as something that is relevant to and for everyone (2008, p.163).

Finally, it should be borne in mind that an approach, a program or a project that is not ostensibly about crime prevention or community safety per se may nonetheless have significant impacts upon crime and antisocial behaviour. This is particularly the case with social policy initiatives in the area of health, education or youth welfare (Homel et al 2004). Simply because the label does not read 'crime prevention' does not mean that it will not contribute positively to reducing or preventing crime. Such is the promise and the value of the social developmental and community capacity building model in this area.

Adopted by the Drugs and Crime Prevention Committee
55 St Andrews Place
East Melbourne 3002
21 May 2012

Appendices

Appendix 1: List of those who gave Briefings to the Committee

Background Briefings

Melbourne 4 April 2011

Name	Position	Organisation
Assoc. Prof. Peter Homel	Research Manager, Crime Reduction and Review Program	Australian Institute of Criminology
Assoc. Prof. Darren Palmer	Convenor, Criminology Program	Deakin University

Melbourne 18 April 2011

Name	Position	Organisation
Mr Rob Spence	Chief Executive Officer	Municipal Association of Victoria
Ms Claire Dunn	Policy Advisor	Municipal Association of Victoria
Ms Clare Hargreaves	Manager, Social Policy	Municipal Association of Victoria
Ms Penny Armytage	Secretary	Department of Justice
Deputy Commissioner Kieran Walshe	Regional and Road Policing	Victoria Police

Appendix 2:   List of Submissions

Submission No.	Name of Individual / Organisation	Date received
1	Mr Geoff Griffiths	05 May 2011
2	Mr Gerard Traynor Volunteer, Morwell Neighbourhood Watch / Safer Communities Group	05 May 2011
3	Ms Naomi Oakley Managing Director U-nome Security	05 May 2011
4	Mr John Thexton Dr Rae Walker Associate Professor in Public Health La Trobe University Ms Eleni Wellings Project Manager, Police and Community Triage Team Project Mr Raul Foglia Clinical Coordinator / Psychologist, Police and Community Triage	20 May 2011
5	Mr Valentine Smith	22 May 2011
6	Mr Andrew Brideson President, Board of Management Neighbourhood Watch Victoria Inc.	23 May 2011
7	Mr Julian Pocock Director, Public Policy and Practice Development Berry Street	26 May 2011
8	Mr Steven Dickson Compliance and Safety Manager Frankston City Council	26 May 2011
9	Mr Peter Sprott Executive Director Crime Stoppers Victoria Ltd	27 May 2011
10	Mr Phil Wheatley Executive Officer Operation Newstart	27 May 2011
11	Mr Craig Kenny Director, Community Programs Local Safety Committee, City of Yarra	27 May 2011
12	Mr Alby Clark Chairman Collingwood Safety Working Group	29 May 2011
13	Mr Bill Horman Immediate Past President, Board of Management Neighbourhood Watch Victoria Inc.	30 May 2011
14	Mr Andrew Brideson President, Board of Management Neighbourhood Watch Victoria Inc.	30 May 2011

Submission No.	Name of Individual / Organisation	Date received
15	Mr Paul Jamieson Community Development Manager City of Greater Geelong	30 May 2011
16	Ms Isabel Calvert Secretary Three Seas Steering Committee / The Dock	30 May 2011
17	Professor John Toumbourou Chief Executive Officer Communities That Care Ltd	30 May 2011
18	Mr Philip Clark and Mrs Mary Clark	31 May 2011
19	Dr Lorraine Beyer Sustainable Communities Planner Macedon Ranges Local Safety Committee, Macedon Ranges Shire Council	3 June 2011
20	Confidential submission	7 June 2011
21	Mr Philip Schier Senior Policy Officer Victorian Local Government Survey	27 June 2011
22	Ms Rhonda Rotherham Division Coordinator Neighbourhood Watch Greater Geelong and Surf Coast Committee	8 August 2011
23	Mr Richard Maugueret Acting Manager, Community Safety City of Casey	10 October 2011
24	Victoria Police	17 April 2012

Appendix 3: Witnesses Appearing at Public Hearings in Melbourne and via Teleconference

Public Hearings — Melbourne

Melbourne 27 June 2011

Name	Position	Organisation
Mr Andrew Brideson	President	Neighbourhood Watch Victoria Inc., Board of Management
Mr Brian Samuel	Secretary	Neighbourhood Watch Victoria Inc., Board of Management
Detective Inspector Myles King	Chief Commissioner's Representative	Neighbourhood Watch Victoria Inc., Board of Management
Mr Bill Horman	Immediate Past President	Neighbourhood Watch Victoria Inc., Board of Management
Ms Maree McPherson	Chief Executive Officer	Victorian Local Government Association
Mr Philip Schier	Senior Policy Officer	Victorian Local Governance Association

Melbourne 9 August 2011

Name	Position	Organisation
Assoc. Prof. Rae Walker	Health Promotion Coordinator	La Trobe University
Mr John Thexton		Independent
Mr Raul Foglia		Independent
Professor Ross Homel	Foundation Professor, Criminology and Criminal Justice	Griffith University
Mr Dean Griggs	Manager, Community Safety and Wellbeing	City of Melbourne
Major Brendan Nottle	Commanding Officer	Salvation Army
Mr Paul Bird	State Director, Victoria	Mission Australia
Dr Lorraine Beyer	Planner, Sustainable Communities	Macedon Ranges Shire Council
Cr Joan Donovan	Council Representative, Macedon Ranges Local Safety Committee	Macedon Ranges Shire Council
Ms Pauline Neil	Coordinator, Youth Development Unit	Macedon Ranges Shire Council
Detective Sergeant Shane Brundell	Macedon Ranges Crime Investigation Unit Representative, Gisborne, Victoria Police	Macedon Ranges Local Safety Committee
Sergeant Geoff Neil	Officer-in-Charge, Macedon Ranges Traffic Management Unit, Gisborne, Victoria Police	Macedon Ranges Local Safety Committee

Melbourne 10 August 2011

Name	Position	Organisation
Ms Jan Shield	Secretary	Victorian Safe Communities Network Inc.
Inspector Alan Dew	Police Liaison Officer	Victorian Safe Communities Network Inc.
Mr Phil Wheatley	Executive Officer	Operation Newstart Victoria
Mr Ross Miller	Chair	Operation Newstart Victoria
Leading Senior Constable Matthew Mudie	Facilitator	Operation Newstart Victoria
Ms Julie Edwards	Chief Executive Officer	Jesuit Social Services
Ms Cath Neville	Strategic Advisor	Jesuit Social Services
Professor John Toumbourou	Chief Executive Officer	Communities that Care Ltd
Mr Julian Pocock	Director, Public Policy and Practice Development	Berry Street
Mr David Hall	Senior Manager, Safe and Caring Communities	Berry Street
Cr Alison Clarke	Mayor	City of Yarra
Mr Ross Goeman	Acting Manager, Community Planning and Advocacy	City of Yarra

Melbourne 24 October 2011

Name	Position	Organisation
Mr Andrew Brideson	State President	Neighbourhood Watch Victoria Inc., Board of Management
Superintendent Tony de Ridder	Strategic Services Superintendent, Chief Commissioner's Representative, Victoria Police	Neighbourhood Watch Victoria Inc., Board of Management

Melbourne 27 February 2012

Name	Position	Organisation
Ms Julianne Brennan	Director Community Crime Prevention	Department of Justice

Melbourne 16 April 2012

Name	Position	Organisation
Deputy Commissioner Tim Cartwright	Deputy Commissioner	Victoria Police
Superintendent Peter Brigham	Community Engagement Division, Media and Corporate Communications Department	Victoria Police
Inspector Tony Langdon	Safer Communities Unit, Community Engagement Division, Media and Corporate Communications Department	Victoria Police

Teleconference
Melbourne 16 April 2012

Mr Jim Maddan	Chair	Neighbourhood and Home Watch Network England and Wales

Appendix 4: Regional Visits and Public Hearings

Dandenong 30 May 2011

Name	Position	Organisation
Inspector Charles Allen	Greater Dandenong Police Service Area	Victoria Police
Inspector Bruce Wemyss	Community Engagement Inspector, Greater Dandenong Police Service Area	Victoria Police
Sergeant Joseph Herrech	Supervisor, Proactive Programs Unit, Southern Metropolitan Region	Victoria Police
Mr Warren Eames	Manager, Community Programs	Youth Support and Advocacy Service (YSAS)
Ms Isabel Calvert	Secretary	Three Seas Steering Committee / The Dock
Mr Tito Agout	Representative	Sudanese Youth Leadership Development Program
Cr Roz Blades	Mayor	City of Greater Dandenong
Mr Mark Doubleday	Director, Community Services	City of Greater Dandenong
Ms Lee Robson	Manager, Community Engagement	City of Greater Dandenong
Mr Kevin Van Boxtel	Manager, Revitalising Central Dandenong	City of Greater Dandenong
Mr Brendan Carins	Acting Coordinator, Community Development	City of Greater Dandenong
Ms Franceyn Cottier	Acting Manager, Consumer, Enforcement and Community Services	Department of Justice
Mr Bruce James	President	Dandenong Neighbourhood Watch
Mr Craig Anderson	Secretary	Dandenong Neighbourhood Watch
Ms Kym Anderson	Member	Dandenong Neighbourhood Watch
Mr Reg Vernon	Member	Dandenong Neighbourhood Watch
Mr Jim Laidlaw	Member	Noble Park Community Action Forum

Frankston 30 May 2011

Name	Position	Organisation
Cr Kristopher Bolam	Mayor	City of Frankston
Ms Jane Homewood	Manager, General Development	City of Frankston
Mr Steven Dickson	Manager, Compliance and Safety	City of Frankston
Inspector Bryan Sharp	Manager, Operation Support	Victoria Police
Leading Senior Constable Reneé Bloomfield	Youth Resources Office, Frankston	Victoria Police
Mr Simon Ruth	Director, Complex Services	Peninsula Health

Mr Mark Whitby	Chief Executive Officer	City Life, Frankston
Mr Geoff Shaw MP	Member of Parliament for Frankston	Parliament of Victoria
Mr Matthew Berry	Electorate Officer	Frankston Electorate, Parliament of Victoria

Geelong 8 August 2011

Name	Position	Organisation
Cr Jan Farrell	Community Safety Portfolio	City of Greater Geelong
Ms Jenny McMahon	General Manager	City of Greater Geelong
Mr Steve Bentley	Place Manager	City of Greater Geelong
Ms Lisa Armstrong-Rowe	Community Development Officer	City of Greater Geelong
Mr John Frame	Chair	Geelong Local Safety Committee
Inspector Carl Peers	Liquor Licensing Division	Victoria Police
Inspector Gary Thompson	Operations Support Manager	Victoria Police
Assoc. Prof Darren Palmer	Convenor, Criminology Program	Deakin University
Mr Darren Holroyd	President	Geelong Nightlife Association
Ms Karina Okotel	Community Lawyer	Barwon Community Legal Service
Ms Rhonda Rotherham	Division Coordinator	Neighbourhood Watch Greater Geelong and Surf Coast Committee
Mr Frank Covill	Member	Geelong Local Safety Committee
Mr Stephen Fisher	Quality Assurance Officer	Geelong Taxi Network
Ms Jane Lonzarich	Chairperson	Geelong South Public Tenants Group

Ballarat 18 October 2011

Name	Position	Organisation
Mr Peter Appleton	Acting Director, People and Communities	City of Ballarat
Cr Des Hudson	People and Communities Portfolio	City of Ballarat
Cr John Philips	People and Communities Portfolio	City of Ballarat
Cr Cheryl Bromfield	Deputy Chair, Community Safety Advisory Committee	City of Ballarat
Ms Jeannie King	Director, Student Connect	University of Ballarat
Mr Doug Fisher	Member, Ballarat PSA Neighbourhood Watch Committee	Neighbourhood Watch
Ms Lindsay Florence	Chair, Ballarat PSA Neighbourhood Watch Committee	Neighbourhood Watch

Appendix 5: Witnesses Appearing at Interstate Meetings, Site Visits and Public Hearings

Perth 20 June 2011

Name	Position	Organisation
Professor Steve Allsop	Director	National Drug Research Institute, Curtin University
Professor Dennis Gray	Deputy Director	National Drug Research Institute, Curtin University
Assoc. Prof. Ted Wilkes	Associate Professor	National Drug Research Institute, Curtin University
Assoc. Prof. Tanya Chikritzh	Associate Professor	National Drug Research Institute, Curtin University
Mr James Alex	Acting Director, Strategy and Performance	Western Australia Police
Mr David Wray	Assistant Director	Western Australia Office of Crime Prevention
Superintendent John Leembruggen	Community Engagement Division	Western Australia Office of Crime Prevention
Mr Peter Jones	Acting Executive Director, Regional and School Bus Services	Transperth System, Public Transport Authority
Ms Keryn Reid	Program Coordinator, Graffiti Team	Western Australia Police
Ms Denise Lofthouse	Manager, Capability and Development, State Intelligence Division	Western Australia Police
Mr Mark Padget	Leading Intelligence Analyst, State Intelligence Division	Western Australia Police
Ms Carole Shepherdson	Strategic Intelligence Analyst, State Intelligence Division	Western Australia Police

Perth 21 June 2011

Name	Position	Organisation
Mr Michael Wood	Coordinator, Safer Vincent Crime Prevention Partnership	Town of Vincent
Assistant Commissioner Wayne Gregson	Assistant Commissioner, Judicial Services	Western Australia Police
Senior Sergeant Sue Parmer	District Coordinator, Community Engagement Division	Western Australia Police
Mr Mat Jovanou	Project Coordinator, 'Eyes on the street' Program	Western Australia Office of Crime Prevention
Senior Constable Steve Harrison	CCTV/Blue Iris Program	Western Australia Office of Crime Prevention
Mr David Wray	Assistant Director	Western Australia Office of Crime Prevention
Mr Bernie Durkin	Executive Manager, Strategic Projects	Western Australia Office of Crime Prevention
Mr Brian Scully	State Coordinator Neighbourhood Watch	Neighbourhood Watch State Office
Ms Deborah Costello	Chief Executive Officer	Injury Prevention Council of Western Australia

Ms Jody Niven	Manager, Community Safety Programs	Injury Prevention Council of Western Australia
Ms Maria Orifici	Manager, Health Promotion	North Metropolitan Public Health Unit

Perth 21 June 2011 — Evening Community Walk

Name	Position	Organisation
Mr Garry Dunne	Director, Service Units	City of Perth
Ms Lesley Murray	Principal Social and Community Planner, Sustainable Community Development	City of Perth
Mr Bill Strong	Coordinator, Safety and Security	City of Perth
Ms Jane Hannaford	Community Safety Planning Officer, Compliance Services	City of Perth
Acting Inspector Dave Hooper	City Watch Surveillance Centre	WA Police (Perth)
Ms Wendy Earl	Manager, Economic Development	City of Perth

Perth 22 June 2011

Name	Position	Organisation
Mr Garry Dunne	Director, Service Units	City of Perth
Mr Dennis Stevens	Manager, Compliance Services	City of Perth
Ms Wendy Earl	Manager, Economic Development	City of Perth
Ms Lesley Murray	Principal Social and Community Planner, Sustainable Community Development	City of Perth
Mr Bill Strong	Coordinator, Safety and Security	City of Perth
Ms Jane Hannaford	Community Safety Planning Officer, Compliance Services	City of Perth
Ms Elaine Clucas	Coordinator, Environmental Health, Compliance Services	City of Perth

Sydney 19 September 2011

Name	Position	Organisation
Mr Brendan Thomas	Assistant Director-General, Crime Prevention and Community Programs	New South Wales Department of Attorney General and Justice
Dr Tania Matruglio	Assistant Director, Crime Prevention Division	New South Wales Department of Attorney General and Justice
Assistant Commissioner Carlene York	Assistant Commissioner, Northern Region Commander	New South Wales Police Service

Name	Position	Organisation
Superintendent Commander Helen Begg	Operational Programs, Sydney	New South Wales Police Service
Chief Inspector Joshua Maxwell	Human Resources, South West Sydney	New South Wales Police Service
Inspector Leith Kennedy	Project Officer Customer Service and Programs, Sydney Metropolitan	New South Wales Police Service
Mr Garner Clancey	Adjunct Lecturer	Sydney Institute of Criminology, University of Sydney
Professor Don Weatherburn	Director	New South Wales Bureau of Crime Statistics and Research
Ms Margaret Southwell	Chair / Community Development Officer	New South Wales Local Government Community Safety and Crime Prevention Committee / Community Development, Bankstown City Council
Mr John Maynard	Senior Project Coordinator, Safe City	City of Sydney
Mr Rodger Watson	Deputy Director	Designing Out Crime Research Centre, University of Technology, Sydney
Ms Olga Camacho-Duarte	Postdoctoral Research Fellow	Designing Out Crime Research Centre, University of Technology, Sydney

Appendix 6: List of Questions circulated to Neighbourhood Watch Chapters

- What does your chapter understand by the concept of crime prevention? What areas does it encompass?

- What does the chapter consider its role to be in crime prevention for their local districts?

- How does the chapter determine what the needs and priorities are with regard to crime prevention in their areas?

- What locally initiated projects are run by the chapter. Please provide information on each local project. (This would include a brief description, organisations involved in their delivery, who finances the projects and how projects are prioritised)?

- How does Neighbourhood Watch reach out to or involve local community or private sector organisations in their planning and delivery of crime prevention programs?

- How is success measured and how successful are these projects?

- Have there been any formal evaluations of these programmes? If they are available could the Committee have a copy?

- What are the specific community safety needs in your community? Are they varied across the division? How are these particular and diverse needs addressed?

- What challenges are faced in operating Neighbourhood Watch programmes generally in the area?

- What challenges are faced in operating specific programmes and state wide projects?

- What degree of support is provided by local and state authorities?

- How successful do local community groups think that Neighbourhood Watch is in their local area?

- What weaknesses if any exist in the current Neighbourhood Watch Model?

- What new directions could Neighbourhood Watch take to improve outcomes?

Appendix 7: List of Neighbourhood Watch Chapters that answered Questions

Name of Neighbourhood Watch Chapter	Date received
Banyule (and Nillumbik)	31 May 2011
Cardinia	31 May 2011
Glen Eira	31 May 2011
Greater Dandenong	28 May 2011
Greater Frankston	23 May 2011
Greater Geelong & Surf Coast	30 May 2011
Manningham	23 May 2011
Maroondah	23 May 2011
Mildura	23 May 2011
Monash	26 May 2011
Moreland & Hume	28 May 2011
Morwell	28 May 2011
Somers	23 May 2011
Western Division 2 (Warrnambool/Moyne & Southern Grampians/Glenelg)	26 May 2011
Whitehorse	28 May 2011
Whittlesea	26 May 2011

Appendix 8: List of Conferences and Seminars attended by the Committee and staff

Name of conference or seminar	Date
Local Government Professionals (LGPro) — Special Interest Group for Community Safety Forum, LGPro, Melbourne.	16 November 2011
Crime prevention and policy: New tools for contemporary challenges, Conference sponsored by the New South Wales Department of Attorney-General and Justice in partnership with the Australian Institute of Criminology, Sydney.	23–24 November 2011
'Information Session for potential applicants for the Reducing Violence against Women and their Children Grants' held at Treasury Theatre, 1 Macarthur Place, East Melbourne.	14 March 2012

Appendix 9: Range of Crime Prevention and Community Safety Approaches and Programs

Action or Intervention	Description	Examples
Arts development project	An arts development project is one that uses art (including visual art, theatre, dance etc.) as the medium for social or community development	• Urban art projects • Theatre workshops
Awareness campaign	An awareness campaign aims to provide information to a target group to raise awareness of specific issues, crimes, services and/or preventative measures	• Marketing and advertising campaigns, including the distribution of material with crime prevention advice • Distributing information about crime and security • Distributing road safety material to drivers
Community involvement/ engagement projects	Community involvement or engagement projects seek to change the social structure of particular communities, through community mobilisation, increasing community bonds and informal social controls	• Community events which encourage individuals to engage with one another
Community patrol and/ or community policing project	A community patrol is a group of people that actively patrol their community, possibly offering an outreach service to provide information and assistance to members of the community (including referrals to support services), safe transport, reporting incidents and information to police and in some instances provide a security service to help maintain social order	• Local government security patrols • Neighbourhood Watch • Eyes on the Street
CPTED / Urban renewal	CPTED or urban renewal projects seek to reduce the opportunities for crime through the design and management of the built and landscaped environment. This includes strategies that involve modifying the built environment to create safer places that are less crime prone, or to make people feel safer	• Integration of CPTED principles into town planning • Development of CPTED policy • CPTED audits of public spaces • Urban regeneration initiatives
Diversionary activities project	Diversionary activities attempt to divert people away from engaging in criminal or antisocial behaviour by providing alternative activities in a safe environment that are rewarding, challenging and age appropriate. These activities can reduce boredom or reduce the opportunity to engage in less desirable behaviour and can also have a socialising effect. These activities can include sport, art, media projects, music and camps (see sub classification)	• After school, weekend and vacation sport and recreational activities • Youth drop in centres • Establishing recreational facilities such as skate parks • Music festivals
Education-type project	An education-type program is any structured set of activities that aim to deliver information to the target group with a view to improving their skills or knowledge. Unlike awareness campaigns, education type projects rely on the active participation of the recipient. This can include community education and workshops, vocational education and training, professional development, strategies that aim to improve school performance and drug and alcohol education	• Providing security and/or community safety advice to seniors, business owners, victims of crime, young people, community groups or CALD communities • Drug and alcohol education in schools • Road/bike safety education in schools

Action or Intervention	Description	Examples
Employment project	An employment program may actively seek or assist an individual to find employment, or provide vocational/ job skills training that will increase the opportunities for employment available to the individual	• Mechanical skills workshops • Projects that help young people to develop resumes and application for employment
Mentoring project	Mentoring is when a more experienced person takes on a role advising a less experienced person. Mentoring programs as a crime prevention strategy are characterised by contact between individuals that have had contact with the criminal justice system, or are 'at risk' of becoming involved in offending or antisocial behaviour, with positive role models. These role models are usually older and more experienced and provide support, guidance and encouragement to the less experienced young person	• Projects that engage members of sporting clubs to mentor young people
Personal development project	Personal development strategies seek to address those risk factors relating to the individual and their social environment, such as social skills, life skills and parenting skills. Early intervention or developmental intervention projects often incorporate personal development strategies	• Parenting course and support programs for young parents
Security related infrastructure	Capital infrastructure projects that draw on security measures such as closed-circuit television (CCTV), street lighting, and/or access control (i.e. fencing)	• Installation or upgrade of CCTV systems, fixed and mobile • Initiatives to improve street lighting
Service coordination	Service coordination includes projects that specifically aim to improve the way in which various organisations work together to address crime problems or to provide services to offenders, victims or those at risk of becoming an offender or victim of crime. They may involve a range of other interventions, but have as their primary goal improving the way agencies work together	• Crime prevention committees • Projects that work with police to develop referral mechanisms to improve access to services for victims of domestic violence • Audits/promotion of existing services
Support services	Support services aim to provide some type of customised support for individuals (typically on an individual basis but also in small groups) that are victims or offenders of crime, or at risk of becoming a victim or offender. This often involves individual case management or an assessment of an individual's needs, often with a view to improving access to essential services (such as counselling, emergency accommodation etc.) by way of referrals	• Support services for victims of domestic violence • Outreach services for young people • Counselling for people with substance use problems
Target hardening	Target hardening seeks to increase the effort associated with committing an offence, usually through the alteration of the physical environment or surroundings to make specific crimes more difficult. Target hardening may also serve to decrease the rewards associated with crime (e.g. through property marking) and in some cases increases the risks associated with criminal activity	• Provide property marking services • Security audits for small business • Providing rebates for security alarms and devices • Rapid removal of graffiti

Source: Adapted from Morgan & Homel 2011, *Understanding the CSCP Planning Process*, pp.35–36.

CRIME PREVENTION STRATEGY TEMPLATE

1. CRIME PROFILE

(see Section 3.1 in the Crime Prevention Planning Guidelines)

1.1 Local Crime Priorities

- Identify your local priority offences. Your crime prevention strategy should only focus on 1 or 2 priority crimes.

- The following criteria should be used to identify your priority offences:

- **Total number of offences** – Are there enough offences to warrant the selection of the offence as a priority?

- **Trend** – Has the offence increased over the past 36-month period?

- **State ranking** – Where does your LGA rank in NSW for the offence?

- **Comparison analysis** – How does your trend compare to broader NSW or other areas with similar demographics?

- **Capacity** – does your Council and community have the necessary services, infrastructure, expertise and commitment necessary to impact on the offence? Is there a realistic chance that a strategy led by Council can reduce this offence?

To assist with your crime data analysis, the Bureau of Crime Statistics and Research website has a number of online tools that can help you to identify your priority offences. These tools include:

- **Crime trends tool – This tool allows you to identify the crime trend for various offences within your LGA, over any period from 2 – 10 years.**

- **LGA ranking tool – This tool allows you to see where your LGA ranks (in NSW) for various offences.**

- **Offences by premise type – This tool allows you to identify where major crime occur, by premise types (e.g. licensed premises, residential address, outdoor public space etc).**

1.2 How the priority crimes were selected

Input received from police intelligence and any other relevant sources should be included here.

Summarise relevant advice from your Police Local Area Command for your priority offences:
- Hot spots (where the majority of the offences geographically occur).
- Priority times and days (when the majority of offences committed).
- Victim and offender profiles (demographics for victims and offenders).
- Any Police operations or strategies designed to reduce your target crime (subject to your Police Local Area Commander's consent).
- Identification of unique factors that are contributing to the high offending rate.

You may wish to present this data in the following format:

Offence	Hot spots	Priority times	Victims and Offenders

1.3 Situational analysis:

Identify the key points from your situational analysis here.

Document any environmental factors that contribute to levels of offending in the area. Consider:
- Whether the design and maintenance of the environment makes it easier for crime to occur.

- Whether the presence of transport or lack of transport contributes to the incidence of offending.

- If the number of people using the environment make it easier for the offence to be committed.

- If the proximity of licensed premises or other businesses or attractions influences the levels of crime in the environment.

1.4 Stakeholders

Summarise any information provided from stakeholders and set out any commitments from them in this section.
Include any relevant information from stakeholders that provides further insight into factors that influence the incidence of crime in the environment you are targeting. This would include input from service providers or businesses in the area you are targeting and/or those that interact with people who are at risk of experiencing crime in the environment.

2. Actions and Implementation

In this section include a brief overview of any activities, projects and actions that you will be implementing with partners or with your own funding in addition to the Action Plan in Section 4.

(see Section 4 in the Crime Prevention Planning Guidelines)

These definitions will assist you to develop your action plan.

Target Offence: The target offence is the crime that you are focusing on.

Project: Describe how you intend to impact on the target offence. For example if you are targeting Assault, you might develop a project that aids in dispersing patrons leaving licensed premises after 10.00 p.m. on Friday and Saturday nights.

Rationale: The rationale should detail the reasons why the strategy is appropriate and why it is believed it will impact on the target offence. In the case of Assault it might be "75% of assaults are alcohol related and occur outside licensed premises. Research suggests that the provision of improved transport options along with the enforcement of responsible service of alcohol can reduce the incidence of these types of offences".

Lead Agency & Partners: If you nominate project partners, ensure that you consult and negotiate with them to seek their support and to secure their commitment.

Objective: The pre-specified intended outcomes of a program, process, or policy. Objectives tend to be more specific than goals. Eg. "To achieve a 10% reduction in the incidence of alcohol related assaults in hot spots identified by police between the hours of 10pm and 3am on Friday and Saturday nights".

Expected Outcome: The desired longer-term impact, usually expressed in terms of broad socio-economic consequences, which can be attributed to the project.

Performance Measures Involves ongoing data collection to determine if a program is implementing activities and achieving objectives. It measures inputs, outputs, and outcomes over time to objectively measure the degree of success a program has had. In general, pre and post comparisons are used to assess change.

Refer to 4: Crime Prevention Action Plan template.

3. Monitoring and Evaluating

Describe how your strategy will be monitored, who will be responsible for the monitoring, what information will be collected and how it will be used to evaluate the success of the Crime Prevention Strategy. (see Section 5 of the *Crime Prevention Planning Guidelines* and the Monitoring and Evaluation tool)

Monitoring

- Identify the performance indicators you will use to monitor progress.
- Identify timeframes to assist you in monitoring if your project is on track.
- Identify the role of project partners that will assist with this process.

Evaluation and data collection

- State what data will be collected and analysed – ensure you monitor any changes in baseline data.
- Identify how you will consider impact on risk factors as well as actual incidence of crime.
- Explain how you have isolated the perceived impact of your strategy from other activity in the area.

4. Crime Prevention Action Plan

-
Target Offence:
Project:
Rationale:
Objective:
Lead Agency & Partners:
Expected Outcome:

Action	Performance Measures	Time Frames	Funding required	Milestones

Appendix 11: Copy of the Survey developed by the Australian Institute of Criminology for the Drugs and Crime Prevention Committee

The Victorian Parliamentary Drugs and Crime Prevention Committee is currently conducting an Inquiry into the nature and extent of locally based community safety and crime prevention strategies and initiatives. The Australian Institute of Criminology (AIC) has been commissioned by the Committee to assist in the inquiry through the distribution and administration of this survey.

The purpose of the survey is to ask councils and shires to identify all local crime prevention initiatives in their area and answer specific questions in relation to their operation and effectiveness. The results of this important benchmarking research work will form the framework for the Committee's Final Report and recommendations.

It is estimated that the survey will take approximately 30 minutes to complete. The Committee requests that in the interests of efficiency and ensuring that the most complete information is collected, the most appropriate person within your organization is designated to complete the survey.

The Committee would appreciate it if you could complete the survey by the close of business on Friday 23 September 2011 so that the AIC can undertake the analysis and present the findings to the Committee in a timely way.

If you have any queries of a general nature regarding the Inquiry please contact: Sandy Cook, Executive Officer on 86822810 or sandy.cook@parliament.vic.gov.au

How to complete this survey.

The survey has a total of 52 questions. Some of these are free response questions. If at any time you wish to change or edit an answer to a previous question, simply navigate to that page using the back arrow on the internet browser.

If you are choosing to fill this survey out offline – once completed, please save a copy and return it via email to Georgina Fuller at georgina.fuller@aic.gov.au

If you have any queries about the survey please contact Peter Homel at the AIC on 02 9560 2109 (email: peter.homel@aic.gov.au) or Georgina Fuller on 02 6260 9280 (email: georgina.fuller@aic.gov.au).

Question One. Broadly speaking, there are two common approaches to crime prevention known as social and environmental. These two approaches are generally used in combination but strategies and programmes may emphasise one approach or the other. Environmental measures can involve activities such as;

- improved security through strengthening locks;
- improving surveillance;
- improving street lighting;
- installing closed circuit television;
- putting locks on windows;
- introducing safer money handling procedures; and,
- limiting the amount of money held on premise.

The social/structural approaches may include action to improve housing, health and educational achievement as well as improved community cohesion through community development measures.

On the scale of 1 to 5, please indicate the extent to which you would broadly describe the emphasis of the crime prevention strategies and programmes in your area as either mainly social or environmental.

| 1. (mainly social) ☐ | 2. ☐ | 3. ☐ | 4. ☐ | 5. (mainly environmental) ☐ |

Question Two. From your experience, describe three problems that community organisations face in implementing, operating and managing crime prevention and community safety programmes/initiatives.

Problem 1

Problem 2

Problem 3

Crime and community safety issues

Question three. What are the main crime and community safety issues in your local government area? *Tick all that apply*

Alcohol related problems ☐

Armed violence ☐

Assault ☐

Corruption ☐

Domestic, family or gendered violence ☐

Hate/racially motivated crimes ☐

Homicide ☐

Illegal substance abuse ☐

Juvenile/youth offending ☐

Offensive behaviour ☐

Organised crime ☐

Public disorder ☐

Road safety ☐

Safety in schools ☐

Street and illegal prostitution and soliciting ☐

Street gangs ☐

Theft (commercial or residential) ☐

Vandalism and graffiti ☐

Other – please specify

Question four. What data resources are used to identify and evaluate the main crime and community safety issues in your local government area? *Tick all that apply*

Police statistics	☐
The Australian Bureau of Statistics	☐
Community survey	☐
None	☐

Other – please specify

Question five. Is the data necessary to identify crime and community safety issues in your local government area easy to access?

Yes	☐
No	☐

If no, why not?

Question six. How difficult is it to collect and collate the information needed in order to identify crime and community safety issues in your local government area?

Not difficult	☐
Moderately difficult	☐
Difficult	☐
Very difficult	☐
Impossible	☐

Question seven. Is there a process in place to monitor, refresh and/or update this information?

Yes ☐

No ☐

If yes, how often?

Question eight. What other departments, bodies, committees or agencies (government and non-government) are responsible for implementing crime prevention and/or community safety strategies in your local government area? *Tick all that apply*

Police ☐

Courts ☐

Schools/other educational institutions ☐

Private sector ☐

Community associations ☐

Non-government organisations ☐

Other – please specify

Question nine. Who are the main sources of crime prevention and community safety funding in your local government area? *Tick all that apply*

Own organisation ☐

Federal Government ☐

State Government ☐

Local Government ☐

Private sector (including business sponsorships) ☐

Community associations (e.g. Chamber of Commerce) ☐

Private donations/benefactors ☐

Other – please specify

Crime prevention and community safety strategy

Question ten. Does your organisation have a formal crime prevention and community safety strategy?

Yes ☐

No ☐

If no, why not?

Question eleven. Describe the key elements of your organisation's crime prevention and community safety strategy. *Note: if your organisation does not have a crime prevention or community safety strategy, please fill in with N/A.*

Aim

Target crime/community safety issue

Methodology *(how is this strategy implemented)*

Target population

Question twelve. Name any other departments, bodies, committees or agencies who were involved in the formulation of your organisation's crime prevention/community safety strategy (e.g. Ministry of Justice, local/state police, community groups (such as Neighbourhood Watch), non-government organisations).

None ☐

Question thirteen. In general, what was the extent of the other agency/agencies involvement in the formulation of your organisation's crime prevention and community safety strategy? *Tick all that apply*

Consultation ☐

Funding ☐

Joint strategy implementation ☐

No involvement from external agencies ☐

Other – please specify

Question fourteen. How would you rate the value of their contribution?

Very useful ☐

Useful ☐

Not useful ☐

Detrimental ☐

If not useful or detrimental, why?

Question fifteen. Was the strategy formulated with input from the community and/or target population?

Yes ☐

No ☐

If no, why not?

Question sixteen. How did your organisation gather information relating to the community and/or target population's view on crime prevention and community safety? *Tick all that apply*

Community survey ☐

Public meetings ☐

No involvement from community or target population ☐

Other – please specify

Question seventeen. Did your organisation consider the needs of specific populations (for example, Indigenous peoples, women, youth, young offenders, culturally and linguistically diverse communities) in the formulation of its crime prevention and community safety strategy?

Yes ☐

No ☐

If no, why not?

Question eighteen. If yes, which specific populations did your organisation consider when formulating its crime prevention and community safety strategy? *Tick all that apply*

Indigenous people ☐

Women ☐

Youth ☐

Juvenile offenders ☐

CALD communities *(culturally and linguistically diverse)* ☐

Seniors ☐

Other – please specify

Question nineteen. What research informed your organisation's crime prevention and community safety strategy? *Tick all that apply*

Community safety audit ☐

Academic research ☐

Crime statistics ☐

Other – please specify

Question twenty. Was this research easy to access?

Yes ☐

No ☐

If no, why not?

Question twenty-one. Did your organisation encounter any key problems or issues when formulating its crime prevention and community safety strategy?

Yes   ☐

No   ☐

Question twenty-two. If yes, describe three key problems or issues encountered by your organisation during the formulation of the crime prevention and community safety strategy.

Problem 1

Solution

Problem 2

Solution

Problem 3

Solution

Question twenty-three. How does your organisation's strategy encourage or facilitate crime prevention or community safety programmes in your local government area? *Tick all that apply*

Funding ☐

Direct implementation of programmes/initiatives ☐

Research ☐

Other – please specify

Crime prevention and community safety programmes

Question twenty-four. Outline the key crime prevention and/or community safety programmes or initiatives administered by your organisation. *Note: There is space for up to ten programmes or initiatives. Fill out only the number that apply.*

Name of initiative/programme 1

Focus

Does this initiative/programme target the needs of specific communities? Which ones?

How was the initiative/programme implemented *(the main methodology)*

Funding amount

Is this initiative/programme to be ongoing? Y/N

Describe the involvement of specific external agencies (e.g government departments, community groups, non-government agencies).

Name of initiative/programme 2

Focus

Does this initiative/programme target the needs
of specific communities? Which ones?

How was the initiative/programme implemented
(the main methodology)

Funding amount

Is this initiative/programme to be ongoing? Y/N

Describe the involvement of specific external
agencies (e.g government departments,
community groups, non-government agencies).

Name of initiative/programme 3

Focus

Does this initiative/programme target the needs
of specific communities? Which ones?

How was the initiative/programme implemented
(the main methodology)

Funding amount

Is this initiative/programme to be ongoing? Y/N

Describe the involvement of specific external
agencies (e.g government departments,
community groups, non-government agencies).

Name of initiative/programme 4

Focus

Does this initiative/programme target the needs of specific communities? Which ones?

How was the initiative/programme implemented *(the main methodology)*

Funding amount

Is this initiative/programme to be ongoing? Y/N

Describe the involvement of specific external agencies (e.g government departments, community groups, non-government agencies).

Name of initiative/programme 5

Focus

Does this initiative/programme target the needs of specific communities? Which ones?

How was the initiative/programme implemented *(the main methodology)*

Funding amount

Is this initiative/programme to be ongoing? Y/N

Describe the involvement of specific external agencies (e.g government departments, community groups, non-government agencies).

Name of initiative/programme 6

Focus

Does this initiative/programme target the needs
of specific communities? Which ones?

How was the initiative/programme implemented
(the main methodology)

Funding amount

Is this initiative/programme to be ongoing? Y/N

Describe the involvement of specific external
agencies (e.g government departments,
community groups, non-government agencies).

Name of initiative/programme 7

Focus

Does this initiative/programme target the needs
of specific communities? Which ones?

How was the initiative/programme implemented
(the main methodology)

Funding amount

Is this initiative/programme to be ongoing? Y/N

Describe the involvement of specific external
agencies (e.g government departments,
community groups, non-government agencies).

Name of initiative/programme 8

Focus

Does this initiative/programme target the needs
of specific communities? Which ones?

How was the initiative/programme implemented
(the main methodology)

Funding amount

Is this initiative/programme to be ongoing? Y/N

Describe the involvement of specific external
agencies (e.g government departments,
community groups, non-government agencies).

Name of initiative/programme 9

Focus

Does this initiative/programme target the needs
of specific communities? Which ones?

How was the initiative/programme implemented
(the main methodology)

Funding amount

Is this initiative/programme to be ongoing? Y/N

Describe the involvement of specific external
agencies (e.g government departments,
community groups, non-government agencies).

Name of initiative/programme 10

Focus

Does this initiative/programme target the needs
of specific communities? Which ones?

How was the initiative/programme implemented
(the main methodology)

Funding amount

Is this initiative/programme to be ongoing? Y/N

Describe the involvement of specific external
agencies (e.g government departments,
community groups, non-government agencies).

Question twenty-five. To what extent are your organisation's initiatives/programmes a direct
response to;

	Not at all	Slightly	Moderately	Very much
Local government policy	☐	☐	☐	☐
State government policy	☐	☐	☐	☐
Federal government policy	☐	☐	☐	☐

Question twenty-six. In general, how are external agencies involve in the crime prevention/
community safety initiatives or programmes administered by your organisation? *Tick all that apply*

Data sharing	☐
Funding	☐
Joint programme management	☐
Personnel	☐
Not involved	☐

Other – please specify

Question twenty-seven. Overall, how would you rate the contribution of external agencies to the implementation and management of crime prevention and community safety initiatives/ programmes?

Very useful	Useful	Not useful	Detrimental
☐	☐	☐	☐

Question twenty-eight. If not useful or detrimental, why was this the case?

Question twenty-nine. Did your organisation consider the needs of specific populations (for example Indigenous people, women, youth, young offenders, CALD communities) in the formation of its crime prevention/community safety initiative or programme?

Yes ☐

No ☐

Question thirty. If yes, which specific populations did your organisation consider when formulating its crime prevention and community safety initiative/programme? *Tick all that apply*

Indigenous people ☐

Women ☐

Youth ☐

Juvenile offenders ☐

CALD communities *(culturally and linguistically diverse)* ☐

Seniors ☐

Question thirty-one. Describe three key problems and solutions your organisation has faced in the implementation, operation and management of crime prevention and community safety initiatives or programmes?

Problem 1

Solution

Problem 2

Solution

Problem 3

Solution

Question thirty-two. Were other initiatives, programmes or approaches proposed?

Yes   ☐

No   ☐

If yes, what were the main reasons why these were rejected?

Effectiveness and evaluation

Question thirty-three. What are the results, to date, of the crime prevention and community safety strategy? *Tick all that apply*

Decrease in crime rates   ☐

Increase in perceptions of community safety   ☐

Greater community cohesion   ☐

No results currently available   ☐

Other – please specify

Question thirty-four. Who is/has been monitoring the results? *Tick all that apply*

Own organisation   ☐

Other government department   ☐

Non-government organisation   ☐

Police   ☐

Other – please specify

Question thirty-five. Has the crime prevention and community safety strategy been evaluated?

Yes ☐

No ☐

If no, why not?

Question thirty-six. If yes, what type of evaluation was conducted? *Tick all that apply*

Process/implementation evaluation

(Focuses on how well the programme or initiative was executed and run. Minimal focus on outcome.)

Impact evaluation

(Focuses on identifying the extent to which changes can be attributed to the programme or initiative)

Other – please specify

Question thirty-seven. Who conducted the evaluation? *Tick all that apply*

Own organisation ☐

Other government department ☐

Non-government organisation ☐

University ☐

Other – please specify

Question thirty-eight. Has the strategy been found to be cost-effective for the community?

Yes ☐

No ☐

Cost-benefit analysis has not been conducted ☐

If not, why not?

Question thirty-nine. What were the three key findings of the evaluation of your organisation's crime prevention and community safety strategy?

Finding 1

Finding 2

Finding 3

Neighbourhood Watch

Question forty. Is there a Neighbourhood Watch chapter in your local government area?

Yes ☐

No ☐

Don't know ☐

Question forty-one. What are the main initiatives/programmes run by Neighbourhood Watch in your local government area? *Tick all that apply*

Advising community members on security measures (i.e. improving home security systems)   ☐

Building bridges between different community groups   ☐

Campaigning for and organising improvements to the geography of the local area   ☐

Campaigning for and organising improvements to the geography of the local area   ☐

Disseminating information related to crime and community safety issues   ☐

Liaising between the community and police   ☐

Maintain partnerships with crime and community related organisations (i.e. councils, churches, youth groups, police, fire and emergency services, local business etc)   ☐

Operating initiatives designed to empower neighbours to look out for each other and each other's property   ☐

Organising graffiti clean ups   ☐

Provide activities for young people   ☐

Recognising specific crime and community safety issues   ☐

Securing funding for crime prevention and community safety initiatives   ☐

Other – please specify

Question forty-two. To what extent do you agree that there is an ongoing role for Neighbourhood Watch within your organisation's crime prevention and community safety strategies/initiatives?

Strongly agree ☐

Agree ☐

Disagree ☐

Strongly disagree ☐

Neither agree nor disagree ☐

If disagree or strongly disagree, why?

Question forty-three. Does your organisation involve Neighbourhood Watch in any of its crime prevention or community safety initiatives/programmes?

Yes ☐

No ☐

If no, why not?

Question forty-four. If yes, outline the nature of Neighbourhood Watch's involvement in three key initiatives/programmes

Name of initiative/programme 1

How was Neighbourhood Watch involved?

Name of initiative/programme 2

How was Neighbourhood Watch involved?

Name of initiative/programme 3

How was Neighbourhood Watch involved?

Contact details

Name of organisation:

Organisation's website:

Contact's name:

Contact's position:

Contact's position:

Contact's email:

Contact phone:

Local government area:

Choose an item.

How would you classify your local government area?

Urban	☐
Rural	☐
Outer interface (i.e. city fringe)	☐

Thank you for completing this survey.

If you have any questions regarding the general nature of the inquiry, please contact:
Sandy Cook, Executive Officer on 86822810

If you have any queries regarding the survey, please contact either Peter Homel at the the AIC on 02 9560 2109 (email: peter.homel@aic.gov.au) or Georgina Fuller on 02 6260 9280 (email: georgina.fuller@aic.gov.au)

Appendix 12: Examples of Successful Department of Justice Partnership Programs

Court Integrated Services Program

The Court Integrated Services Program (CISP) was established in November 2006 by the Department of Justice and the Magistrates' Court of Victoria, to assist in ensuring that the accused who have been charged but not yet convicted or sentenced receive support and services to promote safer communities through reduced rates of re-offending. The program currently operates at the Latrobe Valley, Melbourne and Sunshine Magistrates' Courts.

CISP aims to:

- provide short-term assistance before sentencing for the accused with health and social needs

- work on the causes of offending through individualized case management support

- provide priority access to treatment and community support services

- reduce the likelihood of re-offending.

The CISP provides

- a multi-disciplinary team-based approach to the assessment and referral to treatment of clients

- three levels of support based on the assessed needs of the client; this may include case management for up to four months

- referrals and linkages to support services including drug and alcohol treatment, acquired brain injury services, accommodation services, disability and mental health services, as well as the Koori Liaison Officer program.

Regional and Local Aboriginal Justice Advisory Committees

In this program Koori communities work in partnership with justice agencies to design and implement local solutions to justice issues. In particular, Regional and Local Aboriginal Justice Advisory Committees:

- advocate for and promote improved justice outcomes and Koori justice initiatives to both Koori communities and government agencies

- develop and implement regional justice plans that address Koori over-representation [in the criminal justice system]

- promote and participate in cross-agency and partnership forums, such as the Aboriginal Justice Forum, and other initiatives to address Koori disadvantage

- work with other regional Koori advocacy groups

- monitor and comment on Koori contact with the justice system at a regional/state-wide level

- promote and nurture the Local Aboriginal Justice Action Committees, providing advocacy for them at the regional level

- participate in the assessment process for government grant funding applications for Koori justice-related programs

- aid in the successful delivery of Koori programs under the Victorian Aboriginal Justice Agreement(AJA).

Justice for Refugees Program

This program works with refugee, ethnic and NESB [non-English-speaking background] advocate groups in partnership to assist newly arrived communities to address over-representation in the criminal justice system by members of refugee communities.

Reducing Weapons Related Violence – Knives Scar Lives

The Department of Justice works in partnership with community groups, sport groups, and industry to raise awareness of the risks of carrying and using knives.

Graffiti Clean-up and Removal

The Graffiti Prevention and Removal Grants program is a Community Crime Prevention Program initiative, which funds councils to partner with communities to prevent and remove graffiti.

There are a number of other preventative measures for councils and communities to consider:

- graffiti hotlines, with dedicated phone numbers for residents and businesses to report graffiti

- free or discounted graffiti removal services for residents and retailers

- free or discounted graffiti removal kits, paint and anti-graffiti coatings

- support for community groups interested in addressing graffiti, including Adopt-a-Space and Care-for-an-Area projects

- education and diversionary programs to help raise young people's awareness of the impacts of graffiti.

Adopt-a-Space and Care-for-an-Area projects commonly develop from a community concern about a particular location, such as a local park, street, bus shelter, shopping strip. Community members rally together to clean-up and maintain the area.

Source: Department of Justice website – http://www.justice.vic.gov.au/home/

Appendix 13: Victoria Police Crime Prevention Programs

As community safety is predicated on confidence in police and connectedness to wider society, some of the following examples are initiatives that seek to build that confidence and connectedness.

A sample of both community safety and crime prevention programs:

* **Residential/business security kits** provided to victims of crime on how to target harden their homes/business was developed and funded by Victoria Police. Additional reprinting costs covered by other stakeholders including CGU/RACV Insurance Co.

* **Crime Prevention through Environmental Design** courses — run by Victoria Police and are self-funded.

* **Remove It/Lock It or Lose It Campaign** - The campaign was designed and implemented by Victoria Police Safer Communities Unit. It was designed to reduce the likelihood of Theft from motor vehicles which became rampant at railway stations and shopping centre car parks. Brochure funded by Victoria Police.

* **Safe Plate** — providing one way screws to motorists to reduce the likelihood of number plate theft and petrol theft. Campaign funded by Victoria Police with some input from key stakeholders including Neighbourhood Watch Victoria, Vic Roads & Bunnings Hardware. This campaign was extremely successful and picked up by other states/territories.

* **Handbag/Purse security campaign** — managed locally by Crime Prevention Officers throughout Victoria. Brochures/training packages funded by Victoria Police with some input from Department of Justice. Costs included shopping centre brochures/posters and visits to educate community.

* **Party Safe Programme** — On line version of 'Party Safe' currently being built and managed by Victoria Police Safer Communities Unit. Build expected to be completed late May 2012. Party Safe will allow general public to report parties *On Line* and will provide them with information on how to conduct a safe party. A poster is printed off informing patrons that the party is registered with Victoria Police. Cost – $86,000 funding received via Department of Justice.

* **High Challenge** — VicPol programme to re-engage with offending young people through challenging activities conducted with sworn officers, in order to build positive relationships and prevent further offending. As can be seen, many of these initiatives stem from diverse parts of Victoria Police.

At the strategic level, there are also many initiatives designed specifically to build confidence, trust and support with communities with strong police participation (and especially with those that are actually or potentially at a disadvantage or at risk of marginalisation):

* **PACMAC. (Police and Community Multicultural Advisory Committee)**

* **The Multi-Faith Council.**

* **The Gay, Lesbian, Bisexual, Transgender, & Queer Reference Group.**

* **Aboriginal Community Liaison Officer Program.**

◆ **New Emerging Community Liaison Officer Program.**

All of these are designed to enhance community perceptions of safety through relationship building, leading to trust, confidence and a clear police mandate.

Programs that are being developed or implemented in conjunction with other departments, agencies or organisations

◆ 'EyeWatch Project. — This program is being implemented in conjunction with Neighbourhood Watch Victoria to bring Neighbourhood Watch into the 21st century. 5 Police Service Areas are currently being trialled including Geelong, Brimbank, Darebin, Yarra Ranges and Hobsons Bay. Localised Facebook pages with local solutions to Crime Prevention and methods on reporting crime. Interactive pages which allow Local Inspectors and crime prevention focussed staff to interact on line with greater community. Provides real time feedback and answers to the community and makes the community feel a part of the Police. Original NSW concept currently on trial here in Victoria with assistance from the NSW Police Force. If this trial is successful — may be rolled out across 54 Police Service Areas.

◆ **Operation Dead Lock** — Proactive programme initiated by Safer Communities predominately looking after the elderly, weak or financially handicapped people in our community. When Police attend the scene of a Burglary or Aggravated Burglary and notice that there are either poor door or window locks or non-existent door locks, Safer Communities Unit is notified who then make contact with Assa-Abloy (Lockwood Company). New door locks are provided and fitted free to this vulnerable group of people.

◆ **Security Audits** — This program has been conducted in conjunction with private industry, local council and community members. Security audits are conducted on homes where members of the public have become repeat victims of crime. Security Audits are conducted by Crime Prevention Officers throughout the state of Victoria. Security audits are also conducted whereby Police members feel that the premises may be subject to repetitive crimes due to location, isolation or vulnerability.

◆ **Property Marking** — theft/burglary reduction campaigns. Funded by Victoria Police with some assistance from Neighbourhood Watch volunteers & private industry — e.g. Smart water system, Data Dot Security, RACV Insurance. 'Mark it in March' campaign where CPOs are supported by NHW volunteers.

◆ **With Indigenous Community & Aboriginal Community Justice Panels** — the Blues & Brothers Murray River Marathon Team entered annually (Koori young people and police joint entries).

◆ **Schoolies Week** — DEECD (Department of Education and Early Childhood Development), local councils, transport, entertainment and accommodation providers, local businesses.

◆ **Safe Streets** — Dedicated project within CBD for reduction and disruption of antisocial behaviour in partnership with Melbourne City Council via its CCTV system.

◆ **Research into perceptions of Safety in our Vietnamese Communities** — Jointly with community representatives, the Australian Research Council (ARC), and a university partner.

- ◆ **Hobson's Bay Community Leadership Programme** — Local Government Area, other emergency services and community leaders. In short, there are many local examples of community engagement, most initiated by local police to meet local needs that they are best placed to identify.

- ◆ **Community Concerns about mussel and pipi harvesting along sections of the Gippsland coast** — jointly with Department of Primary Industry and local residents and conservationists.

- **Community Safety Month** — October is Community Safety Month. Community Safety Month provides Victorians with a chance to take part in activities and events and learn how to make local communities safer places to live and work. Held in October each year, the month aims to promote awareness about a broad range of safety matters, including crime prevention, personal safety, safe work practices and staying safe during an emergency. Community Safety Month was initiated in 1996 by the Victorian Safe Communities Network, which coordinates the project with **support from Victoria Police**. Local communities, groups, schools, regional services, businesses, state and local government departments and agencies, are encouraged to build community safety partnerships by organising safety activities with other groups. The website — **communitysafetymonth.com.au**

- **Elder abuse campaign** was run in conjunction with the Office of Senior Victorians. Similarly 'You are not alone' campaign was also operated by both government agencies. Funding provided by both agencies.

Source: Submission from Victoria Police, to the Drugs and Crime Prevention Committee, Inquiry into Locally Based Approaches to Community Safety and Crime Prevention, April 2012.

Appendix 14: A selection of Neighbourhood Watch and Home Watch programs in the United Kingdom

One of the unique aspects of the Neighbourhood Watch and Home Watch (NW/HW) movement in the United Kingdom is the diverse range of watch groups in existence. Seemingly every aspect of life is covered by some type of community activity that combines intelligence gathering, surveillance and social activities. This Appendix presents a selection of these watch groups and their programs.

Derbyshire boat and canal watch

Usually specialist watch groups operate in partnership with an agency that also has involvement in the area. Thus a NW/HW group in an area of Derbyshire which has high concentrations of boats and canals have combined with water police and British Waterways to guard the canals of East Derbyshire and the boats and barges that use them. The way this watch works is described as follows:

> Members of the Canal and Boat Watch scheme encompass a diversity of people from the boat and canal community, all of whom have an interest and a stake in keeping the canals safe and pleasant places to live and enjoy. They include boat owners and canal bank residents, dog walkers, cyclists, canal enthusiasts and the fishing fraternity. The Neighbourhood Watch group actively seeks opportunities to recruit new members to the scheme. They regularly attend boat festivals and fetes, local libraries and community centres where they hand out a range of general crime prevention and boat safety literature. There are now around 200–300 members signed up to the scheme. Once someone is signed up there is normally a lead individual from the boat or canal community whose contact details are passed onto the police and wardens who will communicate with them in case of any issues (ERS Research and Consultancy 2010a, p.22).

Church, school and university watch

In Leicester the umbrella organisation Police and Community Support Group (PCSG) has established a number of innovative watch groups in response to specific needs and issues within the locality. Church Watch was established in response to a robbery of lead roofing tiles from a local church roof. Volunteers work with church officials to ensure church premises are safeguarded and any suspicious activities are reported. The scheme is now being expanded to other churches in the area.

School Watch, an initiative established in each of the schools within the jurisdiction of the local policing unit, incorporates a range of activities and projects:

> Signs are displayed in and around each school and houses in the nearby area are requested to participate in keeping an eye on the school, particularly during holiday periods. They use different activities and methods to engage the young people in crime prevention and safety. For example, there was an art competition where participants had to depict how they feel about School Watch, offering prizes such as cinema tickets, swimming passes, bike locks and supermarket vouchers. In Eyres Monsell, a deprived area, police have reported a reduction in crime around the area of a school where School Watch has been introduced.

> One of the group's most successful projects, [is] the 100% Attendance Reward Scheme...The impetus for this project came from the police, who wanted to deliver a project to address truancy and anti-social behaviour. The project rewarded pupils with 100% attendance with a trip to the cinema and a goody bag. The project worked with all 12 primary schools [in the local policing area] and was delivered by [the Neighbourhood Watch group] in partnership with police (ERS Research and Consultancy 2010a, p.30).

The PCSG also maintains strong links with the students and staff of Leicester University. The Chair of the NW/HW group attends the University of Leicester Community Liaison Group on behalf of the organisation and these meetings provide NW/HW with the opportunity to have input into crime prevention issues relating to the many students in the area. NW/HW also works with the Students Union and invites criminology students 'to attend Neighbourhood Watch group meetings and assist the members in delivering local community projects' (ERS Research and Consultancy 2010a, p.31).

Rural watches

There are a number of NW/HW groups throughout England and Wales that address crime and safety issues for people living in the rural areas of the country. Rural communities are often isolated from mainstream services and from people living and working in the local areas. 'This isolation can lead to the community feeling vulnerable to crime and a lack of police presence or means of communicating crime warnings and prevention messages can intensify this fear' (ERS Research and Consultancy 2010a, p.36). Rural Watch meetings are often held in farms and properties across the rural districts. As discussed below, they often act as social occasions in addition to providing information and feedback on crime in the area. Rural Watch schemes such as the one operating in East Hertfordshire often equip members with pager systems to report rural crime to police and other members of the Watch. These schemes are:

> [t]argeted at those members of the rural community who are out and about in the countryside on a daily basis, such as farmers, game keepers, horse riders and milkmen. These people can act as the eyes and ears of the countryside and if they spot something suspicious they can use the pagers to communicate what they see to police and others in the area (ERS Research and Consultancy 2010a, p.38).

The Borderwatch group in Richmondshire involves about 50 volunteers spread across four 'beat areas' to help combat rural crime. Each area has its own watch coordinator and an attached police officer to work in support. 'Volunteers offer detailed local knowledge, being aware of people and vehicles from outside the area and knowing on which land people are allowed to be and which they are not allowed to be' (ERS Research and Consultancy 2010a, p.108).

Harborough Be safe

Some NW/HW schemes in England have specific projects outside the usual remit of intelligence gathering and crime reporting. For example, the Harborough Be Safe program in Market Harborough, Leicestershire, assists the elderly and particularly victims of crime by providing a free of charge service to improve home security in addition to offering one-to-one support on security and crime prevention matters, particularly in the area of 'distraction burglaries'.[1] This program provides the following services:

> The team of volunteers will fit enhanced security equipment to the homes of elderly people who have been the victims of crime, as well as for vulnerable people who need improved home security to reduce the likelihood of being burgled. This includes door chains, door bars, door viewers, letterbox visors, memo minders and smoke alarms. In cases where the team does not have the equipment necessary to address a specific issue, they will try to source it or come up with a solution. Every attempt is made to visit a victim of a distraction burglary on the same day or within a couple of days of receiving the referral (from agencies including social services, victim support, age concern) but given that the scheme is run by volunteers this is not always possible. However, the scheme has the support of a locksmith who volunteers his time to respond to the most vulnerable people within six or seven hours of being informed (ERS Research and Consultancy 2010a, p.27).

In addition, Harborough Be Safe gives presentations to local groups on crime prevention and safety awareness matters and produces a calendar each year on crime prevention in partnership with other agencies such as the Leicestershire Constabulary, Victim Support and Aged Concern.

---

1   Distraction burglaries can be characterised where a person uses a falsehood, distraction or trick to gain entry to a residence in order to commit a burglary.

Valleys and Vale Neighbourhood Watch Association (VVNWA)

The VVNWA is based in Stroud in rural Gloucestershire and works in partnership with the Stroud and District Access Group to support local residents who are impaired, disabled or housebound. This group started in response to the needs of a number of disabled residents, one of whom had already been a member of NW/HW:

> Due to the cross-membership with Neighbourhood Watch links with the VVNWA were established at an early stage. VVNWA has provided people with security markings on mobility scooters and wheelchairs, produces its newsletter in yellow and black to make it accessible for visually impaired people, and provides its membership handbook on DVD (ERS Research and Consultancy 2010a, p.90).

Kids Watch and Junior Watch

Across England and Wales a number of NW/HW offshoot groups have been established catering for children. For example, the Junior Neighbourhood Watch (JNW) scheme in Stockton on Tees consists of five groups representing five primary schools in the local area. Approximately 20 students from each school attend their JNW group 'during which they can participate in creative activities around citizenship, personal safety and the impacts of crime' (ERS Research and Consultancy 2010a, p.57). The project arose from the police and local Neighbourhood Watch groups being keen to engage with young children and encourage and assist them to report antisocial and criminal behaviour in their community:

> The participating children initially learnt about what they should do if they see any suspicious or antisocial behaviour near school premises. During the school holiday period the school building was subjected to a higher risk of vandalism and the JNW used the theme of protecting the school building to arouse the interest of the children (ERS Research and Consultancy 2010a, p.57).

The JNW is coordinated by a project manager on a voluntary basis. Each school has an appointed staff member to oversee activities which generally take place once every two weeks for one hour, although some activities have taken place on a weekend. The five schools include children from a range of educational, ethnic and socioeconomic backgrounds (ERS Research and Consultancy 2010a, p.57).

Interest in joining the group is generated by the project manager supported by the Police Liaison Officer. Together they conduct a school assembly in which they select their representatives and promote the concept and types of activities on offer.

The activities of each of the JNW groups take place both in the classroom and the community. Knowledge acquired is not restricted to the members of each JNW, with information regularly communicated via class and school presentations. The groups also undertake home-based tasks, applying knowledge in their home environment and passing on knowledge to friends and family members (ERS Research and Consultancy 2010a, p.58).

Where possible, some activities allow for the different school Watches to undertake activities jointly, enabling children from a variety of backgrounds who may otherwise not meet to work together, reflecting the community cohesion that the project wishes to promote outside of the classroom.

A high level of interest has been generated from staff and children within engaged schools. Similar programs have been established throughout Britain including a Kids Neighbourhood Watch in Hull for those young people aged 16 and under. As a first project the young members of this group raised a petition to the LGA which led to the installation of bus shelters in the district (ERS Research and Consultancy 2010a, p.119).[2]

---

2   In addition to these specialist 'Watches', there are many other forms of NW/HW operating throughout the UK, including Business Watch, Golf Watch, Caravan Watch and Farm Watch.

Bibliography

Anderson, J & Tresidder, J 2008, *A review of the Western Australian community safety and crime prevention planning process: Final report*, Australian Institute of Criminology, Canberra.

Aos, Steve, Phipps, Polly, Barnoski, Robert & Lieb, Roxanne 2001, *The comparative costs and benefits of programs to reduce crime*, Washington State Institute for Public Policy, Washington.

Aos, Steve, Lieb, Roxanne, Mayfield, Jim, Miller, Marna & Pennucci, Annie 2004, *Benefits and costs of prevention and early intervention programs for youth*, Washington State Institute for Public Policy, Olympia.

Aos, Steve 2010, *Fight crime and save money: Development of an investment tool for states to study sentencing and corrections public policy options*, Washington Institute For Public Policy, Washington.

Aos, Steve 2011, 'Benefit-cost analysis in the real world: How the Washington State Legislature is using evidence-based information to lower crime rates and cut crime costs', paper presented at the *Crime prevention and policy: New tools for contemporary challenges conference*, Sydney 23 November.

Armstrong, A & Francis, R 2003, 'Difficulties in evaluating crime prevention programs: what are some lessons for evaluators of community based programs?', Paper presented to the *Evaluation in Crime and Justice: Trends and Methods Conference* convened by the Australian Institute of Criminology in conjunction with the Australian Bureau of Statistics, Canberra, 24–25 March.

Auer, MR 2011, 'The policy sciences of social media', *Policy Studies Journal*, vol. 39, no. 4, pp.709–736.

Australian Attorney-General's Department 2011, *Tip sheet 11: Challenges for local crime prevention in rural and remote communities*, Canberra.

Australian Institute of Criminology (AIC) 2003a, 'Understanding situational crime prevention', *AICrime Reduction Matters*, no. 3, June, p.1.

Australian Institute of Criminology (AIC) 2003b, 'Measuring crime prevention program costs and benefits', *AICrime reduction matters*, no. 15, p.1.

Australian Institute of Criminology (AIC), 2004, 'Why local government has a major role in crime prevention', *AICrime reduction matters*, no. 19, February, p.1

Australian Institute of Criminology (AIC) 2005, 'The market reduction approach to reducing property crime', *AICrime Reduction Matters*, no. 32, April, p.1.

Australian Institute of Criminology on behalf of the Australian and New Zealand Crime Prevention Senior Officers' Group 2012, *National Crime Prevention Framework*, AIC, Canberra.

Australian Institute of Criminology (AIC) n.d., 'Challenges for local crime prevention in rural and remote communities', *Tip Sheet 11*, AIC, Canberra.

Australian National Council on Drugs (ANCD) 2001, *Structural determinants of youth drug use*, A report prepared by National Drug and Alcohol Research Centre, UNSW in collaboration with Spooner, C., Hall, W. & Lynskey, M., ANCD Research Paper 2.

Ayling, J 2007, 'Force multiplier: People as a policing resource', *International Journal of Comparative and Applied Criminal Justice*, vol. 31, no. 1, Spring, pp.80–93.

Babor, T, Caetano, R, Casswell, S Edwards, G, Giesebrecht, N, Graham, K, Grube, J, Gruenewald, P, Hill, L, Holder, H, Homel, R, Osterberg, E, Rehm, J, Room, R & Rossow, I 2004, *Alcohol: No ordinary commodity – Research and public policy*, Oxford University Press, Oxford.

Baker, J 1998, *Juveniles in crime – Part 1: Participation rates and risk factors*, NSW Bureau of Crime Statistics and Research, Sydney.

Bayley, D 1986, *Community policing in Australia: An appraisal*, Working paper, National Police Research Unit, South Australia.

Beck, U 1992, *Risk society: Towards a new modernity*, Sage, London.

Beck, U 1998, 'Politics of risk society', in J Franklin (ed.), *The politics of risk society*, pp.9–22, Polity Press, Cambridge.

Bennett, T 1990, *Evaluating Neighbourhood Watch*, Aldershot, Gower.

Bennington L & Cummane, J 1999, 'Partnering relationships in the public sector', *The Quality Magazine*, pp.8–15.

Berry, G, Briggs, P, Errol, R & Van Staden, L 2011, *The effectiveness of partnership working in a crime and disorder context*, Research Report No 52, Home Office, London.

Bessant, J, Hil, R & Watts, R 2003, *Discovering risk: Social research and policy making*, Peter Lang, New York.

Brantingham, PJ & Faust, F 1976, 'A conceptual model of crime prevention', *Crime and Delinquency*, vol. 22, pp.130–146.

Brantingham, PL, Brantingham, PJ & Taylor, W 2005, 'Situational crime prevention as a key component in embedded crime prevention', *Canadian Journal of Criminology and Criminal Justice*, vol 42, no 2, pp.271–292.

Brinkerhoff, JM 2002, 'Assessing and improving partnership relationships and outcomes: A proposed framework', *Evaluation and Program Planning*, no. 25, pp.215–231.

Buckland, G & Wincup, E 2004, 'Researching crime and criminal justice', in J Muncie & D Wilson (eds), *Student handbook of criminal justice and criminology*, pp.37–48, Cavendish Publishing, London.

Buckley, L 2010, *An evaluation undertaken by Crime and Disorder Reduction Partnerships in the North West which aimed to engage young people in crime prevention and reduction initiatives*, Undertaken on behalf of Neighbourhood and Home Watch North West, University of Central Lancashire.

Cahalen, E n.d., *A critical time to support Neighborhood Watch*, Montgomery County, Maryland USA. Accessed at http://www.usaonwatch.org/resource/publication.aspx?PublicationId=31

Cameron M & Laycock G 2003, 'Crime prevention in Australia', in A Graycar & P Grabowsky (eds), *The Cambridge handbook of Australian criminology*, pp. 313–331, Cambridge University Press, Cambridge.

Cameron, M & MacDougall, C 2000, 'Crime prevention through sport and physical activity', *Trends and Issues in Crime and Criminal Justice*, no. 165, September, Australian Institute of Criminology, Canberra, pp.1–6.

Carr, P 2005, *Clean streets: Controlling crime, maintaining order, and building community activism*, NYU Press, New York.

Carrington, K & Scott, J 2008, 'Masculinity, rurality and violence', *British Journal of Criminology*, vol.48, pp.641–666.

Catalano, P 1999, 'A review of the Commonwealth's National Crime Prevention Initiative', *Current Issues in Criminal Justice*, vol. 11, no. 1, pp.79–87.

Cherney, A 2004, 'Crime prevention/community safety partnerships in action: Victorian experience', *Current Issues in Criminal Justice*, vol. 15, no. 3, pp.237–252.

Cherney, A 2007, 'Crime prevention in Australia: Beyond "What works?"?', *Australian and New Zealand Journal of Criminology*, vol.40, no.1, April, pp.65–81.

Cherney, A & Sutton, A 2007, 'Crime prevention in Australia: Beyond 'what works?' *The Australian and New Zealand Journal of Criminology*, vol. 40, no. 1, pp.65–81.

Chikritzhs, T, Gray, D, Lyons, Z & Saggers, S 2007, *Restrictions on the sale and supply of alcohol: Evidence and outcomes*, National Drug Research Institute, Curtin University of Technology, Perth, Western Australia.

Chisholm, J 2000, 'Benefit-cost analysis and crime prevention, *Trends and Issues in Crime and Criminal Justice*, no. 147, February, Australian Institute of Criminology, Canberra, pp.1–6.

Clancey, G 2011, 'Crime prevention programs/initiatives found to be particularly valuable and relevant in Australia', Paper presented at the *Crime Prevention and Beyond Forum*, Sydney Institute of Criminology, University of Sydney, 23-26 January.

Clarke, R 1995, 'Situational crime prevention', in M Tonry & D Farrington (eds), *Building a safer society: Strategic approaches to crime prevention*, pp.91–150, University of Chicago Press, Chicago.

Cohen, S 1996, 'If nothing works, What is our work?', *Australian and New Zealand Journal of Criminology*, vol. 27, pp.2–18.

Commonwealth of Australia 2003, *Early intervention: Diversion and youth conferencing*, Australian Government's Attorney-General's Department, Canberra.

Crawford, A 1998, *Crime prevention and community safety: Politics, policies and practices*, Longman, London and New York.

Crawford, A 2006, 'Fixing broken promises?: Neighbourhood wardens and social capital', *Urban Studies*, vol.43 no.5–6, pp.956–976.

Crime Research Centre, 2008, *Evaluation of the 'Eyes on the Street' program*, Report prepared for the Office of Crime Prevention, Crime Research Centre, University of Western Australia, Perth.

Cunneen, C 2004, 'The political resonance of crime control strategies: Zero tolerance policing', in R Hil & G Tait (eds), *Hard lessons: Reflections on governance and crime control in late modernity*, pp.151–169, Ashgate, Aldershot UK.

Dalgleish, D & Myhill, A 2004, *Reassuring the public: A review of international policing interventions*, Home Office Research Development and Statistics Directorate, London.

Davids, C 1995, 'Understanding the significance and persistence of Neighbourhood Watch in Victoria', *Law in Context*, vol. 12, no. 1, pp.57–80.

Davies, A & Jenkins, R 2010, *Civil society gains a new resource: Reporting the development of the Neighbourhood and Home Watch Network*. Accessed at http://www.ourwatch.org.uk/ resource_centre/document_library/civil_society_gains_a_new resource

Davis, M 1990, *City of Quartz: Excavating the Future of Los Angeles*, Vintage Books, New York.

Day, A, Howells, K & Rickwood, D 2003, *Victorian juvenile justice rehabilitation review*, Report prepared for the Department of Human Services, Victorian Government Printer, Melbourne.

Day, A, Howells, K & Rickwood, D 2004, 'Current trends in the rehabilitation of juvenile offenders', *Trends and Issues in Crime and Criminal Justice*, no. 284, October, pp.1–6.

Dempsey, JS & Forst, L, 2010, *Police*, Cengage Learning Inc, New York.

Department of Justice (DOJ) (Vic), 2010, *Evaluating the Neighbourhood Justice Centre in Yarra 2007–2009*, DOJ, Melbourne.

Department of Justice (Vic) 2011, *Annual report 2010–2011*, Department of Justice, Melbourne.

Department of Justice & Community Safety (ACT) 2004, *Crime victims and the prevention of residential burglary*, Report of the ACT Burglary Victims Response Project 2004, ACT Department of Justice & Community Safety, Canberra.

Department of Planning and Community Development (Vic), *Safer Design Guidelines for Victoria*. Accessed at: http://www.dpcd.vic.gov.au/planning/urbandesign/guidelines/safer-design-guidelines

de Ridder T & Johns R 2008, Review of Neighbourhood Watch, final report with recommendations for consideration, Victoria Police, Melbourne.

Dossetor, K 2011, 'Cost-benefit analysis and its application to crime prevention and criminal justice research', *Technical and Background Paper no 42*, Australian Institute of Criminology, Canberra.

Dowds, L & Mayhew, P 1994, 'Participation in neighbourhood watch: Findings from the 1992 British Crime Survey', *Home Office Research Findings*, p.11.

Drake, Elizabeth K, Aos, Steve & Miller, Marna G 2009, 'Evidence based public policy options to reduce crime and criminal justice costs: Implications in Washington State', *Victims and Offenders*, vol. 4, pp.170–196.

Drugs and Crime Prevention Committee 2006, *Inquiry into Strategies to Reduce Harmful Alcohol Consumption*, Final Report, volume 2, Parliament of Victoria, Melbourne.

Drugs and Crime Prevention Committee 2009, *Inquiry into Strategies to Prevent High Volume Offending by Young People*, Final Report, Parliament of Victoria, Melbourne.

DuBow, F & Emmons, D 1981, 'The community hypothesis,' in D Lewis (ed.), Reactions to crime, Sage, Beverly Hills, CA.

Dussuyer, I 1991, 'The Good Neighbourhood Program', Paper presented at the *Seventh Annual Conference of the Australian and New Zealand Society of Criminology*, Melbourne, 2-4 October. Unpublished.

Dwyer, P & Wyn, J 2001, *Youth, education and risk*, Routledge/Falmer, London.

Edgar, L, Marshall, C & Bassett M, 2006, *Partnerships: Putting good governance principles in practice*, Institute on Governance, Ottawa.

Edge, S 2007, 'The good neighbours who fought back', *The Daily Mail*, 24 February, p.43.

Ekblom, P & Tilley, N 2000, 'Going equipped: Criminology, situational crime prevention and the resourceful offender', *British Journal of Criminology*, vol. 40, pp.376–398.

Ergas, Henry 2009, 'In defence of cost-benefit analysis', *Agenda*, vol. 16, no. 3, p.33.

ERS Research and Consultancy 2010a, *Showcasing Neighbourhood and Home Watch achievements*, Newcastle upon Tyne, UK.

ERS Research and Consultancy, 2010b, *Exploring barriers to participation in Neighbourhood and Home Watch schemes*, Newcastle upon Tyne, UK.

Felson, M 1995, 'Those who discourage crime', *Crime Prevention Studies*, vol. 4, pp.53–66.

Fleming, J 2005, 'Working together: Neighbourhood Watch, reassurance policing and the potential of partnerships', *Trends and Issues in Crime and Criminal Justice*, no. 303, September, Australian Institute of Criminology, Canberra, pp.1–6.

Foucault, M 1979, *Discipline and punish: The birth of the prison*, translated from the French by Alan Sheridan, Penguin, Harmondsworth.

Geason, S & Wilson, P 1992, 'The approach: Situational crime prevention', in *Australian Institute of Criminology, Crime Prevention Series – Preventing Retail Crime*, Australian Institute of Criminology, Canberra, pp.7–11.

Gelb, K 2006, *Myths and misconceptions: Public opinion versus public judgement about sentencing*, Sentencing Advisory Council, Melbourne.

Gelb, K 2008, *More myths and misconceptions*, Sentencing Advisory Council, Melbourne.

Gellately, R 2002, *Backing Hitler: Consent and coercion in Nazi Germany*, Oxford University Press, New York.

Goethe, W von 1971 translated by R.J. Hollingdale, *Elective affinities*, Penguin Books, London.

Goodnow, J 2006, 'Adding social contexts to developmental analysis of crime prevention', *Australian and New Zealand Journal of Criminology*, vol. 39, pp.327–338.

Gottfredson, D & Soule, D 2005, 'The timing of property crime, violent crime, and substance use among juveniles', *Journal of Research in Crime and Delinquency*, vol. 42, no. 1, February, pp.110–120.

Government of Western Australia 2000, *Safer W.A. Together against crime: A partnership between the community, police, state and local government*. Accessed 13 July at: http://www.saferwa. wa.gov.au/html/fs04pub.htm

Gray, D & Wilkes, D 2010, *Reducing alcohol and other drug related harm*, Resource Sheet No 3, Closing the Gap Clearing House, Australian Institute of Health and Welfare, Canberra.

Graham, K & Homel, R 2008, *Raising the bar: Preventing aggression in and around bars, pubs and clubs*, Willan Publishing, Devon UK.

Hicks, C 1993, *Community crime prevention: toward safer communities*. Accessed 9 September 2011 at: www.aic.gov.au/publicationsprevious%20series/.../1-27/~/.../hicks.ashx,

Hil, R 1996, 'Crime prevention and the technologies of social order – A response to Phillip Hill and Adam Sutton', *Just Policy*, no. 6, May, pp.59–61.

Hill, P & Sutton, A 1996, 'Crime prevention: Not just Neighbourhood Watch and street lighting', *Just Policy*, no. 6, May, pp.54–58.

Holloway, K, Bennett, T & Farrington, DP 2008, *Crime prevention research review no.3: Does Neighborhood Watch reduce crime?*, US Department of Justice Office of Community Oriented Policing Services, Washington DC.

Home Office 2010, *Policing in the 21st century: Reconnecting police and the people*, Home Office, London.

Home Office 2011, *A new approach to fighting crime*, Home Office. London, UK. Accessed 10 June at: http://www.homeoffice.gov.uk/publications/crime/new-approach-fighting-crime

Homel, P 2004, 'The whole of government approach to crime prevention', *Trends and Issues in Crime and Criminal Justice*, no. 287, November, Australian Institute of Criminology, Canberra, pp. 1–6.

Homel, P 2005, 'A short history of crime prevention in Australia', *Canadian Journal of Criminology and Criminal Justice*, vol. 47, no. 2, pp.355–368.

Homel, P 2005, *Regional organisation for crime prevention delivery*, Australian Institute of Criminology, Canberra.

Homel, P 2006, 'Joining up the pieces: What central agencies need to support effective local crime prevention', in J Knutsson & RV Clarke (eds), *Putting theory to work: Implementing situational crime prevention and problem oriented policing, Crime Prevention Studies*, vol 20, pp.111–138, Criminal Justice Press, New York.

Homel, P 2009a, 'Improving crime prevention knowledge and practice', *Trends and Issues in Crime and Criminal Justice*, no. 385, November, Australian Institute of Criminology, Canberra, pp.1–6.

Homel, P 2009b, 'Lessons for Canadian crime prevention from recent international experience', *Revue de l'IPC/IPC Review*, vol. 3, March, pp.13–39.

Homel, P 2010a, 'Delivering effective local crime prevention: Why understanding variations in municipal governance arrangements matters', in M Idriss et al (eds), *2010 International report on crime prevention and community safety: trends and prospects*, pp.118–119, International Centre for the Prevention of Crime, Montreal.

Homel, P 2010b, 'The ghost of crime prevention future', Paper presented at the Sydney Institute of Criminology, Crime Prevention Seminar. Accessed 10 May 2010 at: http://sydney.edu. au/law/criminology/seminars_events/past_events.shtml#crime

Homel, P 2011, 'How do I know it worked? Measuring the effectiveness of crime prevention in Australia', Paper presented at the *Crime prevention and policy: New tools for contemporary challenges* conference, Sydney, 23–24 November.

Homel, P, Nutley, S, Webb, B & Tilley, N 2004, *Investing to deliver: Reviewing the implementation of the UK Crime Reduction Programme*, Home Office Research Study 281, Home Office, London.

Homel, R 2005, 'Developmental crime prevention', in N Tilley (ed.), *Handbook of crime prevention and community safety*, pp. 71–106, Willan Publishing, Cullompton, Devon.

Homel, R, Hauritz, M, Wortley, R, McIlwain, G & Carvolth, R 1997, 'Preventing alcohol-related crime through community action: The Surfers Paradise safety action project', in R Homel (ed.), *Policing for prevention: Reducing crime, public intoxication, and injury*, pp.35–90, Criminal Justice Press, New York.

Homel, R, Freiberg, K, Lamb, C, Leech, M, Carr, A, Hampshire, A, Hay, I, Elias, G, Manning, M, Teague, R & Batchelor, B 2006, *The Pathways to Prevention Project: The first five years 1999–2004*, Mission Australia and Griffith University, Brisbane.

Homel, R & Homel, P 2012, 'Implementing crime prevention: Good governance and a science of implementation' in B Welsh & D Farrington (eds), *The Oxford Handbook on Crime Prevention*, Oxford University Press, Oxford.

Homel, R & McGee, T (forthcoming), 'Community approaches to preventing crime and violence: The challenge of building prevention capacity', in R Loeber & B Welsh (eds), *The future of criminology; Essays in honour of David* Farrington, Oxford University Press, New York.

Hope, T 1996, 'Community, crime and inequality in England and Wales', in T Bennett (ed.), *Preventing crime and disorder*, pp.51–62, Cropwood series, University of Cambridge, Cambridge.

Huck, S & Kosfeld, M 2007, 'The dynamics of Neighbourhood Watch and norm enforcement', *The Economic Journal*, no. 117 (January), pp.270–286.

Hughes, G 1998, *Understanding crime prevention: social control, risk and late modernity*, Open University, Buckingham.

Husain, S 1988, *Neighbourhood Watch in England and Wales: A locational analysis*, (Crime Prevention Unit Paper 12), Home Office, London, UK.

Injury Control Council of Western Australia, (ICCWA) 2011, *Community violence prevention strategy in the north metropolitan area*, ICCWA in conjunction with the North Metropolitan Area Health Service, Perth.

Institute of Public Affairs Australia (IPAA) 2002, *Working together – Integrated governance: Final report*, IPA. Accessed at Hittp://www.ipaa.org.au/12_pdf/national_research_final.pdf

Institute on Governance 2003, *Principles for good governance in the 21st century*, Institute on Governance, Ottawa, Canada.

International Centre for the Prevention of Crime (ICPC), 2003, *Crime prevention and indigenous communities, current international strategies and programmes, Final Report*, ICPC, Montreal.

International Centre for the Prevention of Crime (ICPC) 2008, *International report on crime prevention and community safety*, ICPC, Montreal.

International Centre for the Prevention of Crime (ICPC) 2010, *Crime prevention and community safety: Trends and perspectives*, ICPC, Montreal.

International Centre for the Prevention of Crime (ICPC) 2010b, *International report on crime prevention and community safety*, ICPC, Montreal.

International Centre for the Prevention of Crime (ICPC) 2011, *Public-private partnerships and community safety: A guide to action*, ICPC, Montreal, Canada.

Jacobs, J 1961, *The death and life of great American cities*, Sage Random House, New York.

Jacobs, K 2010, 'The politics of partnerships: A study of police and housing collaboration to tackle anti-social behaviour on Australian public housing estates', *Public Administration*, vol. 88, no. 4, pp.928–942.

Jeffries, S, Payne, J & Smith, RG 2002, *Preventing crime in Australia 1990–2002: A selected register of crime prevention projects*, Australian Institute of Criminology, Canberra.

Jobes, PC, Barlcay, E, Weinand, H & Donnermeyer, JF 2004, 'A structural analysis of social disorganisation and crime in rural Ccommunities in Australia', *The Australian and New Zealand Journal of Criminology*, vol. 37, no. 1, pp.114–140.

Joseph Rowntree Foundation. 2003 *Developing people – regenerating place: achieving greater integration for local area regeneration*, York. Accessed at http://www.jrf.org.uk

Judd, B, Samuels, R & Barton, J n.d., 'The effectiveness of strategies for crime reduction in areas of public housing concentration', *Social City*, Australian Housing and Urban Research Institute. Accessed at http://www.fbe.unsw.edu.au/cityfutures/publications/presentations/soacjuddsamuels.pdf

Kang, Ji Hyon 2011, 'Participation in the community social control, the Neighbourhood Watch groups: Individual- and neighbourhood- related factors', *Crime & Delinquency*, February, pp.1–25.

Kelly, P 1999, 'Wild and tame zones: Regulating the transition of youth at risk', *Journal of Youth Studies*, vol. 2, no. 2, pp.193–211.

Kelly, P 2000, 'The dangerousness of youth at risk: The possibilities of surveillance and intervention in uncertain times', *Journal of Adolescence*, vol. 23, no. 4, pp.463–476.

King, M 1988, How to make social crime prevention work: The French experience, NACRO, London.

Lane, M & Henry, K 2004, 'Beyond symptoms: Crime prevention and community development', *Australian Journal of Social Issues*, vol. 39, no. 2, May, pp.201–213.

Laycock, G & Tilley, N 1995, *Policing and Neighbourhood Watch: Strategic issues*, (Crime Detection and Prevention Series, Paper No. 60), Home Office, London, UK.

Leach, P 2006, 'Regimes of insecurity? Citizen security initiatives as regulatory', paper presented at the *Australian and New Zealand Society of Criminology Conference*, Hobart, Tasmania, 7-9 February.

Lester, A 2001, 'Crime reduction through product design', *Trends and Issues in Crime and Criminal Justice*, no. 206, May, Australian Institute of Criminology, Canberra, pp.1–6.

Lievore, D 2003, *Non-reporting and hidden recording of sexual assault: An international literature review*, Australian Institute of Criminology for the Commonwealth Office of the Status of Women, Barton, A.C.T.

Loxley, W, Toumbourou, JW, Stockwell, T, Haines, B, Scott, K, Godfrey, C, Waters, E, Patton, G, Fordham, R, Gray, D, Marshall, J, Ryder, D, Saggers, S, Sanci, L & Williams, J 2004, *The prevention of substance use, risk and harm in Australia: A review of the evidence*, prepared for National Drug Research Institute and Centre for Adolescent Health, AGPS, Canberra.

Macrae, L, Paetsch, J, Bertrand, L & Hornick, J 2005, 'National police leadership survey on crime prevention through social development', Paper prepared for National Crime Prevention Centre by Canadian Research Institute for Law and the Family, Calgary.

Makkai, T 2004, 'Director's introduction to Homel, P, "The Whole of Government Approach to Crime Prevention"', *Trends and Issues in Crime and Criminal Justice*, no 287, November, Australian Institute of Criminology, Canberra, pp. 1–6.

Manning, M, Homel R, & Smith, C 2006, 'Economic evaluation of a community based early intervention program implemented in a disadvantaged urban area of Queensland', *Economic Analysis and Policy*, vol. 36, no. 1/2, September, pp.99–119.

Mayhew, P, Aye Maung, N & Mirrilees-Black, C 1993, *The 1992 British Crime Survey*, Home Office Research Study No 111, HMSO, London.

McConville, M & Shepherd D, 1992, *Watching police, watching communities*, Routledge, London.

McKendry, B. 2003, 'Crime prevention works: Practical approaches to community safety', Presentation to the Victorian Safe Communities Network First Annual Conference, 31 October. Accessed 4 July 2011 at: www.vscn.org.au/pages/documents/conf2003/

McMillan, E 1991, *An overview of crime prevention in Victoria*, Proceedings of the National Overview on Crime Prevention Conference, Australian Institute of Criminology, Canberra, 4–6 June, Accessed at: http://www.aic.gov.au/publications/previous%20series/proceedings/

McMillan, E 1992, *An overview of crime prevention in Victoria*, at http://www.aic.gov.au/publications/previous%20series/proceedings/1-27/~/media/publications/proceedings/15/mcmillan.ashx

Midford, R 2004, 'Community action to reduce alcohol problems: What should we try in Australia?', *Centrelines*, Newsletter of the National Centres for Drug and Alcohol Research, National Drug and Alcohol Research Centre, Perth, pp.3–4.

Morgan, A & Homel, P 2011, 'A model performance framework for community based crime prevention', *Technical and Background Paper no. 40*, Australian Institute of Criminology, Canberra.

Morgan, J 1991, *Safer communities: The local delivery of crime prevention through the partnership approach*, Home Office, London.

Morris, L, Sallybanks, J & Willis, K 2003, 'Sport, physical activity and antisocial behaviour in youth', *Australian Institute of Criminology Research and Public Policy Series*, no. 49, Australian Institute of Criminology, Canberra.

Morris, L, Sallybanks, J, Willis, K & Makkai, T 2003, 'Sport, physical activity and antisocial behaviour in youth', *Trends and Issues in Crime and Criminal Justice*, no. 249, April, pp.1–6.

Mukherjee, S & Wilson, P 1987, 'Neighbourhood Watch: Issues and policy implications', *Trends and Issues in Crime and Criminal Justice*, no.8, November, Australian Institute of Criminology, Canberra, pp.1–7.

National Crime Prevention Framework, 20011, Accessed at http://www.aic.gov.au/crime_community/crimeprevention/~/media/aic/ncpf/ncp_framework

Newman, O 1972, *Defensible space: People and design in the violent city*, Architectural Press, London.

New South Wales Government 2008, *New South Wales Crime Prevention Framework*, Department of Premier and Cabinet, New South Wales Government, Sydney.

New South Wales Law Reform Commission 2001, *Surveillance: An interim report*, report no. 98. Accessed 29 April 2011 at: www.agd.nsw.gov.au/lrc.nsf

New South Wales Police Force, *Safer by design*. Accessed 29 August 2011 at: http://www.police.nsw.gov.au/community_issues/crime_prevention/safer_by_design

Norris, C & Armstrong, G 1999, *The maximum surveillance society: The rise of closed circuit television*, Perpetuity Press, Oxford.

Nutley, S & Davies H 2001, 'Developing organisational learning in the NHS' *Medical Education*, no. 35, pp.35–42.

Nutley, S, Davies H & Walter, I. 2002, *Evidence based policy and practice: Cross sector lessons from the UK*, Economic and Social Research Council (ESRC), UK Centre for Evidence Based Policy and Practice, Working Paper 9. Accessed 22 August 2011 at: http://www.kcl.ac.uk/content/1/c6/03/46/00/wp9b.pdf

O'Toole, S 2002, 'The politics of punishment', *Alternative Law Journal*, vol. 27, no. 5, October, pp.242–243.

Painter, K & Farrington, D 2001, 'Evaluating situational crime prevention using a young people's survey', *British Journal of Criminology*, vol. 41, pp.266–284.

Parliament of Australia 2005, *An overview of the effectiveness of closed circuit television (CCTV) surveillance*, Parliamentary Library Research Service, Parliament of Australia, Canberra.

Prenzler, T & Sarre, R 2010, *An overview of security industry OH&S in Australia*, Report to the Australian Security Industry Association Limited, Sydney.

Randolph, B & Judd, B 2000, 'Community renewal and public housing estates', *Urban Policy and Research*, vol. 9, no. 1, pp.91–104.

Rhodes, RAW 1997, *Understanding governance*, Open University Press, Buckingham.

Rollings, K 2008, *Counting the costs of crime in Australia: a 2005 update*, Research and public policy series no. 91, Australian Institute of Criminology, Canberra. Also accessed at http://www.aic.gov.au/publications/rpp/91/index.html

Rosenbaum, DP 1988, 'Community crime prevention: A review and synthesis of the literature', *Justice Quarterly*, vol. 5, pp.323–95.

Saltz, R 2005. 'What is "evidence" and can we provide it?', in T Stockwell, PJ Gruenewald, JW Toumbourou & W Loxley (eds), *Preventing harmful substance use: The evidence base for policy and practice*, pp.313–323, John Wiley and Sons Ltd, Chichester, England.

Sampson, R & Laub, J 2005, 'A life-course view of the development of crime', *The Annals of the American Academy*, vol. 602, pp.12–45.

Sentencing Advisory Council of Victoria 2011a, *Alternatives to imprisonment: Community views in Victoria*, Sentencing Advisory Council of Victoria, Melbourne.

Sentencing Advisory Council of Victoria 2011b, *Does imprisonment deter? – A review of the evidence*, Sentencing Advisory Council of Victoria, Melbourne.

Sherman, LW 1997, 'Policing for crime prevention', in LW Sherman, DC Gottfredson, DL MacKenzie, J Eck, P Reuter & S Bushway (eds), *Preventing crime: What works, what doesn't, what's promising*, chapter 8, US Office of Justice Programs, Washington, DC.

Skogan, K 1988, 'Community organisations and crime', in M Tonry & N Morris (eds), *Crime and justice: A review of research*, pp.39–78, University of Chicago Press, Chicago.

Smith, M & Cornish, D (eds) 2003, 'Theory for situational crime prevention', *Crime Prevention Studies*, vol. 16, Criminal Justice Press, Monsey, New York.

Smyth, R 2011, *Costs of Crime in Victoria*, Discussion paper, Department of Economics, Monash University, Melbourne. Accessed at http://www.buseco.monash.edu.au/eco/research/papers/2011/2511costsofcrimesmyth.pdf

Solomon, E 2009, 'New Labour and crime prevention in England and Wales: What worked?', *Revue de l'ICP/ICP Review*, vol 3, March, pp.41–65.

Spindler, S 1994, 'The rehabilitation of prisoners as an aspect of crime prevention', *Criminology Australia*, November, pp.21–25.

Springall, L 2002, *Rhetoric and reality...A flexible framework for crime prevention evaluation in Victoria*, Paper presented at the Crime Prevention Conference convened by Australian Institute of Criminology and Commonwealth Attorney-General's Department, Sydney, 12–13 September. Accessed 11 July 2011 at: http://www.aic.gov.au/crime_community/crimeprevention/localgovt/vic.aspx

Squires, P 1999, *Criminology and the 'community safety' paradigm: Safety, power and success and the limits of the local*. Accessed 31 August 2011 at: http://www.britsoccrim.org/volume2/012.pdf

Stark, A & McCullough, J 2005, *Engaging communities in community renewal: Challenges, success factors and critical questions*. Accessed 31 August 2011 at: http://www.engagingcommunities2005.org/abstracts/McCullough-Julie-Ann-final.pdf

Stephenson, M, Giller, H & Brown, S 2007, *Effective practice in youth justice*, Willan Publishing, Devon.

Surveillance Studies Network 2006, *A report on the surveillance society*, Full report for the Information Commissioner by the Surveillance Studies Network (Editor: David Murakami Wood), Surveillance Studies Network, London.

Sutton, A & White, R 1995, 'Crime prevention, urban space and social exclusion', *Australian and New Zealand Journal of Sociology*, vol 34, no. 2, pp.82–99.

Sutton, A, Cherney, A & White, R 2008, *Crime prevention: Principles, perspectives and practices*, Cambridge University Press, Port Melbourne.

Toumbourou, J 1999, 'Implementing Communities that Care in Australia: A community mobilisation approach to crime prevention', *Trends and Issues in Crime and Criminal Justice*, no. 122, July, Australian Institute of Criminology, Canberra, pp.1-6.

United Nations Council for Economic and Social Development (UN–ECOSOC) 2002, *Guidelines for the prevention of urban crime: Resolution 1995/9*. Accessed 10 June 2011 at: http:www.un.org/documents/ecosoc/res/1995/eres1995-9.htm

United Nations Office on Drugs and Crime (UNODC) 2010, *Handbook on the crime prevention guidelines: Making them work*, UNODC at www.unodc.org

Van Dijk, J & De Waard, J 1991, 'A two dimensional typology of crime prevention projects', *Criminal Justice Abstracts*, vol. 23, pp.483–503.

Waller, I 2006, *Less law, more order: The truth about reducing crime*, Praeger Imprint Series, Westport, CN.

Watts, R Bessant, J & Hil R 2008, *International criminology: A critical introduction*, Routledge, London and New York.

Welsh, Brandon C & Farrington, David, 2005, 'Evidence-based crime prevention: conclusions and directions for a Safer Society', *Canadian Journal of Criminology and Criminal Justice*, April, pp.337–354.

Western Australia Police 2011, *Crime prevention strategy 2011–2014*, Western Australia Police, Perth.

Whitzman, C 2005, 'Social planning and crime prevention: Some lessons from innovative practices', *Australian Planner*, vol. 42, no. 3, September, pp.32–35.

Williams, J, Toumbourou, J, Williamson, E, Hemphill, S & Patton, G 2009, *Violent and antisocial behaviours amongst young adolescents in Australian communities*, Australian Research Alliance for Children and Youth, October.

Williams, P 2001, 'Illicit drug use in regional Australia, 1988–1998', *Trends and Issues in crime and criminal justice*, no. 192, February, Australian Institute of Criminology, Canberra.

Wilson, J & Kelling, G 1982, 'Broken windows', *The Atlantic Monthly*, vol. 249, no. 3 (March), pp.29–38.

World Health Organization (WHO) Programme on Substance Abuse 1992, *Proceedings of the International Consultation on Solvent Abuse*, WHO, Geneva, 7 December, p.3.

World Health Organization (WHO) 2009a, *Preventing violence through the development of safe, stable and nurturing relationships between children and their caregivers*. Accessed 20 June 2011 at: http://www.who.int/violence_injury_prevention/violence/4th_milestones_meeting/publications/en/index.html

World Health Organization (WHO) 2009b, *Changing cultural and social norms that support violence*. Accessed 20 June 2011 at: http://www.who.int/violence_injury_prevention/violence/4th_milestones_meeting/publications/en/index.html